Negotiating While Fighting

HOOVER ARCHIVAL DOCUMENTARIES

General editor: *Milorad M. Drachkovitch*

The original documents reproduced in this series (unless otherwise indicated) are deposited in the archives of the Hoover Institution on War, Revolution and Peace at Stanford University. The purpose of their publication is to shed new light on some important events concerning the United States or the general history of the twentieth century.

Negotiating While Fighting:

The Diary
of Admiral C. Turner Joy
at the Korean Armistice Conference

edited and with an introduction by
Allan E. Goodman

foreword by
General Matthew B. Ridgway
U.S. Army (Ret.)

HOOVER INSTITUTION PRESS
Stanford University   Stanford, California 94305

Hoover Institution Publication 175

© 1978 by the Board of Trustees of the
Leland Stanford Junior University
All rights reserved
International Standard Book Number: 0−8179−6751−6
Library of Congress Catalog Card Number: 77−7/565
Printed in the United States of America

Contents

Foreword

In 1955 the book *How Communists Negotiate*, by the late Admiral C. Turner Joy, United States Navy, was published by the Macmillan Company. At his request I wrote the foreword of which the following is an extract:

> Throughout my tenure as Commander-in-Chief, United Nations Command, Admiral C. Turner Joy was the Commander of Naval Forces in the Far East. He served as Senior Delegate to the Korean Armistice Conference during my period of responsibility for the armistice effort.
>
> I could not overstate the value of his calm advice, his skillful performance, and his loyal personal support during that trying time. His qualities of absolute integrity, deep sincerity, and intelligent devotion to the best interests of freedom shone brightly through all the dark shadows of our negotiations with the Communists at Kaesong and Panmunjom. His power of penetrating analysis was superb. No one could have more ably represented the United States in that conference.
>
> Admiral Joy's analysis of Communist techniques is drawn from the experience of ten arduous months of confronting the Communists almost daily. The negotiations he conducted covered the entire spectrum of Communist interests and objectives—political and military—in Korea and world-wide. I know of no citizen of the free world who could speak of Communist negotiating tactics from a broader base of practical knowledge.

That book placed before the world, in condensed form, the essence of his unabridged diary, which the Hoover Institution on War, Revolution and Peace is now making available to the public. At the Institution's request, endorsed by Admiral Joy's widow and son, I undertook to write this foreword.

Some time after publication of *How Communists Negotiate* there occurred an apparent concerted effort severely to limit public distribution and particularly to curtail its circulation among policy-makers in the Executive branch of our government. While I was given some information about this unexplained occurrence by an individual who purported to have substantiating facts, he did not reveal, if indeed he knew, either the source or motivation, and at this writing, I know neither the one nor the other.

However, the full diary is now being published, and since it is of such great potential value, I feel it essential that this foreword to the diary include a verbatim extract from the one I wrote for *How Communists Negotiate*.* Further, since the diary reveals in full detail the various matters on which differences developed between the authorities in Washington, i.e., the Executive branch (the White House, the Departments of State and Defense, and the Joint Chiefs of Staff) on the one hand, and those in the field, i.e., my Headquarters in Tokyo and the U.N. Delegation in Korea on the other, I deem it important also to include the inscription in Admiral Joy's handwriting in the copy of his book, which he sent to me. His words will evidence the almost invariable agreement that developed between Admiral Joy's views and mine.

> To: General Matt Ridgway whose superlative leadership and staunch support of the Delegation's efforts in Korea were an inspiration to all of us who were privileged to serve under his command. With profound admiration and affectionate best wishes.
>
> [signed] Turner Joy

The unchanging purpose of Communist negotiators is to achieve at the conference table, the objectives that their use of force has failed to attain. Our repeated failure to recognize this truth and to act upon it, led us into innumerable difficulties in Korea, and later in Vietnam. It is fervently to be hoped that the hard lessons so painfully apparent will at long last be applied to our benefit at the adversary confrontations we shall inevitably face in future negotiations— negotiations in which our participants must rely on "more steel and less silk, must know that they have much to gain by standing firm, and everything to lose by compromising" (Admiral Joy's words), and must ever remember that firmness and the will to stand on your positions are all that Communists respect. We MUST negotiate, BUT we MUST obtain fully compensating concessions for any the U.S. is willing to make.

We are, and shall long continue to be engaged in a crucial struggle with the leadership of the USSR, an implacable adversary unalterably opposed to our concepts of the freedom of the individual and of human dignity, and openly dedicated to the triumph of its system of government in the irreconcilable conflict between capitalism and socialism. It is an unceasing contest, waged by the Soviet Union to date, more by economic, political, and psychological than by military means—a contest of nerves and determination in which Soviet doctrine

---

*A paperback edition of *How Communists Negotiate* was published in 1970 by Fidelis Publishers, Inc., Santa Monica, Calif. I had no knowledge of this edition until after it appeared; my foreword in the original edition was deleted, and one by Vice Admiral R. E. Libby, U.S.N. (Ret.) was substituted, for what reason I do not know.

The publisher of this new edition issued a statement that: "This book has been all but unobtainable."—M.B.R.

permits no compromise, and supporting which is the tremendous military capability of the Soviet Union for practicing coercive diplomacy, and ultimately, IF IT SHOULD SO CHOOSE, to employ that awesome capability.

Examination of this authentic diary of the Korean Armistice negotiations over the ten months in which its author, Admiral Joy, was chief of the U.S. Delegation, will reveal the full stature, the superb performance, and the sterling character of this great American. He, his principal assistants, all of whom are named in the accompanying documents, and his staff rendered conspicuously superior service in their dedicated and untiring efforts to accomplish their extremely difficult mission under the most trying and exasperating conditions.

In his excellent introduction to the diary, Professor Allan E. Goodman, the editor, states that he would like "to believe that the reading of it will help those concerned with the theory and practice of diplomacy generally to understand better how what is done at the conference table may encourage an adversary to prolong a conflict rather than end it." I would merely add my hope that those of the Executive branch of our government responsible for the policy decisions governing our negotiating delegations, and our negotiators themselves, will study and digest the record which a dedicated, selfless American has bequeathed them. The Hoover Institution on War, Revolution and Peace has rendered a great service in publishing this document.

M. B. RIDGWAY
Pittsburgh, Pa.   *General, U.S. Army*
Retired

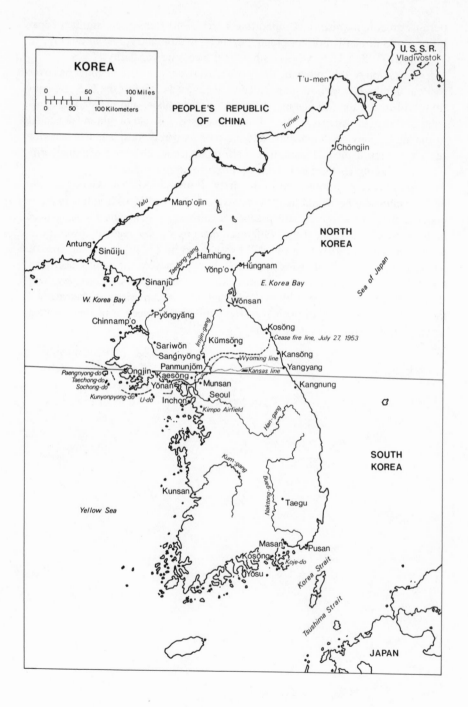

KOREA

0　　　50　　　100 Miles
0　　50　　100 Kilometers

PEOPLE'S REPUBLIC
OF CHINA

U. S. S. R.
Vladivostok

T'u-men

Tumen

Chöngjin

Yalu

Manp'ojin

NORTH
KOREA

Antung

Sinŭiju

Taedong-gang

Hamhŭng

Yŏnp'o

Hŭngnam

Sinanju

E. Korea Bay

Sea of Japan

W. Korea Bay

Wŏnsan

Chinnamp'o

Pyŏngyäng

Imjin-gang

Kosŏng

Cease fire line, July 27, 1953

Sariwŏn

Kŭmsŏng

Sanónyŏng

Kansŏng

Panmunjŏm

Wyoming line

Paengnyong-do

sOngjin

Kaesŏng

Kansas line

Yangyang

Taechong-do
Sochong-do

Yŏnan

Munsan

Kangnung

Kunyonpyong-do

U-do

Inchon

Seoul

Kimpo Airfield

Han-gang

SOUTH
KOREA

Kum-gang

Naktong-gang

Kunsan

Taegu

Yellow Sea

Masan

Pusan

Kosŏng

Koje-do

Yŏsu

Korea Strait

Tsushima Strait

JAPAN

Editor's Introduction

Americans negotiate to end warfare; Communists use negotiations to protract it. To a Communist negotiator, warfare and armistice alike have the same objective—victory. Nowhere has this been clearer than when the United States has been at war in Asia. In Korea, as later in Vietnam, our adversaries sought through negotiating what they had not gained through fighting.

In both cases, the fact that there were negotiations, and that these were protracted, encouraged a war-weariness that American presidents could not ignore. War-weariness gave rise to controversy over war aims. As war aims were adjusted to respond to domestic criticism, concessions were made at the conference table. These concessions, instead of encouraging the adversary to respond in kind, encouraged intransigence in the expectation that other concessions would follow. In the process, the American negotiator was instructed to seek less than had been achieved in the fighting while the adversary relentlessly sought to gain at the conference table what it could not on the battlefield.

The diary of Vice Admiral C. Turner Joy, the first head of the U.N. delegation to the Korean Armistice Conference, records one American's view of how difficult it is to negotiate while fighting. It is an account of the frustrations of the United Nations Command delegates in negotiating with, on the one hand, the North Korean and Chinese Communist delegates to the Korean Armistice Conference, and, on the other, with the White House, the State Department, and the Joint Chiefs of Staff. To Admiral Joy, a major problem with the negotiations stemmed from Washington's need to be responsive to demands that the United States should, as one editorial at the time put it, "Save lives, not face" by concluding the negotiations as rapidly as possible. In his own view, neither lives nor face would be saved, nor would the conference proceed rapidly, unless and until the U.N. Command made clear its basic position and stood firm thereafter. Only such firmness, Joy believed, would induce the Communists to agree to a cease-fire that would last.

As the diary shows, Joy was not permitted to follow his belief. Consequently, the U.N. Command's position tended to appear to the Communists as constantly open to change. Joy wanted to lay his cards on the table at the outset in order to discourage Communist hopes that time and their intransigence would erode

American resolve and generate unilateral concessions. Instead, Joy was instructed to reveal the U.N. position only an element at a time. While his strategy
was geared to the probability that the fighting as well as the negotiations would
be protracted, Joy received and necessarily obeyed instructions from Washington which assumed that "peace might be just around the next corner."[1]

In his own memoir published in 1955, Joy reviewed the course of the negotiations with a view to extracting the pertinent lessons about Communist negotiating
behavior. But in the following passage he took an especially critical look at the
U.S. approach, and it provides the context in which his diary should now be
read:

> We learned in Korea that crystallization of political objectives should precede
> initiation of armistice talks. All personnel in the United Nations Command dele-
> gation were aware of the chameleon-like character of American political objec-
> tives in Korea. United States forces entered Korea, in accord with political
> objectives, to prevent an impending collapse in the South Korean Government
> and to help repel aggression against South Korea. When the North Korean ag-
> gressor was thrown back north of the 38th parallel from whence he came, these
> two political objectives had been secured. Then United States policy shifted to the
> intent to unify Korea. Accordingly, United Nations Command forces swept north
> of the 38th parallel, headed for the Yalu. When the Red Chinese plunged into
> the fray, the controlling political objective of the United States became a desire
> to avoid all-out war with China. When the Soviets suggested an armistice, the
> political objectives in Korea became an honorable cease-fire. During the armistice
> negotiations, we took on a political objective of gaining a propaganda victory
> over Communism in respect to prisoners of war. Thus the political objectives
> of the United States in Korea weather-vaned with the winds of combat, accom-
> modating themselves to current military events rather than constituting the goal
> to be reached through military operations. Consequently, the delegation, and
> indeed General Ridgway, never knew when a new directive would emanate from
> Washington to alter our basic objective of obtaining an honorable and stable armis-
> tice agreement. In such circumstances it is most difficult to develop sound plans,
> to present one's case convincingly, to give an appearance of unmistakable firm-
> ness and finality. It seemed to us that the United States Government did not
> know exactly what its political objectives in Korea were or should be. As a result,
> the United Nations Command delegation was constantly looking over its shoulder,

---

1. This illusion was later well described by Joy's superior, the commander in chief of the United
Nations Command, General Matthew B. Ridgway, in the following terms: "I was not unfamiliar
with the Communist tactic of trying to wear down an opponent through endless and pointless
argument . . . but I could not begin to foresee the wearying months of fruitless discussion that
lay ahead. . . . It seemed to me, with a cease-fire faintly visible on the horizon, that I should do all I
could to keep our losses at a justifiable minimum. . . . When the first anniversary of the opening of
hostilities arrived, I thought peace might be just around the next corner. Yet there were still two years
and many lives and much blood between us and this constant dream of every soldier." *The Korean
War* (Garden City, N.Y.: Doubleday, 1967), pp. 182−83.

fearing a new directive from afar which would require action inconsistent with that currently being taken.[2]

The diary Joy wrote during his ten months in Korea constituted the evidentiary base on which he reached the conclusion that the negotiating "strategy" he was instructed to follow protracted both the armistice conference and the war.

The initiative that led to direct negotiations between the U.N. Command and the Communist side came from a Soviet proposal in late June 1951.[3] The negotiations of the Korean Armistice Conference opened on July 10. They were to extend to the signing of the armistice document on July 27, 1953. To President Truman and his advisers, the Chinese entry into the war in late 1950 and the mounting U.S. casualties—fully 45 percent of all U.S. casualties were to occur during the negotiating-while-fighting period—had made a negotiated settlement, not military victory, essential. To push for military victory might escalate the conflict into a world war, while to fail to end it through negotiations would constitute a setback for U.S. foreign policy and encourage subversive Communist movements elsewhere. Stalemating the enemy was, therefore, essential to keeping a limited war limited and hastening, Truman believed, fruitful negotiations.

The negotiations, however, were repeatedly deadlocked over three basic issues. The first concerned the withdrawal of all foreign forces from the peninsula. This was sought by the Chinese Communists, who claimed their soldiers were "volunteers" and hence not liable to a withdrawal provision. The U.N.

---

2. *How Communists Negotiate* (New York: Macmillan, 1955), pp. 173–74.
3. In preparing this introduction I learned some new details on the origins of the Soviet initiative from Paul Nitze who was director of the State Department's Policy Planning Staff in 1951. About a month before the Soviet representative to the U.N., Deputy Foreign Minister Jacob Malik, proposed armistice talks (during a June 23 broadcast of the "Price of Peace" radio program), Thomas J. Cory (an advisor to the U.S. delegation to the U.N.) telephoned Nitze and asked for an urgent appointment. The following day in Washington, Cory described to Nitze a conversation that he had had with Semen Tsarapkin, the Soviet deputy U.N. representative. Tsarapkin, Cory said, after a long denunciation of the U.S. and its actions in Korea, concluded with a few sentences that indicated that Moscow might be ready to support armistice talks on Korea.
Nitze immediately informed Dean Acheson. Both were puzzled by the channel of communication Moscow had chosen and the implied change from the previous Soviet line. They decided to enlist George Kennan's help (Kennan was not then part of the government). Kennan agreed to explore with Malik, on a purely personal basis, whether the Soviet government might now take a favorable view toward Korean armistice negotiations. Kennan did so, indicating that it was his personal view that the U.S. government would react favorably if Moscow were interested. Malik said that he was about to leave for consultations in Moscow and would inform Kennan if there were any change in the Soviet attitude toward armistice talks when he returned. U.S. planning for the talks really began, Nitze recalled, on the strength of the Cory-Tsarapkin conversation, and Malik's non-denial of the possibility that the Soviet Union might be interested. Malik never did inform Kennan; his June 23 broadcast took place with no further communication to Kennan or the U.S. government.

Command maintained, of course, that Chinese withdrawal was a prerequisite to a cease-fire. The second source of deadlock concerned the boundary between the two Koreas. The North Korean and Chinese Communists wanted the 38th parallel as the boundary, while the UNC argued for the battle line to avoid recognizing the 38th parallel as anything more than a temporary demarcation. The third issue involved the procedures to be followed in repatriating prisoners of war. The Communists initially wanted all POWs automatically repatriated, while the UNC sought a process permitting those North Korean and Chinese soldiers who wanted to remain in the South to do so.

From the outset, it was also clear that the UNC and the Communist delegations viewed the scope of the talks differently. The U.N. side sought negotiations strictly confined to the terms of an armistice. The nine-point agenda it submitted (*see* diary, July 7, 1951) called for "limitation of discussion at this and all subsequent meetings to purely military matters related to Korea only" and implied the necessity for a complex truce-supervision system to assure that the cease-fire would last. The Communist agenda suggested negotiations for a political as well as a military solution to the war.

The basic agenda as adopted on July 25 included the following points or, as Admiral Joy refers to them in the diary, "items":

1. Adoption of the agenda.

2. Fixing a military demarcation line between both sides so as to establish a de-militarized zone as the basic condition for cessation of hostilities in Korea.

3. Concrete arrangements for the realization of cease-fire and armistice in Korea, including the composition, authority, and functions of a supervisory organ for carrying out the terms of cease-fire and armistice.

4. Arrangements relating to prisoners of war.

5. Recommendations to the governments of the countries concerned on both sides.[4]

The negotiations began in a teahouse located behind Communist lines at Kaesong. Admiral Joy saw in this bleak place, surrounded by heavily armed North Korean "guards," an indicator of how the Communists would approach the talks. "What irked me more than anything," he wrote after the first meeting, "was . . . that the entire conference area is continually heavily guarded and no real freedom given the UN Delegation. The reason is obvious—we are considered the vanquished suing them for an armistice."

The proximity of the war, moreover, increased the chances that the negotiators themselves might come under attack, as indeed they did. In protest over being accidentally strafed, the Communists broke off the talks on August 23. They did

---

4. *How Communists Negotiate*, p. 27. *See* diary, July 16–25, for the revised agenda adopted July 26.

not resume until October 25, at a new site—the no man's land of the battle line at Panmunjom.

By November 27 the negotiators had reached agreement that the cease-fire line would be coterminous with the battle line rather than the 38th parallel, but further agreements were long in coming and the issue of POW repatriation remained unsettled until April 11, 1953—five weeks after the death of Stalin. It was then that the proposal allowing POWs who did not wish repatriation to be demobilized to a neutral nation was accepted in principle by the Communist side.

This turning point, many believe, came as a result of considerable U.S. pressure on the Soviet Union's new leaders to persuade the North Koreans to reach a negotiated cease-fire. The origin of this policy of pressure lay in General Dwight D. Eisenhower's pledge that, if elected president, he would go to Korea and then develop a plan to end the war. He visited the peninsula on December 2−5, 1952, and concluded that "we could not stand forever on a static front and continue to accept casualties without any visible results."[5] Eisenhower was increasingly appalled thereafter as president that U.N. forces were sustaining heavy casualties for little, if any, gain.

Counting on the fear that the prospect of atomic war was likely to create in the minds of North Korea's allies, he considered that "one possibility to break the deadlock in the negotiations was to let the Communist authorities understand that, in the absence of negotiating progress, we intended to move decisively without inhibition in our use of weapons, and would no longer be responsible for confining hostilities to the Korean peninsula."[6] Dropping words rather than bombs worked. By June 8, 1953, the negotiators had agreed to give a neutral commission responsibility for the POWs not seeking repatriation. They also agreed that the POWs' country of origin would be given a period of ninety days in which to appeal to them to return before they would actually become parolees in another country.

These procedures were still not to the liking of the South Koreans, who favored continuing the war, carrying it northward, and simply releasing those anti-Communist POWs who wanted to remain in the South. The last course was taken by South Korea's President Syngman Rhee on June 18 and led to yet another breakdown of the talks. Only after substantial U.S. pledges to assist the Republic of Korea in rebuilding the country and its army did the Rhee government agree to accept the truce agreement.[7]

The armistice permitted the U.N. Command to remain in South Korea, established the battle line as the dividing line between North and South Korea, and left the repatriation of POWs to a neutral nations' commission—all objectives sought by the U.N. side. While Eisenhower "viewed the outcome

5. *Mandate for Change* (Garden City, N.Y.: Doubleday, 1963), p. 95.
6. Ibid., p. 181.
7. Ibid., pp. 181−87.

with a measure of satisfaction,'' he also observed that ''this was tempered by the haunting doubt that any peaceful negotiation could reunite Korea until the basic conflict between the Free World and Communism would one day be resolved.''[8]

While the administration doubted whether the armistice would lead to a political settlement on the Korean peninsula, in the academic community others were busily engaged in extracting the lessons of the Korean experience. Harvard professor Henry Kissinger summarized the conclusions of many when he wrote:

> Our decision to stop military operations, except those of a purely defensive nature, at the *very beginning* of the armistice negotiations reflected our conviction that the process of negotiation operated on its own inherent logic independently of the military pressures brought to bear. But by stopping military operations we removed the only Chinese incentive for a settlement; we produced the frustration of two years of unconclusive negotiations. In short, our insistence on divorcing force from diplomacy caused our power to lack purpose and our negotiations to lack force.[9]

Thus was the Korean experience full of lessons about the relationship between fighting and negotiating that would ultimately go unheeded. It is a small but interesting happenstance that one of the destroyers allegedly attacked by North Vietnamese patrol boats in the Gulf of Tonkin was the *Turner Joy*. That incident deepened U.S. involvement in another limited war in Asia—something Joy would have recommended against. For during his term as senior delegate at the Korean Armistice Conference he had recognized that self-imposed limitations encouraged the adversary to continue fighting, weakened support for the war effort at home, and protracted the fighting.

Joy's ten months as senior delegate for the U.N. Command ended with his being given another assignment, which he desired. By then he had won authority from the Joint Chiefs of Staff to stand firm. On April 28, 1952, he submitted to the Communists what was termed the UNC's final package proposal:

> I told the Communists that that was the end of negotiating; thenceforward the question was simply one of take it or leave it. For our part, there were to be no more concessions, no substantive changes in the draft armistice agreement. That was it. . . . I departed the Korean Armistice Conference for assignment as Superintendent of the United States Naval Academy on May 22, 1952. Major General William K. Harrison of the United States Army replaced me as Senior Delegate. Though General Harrison is an unusually able officer whose skill as a negotiator is beyond question, there was really nothing left to negotiate.[10]

The reading of Admiral Joy's diary does not indicate that in preparing for the negotiations he profited from any in-depth official analysis of Communist nego-

---

8. Ibid., p. 191.
9. *Nuclear Weapons and Foreign Policy* (New York: Norton, 1957), pp. 50–51; emphasis in original.
10. *How Communists Negotiate*, pp. 156, 161.

tiating style to serve as his guide. One may assume, therefore, that a book containing reminiscences by senior U.S. military officers concerning their dealings with Soviet officials during World War II, attracted his sustained attention and led him to make extensive notes from it.[11] The essence of what Joy learned from this "preparation," I think, can best be summed up by quoting from passages that he apparently wanted to keep constantly in mind:

> It is almost axiomatic that the vigor, vindictiveness, spleen and outright dishonesty of the Soviet argument increases in direct ratio with the weakness of its position.

> They would agree to a matter one day and repudiate the agreement the next, evidently having communicated with Moscow in the meantime, without any appearance of embarrassment at the inconsistency and with the blandest suavity of manner.

> After trying up to a certain point and finding that the demand cannot be put through the Soviet representative has often given in, only to turn to the next item in dispute, over which a similarly prolonged period of deadlock ensues.

> The principal lesson of these negots. [negotiations] is that in dealing with the Soviet Union there is no substitute for power.

As these passages suggest, Joy knew what to expect and based on this had conceived what he thought would be an appropriate negotiating strategy.

What had gone wrong? Joy's answer to this question is contained in the speech he delivered at Winston-Salem, North Carolina, on April 29, 1953, that precedes the text of the diary itself.

Admiral Joy kept a diary during his participation in the negotiations, first at Kaesong and then at Panmunjom, because he believed that only by recording the events of each day and his impressions at the time would he be equal to his Communist adversaries. Doubtless, too, this private diary gave him a ready reference aside from the official records, and the act of writing it by hand sorted out and impressed on his memory the points he wished to have immediately and correctly available. It is the verbatim text of the diary that is printed here. It greatly supplements the more thematic presentation given in his aforementioned book, which nonetheless is very valuable for reading in conjunction with it. Here, without discussion or hindsight, is the immediacy and suspensefulness of a day-to-day record of events as they happened.

The diary, presented to the Hoover Institution Archives by Captain C. Turner Joy, Jr., USN (Ret.), on November 6, 1974, consists of 1,024 pages, on 5½ x 8½ inch sheets, written in ink and gathered in three black leather ring-binders. There are also 11 sheets, 3½ x 6½ inches, on which Joy began the diary in

---

11. Raymond Dennett and Joseph E. Johnson, eds., *Negotiating with the Russians* (Boston: World Peace Foundation, 1951). Joy used thirty-one sheets of diary paper for copying extracts; they are kept with the diary at the Hoover Institution Archives.

pencil; these sheets cover the period from July 1 through July 10, 1951, when the final preparations were made for the opening of the conference. Joy also prepared a summary calendar of events as another reference tool and this is printed here at the end of the diary. Where deemed necessary or convenient for clarifying the text, editorial insertions are supplied in brackets; all words in parentheses are Joy's own. The printed version of this diary conforms as closely as possible to the original handwritten version, including spelling, punctuation, capitalization, and format. An exception is in the dates of each entry (month, day, and year), which have been arranged in a consistent format for the reader's convenience. Joy has emphasized material in his diary by the use of underlining, check marks in the margins, and both underlining and check marks. Indication of this emphasis is shown by the use of italics, boldface type, and boldface italics.

Since the diary simply plunges in, it will be helpful to know the way business was conducted at the conference. Joy described the staffing procedures in his book:

> As a general matter, we attempted to secure agreements on broad principles at the plenary sessions of full delegations. This being done, we arranged for meetings of subcommittees of delegates to expand upon the general principle that had been established in plenary sessions. We then had groups of staff officers discuss the finer details of the agreements reached by the delegates. Our liaison officers were charged to attend to "incidents" and to make arrangements governing the conditions of meetings. In the case both of the United Nations Command delegation and of the Communist delegation, the liaison officers were also notably active as staff officers.

> The United Nations Command delegation followed a practice of "staffing" all formal statements uttered in the armistice conference by delegates. Each day staff officers prepared a number of proposed statements for use by the delegates. These were considered and discussed by the delegates and staff officers in meetings at our camp at Munsan, before proceeding to Panmunjom for the day's events. The statement finally worked out was almost never the work of any one individual. It was the product of careful editing by all delegates and final approval by the Senior Delegate. Thus the benefit of all the fine intellects available to the delegation was used to the fullest.

> Subsequent to each day's meeting with the Communists, the United Nations Command delegates and staff officers gathered in my tent at Munsan, to discuss the steps to be taken the following day. When a basic decision was reached, staff officers prepared implementing statements for use on the morrow.[12]

Charles Turner Joy was born in St. Louis, Missouri, on February 17, 1895. A graduate of the U.S. Naval Academy in 1913, he held his first commission on the battleship *Pennsylvania,* which escorted President Wilson's ship to the Paris

---

12. *How Communists Negotiate*, pp. 168–69.

Peace Conference. After advanced training in engineering, Lieutenant Joy was posted to the staff of the commander of the Yangtze Patrol in China, where he served from 1923 to 1925. He met and married Martha Ann Chess at Hankow in 1924. Both their sons have followed military careers, C. Turner Joy, Jr., in the Navy and David Duncan Joy in the Army; their daughter, Mrs. Mary M. Joy Roll, appears briefly in the diary, as does "Dunc."

During World War II, Joy served on the *Lexington* and the *Louisville* in the Pacific, headed the Navy's Pacific Plans Division in Washington, and as rear admiral headed Cruiser Division 6 as it supported the drive toward the Japanese homeland. After the war he spent a year commanding Task Force 73 in Chinese waters and then was appointed commander of the Naval Proving Ground at Dahlgren, Virginia.

Joy became a vice admiral in 1949 and had command, headquartered in Tokyo, of the U.S. Naval Forces, Far East. This command grew to four hundred ships by the end of 1950 and was reponsible for all naval operations in the Korean War. After service at the Armistice Conference, Joy was superintendent of the U.S. Naval Academy. He retired in 1954 and died of leukemia on June 6, 1956.

I began editing the Joy diary while a National Fellow at the Hoover Institution in the spring of 1975. The introduction was written that fall, after I joined the Office of Political Research of the Central Intelligence Agency. However, this book is in no way sponsored by that or any other U.S. government agency, and the opinions and analyses contained herein should not be construed as reflecting official U.S. views.

I am grateful to Milorad M. Drachkovitch and Dennis Bark, Archivist and Assistant Director, respectively, of the Hoover Institution, for their support of my preparation of the manuscript of this book, and to Charles Palm, Deputy Archivist, and Jesse Phillips for their valuable editorial advice. C. Turner Joy, Jr., provided information about his father and the officers associated with him. I had the benefit also of discussions with Alexander George and with Herbert Goldhamer, and of research assistance in Washington from Dean Allard of the Operational Archives Branch, Naval Historical Center. Jeanne Nickerson and Linda Leiss prepared the typescript from the hand-written diary, an exacting task faithfully performed. My gratitude to all of these, of course, does not relieve me of responsibility for the result.

I should like to consider this book as being dedicated to the memory of C. Turner Joy, and to believe that the reading of it will help those concerned with the theory and practice of diplomacy generally to understand better how what is done at the conference table may encourage an adversary to prolong a conflict rather than end it.

Washington, D.C. ALLAN E. GOODMAN

Photographs

Kaesong, initial site of the Military Armistice Conference between the United Nations and Communist delegations, July 1951. (*U.S. Air Force*)

The initial group of senior United Nations officers at the armistice talks (*left to right*): Rear Admiral Arleigh A. Burke, USN; Major General Paik Sun Yup, commander of Republic of Korea I Corps; Vice Admiral C. Turner Joy, USN, team leader; Major General Laurence C. Craigie, USAF, Far East Air Forces; and Major General Henry I. Hodes, USA, deputy chief of staff, Eighth Army. (*U.S. Air Force*)

North Korean Communist delegates at Kaesong: Lieutenant General Nam Il, senior delegate, followed by Major General Lee Sang Cho and Major General Chang Pyong San. (*U.S. Air Force*)

The conference area at Panmunjom, site of the armistice talks after the transfer from Kaesong in October 1951. Meetings were held in the two large tents in the center; the darker tents at the right were for the use of the delegates. (*U.S. Army*)

At the United Nations base camp, Munsan, November 8, 1951: arrival of General Matthew B. Ridgway, commander in chief of the United Nations Command, met by Vice Admiral C. Turner Joy, senior United Nations' delegate to the Military Armistice Conference. (*U.S. Army*)

The United Nations Command delegation at Panmunjom, February 6, 1952 (*left to right*): Major General Yu Chae Heung, Republic of Korea Army; Major General William K. Harrison, USA; Vice Admiral C. Turner Joy, USN; Major General Howard M. Turner, USAF; Rear Admiral Ruthven E. Libby, USN. (*U.S. Army*)

United Nations Command delegates and staff officers in a daily meeting at the Munsan base camp. (*U.S. Army*)

February 1952: political demonstration by internees at the United Nations prisoner-of-war compound, Koje-do. (*U.S. Army*)

Texts
by Admiral Joy

The Korean Truce Talks as I Saw Them

by Vice Admiral C. Turner Joy, USN

An Address to be Delivered in Connection
with Armed Forces Day at
Winston-Salem, North Carolina

On May 22, 1952, nearly a year ago, when I turned over my job as senior delegate of the UNC Delegation to Major General Harrison, the wording of only one paragraph, in an armistice document containing sixty-two paragraphs, stood in the way of an honorable agreement. That controversial paragraph, as you know, deals with the much publicized prisoner of war issue. After a bitter verbal battle lasting over ten months all paragraphs but that one had been agreed upon.

The story of our battle in reaching agreement on the sixty-one paragraphs is much too long and involved to tell you tonight. But the story of *why* our battle was so long and bitter and *why* we could not reach agreement on the prisoner of war question is much more quickly and easily told. I shall confine my remarks primarily to the latter story in the hope that it will give you an insight into the difficulties of trying to negotiate with the Communists.

Now if you remember, when Jacob Malik, Soviet representative in the United Nations, made his proposal for a Korean truce on June 23, 1951, many people believed the Communists wanted an Armistice badly enough to agree on reasonable terms. I was one of them. Their armies had taken a beating on the battlefield the month before when they had attacked in strength. In that abortive May offensive they had suffered some 200,000 casualties. The Eighth Army had counterattacked and was slowly pushing them beyond the 38th parallel. Though by no means decisively defeated, the Communists were in a bad way and needed a cease-fire to repair their battered war machine.

Consequently, since we were negotiating from a position of military strength, it did not surprise me too much when we of the UNC Delegation made progress in those earlier days of the Armistice Conference. To be sure it was slower progress than anyone had expected, due mainly to irritating interruptions and Communist intransigence, but it was progress nonetheless. For example, it took only ten meetings to reach agreement on an agenda for the Conference in spite of a wide difference of opinion as to the wording and contents of the agenda.

The first of these agenda items reads as follows: "The fixing of a military demarcation line between both sides so as to establish a demilitarized zone as a basic condition for the cessation of hostilities in Korea."

On July 26 when the two delegations began the main discussions on this item the Communists were adamant in their insistence that the demarcation line separating the two forces must be none other than the 38th parallel. Our own position was that the demarcation line should be based generally on the battle line, which, as you will remember, was considerably north of the 38th parallel in all areas of military significance. We were not of a mind to save Communist face by withdrawing from hard-won ground above the 38th parallel thus erasing any penalty for their war of aggression. The Communists presented many arguments in support of the 38th parallel, none of which were any good and all of which were refuted many times. Some were downright ridiculous. For example, they contended that since the war started on the 38th parallel it should end there. When their arguments failed them they took refuge in vituperation, insults, and rage. You could always tell their estimate of the progress they were making from the amount of obnoxious propaganda that blared forth on the Communist radio and in their press. When they were not doing so well it intensified. I presume this was their idea of putting pressure on their opponents.

Finally the Communists had to accept the fact that no amount of vituperation or rage was going to make us agree to the 38th parallel. In order to gain time to figure out their next move they created a fake incident on August 22, charged us with a violation of the Conference neutral zone and then recessed the talks. This recess lasted for two months. During this period the Eighth Army launched a number of limited offensives that were costly in territory for the enemy. At the same time it was announced that as the battle line moved north so would the demarcation line. The enemy began to see the light and requested a resumption of the talks. At General Ridgway's insistence they also accepted a new conference site at Panmunjom, a site more acceptable to us than Kaesong.

When the talks were resumed on October 25, we had heard the last of the 38th parallel. The enemy had come around to our idea that the battle line should be the basis for the demilitarized zone. However there was an important difference. The Communists wanted to fix the *then* existing battle line as the FINAL demarcation line between both sides. Their strategy was obvious. If the line were fixed, once and for all, there would be no reason for the Eighth Army to push them further north because we would have to give them back the territory we had gained when and if an armistice was signed. In short, the Communists wanted a *de facto* cease-fire then and there as a relief from the Eighth Army's pressure.

But we insisted that the demarcation line be the battle line as of the time of the signing of the armistice. We realized if the line were fixed permanently before completion of the negotiations the Communists could stall to their hearts content over the remaining items of the agenda. General Ridgway and the delegation felt very strongly that this was a situation calling for more steel and less silk. We felt certain the Communists would eventually give in on this point, thus assuring us of the retention of the negotiating initiative and of continuing pressure by the Eighth Army.

However, orders came through to agree to the then existing battle line as a provisional demarcation line with a thirty-day time limit. This was done in a plenary session on November 27. Presumably the decision had been made on the basis that it would serve as an incentive for the Communists to show good faith by speeding up agreement on honorable and equitable terms. Instead of showing good faith they dragged their feet at every opportunity and used the thirty days of grace to dig in and stabilize their battle line.

In retrospect, I believe this was the turning point of the Armistice Conference, and a principal reason progress slowed to a snail's pace from then on. In demonstrating our own good faith we lost the initiative, never to regain it. We were no longer negotiating from a position of strength but from a position of military stalemate. And slowly before our eyes that which we wanted most to avoid began to happen—the balance of military advantages began to shift in favor of the enemy. The end of the thirty-day time limit was just another date on the calendar. No one wanted to launch another ground offensive because the psychological handicap would be too large to overcome. The impetus was gone. And if the UNC did launch an offensive it would be with the foreknowledge that the price would be extremely high because of the time the enemy had been given to prepare.

Rather late, and yet comparatively early, in our efforts to end the war, we had to learn that in negotiating with the Communists there is no substitute for the imperative logic of military pressure. In other words, we learned that progress in negotiating with them is in direct proportion to the degree of military pressure applied.

In order that you may better understand why it is so difficult to do business with the Communists, I want to tell you at this point something of what we learned about their personality during the debates on the demilitarized zone. I have already told you how they take refuge in vituperation, rage and insults when their arguments fail them.

One of their most noticeable characteristics is a deep feeling of inferiority. We ran into it at every turn. One day General Nam Il, their senior delegate, called attention to the fact that I had spoken for seventy minutes. The next day, not to be outdone, he spoke for 110 minutes. On the first day of the Conference we placed a small standard with the United Nations flag in the center of the table.

When we returned from a recess we found a North Korean flag flying from a standard several inches taller than ours. The day after I drove to Panmunjom for the first time in an Army Chevrolet sedan, Nam Il who had always ridden in a jeep before, arrived in a captured Chrysler. They could never match us with helicopters, however, and I think that really bothered them.

Another obvious characteristic is their hatred and suspicion of capitalism and the free world. One day during a period of silence when we glared at each other across the table for two hours and ten minutes without saying a single word, I noticed that our own General Paik, the South Korean delegate, was valiantly striving to restrain his anger. After the meeting I asked him what had been the matter. He said that North Korean Major General Lee Sang Jo who sat opposite him had passed a note to Nam Il. The note written in red crayon and in Korean characters large enough to read across the table said: ''The Imperialist errand boys are lower than dogs in a morgue.'' To a Korean this is the worst of insults.

Still another characteristic was their apparent lack of latitude in negotiating. They were mere puppets who were bound hand and foot by the explicit instructions of their superiors. The vehemence with which they attempted to carry out instructions was no doubt inspired by the instinct of self-preservation. Presumably, they were afraid of their necks if they failed. They never gave an immediate definite answer to any of our proposals no matter how minor. Instead they would invariably say: ''We will study your proposition and let you know later.'' Judging from the time it took to get an answer we could generally guess whether the matter was referred to Peiping or Moscow for a decision. Naturally this was very time-consuming. Incidentally it soon became evident that the Chinese were the real bosses at the Conference table. Nam Il never said anything of importance without first getting the nod from General Hsieh Fang, one of the two Chinese members of the opposing delegation and the smartest one of the lot.

As soon as the question of the demarcation line was settled we plunged into discussions of the next topic on the agenda which read: ''Concrete arrangements for the realization of cease-fire and armistice in Korea, including the composition, authority, and functions of a supervisory organ for carrying out the terms of cease-fire and armistice.''

It took 155 days of meetings with the Communists to boil down the unsolved issues under this topic to two, namely; (1) a ban on the construction and rehabilitation of airfields during the armistice, and (2) the composition of the Neutral Nations Supervisory Commission for carrying out behind-the-lines inspection. We had nominated Norway, Sweden, and Switzerland as members of this commission, whereas the Communists had nominated Poland, Czechoslovakia, and (believe it or not) the USSR. We accepted the first two, but of course categorically rejected the Soviet Union as a neutral. Before leaving this subject I would like to give another illustration of what it is like to deal with the Communists. When the Communists originally proposed that behind-the-lines inspection be done by representatives of neutral nations, they stated, and we agreed, that the criterion for nations selected should be their acceptability to both sides. When they nominated the USSR, we rejected the nomination as unacceptable. The Communists then blithely repudiated their agreement and said that what they actually meant was that all nations nominated should automatically be acceptable to the other side. We emphatically rejected the new interpretation.

The main reason it took so long to narrow the unsolved questions down to two lay in the wide divergence between ourselves and the Communists in our approach to this topic of the agenda. We considered it most important and the real heart of the armistice agreement. On the other hand we soon learned that all the Communists wanted was a simple cease-fire, as distinguished from a bona fide armistice with suitable supervision and adequate safeguards. Nam Il's plan for a truce was a model of simplicity. The shooting would stop and both sides would withdraw from the demilitarized zone. In short we were to assume the millenium had arrived, that the Communists had forsaken their warlike intentions for all time. I proposed that, in addition to the arrangements for a simple cease-fire, the military capabilities of both sides remain frozen during the armistice and that an adequate system of inspection and supervision be instituted. Our proposal represented the difference between a simple cease-fire and a reasonably stable armistice and judging by the loud and violent resistance over many months, that difference made all the difference in the world to the Communists.

In order to speed up the snail's pace progress, I proposed simultaneous discussions by two different sub-delegations on this item and the next item of the agenda, namely: "Arrangements pertaining to Prisoners of War." The Communists, of course, protested but in the end reluctantly agreed and on December 11, 1951, we began the long-drawn-out negotiations on the prisoner question.

At the initial meeting of the sub-delegation handling the POW question the Communists made another one of their malevolently naive suggestions. They said: "In order to reach a quick agreement on this item of the agenda we think it best to release all prisoners of war after the armistice and let them go home soon." This was a little too simple for us. What did the Communists mean when they said all? Did they mean only the 110 prisoners they had reported to Geneva? Or did they mean roughly 70,000 they had boasted over the radio as having captured during the first nine months of the war? We had no means of knowing and they refused to tell us. They wanted us to agree to the principle of an all for all exchange of prisoners before they would exchange lists of names. Of course, we refused to buy a pig in a poke. We insisted on an exchange of lists of prisoners' names so we would know what we were talking about.

Finally our sub-delegation wore them down and they agreed to exchange the lists of names. We handed them a list containing about 132,000 names and they handed us one containing only 11,559. Their list included only 3,198 U.S. personnel or hardly 27 percent of the number of U.S. personnel missing in action.

We were, of course, dumbfounded at the paucity of the list handed us. When we demanded an explanation as to what had happened to the large number of prisoners they boasted as having captured they blandly said that they had died or had been released at the front and were home leading peaceful lives. What they probably meant was that more than 50,000 captured South Korean soldiers had been impressed into their armies.

The details of what went on during the next several months on this prisoner of war question are numerous and involved. Let me summarize by saying that the UNC proposed initially to return to the Communists every one we held who wanted to go back to their side. In other words we proposed the principle of voluntary repatriation. As you know, there had been thousands in our POW camps who had already indicated they would rather die than go back to their former masters. Subsequently we modified our position to one of no forced repatriation, that is, only those who would forcibly resist returning to Communist control would be permitted to stay on our side.

In the long weeks and months of debate, the Communists presented only two objections to voluntary repatriation. They claimed it was contrary to the Geneva Conventions and that it was a "sinister scheme" to "forcibly detain large numbers of prisoners of war." It was very odd to hear the Communists piously quoting from the Geneva Conventions after they had systematically and deliberately broken every rule in the book during the war.

The debate wore on. Finally in the latter part of March the Communists indicated they would be willing to seek a solution to the prisoner question on the basis of "round numbers" to be returned. The implication was that if a sufficient number of people held by us elected to go north, or indicated they would not forcibly resist going north, the Communists would accept the figure. We pointed out that the only way to arrive at such a "round number" would be to screen the prisoners the UNC had in custody and thus determine their attitudes. When the Communists tacitly agreed on April 4 the screening operation was set in motion.

By the time we undertook to screen the prisoners, then, the three major stumbling blocks in the way of an armistice were the ban on airfields, the composition of the neutral nations commission, and the basis of prisoner repatriation.

To the unqualified amazement of everyone at our base camp the screening of prisoners revealed that only an estimated 70,000 persons in our custody would return to the Communist side without the application of force. When this figure was presented to the Communists they replied with a torrent of vituperation while their propaganda machine shifted into high gear. The die was cast. The time had come for a showdown. I called for a plenary session and on April 28, for the first time in more than two months, the full delegations met.

In that meeting I did what I had wanted to do for a long time. I presented a package proposal embodying our final effort to reach agreement. This compromise solution, originated in Washington, was incorporated in the draft of an entire armistice agreement consisting of sixty-two paragraphs. The crux of the solution was that we agreed to omit the paragraph prohibiting the construction of military airfields during an armistice provided the Communists would give in on the prisoner of war issue. In the paragraph designating member nations of the Neutral Nations Supervisory Commission we compromised by omitting our nominee Norway and their nominee the USSR.

I pointed out to Nam Il that our offer would have to be accepted in toto or rejected in toto. It was not subject to piecemeal negotiation—in fact it was not subject to negotiation at all. After ten long months we had reached the end of the line. It gave me a feeling of relief and satisfaction, I can assure you, to be able to lay our final offer on the table.

The Communist reception of our final package proposal was typical. They blandly said in effect: ''We have told you all along that the airfield question was an internal affair of ours and therefore none of your business. We are glad you saw the light. If you would only be reasonable on the POW question the armistice would be in the bag.'' This is the way they negotiate. As we understand negotiation it is to give something and get something in return. In other words both parties work from opposite ends towards a common goal, the process commonly known as quid pro quo. The Communist idea is what Secretary of Defense Lovett accurately described as ''quid pro quid.'' You offer a concession in exchange for one on their part and they take your concession as a fait accompli. But they even go further than that. To them the very fact that you offer a concession is a sign of weakness, and shows that their will is stronger than yours. Their attitude seems to say: ''Let's sit back and wait them out and maybe they will give some more.'' I am sure they regard our willingness even to continue a discussion as a sign of weakness. As long as we continue to talk they assume our position must not be too firm. That is why I strongly recommended to higher authority before I left the Far East last June that the UNC recess the Conference indefinitely to emphasize the finality of our package proposal. As you know this was finally done on October 8 of last year.

Between the time I presented our final proposal and the time of the Koje-do prison camp riots, some ten days, the Communists were in bad shape from a propaganda standpoint. They had lost tremendous face in the fact that only 70,000 out of some 132,000 of their people were willing to return to their control without the application of force. And they did not dare to accept our offer to verify the results of the screening by participating in a joint rescreening after the armistice. Then came the Koje-do riots, which lent an air of plausibility to their contention that the UNC was forcibly detaining their people. The incidents were made to order for the Communist propaganda mill, which immediately went on a twenty-four-hour day, seven-day week basis. We always suspected that these riots were deliberately instigated by the Communist Delegation itself through its underground. Later this was proved to be so.

My last two memorable weeks at Panmunjom convinced me that the Communists were not interested in reaching a fair and humanitarian solution to the prisoner of war question. I say this because of their vicious propaganda statements. Replete with distortions and falsehoods, these statements were designed solely to lend credibility to their claim that the UNC was forcibly detaining their people. The statements were directed almost entirely to the emotions of the Communist world and not to the intelligence of their opponents. The Communists just could not face or accept the fact that large numbers of their people including their so-called volunteers would rather die than return to Communist control. Furthermore, the principle of voluntary repatriation symbolized the fundamental difference between the free world and the Communist world. As you know in the free world the individual counts for everything; in the Communist world the individual counts for nothing and the state for everything. There is no such thing as individual free choice in the Communist world.

Many people have asked me my opinion as to what lay behind the Communist actions at the truce talks. I believe it is as simple as this. They entered into the negotiations, not with sincerity and high purpose, but rather to gain time to repair their shattered forces and to try to accomplish at the conference table what their armies could not accomplish in the field. In short they used the talks as a tactical maneuver. When they had regained their strength they were interested in an armistice only on their own terms.

The net result of my ten months of meeting with the Communists convinces me beyond the shadow of a doubt that in dealing with them there is no substitute for power. As I have said publicly before, and as I say again, the only way to negotiate with them is through patience and unmistakable firmness backed up by military force and the willingness to use that force. Nothing else makes sense to the Communist mind. They are not impressed by logic nor are they remotely concerned with morality. Their guiding precept is that the end justifies the means. The only arguments they understand are our Army, Navy, and Air Force. The only factor that impresses them is our military power in being. And the only real persuader we have is our willingness to use that power. It is idle and foolish to think otherwise; in fact, it may be suicidal from the national standpoint.

I have taken many words to say what is summarized in only three words in the theme for Armed Forces Day this year. That theme is "Power for Peace." We must not allow ourselves to be lulled into a false sense of security by honeyed and hollow words of peace from behind the Iron Curtain. And we must not forget that the best insurance for peace is the same today as it has always been in the past—a strong National Defense.

April 29, 1953

Diary, July 1-10, 1951

July 1 [1951]. 0900: Conference with Ridgway on question of cease fire meeting with Commies. Discussed agenda and procedures, time & place. Wonsan harbor on Jutlandia. Primary purpose of U.N. delegates at 1st meeting is to determine in their own minds whether or not the enemy delegates appear to be acting in good faith and appear willing to seek agreement on the conditions for bringing about a cessation of hostilities and of acts of armed force in Korea, under conditions which will provide assurances for the security of the forces of both sides and against the resumption of hostilities or acts of armed force in Korea for an extended period.*

Arrived at agenda which follows and which was transmitted to JCS.

a. Adoption of agenda.

b. Limitation of discussion at this and all subsequent meetings to purely military matters related to Korea only.

c. Cessation of hostilities and acts of armed force in Korea under conditions which will assure against resumption of hostilities and acts of armed force in Korea.

d. Agreement on a demilitarized zone across Korea.

e. Composition, authority and functions of Military Armistice Commission.

f. Agreement on principle of inspection within Korea by military observer teams, functioning under Military Armistice Commission.

g. Composition and functions of these teams.

h. Agreements pertaining to Prisoners of War.

Ridgway particularly pointed out that:

a. 1st meeting was primarily to determine good faith of enemy, and,

b. To see if Commies will accept agenda.

---

*The printed version of this diary conforms as closely as possible to the original handwritten version, including spelling, punctuation, capitalization, and format. An exception is in the dates of each entry (month, day, and year), which have been arranged in a consistent format for the reader's convenience. Joy has emphasized material in his diary by the use of underlining, check marks in the margins, and both underlining and check marks. Indication of this emphasis is shown by the use of italics, boldface type, and boldface italics.—Ed.

Other points stressed:
1. 38th parallel has no military significance.
2. Primary consideration is safety and security of U.N. Forces.
Agenda referred to Washington for approval.

July 2. 0930: Met with Ridgway, O. P. Weyland and Hickey to discuss Commie reply to CinCUNC's despatch proposing armistice conference. Main objection was that Commies proposed, first cease fire then negotiations, which would greatly facilitate their offensive build up since they would be free to continue build up while negotiations were taking place. Another objection was the delay until 10−15 July for 1st meeting. Kaesong proposed by Commies for meeting which though not as desirable as Wonsan offered no serious objections. CinCUNC's objections referred to Wash [Washington] for approval.

Since meeting is to be Kaesong, Ridgway brought up desirability of perhaps an Army officer acting as Senior representative. After discussion this was vetoed because most desirable Army officers were too involved with fighting and could not be pulled out of the front lines.

Spent remainder of day conferring with Kiland on set up at Inchon and with others on various details such as Logistic support of delegates, communications, Public Info, etc.

July 3. 1030: Held conference in my office with Burke, Hodes and Craige [*sic*] (Briggs present) to discuss procedures of 1st meeting. Points discussed were: No. [number] in party for Kaesong, procedural matters including introductory remarks, agenda.

1200. Ridgway's reply to Commies setting up preliminary meeting by liaison officer was broadcast on radio. Agreed to use of Kaesong for conference and July 10th for date.

1600. Conference with Ridgway on G-2 matters in which startling info on Soviets preparation for war was disclosed.

After briefing on Soviet capabalities [*sic*] some questions on peace negotiations were discussed including slight changes in agenda.

Read Wash despatch (JCS) which gave correct version of Commie reply to CinCUNCs original communication. This despatch approved agenda.

July 4: Ridgways despatch to Commies concerning preliminary meeting which proposed liaison officers meet on 5 July. It was not expected reply would be forthcoming in time to hold meeting on that date.

1230. Attended GHQ reception at GHQ club later about 1300 to American club.

1800. Attended reception at Sebalds [William J. Sebald, Acting U.S. Political Adviser to the supreme commander, Allied Powers]. Kislenko [Major

General A. P. Kislenko, Soviet member of the Allied Council for Japan] was there and being introduced by Army officer to many of guests. Noticed how many foreigners (not US) fawned on him.

Reply received from commies proposing preliminary meeting of liaison officers on 8 July.

July 5: Ridgway accepted Commie proposal for initial meeting on 8 July.

Discussed many moot points that might be raised at conference with Paul Nitze and Burke. Nitze left list of debatable questions that might come up. These were turned over to Wright to puzzle out with JSPOG.

Luncheon at Embassy for Governor Dewey, who appeared to be a very likeable chap. Much concerned about civil defense of N.Y. state.

Nitze left for U.S. in afternoon.

July 8. 1215: Met with Ridgway to discuss agenda items and my introductory remarks which were approved.

Agenda items same as before except "Authority for Int. [International] Red Cross to visit P.W. camps" included and "Arrangements for press Coverages & releases" was stricken out. Also discussed such matters as trip over to Korea which was set up for 10:30 tomorrow as Commies had agreed to first meeting at 1000 on the 10th.

Evening. Read JSPOG paper on studies of agenda items which I did not think was complete enough, as initial & minimum conditions were insufficiently covered.

July 9−14: Left Tokyo at 1030 morning of the 9th for Seoul with Ridgway and party arriving Seoul about 2:30 pm. Thence to base camp just south of Imjin River. Delighted to find on arrival that Duncan was around the corner in charge of the telephone switchboard. Spent remainder of day going over procedure for opening day and getting squared away in camp. My tent luxurious with wooden deck, cot with mosquito netting, wash stand and mirror etc.

July 10: Took off from base camp to arrive over Imjin river at 1000. Royal send off by R- and press. Dunc also put in an appearance. Read short statement prior leaving as follows: "We the delegation from the UNC are leaving for Kaesong fully conscious of the importance of these meetings to the entire world. We are proceeding in good faith, prepared to do our part to bring about an *honorable* armistice under terms that are satisfactory to the UNC.["] Newsmen called out "Good luck to you Admiral."

Upon arrival at Kaesong we were met at the Helicopter landing area by a N.K. Reception committee who took us to a stone house on the side of a hill reserved for U.N. House totally devoid of any conveniences and surrounded by guards with tommy-guns. We were informed meeting not scheduled to start until 1100. About 15 mins. before appointed time proceed in jeeps to meeting place. Armed troops noticed in doorways of houses enroute. About 4 sentries with guns standing at entrance to conference grounds. When our jeep attempted to proceed up driveway our way was blocked by a soldier with a tommy gun who motioned us along grass road.

We met the Commie Delegates in a small antiroom before proceeding to main conference chamber. They were stiff though polite and barely bowed as did we. Nam Il impressed me as a smart and shrewd young man. His history shows he is a thoroughly indoctrinated Communist. He is in his 30's so I'm told.

After assembling in conference room and exchanging formalities & credentials, I lead off with my speech, which Nam Il followed by a dissertation giving in effect the communist delegation's agenda. After introduction of our written agenda I asked Commies for a written copy of theirs which they could not produce. They then asked for 3½ hr recess.

We returned to UN house for lunch & talks. During interval we attempted to send courier back to inform Ridgway of our progress. Delay in getting his clearance necessitated calling off idea. After lunch Commie agenda was presented and much argument ensued in attempt to get them to generalize their agenda which they flatly refused to do. They also attacked our #2 Item (Red Cross) and its place on agenda.

After further wrangling which got nowhere except Commies definition of foreign troops the meeting was adjourned to following day. After arrival back at camp U.N. delegation spent rest of day drafting despatch to JCS and planning papers for next day.

A really hectic day.

NOTES: In Nam Ils opening speech on 10 July this was one of his basic proposals "To establish 38th parallel as the milt. [military] demarcation line, the armed forces on both sides to withdraw 10 kilometers from the 38th parallel, and simultaneously complete the withdrawal with a definite time limit, leaving evacuated area as a demilitarized zone, *and the civilian administration shall be restored as it was before June 25 1950.["]*

On 11 July Nam Il said did not consider 38th as imaginary line since line existed before & war broke out on that line. Therefore cease fire must be concluded on that line.

On 15 July he said again "It is only when 38th parallel has been established as dem line between both sides that question of armistice is possible."

Same emphasis on 38th parallel on 17 & 18 July.

SOME THOUGHTS: They knew what they were after and they were clever and ruthless in the way they pursued their objectives. Contradiction meant nothing to them, nor did they hesitate (blush) to twist and distort our statements and arguments to suit their purpose. Their basic dishonesty was shown by the way they would take our hypothetical viewpoints (arguments) and quote us as saying that those same hypothetical viewpoints represented our real beliefs. Whenever they were stumped for a good refutation of our arguments they would baldly assert that we were wrong. Later they would contend that this same assertion completely refuted our argument.

Diary, July 10, 1951–May 22, 1952

July 10 [1951]: Took off from Base Camp at Munsan Ni in helicopters to arrive over Imjin river at 1000. Royal send off by Ridgway and press. Dunc also put in an appearance. Read short statement prior to leaving as follows: "We the delegation from the UNC are leaving for Kaesong fully conscious of the importance of these meetings to the entire world. We are proceeding in good faith, prepared to do our part to bring about an honorable armistice under terms that are satisfactory to the UNC.["] Newsmen called out "Good luck to you Admiral."

Upon arrival at Kaesong we were met at Heli landing area by a Commie reception committee who took us to a stone house on the side of a hill, which was to be our Hdqtrs. House totally devoid of conveniences and surrounded by guards with tommy guns. We were informed meeting not scheduled to start until 1100. About 15 mins before appointed time proceeded in jeeps to meeting place. Armed troops noted in doorways of houses while enroute. About 4 sentries with guns standing at entrance to conference grounds. When our jeep attempted to proceed up driveway our way was blocked by a soldier with a tommy gun who looked us over before allowing us to proceed. We met the Commie delegates in a small ante room before proceeding to the main conference chamber. They were stiff though polite and barely bowed as did we. Nam Il impressed me as a smart and shrewd young man, very sure of himself. His history shows he is a thoroughly indoctrinated Communist, having served in the Soviet Army. Age about 35.

After assembling in the conference room and exchanging formalities and credentials I lead off with my introductory speech outlining our mission and emphasizing that UNC delegation would act in good faith. Nam Ils dissertation which followed gave in effect their agenda containing their two basic proposals based on Maliks proposal of June 23d. They were: withdrawal from 38th parallel [to a] distance of 10 kilometers and withdrawal of armed forces of all foreign countries from Korea as early as possible. Chinese Chief Delegate then gave short speech agreeing with Nam Il.

After introduction of our written agenda I asked Commies for a written copy of theirs which they could not produce. They then asked for 3½ hr recess. Time then 12:25. UNC Del [delegation] returned to UN house for lunch and discussion. During recess we attempted to send courier back to inform R of our progress. Delay in obtaining his clearance necessitated calling off idea. Upon reconvening at 1600 we continued to press for their agenda which they finally produced in 3 smooth copies, Korean Chinese & English. At this point four photographers dashed in and commenced taking pictures. We protested and after some delay they were withdrawn. We also protested delay of our courier. Commies apologized. We then proposed introduce 20 pressmen at subsequent meetings. Commies agreed—the first agreement! Nam Il later backed down on this agreement stating he had received no reply from his supreme Cmdr [commander]. Much argument ensued in our attempts to get Commies to generalize their agenda which they flatly refused to do. They also attacked our Item 2 (Red Cross[)] and its place on the agenda. After further wrangling which got nowhere except to bring out Commies definition of foreign troops we adjourned at 1815. An interesting high light occurred when Nam Il defined "Foreign troops" as "We mean all troops who are here under the permission of their governments so the foreign troops under the name of UN in Korea they are all foreign troops." A short time later the NK Chief Delegate stated, "By foreign troops we mean those troops not Korea[n], not in Korean Armies."

Attitude of Commie delegates can be summarized as follows: UNC Del felt that the Communist delegates believed prior to todays conference that acceptance could be obtained of a cease fire solution along the 38th parallel and the prompt withdrawal of all foreign troops from Korea. They have refused thus far to deviate from their stand. Too early to determine whether this is final or only initial party line. No major concessions and a few minor ones were made by Commies. It was obvious NK's had final say.

Nam Il is dominant figure on Commie side.

What irked me more than anything was to note that entire conference area is continually heavily guarded and no real freedom given UNC Delegation. The reason is obvious—We are considered the vanquished suing them for an armistice.

July 11: My instructions from R for this meeting included informing senior Communist Delegate that UNC cannot accept restrictions enemy has imposed. Our requirements: (1) Freedom of movement during daylight hrs to, from and within conference site. (2) presence of newsmen of major import [importance]. Must be admitted to conference site without further delay.

Conference convened at 1000 k[H]. Commies began by reiterating that they do not plan any restrictions on UNCD. Their concern mainly for our safety. After we pressed the issue of free transit Commies agreed to let properly marked vehicles move if they are notified of departure from Imjin River. Our discussion centered on admission of newsmen, disinterest in imaginary line with no milt. [military] significance, impossibility of including withdrawal of non Korean troops, explanation of our agenda. Commies discussed, our Red Cross item, priority of items. They could not see how armistice could be guaranteed without foreign troop withdrawal. They insist 38th parallel as dem [demarcation] line & withdrawal of troops are basic and inseparable. UNCD asked if Commies were willing to broaden their agenda item concerning the establishment of dem [demilitarized] zone on 38th since this only one line and there are many possible lines & zones. Quickly asked what line did we suggest. Also stated they did not consider 38th an imaginary line since line existed before and war broke out on that line. Therefore cease fire must be concluded on this line & must be on agenda. We closed meeting on press problem stating we insisted on bringing them. I asked for answer by 120730 [July 12, at 0730 hrs]. Nam Il reacted with considerable agitation inquiring if this meant UN wanted to discontinue meetings. He was advised that we wished to continue meetings but would recess until sessions can be resumed with newsmen present in conference area.

Nam Il remained dominant figure. sure of himself. Kept notes himself & talked directly from notes without prior consultation [with] other delegates. In a few instances he conversed with the 2nd ranking NK delegate on matters & through a Chinese interpreter to Gen Teng Hua. On matters relating to security of personnel he asked & received advice from Hsieh Fang, 2nd ranking Chink [Chinese] evidently in command of CCF in immediate area. CCF members appeared as junior and silent partners. NK delegates sensitive to any proposition concerning inspections or rpts. by Int Red Cross. Noticeable anxiety in NK group when my press statement was misunderstood to mean termination of future discussions.

July 12: Commie liaison officer advised ours at 0730 that they would welcome press when agreement on negotiations reached. We advised him convoy with pressmen already enroute. Our convoy was halted at Pan Mun Jom at 0830. When convoy Cmdr [commander] requested instructions R advised him remain until 0930 and if at that time all vehicles and personnel were not allowed to pass convoy was to return. I then dispatched msg [message] to Nam Il advising him that I "was prepared to return with delegation and continue discussions which were recessed yesterday upon notification from you that my convoy, bearing personnel of my choosing including such press representatives as I consider necessary will be cleared to conference site."

We remained in camp.

July 13: Msg from Ridgway to Peng Teh-Huai released to press. Gist of msg. R reviewed selection and his acceptance of Kaesong. Said "evident that equality of treatment so [the word "successful" was written here by the author and crossed out by him, substituting "essential"] essential to conduct of negotiations is lacking." Brought out restrictions imposed on delegation & armed guards. Also refusal to agree to pressmen at conference site. Said he was ready to resume conference when assurances received Commie delegation would proceed in like spirit. Stated few and simple assurances: Conference site free of armed guards, complete reciprocity of treatment to include freedom of movement, freedom in selection of UNC delegation party to include representatives of press. Proposed 5 mile circular area centered at Kaesong as neutral zone and that area of site and roads thereto used by both delegations be free of armed personnel. No hostile acts within zone.

In reply to msg from Nam Il asking for [two words crossed out; now illegible] meeting this date I sent msg saying in effect CinCUNC was communicating with his bosses & that we desired continue recess until further notice.

July 14: Remained in camp. Received reply to Ridgways msg. to Kim Il Sung & Peng Teh Huai: which in essence agreed to R's demands. Contended problem of press was minor & not related to neutral zone. Limits of conference area & other details to be left to delegates. I then sent msg to Nam Il proposing meeting of delegations at 1400 tomorrow. Nam Il replied he would welcome us at that time.

July 15: Commies agreed to all proposed requirements for neutral zone. (1) 5 mile radius area (2) Refrain from hostile acts (3) All armed personnel to be removed except those necessary for MP duty (4) No armed personnel in conference area ½ mile radius from conference house (5) Main road from Pan Mun Jom to conference area to be free of armed guards & UNCD to have unrestricted use of this road during daylight hrs without notification. After agreeing on this Nam Il spent 45 mins criticizing UNC agenda and justifying their own. Stressed again 38th parallel. We agreed to remove Red Cross item from agenda and discuss it under topic Prisoners of War. Also agreed to remove item which stated only military matters in Korea would be discussed since Commies had assured us that this was their intention. We further explained that we could not accept any particular military dem [demarcation] line as an item for discussion as a basis for establishing agenda.

Our opponents seemed willing and anxious to get down to business as if they wanted to show results or determine our position as quickly as possible. When I told of being stopped by guard on road Chinese appeared annoyed. Chinese appeared particularly impressed by argument pointing out difference between line of parallel and defensible line.

We requested that location of POW Camps be given to Red Cross. & that representatives be allowed to visit them.

July 16: Morning session of 50 mins entirely taken up by UNCD laying foundation for presentation of revised agenda. Upon receipt of agenda from UNC

Del. they asked for 2 hr recess. Afternoon session 45 mins consisted of discussion of our revised agenda by Commies. Concession made by them when they agreed to eliminate 38th parallel specifically from agenda. Offered a revised version to our Item 2 but remained adamant on Withdrawal of Troops. Our revised agenda. (1) Adoption (2) Establishment of a demilt [demilitarized] zone as a basic condition for cessation of hostilities (3) Concrete arrangements for cease fire & armistice which will insure against a resumption of hostilities & acts armed forces in Korea pending a final peace settlement. 3(a) Milt Armistice Commission 3(b) Milt Observer Teams. (4) Arrangements relating to POWs. By their comments Commies appeared interested in arriving at agenda. Several concessions on their part indicated their interest. They continue to contend that withdrawal of troops is the guarantee against resumption of hostilities. We pointed out no foreign troops were in Korea when war broke out. Commies appeared anxious to get down to substantive discussions.

July 17: Based on revised agenda submitted by UNC delegation Commies submitted proposed agenda which approached our views more closely than past Commie agenda—except for withdrawal of foreign troop item. This was it (1) Adoption (2) Fixing a dem [demarcation] line between both sides so as to establish a dem [demilitarized] zone as a basic condition for cessation of hostilities in Korea (3) Withdrawal of all armed forces of foreign countries from Korea to insure against resumption of hostilities and acts of armed force in Korea (4) Concrete arrangements for realization of cease fire and armistice in Korea, including the composition, authority & functions of a supervisory organization for carrying out terms of cease fire and armistice (5) Arrangements relating to POW's Nam Il in presenting his agenda adopted positive manner. His approach however was to present firm statements rather than to argue or discuss problem in detail. Concluded that Commies still desire to reach early agreement on agenda in spite of delays today. Too early to predict whether withdrawal of troop item will be breaking point. During meeting today senior Commie Delegate complained that his outpost at Pan Mun Jom had been fired on by UN Patrol of 16 July. Our investigation showed this had no basis in fact.

July 18: I took up each item on Commie agenda separately accepting their wording of item 3. Suggested minor change in wording of item 2, dem [demilitarized] zone. Stated their item 3 ref [reference] withdrawal of troops would not be discussed. Four agreed items were then proposed as agenda. During pm. Nam Il opened discussions with statement they considered great diff [difference] in principle between agenda UNC proposed and theirs. Said they intended use 38th as basis for their negotiations. Adamant about their troop withdrawal item. Questioned us considerably about our proposed change of "fixing lines" which we had inserted in item 2. They tried to get our views on our dem zone. We said we would agree to Commie wording for item 2 but that we reserved right to establish dem zone in our own way. In making its reservation regarding non inclusion of specific mention of an armistice commission and observation teams with unrestricted access to all of Korea. UNC delegation said we would insist on discussing later[.] Nam Il reacted strongly, apparently sensitive to inspection idea, saying he could not accept such substantive details at this time.

July 19: Upon being asked what we thought of their item 3, withdrawal of foreign troop item, I answered our position was clear—it was unacceptable & recommended four items mutually agreed upon be adopted for agenda. Nam Il replied with prepared speech which was obviously for propaganda purposes, saying foreign troops were source & continuance of war in Korea. Fact we refuse to discuss it shows our lack of sincerity. Following his speech we reiterated item was unacceptable and again recommended 4 item agenda be adopted. Session lasted 2 hrs 20 mins. Believe Commies are using propaganda tactics in endeavor to create enough political pressure to force us to accept topic as agenda item.

July 20: Weather and swollen streams prevented our getting up to Kaesong. I expressed regrets thru liaison officer and scheduled meeting for 1000 July 21st.

July 21: Upon being asked our views on their item 3 I responded with argument that Commies views had not changed UNC opinion concerning this matter. I held firm that 4 item agenda all that was needed for discussion of military armistice. After discussing with Chinese Nam Il read from prepared statement consisting of arguments which had been presented in previous meetings. This speech touched on doubt of UNC good faith, the need for guaranteeing the armistice, the principle of the 38th parallel and a statement that although certain political actions must be passed to future conferences, this should be done by resolution at this conference. and therefore must be on agenda. I then made statement concerning diff [difference] between an armistice and a peace settlement & recommended Commies reconsider their stand. Nam Il then proposed recess until 1100 k[*sic*] 25 July to which we agreed after ½ hr recess.

KAESONG

July 25: After recess called by Commies on 21 July we reconvened in morning (1000). Nam Il proposed new Item 5 on agenda which read "Recommendations to govts of countries concerned on both sides." He further contended we could discuss items agreed upon before taking this up. He was asked whether he would sign armistice agreement before discussing item but evaded question saying that depended on our good faith. I could hardly blame him.

In proposing item he made remark that the question of recommending withdrawal of troops could be brought up appropriately as recommendation for consideration at a higher conference within a definite time limit.

We requested recess until 1400 following day.

Upon return to camp held telecon [telephone conversation] with Ridgway and recommended approval of item. He concurred.

July 26: Agenda was adopted formally. I cautioned that this did not bind UNC delegation to any specific agreement but that we would discuss item in good faith when it was reached. (This was in accord with Ridgways instructions)

Nam Il wanted to begin substantive discussions right away but I countered with proposal to settle procedural matters first which evidently they had not considered but which they later agreed upon in principle. Gist of this—to settle each item first before proceeding to next and to let liaison officers work up exact wording of text of each article of Armistice agreement.

Nam Il after saying he would later give his opinion as to our procedural proposal then launched into the old song and dance about the 38th parallel as the only logical demarcation line. Asked for our stand on Item 2 but we countered saying we preferred to wait until tomorrow.

July 27: Met at 1000. Commies agreed in principle with our procedural proposals saying that if they found other procedures that would expedite proceedings they would propose them at proper time. I invited attention to incorrect wording in our proposed preamble of NK & CCF forces. We both named liaison officers who would work out specific wording of each Article of Arm [Armistice] Agreement when substance of article was agreed upon by delegates.

I then launched into a rebuttal of Nam Ils argument of yesterday for a zone based on the 38th parallel, saying that just because war started on 38th was no reason it should end there.

Following rebuttal I gave our presentation of the UNC's conception of where the demilitarized zone should be, pointing out that the zone should be based on military realities. Also contended all factors of our ground sea & air power should be taken into consideration. We were giving up great advantages (sea & air) for which we should be compensated. This seemed to anger Commies greatly.

July 28: Entire day spent in debate over location of demilitarized zone. Nam Il delivered attack on UNC proposed zone reiterated 38th as only basis. UNC gave rebuttal in afternoon attacking 38th parallel as basis for zone.

Nam Ils attack in morning was bitter in nature claiming we were arrogant, etc. Used may [many] vulgar adjectives. My rebuttal in p.m. forceful and temperate, which seem[ed] to mollify their tone. Explained that when we had to have a defensive line to compensate for our withdrawal of our air and sea forces we did not mean we would continue operations with air & navy while an armistice was being held on ground.

July 29: Entire day again spent in debate over location of demilitarized zone. NO progress.

July 30: Same as day before session lasting 3½ hrs. Commies showed little interest in UN's arguments for demilitarized zone based on battle line as I read paper after paper on the subject. Upon my return to camp I asked for telecon with Ridgway. Explained their adamant stand and 4 courses of action open to us. (1) Keep on present tactics (2) Propose shifting to Item 3 (3) Propose final stand of our demilitarized zone (4) Recess for several days during which Washington comes out with strong statement on 38th parallel. Delegation recommended course (1) but that CinCUNC ask Wash [Washington] to make strong statement. Ridgway loath to ask Wash because of [Defense Secretary George C.] Marshalls statement: we must have strong defensive line, and AP dispatch saying we would not agree on 38th. I told Ridgway in future I was going to cut meetings short and end up with strong note saying "the 38th parallel is totally unacceptable to UN Command.["]

July 31: Met at 1100. Answered Nam Ils question of previous day about demarcation line we proposed. Said essentially our zone would not be changed unless Armistice agreement is excessively delayed and delay is accompanied by appreciable change in battle lines. Rebutted his remarks of yesterday that we think in terms of war while they think in terms of peace. Gist of my remarks; our defensive lines proposed—insurance against war. I then got into quite a verbal battle with Nam Il on the subject of "would be aggressor." Finally concluded meeting by strong statement that 38th parallel as basis for demilitarized zone was totally unacceptable to UNC[.]

Aug. 1: Met at 1100. I rebutted his five major points on the 38th parallel one by one saying I have looked for military logic and have found nothing more than political thinking[.] I then launched into a definition of a military armistice saying we apparently had been talking about different types of armistices—they about a magic type which would solve all problems of Korea—we about a military armistice. Said we continue to insist on a demilitarized zone with suitable defensive positions to south for U.N. troops. Ended by saying again 38th parallel totally unacceptable to UNC. I made one statement "when you cease discussion of the wholly unacceptable line of demarcation you have proposed I am confident we can agree on a demil [demilitarized] zone." Nam Il then asked "You mean if we insist on the 38th parallel, no problems can be discussed any more in this conference."

Recessed at 1325[.]

Aug. 2: Met at 1100. Nam Ils opening statement showed three main things (1) He seemed to think that he has refuted our argument for compensation due to withdrawal of our air and navy (2) Commies are very touchy about our proposed zone because they contend it reaches far into their territory (3) They believe we have evaded the topic of a demarcation line in proposing our zone. My question "Do you or do you not agree that the security of his forces is the duty of each Comdr during an armistice" put Nam Il in a tight corner which he tried to get out of by saying the immediate solution of this question is to make the 38th parallel the milt demarcation line. I accused him of dodging the question. I ended the day at 1224 by saying again that the 38th was totally unacceptable to the U.N.C.

Aug. 3: 18th session. Answered points brought up by Nam Il in yesterdays meeting (1) Unfairness for UNC to be compensated for cessation of air & navy effectiveness (2) seeking a defensible line deep in their territory (3) Our lack of sincerity & good faith (4) Our alleged attitude of victors (5) Evaded topic of demarcation line (6) Our dem. line was a fabrication. We then received Nam Ils 108 min speech which reviewed his illogical position. My next statement reiterated again our contention that 38th parallel does not meet any conditions for an acceptable military armistice. & was therefore totally unacceptable to UNC. Session lasted 2 hr 50 m.

Aug. 4: 19th session. Reconvening at 1100 I started the ball rolling by answering Nam Il's questions of yesterday. Stripped of their rhetoric the questions were (1st) On what grounds do you still insist on your proposed milt dem [military demarcation] line (2nd) What reason do you have for refusing to abandon your proposed dem. line. (3d) What reason do you have for opposing our proposed dem. line. We offered to discuss our zone on map. This was refused. During recess for lunch company of Chinese soldiers was noted marching along road in conference area. I noted this for the record before signing off for the day and reported occurrence to Ridgway upon returning to camp. Upon receiving rpt Ridgway directed us to remain in camp while he dispatched strong note of protest to Kim Il Sung and Chinese General.

Aug. 5: Remained in camp exchanging despatches with Ridgway about neutrality violation. Had telecon with him in midst of terrific downpour of rain. Our msg mainly concerned with giving him all details of neutral zone violation which formed basis of his protest to Commies.

Aug. 6: Commie reply to Ridgway received. In effect admitted violation and assured it would not happen again. Inferred it was trivial accidental matter. Upon request from R. for recommendation we suggested Commie explanation be accepted. Later in morning we were summoned by R to proceed to Tokyo for conference in connection with reply to Commies explanation. Evident from R's despatch he was thinking about demanding Commies agree to joint inspection team or shift of conference site to another locality. While enroute to Tokyo where we arrived about 5:15 pm. Delegation came to unanimous conclusion we should capitalize on incident by trying to break deadlock on 38th parallel. Our opinion was that incident showed conclusively we could not rely on Commies good faith in any agreement hence we must have secure defensive lines which 38th parallel did not provide. Went straight to Dai Ichi Bldg [Headquarters, Supreme Command, Allied Powers] on arrival where R was already in conference with his staff drafting msg to J.C.S. R had not thought of our idea but accepted it and we left conference with thought main emphasis to JCS would be on thought that incident could be used to attack Commies stand on 38th.

Aug. 7: Was astounded at msg which was released to J.C.S. It was weak and only incorporated our idea in a brief short paragraph that made no reference to 38th. At 1030 when we met with R quite a battle ensued in which our position was again made clear. R. saw our point and we were in process of redrafting GHQ msg to JCS when msg was received from JCS which in effect disapproved inspection teams and suggested R accept Commies explanation. No mention was made of the idea contained in the brief short para—and no wonder—doubt whether J.C.S. ever got the idea from way msg was framed. I spent rest of day loafing and at 4 pm had a swim in Craigies pool. Informal dinner that night at my house—delegates, Murray and Briggs.

Aug. 8: Left Tokyo at 900 in Connie [Constellation aircraft] along with delegation party and Mr [Richard Gardener] Casey the Australian minister for foreign affair[s] and a most interesting gent who seemed concerned over Japan's economic future. Arrived Seoul 1230 where was met by Mayor of Seoul who presented me with a large bouquet of flowers. Said good bye to Casey and then proceeded to CinCUNC (adv) [advance headquarters] by helicopters. Had short conference with delegation on papers for next meeting.

Aug. 9: Spent day talking with delegation about next meeting. Answered Nam Ils blast about UN air violation and looked over 8th Army's report on alleged violation of neutral zone by UN patrols. Report clearly showed no patrols anywhere near scene of alleged violation. Although Kim Il Sungs reply to Ridgway was deliberately provocative we recommended that it be accepted so that conference might proceed.

Aug. 10: In accord with R's instructions sent msg to Kaesong we would resume meetings at 1330. Spent morning going over strategy and preparing rpts for delivery to Nam Il on alleged violations. Rains have been so violent lately that it has been impossible to bridge Imjin. Consequently when we arrived at Kaesong we had to use Russian jeeps for transportation from helicop[ter] field to conference house. Commies capitalized on this by taking many pictures of us in jeeps. Conference opened by Nam Il asking whether we had given up our proposal. I then gave him our tough stand answer ending up by saying "we will not discuss further the 38th parallel as military dem [demarcation] line." Nam Il was touchy about our ref [reference] to aggressive war. Nam Il then countered with the usual line about his "just & reasonable proposal," trying also to make out that our air & navy were wantonly bombing and that his proposal reflects the military realities. He asked whether we were trying to deprive him of right to insist on 38th. I of course answered we did not but that we would be unresponsive to any further efforts on his part to engage us in discussion of 38th. Then came 2 hrs & 11 min of silence since no one had anything else to say. We then proposed shifting to item 3 which Nam Il turned down on flimsy excuses. On our proposal we recessed to meet again at 1100 tomorrow.

Aug. 11: At 1100 Nam Il opened with proposal that liaison officers meet again to discuss & agree upon draft of detailed provisions of neutralization[.] We asked for proposal in writing & said would consider it and answer later. I then pointed out that violation of neutrality guarantees was directly connected with item 2 since if we could not rely on their pledged word, how could we rely on it with ref to security of our forces during an armistice. Therefore we must rely on strong defensible positions. After brushing this aside as a matter for liaison officers Nam Il launched into his main speech which was primarily a re-hash of former statements. Ended up with old song that zone based on 38th parallel is fair & reasonable & ours untenable. I then came up with the "superior force" paper ending with question we would welcome an exposition of your conception of a dem [demilitarized] zone based on present battle line. Nam Il as much as refused saying 38th parallel appears on map. After lunch Nam Il took off again and accused us of not daring to make our line public. I ended the day with the arrogant speech which they were by no means too happy about although Nam Il did not admit we frightened them.

Aug. 12: Nam Il started on a lengthy blast attacking our proposal for the demilitarized zone based on the general area of the battle line. Accused us of being arrogant for insisting on a dem. [demarcation] line deep in their positions[.] Dared us again to make public our proposed zone. Their motive for this may be to build up a golden bridge by which they can show the world eventually, (if they agree to our zone) that we were forced to give up our original position. Nam Il ended up his tirade by asking 5 questions which we later said we would study in detail along with the map he gave us. I then launched into his proposal of yesterday with regard to the meeting of the liaison officers to discuss details of neutralization of Kaesong handing him answer to his of yesterday. Ended day by again saying we would not discuss 38th. Suggested again going to item 3 or 4 or both. Nam Il replied his stand on 38th still unshakeable. In general Commies willingness to discuss & ask questions about our zone was more encouraging than heretofore. Is it the beginning of their retraction from the 38th or are they still determined to have the 38th or no armistice?

Aug. 13: I started the ball rolling by answering the 5 questions Nam Il asked yesterday. Nam Il then asked "dont you see that present battle line you maintain is result of the cooperative action of your ground, air & naval forces." Nam Il also asked for clearer answer to question 4 no doubt for the one purpose of getting a different proposal from us than our original one. Nam Il complained, after I had explained our answer was clear enough, that he would like a more direct answer. He then wound up with the usual line that our proposal was absurd & arrogant while his was fair & reasonable. Also said in prepared statement that our answers were unsatisfactory which made me so mad that I wound up the day after giving him our map which showed our conception of location of battle line, somewhat north of his. Results—no progress although Commies appear to continue interested in any new proposal we might offer.

Aug. 14: Nam Ils arrogant and lengthy speech starting the days proceedings showed that he had given scant attention to the (ours) replies to his five questions, probably because we did not propose any new location for our demilitarized zone. We feel however that the next move is up to them. They should show a real interest in a zone based on the b.l. [battle line] and make a counter proposal before we should relax from our original stand. Nam Ils lengthy speech again petulantly blasted our wanton bombing & proof that our air effort is hurting them. He used "arrogant and absurd," when referring to our proposal, 19 times in 1 hr & 12 min. By bald assertions unsupported by any basis in fact he tried to accuse us of causing the deadlock. After Nam Il had finished I went ahead with a scathing denouncement of the Commie charge that we were blocking progress, pointing out that they were trying to gain at the conference table what they had lost in battle. I then took up his question "Do you not see that the b.l. which you have at present is result of combined actions of your land, sea & air forces." I went on to say "No" only a portion of our air & naval ops.

[operations] directly support ground forces. We again pointed out advantages accruing to Commies from withdrawal of our air and navy which necessitated good defensive positions for UN forces. We also again answered question 4 saying we had made two proposals to Commies, one the original proposed dem [demilitarized] zone and, two, a proposal to be receptive to proposed adjustments.

Aug. 15: Nam Il again started off on one of his tirades, first accusing us of making two proposals when in fact there was only one. He then attempted to refute our argument concerning air & navy effectiveness claiming total effect was reflected in ground forces position. More reference to indiscriminate bombing[.] In fact I thought his speech was even more arrogant than the one of the day before. He and his infamous cohort Lee [Sang Cho] actually sneered at us[.] They seemed smug and complacent about something which we cannot evaluate (telling JCS in despatch). We ended with the proposal that in an endeavor to break the deadlock, each delegation appoint one delegate to membership in a joint sub committee of the delegation to exchange views on item 2 and to make recommendations. Recs must be approved by the two delegations before being agreed to. Chinese seemed interested more so than Nam Il & Co. I'm curious however to see whether they will try to dodge this additional attempt of ours to break the deadlock. We meet later (at 1300) tomorrow; does this late time proposed by the enemy mean anything?

Aug. 16: When I asked for Nam Ils answer to our proposal, he started in with the same old line blasting our reasons for a strong defensive line viz air & navy superiority. His tone however appeared less belligerent and arrogant than usual, though he did harp on our refusal to discuss the 38th. Evidently this sticks in his craw. He did not however reiterate that their stand was unshakeable nor did he say that they would refuse to discuss our zone, something I half way expected. Had he done so the dead lock would have been almost impossible to break. Finally he ended up by agreeing in principle to our sub-committee proposal. After a 30 min recess, we agreed to his proposal for a sub-committee—two delegates & two assistants from each side. Hodes & Burke will start off meeting at 1100 tomorrow. Mudgett staff asst [assistant] & Underwood the interpreter. Site of meeting undetermined, may be they are looking for a round table. Days work encouraging, shows they still want to talk. Sub-Com [subcommittee] idea provides them with a golden bridge—I hope. Some rumor spreading among correspondents that they will come off 38th and take up battle line. But I'm keeping my fingers crossed.

Aug. 17: Sub-delegation met very informally around two foot round table. Hodes explained possible ways to break dead lock and tried to get agreement on 3 points (1) Milt Armistice has nothing to do with ultimate territory arrangements in Korea. (2) Demilitarized zone should be positioned so that balance of milt advantages at time of Armistice is not upset. (3) Each side should have defensible positions.

They contended: (1) 38th only sound solution (2) B.L. [battle line] does not represent milt situation. (3) Their ground forces can push us south of 38th at any time and therefore balance of power is now on their side (4) We should accept their word as a guarantee they will not attack during an armistice (5) A & N [air and naval forces] have some minor effect but only on position of B.L.

Sub delegation made it plain UN, UNC our main delegation and our sub deleg [delegation] would not accept 38th as a milt. dem. [military demarcation] line.

It was concluded they expect to milk us for as much info as possible before giving up 38th or breaking the conference. Chinese apparently prefer sub deleg [delegation] method of meeting because they can then talk. Hsieh Fang spoke frequently and poured oil when waters got troubled. Maybe Chinese will be willing to discuss some zone other than one based on 38th but evidence of that extremely slight so far.

Aug. 18: Commies produced map outlining UN zone 38th parallel zone and BL [battle line]. 38th zone had been modified by a so called adjustment on their part which in reality was no concession at all. Gave us some ground about 4 Kms in east while they took same amount in west. Their only real argument, which they continually repeat, proposes equal exchange of real estate along 38th which has no bearing on present situation. They continue to insist that basic principle in an armistice was pledged word of each side not to resume hostilities and that demilitarized zone itself provided all necessary additional security. The UNC Del (sub) [sub delegation] agreed that that [*sic*] the pledged word was an important principle but maintained that neither it nor the demil. [demilitarized] zone in themselves provided the security we demand for our troops and that adequate defensive positions were also essential. The UNCD stressed on numerous occasions the necessity for maintenance of balance between the two forces during the armistice and stressed the principle that neither side improve its military position. This is a requirement the Commies refuse to admit. They proposed that we (1) drop from the map the UNC proposed zone (2) drop hypothetically the 38th though remembering it is still their basic proposal (3) drop the B.L. (4) start fresh with the UNC placing on the map a new zone completely unrelated to any of lines formerly on map. UNC countered with suggestion that Commies place on the map their concept of such a zone. Commies refused. UNCSD then suggested flip coin to determine who would place zone related to B.L. on a clean map. In refusing this request they stated flatly they had no proposal in mind except one based on 38th. Evidently they realized what a spot they would be in if they lost and couldn't make a proposal. Discussion then centered on UNCD attempting to get an agreement on fundamentals without success. In replying to question on milt. [military] balance Commies stated only line representing true military balance was 38th. UNCSD then asked 3 times: "Is any zone not based on 38th acceptable to you?" They beat around bush and would not give direct answer. UNCSD then asked: "you have led me to believe you are here to negotiate an armistice only if it is based on 38th. Is my impression correct?'' After fumbling Commies finally replied by stating that their basic principle was to retain 38th but that this am. they had proposed some adjustments. They added that they still believed their first proposal was fair & reasonable but they did not mean they refused to discuss a solution better than theirs. Stated "your proposals to date continue unacceptable." UNC then proposed sub committees to discuss Items 2, 3, & 4. Useless said Commies until 2 was settled. UNC again stated it should be made clear we will not accept 38th. Commies replied it should be perfectly clear they would not accept UNC proposal or any adjustments thus far proposed. UNC then attempted to determine if any proposal other than 38th would be acceptable. Commies would not reply directly but indicated only zone on 38th would interest them. They added if we would drop our exaggerated demands for compensation of air & naval withdrawal we could then see the 38th as "just and reasonable" offer. In reply to question by UNC Commies indicated width of zone immaterial, it could be 5 or 100 kilometers.

Conclusion: There is clear indication Commies have no authority to make a specific proposal other than 38th zone. They are authorized hypothetically any such proposal we might put up for discussion. They are utilizing sub-del meetings to milk us for info and to resist our efforts to obtain info in return. We are in the same position as the full delegation.

Aug. 19: It was decided this morning that something drastic should be done to break the deadlock by convincing the Commies we would never accept the 38th. Accordingly it was decided that Craigie and I should proceed (with Kinney, Galloway and Mudgett) to Tokyo to try and sell the ultimatum idea to Ridgway stopping enroute at Van Fleets Hdqtrs to get his ideas. Spent 2 hrs with him. His idea of an armistice is to stop fighting in present positions with only a narrow zone and let the GI's with rifles be the inspectors. He did not think inspecting teams behind the lines practicable. Believed our ultimatum good solution but suggested it be timed for early September to coincide with limited offensive in eastern sector of line, designed to straighten out our lines. Weather would also permit more effective air support then. I liked his straight forward practical approach to the problem—a real soldier's viewpoint.

On our way to Tokyo, Craigie Kinney and I worked out our ultimatum proposed for submission to Ridgway. Briefly our proposal contended time was working for the Commies as the talks progressed. They had no real incentive to abandon the 38th since they knew they could always get a better proposition than our original one. If they really wanted an armistice the only way to jar them loose from the 38th was an ultimatum proposing our final and minimum position based on the B.L. [battle line]. Commies can exploit their initiative by stalling until public opinion in U.S. and in allied countries demands solution. Already signs of impatience (Sioux Falls editorial about stop saving face and save lives).

Our proposal: On 30 Aug, delegation will announce that present line of contact is its final position reference a demarcation line, and a demilt. zone of ___ kms width centered on line of dem. [demarcation], is its final position on our zone. If Commies merely reiterate 38th parallel as mandatory CinCUNC will be notified by UNC Del that time for forceful action has come. On 1 Sept we will not return to Kaesong. On 1 Sept CinCUNC or I will announce that unless in 4 days Commies state willingness to accept our proposal we will consider they have served notice by silence or rejecting our fair proposal they have no sincere desire for an armistice at this time. We will state that UNC delegation will return to Kaesong any time Commies are ready to accept. We arrived Tokyo shortly after 1700. arranged conference with Hickey at 0830 following morning.

Forgot to mention that while with Van Fleet, Briggs phoned to report no progress at Kaesong and that meeting had broken up early.

Aug. 20: Hickey appeared to endorse our ultimatum idea strongly though he seemed to take a different viewpoint when we later discussed it with R. I'm afraid we didn't entirely sell it to R though he appeared much interested and promised he would consider it seriously. He believes JCS would not go along since they turned down a similar proposal from him. I pointed out that our proposal was not suddenly given to the JCS as was his, and that our plan permitted a build up propaganda wise to educate the public to a possible break. Furthermore if Commies really wanted an armistice they would accept. If they didn't the conference was doomed to failure anyway and our proposal would smoke out their real intentions. We all agreed the timing was important, probably JCS would never agree to such action at time of Japanese peace treaty signing at S.F. [San Francisco]. All of us speculated on Soviets motive for stalling if they really wanted an armistice at Kaesong. There is of course no real answer.

That evening a new crisis arose. Yesterday a Commie patrol had been ambushed within the neutral zone not far from Pan Mun Jom with result platoon leader was killed. Nam Il had transmitted an angry note to me demanding an explanation. I told Hodes in a msg to inform Nam Il over my signature that I would reply fully when result of investigation was known to me and that preliminary report did not substantiate the charges he made. From the press release Hodes made, it looks as if the incident was caused by a band of partisans since most of the assailants were in civilian clothes. It may have been instigated in an attempt to sabotage the conference.

Aug. 21: Had conference with R, Craigie, Hickey & Mudgett in R's office to decide on our final position of the demilt. [demilitarized] zone based on the B.L. [battle line]. Decisions made: (1) Zone would be 4 kms wide (minimum) (2) Would only be proposed in plenary session of delegation and then only if Commies agreed in sub Del meeting to get off 38th parallel (3) Our present final position can be used in sub-Del if good opportunity offers (4) Plenary session would only be convened if Sub-Del submitted recommendation to discuss zone based on B.L. as ways and means to break dead lock (5) JCS would be sounded out to see if they approve of narrow zone based on line of contact. (6) G.H.Q. would take action to relieve ROK patrols across Imjin by U.S. patrols (7) We cannot suggest zone based on line of contact until it has been approved by JCS (8) Weyland and I will take up question of keeping Craigie & Burke on until conference is over.

Results of conference on 20th. Burke presented UNC position arguments for demilt. zone in general area of B.L. Stated necessity for maintaining present even balance of military effectiveness in order to present [prevent] one side from gaining strength and other losing strength thereby encouraging violation of armistice. Pointed out that Commie proposal would almost double length of line; that area we would require in west would be in-definite and that in east we would be required to retire from defensible positions to indefensible ones far to the south. (A very good presentation that might well be given again) Lee [Sang Cho] stated that difference of opinion resulted from fact that we viewed question from standpoint of maintaining military balance while they viewed it from standpoint of milt. realities and living up to international agreements. He drew distinction between line of contact and general area of B.L. and stated that as long as we adhere to our position that demilt zone must be in latter area no progress could be made. (Note: this sounds encouraging but still is not a definite proposal)

Upon return to camp at 1830 and after discussing our trip to Tokyo, I was told conference today was as unproductive of results as one yesterday. Commies continued to milk us for info without making a definite proposal themselves. They appear to desire that UNC sub delegation propose B.L. as milt. line of demarcation but will not submit such a proposal themselves. This interest may indicate possible acceptance by them but it may only be attempt to maneuver us into proposing more favorable position for them and starting again from there. Hsieh seemed quite serious and perturbed that agreement was not in sight. The $64 question seems to be whether or not we should at this time submit another proposed zone. This of course depends on the sincerity of the Commies. If we were convinced of their sincerity to seek an armistice we would have nothing to lose and something to gain by proposing another zone. However we should by no means propose our minimum or final position since this would leave us in a non bargaining position.

Aug. 22: 6th sub del meeting. Craigie & Hodes. Discussions followed same trend as that of former meetings & concluded with an exploration of the principle of adjustments to the B.L. as a means of establishing the military demarcation line. Lee several times made statement that no progress could be made until UNC delegation gave up not only the concept under which the UNC is compensated on the ground for its air & navy but also any plan based upon line of contact. Hsieh on other hand said no progress could be made until UNC gave up at least its first proposal. Not known whether their [*sic*] is difference in statements between the two. Both parties agreed to broad principle that adjustments could be made to L of C [line of contact] by withdrawals and advances by both sides in such a way as to fix a milt. dem. [military demarcation] line. Not yet known why Commies pressed for agreement on this principle.

At 2330 Commie liaison officer called by radio phone, in an agitated voice, saying conference site was bombed and straffed [*sic*] at 2320. Requested senior UNC liaison officer to investigate immediately. Colonels Kinney and Murray set out by jeep arriving Kaesong about 0145. Upon their arrival Colonel Chang stated UNC aircraft had attacked neutral zone at 2320, the attack including strikes within immediate conference area. Commies produced two marble size bits of metal which allegedly hit jeep of senior Commie delegate. On inquiry they did not know how many bombs were dropped or how many passes were made. Chang stated all present, which included Commie liaison officers, staff assistants, news reporters and photographers, had heard aircraft. On being questioned by Kinney one soldier said he saw aircraft with lights on—headlights. Kinney and Murray were escorted to within 100 yds of UNC Del house and there were shown rumpled piece of rolled metal about 18″ × 30″ covered with oil and lying in road. Chang asserted this was napalm bomb although no bomb crater or scorched earth nearby. Piece of metal appeared to be part of a tank of some sort. About 25 yds away was minor depression in earth, perhaps 6 inches deep and approx 24″ in dia [diameter], clearly not a bomb crater. Near residence of Commie Delegates, 3 other pieces of metal were shown. Flush riveting. Two of these appeared to be pieces of UNC aircraft. Each piece about 1 foot square Third piece fin of rocket. No craters or furrows present. On return to conference house Kinney asserted evidence plainly not result of UNC bombing. Pointed out no damage to any structure, person or even crop. Chang immediately announced, from written notes, that there would be no further meetings. Kinney inquired if Chang meant sub-Del meetings as well as liaison meetings. Chang replied "all meetings were off" from this time. UNC liaison officers departed to return to camp. Halfway to Pan Mun Jom they were overtaken by Chang & Tsai and asked to return to Kaesong to view more evidence. After protesting rain & darkness precluded satisfactory investigation they returned to Kaesong. 2 more pieces of flush riveted metal were pointed out in area near Commie Del residence. Hole nearby clearly not bomb crater. Final piece of metal also flush riveted and was lying in only small amnt liquid possibly poor grade napalm. 3 or 4 scorched areas about 15″ square inches [*sic*] each nearby. Although Kinney requested investigation be continued in morning in better light, Chang refused saying investigation was concluded & that metal pieces would be removed for analysis.

Investigation by Air Force did not disclose that any of our aircraft had operated in vicinity during time of incident. Bogie reported to west of Kaesong 6 mins before 2320, proceeding about 180 kts [knots] being investigated.

Whether or not this was a manufactured incident is debatable. From the agitated demeanor of the liaison officers and the fact that a number of Commies claimed to have heard the aircraft, plus the fact that one soldier saw the "headlights" of a plane, it is reasonable to assume that some aircraft was in the immediate vicinity of Kaesong. The location of a blip to the west of Kaesong shortly before the incident tends also to support the belief that an airplane had been in the area. The question is: what airplane and why was it there? Could it have been a ROK? In breaking off the talks do the Commies have a permanent break in mind? Only time will tell.

Aug. 23: At 0900 Colonel Lee transmitted my reply to Nam Il concerning incident of 19 August. Gist of my report: that no UNC forces were involved, rather the ambuscade on CCF patrol was carried out by a group of partisan irregulars. No evidence exists that this group came from without zone. My ltr [letter] contended responsibility for control of irregular partisan groups within neutral zone rests with Nam Il. I also pointed out that the formation of a joint inspection committee to examine into conditions within neutral zone was now more strongly indicated than it was when I originally proposed such a committee on 14 Aug.

Aug. 24: A.M. Sent Colonel Lee to Pan Mun Jom for msg [message]from Kim Il Sung and Peng Teh-Huai to Ridgway. Gist of msg. Accused UNC of murdering platoon Commander in ambush incident of 19 August and of attempting to murder Commie delegation by bombing and strafing on 22 August. Said "since your side has wantonly undertaken such provocative acts outside of the conference room, while within the conference room you have persistently insisted upon your arrogant proposal of pushing the milt. dem. [military demarcation] line into our positions to stall the negotiations, it is already crystal clear what good faith you could have in the armistice negotiations" Ended by contending "responsibility rests entirely with your side" & "we await a satisfactory reply."

Spent pm drafting recommended reply for R. Our msg reviewed the alleged incidents that had occurred previous to the current one, disclaiming responsibility on the part of UNC Forces. It charged that bombing incident was a fabrication and demanded change of site of conference as condition for resuming negotiations. It ended by reaffirming and clarifying our stand on line of demarcation.

Aug. 25: Received R's msg to JCS which he sent for their approval. MSG based on following analysis: (a) bombing incident was a complete and premeditated fabrication. (fabrication attested to by investigation. Premeditation by immediate announcement from written notes by Commie liaison officer that meetings were off. Obviously decision must have been made in advance at highest level.)

(b) Commies have announced that negotiations are suspended pending a satisfactory reply to allegation. (c) Possible motivation: (1) Commies desire an excuse to bring an end to negotiations with object of seeking to fix blame for the cessation on UN. Possible that with no desire for an ultimate peace in Korea they have accomplished their original program during time negotiations have now run. This borne out by tactical ops [operations] now in progress and pending. Suspension can well be the preliminary to a complete break when they choose. (2) Incident is designed to provide a stalling procedure to mesh timing of Kaesong talks with global events such as Jap peace treaty conference & Russian peace offensive (3) Commies desire a suspension based on manufactured incidents in order to strengthen their propaganda position and regain the initiative in the conduct of negotiations. Note: Another motive, not mentioned by R., is, I believe important—the motive of revenge for causing them to lose face by admitting the armed troop violation on Aug 4th which they claimed was trivial and unimportant.

R's answer was broadcasted by Allen at noon and a certified copy sent up by me to Pan Mun Jom via helicopter. Colonel Lee, General Paik's aide, who took it up, presented it to Colonel Chang with a speech in English to the effect that he had the honor to deliver certified copy of General R's reply to Kim Il Sung and Peng Teh Huai. Chang then said rather petulantly, why don't you speak Korean? Lee thereupon drew himself up and replied vehemently: "I will speak in whatever language I please. That is what we are fighting for; freedom of speech.["]

Aug. 26 (Sun): Speculation is rife in camp as to reasons for course of action which Commies have elected to follow with reference to the alleged 22 August violation of the neutral zone. Some of the more plausible ones follow: (1) Commies desire to regain face lost as a result of 4 Aug conference area violation and the attendant capitulation in the face of General R's strong demands (2) Commies desire to give firm impression to UN countries that they are not afraid to break conference and thus improve bargaining position at conference table (3) Commies have finally become convinced that UNC Del has firm instructions never to accept 38th as M.DL [military demarcation line]. Their Moscow–Peking policy does not permit acceptance of armistice terms which do not include the "face saving 38th." They must therefore break off discussions.

On the other hand Dr. Goldhammer of Rand believes (a) the discussions are not in imminent danger of breaking down (b) that the Commies are genuinely interested in an armistice and will settle for terms short of the 38th parallel.

Aug. 27 (Mon): Worked on Final statement to be used as a radio broadcast in event Commies broke off talks. Statement was about a 20 min review of our troubles at Kaesong in trying to negotiate an armistice. First took up Commie stand on 38th parallel zone, then our arguments for a zone based on present battle line. Also went into the steps we took and proposals we made in our attempts to break the dead lock. Then took up a review of the incidents which violated the neutrality of the conference area. The final close out ended: "With the security of our fighting men, and the honor and survival of the UN clearly in the balance, God helping us, we could choose no other course."

Late in p.m. received msg from R. that he would like to see me at Kimpo [Airfield, near Seoul] at 1815. Hodes and I made trip but R did not show up until 1900. Had 20 min talk with him in which he told me final broadcast announcing permanent break off would be made by him. He and JCS had been thrashing out his final statement. He also announced General Paik would remain permanently with his Corps and not return to conference as he was sorely needed in fighting.

Aug. 28 (Tues): Worked with other delegates on msg to R. proposing reply to Kim Il Sung's msg to R. Our despatch to R in 4 parts. Part 1, compiled mainly by Dr. Golhamer, anylized [*sic*] the Commie msg as (1) desiring to continue the armistice talks and (2) as conciliatory (from Commie standards). Part II was proposed reply which refuted Commies "demand" that investigation of Aug 22nd bombing and strafing incident be renewed and ended up by proposing representatives get together to discuss ways & means to avoid further interruptions to conference. Part III Gave delegates reasons for Part II and Part IV was our proposed press release.

R's tentative msg which he sent over to us for comment was much briefer that [than] our proposed reply. It simply said there was no purpose in having a re investigation of incident of 22 Aug and proposed representatives meet to continue conference.

Aug. 29 (Wed): R's reply to the Commies, as modified and approved by the JCS was delivered by Colonel Lee to Commie Liaison officer at Pan Mun Jom at 0930. Delivered msg read as follows: "On the night of 23 August your liaison officer, Colonel Chang, specifically refused the request of my liaison officer to continue the investigation during daylight & to leave all of the alleged evidence in place. The offer you now make to permit a re-investigation after this lapse of time could serve no purpose other than to continue this unjustifiable delay in the armistice negotiations.

["]As stated in my previous msg of 25 Aug, when you are prepared to terminate the suspension of armistice negotiations, which you declared on Aug 23, I will direct my representatives to meet with yours, with a view to seeking a reasonable armistice agreement[.]"

Camp is divided in conjectures as to what Commie reaction to this msg will be. Some believe Commies will be more conciliatory in next msg. Dr. Gold-hamer still convinced they desire an armistice[.] Others believe there is little chance of their acceding to R's proposal that representatives meet again, without at least guarantees from R that incidents will not re occur.

"Robby" [Lt. Gen., Sir Horace Robertson] dropped in for dinner. He believes Commie stalling of Kaesong talks closely allied with S.F. [San Francisco] peace conference and that Soviets are prepared to initiate World War 3 when Jap peace treaty is signed. I still dont believe Russians are ready for war[.]

Aug. 30 (Thurs): Not much of interest. Radio broadcast from Peking called R a liar and denounced his statement that Col Chang refused to allow Kinney to continue investigation during day light. Radio said it was quoting a special correspondent at Kaesong. Therefore not considered official.

Went over Dr. Goldhamers paper which offers the opinion that Commies are agreeable to giving up the 38th parallel. If talks are resumed believes we will be in a good position to get favorable buffer zone for UN.

Col Lee sent up to Pan Mun Jom in response to Commie request. Brought back protest from Nam Il which claimed that at 02:40 Aug 29 aircraft dropped flare in vicinity of conference site. *Demanded* that culprits be severely punished & that we ensure against recurrence.

At same time Lee was given verbal protest that our armed personnel had attacked Commie Milt Police in vicinity of Ch'ongdam-dong.

Aug. 31 (Fri): Recd rpt from General Everest that preliminary investigation revealed that 2 RB-26 aircraft dropped two photo flash bombs at 03:40 approx 20 to 25 miles N of Kaesong. Bombs make loud noise and can be seen for great distances. At approx same time 4 C-47 aircraft dropped flares in area 50 mi north of Kaesong.

Lem Shepherd visited me and stayed for lunch. While in my tent Edwards delivered Nam Ils ltr of protest about shooting incident. Ltr claims at 0600 yesterday Commie police personnel were attacked by more than 10 uniformed SK troops who "murdered" two (2) Commies & wounded another before escaping. Demanded that culprits be severely punished and that we ensure against recurrence.

Sept. 1 (Sat): Another alleged bombing incident on the part of the UNC reported. Incident took place at 12:30 this am. Sent Kinney & Murray, Ordnance officer & Operations officer from 5th Air Force along with 5 newspaper men photographers & interpreters (Total 15 in party) up to Kaesong to investigate. Party left camp about 1100 and returned at ___ [sic].

Muccio arrived at 12:45. After lunch we discussed Paiks release from delegation and how it would be best to announce it to press. As result I sent msg to Ridgway suggesting only that appointment of Lee as alternate for Paik be announced and that no direct announcement of Paik's return to his Corps be made. Muccio was afraid, and I concurred, that if announcement was made that Paik was relieved it would create misgivings in eyes of Korean people.

Murray & Kinney etc returned about 1700 with the news that evidently two 500 lb bombs had been dropped. Location was 2.9 miles from delegates house. When Kinney asked why they (Commies) had said bombs had been dropped in vicinity of delegates residence Chang replied delegates had moved. Kinney then pointed out only Commies knew they had moved therefore bombs must have been dropped by a plane which knew of place to which delegates had moved. All civilian witnesses obviously coached. Said they knew it was an American plane from sound plane made! Air Force radar had picked up blip (unidentified) at time alleged bombing took place. Blip had suddenly appeared over Kaesong for brief moment, showing plane had come in low and gained alt [altitude] briefly to drop bomb. Bomb fragments from American bomb probably captured at Pyongang [Pyongyang].

Sept. 2 (Sun): About noon Peking radio transmitted Peng's & Kim's reply to R. Msg mentioned bombing incident of yesterday. Said world will "not believe such preposterous lies & denials on your part." Ended by saying "If you do have the intention to resume the Kaesong talks in order to seek a just and reasonable armistice agreement, you should agree to the following demands of our side: namely your side must conscientiously and responsibly deal with the series of grave provocative incidents from Aug 22 to Sept 1st and must thoroughly guarantee that there would be no recurrence of similar acts which violate the Kaesong neutralization agreement, so that the armistice meeting can be resumed."

In our proposed reply sent R we suggested that our representatives meet immediately to discuss the selection of a new site. In event JCS do not approve idea of a new site we proposed "that our representatives meet to discuss ways and means for insuring the conference talks at Kaesong against further interruptions."

Sept. 3 (Mon): Decided to return to Tokyo. Just before leaving had call from Commies to send liaison officer for msgs. Three long letters received from Nam Il, two on alleged violations of neutral zone by our forces and one on parachute flare incident. Took off for Tokyo without attempting to answer ltrs beforehand. Arrived Tokyo shortly before eight p.m. Family arrived home from Karuizawa about ½ hr before me.

Sept. 4 (Tues): Conference with R at 0900 to go over reply to Kim & Peng. Burke Craigie & Briggs also attending. We suggested re wording of msgs GHQ had worked out. Ours more factual. Two msgs; one if J.C.S approved idea of proposing new site, other if answer in negative. R's msg to JCS strongly recommended he be given this authority. His basis—safety of UNC delegation and prevention of recurrence of incidents. P.M. Golfed with Robertson, Craigie & Muse. Had Martin, Kiland, Hill, Ammon John Roper & Ofstie for dinner.

Sept. 5 (Wed): Forgot to mention yesterday of three msgs. I sent in answer to Nam Il's[.] All very short. Acknowledged his in first sentence, disclaimed any responsibility for UNC in alleged incidents in second.

Conferred with Craigie & Burke concerning observation teams and paper on subject to be submitted to R. In view J.C.S stand on unrestricted inspection we felt it was necessary to find out whether J.C.S desired delegation to press for this point if Commies were adamant against it. Was it a breaking point? We felt it was not—that we should give, provided of course we ever got past item 2. We also felt we should have an early decision from J.C.S since the zone and inspection were related. With a wide zone we would not really need unrestricted inspection; with a narrow zone we would need some inspection behind Commie lines to insure against surprise attack. Also discussed ultimatum idea for item 2. Decided we should have that authority if upon resuming talks we got nowhere on item 2.

P.M. at office catching up on what Navy has been doing. Discussed Apache operation, Jap navy, dependents, etc.

Sept. 6 (Thurs): J.C.S msg giving R. authority to propose new conference site was received. At 0900 had conference with R. to decide on his reply to Kim & Peng. Gist of his reply follows: 1st para. denounced charges as false and said "you have again impugned the good faith of the UNC." Investigations have indicated our forces did not violate any agreements. Guarantees R has made remain effective. Called upon Commies to cease despicable practices & get on with conference. Ended by saying "when you decide to terminate the suspension of armistice negotiations which you declared on Aug 23 I propose that our liaison officers meet at the bridge at Pan Mun Jom to discuss selection of a new site where negotiations can be continued without interruptions."

Spent rest of morning with JSPOG group discussing new conference sites and paper thereon to serve as guide for liaison officers. Any new site would have objections but we believe following would be acceptable (1) neutral ship (2) Island off coast (3) Hongkong—(Kowloon on Chinese-Br [British] boundary) (4) site at Pan Mun Jom. Also discussed inspection paper and agreed to meet again tomorrow at 0900 to continue on ultimatum on Item 2 proposal. Golfed in p.m. with Garey, Allen & Col. Gillespie.

Sept. 7 (Fri): Met with Craigie, Burke and others at JSPOG office to go over final draft of paper on unrestricted inspection and discuss paper concerning new conference site. Conference with R, Ofstie, Weyland & Hickey at 10:30. in which release of Burke and Craigie was discussed. R firm in his views they must be held until armistice talks are over. Later I replied in a Joy to Fechteler despatch that R felt strongly Burke could not be released at this time—issues at stake too important to break up good smooth working team. At 1130 Craigie and I discussed unrestricted inspection paper with R who agreed with our views (or seemed to) that JCS stand on subject should be re-examined in event we can get by hurdle of item 2. Basic question "is unrestricted insp. [inspection] a breaking point?"

Rec'd two short ltrs from Nam Il saying in effect my short replies concerning shooting (murder) incidents of 19 Aug & 30 Aug, & parachute flare incident of Aug 29 were "absolutely unsatisfactory."

After lunch discussed ultimatum on item 2 with Pinkie Wright who agreed to strengthen his paper, which in effect did not present the idea as an ultimatum to R. An ultimatum would be the final step in a series starting with renewed negotiations by sub del committee for several days, followed by plenary sessions of 2 or 3 days at end of which we would give Commies our "take it or leave it" stand. It was also agreed that it would be better for R to give the ultimatum to the Commies.

Sept. 8 (Sat): Discussed new conference site paper with JSPOG group including Kinney & Murray who had returned from Korea. If Commies agree to R's proposal first step would be to get them to agree on certain criteria or characteristics for site—non conducive to incidents, etc. Sites preferred in order of priority—neutral ship, island off west coast, neutral territory, and site between lines (Pan Mun Jom)[.] Called Galloway & asked him to send back Hickman with study of paper approaching incidents from a legalistic viewpoint. This paper to be basis for an eventual press release. Rest of day spent at my Hdqtrs and at home. Went over several matters with Martin; Tomlinson & Spore. Also his visit with Van Fleet.

Sept. 9 (Sun): Conference at JSPOG Burke, Craigie, Briggs, Latoweski [*sic*], Briggs [*sic*]. Hickman, Kinney & Murray. concerning final draft of unrestricted inspection paper, new conference site paper & Hickman's legalistic studies. Most of discussion centered on conference site and what conditions should we insist upon if Commies refused to consider any place other than Kaesong. Possibility of Port Arthur considered but this was thrown out since its status is obscure; ostensibly it is under Chinese control. Hickman given job of revising his incident studies and submitting outline of what paper would include. Released short msg to press concerning Nam Ils last two short letters, which said in effect that Nam Il's charges had previously been proved baseless and were not worthy of a reply. Afternoon at home.

Sept. 10 (Mon): Conference again at JSPOG to discuss paper for submission to R. on subject of renouncing neutrality of Kaesong neutral zone. Reasons—Zone breeds incidents, is military liability since it provides sanctuary for enemy troops. Msg to JCS in order however if we are to abrogate neutrality agreement[.] Also went over paper to be used as guide for liaison officers if and when they meet with enemy liaison officers to discuss new conference site. Paper limits discussion to neutral ship, island off coast and site between lines. Latter is a stickler because of question as to immunity from attack for delegation parties.

Forgot to mention I was called at 0500 today concerning another alleged strafing attack by UN aircraft on zone. I concurred in Burkes msg to Galloway that we should investigate incident. Darrow & Levie given job, going up to Kaesong at 0900.

Burke Craigie and I talked to R. about neutrality msg to JCS. He is in favor of withdrawing neutrality[.]

Rec'd short letter from Nam Il complaining about alleged UN invasion of air over neutral zone, over 100 (actually 139) sorties since Sept 1[.]

Sept. 11 (Tues): Worked at JSPOG over proposed msg to JCS concerning abolishment of Kaesong neutral zone. At 10:30 conferred with R who took proposed msg to rework. Guide to liaison officers on discussion of new conference site was finally approved. Order of preference—ship, island off Onjin [Ongjin] Peninsula, site on Pan Mun Jom bridge. At 1600 again conferred with R to smooth up msg to JCS in final form. First part of msg devoted to reasons why Kaesong zone should be terminate[d]—basis for incidents, provides enemy with a material milt. advantage refuge for Commie troops, enemy continues to stall & fabricate new allegations under cover of zone whose neutrality we respect. Msg proposed statement to Kim & Peng informing them that 24 hrs after statement was delivered immunity from attack will terminate, giving as reason zone not needed any longer. R would indicate willingness to dispatch liaison officers to meet with theirs to make arrangements for resumption of negotiations.

5th A.F. [Air Force] rpt into strafing incident showed a B-26 had been over Kaesong at time Commies contended incident occurred (about 0300 yesterday a.m.) and had actually strafed some lights. Agreed with R that we should make a clean breast of our responsibility and send note to liaison officers for transmittal to Commie liaison officers admitting our guilt and saying appropriate disciplinary action was being taken. Also get out press release & dispatch reporting violation to J.C.S. Burke & Craigie remained to work up necessary papers.

I Also released terse dispatch to Darrow (senior off [officer] remaining at camp) for delivery to Nam Il on subject of 139 sortie protest, inviting his (Nam) attention to my ltr to him of Sept 2 and asserting this answered his. & no further comment necessary.

Sept. 12 (Wed): Msg that was sent to Darrow for delivery to Nam Il follows: "The UNC Air Comdr has reported to the UNC delegate that at about 0130, 10

Sept, an aircraft was located in the Kaesong area. A continuing radar plot of the flight of the aircraft coupled with normal identification procedures revevealed [*sic*] this a/c [aircraft] to be one of the UNC. Subsequent interrogation of the pilot disclosed that he had made a strafing attack at about 0135 on targets which through faulty navigation he had incorrectly identified.

["]Based upon this info & the investigation conducted by the UNC liaison officers today the fact that an a/c of the UNC strafed within the limits of the Kaesong neutral zone on 10 Sept is accepted.

["]The UNC regrets this violation of the agreed neutrality which resulted from the pilots error in navigation. Appropriate disciplinary action is being initiated. It is noted no damage resulted from the attack[.]"

Kim & Peng replied to R in a lengthy msg, saying that his ltr. was unsatisfactory & unacceptable. Reviewed incidents accusing UNC of trying to shift blame for suspension of talks on Commies. & escape responsibility. Since we cannot deny them we are trying to divert attention by proposing change in conference site. Also we are trying to evade responsibility for agreement violations & create pretext for breaking off negotiations. Ends by demanding that we put an end at once to incessant acts of violations of agreement. Otherwise will have to bear entire responsibility for delay & obstruction in progress of negotiations and their consequences.

Worked over proposed reply in the evening.

Sept. 13 (Thurs): Smoothed up proposed reply in JSPOG, to Kims & Pengs ltr to R. After acknowledging ltr our proposed reply went on to point out that each of Commies allegations of violation of neutral zone had been carefully investigated. UNC's objective attitude towards incidents clearly demonstrated by our acknowledgement of fact that UNC aircraft had strafed Kaesong on 10 Sept through accident. Evidence supplied by UNC radar, plus investigation, determined this fact. Our proposed reply then went on to say that UNC has never guaranteed that its a/c [aircraft] will not fly over zone. Liaison officers were discussing matter when talks were suspended. Although no agreement existed UNC planes have employed every reasonable precaution to avoid flights over Kaesong area. Concerning proposal for a new site we pointed out that this was clearly a constructive step towards freeing armistice talks from interruption. Ended msg. by saying "When you are ready to terminate the suspension of the armistice negotiations which you declared on 23 Aug I am prepared to order my liaison officers to Pan Mun Jom to discuss conditions that will be mutually satisfactory for a resumption of the armistice talks.["]

Although Ridgway liked and accepted the proposed reply it was decided not to send it until Commies had a chance to answer my acknowledgment of the 10 Sept strafing incident. Craigie Burke & I also discussed ultimatum msg to J.C.S which R accepted with mods [modifications] proposed by us. These mods had to do with proposed course of action, i.e. in what steps we would lead up to springing ultimatum to Commies. first sub-del meetings, then plenary sessions and lastly the delivery of the ultimatum by CinCUNC on the demilt [demilitarized] zone. Discussed also JCS msg in reply to R's which requested authority to abrogate neutral zone. JCS told R in effect to wait another week and bring matter up again. Seemed to think in view my msg to Nam Il acknowledging our guilt in strafing incident that this was not the time to announce abolishment of zone.

Sept. 14—17: At Karuizawa

Sept. 18 (Tues): Returned to Tokyo last night to read R's reply in Stars and Stripes to Commies ltr of 12 Sept. It was much shorter than our proposed version which I understand will be used as press material. Gist of it was to effect "that allegations contained in your ltr have been thoroughly investigated establishing fact that UNC forces were not involved except for one incident occurring 10 Sept. Investigations demonstrate objective and responsible attitude of UNC towards violations of agreements concerning neutral zone." Ends up by saying "if you are now disposed to terminate suspension of armistice negotiations which you declared on 23 August I am still prepared to order my liaison officers to meet with yours at Pan Mun Jom to discuss conditions that will be mutually satisfactory for a resumption of armistice talks."

Sept. 19 (Wed): Another "incident" which was somewhat ludicrous. Four ROK medics sent on mission to spray DDT on advanced billets became lost & wandered into Pan Mun Jom where they were picked up by Commies who telephoned camp asking our liaison offs. [officers] come to Kaesong. Edwards, senior of our party which went up to investigate, convinced Commies that ROKs were harmless, since they carried no arms, and should be released which was done. Edwards reported Col Chang was much more friendly than usual. which may be a good sign.
Spent most of day at my Hdqtrs.

Sept. 20 (Thurs): Spent entire morning at GHQ considering proposed reply to Gens [Generals] Kim & Pengs ltr to Gen R, dated 19 Sept. Korean & Chinese versions somewhat different. Gist of Korean version: "You have ack. [acknowledged] fact that UN acft [aircraft] machine gunned Kaesong zone on 10 Sept. But you still deny many incidents of air & ground violations. Denials cannot do away with evidence we hold. Therefore you must proceed with a responsible disposition of these incidents[.]"
"In view your expression of regret of recent violation and your statement that you would take a responsible attitude. & so that as yet unsettled incidents shall not continue to hinder progress of negotiations we propose delegations immediately

resume negotiations in Kaesong[.]'' [*sic*] No necessity to discuss again conditions for resumption of negotiations[.]''

[''*]Regarding question of disposition of above mentioned unsettled incidents &
guarantee of strict agreements re. neutralization of Kaesong zone, we propose that
at first meeting there be established under mutual agreement a suitable organization for taking chg [charge] of such functions. Of course, all agreements of this
organ. [organization] will be effective only upon ratification of delegations of
both sides.

[''*]If you agree, we hope that you will immediately order your liaison offs. to
meet ours to discuss time & date for resumption of negots [negotiations] in
Kaesong.''

At conf.[conference] with R in p.m. it was decided that reply would disclaim
necessity for reviewing & rehashing past incidents & would hold out for new
conference site. Would end up by saying Liaison offs would meet theirs at Pan
Mun Jom to discuss conditions for resumption of negotiations. More conferences
tomorrow[.]

Sept. 21 (Fri): Following msg approved by R in reply to Kim & Peng's of 19th.
"Your msg of 19 Sept, received 20 Sept, has been noted. I flatly reject your
suggestion therein that there are instances of alleged violations of the Kaesong
neutral zone which remain unsettled. Each of the several cases wherein you
reported an alleged violation of the zone and requested an investigation was
investigated fully at the time. Where UN forces were responsible, the fact was
reported. Where UN forces were not involved you were so advised. All cases
were settled definitely and my representatives will be guided accordingly. Again
I emphatically reject the baseless charges repeated in your ltr that alleged
violations of the Kaesong zone by the UNC forces made it impossible to continue
the negotiations. The responsibility for the inexcusable interruption in the
armistice conference is completely yours.''

"In your msg you arbitrarily dismissed the need to discuss conditions incident
to the resumption of negotiations in spite of the obvious fact that the armistice
discussions have been interrupted for prolonged periods because of incidents or
alleged incidents. I have therefore given instructions to my liaison officers to
insure that this vital subject receives careful attention in order to minimize the
likelihood of further interruption.''

[''*]Since you are now ready to terminate the suspension of armistice talks which
you declared on 23 Aug. my liaison officers will be at the bridge at Pan Mun Jom
at 1000 on 24 Sept to meet your liaison officers and to discuss conditions
mutually satisfactory for a resumption of the armistice talks.''

At the 0945 conference which approved the above we also discussed the
proposed guide for our liaison officers and the memo Kinney is to hand to Col
Chang, which needed revision.

Sept. 22 (Sat): J.C.S came thru with a msg. which in effect turned thumbs down on par [paragraph] 2 & 3 of R's proposed reply to Commies. In conference with R. attended by Craigie Burke Hickey Wright & others we went over our proposed reply to JCS requesting re-consideration. This msg to JCS pointed out that it was obvious Commies desired to establish certain principles & facts & to induce a reply which could be made to appear as agreement thereto by UNC[.] Said also "In my opinion the omission of the 2nd and 3d paras. of my proposed msg will completely abrogate the posit [position] we have established and will assist the Commies in their efforts to maneuver UNC into the position desired by them.["]

Sept. 23 (Sun): J.C.S came thru with an approval of R's reconsideration msg to them. but telling R to tone down his par [paragraphs] 2 & 3. Reply to Commies which went out at 1800 today approx as follows: "Your suggestion therein that there are instances of alleged violations of Kaesong neutral zone which remain unsettled is rejected. Each of several cases wherein you reptd [reported] an alleged violation was fully investigated. Where UNC forces were responsible, the fact was rptd. Where UNC forces were not involved you were so advised and the cases closed. I have so instructed my representatives." Rest of msg about the same as before.

Sept. 24 (Mon): Met at 0830 JSPOG to discuss JCS suggestion that new proposal to Commies on demilt.[demilitarized] zone be made when talks are resumed. Zone to be of 4 kms in width and based strictly on b.l. [battle line] or in effect our minimum position. We felt that any such drastic concession would indicate weakness on our part and encourage Commies to stall again through the use of other incidents in order to get further concessions from us. However we recognized desirability of presenting a new proposal, this proposal to be a clarification of last position taken by UNC sub committee. It would be in nature of our former min. [minimum] position. Ridgway agreed at conference with him at 0930. Also agreed with us that our proposed msg to JCS on unrestricted inspection be held up until we are sure of returning to Korea. Our ultimatum msg like wise.

Rec'd Kinney & Murray's rpt of their 1000 meeting at Pan Mun Jom with Chang. They proceeded to Kaesong for talks. Chang disavowed authority to discuss other than time or date. Kinney presented him with written memo on proposal to change conference site asking for authorized answer tomorrow at 1000 when Kinney & Murray would return to Kaesong unless advised otherwise by Chang. He recommended no reply to Kim & Pengs msg of this morning until present phase of liaison meetings is over.

Kim & Pengs reply of this date to R's of yesterday reiterated their former stand. Said "We have already instructed our delegates to put forward our demands for the appropriate machinery which should be set up by mutual agreement after resumption of Kaesong talks in order to deal with these unsettled incidents." — — — "Our side has always requested that a strict agreement on the neutrality of the Kaesong area be worked out to avoid future interruptions. However, our liaison officers do not have authority to stipulate these concrete & strict conditions that must be mutually agreed upon; it is necessary that agreement thereon be made by our delegates. In order not to affect the armistice negotiations we have proposed that the first meeting upon the resumption of negots. [negotiations] at Kaesong an appropriate machinery should be set up thru mutual agreement to settle these problems."

Sept. 25 (Tues): At liaison offs [officers] meeting Communists continued their refusal to discuss conditions mutually satisfactory for a resumption of Armistice talks. Met with R. & others to discuss drafting msg to JCS requesting that R. be authorized "to refuse categorically to send my delegation back to Kaesong & to insist upon a new and satisfactory conference site within which security for both sides can be assured beyond reasonable doubt[.]" Msg based reason for this request that Commies are dodging & evading UNC positions. Their purpose is to force the UNC Del to hold at least one more meeting at Kaesong. Pointed out that Jap leaders say only way to handle Commies is to continue to take strong positions and not to be in too much of a hurry. Ceaseless flow of protests & propaganda would keep UNC in role of a defendant if we return to Kaesong. R's view that UNC Del should agree to a resumption of conference only under conditions fully acceptable to us. Time working to Commie disadvantage[.] Agreement on Kaesong issue would constitute deplorable abandonment of all we have so far achieved, would surrender initiative and subject us to further outrageous demands & ridicule of U.S. & world opinion.

Sept. 26 (Wed): Telecon with Wash [Washington] from 08:15 until 12:00. Present Wash: Collins, Bolte, Mr Merchant, Bohlen & Nitze. Present CinCFE Ridgway, Hickey, Joy, Craigie, Burke, Wright, Briggs, Galloway, Hickman Moorman. Wash started off. State & JCS feel that every effort should be made to arrange a meeting of principal negotiators as soon as possible in order that real intention of Commies may be revealed. Present liaison off [officer] discussions not likely to be productive. Suggested extraordinary meeting of principal negotiators at suitable place vicinity front lines. Great importance would attach to initial posit [position] adopted by UNC at such a meeting. Should not resume old bargaining position as to demilt [demilitarized] zone. Would be retrogression from last sub Del meeting. Many advantages would accrue to picking up from point where talks broke down. Adm Joy should at once make a proposal in writing on a map. If Commies do not arbitrarily reject our proposal but indicate they need time for consultation, principals could then proceed to discuss site for next meeting. Then asked clarification on our minimum position; what site as alternative for Kaesong; conditions to insure neutrality of site to avoid recurrence of trumped up charges. Wash went on to say "single issue of our refusal to return to Kaesong would be disadvantageous to us as definitive breaking point of negots [negotiations]. We cannot tell whether or not Commies would in fact break on this point but we do not believe we should continue to insist on change of site as precondition for meeting of principal delegates to point where risk seems great that Commies will break. — — — We emphasize importance of full delegation meeting promptly under min. [minimum] safety conditions acceptable to you in order to get into Commie hands in writing modified posit [position] on line of dem [demarcation]. One factor in our respective attitudes on negotiating tactics is estimate of Commie attitude to Armistice. We take it that you are satisfied that "an early Armistice is for Commies a matter of urgency[.]" We here are still in doubt as to degree to which in fact Commies desire or feel need of Armistice. Hence we think it important to ascertain their intentions by move on our part.

Tokyo's rmks [remarks]. First sent Chang's reply to Kinney saying "Del our side ready to meet with yours at 1000 Sept 26th. As you are aware my Cmdrs have proposed to your CinC that dels. both sides should resume negots. in Kaesong immediately without need to discuss conditions for resuming negots. I am only authorized to discuss date & time for resuming talks. Should your side be adverse to resuming armst. conf. [armistice conference] on 26th it is requested you inform me specifically to that effect & I shall be prepared to continue to consult with you at 0900 Sept 26 about date & time for resuming conference." Kinney rpld. [replied] "I shall meet you at 1000 today in accord my msg to you" at which time they met. We went on to say to Wash "The subject of 1st priority is an acceptable arrangement for the meeting of the principal delegates. This must be accomplished before serious consideration of UNC position on Item 2 of agenda is pertinent. I consider max [maximum] concession that can be made towards effecting a meeting of the principal delegates is to propose a meeting at some place between b.l.'s [battle lines] (under no circumstances at Kaesong) for the specific & single purpose of discussing conditions mutually satisfactory for a resumption of armistice talks. Believe we failed to make clear it was our intention in first substantive meeting to present proposal which embodied aspects most favorable to Commies as presented in sub-comit [committee] meeting of Aug 22. This actually complies with a request made by Commies at sub-comit meeting at which they expressed confusion at the many alternative adjustments informally discussed by UNC sub Committee. It would in our opinion pick up discussion at point where talks broke down. To do otherwise would indicate to Commies that they gained great advantages by long recess they initiated. Following seem to be determining factors in reaching decision on your proposal. 1st to comply with your instrs we must avoid agreement on any zone which endangers Kansas line. Line of 4 kms. described above would be our absolute min position. 2nd since it would be the min position it must be made clear to

Commies at or about the time this proposal is made that it is a 'take it or leave it' proposal. In other words it will be an ultimatum on which we much be prepared to break[.]''

Upon receipt of note that UNC Liaison Offs were coming to K. at 1000 Chang replied: ''Since you did not come at 0900 I am prepared to meet with you at 1000 today to discuss date & time for resuming negots at Kaesong.'' They are certainly persistent devils!

I then spent from 1301 to 1700 with JSPOG Burke & Craigie preparing despatch to JCS. essentially as follows: Part 1 Conference site. Meeting place should be between forward elements of both sides at a point not dominated by either side. Intend propose location along line of contact in vicinity Songhyon-Ni [Sangnyong?]. This would minimize difficulties both sides have experienced at Kaesong. Condition 1000 yd circular area. No armed personnel in area. Refrain from acts of armed force within conference area from 0800 to 1800 daily & along selected routes of approach to conf. [conference] area from Kaesong & Munsan Ni daily from 0800 to 1800. Free access from 0800 to 1800 daily. Patrols from each side, manned & armed as mutually agreed to patrol along outer boundary of area from 0800 to 1800. Area of patrol by mutual agreement.

Part 2 Demilitarized Zone (A)(1) Armistice concluded must leave us in secure possession of Kansas line; we must have security zone of adequate depth; present line of contact if adopted as median line of 4 kms zone would provide this essential security zone and, except in center of present front, no rpt [repeat] no more. (2) In center of our present posit we could withdraw somewhat to south of line of contact without essential encroachment on min necessary security zone. (3) Withdrawal from center would only be contemplated as part of an exchange by which UNC would acquire control of part of Yonan Peninsula. (4) Hence 4 km zone based on present line of c [contact] as median should be accepted as our min. posit. (5) At initial meeting propose to present 20 km zone roughly sketched out by Hodes at last sub-del meeting as possibility for discussion. (B) Pointed out any concession to Commies on zone during 1st meeting will be equivalent to making first of series of blackmail payments. Must not let Commies dictate all imp. [important] moves. UNC tactical position is too strong for us to appease. Time working for us.

Part 3. Recommended Courses of Action. (a) state to Commies thru liaison offs. that our Del will be at Songhyon Ni at earliest possible time. (b) If Commies agree to meet at Songhyon-Ni UNC Del will attempt to limit discussion to conditions for resumption of armistice conference & substantive items of agenda & definitely refuse to discuss past incidents. (c) If Commies insist upon discussing past incidents UNC will nevertheless read paper and present map giving posit of demil zone (Hodes rough sketch) (d) If Commies refuse to meet at Songhyon Ni abrogate neutral zone unless you have directed otherwise.

2 [sic]. If these rec [recommended] courses of action approved, I intend to

send following to Commies: "Since you have not seen fit to give your liaison offs sufficient authority to permit satisfactory conditions to be arranged for the resumption of armistice talks, I submit following proposal directly to you. I believe this proposal provides for arrangements that can be mutually satisfactory to both sides."

"I propose that both delegations meet as early as possible at a point approx midway between the b.1.'s in vicinity of Songhyon-Ni."

"It would, of course, be agreed by both sides that this meeting place would be kept free of armed troops and that both sides would abstain from any hostile acts or exercise of authority over members of other side in their passage to this point or while they are there."

"I propose that upon resumption of del. meetings at this point, both dels. be prepared to return to the discussion of Item 2 of Agenda immediately following any discussion that may be needed to clarify physical & security arrangements at the meeting place."

"If you concur, I will arrange to have our liaison offs. meet to discuss immediate erection of the necessary physical facilities."

Part 4 Conclusions. "I regard the issue of resumption of Del. meetings at Kaesong as the most fundamental of any so far faced. I regard retreat on this issue as surrender, which will enormously multiply our difficulties in all subsequent Armistice discussions here."

I finally got home about 1845. What a day!

Sept. 27 (Thurs): JCS came thru with approval of Part 1; Rec [recommended] Part 3 paras 1a & b approved and proposed despatch to Commies with minor mod [modification] approved. J.C.S went on to say "Although this course of action will make it still more difficult to return to Kaesong, if Commies insist on Kaesong you will not make this issue a final breaking pt [point] nor abrogate neutrality of Kaesong without further ref [reference] to Washington. Action on your other rec. courses of action will be sent you soonest."

Kinney sent following msg to Chang. "In reply to your proposal that the dels. [delegations] meet on 27 Sept, I am instructed to inform you that it is Adm. Joy's desire that the Dels. meet as soon as conditions mutually satisfactory for the meetings have been arranged, including fixing the time & date of the meeting of the delegates. To that end unless I hear from you to the contrary, I will meet with you at 1000 27 Sept." To which Chang replied "Since your side has, for 3d time rejected the proposal of our side to resume negots [negotiations] by refusing to come to K at 1000 Sept 27 to proceed with armistice negots, I am prepared to continue to consult with you at 1000 Sept 27 on the date & time of resumption of Kaesong negots. and only on the question of the date & time of resumption of Armistice negots at Kaesong."

Kinney stalled off going to Kaesong at 1000 and instead went up later to deliver msg for Kim & Peng (signed by Ridgway) which had been approved by JCS. We spent some time deliberating on who would sign msg R or myself. Finally decided on R. because it would have more weight and avoid possibility of having Nam come back saying he had no authority to meet at any place other than Kaesong. Would also take Kinney off the hook and make it more difficult for JCS to turn down R's request for authority to refuse to return to Kaesong.

I then had short talk with R about responsibilities. R said Kinney exceeded his authority in saying he had broad authority to arrange for resumption of negots & conference site. I said I would send Burke back to keep tight reign on things. Burke leaves tomorrow. We discussed papers to prepare. Position on Demilt [demilitarized] zone is one & Conditions for resuming negots at K [Kaesong] another. Later in pm I had conference with Burke & Craigie over article in Times which said Commies proposal for setting appropriate machinery for settling past & future incidents was same as we had previously proposed for regulating & inspecting neutrality zone. They concurred with me that N.Y. Times & other papers should be set straight thru Brig. Gen. Allen.

Sept. 28 (Fri): Nothing special except golf game in p.m. with Craigie Muse & Garey. While on links word came thru Ridgway wanted to see me at 1800 at Embassy. along with Craigie. Upon arrival there also found Hickey. R's purpose of conference—that we all agreed on firm stand he would take with Bradly & Bohlen about returning to Kaesong. I was not too pleased with his paper outlining concessions UNC had made to Commies. Felt that it showed Delegation had given in to Commies too much. when in fact we had now major victory. over foreign troop withdrawal issue which we had kept off agenda.

Sept. 29 (Sat): Conference with R, Bradley Bohlen, Hickey & Craigie over our next move. Bohlen definitely felt only way we could determine Commie intentions was to reenter negotiations with a definite proposal in writing, accompanied by a map, showing our "near" final position on the demilt. zone based on B.L. [battle line]. This would not be a concession from Hodes last posit [position] at sub del meeting since we would not abandon our posit of refusing to negotiate on basis of 38th parallel. Bohlen & Bradley both agreed we could not go back to Kaesong. Following decisions made on basis Commies reply to last R msg refused proposal for Delegations to meet at Songhyon-Ni. (1) By ltr of transmital to Peng & Kim R would propose sub del meet at place of Commie choosing between B.L. to discuss our "near" final position on Item 2 which would be Basis for Discussion. This position would show mutual withdrawal from L of C. [line of contact] but would not be final position which would not be proposed until later meetings and then only on a take it or leave it basis. If our final or min [minimum] position was unfavorably received we could then walk out of the conference. By 1000 tomorrow we were to have ready map showing (1) "near" final position (2) final position and Kansas line. (3) Ltr of transmittal to Commies (thru liaison offs) and (4) Courses of action.

Had lunch with Bohlen & Craigie at Air Force Club and then attended conference at JSPOG with Craigie to assign work on papers to be ready by 0830 tomorrow when we would meet prior to Conference. Courses of action to be divided in two parts (A) If Commies refuse to meet at Songhyon Ni and (B) If they agree to meet there.

Bradlys, Bohlen, LeFevres, Trivett, Dr Skinner, Pelley, Craigies, & Eric Pollock came for Kts' [cocktails].

Sept. 30 (Sun): After meeting at JSPOG to go over papers met with R, Bradley, Bohlen Craigie and Hickey at 1000 to go over map with zone we would propose if and when it was decided to present same to Commies. Map showed 4 km zone based on present line of contact with compensating and mutual withdrawals. It was not our min. or "take it or leave it" position. It also showed outpost line needed to secure Kansas line. We withdraw on extreme east and in center whereas Commies withdraw in vicinity of Kaesong. Bradley asked R if from our own military standpoint an early armistice was necessary. R said no it was not urgent. It was therefore agreed that we would not be in a hurry to meet with Commies or to present our new UNC proposed zone. Based on supposition that Commies would not agree to our proposal to meet at Songhyon-Ni it was decided to counter Commie refusal only with suggestion that they propose a site between the b.ls. [battle lines] acceptable to us. If this does not get them out of Kaesong and if it should become evident they were on the point of breaking off the negots permanently we would then propose, thru the liaison offs, our new zone as a "basis for discussion." In this proposal we would unequivocally refuse to return to Kaesong, which would require approval from J.C.S. R has authority to continue insistence on new site as long as he does not categorically refuse to return to Kaesong. Bohlen made it clear public would support non return to Kaesong but our support would not be as solid if conference broke without our having presented our reasonable and new demilt zone, instead of only the original 20 mile version. We also discussed unrestricted inspection and agreed to send our previously drafted despatch on subject to JC.S. after R has reviewed it again. Discussed also prisoners of war and some of the knotty problems connected therewith—including what to do with PWs who do not wish to return to Commie side. No decisions reached.

Bradley emphasized that their visit was mainly for exchanging views and not to make decisions. The difference in their thinking from ours is that Wash [Washington] was of opinion an armistice was a matter of urgency for us, whereas it actually is not as R explained. Time & the approach of winter is working to our advantage. Therefore it is better from our standpoint not to hurry a meeting of the delegations.

Bohlen asked our view on the desirability of having Kirk [Allan G. Kirk, U.S. ambassador to the Soviet Union] interview Stalin before he (Kirk) left Moscow. Kirk to caution Stalin war might well spread unless Korean war concluded. Kirk must be careful not to threaten. We allowed that it might help and R said he thought it a good idea, but we must not show undue eagerness.

It was decided Craigie would make trip to Korea tomorrow with R Bradley & Bohlen to interview Van Fleet regarding proposed zone. After he telephoned back result from Seoul msg was to be sent to JCS giving coordinates of new UNC zone in order that we might have early approval should Commies suddenly accept R's proposal to meet at Songhyon-Ni.

Oct. 1 (Mon): No business concerning armistice negots. Remained all day at my Hdqtrs catching up on Navy business. Saw Jack Clark & Hill. Latter to give briefing tomorrow on Operation Wrangler. Galloway phoned to say new 4 km zone approved by Van Fleet & Hodes with minor modification & would be passed on to J.C.S. Nothing from Commies in reply to R's proposal to meet at Songhyon-Ni. Attended Hahn's [a Navy combat artist] exhibit of his sketches at Readers Digest Bldg.

Oct. 2 (Tues): Following msg sent to JCS last night after Craigie called from Seoul:

"1. In event exchanges with Commies result in agreement on a site other than Kaesong, UNC Del at first substantive session will immediately propose as the basis for discussion a 4 km demilt zone based on the following median line. — — — This line gives us some negotiating flexibility without jeopardizing line Kansas in event Commies accept it as basis for discussion. In event this line of C [contact] undergoes any appreciable change prior to submitting this proposal the location of the demilt zone will be adjusted accordingly.

"2. In event Commies continue their present intransigent stand relative to Kaesong, but there is no indication that a break is imminent, I plan to continue pressing for a new site without categorically foreclosing on Kaesong at that time.

"3. In event Commies continue their present intransigent stand on Kaesong and in addition it is estimated they are about to break on this issue, I intend to send following msg to Commies, with a map describing the proposed zone as indicated below. 'Your ltr to me acknowledges my ltr to you of 27 Sept. but rejects my proposal for meeting of our two delegations at Songhyon Ni. I have already made clear to you my views regarding the unsuitability of Kaesong as a conference site; equality of entry & control has not been and cannot be assured there.

"I repeat that the UNC has been and still remains willing to effect an honorable milt. armistice. Therefore, I propose that the negots be resumed at a meeting of the sub-dels. to discuss agenda item 2 and that it be agreed in advance by both parties to accept the attached map as the basis for discussion of Agenda Item 2.

"You will note that this basis for discussion envisages a demilt zone generally along present line of C. It requires compensating withdrawals in some places and mutual withdrawals in others in order to establish the demilt zone.

"If you concur in the above as the basis for discussion, I propose that the armistice negots be resumed at a place selected by you and acceptable to us midway between the present b.ls.

"The above proposals are submitted to you in an effort to secure an early resumption of negots. [There is a sentence crossed out here, identical to the one which follows except for the last word, which is "negots" instead of "talks"] If you accept my liaison offs. will meet with yours to discuss the new location and to arrange for the facilities required for the resumption of the talks.

"4. Copies of my msg to Kim & Peng together with photo copies of the map, will be issued to the press simultaneously with the release to the Commies in event this msg is sent under conditions visualized in para 3.

"5. Accomplishment of the above should make clear to world opinion that the UNC is prepared to establish a demilt zone based on the principle of mutual withdrawal from present l of c [line of contact]."

"6. Bradly [*sic*] & Bohlen concur. Your approval requested."

Oct 3 (Wed): Still no word from Commies. Attended watch committee conference at GHQ at 0900. At 1000 R. had short conference with his principal Tokyo Generals Bradley, Bohlen, Weyland & myself. Bradley led off with remarks on his trip to Korea—very pleased with what he saw. Complimented Command. Bohlen then took over with resume of State Dept's position on world problems. Keen and careful attention given to Korean war which he considered key to future trend of events. Expansion of war might lead to World War III though he believed Stalin spent 23 hrs of 24 worrying over internal situation in Russia and security of "the Party", and not to long range planning for World War III. Stalin is a great opportunist. The Russians are like a vulture on a fence waiting to pounce on a weak animal. Iran a very tender spot but trouble not caused by Soviets. It is an emotional and hysterical nationalistic movement. Also fraught with danger economically since Britain needs vital middle east oil.

Upon termination of conference I gave R our revised msg for JCS concerning our views on the question of unlimited inspection and asked R to bring up point of Burke & Craigie's retention until negots are over.

Saw Bradleys' & Bohlen off at Haneda [airfield at Tokyo] at 1900. Bradley said to me: "Keep up the good work."

Oct. 4 (Thurs): Commies replied to R's ltr of 27th. Gist of their reply. Saw no reason for our proposal to change conference site[.] Accidental incident of 4 Aug (armed troop violation) disposed of satisfactorily. Suspension talks since Aug 22 due to UNC violations. "When you admitted violation on 10 Sept and showed you were ready to make responsible disposition we proposed meetings be resumed." Immed. [immediate] problem is to resume negots. at Kaesong immediately and by regulating strict neutrality agreement guarantee that incidents will not occur again. Cant strike aside issues & bring up new problem of changing site. UNC unreasonable proposal is only to make new excuse to delay negots. If UNC had same sincere & responsible attitude as we have it would not be difficult to arrive at reasonable results. "Therefore I propose delegations immediately resume conference at Kaesong organize appropriate machinery and establish strict agreement on neutralization of zone, & guarantee smooth progress of negots by its enforcement." Ended by suggesting liaison offs meet immed. to discuss matters concerning resumption of conference at Kaesong.

Noticeable concessions on part of Commies are (1) Dropping of their insistence that past incidents must be responsibly settled (2) giving liaison offs. power to discuss conditions for resumption of conference.

Our reply to above was short and to the point. R cut down UNCD proposed reply to following: "I have already made clear to you my views regarding the unsuitability of Kaesong as a conference site. Events have proved that equality of movement and control has not been and cannot be assured there. Satisfactory conditions for resumption of the Armistice talks can only be insured by moving the conference site to an area which is not under exclusive control of either side.

"Since you reject my suggestion to meet at Songhyon-Ni, I propose that our Dels. meet at a site selected by you and acceptable to me approx midway between our respective front lines where the Armistice discussions can be promptly resumed, under the conditions stated in my msg to you of 27 Sept."

Some discussion centered on our sentence containing "can only be assured" since this could be interpreted as an ultimatum. R felt msg would be weakened by substituting "best" for "only". At any rate msg is on border line while definitely not refusing to return to Kaesong.

After considerable discussion msg to J.C.S. requesting guidance on question of insistence on unlimited inspection. Gist of msg follows. Points out JCS now require free & unlimited access to all Korea by teams of observers to insure terms of Armistice are carried out. In view Commies known position against observation of activities under their direct control UNC requires clarification on degree of inspection UNC must insist upon. What we want is sufficient freedom of access and right of inspection in areas outside demilt zone to insure that there is no build up of troops or supplies in such quantities as would if continued substantially impair security of UNC as that security existed when Armistice became effective. Depending on agreement reached on Agenda Item 2, UNC may find it desirable to accept less than ideal solution on inspection unless UNC is authorized to break negots on this point. If this not case it might be desirable to consider alternate positions on inspection. In R's view minimum rights of inspection consistent with reasonably safeguarding security UNC would be about as follows:

(a) Observation by Joint Observer Teams at ground sea & air ports of entry and communication centers thruout all Korea as mutually agreed to by two Dels, together with freedom of movement for above teams over principal lines of communication thruout all Korea.

(b) Joint aerial observation & photo reconn over all Korea.

(c) Complete joint observation of demilt. zone.

Final position. Same as above except omit (b)[.]

Oct. 5 (Fri): Command conference with R at 10:30. Discussed frigates (10) for Japan and Ryukan [*sic*] Coast Guard (2). R wants memo showing our views as to what organization Jap Coastal Security Force should be under until Peace Treaty is signed. We believe should be initially under MSA for fiscal support and as a cover but when Treaty is signed it should be a separate agency. He (R) will take matter up with [Prime Minister] Yoshida when our views are known in order that we may be able to contact some Jap in authority to start planning set up for organization.

Oct. 6 (Sat): Nothing special. Golf in p.m. with Robertson, Muse & Craigie. I took all the money[.]

Oct. 7 (Sun): Commies reply to R's ltr of 4th was delivered in p.m. Gist of it. Complained no reason for changing conference site unless UNC wishes to evade responsibility of disposing of continuous provocative actions by which UNC violated Neutral Zone agreement. You (UNC) cannot evade responsibility. But in order to test UNC good faith we propose. (1) Scope of neutrality of Conference site be expanded to a rectangular zone to include Kaesong & Munsan (2) Conference site be moved to Pan Mun Jom (3) Both sides assume responsibility of protecting conference site. Also propose resume conference immediately and that at first meeting after resumption make regs [regulations] concerning expansion of Neutrality zone and principle concerning security of site[.] Establish machinery to discuss concrete & strict regs, and that by guaranteeing their enforcement smooth progress of negots be assured. *After* you agree our Liaison offs meet with yours to discuss matters concerning resumption of conference.

Oct. 8 (Mon): Spent all day, practically, at Dai Ichi Bldg framing reply to Commie msg which in final form follows: (1) "Your msg of 7 Oct has been received. I refer you to my previous msgs and again categorically state that the responsibility for the delay in the negots [negotiations] during the past several weeks is yours.

2. "In my msgs to you of 27 Sept and 4 Oct, I stated the fundamental condition which must exist in order to insure equality of control & equality of movement from & within the conference site. That condition is, I repeat, that the conference site be situated approx midway between our respective front lines. Only so, can each side be expected to discharge its share of responsibility for the security of the approaches to the conference site and of the site itself.

3. "In regard to your proposed expansion of the neutral zone, it is my view that all that is necessary is a small neutral zone around the new conference site, with Kaesong Munsan and the roads to Pan Mun Jom from Kaesong and Munsan free from attack by both sides.

4. "In the belief that a site in the immed vicinity of Pan Mun Jom will meet the fundamental condition of equality of movement & control and that you will share my views regarding its neutrality I am instructing my liaison offs. to meet with yours at 1000 10 Oct for the purpose of discussing matters concerning the resumption of negots by our resp. [respective] delegations.[''']

Oct. 9 (Tues): Finally approved in conference with R instrs. to Liaison offs [officers]. These included (a) Selection & joint control of conference site (b) Physical facilities at conference site (c) Security of both Dels in their respective housing areas in Kaesong and Munsan and on the roads there from to Pan Mun Jom.

In order that UNC can exercise equality of control & movement to new conference site, 8th Army has been instructed to be prepared to occupy with a security force the high ground to east of and dominating Pan Mun Jom at any time subsequent to 1000 10 Oct '51. In your discussion with Commies liaison offs should inform them of general area in which UNC security troops are to be moved forward to posits [positions] formerly occupied on 17 July and subsequently withdrawn by UNC order. These troops are to provide the UNC participation in the protection of the conference site.

Also discussed with R despatch from Vandenberg which again asked that Craigie be relieved (to get 3 stars). Agreed with R that Craigie be released two weeks after Turner reports. I also asked that Nuckols be returned to Korea with Delegation. We then discussed presentation of item 2 at first meeting. It was agreed that our new proposal be presented as "a basis for discussion" which would be better than merely as a proposal, since we could then walk out if Commies stuck to the 38th parallel (tactics suggested by Bradley and Bohlen).

Ridgway wants the security troops moved in to occupy the high ground before main Dels meet and Commies so informed.

Oct. 10 (Wed): Met Radford and party at Haneda at 0900. Proceeded my qtrs for short discussion with Raddy before leaving for Korea. At 1100 departed Haneda for Kimpo with Craigie, Briggs & Wagner in P2V [twin-engine patrol bomber]. Arrived Munsan shortly after 1500. Had conference immediately to learn results of liaison officers meeting in morning. Murray reported Commies had already erected a tent in a field opposite village of PMJ [Pan Mun Jom] where they had their meeting. Commie instructions only permitted them to discuss arrangements for a site and time & date for meeting of main Dels. Refused to discuss our proposal for Restricted areas at Kaesong & Munsan and security arrangements other than at conference site itself, saying these were matters for main Dels and beyond their authority. Chang refused to accept our map showing circular areas around Munsan & Kaesong but Chinese took it up before meeting broke up. They arranged to meet again tomorrow. Later in evening we sent a msg to Tokyo saying that liaison officers would continue on present tack trying to button up all arrangements before Dels meet. Would continue this way for several days and then if unsuccessful in reaching agreement would agree to Dels meeting to thrash out matters which could not be settled by liaison officers.

Oct. 11 (Thurs): Had meeting in my tent with Craigie, Burke & Goldhamer to discuss whether new UNC zone proposal would be introduced as a proposal or as a basis for discussion. Agreed latter implied greater bargaining latitude and that zone would initially be introduced as a proposal. Later we could propose it as a basis for discussion and walk out if it were not accepted as such. Since R understands new zone will be introduced as basis for discussion it will be necessary to advise him of our intentions to introduce it as a proposal.

We had considerable discussion as to when the UNC proposal should be presented. Should we wait to see what Commies have to offer or should our proposal be presented at earliest possible moment? Or at earliest convenient moment? On the whole the reasons for trying to maneuver the Commies into speaking first do not seem very compelling. Craigie & Burke feel we should deal with procedural matters first (security arrangements, etc.) before presenting our new item 2 zone. It would create an impression of anxiety for UNC to rush into presenting the proposal. To rush would make Commies suspicious.

Oct. 12 (Fri): Liaison officers met again at 10:00. Commies presented proposed draft agreement for permitting delegations to meet which included most of our conditions but not our proposal for a Kaesong restricted area of 3000 yd radius. Agreed to circular area for Munsan and stipulation that each side refrain from attacking road to Pan Mun Jom. Conference site area conditions also mutually agreed upon. At noon recess we went over with Murray Commies proposed draft agreement for resumption of Delegation meetings, correcting certain items and suggesting an additional para [paragraph] for submission to the Commies in the afternoon session. This para outlined our proposal for the Kaesong Restricted area. Murray told Commies as soon as they agreed to our proposed additional para. he would be in a position to make a definite committment [*sic*] as to time & date for UNC Del to meet with Commies. He reported Commies still appeared anxious to have Dels. meet as soon as possible.

Sent a msg to R outlining our proposed course of action with regard to introduction of new demilt. [demilitarized] zone. Zone would be proposed as a "solution" to Item 2 of the Agenda—a new, specific, concrete solution. In presenting the proposal it is not planned to propose also that it be made the sole basis for discussion. Under present circumstances UNC firm insistence on the acceptance of its proposal seems preferable to permitting the discussion to become sidetracked into lengthy argument on the limits of discussion. Later if Commies show complete recalcitrance the UNC can insist on its proposal being the sole basis of discussion and if necessary support its insistence by an ultimatum.

Murray does not think Commies will agree to our proposal concerning Kaesong Restricted area and will continue to press that matter be settled by Delegations. This brings up question as to how we should go about it. My opinion is that we should come out with flat statement at 1st meeting that we will not recognize the old neutral zone—only area similar to one around Munsan. After making that statement it is my opinion we should then go ahead with proposal for new zone.

At 1915 Commies phoned to report another neutrality zone violation by UNC aircraft at 1725[.] Requested investigators proceed PMJ [Pan Mun Jom]. I sent up Darrow & Edwards with instructions to tell Commies we would hold investigation during daylight.

Oct. 13 (Sat): Darrow reported at my tent around midnight last night upon return of his investigating trip to P.M.J. Incident occurred about 1 mile above PMJ by 3 planes, evidently jets, which straffed [*sic*] road when proceeding from NW to SE. One boy about 12 yrs old killed and his baby brother, age 2, whom he was carrying was injured in the arm. Darrow believes incident was bona fide. Another location to NW where another incident was alleged to have taken place was not investigated. Darrow & party will return today at 0900 to continue investigation during daylight. He will advise whether Commies indicate desire to continue with liaison officer talks scheduled for 1000.

I am much concerned over implications this will have on resumption of negotiations[.] No doubt Commies will make capital of the incident but the main question seems to be will they again suspend negots on the pretext that we are showing bad faith? At any rate I am convinced we should wait no longer before resuming main Del. talks. Have instructed Kinney to draw up msg to R. advising him we will meet tomorrow unless otherwise directed. Decided later to hold up msg pending report of investigators. Others seem to think we would weaken our position by sending it. Therefore I decided to wait until Darrow returned to see attitude of Commies.

Upon return Darrow rptd. investigation went off smoothly with no untoward antipathy shown by Commies. In fact arrangements were made for liaison offs to meet again tomorrow to continue talks.

Recd msg from R which laid down the law that full agreement on all items of our proposed conditions for resuming Delegation meetings was considered essential to successful continuation of negots and should be reached prior to discussion of substantive agenda items. Commies have balked on our requirement that present Kaesong neutral zone be abrogated and new Restricted area of 1½ miles radius be substituted therefore. They do not like our stipulation that each side is not responsible for partisan activity. They continue to contend that these questions should be settled on delegation level and not by liaison offs. We hold that we will not discuss date & time for resumption of negots until conditions are properly settled.

Oct. 14 (Sun): Liaison offs met for very short period. Rptd Commies were frigid and much less cordial. Referred to incident of Fri pm and asked what we had done about it. Kinney answered that matter was still under investigation. No progress.

I called Hickey in afternoon to find out when reply to their protest about strafing incident would be ready for delivery. He said it would be over soon. I also said we would continue to attempt to get an agreement on conditions for resumption of negots on liaison level as I thought we stood a better chance of getting somewhere on that level than at Delegation meetings. He replied "use your own judgment."

Msg from R to Kim & Peng said in effect that he accepted responsibility for the strafing incident and that prompt disciplinary action was being taken.

Had quite a long session with the boys on the question of whether it would be better to resume Delegation meetings and thrash out an agreement for security etc on that level or to continue as at present on the liaison level. Consensus of opinion seems to be that we are in a better bargaining position by trying to reach an agreement on the liaison level. I am concerned however as to the public reaction if we delay too long in resuming negots. At the same time we are not likely to get anywhere on the Delegation level and may even get sidetracked on the question of past incidents.

Oct. 15 (Mon): Hiked up mountain in the morning with Craigie, Muse, Hill, Latosheski [sic][.] Beautiful day, took numerous colored pictures. It was a tough climb and I was pretty winded when we reached the top.

Liaison officers reported Commies, particularly Col Tsai, were most interested is [in] the proposal by Kinney that certain items of our proposed agreement be treated as understandings and that they not appear in the draft agreement to be signed and ratified by the Delegations. In other words they would be handled separately, possibly in a letter exchange between Nam Il and myself.

While discussing future courses of action with the boys in my tent Jacoby came up with the idea that the sub Delegation take over if an agreement cannot be reached on the liaison level within a reasonable length of time. Craigie and Burke are against this but can offer no better solution. I am of the opinion that it has considerable merit for the following reasons: (a) It is a compromise and not a complete surrender, which would be the case if we agreed to settle all differences on the Delegation level. (b) It begins again where we left off on August 22nd. (c) Since the sub Del meetings are held informally without records, they would not be a good forum for bringing up past incidents[.] (d) It would be just as speedy a method as by the liaison offs. (e) Since it is a compromise the commies would have difficulty in refusing. It would also be difficult for them to refuse their sub delegates the necessary authority. (f) By proposing such a compromise our position in the eyes of the free world would be strengthened. It would show our people that we are doing every thing possible to get on with the talks and the substantive issues at stake. (g) I could make this proposal to Nam Il thru the liaison officers. If it did not go over R. could propose it to Kim & Peng.

At any rate I agree with them (the boys) that we continue to thrash the matter out on the liaison officer level for several days or a week at most[.]

After thinking matter over and in view of the opposition by the majority I decided to accompany Craigie and others to Tokyo tomorrow to obtain R's approval of continuing present course of action for approx a week longer and then going to the sub Del. level which I am convinced is the most reasonable course of action next to pursue[.]

Oct. 16 (Tues): Took off from Seoul municipal air port in Gen Everest's B-17 at 10:15 arriving Tokyo about 1330. Pretty bumpy trip over mountains as we came direct. All of us which included Craigie, Galloway, Muse & Darrow conferred with Hickey & R from about 1700 to 1800. I told R that the Del [delegation] unanimously recommended continuing in our attempt to obtain an agreement on the liaison officer level for another week as long as some progress was being made. R. agreed and approved of this course of action. Hickey then asked ''what next'' whereupon I spoke up for the sub-del idea giving some of the reasons and inviting attention that it was a compromise. I also pointed out that I did not have the full support of the delegation but that noone had advanced a better solution. Craigie started to give reasons why he did not like sub Del course of action but was not very convincing. At first R was inclined to go along with the Sub-del idea. Later he said he would reserve decision, no doubt because he saw there was a difference of opinion in the delegation. As we were talking a phone call came through from Munsan requesting authority to increase restricted area around Kaesong and Munsan to a circular area having a radius of 3 miles instead of 1500 yds, should it be found necessary to compromise. R gave his approval.

Oct. 17 (Wed): Had short chat with VAdm [Vice Admiral] Russel RN [Royal Navy; Sir Guy Russel, CinC FEast in 1951−52] at 0900, who came out to Qtrs [quarters] 404 to see me. He seemed well satisfied with his visit to the Fleet.

Asked if Scott Moncrief [Admiral Sir Alan; Commander Fifth Cruiser Squadron, Royal Navy] could return to Hongkong upon conclusion of the Armistice, to which I gave a tentative affirmative. The R.N. ships could remain in Korea for as long as needed. Phone from GHQ asked me to see R before I shoved off again for Korea, which I had planned to do at 1000. R only wanted to know if I had anything else to bring up before I left. I had nothing special except to put in another plug for the sub Del course of action should we continue to run up against a stone wall on the liaison officer level. I also asked that all CinCUNC despatches to DA. concerning the armistice be sent to us for info.

Took off from Haneda at about 1035 in P2V with George Muse arriving Kimpo at 1410. and at Munsan about ¾ hr in advance of Radford.

Liaison offs. returned shortly after Radford arrived to report some progress. Chang proposed that an understanding on the subject of armed forces be entered into by liaison offs. The term "armed forces of both sides" in the agreement includes only the armed units and armed personnel under the control of or inspired by either side. This disposes of the partisan item of our proposed agreement since 2nd sentence of Chang's proposal reads[.] "Neither side will be responsible for an incident unless it is definitely established thru joint investigation that the persons responsible for that incident are not inspired by or subject to the control of either side." Chang's proposal also agreed that "all previous security agreements and agreements regarding the Kaesong conference site area and neutral zone are superseded by the agreement of security arrangements for the entire duration of the armistice negotiations when the latter agreement is *stipulated* by the delegations of both sides." Little other progress was made.

Oct. 18 (Thurs): Liaison offs had morning session only. Kinney gave chang [*sic*] a proposed revision to Chang's "understanding" statement of yesterday. Note: Word stipulated should be clarified since (as used above) it connotes that final agreement will not be drawn until delegations meet. Kinney also submitted a revised UNC proposed agreement having 8 parts. Points which Commies still dispute, (1) They will not agree to reducing area around Kaesong to 3 miles; they still want 5 miles. They also want a 3 mile zone along the road, instead of only agreeing to refraining from acts of armed force against road itself. They also balk at the phrase "acts of armed force" and want to make it hostile acts which would include prohibition against aircraft flying over the Kaesong & Munsan restricted areas. We are insisting on the right of aircraft to fly over these areas as long as they do not attack them. Some progress made I believe.

Oct. 19 (Fri): Liaison officers made more progress today. Commies agreed to a 3 mi radius restricted area at Munsan and Kaesong but continue to insist on the inclusion of the phrase "agrees to refrain from hostile acts" instead of the one we proposed—"acts of armed force." They continue to contend that hostile acts includes over flight of aircraft whereas we hold such flights should be permitted since they can do no harm unless they actually attack. Commies also continue to insist on corridor for road but propose reducing width on each side from 1½ mi to 1 mi. Tomorrow Kinney will suggest 200 meters and agree that over flight of aircraft will be avoided as much as possible but not guaranteed.

Craigie with his relief Turner and the others returned from Tokyo.

Oct. 20 (Sat): Liaison officers narrowed disagreements to only one—the question of overflight of aircraft in connection with the Kaesong area[.] They (the Commies) continue to contend that the term "hostile acts" includes such over flight. The road corridor question was settled by the Commies agreeing to 200 meters on each side of the road. Kinney and Murray both believe that a final agreement may be reached tomorrow.

Oct. 21 (Sun): Morning session of liaison officers resulted in agreement on item 1 of the understandings which now reads: "The term armed forces as used in the agreement includes only the armed units and armed individuals under the control of or prompted either overtly or covertly by either side. When the factual findings of joint investigation prove beyond reasonable doubt that the persons responsible for the incident are under the control of or prompted either overtly or covertly by either side, that side shall not evade its responsibility for the incident.["]

Understanding #5 was cleared up and agreed to by beginning para with words, "Except under weather and technical conditions beyond control; the military aircraft of both sides shall not fly over, etc[.]"

It was agreed that Korean, Chinese and English versions of the draft would be exchanged at 0800 tomorrow and that liaison officers would sign the drafts at 1000.

Oct. 22 (Mon): Draft agreements were sent up to Pan Mun Jom at 0800. Liaison officers met at 1000 and signed agreement on matters concerning resumption of conference by Delegations. No difficulties encountered. Kinney informed Commies that UNC security troops would be moved forward to positions just east of PMJ (on high ground) to prevent any irresponsible elements operating near this area. Said he would have to consult senior delegate as to time & date for first meeting of delegations. Chang wanted us to meet tomorrow at 1100[.]

At 1400 I transmitted signed agreement by ltr to Nam Il. Ltr also agreed to understandings reached by liaison officers, and said they had same force as agreement itself. Requested Nam Il return signed English & Korean copies. Upon ratification we would meet to proceed with item 2 of agenda at 1100 the day after the agreement was returned signed. Requested Nam Il to indicate in his reply that he also agreed to understandings.

Had short conference in my tent after supper to outline course of action we would follow at first meeting. It follows[:]

1. If Nam Il asks what we have to say I will immediately read our paper on proposed solution to item 2 of agenda.

2. If he gets floor first and

(a) proposes B. L. [battle line] solution more favorable to us than ours I will call a recess to consider it and frame a reply.

(b) proposes B.L. solution about same as ours, I will likewise call a recess

(c) proposes a B.L. solution much less favorable to us than ours I will immediately counter with our proposal

(d) launches into harangue on past incidents I will brush him off with Hickman's short paper and then immediately propose our solution.

Oct. 23 (Tues): No word from Commies. Press release has notified the world that I have ratified the liaison officers agreement and sent it up to Nam Il for his signature. All that stands between a meeting of the two delegations is an O.K. from him. It will put him in a bad light if he refuses to sign until Delegations meet.

Had a conference in my tent concerning the demilitarized zone we shall propose. Burke and Craigie wish to ask for pushing the median line above Kaesong at the expense of withdrawal in the center. Hodes is not in favor. I have no objection to requesting authority to push line up slightly to take in good defense positions on high ground but am against trying to grab off a large area without compensating the Commies in the center.

Jack Clark dropped in to see me for an hour in the afternoon and Robbie came for dinner and to say good bye. He is leaving for his new job in Australia, in charge of recruiting, about 8 Nov. His address will be Victoria Barracks, Melbourne.

Oct. 24 (Wed): Nam Il replied today at 1000 with signed agreement. His letter of transmittal acknowledged that the understandings reached by the liaison officers had same force as the agreement for the resumption of the negotiations. He proposed that we meet tomorrow at 1100 to which we replied in the affirmative.

Held conference in my tent on plan advocated by Burke & Craigie to extend our proposed zone considerably to northward in Kaesong area. Hodes dead against it. In the end it was decided not to send Gen Ridgway a despatch recommending a revision of presently authorized zone, which would only be used if Commies were softhearted and made a proposal more favorable to us than ours[.]

Oct. 25 (Thurs): At 1100 met with Commies at Pan Mun Jom. Nam Il started the proceedings by introducing General Pien Chang Wu who took the place of Tung

[Teng] Hua and Major General Chung Too [Tu] Whan [Hwan] who took the place of Maj Gen Chang Pyong San. I then presented the credentials of Maj Gen Hyong Keun Lee [Lee Hyung Koon] who took Paik's place. Following these formalities Nam Il proposed that a joint office of Liaison officers be set up to be responsible for the details of security arrangements for the inspection of the observance of the agreement by both sides, for the investigation of violations of the agreement, and for the handling of administrative matters. I said we would give our answer later. I then followed by a short statement commending the liaison officers and asking if they had any proposals to make regarding item 2 of the agenda. Nam Il replied by proposing the question be referred to the sub-delegation. After asking for a 20 min recess we returned to announce our agreement with both proposals, suggesting that the sub-dels meet that afternoon. Nam Il suggested 1400 to which I agreed. I appointed Hodes & Burke. Meeting recessed at 1159.

Sub Del meeting, with Hsieh & Lee [Sang Cho] as delegates for the Commies, convened at 1400. After preliminary sparring during which Hodes attempted to get them to submit a proposal, Lee said following which is significant: "Both sides should give up previous stand and approach problem anew." When Lee held firm that it was up to UNC to make a new proposal which would be a reasonable and acceptable solution Hodes recessed for 30 mins. Upon returning he presented our "fair and reasonable" solution which provided for Commies advancing in the East & Central sectors while the UNC advanced in the west. Otherwise the 4 km zone generally follows the battle line. Our solution also pointed out that "should the conference continue for some time, it is entirely possible that what is a just and reasonable b.l. solution now will not be so at a later date." This last is meant to be a veiled threat to hurry up and decide or else. When Lee said "we do not consider it fair just & reasonable" Hodes jumped at him asking why not. Lee then, more conciliatory, said they would study the "solution" and give their views tomorrow at 1100.

The most significant thing about this meeting was the fact that the Commies made no mention of the 38th parallel. They have evidently abandoned any future attempt to get us to settle on the 38th[.]

Oct. 26 (Fri): I decided to fly to Tokyo to see Molly off as well as to take up several matters with GHQ. Had very uncomfortable trip over as B-17's heating system was not working properly. Arrived shortly before 1500. Discussed Dr Goldhamers status with Hickey (Craigie & Turner also present) who told me R did not approve his attending conferences at Pan Mun Jom. Basis for his disapproval—it was strictly a military conference. State Dept had previously turned down any of their representatives from attending. I pointed out that Goldhamer was working for the military as an operational analyist [*sic*] and was therefore in a different status. Craigie will take matter up with R later on.

Report from sub-del meeting today. Lee objected our proposal on grounds (1) Dem [demarcation] line lies almost entirely north of l of c [line of contact] and within Red positions (2) UNC would withdraw only on east coast and slightly in area Kumsong (3) Commies would withdraw 1500 square Kms & UNC only 600[.] Strong objection to Commie withdrawal in Kaesong area. Commies then proposed their line of dem which was well south of line of contact along 95% of battle line (av 15 miles) and crossed l of c in vicinity Kaesong. UNC would withdraw to dem line to east of crossing and Commies to west of crossing. Area evacuated would be demilt. [demilitarized] with each side responsible for civil admin. [administration] in area evacuated by it. Their line of dem cuts across Onjin & Yonan peninsulas which are meaningless to us. During discussion which followed it was apparent that there was basic disagreement as to actual location of l of c. Hodes rejected Commie proposal pointing out it would require UNC to withdraw relatively great distances along about 95% of b.l. [battle line] and that Commie withdrawal on west would not really be a withdrawal. Sub Del procedure for 27 Oct planned as follows. (1) Again strongly refute and reject Commie proposal outlining all reasons therefore (2) attempt to get agreement on l of c. (3) repeatedly suggest acceptance our proposal (We are prepared to sit out this proposal as long as it is deemed advisable.[)]

Oct. 27 (Sat): Golfed p.m. with Robbie, Craigie & Muse and attended dinner for Collins & Anna Rosenberg [U.S. Assistant Secretary of Defense] in evening. Only chance to talk to R. & Collins. Asked them to be patient—we would eventually wind up with a just & reasonable armistice.

Report from Munsan. am and pm sessions resulted no progress. Hodes again gave reasons why their proposal unacceptable & why ours was [*sic*]. Much discussion Kaesong area. Commies rejected our good reasons. Hodes proposed discussion location l of c [line of contact][.] They refused but finally agreed present their concept tomorrow. Sub del believes Commie proposal probably a bargaining one. They apparently hope for a compromise someplace between proposals and our adamant stand comes as a rude shock to them. Their milking technique failing.

Oct. 28 (Sun): Saw Molly off on Marseillaise at 1330. About 25 of her friends on hand. Much champagne. Beautiful ship; girls each had roomy outside staterooms sharing bath. Cost $650 per which includes everything. They arrive Marseille [*sic*] Nov 28.

Report from Munsan. Discussions centered mainly on lines of contact. Commie version considerably south of ours. Also discussed relative merits of proposals. Ours alleged as unfair because based on their version of line of C. UNC forces advance 1025 sq Kms more than they withdrew. Tried unsuccessfully to get categorical answer that this was only reason for their rejection. We believe they may eventually accept l of c as milt. dem. line. They connected 38th to their proposal today but in connection eventual solution to Korean problem. Perhaps some progress.

Oct. 29 (Mon): Had breakfast with [Gen. Clifton B., USMC] Cates at my qtrs. He is much concerned because Marines not getting proper air support. Expects to take matter up on JCS level upon return to Wash. [Washington]. He is retiring in Jan. Lem Shepherd his probable relief. Left Tokyo 1000 in old Bataan arriving back in camp shortly before 1500.

Report from sub-del. Evident that agreement can be reached on location of l of c [line of contact]. Before continuing to define exact location UNC sub-del insisted that it was first necessary to determine objective in locating l of c. Commies stated that reason was to compare two proposals. Whereupon Hodes pointed out it did not matter where l of c was in their proposal since their line of [Joy had written "contact," then crossed it out and written "demarcation"] demarcation in west was entirely without merit because UNC gained nothing and dem was meaningless. Any offer of compensation by relocation of line of demarcation in west was entirely without merit because UNC gained nothing and Commies lost nothing by such relocation. Apparent Commies wanted reach agreement on location of l of c either to compromise on demilt. zone along l of c or to show our proposal was not a fair acre for acre exchange and that their proposal was fair. They give every indication of accepting a reasonable solution to location of l of c. It will be hard to convince them of merits of our Kaesong proposal unless it can be obtained on acre for acre exchange but tomorrow we'll concentrate on that.

Forgot to mention I had to give Maj Gen Lee [Hyung Koon] (who also went to Tokyo with me) a stern talking to on the plane coming back, disapproving his request to go to Pusan to see Pres [Syngman] Rhee. He wanted to tell the President his position. I told him he was subject to R's orders only and that only proper channel for communicating with Rhee was through R. If he continues to worry and pester me about his anomalous position as a member of the delegation, I shall have him relieved.

Oct. 30 (Tues): During morning session considerable time was spent attempting to point out why UNC proposal is equitable and reasonable in contrast to meaningless Commie proposal. Commies referr ed to fighting in Yonan and Onjin peninsulas[.] UNC asked for location of l of C [line of contact] in this area in order establish future trading position. Commies refused to indicate contact line but continued to maintain there were battles in the area from which they would withdraw their troops. UNC delegates pointed out that situation in Onjin & Yonan areas was identical to those in Wonsan[,] Chinampo and other areas in that there was no line of ground contact on those peninsulas. Discussion then shifted to islands [held by UNC; for names see entry for February 22, 1952]. Commies maintained UNC withdrawal from islands should not be considered in settlement to be made along main battle position. Thereafter discussion was directed to meaningless[ness] of Commie line of demarcation in the west and consequent basic lack of soundness in their position. During pm line of contact was discussed. Commies refused to agree that Kaesong merited special consideration on grounds that they had occupied area without combat as result armistice security arrangements. Commies gave long speech of self adulation.

Estimate made in our summary of yesterday was overly optimistic. Commies insist their l of c is correct. They would not modify it today but did admit it was based on info. several days old.

Commies continue to urge their original proposal without visible signs of weakening. Their presentations in support of it today were not good, but they are not yet exhausted. UNC will continue to pound home superiority of UNC proposal over Communist one.

My own concern at this time is possibility JCS may force us into compromising with the Commies on the location of the demilt zone. This would be disastrous in that it would weaken seriously our position in future negotiations over the other items of the agenda. Our despatches might therefore be a little more optimistic in order that the JCS may not become impatient.

Oct. 31 (Wed): Hsieh Fang did major part of talking in morning to disprove our claims to Kaesong area. Not once did he or Lee [Sang Cho] mention Commie proposal. They had two objections only to our proposal[—]Our insistence on Kaesong and the overall inequality in withdrawals and advances. UNC delegates presented all arguments as to why demilt zone should pass north of Kaesong including UNC withdrawal from other areas and islands, Commies acceptance of Kaesong by default and provision for defensive positions for Seoul. A significant statement by Lee was, "especially we hope you will give up your demand for the Kaesong area." "This will contribute to our progress and is the key point to the solution of our problem."

At pm session, Lee read a carefully prepared speech the first part of which vehemently criticized the UNC sub-del attitude and the UNC proposal. He stated that the UNC proposal was absolutely unacceptable and defended their original proposal. As the closing part of his statement he submitted a new proposal to the effect that both sides withdraw 2 kilometers from the adjusted line of contact. Their zone generally runs just south of ours except in Kaesong area where it runs considerably south, even of Pan Mun Jom. When compared with our version of l of c [line of contact] we would withdraw approx 560 sq. kms more than they.

Under Commie proposal zone is subject to changes in l of c before signing of armistice. The statement referred to minor adjustments based on terrain. It is not yet clear whether these adjustments are incorporated in given line or whether they are open to discussion. Since Commie zone is based on their version of 1 of c. UNC tactics for tomorrow are (1) to get agreement on 1 of c, and (2) to determine by adjustments how close we can bring the Commie proposal to ours.

I feel definitely that the ice is broken and that agreement on the demilt zone is in sight. Do not feel we should hold out too long for Kaesong but it is possible we may be able to convince them of the logic of including Kaesong in the demilt zone, perhaps as the capital.

Correspondents on the press train cannot understand our insistence on Kaesong. It is difficult to explain since our real reason is that Kaesong would be a sop to the ROK government (as it was once the capital of Korea)[.]

I sent msg to R for info only pointing out we might need guidance on item 2 in near future. Msg. dwelt mainly on our view that Kaesong area may be unobtainable unless we are prepared to make a major concession in another area. Sub del believes Commie proposal a bargaining one in spite of their insistence that it is final. Sub del further believes that an agreement can be reached somewhere between our proposal and theirs. We feel that sub-del must be prepared at any time to modify our proposal either in Kaesong area or in eastern section.

Nov. 1 (Thurs): UNC delegates opened morning session with detailed refutation of Commie proposal of yesterday. Commies feigned surprise at strong rejection to their proposal; attempted to get UNC del to take recess until tomorrow for purpose of further study of their proposal. UNC delegates made it very clear that the proposal had been given thorough study and that no additional time for study was needed. Afternoon session brought additional arguments on relative merits of two proposals.

While Commies reiterate that their proposal is final the delegation believes that the UNC demand for the Kaesong area is the crux of their objection to UNC proposal and that almost any compromise which does not require them to forfeit Kaesong would be acceptable. Sub del believes we should continue to take advantage of the momentum gained during past 7 days. for the present at least.

Recd msg from R quoting JCS msg to him. Gist of msg. JCS do not feel current offer should be regarded as "final" subject only to "minor changes." Our min posit. [minimum position] is maintenance of security of line Kansas, to include an adequate oplr [sic]. JCS understanding is UNC concept of demilt zone provides negotiation flexibility without jeopardizing this min. posit. JCS recognize it is difficult to UNC to surrender hard earned ground and do not consider UNC should do so unless negots seem likely to fail on an issue which does not involve UNC min posit. R added that our press releases should not be such as to make it difficult for us finally to settle on a compromise posit *if so directed.*

Nov. 2 (Fri): Morning session devoted to (1) Commie prepared statement upholding their proposal and denouncing our proposal as unfair, etc, with emphasis on Kaesong area. (2) In order to clarify a remark of Lees to the effect that their proposal was their max. [maximum] effort we asked, "Is that an ultimatum." Lee would not give a direct answer and developments indicated clearly that he did not want to infer that he was issuing an ultimatum. (3) Demonstration on our part by referring to the map to consider certain adjustments closely coinciding or coinciding exactly with their zone in the eastern ¾ of the b.l. [battle line]. The afternoon session began with a firm re-statement of our position with emphasis on its fairness and our requirement for the Kaesong area. Hsieh of course refuted again all arguments to our justification for this area. The Commies insist on avoiding all consideration at this time of islands as an additional bargaining point, possibly with the intent of having us drop them at a later day as unimportant. Although no visible progress made today, this was only second day after their proposal and therefore too soon to expect any sign of Commie weakening.

In order to avoid impasse in discussions of demilt zone R authorized me to continue support of our proposal except in west where alteration may be made to place Kaesong in demilt. zone. If we feel it necessary to give up Kaesong to insure continuation of negots, southern boundary of demilt zone should permit UNC to place an oplr [*sic*] on west bank of Imjin. Because of impact on ROKs we must not give up Kaesong without final clearance from R.

The $64 question is—how long should we hold out on our original proposal? The longer we hold out before advancing proposal to include Kaesong in neutral zone the better will be our chance to make this compromise stick. At the same time I feel the Commies will remain adamant on their b.l. proposal and the negots will be deadlocked until we make a counter proposal. After all the Commies have made two proposals against our one. The next move seems up to us.

Nov. 3 (Sat): After long debate over Kaesong issue principally, with UNC laying stress on concession we make giving up islands north of demilt zone and in territorial waters, we took a new step. Carefully phrased as a matter for discussion purposes only, we asked what the Commies would think of projecting a 4 km wide corridor from the UNC proposed zone (25 Oct) roughly south to include Kaesong so as to bring Kaesong into demilt zone. Commie action was strongly negative, with Hsieh Fang answering question by stating his delegation would never accept a solution which left Kaesong either in UNC control or in demilt. zone.

Commies seemed very anxious to obtain agreement on the principle that the zone be based strictly on l. of c. [line of contact]. We agreed in general but emphasized appropriate adjustments were mandatory. Commies rejected this interpretation. Thus meeting ended with no agreement on any general or specific point.

Since it is becoming increasingly evident that the Commies are going to adhere strictly to their b.l. [battle line] proposal, and since we do not have authority at present to a demilt. zone based strictly on the b.l., I sent a msg to R outlining our tactics tomorrow. Msg was to effect that Hodes would revert to our original 25 Oct proposal after telling Commies "I have nothing to add to what was said yesterday. It is clear to me that the Kaesong area is the main point at issue. Yesterday our side tried to explore a possibility that might provide a solution for our disagreement in this area. We gather that you were not interested in such a suggestion."

Nov. 4 (Sun): In morning session of sub del. Commies advanced so called new proposal requiring each side to withdraw 2 kms from 1 of c [line of contact] without any adjustments whatsoever. They argued this was a new proposal since it dropped their former claims to the Kosong & Kumsong salients. Hodes pointed out that this solution merely eliminated territory Commies previosuly asked for without compensation. Burke inquired whether the Commies had taken into account UNC withdrawal from the islands held in territorial waters of Korea. Commies stated our withdrawal from islands was comparable to their elimination of patrol activities in UNC rear areas, and that they had considered our withdrawal from islands in their overall consideration of the demilt zone. When pressed for detailed compensation for UNC withdrawal Commies asserted that the islands were unimportant and could not be measured in kilograms and kilometers. The Kaesong problem was rehashed with UNC again stating that the Kaesong area was under the control of neither side in early July. Fruitless discussion followed as to where the UNC & Commie troops were located in early July. Commies consistently held to view that Kaesong either in demilt zone or under UNC control was unsatisfactory.

A short afternoon session was confined to statements by both sides that they had nothing further to offer at the time.

Special note: Hodes and Burke now believe Hsieh Fang is the real brains behind the Commies negotiations. Very smart, doesn't miss a trick. Lee comparatively dumb—sticks strictly to the party line. All his speeches much the same. That has also been my impression from reading record of proceedings.

Nov. 5 (Mon): Commies opened sub-del meeting with prepared statement on their proposal which they described as as [*sic*] a strict settlement on the 1 of c [line of contact] with appropriate adjustments, or in event adjustments could not be agreed upon, a withdrawal of 2 kms from 1 of c by both sides without major adjustments. UNC delegates explored the proposal thruout morning reaching conclusion that Commies would agree that as a matter of principle adjustments in the line were desirable and that in general such adjustments would be equivalent, but that each case would have to be decided on its own merits. In p.m. UNC presented following proposal or statement. "Sub delegations agree: (1) To accept principle that the milt. dem. [military demarcation] line and the demilt [demilitarized] zone will be based on the actual l of c at the time of the signing of the armistice with appropriate adjustments. (2) That the zone be approx 4 kms in width. (3) To establish a committee of 3 officers from each side the function of which shall be to determine to the satisfaction of both sides the actual line of contact as of any specific further date and to be prepared to provide to the delegations such an agreed line at such time as it may be needed for the purpose of accurately determining the milt. dem. line and the demilt zone prior to the finalization of the armistice agreements. (4) To rpt their agreements to the plenary session of the dels. with the recommendation that the latter proceed to the discussion of other items of the agenda leaving the finalization of the agreement on agenda item 2 until such time as it is possible to settle it definitely in order to reach agreement on all questions in Korea at earliest possible date."

Commies immediately set about exploring meaning of "appropriate adjustments" asking first, does this mean that you drop your demand on Kaesong, then trying by more diplomatic questions to get same info. UNC delegates took the position that what was or was not an appropriate adjustment could be determined only in relation to a specific l of c; that is the line on the date the agreement is finalized. Commies expressed a tentative conclusion that although both sides used the same words in describing the principle upon which agreement was sought, there was no actual agreement. They took the proposal home for study.

Nov. 6 (Tues): Sub-del reports as follows on meeting this date: Communists presented long prepared statement rejecting our proposal of yesterday on basis agenda item 2 must be finally solved before going to other items. Communists now want to determine present l of c [line of contact] and make that line final line of dem. [demarcation] of demilt. zone regardless of the time the milt armistice is eventually signed or the actual l of c at that time. This concept is in complete disagreement with that they have previously said and with our own views. We pointed out that terms of armistice depends [*sic*] on conditions at time of signing of armistice and that tentative agreement reached on each item might be modified if conditions on which tentative agreement was based changed significantly. No indications their future action.

We will continue to press for an agreement on our proposal. We do not intend agree to permanently fixing demilt zone until armistice is signed.

Nov. 7 (Wed): **Sub-del reports that crux of todays session came during late afternoon when Lee read from a statement formally proposing the**

following. While Lee was reading, Commie representatives outside conference tent handed typed copies to UN correspondents.

"The sub del of the KPA and the Chinese Peoples Volunteers formally proposes:

(1) To decide upon the principle that the existing actual line of contact be made the milt. dem. [military demarcation] line, and that both sides withdraw 2 kms from this line so as to establish demilt. [demilitarized] zone.

(2) In accord. [accordance] with above mentioned principle, the sub committee start immediately to check the existing actual line of contact on the 250,000 to 1 map, so that this line agreed by both sides may be fixed specifically as the milt. dem. line, and that the 2 lines 2 kms away on both sides of this line be made the southern & northern boundaries, marking the demilt zone.

It also proposes the following understandings be reached:

(A) When fixing specifically the existing actual line of contact as the milt dem line, the side which proposes to make an adjustment should give up its proposal for adjustment if the other side is not agreeable.

(B) As soon as the sub-committee has in general determined the location of the milt dem line and the demilt. zone on the 250,000 to 1 map, it should submit to the plenary conference this specific proposal of the milt. dem. line & demilt zone agreed upon by both sides, and recommend that the plenary conference proceed immediately to the discussion of the other items of the agenda, while leaving the work of specifically marking the location of the line & zone to the committee of staff officers to be formed by both sides.

(C) In view of fact that it would be clearly inexpedient to alter the specific location of the milt dem line in accord with minor changes each day in the actual l of c [line of contact], if armistice negots. proceed rapidly and no major change occurs in the actual l of c prior to signing of armistice agreement, the line & zone preliminarily defined by both sides does not have to be revised. Otherwise, both sides reserve right to propose, prior to signing of agreement, revisions of the milt. dem. line and the demilt. zone corresponding to the changes on actual l of c."

The proposal is no more than than [sic] a formalization of proposals discussed informally earlier. It was rejected on the grounds that fixing the dem line & the demilt zone on the basis of the current l of c with provision for changes subject to veto by either side would in effect constitute an immediate cease fire on the basis of agreement on only one item of the agenda. Regardless of the time spent on other agenda items and of the changes which might occur in the l of c as result of milt. ops. between fixing of line & signing of armistice no changes could occur in the dem. line since the consent of the other side would be necessary. Thus the agreement to this proposal would provide an insurance policy under which Commies would be insured against effects of UNC milt ops during discussion of other agenda items.

JCS msg [message; in the margin CTJ penned "JCS 86291"] received today said in effect that line proposed by Commies is one JCS would rather accept than let negots break down or reach stalemate. Consequently if Commies flatly reject our latest approach and negots on that point appear fruitless, "the quicker we accept a compromise, the less it will appear as an important back down both here (Wash) [Washington] and as far as Commie propaganda is concerned." JCS go on to say

"Thru out we have taken as basic principle that dem line should be generally along b.l. [battle line]. Commies now appear to have accepted this principle. We feel that in general this adequately meets our min. posit [minimum position] re. demilt. zone.

"Judging from press reaction here it would be hard to make the people understand why negots broke down, if such should happen, over Kaesong in face of recent Commie concessions[.] This has been mentioned several times in last few days both in radio and press.

"If your latest proposal to postpone agreement on a line and zone is rejected completely by Commies, and further negots along this approach appear fruitless, early agreement generally along proposed Commie line in Kaesong area is advisable.

"Moreover JCS are concerned over latest Commie proposal (taking present l of c as final line) since agreement to such proposal would have practical effect of curtailing further UN ground advances beyond agreed l of c. This would be militarily unacceptable unless agreement on all other agenda items also was reached shortly thereafter. Accordingly, though latest Commie proposal insofar as location of demilt. zone is concerned meets our basic position and is thus acceptable such acceptance must be qualified by a time limitation for completion of all agenda items, preferably a definite period in which major forward UN ground ops. are not otherwise contemplated. It would be stipulated that in event agreement is not reached on all agenda items within the definite period specified, location of the demilt. zone is subject to revision."

Nov. 8 (Thurs): UNC delegates opened refuting Commie proposal of 7 November principally on grounds that fixing a zone on the basis of the current l of c [line of contact] with provisions for changes subject to veto by either side would in effect constitute an immed. [immediate] cease fire on the basis of agreement on only 1 item on the agenda. In replying to these objections Commies expressed views on "adjustments" which were inconsistent with the phraseology of their proposal. In an effort to develop a meeting of minds on the question of "adjustments," UNC delegates invited Commies to go to the map to develop a milt. dem. [military demarcation] line based on the existing l of c. In the course of this, the UNC formally proposed a compromise on the Kaesong area with the dem. line passing thru the city. Lee opposed this with usual arguments. Hsieh seemed less positive. This discussion revealed that in terms of area, Commies were offering only about 50% of equivalent value in exchange for adjustments in Kaesong & Kumsong areas.

Following Commie refusal of a compromise in Kaesong area, UNC reiterated its proposal of 5 Nov, stating that it is sufficient for the present to reach agreement on the principle that the dem. line and demilt zone will be based on the l of c. as of the date of the finalizing of the agreement. We recommend that no further time be wasted in trying to determine a pre determined milt. dem. line & demilt. zone based on the existing l of c as this step is entirely unnecessary. Sub Del feels that Commies are anxious to get an agreement on a tentative demilt. zone even if it is understood that it will be revised to conform with any changes in the b.l. [battle line]. Commies took proposal home for study.

R spent night at Munsan with us. Purpose of his visit was to get our views on future courses of action and frame msg replying to JCS msg. outlined in yesterdays notes. Gist of msg finally sent. Concurred with JCS opinion that it would be better to accept Commie proposal of settling on existing l of c than let negots break down. Also concurred it would be hard to make people understand break down over Kaesong. Pointed out that Commies had not yet accepted principle that dem. line should be generally along b.l. at time armistice is signed although they had provided for revision if major change occurred. Did not like J.C.S idea of definite time limit. Then pointed out why we felt the way we did about Kaesong (1) Kaesong viewed in different lights from rest of line for following reasons. (a) our possession of it would be viewed in Asia as damaging to Commie prestige and enhancing our own. (b) When negots began Kaesong was in no mans land. We felt we were entitled to assume that if Kaesong had not been neutralized in July l of c would now pass thru it.

R's views at moment summarized as follows:

(a) Our sub del has retained initiative having presented to Commies on 5 & 8 Nov two alternatives acceptance of either of which would leave us on firm ground. These are:

(1) Proposal outlined in notes of 5 Nov.

(2) On 8 Nov a predetermined zone based on present l of c in such a manner that UNC withdrawals from Kosong & Kumson[g] areas would be compensated by equal Commie withdrawal in Kaesong area, with city of Kaesong in demilt zone. This predetermined zone is of course subject to revision based on changes in l of c occurring prior to signing of armistice.

(b) We must be prepared, however, to make known our decision with respect to Kaesong before our concession of this city damages our prestige and prejudices our position on other agenda items.

(c) feeling that public opinion in Asia accords far more importance to Commie retention of K. [Kaesong] than UN public opinion would accord to its loss, I am prepared to concede our K position at such time as I am satisfied there is no reasonable chance of our obtaining early Commie agreement to our possessing it or to its demilt [demilitarization]. In doing this I would [,] of course, then stand inflexibly on principle that l of c as of the effective date of the armistice must be the line of dem.

(d) Subject to your contrary instrs [instructions] I shall follow course outlined above making intensive effort here to make our positions and major supporting reasons for each crystal clear to public opinion.

Nov. 9 (Fri): Commies opened sub Del meeting of 9 Nov saying that inasmuch as agreement on adjustments could not be reached we should agree to a dem [demarcation] line based on existing l of c [line of contact] without adjustments. UNC stated as a general principle adjustments were desirable and it was so recognized by both sides and that demilt [demilitarized] zone should be based on l of c at time of armistice. It then asserted the superiority of the UNC proposal of 5 Nov over that of the Commies since it renders it unnecessary and undesarable [*sic*] the step of determining a provisional dem zone based on the existing l of c which is subject to change prior to signature of the armistice. Commies attempted to refute this as a departure from the agenda and reasserted the superiority of a tentative agreement on the basis of the existing l of c. UNC in closing reasserted the superiority of the 5 Nov proposal and recommended that it be studied further both by itself and in relation to Commies proposal of 7 Nov and UNC compromise proposal of 8 Nov. Note: It was very clear today that Commies want a dem line on basis of existing l of C even though it is subject to revision on the date of signing. It is far from certain that they want it badly enough to agree to accept the UNC compromise proposal of 8 Nov in return therefor.

At the request of R I went to Seoul today (with Turner) to meet R & Muccio at Eusak's advance Hdqtrs. R's purpose was to acquaint Muccio with his decision to give up our position on Kaesong if sub-del continues to run up against a stone wall on our Nov 8th proposal. Muccio said he was not concerned with ROK reaction as much as the effect our withdrawal from the Kaesong position would have in Asia. Our prestige would suffer thruout Orient and Commie world would interpret it as a victory for them. We also discussed the [South] Korean delegate Maj Gen Lee. He is not as staunch a fellow as Paik. Is always complaining about his difficult position.

Upon return to camp and after talking to Hodes and Burke we sent following msg to R at 9th Corps C.P. where he was spending the night.

"Commies today made it very clear that they recognized UNC was applying pressure to obtain Kaesong or place it in demilt zone. They stated they had no intention of accepting a solution similar to our compromise proposal of yesterday or our 5 Nov proposal which included the phrase "appropriate adjustments" since both meant in essence the same thing.

"UN sub Del estimates it would require considerable time to gain acceptance of either.

Commie sub Del stated many times today they prefer no adjustments or only local adjustments to any other provision for adjustments. UNC sub-del felt Commies several times were on verge of proposing formally that solution as one modification to our 5 Nov proposal.

"Sub del plans tomorrow offer 5 Nov proposal modified by substituting "minor local adjustments" for "appropriate adjustments" to the b.l. [battle line].

Reasons for rec. [recommended] course of action:

(a) Retention of initiative and preventing necessity of having to accept a similar Commie proposal.

c. We will then be in a firm milt [military] defensible posit [position] and can show such firmness indefinitely in debate.

b. Belief that Commies will not agree to either our proposal of 8 Nov or 5 Nov at least for a relatively long time. ["c" appears before "b" in diary]

d. There is always possibility that, since Commies appear eager to publish some sort of milt. dem line & demilt zone, they will prefer the 8 Nov compromise or some proposal more favorable to us than the exact present l of c to the proposal we plan to use 10 November."

Nov. 10 (Sat): High light of todays sub del meeting came in late afternoon when Lee introduced a "new" proposal. Stripped of rhetoric and propaganda it was substantially the same as their proposal of 7 Nov. It was substantially as follows:

"(1) To decide upon the principle that the actual l of c [line of contact] between both sides be made the milt. dem. [military demarcation] line, and that both sides withdraw 2 kms from this line so as to establish the demilt. zone.

(2) In accord with the above mentioned principle, the sub committee check immed [immediately] the present actual l of c so as to fix the present l of c agreed upon by both sides as the milt. dem line, and to fix the two lines 2 kms away on both sides of this present actual l of c as the southern & northern boundaries marking the demilt zone.

(3) After the armistice agreement is fully agreed on and prior to the signing of the armistice agreement, the sub-com [committee] shall make revisions to the above mentioned milt. dem. line and demilt zone, corresponding to the changes which may have taken place in the actual l of c between both sides.

"The sub-del of the Korean People's Army & CPV proposes specifically that the sub-committee report to the plenary conference the above mentioned three resolutions as soon as they are adopted, and recommend that the plenary conference proceed immediately to the discussion of the 3rd item of the agenda, and leave the specific work of checking the actual l of c, of fixing the present actual l of c mutually agreed upon as the milt. dem. line. and of fixing accordingly the demilt zone to be carried out by this sub committee concurrently.

The UNC sub-del counterproposed the following:

"In order to establish a demilt zone as a basic condition for the cessation of hostilities in Korea the sub dels recommend the establishment of a milt. dem. line located at the actual line of ground contact a [at] the time of the signing of the armistice agreement, and the creation of a demilt zone of 4 kms in width by the withdrawal of each side for a dist [distance] of 2 kms from agreed dem line; the milt dem line and the boundaries of the demilt zone being subject to such minor local adjustments as may be considered mutually desirable."

The UNC sub-Del stated, immediately after making the above proposal, that the plenary sessions of the delegations could now proceed to the discussion of other items of the agenda, leaving the determination of the specific location of the milt. dem. line and the boundaries of the demilt zone until immediately prior to the signing of the armistice.

Todays session closed without agreement[.]

Following despatch was passed to us by CinCUNC from JCS [CTJ penned in margin: "JCS 86654"]:

"Approved course of action outlined in R's despatch to JCS, however JCS reserve judgment for present on advisability of taking inflexible position in regard to our proposal of today. Accordingly, while you should continue to press for acceptance of this principle, this should not constitute a final UNC position.

"We (JCS) feel here that early agreement on principles governing selection of line of dem satisfying our major requirements has considerable importance. Possibility exists that having made substantial concessions on location of line, Commie resistance may considerably stiffen and even revert to 38th parallel position."

In my humble opinion this is a helluva wishy washy despatch[.] If this is the sort of backing we are going to get woe betide us in the days ahead.

Nov. 11 (Sun): At 0800 today I delivered a statement to the correspondents aboard the press train at Munsan-ni. This is the beginning of an intensified public education program ordered by R. The gist of the statement which, according to Nuckols, was well received is about as follows: It outlined the objectives of the UNC delegation namely: (1) Establishment of a demilt [demilitarized] zone that will reflect the milt [military] situation on the day the armistice is signed. (2) Complete & adequate security for UNC combat forces & UNC rear areas during suspension of hostilities (3) Concrete arrangements that will prevent buildup of milt forces beyond the level existing at the time the armistice is placed in effect (4) Quick & satisfactory arrangements relating to POW's statement ended up comparing our latest proposal with Commies latest, explaining why theirs in effect was a defacto cease fire whereas we wanted to retain flexibility of milt action by deferring determination of the final dem. [demarcation] line & zone until just prior to signing of armistice agreement.

I told the press that whenever I had any important statements to make I would in future follow today's procedure.

The sub Del reports the following on todays meeting:

Morning session opened with UNC representatives submitting proposal of 10 November in complete resolution form and pointing out that it was a concrete, specific and complete solution to item 2 of the agenda. We called for its acceptance today and a plenary session of the delegations tomorrow.

Lee insisted at great length that UNC proposal did not constitute the required compliance with the agenda item.

Hsieh characterized our proposal as a step forward but pointed out the main difference between the present UNC and Commie proposals i.e. that theirs calls for a provisional dem. line now while ours does not. He elaborated on the objection raised by Lee; contended that our proposal was not in accord with our previous proposals; and, referring to statements in American press that Commies were seeking this method of relieving milt pressure on them, asserted that this worked both ways[.]

At afternoon session Lee rptd [repeated] usual statements that UNC proposal was not specific, not logical and did not fulfill requirements of item 2 whereas Commie proposal did.

I sent msg to R suggesting a msg be sent to JCS along following lines[—]msg to show difference between our proposal and Commies'. My suggested msg ended about as follows: "It is considered here to be of highest importance that Commies be forced to accept UNC battle line proposal. If Commies insist on having some sort of definite or interim zone established now the delegations position would be considerably strengthened if it could point out that it has already offered such a proposal in the UNC proposal of Oct 25 as modified by later concessions in the Kaesong area. The delegation could then place before the Commies the alternatives of (a) a b.l. solution in the UNC version or (b) a zone to be decided on now but conforming to the last zone presented to the Commies, i.e., with Kaesong in demilt zone. A strong insistence that the Commies must choose between these two would in all likelihood speed up considerably their choice of the UNC version of the b.l. solution.

"**UNC would be able to settle Item 2 of agenda in a much more satisfactory fashion if JCS would provide authorization as follows: That UNC be authorized to stand firmly for a settlement in terms of either its proposal of yesterday or its proposal of Oct 25 modified by compromise concession on Kaesong area, and that the delegation be authorized to insist on either of these two solutions.**"

Nov. 12 (Sun): Commies continued to attack UNC proposal of 10 Nov on ground that it does not adhere to agenda approved by both delegations and allege UNC attitude forecasts later UNC abandonment of other agreements. Also accuse UNC of being inconsistent since earlier proposals include demilt zones defined on a map.

UNC repeatedly pointed out that its current proposal fixed the line of dem [demarcation] and demilt [demilitarized] zone completely; that all that remained was determination of final l of c [line of contact]; that it carried out full intent of item 2; and that it differed from former UNC proposals in that it did not require correlation of adjustments other than admin [administrative] adjustments.

Hsieh attacked motives behind our proposal and alleged UNC making cunning and vicious attempts to set up situation so that we could break down conference in last steps of proceedings. This line of reasoning on his part is believed by sub-del to be significant of his own intentions.

In pm. UNC outlined again at great length the absurdity of Commie proposal which calls for 1st the creation and later the abandonment of a provisional line & zone and compared in detail the two proposals being considered. Commie rebuttal repeated arguments made during morning session and on previous day, and also accused UNC of being afraid of the peace loving peoples of the world and of having a nature which loves smell of gunpowder. Hsiehs attitude in p.m. was more conciliatory and advocated patience in dealing with the armistice problem, but as usual distorted UNC statements in effort to make his points.

UNC sub-del feels from todays discussions that Commies hope that settlement of item 2 alone will accomplish in effect a de facto cease fire now. This impression created by Commie refusal to admit that the revision at the time of the signing of the armistice of their provisional line & zone would then make their proposal similar to that of the UNC, and also by their repeated insistence that their provisional line & zone were prerequisites to settlement of item 2; even though their proposal envisages changes occasioned by subsequent changes in l of c [line of contact].

The UNC sub-del believes it imperative in view of above and of attitude of Commies during past 2 days, that insistence on acceptance of our present proposal be continued. Further, the UNC sub del believes it would be extremely dangerous to accept Commie proposal. It is believed there is no danger of their breaking off conference because they profit by delays.

I sent Gen Turner back to Tokyo today with instructions to talk to R on subject of our initial position on Item 3 which I think is too strong[.] We also should have JCS instructions as to our minimum position on this item. **The Delegation feels unanimously that inspection in the demilt zone is the best we can hope for unless we are willing to break.**

Nov. 13 (Tues): Main argument used today by Commies against UNC proposal of 10 Nov was that it did not meet agenda Item 2 requirements and proposal was therefor illegal. UNC sub-del refuted this argument, offered eliminate phrase ''minor local adjustments'' but Commies not interested.

Commies propounded questions designed to ascertain whether UNC would be willing to stop fighting on present l of c [line of contact]. When advised that location of any cease fire line would depend upon the location of the l of c when armistice was signed, Commies asked why our present proposal differed from our previous ones in not providing a present line & zone. It was again explained that our previous proposals were based upon adjusted lines which had to be specifically spelled out while present proposal is based exclusively on l of c as it may exist on the date of the signing of the armistice and therefor requires no predetermination.

UNC query as to whether Commies expected a withdrawal and cease fire to follow upon reaching agreement on item 2 alone was given equivocal answer which indicated no intent to require immediate withdrawal but avoided reference to cease fire. An indicated objection to our proposal was the fear that disputes on the location of the l of c at time of signing of armistice would possibly result in UNC breaking off negots at that late date with the obvious implication that under their proposal unresolved disputes on proposed revisions would still leave the agreed provisional milt dem [military demarcation] line as the one to be used in the armistice agreement.

Commie reps. [representatives] stated that they would not accept our proposal, that under it we would be able to delay final agreement on the armistice until l of c was most favorable to us. Of course this argument also applicable to Commie proposal.

Commies repeatedly demanded that UNC state now, in solution to item 2, the line at which it desire fighting to stop, insisting that this would have followed from any of our previous proposals. UNC sub Del repeatedly stated that fighting would stop when complete armistice was agreed to on the l of c at that time. Further stated that establishment demilt zone now on present l of c would encourage delay in agreement on subsequent agenda items. The important point is achievement of complete armistice agreement[.]

Both Commie delegates appeared to lose their tempers, perhaps intentionally[,] as meeting continued for 5 hrs without recess.

UNC sub Del. has been unable to unearth real reason for Commie refusal accept our proposal. Whatever it may be, it is of high importance to them since their stated objections, while completely illogical, are gaining in vehemence and vituperativeness.

Nov. 14 (Wed): **Shin Turner returned from Tokyo and gave me results his discussions with R. Showed me despatch R had received from JCS [CTJ penned in margin: "JCS-86804"] and R's reply thereto. Gist of JCS despatch: Urged acceptance of Commie proposal earliest "with understanding that agreement as to this line will remain valid for definite period during which remainder of agenda must be accomplished." Suggested this be**

approx one month. Make clear to Commies that if no settlement reached end of this period, agreement with respect to location of median line no longer valid. JCS do not consider agreement as above on Item 2 would imply cease fire. Ground action could still continue. Air & naval action unaffected.

R's answer requested reconsideration. Pointed out in every instance in which UNC has been permitted to stand pat on their requirements there has been eventual agreement by Commies. Continued patience & resistance will gain us this point. R pointed out clearly our concern over giving Commies de facto cease fire on ground. even though no signed armistice. They may want this to delay indefinitely on subsequent agenda items or to increase their bargaining powers in remainder of negots because of lessening milt. pressure on them. "The vital difference between the UNC and Commie proposals rests in the intent behind the Commie insistence on a dem [demarcation] **line based on present l of c** [line of contact] **despite their pretended agreement that the present b.l.** [battle line] **has no legal relevance for the final settlement of Item 2." R then quoted some of Hodes remarks to stress instability of Commie position and gave basic reason for his (R) belief that Commies must eventually concede our position.**

"R" ended his msg by saying he felt premature acceptance of present l of c as proposed by Commies must inevitably delay the possibility of obtaining an acceptable and honorable armistice. "I feel there is substantial probability that announcement to Commies of course you have directed will increase Commie intransigence and weaken our future positions on every substantive point. Having grown up with this developing situation, I have a strong inner conviction that more steel and less silk, more forthright Amer. [American] insistence on the unchallengeable logic of our position, will yield the objectives for which we honorably contend. Conversely I feel that the course you are directing will lead step by step to sacrifice of our basic principles and repudiation of the cause for which so many gallant men have laid down their lives. We stand at a crucial point. We have much to gain by standing firm. We have everything to lose thru concession. With all my conscience I urge we stand firm."

Following msg sent to R when sub del returned:

"UNC opened session by querying Communists as to how Commie proposal would prevent a break off of negots at the last minute, or prevent stalling to obtain a favorable l of c, objections which they had raised to UNC proposal. **Commies stated that agreement on milt. dem line in the solution of agenda item 2 would constitute a "de facto cease fire"**; that this was an "unavoidable result" of agenda item 2. They still insisted that changes in the l of c after agreement on the milt. dem. line would be reflected in revisions to be made prior to the signing of the armistice although if one side tried to make changes in accord. their legal right it would be an indication of bad faith and insincerity and prove that that side did not want an armistice.

"UNC repeatedly asked whether this de facto cease fire was expected to apply to air & navy as well as ground. Commies finally indicated, without specifically so stating, that they expected a complete cease-fire on the ground, in the air and at sea as a demonstration of our good faith. Chinese representative delivered lengthy tirade in which he asserted that our former proposals necessarily included a de facto cease fire and that this was because we would have gotten all we wanted by negots; that under our present proposal we intend to get by force of arms what we have been unable to win by negots. His statement was replete with accusations that UNC did not desire to end hostilities and with anger directed at UNC position, that in order to preclude stalling on other items UNC would not put itself in a position where it could not continue to conduct milt. ops. [military operations] up until such time as a complete armistice is agreed upon and signed.

"Commies said de facto cease fire would have no binding legal force but that any milt activities of either side after agreement on item 2 was reached would be an indication of that side's desire for an armistice; but that it was to meet UNC insistence on the right to continue hostilities that they had included the 3rd para in their proposal.

"UNC asserted that Commie proposal had apparently been purposely drawn so as to be open to the construction now being given it while not so stating on the surface; pointed out that it had required many questions over several days, the answers to all of which had been evasive prior to this morning to bring Commies intent out into open; and stated UNC wanted an armistice but that it wanted a complete one, including all of the items on the agenda, and that it did not want to set up a situation whereby those other items might never be solved.

"Commies summarized their position substantially as follows; their proposal contemplates a de facto cease fire by all arms; however this is based on good faith only and is not legally binding; in order to allow scope for UNC "military adventures," the 3rd para was added to their proposal; after agreement on item 2, the UNC may change the l of c in accordance with its milt ability; this is equally applicable to both sides; and clarification of proposal was given today only in order to refute our "distorted press propaganda."

"It is belief of sub-del that Commies are pressing for a complete cease fire at the time agenda item 2 only is agreed to. If they get such a cease fire they will proclaim bad faith if any hostile milt ops. of any kind are conducted thereafter regardless of delays or outcome on remainder of agenda items. Careful reading of the principle in the first para of their proposal of 10 Nov permits such interpretation but only during today's discussions have there [sic] points been brought out in the open."

The $64 question at present is, will the JCS adhere to their expressed desire that we accept Commie proposal or will they be governed by R's splendid msg. Hodes & Burke feel definitely that their usefulness is ended if

we are forced to accept Commie terms. The same feeling is shared by me as to my own future usefulness.

Nov. 15 (Thurs): This evening after sub-Del returned the following msg [CTJ penned in margin: "JCS 86969"] was passed to us for info. This is in reply to R's msg to JCS as outlined in my notes of yesterday.

"JCS appreciate views expressed in UR [your] msg and recognize that there are certain disadvantages involved in undertaking action directed by our msg. However from broader viewpoint, they feel these disadvantages are outweighed by desirability of early agreement on agenda item 2.

"Specifically JCS feel: (a) That Commie proposal generally meets our basic position re demilt zone, namely defense of Kansas Line, and in addition provides protection for Wyoming line and the recently improved logistical support of X Corps. Hence agreement with it is no concession on our part. (b) That no major change in our favor in present l of c [line of contact] is likely in next month. (c) That milt pressure on Commies neither will nor should be lessened. (d) that agreement on this agenda item, which is apparently of prime importance to Commies, might well expedite agreement on other items rather than retard them, particularly if we maintain milt pressure.

"JCS reafirm[s] the necessity for agreeing upon all proper arrangements for cessation of hostilities as contained in armistice terms, before any form of cease fire is acceded to. (no relax milt effort until cf. [cease-fire] in arm. [armistice conference] agreed upon)

Accordingly JCS desire that you under take action indicated in JCS 96804 (one outlined in my notes of yesterday). They recognize that certain preparatory work may be necessary, however, they desire that this be done without delay."

On the heels of the above msg the following msg was received from R:

"Desire you press for early settlement item 2 of agenda on basis present l of c a provisional line of dem. [demarcation] with clear understanding that agreement as to this provisional line will remain valid only for definite period during which agreement must be reached on remainder of agenda. Period of 1 mo is suggested. It will be made clear that, if at end of stated period settlement has not been reached on all items of agenda, agreements with respect to location of this provisional line of dem. will no longer be valid, and that a new although not necessarily a different median line will have to be established.

"If Commies raise difficulties about agreeing to location of actual l of c, suggest you attempt to get agreement on basis of map, making such concessions as are not significant, or if this is impossible that you work out such methods of checking line as would be acceptable to you (such as marking & aerial photography) and as will not compel suspension of ops [operations] other than as already provided in Kaesong area.

"You will inform Commie delegation that above is with understanding that both sides will be unrestricted in their ground, naval and air ops. until armistice agreement is accomplished in full. It is desirable that prefactory [prefatory] para of actual agreement on agenda item 2 be couched in terms such as: "The reps [representatives] of the UNC, the NKPA and the CPV do reafirm [sic] their understanding that hostilities will continue until the signing of the armistice document and do agree that — — —. Further, it is desirable that the word "provisional" be used to modify the terms "demilt zone" and "median line" wherever appropriate.

"Attempts to attain objectives of previous 2 paras must be guided by desirability of getting thru with item 2 as promptly as possible."

Report of sub Del meeting of today follows:

Lee opened with usual harangue that UNC proposal on Agenda Item 2 was contrary to spirit of agenda and contrary to previous proposals of UNC. Stated objective of Commie proposal was early cessation of hostilities and to pave way for further agreements.

UNC replied each agenda item has 3 elements where, how & when. UNC proposal fulfills all three. Does not violate spirit of agenda. Asserted Commies yesterday disclosed real but previously concealed meaning of their proposal. This attempt to conceal not conducive to good faith. Stated Commies were seeking cessation of hostilities on basis agreement on 2/5th of agenda. Commies now contradict the earlier statements of their senior delegate and themselves. They themselves recognize these contradictions by phraseology their proposal which admits continuance of operation is legal even though Commies say continued ops would be expression bad faith. Since continuation of these talks cannot be predicted UNC cannot and will not cease milt. action until armistice agreement is reached. The quickest way for Commies to bring about peace and secure their own objectives with respect to location of dem. line is to cooperate fully in a joint venture to work thru remaining items of agenda.

Lee asserted UNC subjective interpretation of Commie proposal resulted in distortion. Yesterday's explanation could have been omitted since proposal is self explanatory. The proposal says that the dem line will be revised. There is no legal restriction on UNC carrying out any milt. adventure until armistice is signed. UNC was seeking hidden motives in proposal only to convince people of world to its own direction. Commies have never mentioned that they are seeking a cease fire prior to signing of armistice and UNC should not assume it. Hsieh continued saying that the determination of the area in which both sides are willing to stop fighting must be a preliminary to settlement of other items.

UNC attacked inconsistencies between Commies expositions of their proposal made yesterday and those made today. Said these shifts gave impression Commies did not know what they intended. Today Commies say cease fire will not come into effect until armistice is signed. If Commies mean that, the l of c at that time becomes milt. dem. line. Then Commies agree with UNC proposal. If not what is purpose of Commie proposal.

Lee replied Commie proposal includes fixing of dem. line. Both sides have come close. As to the when, it must be settled during discussion agenda item 2. Consequently, if neither side develops further milt ops, a defacto cease fire will result even if agreement is not yet signed. However, he added since UNC asks to go on fighting Commie proposal allows for revision of this line.

UNC asked are we trying to settle item 2 as written or according to interpretations placed on it by Commies? Item involves only where, when & how and UNC proposal satisfies all 3. Commies have added to these a provisional dem line & zone not required by item 2.

Today for 1st time during current discussions, Commie delegates particularly Hsieh, showed lack of aggressiveness and little enthusiasm.

Nov. 16 (Fri): Sub Del rpts following:

Commies spent day in attempting to prove illegality of UNC proposal and to obtain info on where UNC was willing to stop fighting. They evaded all attempts to get reasonable or clear answers to such questions as: What is purpose of provisional zone, do you expect a cease fire after agreement on item 2 alone, length of time provisional zone to be effective, would final l of c [line of contact] become the final Milt Dem [military demarcation] line under their proposal. UNC sub Del continued to get definite impression that agreement to Commie proposal of 10 Nov will result in Commie demand for cease fire prior to agreement on subsequent items and possibly long delay in arriving at complete armistice agreement. UNC sub Del is and has been for some time of the opinion that there is absolutely no possibility of obtaining results by means of reasoning or by concession in dealing with Commies. They understand nothing but force.

R's rpt to JCS left out last 3 sentences.

As a result of exchange of msgs between R & delegation, the following proposal will be presented to Commies at an opportune time today:

"The reps [representatives] of the UNC and of the KPA and CPV:

(1) Reaffirm their understanding that hostilities will continue until the signing of the armistice agreement.

(2) Agree that the present l of c as jointly determined by the sub Dels. will constitute a provisional milt dem line, and that 2 lines, 2 kms from this prov. [provisional] milt dem. line, will constitute the southern & northern boundaries of a prov. demilt. zone.

(3) Agree that the above provisional milt. dem line and above prov. demilt zone based upon present l of c shall become effective in any armistice agreement signed within 30 days after this agreement is accepted by the two dels in plenary session.

(4) Agree that, if an armistice agreement is not signed by the end of the 30 day

period, the then existing l of c will be determined jointly by the sub dels and will constitute a new prov. milt. dem. line which will be the median line of a new prov. demilt zone to be effective under such conditions as will be at that time mutually agreed to by the delegations of both sides.''

Nov. 17 (Sat): Morning session & major portion of afternoon session were spent in further discussion of relative merits and demerits of UNC and Commie proposals of 10 Nov. The Commies having given no indication by 1430 that they would abandon their position during this session, the UNC delegates, in compliance with pertinent directives, introduced our new proposal as given in yesterday's notes (Nov 16)[.]

Commies gave preliminary response that proposal seemed to be in accordance with their principles, that if both sides exerted themselves the remaining questions might be resolved soon. However, since this depends on how sincerely we deal with each other, the time element is not a matter of great importance.

Hodes & Burke rptd [reported] **Commies seemed very smug and complacent when our proposal was made. Seemed to be expecting something of the sort. I understand A.P. had word we would set a time limit in a new proposal. Story first appeared in N.Y. Times.**

Nov. 18 (Sun): In todays sub-Del session which lasted only 1½ hrs Commies asked questions to clarify their understanding of UNC proposal made yesterday. They recess for purpose of studying proposal further.

As a result of Commie queries Hodes asked Wright for authority to delete the words from the phrase ''to be effective[''] to end of para or (2) to substitute for the phrase ''under such conditions'' the words ''for such purposes and for such a period.'' We would use these changes only if Commies continue to object to present wording.

CinCUNC answered this as follows: (1) Purpose of wording under discussion was to provide for the insertion of time period of validity and in addition, to provide for insertion of any other clause which might be recommended by some contingency now unforeseen.

(2) Recommend your approach be as follows:

(a) Press for acceptance of para 4 as now written.

(b) If necessary, offer your proposed second alternative—''for such purpose and for such period[.]''

(3) Considered undesirable to agree to proposal deleting entire last sentence of para 4 after word ''zone.'' Deletion of these words leaves proposal strongly implying that the second agreed provisional line & zone will be the final one, regardless of how long the discussions continue thereafter.

Nov. 19 (Mon): In a session which lasted only 1 hr 15 mins Commies sought further clarification on par 4 of UNC proposal, particularly the intent of the word "conditions." When satisfied they proposed a recess until 21 1100 Nov. UNC delegates made inquiry to check Commie understanding of para 1 that hostilities would continue and as to the provisional and tentative nature of the line & zone fixed in accord with paras 2 & 3. Commie reply was "We'll give you our overall reply to your proposal on 21 November."

Upon hearing of recess I decided to return to Tokyo. Left camp at 1530 arriving Tokyo (via Pusan at Gen Ennis request) at 2130.

Nov. 20 (Tues): Conferred with R early 0800 about relieving Burke & Hodes. He agreed with recommendation that they be relieved earliest since they felt that they had outlived their usefulness. He will advise me who will relieve Hodes and agrees to Libby relieving Burke. I then went down to Yokosuka and approached Libby on matter. He is entirely agreeable and will report next Sun or Mon. Sent despatch to Bu Pers [Bureau of Personnel] telling them Libby was being ordered on TD [Temporary Duty] basis as relief for Burke. Was later advised Ferenbaugh, present C.G. 7th Inf. Division would relieve Hodes.

Scratched off annual physical exam [examination] and session with Dentist. Blood pressure higher than last year but otherwise O.K. Doc Goldhamer & Maj Gen Lee came for dinner tonight.

Nov. 21 (Wed): Sub Del reported as follows: Commie reps. [representatives] opened by advising of agreement in principle to UNC proposal but objecting to form thereof. They then presented proposed changes in the form of a new proposal which reads as follows:

"The sub-dels reach the following agreement on Item 2 of the agenda, "Fixing a milt dem [military demarcation] line between both sides so as to establish a demilt [demilitarized] zone as the basic condition for the cessation of hostilities in Korea."

(1) The principle is accepted that the actual l of c [line of contact] between both sides be made the milt dem line, and that both sides withdraw 2 kms. from this line so as to establish the demilt zone.

(2) In accord with the above mentioned principle, the sub dels check immediately the present l of c, so as to fix the actual l of c agreed upon by both sides as the milt. dem. line, with the two lines two kms away on both sides of the milt dem line constituting the southern & northern boundaries of the demilt zone.

(3) In view of the fact that hostilities will continue until the signing of the armistice agreement, if agreements are reached on all the items of the agenda within 30 days after the two delegations approve in the plenary session this agreement and the specific location of the above mentioned milt. dem. line & demilt zone; the milt dem line & demilt zone already fixed shall not be changed regardless of whatever changes that may occur in the actual l of c between both sides; if agreements are not yet reached on all the items of the agenda by the time the 30 days transpire, the milt. dem line & demilt zone already fixed shall be

revised in accordance with the changes which have occurred in the actual l of c between both sides prior to the signing of the armistice agreement."

The UNC reps pointed out in detail the inconsistencies and ambiguities contained in the new Commie proposal, particularly with respect to para 1, most of which were the same as those ascribed to the 10 Nov proposal made by the Commies. Numerous questions intended to clarify the Commie proposal were asked but specific answers could not be obtained.

UNC suggested recess to allow it to study further Commie proposal with a view to rewriting it in clear and unambiguous form and submit revised proposal at tomorrows meeting.

Sub del then sent msg to CinCUNC saying that they intended to present following revisions to Commie proposal tomorrow.

"1[.] The principle is accepted that the actual l of c between both sides (as determined under either para 2 or 3 as appropriate) will be made the milt. dem. line and that at the time specified in the signed armistice agreement both sides will withdraw 2 kms. from this line so as to establish the demilt zone for the duration of the armistice.

"2. In accord with the above stated principle, the sub-dels will determine immediately the present l of c so as to fix it as the milt. dem. line and as the median line of the demilt zone. If the milt. armistice agreement is signed within 30 days after the two dels. approve in the plenary session this agreement and the specific location of the above milt dem line & demilt zone, the line & zone shall not be changed, regardless of whatever changes may occur in the actual l of c between both sides.

"3. In view of fact that hostilities will continue until the signing of the armistice agreement, if the milt armistice is not signed by the time 30 days expire, the milt dem line & demilt zone shall be revised so that the actual l of c between both sides at the time of the signing of the armistice agreement shall become the milt dem line & the median line of the demilt zone." UNC sub del pointed out that reference to withdrawal of troops from demilt zone in Commie proposal may have several connotations. Having once agreed to this part of the principle in their para 1, Commies could demand withdrawal at any time it suited them.

UNC sub del also pointed out that fixing of actual l of c at time of signing of arm. [armistice] agreement as the milt dem line instead of specifying another time limit for approval is believed advantageous over UNC proposal of 17 Nov.

Worked with Darrow, Muse & Herr [sic] over answer to long JCS despatch on subject of inspection (Item 3). Msg asked CinCUNC for his views and said most careful [review] of our (JCS) position in this regard is required. Main purpose of inspn [inspection] & obsn [observation] are: (a) To assure against a resumpt. [resumption] of hostilities and (b) to provide for security of UN Forces. Doubtful that insp mechanism will attain former therefore real concern is scty. [security] of

UN Forces. JCS msg asked a number of questions relative to stationing of observer teams, how handle rpts [reports] of violations, how check rehab. [rehabilitation] airfields, roads etc, what safeguards are envisaged for solving incidents & disagreements. Ended by asking what we would accept if Commies flatly rejected unlimited access & obsn. It is clear to me that JCS will not support a UNC position that is inflexible on unlimited obsn over all Korea, Nor do I believe we should put ourselves in such a position.

Nov. 22 (Thurs): Thanksgiving Day. Left Tokyo with R and the Barkleys in C-54 [four-engine military transport aircraft] at about 0830 arriving Kimpo about 1215 and back at camp via auto about 1430. While enroute R drafted tentative reply to J.C.S msg. I attempted without success to dissuade him from holding out for unlimited obsn. [observation] as our initial stand. Emphasized emphatically importance of UNC Del. knowing our final position before beginning negots on item 3 and need for taking a "take it or leave it" position on our final or min position. V.P. Barkley [U.S. Vice-President Alben W. Barkley] wanted to know when we could expect to sign final arm. [armistice] agreement. I wish I knew.

Upon return to camp Galloway came in with problem. Commies refused to buy revision to para 3 desired by CinCUNC, which read as follows: "In view of fact that hostilities will continue until signing of arm. agreement, if milt [military] arm is not signed by time 30 days expire, the then existing l of c [line of contact] will be determined jointly by the sub-dels. & will constitute a new prov. [provisional] demilt [demilitarized] zone to be effective for such purposes and for such a period as will at that time be mutually agreed by the dels of both sides." Hodes & Burke invited attention that this revision gave Commies more than they had asked. I then called R at Seoul and requested authority to use my judgment in matter, which was granted. Hodes had meanwhile recessed meeting for day when Commies came up with another revised para 3, which read as follows:

"In view of fact that hostilities will continue until the signing of the armistice agreement, if the milt. arm. agreement is not signed within 30 days after the two dels approve in the plenary session this agreement and the specific location of the milt. dem. [demarcation] line and the demilt. zone as determined in the 2nd article, the sub-dels shall revise, after agreements are reached on all items of the agenda, the above milt. dem line and the demilt. zone in accord. with the changes which have occurred in the actual l of c. between both sides prior to the signing of the milt. arm. agreement, so that the revised milt. dem. line will coincide exactly with the l of c between both sides prior to the signing of the milt arm agreement, and constitute the milt. dem. line for the duration of the milt. armistice."

In msg reporting meeting I said that as result of my telephone talk with R. the UNC sub-del on Nov 23 will accept Commie version of para 3 with minor revisions.

Staff offs. meet separately at same time as sub-del to begin determination of actual l of c on map.

Nov. 23 (Fri): Recd msg from R concerning his proposed reply to JCS msg on item 3. Asked for our comments by 1900 today. R's msg came to 2 general conclusions (a) Insistence on principle of inspection is a vital factor in our armistice negots and (b) U.S. Govt must without delay, reach and advise me of its decision on this matter, in order that U.N.C. del may be properly instructed and plot its course. R considered it unacceptable, from the viewpoint of the security of the UN forces, to accept anything less than stipulated in his msg of 4 Oct (see p. 105 [of diary: see entry of that date]).

Our comments on his msg were a recommendation to include following para "It is the opinion of the UNC delegation, based on experience and Commie expressions in sub-del meetings to date that the Commies can be expected to prolong negots and may even break them off if UNC insists on inspection and observation other than in demilt. zone" The reason we recommended this insert is that it provides the JCS our best judgment of the probable outcome of our rec. [recommended] course of action, a pertinent and vital consideration in connection with the general conclusions.

We also rec. that another para of R's proposed msg be reworded as follows: "The recent directed action of the UNC del. in offering the Communists a proposal with the present l of c fixed as the milt. dem. line for 30 days is more advantageous to the Commies than their proposal of 10 November, and has, in my opinion and that of our delegates, substantially weakened our future bargaining potential. I must urge most serious consideration of our view here that the UNC del be given a clear cut decision on how far it can go on agenda Item 3 and still be assured of the support of the U.S. Govt. It is particularly debilitating to our prestige and negotiating position to take firm positions, thereby creating widely publicized issues, only to withdraw from our position under pressure."

In the msg he sent to the JCS, R used our above suggestions but did not make use of another comment which is quoted as follows: "Based on experience with the Kaesong neutral zone and incidents arising therein which could not be settled by joint inspection and which led to acrimonious disputes, the UNC del. desires to submit its opinion that the principle of insp. [inspection] of rear areas could prove in practice to be disadvantageous to the UNC. We feel that the considerations listed in your paras 11 & 12, together with the dubious value of UNC inspection teams in Commie territory, could well result in a net loss to the UNC. Certainly unless national policy is firm and clear on the action to be taken, if any, in event of detected violations of the armistice agreement, the upshot of inspection will be little more than fruitless debate.["]

Agreement was reached by the sub-del on Item 2 of the agenda today. Following is text of recommendation to be submitted to plenary session after location of line of dem. is agreed upon by sub-del.

(1) Same as 1 on p 192 [of the diary; see November 21, ninth paragraph].

2. If the milt. arm. agreement is signed within 30 days after the two dels. approve in the plenary session this agreement and the specific location of the milt. dem. line and demilt. zone determined by the sub-dels on the basis of the above-stated principle and in accord with the present l of c (as indicated in the attached map and explanatory notes), the milt. dem. line and demilt. zone shall not be changed, regardless of whatever changes may occur in the actual l of c.

3. In view of the fact that hostilities will continue until the signing of the arm. agreement, if the milt. arm. agreement is not signed within 30 days after the two dels. approve in the plenary session this agreement and the specific location of the milt. dem. line and demilt zone as determined in par 2 above, the sub-dels shall revise, immediately prior to the signing of the milt. arm. agreement, the above line & zone in accordance with the changes which have occurred in the actual l of c between both sides, so that the revised milt. dem. line will coincide exactly with the l of c between both sides immed. [immediately] prior to the signing of the milt. armistice agreement and will constitute the milt dem line for the duration of the milt. armistice.

Nov. 24 (Sat): At a meeting of liaison officers this date, Colonel Chang, NKA asked for safe conduct for Commie vehicles for del. between Pyongyang & Kaesong. We agreed to providing safe conduct for 6 trucks & 3 jeeps leaving P and K respectively at 0600 daily and following road which leads thru Sariwon and Nanchon-Jon [Namchonjom].

Staff officers met today to determine l of c [line of contact]. Agreement reached on about 50% of l of c. In all cases where differences exist they are based upon enemy dispute of positions held by UN forces. In part, the differences result from enemy's lack of accurate & timely info. In others it appears that he may be attempting to retain particularly desirable positions. UNC staff officers meet Commies again at 1000 tomorrow. In event full agreement is not reached by noon tomorrow UNC sub-del will call for a meeting of the two sub-dels in an attempt to resolve the differences then existing.

Nov. 25 (Sun): Staff officers made progress in getting agreed l of c [line of contact] in today's sessions[.] However, at 1400 eleven points of disagreement remained. Sub-dels [delegations] met at 1500 in an effort to resolve remaining differences. Only one was resolved. The ten remaining points of disagreement concern positions which both sides claim. The UNC is absolutely certain that its info on these locations is correct and up to date almost hourly. The Commies were adamant that their info was current and correct; however, it is well known that it is neither. To agree with Commies in these areas would place the dem [demarcation] line behind positions UNC actually holds.

UNC sub-del offered to fly a joint team to each of the posits [positions] in question but Commies refused. The Commies appeared to expect UNC to capitulate on all points. They became truculent and stubborn and made no effort to attempt to negotiate. Quick agreement on a reasonable l of c is hampered by Commie intransigent attitude. Staff offs meet tomorrow at 1000 to again attempt to reconcile differences.

Nov. 26 (Mon): At todays meeting UNC staff officers reached agreement with Commie counterparts on location of l of c. Meeting terminated at 1930 hrs.

Sub delegations meet tomorrow at 1000 to consider l of c agreed to by staff offs. UNC sub del hopes to secure prompt approval by both sides in order to submit matter to a plenary session of main dels. tentatively scheduled for 1100 tomorrow[.]

After approval of milt dem line, UNC Del intends to press for immed consideration of item 3.

Nov. 27 (Tues): With agenda Item 2 cleared off the books after 37 sub-del and 28 full del meetings, the UNC & Commie leaders plunged into attempting a solution to the 3rd agenda item. at a plenary session.

After UNC presented credentials Maj-Gen Turner as delegate vice [in the place of] Maj Gen Craigie both dels. ratified agreement on Agenda Item 2 submitted by sub-dels. UNC asked that before dels. go to discussion of Agenda Item 3 they entertain a suggestion that would in due course facilitate solution to agenda item 4. The suggestion was that both sides exchange (1) names, nationality and identifying data of POW's (2) location of POW camps and (3) the number by nationality of POW's in each camp.

Nam Il noted this suggestion and went on to make a formal proposal of gen. [general] principles for consideration under Agenda Item 3. These were (1) all armed forces of both sides, including reg. and irregular units and armed personnel of the ground, naval and air forces, shall cease all hostilities from the day of the signing of the arm. [armistice] agreement. (2) all armed forces of both sides shall be withdrawn from the demilt. zone within 3 days after the signing of the arm. agreement. (3) all armed forces of either side shall be withdrawn, within 5 days after the signing of the arm. agreement, from the rear and coastal islands and waters of the other side, with the milt dem. [military demarcation] line as the dividing line. If they are not withdrawn within the stated time limit, and there is no reason for delaying the withdrawal, the other side shall have the right to take all necessary action against such armed personnel for the maintenance of security and order. (4) All armed forces on both sides shall not enter the demilt zone and shall not carry out any acts of armed force against the demilt zone. (5) Both sides shall designate an equal number of members to form an arm. commission to be jointly responsible for the concrete arrangement and the supervision of the implementation of the arm. agreement.

UNC noted this proposal and made an opening statement on agenda Item 3 which rec. [recommended] that following be included in the concrete arrangements. (1) Details of: cease-fire, removal of troops from demilt zone and civil admin [administration] of the demilt zone. (2) Measures which will reduce the possibility of resumption of hostilities. (3) The establishment of a supervisory organization and its joint observer teams to observe in such parts of Korea as necessary.

Nam Il opened afternoon session with prelim [preliminary] response to UNC proposal. He expressed genl [general] agreement with first principle. With respect to the 2nd he expressed fundamental stand of Commies that a "thorough peaceful solution which alone can prevent resumption of hostilities requires the convening of a conference at a higher level to discuss withdrawal of foreign troops and similar matter[s]." He stated this was purpose of agenda Item 5; that purpose of present conference is to attain a milt. arm. [military armistice] and that it cannot solve such questions as those expressed in 2nd principle of the UNC. In this connection, it was notable that in presenting their proposal the Commies ignored the question of joint inspection, and in commenting on the UNC proposal they again ignored the question of joint inspection.

With ref to UNC 3d & 4th principles Nam Il said they corresponded to Commie 5th principle. As to authority of Arm Com. [commission] he said it should be limited to that necessary to supervise implementation of arm terms. In closing, he said dels should seek to reach agreement on subjects within scope of a milt arm.

UNC commented on Commie proposal saying it was inadequate as an expression of principles under wording of Agenda Item 3 and proposed a list of genl. principles to be adopted prior to referring the prob. [problem] to a sub committee for detailed solution. These were:

1(1) [numbers in parentheses refer to CTJ's agenda and numbers preceding them refer to the Communist agenda] There shall be a cease-fire, effective 24 hrs after the signing of the arm agreement, and adhered to by all forces of any type under control of either side.

5(2) There shall be established a supervisory organ. [organization] equally and jointly manned by both sides, for carrying out terms of the arm. agreement.

7(3) There shall be no increase of milt forces, supplies, equipment and facilities by either side after signing of the arm.

6(4) The Milt. Arm. Com. in carrying out its supervisory functions, shall have free access to all parts of Korea, for itself and for the joint obs. [observation] teams responsible to the arm. Com.

2(5) There shall be a withdrawal of forces of each side, air, ground and naval, regular and irregular, from the territory controlled by the other side.

3(6) There shall be no armed forces in the demilt zone except as specifically and mutually agreed by both sides.

4(7) The milt Comdrs [commanders] shall administer their portion of the demilt zone in accord with the terms of the arm. agreement.

Nam Il stated that these 7 principles were only an elab. [elaboration] of the UNC proposal of the morning session to which he had already made a prelim. response. He then proposed recess until 1100 tomorrow to enable both sides to study opinions expressed by other side.

Nov. 28 (Wed): Nam Il opened plenary session with further comment on principles offered by UNC yesterday. He indicated Commie agreement with 1, 2, 6 & 7. He sought clarification of 5, the current wording of which is designed to retain[,] during the period of the armistice[,] coastal islands off N.K. which are now under UNC control.

With respect to the 3rd UNC principle Nam Il contended that in order to achieve a thorough careful settlement of the Korean question, all foreign troops must be withdrawn from Korea. In this event, he said, there will be no question of supplies, equipment and facilities exceeding those existing at the time of the signing. It is because peace can be achieved only by withdrawal of foreign troops said Nam Il that his side wants a conference at a higher level. It is improper to seek a conclusion of such questions in the conference, the objective of which is a milt. [military] armistice. Therefore he said, the UNC 3rd principle exceeds the scope of the present conference and the 4th principle which requires free access for joint observation teams to all parts of Korea is entirely unnecessary. In summary Nam Il opposed the 3rd principle on the grounds that it goes beyond the proper scope of a milt. arm. conference and the 4th principle on the grounds that it is unnecessary.

UNC made a statement on the scope of a milt armistice and stated that insofar as item 3 is concerned the 7 basic principles stated yesterday by the UNC clearly define the scope of the armistice which should be reached. UNC went on to offer an explanation of each of UNC's 7 principles, closing statement with expression of view that these principles constitute a sound basis for solution of agenda Item 3.

Nam Il replied that Item 3 & 4 are beyond the scope of the present conference and that if these matters are discussed it should be under agenda Item 5. The 3rd & 4th principles, he said, are clearly connected with the withdrawal of foreign troops & if this last question cannot be solved neither can the other two. UNC again defined an arm. as a cessation of hostilities under mutually agreed conditions and stated that a cessation of hostilities as a prelude to a settlement of the Korean problem was possible only under an armistice which would prevent either side building up a decisive milt. advantage for its duration. The UNC said it could not agree to an armistice which did not contain min. [minimum] safeguards to prevent the resumption of hostilities & provide for the security of forces.

Nam Il opened pm session with strong refutation of 3rd & 4th principles proposed by UNC. He said UNC seeks to delay solution of K problem thru a prolonged arm. and that to attempt to substitute an arm. for a peaceful settlement is to disclose an unwillingness to settle problem peacefully. He said there is a possibility of an armistice not primarily because there exists a balance of forces but because of the wishes of the peoples of the world, including those of U.S. Moreover he said there is a possibility of further solutions immed. [immediately] after the arm, however setting up a permanent balance of force in Korea will not lead to a peaceful solution. The resumption of host. [hostilities] in K. can be prevented not by a state of balance of war but by the elimination of war thru the withdrawal of foreign troops and subsequent steps for peaceful settlement of the K. problem. Therefore he said, as soon as the armistice is realized, the govts concerned should negotiate the withdrawal of troops and discuss other ways & means for peaceful settlement of K problems and speedily put them into practice. This, he said, is the only real guarantee against resumption of hostilities and the 3rd principle of the UNC is groundless. He said if the UNC insists upon starting broad discussions now on preventing resumption of hostilities his side is in favor of doing so, but the question of the withdrawal of foreign forces within a def. [definite] period must come first. He said again that the concrete measures proposed by the UNC were inappropriate and impracticable and that his side could not agree to the 3d principle and the 4th which follows from it.

Balance of session was spent in defense by UNC of its 3d principle and continuous refutation by Nam Il along lines indicated above. Among significant statements are following. "We hold that all foreign troops should be withdrawn immediately. We are not attempting to increase our forces, but we oppose any attempt to avoid the withdrawal of troops and hamper final settlement of K problem." "Your side seeks to discuss problems beyond the scope of a military armistice but related to the withdrawal of troops. By this means you seek to avoid the withdrawal of troops in the future."

["]The maintenance of an arm thru the maintenance of a balance of forces is not possible. It lies in the sincerity of both sides — — — The basic & permanent solution is the withdrawal of troops. We insist on the withdrawal of all foreign troops. Your side under pretext of maintenance of balance of forces seeks to continue a state of war and evade solution of the K problem.["]

"Principles 3 & 4 are beyond scope of 3rd item of agenda. They are closely related to withdrawal of troops. Without solving the basic quest. [question] of withdrawal these questions cannot be settled. Therefore we completely oppose principles 3 & 4. We insist on carrying on discussion within scope of agenda." Repeated several times in varying forms was the statement that principles 3 & 4 cannot be considered until the problem of foreign troops is settled. When pinned down Nam Il stated that "Withdrawal of foreign troops will settle principles 3 & 4."

In summary the Commie position is that withdrawal of foreign troops will make UNC principles 3 & 4 unnecessary and so far this is the strong stand of Commies on agenda Item 3.

Nov. 29 (Thurs): Nam Il opened session with a statement along following lines. UNC 3d & 4th principles are inappropriate impracticable and absolutely not acceptable. A milt arm. [military armistice] should lead to a peaceful settlement which would render resumption of hostilities impossible. Therefore, the question of withdrawal of foreign troops must be settled before any other matters concerning prevention of a resumption of hostilities are discussed. Its discussion should follow immed [immediately] upon the fixing of the milt. dem. [military demarcation] line. It was at the insistence of the UNC Del that it was agreed to settle a simple milt arm first leaving the question of withdrawal of troops to another conference. However, the UNC Del now insists on extensive discussion of measures to prevent resumption of hostilities under agenda Item 3. We are in favor of doing so. How can resumption of hostilities after the signing of the arm be prevented? The UNC holds that both sides should maintain the level of forces existing at the time of signing. This is to maintain a state of war. To safeguard against resumption of hostilities and to make arm. a bridge to peace, steps must be taken immed. to eliminate the state of war. In other words, discussion must begin immed. on withdrawal of all foreign forces. We agreed to defer this to Item 5. However, since UNC insists upon discussing broad question of preventing resumption of host. [hostilities] under 3rd item, we agree and insist upon starting with the discussion of the withdrawal of foreign troops. We still maintain that the 5 principles proposed by our side provide an adequate solution to agenda Item 3.

UNC Del. stated that deliberations should be limited to considerations within the powers of the respective Comdrs [commanders] to implement; that security of forces, during an armistice could not be left to political considerations beyond their purview. UNC stated it cannot consider any proposal which would omit from the agreement provisions for the security of its forces and the stability of the armistice during its duration. Specifically, it insisted upon provisions against increase in milt. capabilities and provision for observation of the adherence of both sides to such limitations during the period a milt armistice is in effect.

Nam Il replied in the following vein: "To safeguard against the resumption of hostilities steps must be taken immed. to eliminate the state of war and not maintain it. Discussion must begin immed. on the withdrawal of foreign troops. The UNC wants to discuss limitations upon the increase of milt forces. We consider this is not enough. If UNC agrees to discuss conditions to prevent resumption of host. why does it not agree to discuss decrease of milt forces by stages?"

UNC replied that the dels. were to work out a milt. armistice, not write a peace treaty. It said that if an agreement on an arm. can be reached there will be a cessation of hostile acts, but that a peaceful settlement will require further negotiation in which present dels. will not take part[.] UNC said that it was empowered to take only the first step in the process of going from war to peace, that is a milt. arm. It said question of withdrawal of troops must be left to a later conference; that we could make recs. to govts. concerned on this question but do no more. Asserted that discussion on this point should he held under agenda Item 5.

Nam Il replied as follows: UNC says withdrawal of troops is not within scope of 3rd agenda item. But it insists upon discussing extensive measures for preventing resump. [resumption] of host. Withdrawal is essential cond. [condition] to prevent resump. host. After withdrawal there will be no question of increase of forces. If UNC insists on broad discussion of measures for preventing host. under 3rd agenda item, it cannot avoid the question of the withdrawal of foreign trps [troops]. If UNC has the authority to discuss the question of a limit upon the increase of foreign forces in Korea, how is it that it does not have the authority to discuss their withdrawal? Is not the UNC's statement that it is not empowered to discuss withdrawal simply a device for opposing the withdrawal of troops from K. to facilitate the resumption of host. at a time of its own choosing?

Nov. 30 (Fri): UNC opened plenary session clarifying point that the concrete arrangements it seeks are for the duration of the armistice only and that the delegations have no competence to terminate the state of war. In reply to Nam Ils question of yesterday UNC said it had authority to discuss limitation on increase of forces in Korea because govts concerned consider the limitation of forces is a necessary measure to prevent resumption of hostilities during an armistice. However, said UNC, it will not make any comitment [*sic*] at this time concerning ultimate or staged withdrawal of foreign troops since govts concerned consider this question unrelated to a milt [military] armistice. UNC said further, the question is basically not one of authority, it is a question of measures to be taken to insure an effective arm. [armistice]. UNC said it will insist upon principles of limitation of forces and joint observation and that it would not agree to immed [immediate] withdrawal of UNC forces from Korea.

Nam Il replied in following vein. Withdrawal of troops and speedy settlement of K question can prevent hostil. [hostilities] after the armistice. His side is ready to discuss question under Agenda Item 5. The 5 principles he proposed provide reasonable solution to 3d item of agenda, whereas principle and concrete measures of UNC 3d & 4th points are unreasonable and impracticable. UNC insistence on them raises doubt as to its sincerity. Agreement on 5 principles is practicable and would permit plenary session to go on with agenda Item 4 while details are worked out. What is objective of UNC in insisting upon so impractical a principle as your no 4. Under pretext of maintaining balance of forces UNC proposes to interfere in internal affairs of other side. This is inconceivable in a milt armistice. Min [minimum] confidence in the sincerity of the other side which is necessary in an armistice renders such interference unnecessary and unwarranted. His side thought UNC should have recognized such proposals as unreasonable and unattainable but it has nevertheless advanced them. The purpose is to prevent reconstruction and rehab. [rehabilitation] of Korea under pretext of forbidding increase of milt facilities for offensive purposes. Under pretext of striking milt targets UNC destroyed the peaceful towns of Korea. Now under pretext of preventing increase of milt facilities for offensive purpose UNC attempts to keep Korea a heap of ruins.

On one hand UNC wants to refrain from introducing into Korea additional forces. On other it seeks to introduce them under name of replenishment and replacements if there is an armistice. What is need for replenishment and replacements? How are these to be distinguished from an increase of milt forces & equipment? On the one hand the UNC says this is a milt arm. without political consideration. On the other hand it maintains that the supervisory organ [organizations] have free access to all parts of Korea. This is a brazen interference into internal affairs. This is unreasonable and unwarranted and our side cannot absolutely agree to such a provision.

Nam I1 reviewed the 5 Commie principles explaining their meaning. He then returned to the wording of the 5th UNC principle and rejected UNC stand that it retain coastal islands and waters now under its possession during the armistice. UNC responded to Nam Il's comment on Commie 5 principles as follows—It agrees with 1 & 2. It agrees with 3 in part, but UNC must retain coastal islands now under its control during arm. It agrees with principles 4 & 5. However, the 5 principles are not sufficiently broad to be a complete solution to agenda item 3 since they give no thought to question of functions and authority of arm. commission. UNC agrees that plen. [plenary] session lay down gen. [general] principles on Item 3, but these must include functions & authority of commission. The heart of this is the principle of joint inspection.

UNC continued amplifying its views on 3d & 4th principle. In connection with the 3d principle words of para 4e and f of J.C.S. msg 95354 were used. In conn. [connection] with 4th principle it explained joint obs. [observation] as follows: There should be joint obs. teams located at key points thruout Korea such as ports, air fields, and major comm. [communications] centers. In add. [addition] there should be joint aerial obs. of Korea to provide photo & visual checks on conditions related to the arm. By use of aerial observers the Milt. Arm. Com. [Military Armistice Commission] can obtain immediate factual determination of many questions which may arise. Between the 2 methods of obs. air and ground, full coverage of all matters related to the arm. can be obtained.

At UNC suggestion of recess for lunch Nam Il stated he had heard nothing new and that unless UNC had something new for p.m. he proposed recess until 1100 tomorrow.

Dec. 1 (Sat): Plenary session convened 1100[.] Nam Il asked for reply to questions asked yesterday. UNC made a statement setting forth in full its views on rehabilitation and reconstruction in answer to Commie charges that it seeks to limit peaceful reconstruction.

Nam Il replied that he did not consider this a sat. [satisfactory] answer to his question and requested a 15 min recess. Upon returning he made a statement in following vein. UNC 3d & 4th principles are unreasonable, its 5th principle not clear. The 3 are self contradictory and inconsistent with UNC stated positions. On the one hand UNC proposes no introduction of re-inforcements into Korea, on the other it asks for exchange on a man for man basis. To ensure against resumption of hostilities foreign troops should be reduced positively during the armistice. No reason for continued introduction of troops. What reason can UNC have for seeking exchange of troops on man for man basis? Why does UNC want to introduce fresh units & personnel into Korea and what reason does it have for replenishment & replacement? UNC has stated an arm. [armistice] should provide adequate safeguards for security of troops. Yet it demands limitation on reconstruction of milt. [military] facilities during arm. Korean people have right to reconstruct, rehabilitate & reinforce defensive facilities destroyed by wanton bombing. Interference with this right cannot be tolerated. Does UNC seek by this pretext to prevent repair & reconstruction of defensive facilities? What cannot be labeled by UNC as milt fac [facilities] for offensive purposes? UNC holds that arm. negots [negotiations] are strictly milt. and involve no political questions. Yet it insists a supervisory organ [organization] have access to all of Korea, thus directly interfering in the internal affairs of other side. The authority of this organ should be confined to that necessary for carrying out terms of arm. Our side has no intention to interfere in internal affairs of that part of K controlled by UNC. No need for access to all parts of Korea, to carry out the armistice. It would be a flagrant and unwarranted violation in internal affairs which [would] have no justification in a strict milt arm. What is purpose of UNC in this respect? We have fixed a dem [demarcation] line & a demilt [demilitarized] zone to separate the armed forces and provide a definite dem. line with which to cease all hostil and make it difficult for them to be resumed. This was the basic cond [condition] for an arm. Therefore, each side should withdraw its forces in rear of dem. line. This is the inevitable consequence of fixing the line. Yet UNC attempts to retain armed forces on islands in our rear—an obvious violation of spirit of agreement on dem. line. What is object of UNC in this respect? Perhaps it wants to make arm. unstable by retaining forces in our rear. Perhaps it is for some ulterior motive that UNC seeks limitation upon increase in armed force for stated purpose of stabilizing armistice. What object is UNC pursuing?

UNC replied its objective is a just and reasonable armistice which will insure against resumption of hostilities pending final settlement of the Korean problem. UNC stated Nam Il's statement contained no new thoughts; most of which had been refuted previously, none would stand up under examination. UNC then made following statement:

"In order that you may understand clearly our views concerning this milt. arm, I shall make a very imp [important] statement.

"During past 4 days, UNC has stated its position on agenda Item 3 and has explained it in full. Everything in our proposal is as fair to one side as to the other. Every specific principle which we have stipulated is designed to enhance the stability of the milt. arm. and to increase the prospects of an early peace in Korea. All of these principles are strictly military. None are political. We have stated 7 principles upon which the solution of Item 3 of the Agenda must be based. We have listened to your objections to these principles. We now reject these invalid objections categorically.

"You oppose observation by jointly manned teams thruout Korea. You oppose the limitation of forces on both sides, limitations designed to assure that no increase in milt. capabilities occurs on either side during the period of the arm. You have attempted to force out of consideration joint observation of the manner in which arm. terms will be adhered to. You have sought to avoid limitations on milt. capabilities during the period of arm. You have tried to submerge these fair and open arrangements by dragging into discussion the question of withdrawal of foreign troops from Korea. You have done this, knowing full well that withdrawal of forces from Korea is a subject inappropriate to this milt. arm. conference. Here is our answer:

"First, we will continue to insist, as an element of an acceptable armistice agreement that neither side will introduce into Korea any reinforcing milt units or personnel during the arm.

"Second, we will continue to insist as an element of an acceptable arm. agreement, that neither side will increase the level of war equipment & material existing in Korea at the time the arm becomes effective.

"Third, we will continue to insist, as an element of an acceptable arm. agreement, that a milt arm. Commission of mixed membership shall be established to provide supervision over the execution of and adherence to the terms of the arm. arrangements. This commission and its joint observation teams shall have authority to observe at ground, sea and air ports of entry and communication centers thruout all of Korea as mutually agreed to by the 2 delegations, together with freedom of movement over principle [principal] lines of communication thruout Korea. The commission shall likewise have authority to establish joint aerial obs. & photo reconnaissance over all of Korea and complete joint obs [observation] of the demilit. zone.

"Fourth, we will continue to insist that the question of withdrawal of foreign troops from K. is entirely beyond the purview of this milt arm conference and subject to ultimate determination by the govts. concerned.

"We shall continue to insist on the inclusion of the foregoing principles in the arm. With all the earnestness at my command I urge you to cease raising objections to these fair principles. We, and all who seek peace, await your considered answer with the deepest concern.

"Unless you have something new to offer, I suggest we recess until such time as you designate in order that you may carefully study my statement.["]

Nam Il replied he found nothing new in statement and he waited for full response to his morning statement.

Opening p.m. session. [Nam Il said:] The real objective of UNC stand on milt facilities is to deprive one side forever of the right to defend itself while talking about security of forces of both sides. UNC wanton bombardment of peaceful towns has resulted in such serious consequences that Commie side must increase AA [antiaircraft] facilities including construction and improvement of airfields. This is a security necessity—an inalienable right of K people. No interference can be tolerated. UNC should understand this so that progress can be made.

Nam Il went on to make preliminary response to UNC closing statement of morning session as follows: The general principles and concrete measures suggested by UNC are basically contradictory to each other. UNC asserts its principles are designed to enhance stability of arm and increase prospects for peace. Why does it want to retain armed forces in rear of other side after dem. line determined and thus place arm. in state of instability. UNC says its principles are military and nonpolitical. Why does it insist upon free access to all Korea? This is flagrant interference in internal affairs of Dem [Democratic] Peoples Republic of Korea & cannot be tolerated. To insure against resumption of hostilities foreign forces must be withdrawn and peaceful settlement speedily achieved. UNC has no grounds for saying other side is against limiting forces. UNC insists neither side introduce reinforcing armed units and personnel. Why then does it contend that so-called necessary replacements be admitted if it is sincere towards a speedy settlement of the K question? Why replacements after fighting is stopped. Not only should foreign troops not be increased, they should be reduced; not allowed to enter K any longer. If UNC favors restrictions against lifting level of material and equipment why should it seek replacements?

The scope of authority of the Arm Commission should coincide with the specific content of arm. terms. For instance, it should control the demilt zone. Yet UNC, disregarding whatever armistice terms may be agreed to by both sides, demands free access to all Korea to conduct inspections. Why? I request an answer and reserve the right to make further comment following detailed study of UNC proposal.

UNC replied in following manner. With respect to inspection — — — free access by joint obs. teams is necessary for an effective milt. armistice. They will observe milt. matters only. Their function is in no sense political.

With respect to replacements: — — — UNC does not "ask permission" to exchange personnel on man for man basis. It merely informs the other side that it will from time to time remove certain units and individuals replacing them at its own discretion. This procedure will result in no increase in the level of forces in Korea. As guards are changed from time to time so will it change units and individuals[.] It has no intention of removing the guard.

With respect to islands — — — during discussion of Agenda Item 2 other side refused to agree to reasonable adjustments in l of c [line of contact] on grounds that it would not relinquish territory it held. It refused to make any adjustments elsewhere for withdrawal of U.N. forces from the islands. It stated islands were of little consequence. The main and incontestable argument used by the other side was that it physically occupied certain areas and would not give them up under any circumstances. UNC agreed to the reasoning of the other side and to the principle that what it held it kept. Now the other side reverses itself. It wants UN forces to withdraw from territory under its control without adjustments elsewhere. The other side excluded islands from discussion under item 2. UNC will hold these islands unless there is suitable adjustment elsewhere.

Nam Il replied that he thought the 2nd item was closed, the dem line & demilt zone established. Did UNC want to reopen Item 2 of agenda.

UNC replied it had no desire to reopen Item 2—that it had referred to the arguments used there merely to show why it was holding the islands.

Nam Il replied it was not right for either side to have forces in rear of other. UNC insistence on this point means it doesn't want an armistice. His side simply cannot agree to this. Its attitude is absolutely firm.

UNC replied that dem. line and demilt zone are on the mainland[.] They do not nor were they intended to include islands. The other side excluded islands from Item 2 and UNC will hold them unless suitable adjustments are made elsewhere.

Nam Il made statement in general as follows: True purpose of exchange of troops on man for man basis is to continue during arm. the introduction of troops from abroad. True purpose of free access is to interfere directly in internal affairs of DPR of K. True purpose of limitation of airfield reconstruction is to prevent K people from strengthening defensive facilities which are nec [necessary] during an armistice. The demand to retain coastal islands constitutes a direct threat to security of other side & renders resumpt [resumption] of hostilities a possibility. Such proposals and demands are unacceptable. UNC has no reasons to insist on such demands unless it wants to delay negots [negotiations]. Both sides should agree in principle on the points in the two proposals which they have already accepted and jointly work out details while plenary session goes on to item 4.

Nam Il then proposed a recess until 1100 tomorrow. UNC suggested that other side make careful study of last para. of its morning statement. Recessed 1612[.]

Dec. 2 (Sun): UNCD opened plenary session in following vein. Since other side states it is groundless to say that it opposes the limitation of forces during period of arm. [armistice] it is assumed it agrees to UNC 3rd principle. Therefore UNC proposes acceptance of UNC principles 1, 2, 3, 6 & 7 [see entry for November 27, above] by both sides and continued effort to reach agreement on remaining principles.

Nam Il replied that he agreed with principles 1, 2, 6 & 7 but with respect to 3d principle, limitation is not enough; forces should be reduced & withdrawn from Korea. Nam Il went on as follows: there is nothing new "in very imp. [important] statement" made by UNC yesterday. UNC still insists on its unreasonable proposals. It proposes limitation of milt. facilities for its own offensive purposes. True purpose of this is to prevent K people reconstructing their defensive facilities. Yesterday's statement only confirmed this. The restriction is to be placed on the reconstruction of airfields. The K people can never forget the brutal bombing of peaceful towns. They have right to reconstruct during arm. their defensive facilities, including airfields. They will do so to secure their forces and prevent further wanton bombing[.] UNC stresses security of troops. How can it seek to prevent reconstruction of airfields? The K people will never tolerate the slightest interference with such reconstruction. UNC seeks to retain coastal islands. All forces including those on islands should be withdrawn from beyond the dem. [demarcation] line. Retention of the islands by UNC would render arm. unstable. No sophistry on the part of the UNC lifts the obligation which is upon it to withdraw from the islands. As for UNC insistence upon replenishments and replacements, it is inconsistent with your proposal of limiting forces. If UNC really wants to reduce possibility of resumption of hostilities it cannot propose continued entry into K of foreign troops. It çan only withdraw troops. True purpose of insp. [inspection] principle propose [*sic*] by UNC is to interfere in internal admin. [administration] of People's Republic. The authority of the MAC should be contingent upon & consistent with the content of the arm. terms. In any case it is inconceivable that during the arm. and while war is still unterminated, one belligerent should seek obs. [observation] posts in rear of other side, freedom of movement over its lines of comm. [communication] & aerial rec. [reconnaissance]. This is inconceivable[.] Our side seeks no free access to territory under UNC control for purpose of inspection. Neither will it grant such a right to UNC.

UNC replied as follows—The other side objects to routine replacement & replenishment yet it asserts the right to unlimited reconstruction of airfields on grounds they are defensive. If there is no intention of building up forces during arm. why are more air fields needed. Other side seeks to deny UNC right to maintain forces at existing levels, but at same time wants to increase its own offensive potential by unlimited constr. [construction] of air fields. UNC can only conclude that other side desires to use arm. to ready itself for resumption of hostil. [hostilities] at time of its own choosing. If not there is no reason for refusal to accept UNC 3rd principle. Exam. [examination] of objections to 4th principle strengthens this conclusion. Objections to joint obs. on grounds that it is an interference are unconvincing[.] UNC welcomes such obs. as an indication of its good faith and will accept no less from other side. To clarify the meaning of "free access" UNC will amplify its explanation. The joint teams shall have authority to observe at ground, sea and air ports of entry and comm centers, as agreed by both sides, and freedom of movement over principle [principal] lines of comm. It also includes joint aerial obs. & photo rec. This is meaning of "free access." It constitutes no interference in internal admin. UNC has nothing to hide. What does other side object to if it does not in fact intend to violate the arm? The arguments used by the other side to refute UNC 3d & 4th principles only reinforce UNC conviction that these must be included in any arm. UNC retention of the islands is in strict accord with the letter of the agreement on agenda item 2. By mutual agreement the islands were deliberately excluded from consideration under agenda item 2. UNC will retain territory it now holds.

Nam Il opened pm session in following vein—UNC in am presented no new reasons for retaining islands. Since both sides have agreed to dem line why does UNC insist on retaining forces in rear of other side. Arguments used during discussions of dem. line are no longer pertinent. This is test whether UNC is willing to respect agreed dem line. If agreement has value UNC has no ground for its demand. If arm is to be stable what reason can UNC demand have? What is purpose? It is violation of agreement. So long as UNC insists on this the other side cannot take seriously the UNC proposal of restrict. [restricting] introduction of armed forces to enhance stability of arm. If UNC were to abide by letter & spirit of agreement on dem line it would prove that UNC proposal that both sides refrain from introducing into K armed forces and equipment is really designed to stabilize the arm. As for UNC proposals on restrict [restricting] milt facilities and on free inspection, they are an interference in internal admin. of other side & involve political questions[.] They exceed the scope of the negots and are unacceptable. In order that no more time be wasted it is hoped UNC will no longer insist on these two proposals. UNC use of orthodox arguments to persist in these demands implies UNC assumes itself the victor who requires other side to submit. This cannot be tolerated as both sides are on an equal footing. The del. [delegation] of the KPA and CPV shall continue to oppose these proposals. With the greatest sincerity we and all who hope for an early agreement solicit your most serious consideration of this statement.

UNC replied in genl [general] as follows: There is nothing to be gained by further discussion of islands. UNC offered previously to participate in adjustments involving its withdrawal from islands. Other side refused. UNC accepted refusal stating it would retain islands. Other side must now accept consequences of that refusal. To sum up, both sides are agreed [*sic*] on principles 1, 2, 6 & 7. UNC has made it clear that it considers principles 1, 2, 6 & 7 essential. Persistent refusal of other side to accept them only confirms their essentiality. UNC & people of world have been warned by this refusal and that other side seeks in arm not a step towards peace but a period in which to build up its milt. potential. It wishes to do this in secrecy, free of obs. by MAC. In spite of protestation of peace UNC can give credence only to actions. Resistance to these principles indicates an intent to violate them. Thus more than ever, UNC must insist on their inclusion in agreement which binds both sides. No progress can be made until other side alters its views on these principles. The more the other side opposes them the more UNC mistrusts their motives. The Dels. are now separated by 4 points of difference: (1) introduction of reinforcements & limitation of supplies, equipment & facilities (2) joint obs. at principal ports of entry & comm centers as mutually agreed, free movement over comm. lines for joint obs. teams; joint aerial obs. and photo rec. (3) unilateral insistence by other side that UNC give up islands which it will not do without suitable adjustment and (4) unilateral contention of other side that it be free to increase milt capabilities, especially airfields. These 4 points are the basic differences[.] By concentrating on them it might be possible to find a solution.

Nam Il inquired if adjustments in connection with the islands was [*sic*] related to the milt. dem. line.

UNC said it had no desire to reopen agenda item 2, it would retain the islands.

Nam Il again sought clarification & was informed that it did not refer to Item 2.

Nam Il asked if matter of constr. of airfields within his positions was not an internal affair.

UNC replied as follows: Statements of the other side give strong evidence of its intent to use arm. to improve its milt. position. That it should seek enabling provisions in the agreement is incredible. Its statement that it must, during the arm, build up combat air capability, including air field constr, is alien to its protestations of good faith. The other side openly expresses an intent to increase milt. capabilities. It uses the weak pretext of a requirement for increased AA [antiaircraft] facilities, but it alone would determine whether increased capability would be used offensively or defensively. The intended rehab. [rehabilitation] of airfields is an increase in milt. facilities which provides an increased capability. The rebuilt fields would be useful only if air elements were introduced into Korea. Since other side subscribes to principle of non-introduction of reinforcements there is no case for additional airfields. Airfields are not an internal matter when they add to offensive capabilities. The UNC firmly opposes any development of milt airfields.

Nam Il said that nothing new had been said; all had been refuted and that attitude of UNC was delaying conference. He inquired as to whether UNC had any suggestion for the settlement of the 4 outstanding differences.

UNC said it was looking to him for a suggestion in this respect and proposed adjournment. Recessed at 1628.

Dec. 3 (Mon): Nam Il opened plenary session in following vein. The proposals on limitations on increase of milt. [military] facilities and obs. [observation] thruout K. are political questions which constitute direct interference in internal admin [administration] of other side and cannot be tolerated. Matter of defensive facilities is an internal matter. UNC carried out inhuman bombing. It is effective because of inadequate AA facilities. Yet UNC refuses to withdraw its air force during arm. [armistice]. How then can it interfere with sacred right of K people to defend themselves by arranging their defensive facilities? UNC view that the arm. commission have access to all of K. is an unwarranted interference in internal affairs which will not be tolerated. UNC proposal that both sides refrain from introducing into K reinforcements in men & material is inconsistent with its stand on replenishments & replacements. UNC insistence on latter raises doubt as to its sincerity towards former. UNC has no justification for its refusal to withdraw from islands north of dem. [demarcation] line as the dividing line. UNC has only the obligation to withdraw.

UNC replied in following tenor—Statement made by Nam Il only indicates the other side wants not an arm. but a single [*sic*] cease fire under protection of which it could increase its milt. capabilities. As milt. men[,] del. [delegation] of other side should recognize that UNC cannot enter into an arm. which does not involve undertakings by both sides to refrain from attempting to gain a milt advantage during suspension of fighting. As regards joint obs. it would not constitute interference in internal affairs. It would not be a means for intell. [intelligence] info. on such matters as design of weapons. It is necessary, however, that there be joint milt. obs. of key points thruout K. as mutually agreed to by the two sides. UNC does not fear joint obs. but welcomes it because it will not violate an arm. to which it is a signatory. Why does other side fear it? What does it plan to hide.

Nam Il reiterated that milt. facilities and question of obs. are internal questions.

UNC repeated its firm stand in opposition to any increase of milt. fac. [facilities] during arm. and enquired if other side had any suggestion as to a method for resolving the diffs [differences] which were pointed up yesterday by UNC.

Nam Il opened the p.m. session by saying views of both sides had been fully exchanged during last 7 days. He then submitted 2 new principles to add to his original 5 principle proposal. These were: "(6) In order to insure the stability of the milt. arm so as to facilitate the holding by both sides of a political conference of a higher level, both sides shall undertake not to introduce into K any milt. forces, weapons and ammo. [ammunition] under any pretext." ["](7) In order to supervise the strict implementation of the stipulation of para six (6), both sides agree to invite representatives of nations neutral in the K war to form a supervisory organ [organization] to be responsible for conducting necessary inspection, beyond the demilt [demilitarized] zone, of such ports of entry in the rear as mutually agreed upon by both sides, and to report to the joint arm commission the result of inspection.''

Nam Il continued in the following vein: After six days debate no lengthy explanation of these principles is necessary, but the 7 principle proposal is an integral whole, its various paras. being interrelated and inseparable. The new proposal incorporates the reasonable portions of the UNC proposal. It is proposed that the plenary session accept the 7 principle proposal as an over-all agreement for the 3d item of the agenda.

Nam Il then presented the 7 principle proposal in writing. The wording of the 5th principle varied from the original version as previously rptd [reported]. It now reads: ''(5) Both sides shall designate an equal no. of members to form an arm. commission to be jointly responsible for the concrete arrangement and the supervision of the implementation of the *whole* arm agreement, except for the scope of supervision specified in para (6) of this proposal.['']

UNC Del requested a 30 min recess. On its return it stated that it had made a prelim. exam. [preliminary examination] of the new proposal and desired to ask some questions to clarify its understanding of the proposal. A long list of questions was presented. The following are examples: Does item 6 permit unlimited reconstr [reconstruction] & rehab. [rehabilitation] of airfields? Does the term weapons include aircraft? Does item 6 prevent rotation & replenishment of forces? Under principle 7 what nations do you have in mind? Does principle 7 exclude obs of facilities other than ports of entry? Is aerial obs & photo rec. [reconnaissance] included in ''necessary inspection beyond demilt. [demilitarized] zone?['']

Nam Il having indicated that prep. [preparation] of answers to these questions would take time, UNC made a statement as follows: As UNC understands the position of the other side it proposes a compromise between positions held by the two sides. Due to the formal and relatively inflexible nature of the plenary sessions they are not the best medium for negotiatory processes of this nature. UNC therefore suggests reference of the question of acceptable principles to a sub del for resolution. The diffs over agenda item 2 were resolved in this manner[.]

Nam Ils first response was that problem could be turned over to a sub committee only after agreement in principle to the 7 principles he had proposed. He revised this to say that he would give an answer after considering it and proposed a recess until 1100 tomorrow. adjourned at 1616.

Note: Following introduction of Commies new proposal yesterday many other questions were submitted to them by UNC (total of 40 in all). Majority concentrated on their principle 7 (neutral organ). Main fact elicited from answers was that Armistice Com. [Commission] had no authority over neutral organ, which only reported to it result of its findings[.] In other words we would have two emasculated bodies.

Dec. 4 (Tues): Opening plen. [plenary] session at 1100 Nam Il stated he had studied UNC questions and proposal; that such concrete questions could best be discussed in sub-committee. He then stated that he did not oppose UNC proposal of going over to a sub comit [committee] of the delegations.

UNC stated that its suggestion did not imply acceptance of Commie proposal, and that functions of sub-Com. was [*sic*] to resolve diffs between dels. on agenda Item 3 and to rec. to dels. a mutually acceptable solution to that Item. UNC continued, saying that concurrent disc. [discussion] in sub-committee of agenda Items 3 & 4 would contribute materially to progress of negots. UNC proposed appointment of another sub Committee to discuss agenda Item 4.

Nam Il replied that the proposal for discussion of Item 4 would be answered after due consideration & proposed that the sub-committee on agenda Item 3 convene at 1400 today[.]

At 1133 plenary sess. [session] recessed for duration of sub-com meetings subject to resumption on call of either side.

Report of sub commit meeting in p.m. Recd following answers to our questions. (1) Rotation or replacement is impermissible. for the entire duration of arm [armistice]. (2) By milt [military] forces is meant all units & personnel regular and irregular of ground, naval & air forces. (3) By weapons is meant all milt. equipments including a/c [aircraft]. (4) Neither side has right to interfere with or to inspect the reconstruction of any facilities wthin Korea. (5) Replenishments and exchange of any weapons & ammo [ammunition] is impermissible. (6) Supervisory organ [organization] composed of reps. [representatives] of neutral nations shall send to ports of entry in rear agreed upon by both sides, the same kind of reps. for conducting same kind of inspection. Scope of inspec. [inspection] is limited to that prescribed by paras 6 of our proposal. (7) It would be appropriate that the neutral nations be 3 to 5 in number and that they be invited by both sides[.] (8) Regarding list of neutral nations our side will submit our specific proposal after this measure is agreed to by both sides.

Entire session was devoted to Commies providing answers to questions posed by U.N.C. Key points as follows: (1) Commies will accept joint inspec. behind their lines as long as inspectors are from neutral countries. They agree that the composition of the insp. teams will be mixed as between neutrals selected by us and neutrals selected by them. All neutral nations must be agreed upon by both sides. (2) Authority & activity of MAC shall be strictly limited to demilt. [demilitarized] zone, since MAC is to be made up of belligerents. Belligerents cannot be permitted in rear areas. (3) Commies gave no hint as to what neutral countries they have in mind. They said they would give that info later after principle was accepted. (4) Commies deferred answering whether the neutral inspec. organ was to be subject to the authority & direction of MAC. (5) Commies stated that whether inspec was by air or ground methods was to be determined by neutral insp. organ. (6) Whether insp teams would be stationed at ports of entry or go to them from time to time. was to be determined by inspec. organ. (7) All answers by Commies held to strict prohib [prohibition] of replacement, replenishment and rotation except in case of personnel rejoining their units[.] (8) Scope of supervision contemplated in Principle 6 is strictly limited to introduction of forces, weapons and ammo into Korea. Airplanes are considered as weapons[.] (9) Places to be inspected would be determined in the arm. agreement. (10) Except for insp. by the MAC in the demilt. zone and insp of selected ports of entry by the neutral insp organ, all insp. is to be by each side within it's [*sic*] own territory. (11) Commies deferred answers as to what they mean by "coastal" as applied to islands & waters[.]

It was apparent that Commie sub-del had not been instructed completely as to the application of their own proposals, particularly relationship of neutral organ and MAC.

Upon return to camp I sent following msg to CINCUNC. "In order to carry out nec. [necessary] work here on counter-proposal to be made to Commies, key question to which we need an answer from higher authority is whether UNC will or will not accept insp teams composed of nationals from so called neutral countries. It is also imp. [important] to know what authority these teams should have and to whom they should be responsible. *It should be realized that insp. by these neutral teams may be nothing more than a gesture with respect to principle of inspection.* Request guidance as a matter of urgency[.]"

Note: I heard later that above msg. was sent on to JCS without comment by CINCUNC.

Referring to above msg. CINCUNC sent us one which directed us to reintroduce basic UNC principles which he restated as 8 principles instead of our original 7. They were basically the same as our 7 except as follows: (5) reworded to read "Neither side shall increase level of units, personnel, war equip. [equipment] facilities or material existing in Korea at time arm. becomes effective.["] No. 8 read "The arm agreement shall enter into effect when the Milt. Arm. Com. has been organized and is ready to begin the exercise of its functions." Msg ended by admonition to "avoid making ourselves subject to U.S. and world public criticism for obstructing or unduly delaying these negots." Also to "avoid any positive commitment, or posit. [position] which could be construed as commitments, without prior clearance here.["]

Following additional info on Commie posit. rec'd. "MAC and neutral organ are completely independent. Neither is subject to direction of other. MAC may request neutral organ to inspect outside demilt zone. Directive of

neutral organ is armistice agreement itself. Neutral teams may be in place at ports of entry at time of signing of arm.["]

Dec. 5 (Wed): Sub dels convened at 1300. In answer to query, Lee replied his side would agree to invite reps of those nations not directly participating in fighting in K to form neutral insp. organ [inspection organization]. His side would accept members of UN such as Czechoslovakia or Poland, who were not fighting in K. In response to query, Lee replied Switzerland, Sweden and Denmark would be acceptable under stated criteria. Lee said arm. com. [armistice commission] would not direct neutral insp. organ. The two would be parallel organs. Neutral organ would rpt. [report] results its inspections to MAC. Neutral organ is a referee, operating in accord with terms of arm. MAC may request neutral organ to make inspections outside demilt zone. In addition MAC will supervise exchange of POWs and will handle rpts made by neutral insp organ. individual reps. of neutral nations would be selected by govts thereof. The neutral govts will determine whether their reps. are milt [military] or civilian, probably milt. Agreement on neutral nations to be selected can be reached as soon as principle is accepted, in one day, if UNC del is agreeable. As soon as 3d agenda item is completed, neutral nations will be invited during discussion of Agenda Item 4. Personnel from neutral nations can be on hand when arm is signed. Commies refused to answer whether port of entry include airports of entry. Commies evaded answer as to what dist [distance] they had in mind in using phrase "coastal waters and islands." They stated definition of territorial waters under international law was irrelevant. In excluding aircraft from entry to K. during arm, only combatant aircraft are meant. Neutral insp teams may be placed at ports of entry at time of signing of arm.

UNC proposed that a new set of principles to which both sides could agree be discussed and settled one by one. Commies insisted on package of all principles to be considered at once because of inter-relationship.

Part III [*sic*] Tomorrow sub del will first seek answers to the questions on airports of entry and coastal waters. Second we will read categoric positions contained in R's msg (8 principles) and state that Commie proposal ∴ [therefore] not acceptable.

As a result of todays meeting I sent a msg to R suggesting a counter proposal which would propose one *neutral* armistice commission charged also with the responsibility of inspection, pointing out that such an integral organ could be far more effective than the two bilateral organs proposed by Commies.

Dec. 6 (Thurs): Lee declined to say whether word "ports" included airports, or what he meant by word "coastal." UNC stated categorically that airports would be among ports of entry. Lee indicated that all UNC naval forces must be withdrawn south of dem. [demarcation] line. UNC del stated categorically that "coastal" would be interpreted by us as "territorial" as defined in int. [international] law. UNC rejected prohibition of rotation replenishment, replacement within levels existing at time arm. is signed. UNC again proposed step-by-step, principle by principle procedure designed to achieve agreement on at least the core of each principle[.] UNC attempted to gain agreement on core of each principle by phrasing each one so as to eliminate disputed aspects. Commies merely reiterated their own position on each principle, making no effort to reach agreed wording. UNC then presented 8 principles given us by R which have been mentioned previously. Lee commented that there was nothing new in UNC 8 principles which still sought to interfere in internal affairs of his side. This could not be. Lee complained over lack of concrete comment by UNC on his 7 principles. He stated as long as there was no progress on Item 3, his senior delegate would not give an answer to question of sub del for Item 4. If UNC showed sincerity toward Item 3 a sub del on Item 4 could be established. Hsieh Feng asked for UNC comment on Commie proposal, saying he was willing to negotiate a solution. Said UNC was trying to use coercion. UNC induced his side to go into sub-com [committee] by indicate [*sic*] interest in Commie proposal. UNC is stalling, wasting time. He would expect UNC to give formal opinion on Commie proposal tomorrow. Recessed 1335.

I then sent msg to R pointing out that negots were in a condition of stalemate and that to resume progress and regain initiative it was imperative that UNC submit an entirely new counter proposal, preferably one on which we can hold firm to breaking point. Also pointed out that R's 8 principles were little more than a restatement of UNC initial basic principles, consequently they do not constitute a counter proposal. I pointed out that only 2 practicable courses of action seem open: (1) Refuse to accept any proposal other than UNC proposal of this date. This course may lead to a break off. (2) Revise either our own or Commie proposal to reflect following: (a) Insure right of replenishment & replacement within existing levels. (b) Create one neutral organ [organization] to carry out supervisory as well as obs. [observation] functions, incorporating all tasks contemplated for the MAC in the single organ and dropping MAC. Put teeth in inspecting authority of this neutral arm. com. which would report to belligerent Comdrs [commanders]. (c) Drop UNC claims to coastal islands of N.K. (d) Drop prohibition against rehab. [rehabilitation] of air fields, retain prohibition against constructing new air fields. We believe this latter course would insure for UNC all provisions essential to an arm. and it would be exceptionally difficult for Commies to refuse. Arleigh Burke left today.

Dec. 7 (Fri): At sub del meeting this date UNC led off with statement strongly denying Commie charge of stalling, pointing out Commie refusal to undertake simultaneous discussion of Items 3 & 4. After stating UNC was interested in Commie proposal, and considered it a step forward UNC criticized Commie 7 pt. [point] proposal, pt. by pt. UNC indicated general agreement with Commie principles 1 2 & 4 though not with exact wording. UNC rejected prohibition on replacement and replenishment and rejected requirement to abandon islands. UNC line of attack on Commie principles 6 & 7 concentrated on vague relationship of arm. com. [armistice commission] & neutral organ [organization], and the divided, uncertain authority and responsibility. UNC did not attack neutral organ concept as such. UNC insisted on limiting development of air fields. UNC emphasized there are considerable areas of agreement between the two sides. Commies reply again charged UNC was delaying conference. Lee stated his side had never refused simultaneous discussion of Items 3 & 4. Lee complained UNC comments showed plain intent to "interfere in internal affairs" of his side, condemned replacement and replenishment, insisted UNC must withdraw from islands, rejected any inspection of rear areas other than by neutrals. UNC reiterated refusal to consider any proposal designed to bring about withdrawal by attrition. UNC stated its interest "in internal affairs" was limited to increase in milt. [military] capabilities during arm., which we opposed.

In pm session, UNC stated it was still studying neutral nation concept and could not at this time accept or reject it. UNC criticized other features of Commie Principle 7, insisted on single arm. com. rather than dual organs. UNC statement on neutral organ follows:

"You asked for comments on your proposed principle 7. First, as we have previously explained, we maintain that a single supervisory organ, rather than two such organs, should be responsible for supervising the execution of and adherence to all of the terms of the arm agreement. We maintain this single supervisory organ should exercise direct authority over all obs. [observation] activities, whether in demilt. zone or in rear areas. Second, we believe observation should be conducted at comm. [communication] centers as well as ports of entry. Your principle 7 limits observation to ports of entry. 3rd your principle 7 limits the activities of obs. teams to the scope of your principle 6. We have already told you clearly and finally that we will not accept the prohibition on rotation, replenishment and replacement implicit in your principle 6. Therefore, that part of your principle 7 which limits its application to your principle 6 is of course unacceptable.

"As to the question of reps. [representatives] of neutral nations in the role of observers, that matter is under active and continuing study. There are features of this proposal which have definite merit. We are not ready yet to either accept or reject this concept. Certainly, however, the relationship of observer teams to the supervisory organ must be clear and direct.

"The organization supervising the arm. whether a single organ or a dual agency such as you propose, must carry out administrative, judicial and operational functions. By operational functions, I mean obs. at selected points in Korea. Now were this organ. only judicial in nature, it could function successfully under a charter—the arm. agreement—without need for any other directing head. Since the organ. must carry out operational functions such as observation, that part of the overall organ which executes the observation must be subject to direction from some responsible source. It is our belief that the supervisory organ of the arm. as a whole should have the authority and responsibility to direct and control these observation activities. Your proposal does not provide such authority and responsibility to any supervising agency.''

Agreement was reached on substance of UN principles 1 & 2 of our 8 principles. Commies again failed to agree to enter sub-del meetings on agenda Item 4.

Commies pressed vigorously for clear and unequivocal statement regarding neutral organ, insisting that progress of negots [negotiations] was halted until UNC gave some answer on this point. UNC replied answer would be given in due course. Commies indicated this was stalling, deadlocking conference, and insisted on knowing how long would be required for UNC to answer.

"It is considered imperative to the continued progress of negots that we receive guidance re [regarding] the neutral nations as a matter of urgency," ended our rpt for day.

I sent msg to CinCUNC proposing a new solution for breaking current Item 3 deadlock. It was worded to follow general order of Commies' 7 principles, utilizing where appropriate Commie wording. It substituted the principal [principle] of an integral neutral Arm Comm. and inspect. [inspection] teams to supervise the entire arm agreement in place of the joint Com. of the present UNC proposal and the dual set up of the Commie proposal. It did not prohibit the rehab [rehabilitation] of existing air fields & air facilities and requested guidance on this point. Said also that new proposal should[,] subject to decision re. air fields[,] be our minimum position. Our withdrawal would be from islands within territorial waters.

This evening I had Briggs phone Wright to ask what had been done with regard to our suggestion of an armistice com. made up entirely of reps. from neutral nations. Wright said the matter had been dropped as far as he knew[.] I also called Wright urging something be done immediately to get a decision on the matter pointing out what an impossible position the Delegation was in. The next morning I followed this up by phoning Hickey to say if nothing had been passed on about our recommendation re. a neutral Arm. Com. I urged that our views be made known even if R disapproved of them. I again pointed out what a tough spot we were in. This resulted in two blasts from R to me which in effect said to carry out my orders and adopt an intransigent attitude towards Commies in doing so. Our contradictory directives are hard to follow! Since R told us, in a despatch directing his 8 principle proposal, *not* to be intransigent I have been concerned over our present position.

Dec. 8 (Sat): Sub Del meeting this date opened with both sides holding to and insisting upon their respective positions on principles. UNC attempted to get clarification of Commie meaning of "coastal islands and waters." Commies evaded. UNC strongly insisted on its right to retain islands, indicated firm intent to retain them unless appropriate adjustment was made. Commies sought to shift discussion to other principles. UNC insisted on proceeding in order. UNC pointed out wording of agreement in agenda Item 2 contained nothing requiring UNC to give up islands. Asked if Commies had "suitable adjustment" to offer in return for islands. Commies charged UNC delaying, stalling, refusing to show clear attitude on neutral organ [organization] question and alleged UNC is wasting time in order to run out available time by dallying on side issues. After 3½ hr. discussion on islands, ending in stalemate, discussion moved to question of arm. comm. UNC took position against dual agencies supervising armistice. Commies pressed unremittingly for categoric answer to their proposal of neutral nations inspecting organ. UNC reiterated refusal to accept dual agencies in supervision of arm.

UNC recommended Commies give thorough overnight study to UNC 8 point proposal. Lee finished with statement his side would absolutely never agree to interference with internal affairs of his territory. Lee gave no answer on agenda Item 4. Adjourned at 1635.

Dec. 9 (Sun): During todays morning session, UNCD asked Commies again if they had an answer to our proposal for sub-del meetings on Item 4. They replied they did not, that their senior delegate had the proposal under consideration. During the noon recess Gen Turner told press that Commies refused to answer and that it appeared they may be holding this matter as a threat or club over our heads.

Commies insisted steadily on "clear expression['']" of UNC attitude toward neutral inspecting organ [organization]. UNC tried to draw discussion away from this point by discussing islands, replacement & replenishment, and other elements of UNC 8 principles, stating solution of these matters must precede determination of nature of observation teams. Lee returned to inspection question, insisting on neutral inspecting teams. He stated his side would never accept "interference in internal affairs," meaning observation of rear areas by UNC observers. UNC restated its principles, stressing need for effective inspection, single arm. [armistice] supervising authority.

In afternoon, Commies had no new points to make, merely reiterated positions on principles stressing 4 points: (1) Withdrawal by UNC from islands (2) Prohibiting introduction of forces into Korea from abroad, and reducing forces in Korea by stages (3) No interference in internal affairs (4) Only neutral teams observe in rear areas at ports of entry. UNC pointed out there was nothing new in foregoing.

Twice today Lee failed to answer UNC query regarding Agenda Item 4 sub del.

Recd for info msg CinCUNC sent to JCS in which he pointed out difficulty Del was having in maintaining our non-committal attitude towards neutral inspection. In light of situation he recommended JCS consider an arm. Comm [Armistice Commission] of 3 members, 1 representing each belligerent side and 1 a neutral nation. CinCUNC also submitted to JCS our proposal of an arm. com. and its subordinate teams to be composed entirely of neutrals. He did not however point out in his msg that we thought Commies would buy our proposed AC [armistice commission]. He did not make any specific recs. but stated he thought his AC had many more advantages than ours, although advantages were not listed. He ended by asking the probable time during which we must maintain our current position on the issue of "neutral" inspection.

JCS in answer concurred with CinCUNCs views but considered difficulty would be encountered in finding a neutral for CinCUNCs proposed AC who would be acceptable to both sides. JCS reminded CinCUNC of the necessity to establish in the agreement safeguards against their inaction and resulting frustration by the exercise of a veto in MAC or in the teams themselves.

CinCUNC then sent us msg saying above JCS msg "indicates general concurrence with our views. However it does not authorize a change in our present approach to item 3. Therefore you must continue present tactics until final decision is received from highest level."

Dec. 10 (Mon): Sub del opened meeting with Lee inquiring regard neutral organ [organization] proposal. UNC responded with statement advocating immediate initiation of sub-del talks on Item 4 of agenda. Lee replied he would transmit statement to his senior delegate, then repeated his question regarding neutral organ, charging UNC delayed discussion of Item 3 by failing to answer. UNC replied question of neutral organ is under active consideration, answer would be given in due time. UNC inquired if Commies had anything new to propose. Commies answered no. UNC recommended recess until following day. Lee upbraided UNC for failing to answer his question on neutral organ. Lee referred to free insp. [inspection] of rear areas, prohibition of increase of facilities and withdrawal from islands as unreasonable demands of UNC. Neutral nations reps. [representatives] only way inspect rear areas, said Lee, asking UNC opinion on these points. UNC pointed out many unsettled points were not related to question of neutral organ, not dependent upon method of obs. [observation] adopted. Recessed 1140.

Dec. 11 (Tues): As result of strong statement I gave sub-del yesterday to transmit to Commie senior delegate, the Commies have been forced to agree to a meeting of sub-dels on agenda Item 4 at 1300 this date.

Commie sub-del for Item 3 is now composed of General Hsieh Fang and Colonel Chang. North Korean General Lee and Colonel Tsai compose Commie sub-del on Item 4. RAdm [Rear Admiral] Libby and Colonel Hickman will represent UNC for Item 4 while Maj-Gens Turner & Hodes will continue on item 3 until Hodes is relieved by Ferenbaugh.

Meeting on Item 3 opened with UNC again calling for concentration on fundamentals still in disagreement which are not related to or affected by questions of composition of observation teams. **Hsieh Fang rejected this, stating it was well within his rights to insist on a clear expression by UNC relative to all points under consideration before settling any one.** He took a strong stand in favor of withdrawal by attrition and neutral obs. [observation] in rear areas. UNC restated categorically its stand against attrition, attacked indecisive relationships proposed by Commies between supervising authority and observation organ [organization] however composed. Hsieh asked whether UNC would accept neutral observer principle if he accepted "no increase of force" principle of UNC and single directing authority for armistice [sentence emphasized in text by a bold line in left margin]. UNC asked if Hsieh would accept UNC point of view on other disagreements if UNC accepted neutral observer principle. Hsieh declined, reverted to his proposal of 3 Dec, complained of lack of clear UNC statement on neutral organ. UNC inquired if we accept neutral inspecting agency what UNC principles would Hsieh accept. Hsieh failed to respond, merely repeating complaint that UNC would not take a stand regarding neutral organ, and attaking [sic] replenishment principle. Hsieh reiterated Commie stand on all points. Recessed 1650.

Sub comit [committee] on Agenda Item 4 convened at 1300. Commies early in session proposed one simple principle "that both sides release all POWs held by them after signing of arm [armistice]." UNC proposed two general principles: "(1) It is desirable to effect the early regulated exchange of POW's on a fair and equitable basis and under suitable supervision. (2) Suitable provision shall be made to insure humanitarian treatment, safety, and comfort of prisoners preceding and during exchange." Thereafter UNC pressed for acceptance of following prelim. [preliminary] measures [this portion of paragraph emphasized in text by bold line in left margin]: (1) exchange now of POW data requested at plenary session of 27 Nov. and (2) admission now of ICRC reps. [representatives] to P.O.W. camps. Commies made discussion of these & all other "technical matters" contingent upon UNC acceptance of their aforestated simple principle. Commies further indicated disagreement with UNC 1st principle on grds. [grounds] that there was no reason for retaining any POWs after the arm. was signed. UNC finally proposed recess for stated purpose of enabling Commies to reconsider their refusal to exchange POW info now or to permit visits of ICRC reps. Adjourned 1535. Comment: Indications from 1st day are that discussion during subsequent sessions will focus primarily on question of all for all versus one for one, or any other arrangement.

This was a full and important day for despatches, which filled the air all day long. At long last JCS came thru with one of vital importance to us. Gist of it follows: "JCS consider that there are 4 basic issues remaining to be resolved in order to obtain agreement on Item 3: (a) No increase in present str [strength] levels and equip [equipment] stocks versus no introduction of personnel and equip under any pretext. (b) Rehabilitation of facilities, particularly air fields. (c) Status of offshore islands. (d) Neutral obs. teams vs joint teams composed of belligerents and relationship of any such teams to MAC.

"On above issues JCS hold folg. [following] views and you will be guided by them: (a) Rotation must be permitted; accordingly, your present position should be your final posit. [position]. (b) As a final posit you should withdraw objection to rehab [rehabilitation] of facilities other than airfields. (If and when rehab of air fields becomes last obstacle to an arm., refer matter to Wash [Washington]). (c) As a final posit you should agree to withdraw from Korean islands generally north of dem. [demarcation] line extended. (d) As a final posit you should agree to neutral obs. teams composed of personnel of nations whose armed forces are not participating in Korean war, and mutually agreed to by both sides; *however, these teams must be responsible to, and subject to direction and supervision of MAC."*

This was the guidance we had been looking for since Commies made their last proposal—8 days previously. On the 4th we had requested guidance on their proposed neutral obs teams as a matter of urgency!

Upon receipt of JCS despatch quoted above CinCUNC sent us some amplifying instrs [instructions] upon both of which (JCS & his) we built a new proposal of 7 principles for submission to Commies tomorrow. Our proposal was then passed on to R for comment. Since this was not to be our final position we only made a partial concession on the island question. The proposal reads as follows:

"1. All armed forces, ground, sea and air, under control of either side shall cease all hostilities within 24 hrs after the effective date of the arm.

"2. All armed forces under the control of either side shall be withdrawn from the demilt. zone within 72 hrs after the effective date of the arm. Except for such armed forces of a police nature as may be specifically and mutually agreed by both sides, no armed forces of either side shall thereafter enter the demilt zone, nor shall the armed forces of either side commit any acts of armed force against the demilt. zone.

"3. Within 5 days after the effective date of the arm, each side shall withdraw the armed forces under its control, ground, sea, and air, from the territory and territorial waters of each side. If the armed forces are not withdrawn within the stated time limit (unless there is some valid and mutually agreed reason for delaying withdrawal) the other side shall have the right to take all nec. [necessary] action against such armed personnel for the maintenance of security and order.

"4. a. Both sides shall designate an equal number of members to form a MAC which shall be responsible for exercising the supervision of and adherence to the whole arm. agreement. The MAC shall be provided with, and assisted by, observer teams which shall be responsible to, shall report to, and shall be subject to the direction and supervision of the MAC only. The observer teams shall be composed of personnel of nations whose armed forces are not participating in the K war, such nations to be mutually agreed to by both sides.

"b. Observation outside the demilt. zone will be performed only by neutral obs. teams. Obs. within the demilt. zone may be performed by neutral teams, by joint teams selected by the MAC, or by the MAC itself.

"c. Neutral obs teams shall be located at such land, sea & air ports of entry and comm [communication] centers as are mutually agreed to by both sides. These observer teams shall be permitted freedom of movement over principle [*sic*] lines of comm. thruout all of Korea and each side shall afford these teams full assistance in the execution of the duties assigned them by the arm. commission. In addition, such periodic aerial rec. [reconnaissance] and observation and photo flights as are mutually agreed to by both sides will be performed by neutral teams.

"5. Neither side shall increase the level of milt. [military] units, milt. personnel, war equipment, or war material existing in Korea at the time the arm. becomes effective. The rehab, expansion, and improvement of existing airfields and aviation facilities and construction of new airfields and new aviation facilities shall not be permitted.

"6. Each side shall administer in accord with the terms of the arm. agreement that portion of the demilt. zone lying on its side of the milt. dem. line.

"7. The arm shall not become effective until MAC and its observer teams have been organized, are staffed and are ready to begin exercise of their assigned functions[.]"

R agreed with us that a safeguard para [paragraph] on the veto should not be included in list of principles but said we should insist on some such veto safeguard, at least for observer teams, in armistice terms.

Investigation of alleged bombing incident in Kaesong area proved that it was bona fide and probably done by a B-26[.] R acknowledged $\frac{\text{(UNC)}}{\text{(our)}}$ responsibility in a msg to Commie Comdrs and added nec [necessary] disciplinary action was being taken.

Dec. 12 (Wed): #3. UNC opened sub del meeting on [agenda] item 3 with statement denying that Commie proposal of 3 Sept contained any concession to UNC views, then presented revised principles given above.

Hsieh commented as follows: UNC principles are ambiguous as to "day arm. comes into effect, in view of proviso that arm. com. [armistice commission] must be ready to operate before arm. is effective; UNC attempting to delay putting arm. in effect by its ability to withold [*sic*] formation of arm. comm. & staff;

objected to phrase "territorial waters" as irrelevant; dem. [demarcation] line must be basis of withdrawal from rear areas; held to view that obser. organ [observation organization] should be in parallel with arm. comm, not subject to it; directing head of neutral organ shall be from within itself; rejected limitations on facilities and free access for obs. personnel thruout K; UNC had partially exceeded [*sic*] [to North Korean sovereignty over the coastal] islands and only accepted neutral teams as part of supervisory organ.

UNC responded that Hsiehs comments were all invalid and unacceptable. UNC suggested recess until other side could study UNC proposal thoroughly.

In pm session, Hsieh rptd [repeated] his objections to UNC retaining any islands north of dem line; to replenishment and replacement; to prohibition of air field rehab & constr [rehabilitation and construction]; to single arm supervising authority; to observation of points other than ports of entry; to aerial observation and to freedom of movement for obs. teams thruout K.

UNC responded with stiff insistence on acceptance of UNC proposal. Recessed 1640.

#4. UNC opened sub comit [committee] meeting on Item 4 by inquiring if Commies are prepared to exchange POW data and to invite ICRC reps. [representatives] to visit POW camps.

Lee replied important question is immed [immediate] release POWs, not exchange of data.

UNC pointed out Commies misinterpretation of meaning of Item 4. "Arrangements relating to POWs" means all nec. [necessary] arrangements and not merely to a basis for exchange of POW's.

Do Commies refuse to divulge info previously requested at Plen [plenary] session[?] What is their purpose? On what grounds? This not a new issue. UNC has carefully complied with Geneva convention. Commies have not. Have only rptd [reported] 110 POWs to Geneva since war began. Formally propose to exchange data at once.

Lee said basic question is release of POWs. Without solution of this can be little progress. Basic question first then exchange of data. UNC dodges showing its attitude towards this fair principle[.] Why does UNC oppose Geneva convention which says "once hostilities cease, both sides must without delay release all POWs"? Does UNC mean it is unfair to release all POWs held by both sides?

UNC replied why do Commies refuse to exchange POW data as required by Geneva convention. On what grds [grounds] justified? Natural order in discussing things. Exchange of data and arrangements for visitation POW camps by ICRC are first steps. Last fundamental rights of POWs too long withheld. Commies statement they observe convention is mere words. If in fact they are observing Geneva Convention why object to ICRC visitation? What is your answer to our formal proposal[?]

Lee said Commies do not refuse exchange data. Are also prepared to release all POWs 30 days after arm is signed. What is more urgent certainly not exchange of data or ICRC visits. What is UNC aim of retaining part of POWs after arm is signed. UNC must give clear answer to its attitude on release of POW's.

#4. P.M. Using forceful language UNC contd. to press for exchange now of data on POW's and for Commie acceptance of ICRC visitation of POW camps. **Commies evaded answering question on visitation and continued to make exchange of POW data contingent upon UNC acceptance of principle under which all POWs would be released by both sides following signing of arm.** Crux of days proceedings came near end of session when Commies using prepared statement submitted a formal proposal. The proposal follows:

"(1) To decide upon principle that both sides shall release all prisoners of war now in custody of each side.

"(2) To agree that both sides shall release in grps [groups], and complete the repatriation of all POWs in their custody within shortest period possible after signing of arm agreement, and to decide upon principle that these POW[s] who are seriously wounded or sick shall have the priority of being released and repatriated in first group.

"(3) To recommend that PMJ, Kaesong, will be the place for the handing over and receiving of POW by both sides.

"(4) To recommend that both sides will designate an equal no [number] of members to form a POW Repatriation Committee under Arm. Com. [Armistice Commission] to be responsible for dealing with matters related to the handing over and receiving of POW in accord with above stated agreement.

"(5) Once above items are mutually agreed and decided upon, the lists of names of all POW held presently by each side respectively will be exchanged."

#4. In answer to a JCS msg CinCUNC gave following views to JCS on points raised concerning item 4 by JCS.

(1) Discussion of release of non-Korean civilians concurrent with negots [negotiations] for POW exchange is very inadvisable now because it could not be done without raising the highly controversial over all issues of civilian internees & refugees. Question is predominantly political in nature. It is not intended to raise this issue until I have secured a decision on POW question.

(2) **It is highly improbable that Commies would agree to any formula for exchange which involves individual expressions of opinion (whether or not they want to be repatriated) because of extremely adverse affect [sic] that large scale defection would have on world-wide Commie prestige. In accord your recs.** [recommendations] **we shall continue to examine the feasibility of approaching Commies with alternate proposals at an appropriate time provided we have secured POW data.**

(3) I will follow my original planned procedure of seeking 1 for 1 basis of exchange, of demanding that ICRC be permitted to visit all POW camps to render such assist. [assistance] as they can, of expediting exchange of prisoners generally, and of insisting on a group for group basis for exchange to insure return of max [maximum] no. of UNC & ROK personnel. **However I am strongly of opinion that the issue of 1 for 1 exchange will meet with strong Commie resistance and that I may find it nec [necessary] to request authority to agree as a final posit [position] to an all for all exchange to include the forced exchange of those POW's not desiring return to Commie control.**

At our invitation Mr. Bierre of ICRC visited camp today. As result our conference with him we recommended for planning purposes the ICRC in Geneva be advised of strong UNC efforts to get Commies to invite ICRC delegates to visit all POW camps[.]

Dec. 13 (Thurs): Sub del on item 3 met at 1100. Hsieh delivered statement to show "concessions" made by his side. His main theme was "interference with internal affairs." He related this to inspection "thru out Korea" to aerial obs. [observation] and to prohibition on development of air fields. Hsieh argued against UNC retention of any islands outside of territorial waters and north of dem [demarcation] line. This said Hsieh constituted retaining forces in his rear. Hsieh accused UNC of delaying progress by not agreeing to his principles. UNC responded there was nothing new in Hsieh's remarks. Hsieh suggested two fundamental principles be accepted (1) no interference in internal affairs (2) no threat to rear. UNC replied this was agreeable provided UNC interpretation of meaning of these phrases was accepted. UNC emphasized necessity to prohibit air field development and to have thorough observ. including aerial. UNC denied enemy right to islands, denied intent to interfere in legitimate internal affairs. Hsieh contended milt. facilities are internal affairs, approved air obs. & insp. of comm. [communication] centers. UNC suggested Hsieh needed more time to study UNC proposal. Hsieh attacked right of UNC to rotation & replenishment[.] UNC explained rotation would not increase force levels. Recessed 1535.

#4. UNC opened by saying no response can be made to Commie proposal until suitable atmosphere created by exchange POW data & visits of ICRC reps [representatives] to POW camps. Details & basis of exchange cannot be discussed until data upon which discussion must be based is available. Failure of conf [conference] to make progress lies solely in Commies obstinate refusal to disclose essential data. People will ask themselves why Commies ask UNC to agree blindly to their demands as price for handing over data which should have been provided regularly. Visits to POW camps by neutral benevolent agency are sanctioned by custom & usuage [*sic*]. In World War I & II both belligerents exchanged info on POWs & permitted visits to camps. Right of ICRC visits reaffirmed by Geneva Convention of '29 & '49. Although NK not a signatory[,] PAK,

HEN NEN[,] its minister of foreign affairs[,] on 13 July 1950 informed Secty Gen of UN that NK would abide by convention. Also NK made rpts [reports] of POWs to Geneva in Aug & Sept 1950. UNC has agreed to observe GC & has complied. NK not so although it agreed. Only when Commies have complied with UNC request for exchange of data can discussion of release & exchange of POW make progress.

Lee said UNC did not answer question asked yesterday. UNC gave no opinion on Commie proposal. Central question is release POWs. So long as question unsettled why is data nec [necessary]. Conference not to arrange visits to POW camps but to arrange release of POW. Does UNC represent milt. authorities or Red Cross? Is arm [armistice] impossible unless ICRC visits camps? Why does UNC refuse discuss basic principle of releasing POW?

Col Tsai said UNC puts cart before horse—has no reasonable proposal. If UNC does not intend to suspend conf. it should cease unreasonableness & use logic & reason. UNC wants to appear humanitarian. Only a pose. Commie proposal to release all POW a touchstone by which humanitarianism can be tested. UNC would retain POW after arm. Where is it's [sic] humanity. Commie proposal shows real concern for POW. No reason to refuse to discuss it.

Lee asked Does UNC mean it cannot discuss Item 4 until its requests for info are accepted. Do you want to suspend conf?

UNC replied Commies continually misquote Item 4. It means "Arrangements, etc.["] Release & exchange only one of arrangements. UNC does not intend suspend conf. It does intend to have order by procedure. Its 2 logical procedural steps are nec preliminary to further discussion.

Lee ended am session saying if UNC does not abandon attitude no progress will be made[.]

#4. P.M. UNC said Commies are indulging in supposition about UNC intentions towards POW after arm. Commies asked why UNC insists on data exchange now. Reasons are two: UNC needs info as basic data for use in discussion of Item 4. It is required secondly for humanitarian reasons. POWs cannot be exchanged until arm. is signed. In meantime their rights should be observed & families assured they are alive & well. **UNC needs data to appraise effects of its agreement to any proposal.** Cannot buy pig in a poke. Must negotiate with eyes open. Will not be duped by Commie attempt to blackmail it into blind acceptance of Commie proposal. Commies callously ignore fundamental obligation to transmit POW data. Why? Do Commies think UNC desire for an early arm. makes it an early [easy?] mark? UNC wants arm but not at price of everything for nothing. Commies misguided if they think they can wait UNC out and force it to negotiate blindly. Commies tactics effective if their objective is to delay negots.

Lee questioned humanity of UNC for failing to agree to release all POWs after arm. He then revised Commie proposal amplifying it by discussion[.] UNC replied as follows: "You say your para 5 is perfect. It is complete roadblock to any progress. It effectively closes door to any consideration whatsoever by our side on your other 4 proposals. You hold key to both locks on door. 1st lock is your refusal to give us info. now on POWs you hold. 2nd lock is your persistent refusal allow reps ICRC to visit your POW camps." Adjourned 1643.

CinCUNC sent us msg giving JCS views on ICRC and exchange of POW data. Quoted as follows: "JCS concur in my (R) view that public info media should be mobilized to apply pressure on Commie leaders to receive ICRC reps. and are taking steps to make max [maximum] use of approp. media. Suggest you emphasize this in release made to press by you.

"JCS concur in our insistence on provision by Commies of list of POW and their locations prior to *any substantive* [discussion] *on Item 4* and state their intention to *adhere to this posit* [position] *under any circumstances.*"

R then says: "At early time of your choosing, desire that our dels make an announcement to Commies to effect that while UNC is willing to proceed with discussion on item 4, it will not enter into any substantive agreement on that item until provided with list our POW and their locations. In making this announcement of our psn [position], our dels will be instructed to avoid putting it in form of ultimatum which would imply break-off of negots by UNC, if not immed accepted by Commies.["]

Since above was in contradiction to previous instrs. about not discussing item 4 until agreement had been reached about ICRC visits to POW camps and exchange of data, I sent msg to R requesting clarification. Recd reply gist of which follows: "ICRC visits considered non essential. Essential condition which must be met is that Commies furnish list our POW & their locations. Until this condition is met discussion of methods of exchange would seem to be fruitless & even dangerous. Your procedure today indicates that you understand and are applying this point of view.["]

Dec. 14 (Fri): Sub-dels on Item 3 met at 1100. Hsieh restated his case against prohibition of airfields, as an interference in internal affairs. He attacked rotation & replenishment principles as an introduction of reinforcements. He complained UNC would not answer his questions. UNC pointed out quests [questions] he posed had been repeatedly answered. Hsieh pressed matter of weapon replacement, denouncing it as increase of strength. UNC replied no increase was involved, since exchanges were to be made leaving net total same—replacement would be piece for piece, type for type. Hsieh stated UNC intended prolong war, therefore UNC wished to increase forces in K.

P.M. Hsieh pointed out 17 days had passed in discussion Item 3 and dwelt on "concessions" made by his side. Stated UNC proposal Dec 12 unacceptable. Hsieh then made another proposal which differed little from previous one. Differences follow. (1) UNC withdraws from their rear and coastal islands &

waters of other side. (2) "If either side need to rotate its milt [military] personnel in Korea, it shall make request to and require approval of MAC. **No** [number] **of personnel to be rotated not to exceed 5,000 monthly.**" (3) Supervisory organ [organization] of reps [representatives] of neutral nations *entrusted* by MAC shall be responsible outside demilt. [demilitarized] zone. In short their modified items added little and fell far short of our requirements for a MAC.

UNC asked definition of "coastal islands and waters." Hsieh replied evasively. UNC asked wherein new Commie proposal differed from their former proposal in matters of principle. Hsieh pointed to incl. [inclusion] of rotation in his new prin. [principle] 4 and various minor changes in wording. UNC asked if all members of MAC had to agree to rotate and how figure 5000 had been chosen. Hsieh replied 5000 was big enough. Hsieh evaded quest. of approval by MAC. UNC submitted a list of other quests in writing. UNC stated nothing in Commie proposal of today varied from their proposal of 3 Dec, suggested Hsieh study UNC proposal of 12 Dec. further. Recessed 1630[.] Plan tomorrow to reject Commie proposal as no real effort to solve prob [problem].

#4. Lee opened meeting on Item 4 by inquiring as to UNC attitude on Commie 5 pt. [point] proposal. UNC replied it was out of order. Will discuss Item 4 at proper time when suitable atmosphere created. 2 steps nec. [necessary] as prelim [preliminary] to subst. [substantive] discussion Item 4—POW data exchange & visits ICRC. Two requirements must be met before subst. disc. appropriate. Commie obstinate refusal cause for delay.

Commies have indicated they have data. Why refuse to give it now? Is it because they only have handful of names? What is reason? Commies put on notice early in July that UNC considered ICRC visits basic to discussion POW problem. UNC proposed visits as 1st agenda item. At Commie insistence UNC agreed to combine item with overall POW problem (Item 4). On 15 July CinCUNC requested Commies to invite ICRC to visit POWs. **Issue long standing & germane to Agenda Item 4. 4 days ago UNC formally requested Commies to fulfill their moral & legal obligations under Geneva Convention. Will Commies give tangible evidence they are treating POW. according to min [minimum] standards set forth in Geneva convention by inviting ICRC to visit POW? People of world await answer which will clear atmosphere and disperse apprehension as to well being of POW, doubt engendered by Commie continued evasion.**

Lee replied UNC willing to enter disc Agenda Item 4 when two UNC so called two simple demands are accepted. Negots [negotiations] are give and take. UNC demands are unilateral. Demands therefore in violation spirit of Item 4. To be in accord we should first discuss & agree on principle of exchange, then proceed nec. measures such as release of sick & wounded. Why is it UNC as signatory of Geneva Con. is not willing to adhere to para 118 which specifies all POW will be released & repatriated without delay? **How can you say UNC has right to refer Commies to Geneva Conv. when it does not comply with 1st requirement that Conv. UNC legally obligated. Commies are not since they did not sign Conv. Commies respect & honor spirit embodied in Conv. though not signatories. What is reason for UNC to retain POW after arm** [armistice]. **Is this UNC humanitarianism. Are Commies to believe UNC is not willing to carry on armistice if we do not carry out UNC demands which are both unreasonable. In these negots no one party can force other to accept his proposals.**

#4. P.M. **UNC continued refute Lee's statements. Commie Foreign Minister stated on 13 July '50 that NK strictly observes principles of Geneva Convention concerning POW. Word strictly leaves no room for equivocation. Observance involves notification to Geneva of all POW captured**[.] Commies started to observe this principle then stopped. Today Lee states Commies not legally obliged to observe it. **Do they now publicly renounce pledge of Foreign Minister.** Which provisions do they observe & which not? UNC then submitted 4 quests for answer. (1) Do you observe Article which provides furnishing info re: location POW camps. (2) Article which provides for physical welfare of POW. (3) Arts. which provide for prompt reporting of name & iden. [identity] of every POW. (4) Art which provides for granting of all nec facilities for visits to POW by relief societies & specifically recognizes unique & spec. [special] position of ICRC in this regard.

Commies said this am. that neither del [delegation] should make demands which other party cannot accept. What have Commies done? They have said in effect "agree to 5 pt proposal of ours & we will turn over list of POW they propose to release." This is in effect an ultimatum[.] Yet Commies call this fair & reasonable & say because UNC refuses to accept it refuses to negotiate.

Lee replied UNC should not have turned meeting into lecture room on Int. [International] Law. Not for this purpose. UNC distorted statement by Foreign Minister. [This portion of paragraph emphasized by a bold line in left margin.] Where in text that we would abide by all provisions of Gen. Conv? All he means is that he is willing to abide by good spirits embodied in Geneva Conv. Based on statement of Foreign Minister Commies have treated POW well. They have gone further than provisions of Geneva Conv. UNC requested not to misquote statement foreign minister in future. UNC states that it abides by Geneva Conv. If so will it fulfill provisions Art 118 to release POW after arm?

UNC asked again for answer to question, "In what way is our request for POW data unreasonable?"

Gen Lee replied: In relation to lists of names of POW & Red Cross visits to POW camps. Commies are prepared to exchange lists of all names of POWs. But principle of prompt release & repat. [repatriation] of all POW must be det.

[determined] first. **If such a basic principle has not been determined where is need for exchanging lists of names?** What is more imp. to basic quest. of 4th Item. What is more important to POWs their release or ICRC visits? As signatory of Conv. UNC unwilling to observe basic principle, immed release of POW.

Lee then made plea for less formal procedure, more direct discussion, **In course of subsequent discussion he gave a direct answer on ICRC, "as for visits to camps by Red Cross, that is out of question because it is not specified & stipulated in Agenda Item 4["].** While he indicated no weaking [*sic*] on exchange of POW data he spoke of negotiatory procedure in connection with this item.

I sent msg to R. pointing out that although UNC has not as yet given any indication of it's [*sic*] posit [position] on basis of release & exchange of POW, "Commies have assumed that UNC will propose exchange on basis of 1 for 1. On this assumption they are attacking this posit and building up a strong propaganda case against 1 for 1 exchange.

"It now appears that attainment of agreement to exchange on 1 for 1 basis is highly improbable and that UNC would be exposing itself uselessly to adverse propaganda by advancing this as its initial posit.

"UNC Del is therefore considering 2 alternatives to the 1 for 1 proposal as its initial posit in negots. Both are primarily negot posits & do not appear to be acceptable to Commies. They will however, counteract to a large degree the propaganda case of the Commies. Confronted with such proposals enemy might seek exchange on a basis other than all for all. in order to avoid the individual option feature. which could result in adverse publicity to them.

"The first is essentially posit. set forth by JCS in which individual POWs expressing desire not to be exchanged would be permitted to remain under jurisdiction of their captors, in other words a procedure which respected desires of individual POWs. The many disadvantages of this procedure are recognized. We have already rec. [recommended] against it as impracticable. However, an opening proposal of this nature by UNC would avoid trap enemy has set for us, would destroy basis for [paragraph emphasized to this point by a bold line in left margin] his current propaganda efforts and would retain offensive for UNC.

"2nd proposal is a combination of above posit, and the one for one posit. Under this proposal we would try to attain 1 for 1 exchange of all those wishing to return until all POW of one side are exchanged. Of remaining POW those who wish to be repatriated will be returned to other side, while those who do not wish to be repatriated will be released in accord with their individual determination. This proposal based on assumption that UNC holds many more POW than Commies and that there will be sufficient no. of POW held by us to carry out 1 for 1 exchange of all UNC POW held by Commies.

"The negotiatory & propaganda advantages of either of above 2 proposals as initial posit appear to be great. It is difficult to estimate what adverse effect if any such proposals would have on UNC basic objective that nothing must be done to jeopardize return of UNC personnel held as POW by Commies.

"This is submitted for your concurrent consideration & study. Upon completion ours we will make firm recs.[''])

Dec. 15 (Sat): Sub-dels on Item 3 convened at 1100. Hsieh opened by illustrating with a map what he meant by coastal waters and islands, which he described by extending dem. [demarcation] line roughly due east from east coast and roughly SW from W coast. He indicated UNC should withdraw from all islands N of this extended line and waters around them to dist [distance] of approx 25 miles. Hsieh stated MAC would not control neutral supervisory organ [organization], but would merely "entrust" this organ with certain functions. Hsieh stated both sides should accord neutral teams the convenience of traveling over lines of comm. [communication] as agreed upon by both sides. Hsieh stated that rotation requests submitted to MAC must be supported by reasons and data, and must be approved by both sides of MAC. No [number] personnel to be rotated not to exceed 5000 per mo. Hsieh stated that old provincial admin. [administrative] line should divide Han River estuary. Hsieh stated "ports of entry" meant ports agreed by both sides, dodging question of airports. Aerial obs [observation] by neutral teams not nec [necessary] & not permissible. Hsieh stated both sides should make joint efforts to see that neutral organ can be formed and ready to operate immediately after arm. [armistice] agreement.

UNC responded with a statement refuting Commie positions on islands, rotation & replacement, interference in internal affairs, airfields & inspection of rear areas; and asserting firm UNC positions on these pts. [points].

Hsieh accused UNC of refusing to negotiate. UNC denied. Hsieh stated UNC rotation program was needed by UNC to raise morale its troops.

P.M. UNC delivered strong statement emphasizing its insistence on prohibiting increase in milt. capabilities during arm. Hsieh complained of "victor" attitude taken by UNC saying UNC refused to negotiate. UNC stated it was always ready to give serious consideration to any proposal which provided for effective supervision of adherence to arm terms and for prohibition of increase of milt capabilities during arm. Hsieh asked why 5000 per mo. rotation was not enough. UNC stated categorically it would continue rotation & replenishment during arm. & would accept no restrictions except those imposed by requirement not to increase level of forces. Hsieh denounced rotation as defacto increase in forces. Recessed 1600.

#4. UNC opened sub-commit meeting on agenda item 4 as follows: "Two things occurred yesterday of far reaching significance. Their impact on the world would be so detrimental to other side that they may wish to reconsider. **Yesterday was a dark day in the progress of the negots, and in an even larger**

sense. The sanctity of the pledged word reached a new low and the humanitarian aspirations of the people of the world with respect to well being of POW was [sic] dashed.

On that day General Lee, by his interpretation of Foreign Minister Pak's notification of adherence to Geneva Conv., denounced the Convention. On that day General Lee formally refused to permit ICRC to perform its internationally recognized and traditional humanitarian services for the prisoners.

The fact is that the persons entrusted with the admin. [administration] of POWs have failed to comply with a pledge of adherence to the principles of an international convention given by NK Foreign Minister. By means of his interpretation General Lee attempts to nullify retroactively that pledge given 17 mos ago. By means of his wholly unjustifiable interpretation Lee, in effect, denounces his countrys adherence to Geneva Convention. This is a grim responsibility.

Commies stated yesterday that visits to POW camps by ICRC was out of question because it is not specified & stipulated in agenda Item 4. This art. specifies only broad aspects of "arrangements relating to POW." Under this Commies have already proposed 5 Arts, none of which were stipulated in agenda item. UNC does not question these arts. nor will it seek to exclude them from discussion on such flimsy grounds.

For its part, UNC regards services of ICRC as specified in Geneva Conv., an essential element of the arrangements relating to POW. On what logical basis can Commies oppose this?

Commies have in connection with Agenda Item 3 proposed observation by neutrals[.] For many years ICRC has been accorded by international convention a special status as a neutral benevolent society. It is the preeminent neutral. Now, Commies under Item 4 discussions, refuse to permit ICRC entry to prison camps.

Under one item of the agenda Commies propose entry of neutral observers, under another the[y] oppose entry of a neutral of unchallengeable integrity. This is height of inconsistency.

If it is true Commies treat POW more humanely than required under GC should they not, as does UNC, welcome visits by ICRC? This would help you to convince us and the world of compliance. On the other hand, continued refusal only feeds the suspicion that Commie assertions are not entirely factual.

Lee replied in general as follows: I have carefully noted your lengthy statement of today. People of world are well aware as to which issue is more imp. [important]. Because Commies respect basic principles of GC, they treat POWs in best traditional humanitarianism. Moreover they hold that POWs in custody be released after cessation of host [hostilities], that is, when arm is signed. To resolve issues involved in agenda item Commies would like to take up first of all the question of immed. [immediate] release of POW. On this quest. they would like to hear comment.

UNC replied that it regards its two prelim. [preliminary] steps as matters of such imp. that it cannot go on without them. Commies have detailed data on POW held by UNC. This data available during consideration of whole broad problem. Commies may not realize the difficulties of attempting to come to decisions without that data. UNC thinks they do realize it all too well. They are attempting to put UNC in a posit [position] of negotiating in dark. UNC has only 2 lists from you totalling 110 names in contrast to full data held by Commies. Therefore UNC insists on exchange of POW data now. No valid argument to refuse to furnish data on POW. Time has come for Commies to recede from their posit and provide data now.

P.M. UNC contd [continued] to press for entry of ICRC delegates and exchange POW data particularly latter. Commies continued to press for discussion of their 5 Pt proposal. No significant developments.

Recd msg from R. which asked for our comments about making proviso in arm. agreement to permit senior MAC member of either side to assign specific missions to obs. teams and that when assigned they would be executed.

Replied saying we generally concur in seeking to obtain such authority for senior MAC member of either side with some added safeguards. Danger lies in probability that Commie SM [senior member] would saturate capabilities of obs. teams with trifling & specious assignments. Under consideration is plan to assign each team to certain areas outside of which they cannot operate; thereby limiting no [number] teams which can be made available to each senior member. Alternate plan is to reserve ½ of total no of roving obs. teams for senior member each side unless specifically released by him to other side for one assignment only. Specific teams would not be assigned permanently to either side.

In reply to msg from R in which he asked our comments as to an additional initial posit for negotiatory purposes re POW, we sent following: "Delegation recommends following as UNC initial posit on POW matter: "POW shall be exchanged on a person-for-person basis until all POW of of [*sic*] one side have been exchanged. The side which still holds POW shall thereafter release from POW status [prepositional phrase inserted above line] **all remaining POW held by it and repatriate all those who express a desire to be repatriated. Those so repatriated will be paroled to opposing force, such parole to carry with it the condition that the individual will not again bear arms against the side releasing him. Delegates of the ICRC shall be permitted to interview all POW remaining after the person-for-person exchange has been completed in order to insure that their choice is freely made.**"

Also said to R: "The foregoing is essentially the same as suggested in your msg, less the exchange by nationality feature. Final position as to the necessity for exchange by mixed national groups, and, if nec, the optimum nationality ratios required to insure early return of non-K POWs cannot be determined prior to receipt and analysis of list of POWs held by Communists. Exchange by national groups will result in certain admin complications and will in all probability require forced repatriation of some Chinese in lieu of NK, a sufficient no of whom would probably volunteer for repatriation to make up one-for-one total.''

Dec. 16 (Mon): Meeting of sub-dels this date on Item 3 opened with UNC focusing attention to fact delegations were in disagreement on (1) Islands (2) Developments of airfields (3) Aerial observation (4) A single supervising authority for the arm. [armistice] (5) Replenishment & replacement (6) Making the effective date of the arm. coincident with the readiness to operate of the inspecting organization.

Hsieh replied defending his 14 Dec proposal. He attacked replacement and replenishment. Hsieh insisted relation of neutral organ [organization] to MAC be one of reporting only. He opposed restriction on milt. facilities, saying his side had shown consistent, firm attitude against this point from beginning of negots [negotiations]. Hsieh called on UNC not to harbor suspicions of motives of his side, saying his side desired thorough peace. Hsieh took position whether his side did or did not rehabilitate its milt. facilities was strictly the business of his side. Hsieh stated UNC could be sure its attempt to restrict his side thus was categorically and absolutely rejected. As to aerial obs, Hsieh said this was merely a method of observation; and was not needed in connection with observing ports of entry. Hsieh said question of effective date was technical; pointed out that at time of the signing of arm it could be determined whether neutral organ was ready to go. He said this point could be solved by agreement at time of signing. [The remainder of the paragraph is emphasized by a bold line in left margin.] As to islands, Hsieh said they deserved no more discussion. He said: (1) both sides are on equal footing in negots, no victor, no vanquished; and that arm. negots should be clearly separated from political conf. [conference] later, (2) charged UNC sought to gain fruits-of-political conf. while delaying convening political conf. This statement apparently refers to airfields.

UNC charged Hsieh not trying to negotiate, simply insisted on his views. Hsieh said his views were fair & reasonable. UNC repeated charge. Hsieh said UNC had no reason to oppose his principles (1) & (2) above. UNC stated Hsieh either did not want to negotiate or did not have authority to do so. Hsieh asked what UNC proposed as a solution. UNC stated it refused to negotiate between illogic and logic, unreasonableness & reasonableness. UNC denied opposition to peace conference. UNC asked if addition of words, "This restriction means that there shall be no introduction of reinforcing milt forces, equipment, and material" to UNC principle #5 would render it acceptable. Hsieh asked if this meant unlimited rotation and replenishment. UNC replied yes, within "no increase" restriction. Hsieh replied rotation and replenishment meant increase in strength.

UNC asked, on hypothetical basis if UNC offered islands formerly controlled by N.K. what Commies had to offer in return. Hsieh said UNC must withdraw from all islands in his rear. UNC charged Hsieh would not negotiate. Hsieh indicated his side might accept UNC principle 7, if UNC had no intent to deliberately delay effective date of arm. Hsieh said his principles 5 & 6 were a compromise solution. He said there were 2 main points of disagreement. (1) Rotation & replenishment (which he opposed) and (2) restriction on rehab [rehabilitation] of facilities and aerial observation (which he said was totally inappropriate to an arm. conference). Hsieh said it was UNC turn to make a move. UNC stated replacement and replenishment was not a UNC negotiating posit but a firm intent, and that question of restriction had been covered yesterday. Hsieh complained of UNC attitude. Recessed 1530.

#4. Sub-del on agenda Item 4 convened at 1100. UNC pressed during entire session for exchange now of POW data. Commies did not acquiesce and sought answer to question "Is UNC going to release all POW or not?" At close of session UNC placed its own POW lists on table and formally proposed exchange then and there saying if Commies not ready UNC would return with its lists at 1100 tomorrow. Recessed 1310.

Note: Since it is clear that any effort to engage in substantive discussion will only open door to discussion of release & exchange rather than other matters relating to exchange, program for tomorrow involves no change from present procedure. ICRC issue will be kept alive but in subordinate posit.

Dec. 17 (Mon): Sub-dels on Item 3 convened at 1100. General Ferenbaugh seated vice Hodes relieved. Hsieh opened with restatement of (1) rotation & replenishment and (2) rehabilitation of facilities, as crucial points of dispute. UNC reiterated its position on these points. UNC asked for answer to its hypothetical question of yesterday regarding islands. Hsieh said islands was a minor question. Hsieh said rotation and replenishment was [sic] reinforcement, argued lengthily against it. Hsieh said restrictions on facilities and aerial observation were interference with internal affairs and his side unshakeably opposed to them. Hsieh said while his side had made concessions on rotation, UNC had made no concession on rehabilitating facilities. UNC returned to hypothetical question regarding islands. UNC stated rotation and replenishment is [sic] not subject to negotiation, is the firm intent of UNC [not to submit them to negotiation]. UNC asked if Hsieh suggested that in return for UNC conceding islands his side would accept UNC principle 5. Hsieh said UNC withdrawal from islands was obligation of UNC, declined bargain, denouncing as unreasonable. Hsieh said his side absolutely would not tolerate any interference in internal affairs (air field rehabilitation) and absolutely would not accept such restriction, such interference. UNC returned again to hypothetical question of islands, asking for clear answer. Hsieh said question already answered, returned to two points, rotation and replenishment, and rehab. [rehabilitation] of facilities. Hsieh said UNC insisted on rotation and replenishment, his side opposed prohibition of rehab. of facilities. UNC insisted on solution of island question. Hsieh insisted UNC was obligated to withdraw from islands. UNC denied this categorically. After recess for lunch, argument developed as to who needed more time to study proposals of other side. [The following paragraph was entered and then crossed out in the text: Hsieh insisted UNC was obligated to withdraw from islands. UNC denied this categorically. After recess for lunch, argument developed as to who needed more time to study proposals of other side.] Hsieh reiterated he had answered question on islands.

#4. Sub-del meeting on Item 4 convened 1100. Discussion followed pattern set yesterday. Recessed 1300 after Commies indicated they had nothing new to present.

General R arrived about 1700 to discuss the various aspects of the situation and frame a msg to the JCS which would emphasize the issues at stake and reply to a previous msg from the JCS on the subject of POWs. Prior to supper we held a conference, first with the Item 4 sub delegation and then with the delegates for Item 3 during which the major points of disagreement were discussed and the tenor of the msg to the JCS was outlined. After supper R prepared an outline plan for the despatch which was turned over to the two delegations for working up. Kinney was given the job of coordinating and combining the two results. Both sub-dels worked until about 2 am.

Dec. 18 (Tues): Prior to the departure of the sub delegations to Pan Mun Jom Genl R held a conference in my tent for the purpose of reviewing the msg that was completed last night. The gist of the msg follows:

"*Part One.* Following a canvass of the opinions of the del. [delegates] & staff, I submit herewith an analysis which includes:

1. The General Situation [see "*Part Two*" below]

2. Existing major points of disagreement ["*Part Three*"]

3. The final position on each of these major points, which in my view the present and future interests of the U.S. require that we maintain, with the supporting reasons in each case (where a position is in conflict with JCS intrs. [instructions] the facts are so stated) ["*Part Four*"]

4. Conclusions ["*Part Five*"]

5. Recommendations ["*Part Six*"]

Part Two. The General Situation.

1. a. There are several principal elements in the situation as of this date, all of which are indeterminate except one. The single exception is the time remaining of the 30 day period as it affects Agenda Item 2. This period has nine days to run.

b. The indeterminate principle [*sic*] elements are the effect of an extension of this period; the intentions of the Communists with respect to concluding an armistice; and the finality of the several positions which the Communists have taken on the respective existing major points of disagreement. Each of these is discussed in turn.

2. a. Extension of the 30 day period will have a positive [*sic*; negative?] and harmful effect on the mental attitude of our forces in Korea, unless the period of extension is very short and conclusion of the armistice negotiations is clearly imminent. Furthermore, unless this condition obtains, it will have a like effect on public opinion in the U.S.

b. While I state this purely as an opinion, and while I am not in a posit. [position] to gauge its force, I would think it conceivable that such public opinion might result in the U.S. Govt. adopting courses of action in Korea in conflict with its best interests, might incline it to accept a local temporary advantage, rather than an overall far reaching gain.

c. It could be a case of taking the cash and letting the credit go, the "cash" being a temporary lull, a brief interruption in casualty rpts [reports]; the "credit" being safeguards which would provide for max [maximum] recovery of surviving POWs and max insurance against future casualties thru min. [minimum] essential security measures for our forces in Korea today and in Japan tomorrow.

3. The intention of the Communists with respect to concluding an armistice is perhaps the most conjectural of all the variables in the present situation. Opinion has changed 180° several times in the past few weeks, and today there is almost as much on one side as on the other. Whatever be the Communists intentions, it seems probable we are most likely to develop them through a determination of the points on which we will not yield; through prompt announcement of these points in such unequivocal language as to make our purpose crystal clear; and thru reiteration of these positions every day for the remainder of the 30 day period of grace.

4. The finality of the several Commie positions on existing major pts [points] of disagreement can likewise be determined in the same manner.

5. a. Item 3 of the Agenda now under active discussion is not making acceptable progress because of Communist intransigence.

b. Thruout this analysis, in fact thruout our entire negots, the policy directive you have assigned me has been kept clearly in mind, namely the attainment as soon as possible of an arm. on terms acceptable to the U.S.

c. Thruout this analysis & otherwise your directive, that, if negots are broken off the onus must rest on the Communists has likewise been kept clearly in mind.

d. However, these two pts. above deserve comment.

(1) With respect to the 1st, it is axiomatic that the Communists have a like policy objective. Hence, with due respect to the 2nd point, there must come a

time at which our final posits must be stated, and if not accepted, a time at which we must be prepared to continue their reiteration indefinitely until either our patience, or that of the Commies is exhausted.

(2) With respect to both the 1st & the 2nd there is a point at which the law of diminishing returns takes over. While again perhaps presumptuous in attempting to forecast the course of U.S. public opinion, I yet feel that a time must come when, if our final posits continue to be rejected, yet the Commies themselves do not break off negots, that the UNC must do so. I do not of course suggest that that time has yet arrived. I do suggest that if the present course of these negots long continues, it will arrive and the decisions to meet it should be made in advance.

e. Every time that the UNCD abandons a posit which it has strongly held, its future posit & bargaining strength are proportionately reduced. **Communist practices world wide should by now be so thoroughly understood that no reasonable person can any longer be in doubt that the more they gain the more they take**. The more that is yielded to them the more obdurate they become. Only through recognition and application of this well established fact can we hope to bring these negotiations to either a successful conclusion, or to a clear issue warranting their determination by the deliberate decision of the UNC.

Part Three.   Major points of existing disagreement.

Agenda Item 3.

1. Armistice not to be effective until supervising organ [organization] is ready to function.

2. Neutral organ to be subject to direction and control of MAC.

3. Ground (as distinguished from aerial) observation at ports of entry including GROUN[D], SEA & AIR with freedom of movement for observer personnel.

4. Prohibition of rehab. & contr. [rehabilitation and construction] of airfields & aerial obs. [observation] thereof.

5. Rotation, replenishment & replacement.

Agenda Item 4.

6. Basis for release & exchange of POW.

Part IV.   Final posits. on major points of disagreement which in my view the present and future interests of the U.S. require that we maintain.

Agenda Item 3.

1. *Insistence on prohib.* [prohibition] *of constr. or rehab. of airfields.*

The most imp. [important] part of this arm. is the restr. [restriction] on rehab of airfields. Without such a restr. the arm contains no adequately effective provision for the security of our forces, or even for the stability of the arm. itself. The rehab. of airfields during the period of the arm. is inconsistent with the fundamental idea of an arm. The balance of forces and conditions existing at the time the arm is put into effect could be radically altered thereby. The rehab. of enemy airfields is today the greatest potential threat to the security of our forces in K. Tomorrow it could be a similar menace to our forces in Japan.

2. *Insistence on neutral aerial obs. & photo reconnaissance.*

This provision is essential for determination of adherence in terms of Arm, particularly para 1 above. Without aerial obs. of the 97 airfields in N.K., prohibition of rehab. of airfields would have little practicability, and none on new constr.

3. *Insistence on the rotation and replenishment principle, unlimited except by the principle that there shall be no increase in the levels existing at the time the arm becomes effective.* To agree to limit rotation and replenishment to a level beneath that nec. [necessary] to maintain the strength of our forces in Korea would constitute withdrawal by attrition[.] It would be an unmistakable indication of weakness to the Commies[.]

4. *Insistence on including provisions in the Arm. agreement which provide for mandatory action by the MAC & the neutral observer personnel in the execution of tasks assigned in the armistice agreement.* Without provisions making mandatory the execution of tasks assigned the MAC, and the neutral organ, the Commies can block any action by these organs thru refusing to agree. With such provisions included in the arm. agreement, it is not considered necessary to place the neutral organ under the direction & control of the MAC. (This posit varies in wording but not in effect from present JCS instrs)

5. *Insistence on location of neutral observer teams at major ports of entry including ground, sea & air as mutually agreed to by both sides, with freedom of movement over major lines of comm* [communication] *as required.* It is essential that obs. be conducted at a selected no. of major ports of all types and freedom of movement be accorded teams to conduct these observations in order to determine whether enemy is increasing his milt. capabilities by importation.

6. *Basis for Release & Exchange of POWs* (Deduced from Communists statements in meetings to date[)].

a. We believe final position which offers best chance for max recovery of our milt. POWs is all for all exchange confined to milt. personnel only.

b. Although UNC has not as yet given any indication of its posit on basis for release & exchange of POW Commies have assumed that UNC will propose exchange on one for one basis. On this assumption they are attacking this posit. and building up a strong propaganda case against 1 for 1 exchange. Art 118 Geneva Conv. tends to support their all for all argument. In view of this, UNC by formally proposing 1 for 1 exchange will be exposing itself to adverse propaganda. Such a risk would probably reap no productive results, because settlement on a 1 for 1 basis is likely not to be accepted by the Commies and because it seems likely the U.S. public would create an overwhelming demand on the govt. [government] for a concession long before UNC could outsit the Commies on this issue.

c. With respect to inclusion of civilians and forced repatriations:

(1) The only arrangement which gives any reasonable assurance of no forced repatriation is to omit any civilians and insist on a one for one exchange, without nationality considerations, until all POW[s] held by Commies are recovered; thereafter release remainder of POW we hold but repatriate only volunteers. This conflicts with JCS msg and requires your prior authority.

(2) Any tenable position which includes selected civilians will almost certainly entail forced return of some personnel and thereby violate JCS msg.

(3) Therefore JCS decision is required as to which has priority—the return of selected civilians or adherence to principle of no forced return of POW.

d. The repatriation of civilians is a political question. To raise it is to violate the consistent stand of the UNC that the Arm is strictly a military matter.

e. We further believe that if we insist on principle of voluntary repatriation we may establish a dangerous precedent that may react to our disadvantage in later wars with Communist powers. Should they ever hold preponderance of POW, and then adhere to their adamant stand against any form of neutral visits to their POW camps, we would have no recourse, if they said none of our POWs wanted to be repatriated.

f. On assumption civilians have priority there appears to be only one practicable way to proceed:

(1) Offer not to oppose all for all exchange of POW provided as a specified no. of selected civilians are included by Commies. This may well lead to demand by Commies for return by UNC of all civilian internees and refugees in S.K. including S.K. civilian internees once reported to Geneva but since reclassified; that is, they may demand extension of all for all exchange principle to include refugees and internees.

(2) POW shall be exchanged on a person for person basis until all POW of one side have been exchanged. **The side which still holds POW shall thereafter release from POW status all the remaining POW's held by it and repatriate all those who express a desire to be repatriated.** Those so repatriated will be paroled to the opposing force such parole to carry with it the condition that the individual will not bear arms against the side releasing him. Delegates of the ICRC shall be permitted to interview all POW remaining after the person for person exchange has been completed in order to insure that the choice is made freely.

g. The value of the second alternative as a club to secure acceptance of the first depends largely upon the adverse propaganda effect upon the Commies of having a large number of former Commie soldiers refuse to return to their homeland and of having the UNC provide them asylum. **Unfortunately, the second**

alternative, which extends the right of asylum to POWs is so appealing to humanitarian sentiment, that once it is announced and publicized, the demand by our people to stand or fall on this proposal may preclude ultimate abandonment of this position.

h. In view of the many interests involved, negots to accomplish return of civilians would be delicate. It is thought that the UNC should never formally propose alternative 6c(1) above. The sub-del would explore it with as little publicity as possible under the guise of discussing the Communist all for all proposal. We would state that the UNC holds many more prisoners, but that Commies want an all-for-all exchange. If the Commies will include in the exchange a specified no. of civilians from lists to be provided, UNC will not oppose Commie proposal of all for all. Exchange of POW by UNC and POW and listed civilians by the Commies, would be in [*sic*] a one for one basis until POWs and listed civilians held by enemy are exhausted. Delivery of remaining POW held by UNC would be contingent upon satisfactory compliance with terms of agreement by Commies. The club would be exposed but not wielded.

Part V. Conclusions

Agenda Item 3.

1. The question of whether the enemy will or will not agree to an armistice containing a prohibition on increasing milt. capabilities (air facilities) during the period of the arm. is perhaps the gravest question posed by the Armistice negotiations, *and in the unanimous opinion of the delegation is the key question on which the fate of the armistice hinges. If the enemy will not accent [assent],* or will long delay an arm. which contains a prohib. against airfields, the question arises why the enemy is so seriously concerned with airfields. The answer to that question may indicate the intentions of the enemy. The only way that crucial question can be decisively answered is to press the enemy to a point of ultimate decision and choice—an armistice or airfields. If his choice is the latter, then his intention to take over all of Korea (accepted in National Intell [Intelligence] estimate No 55) includes the determination to project his air power thruout the peninsula.

2. The choice between permitting UNC POWs to volunteer for repatriation and attempting to secure the return of UN and ROK civilians, needs to be made because it is the opinion here that both cannot be achieved in the same UNC proposal.

Part VI. Recommendations.

1. That final positions outlined in Part IV above be approved soonest without qualification and that UNC Delegation be authorized to announce them as such to the Commies and to the world at times of my choosing.

2. That current JCS instrs in conflict with the above be rescinded''

signed Ridgway.

Considerable discussion occurred during the am. between Van Fleet, R, myself and others over the above msg. (Van Fleet had come up from Seoul to see R).

V.F. contended it was much too stiff and that if we held out for it we would get no armistice. It was pointed out that the primary purpose of the msg was to put the whole question up to the JCS in order to get a firm discision [*sic*] out of them as to our final positions.

Muccio also was present. He, R and Maj Gen Lee held a private conference during which Lee voiced his concern over the return of the ROK civilians. Implied he would have to withdraw from the delegation if we did not attempt to get them back. He said however if we failed in our attempts to have them returned with POWs he would be agreeable to having the question brought up under agenda item 5.

During the morning Libby sent back word the Commies had agreed to give us this POW data at 3 pm.

I saw R & Muccio off at 2 pm.

Libby returned with the list at 3:30 pm. The list contained the following tentative nos:

U.S. 3198 (3 rptd as Japs probably Nisei)

Other U.N. Turks 234, French 10, Netherlands 1, Philippines 40, South Africans 4, Greeks 1, U.K. 919, Australians 6, Canadians 1.

Meeting on Item 3 opened 1100. Hsieh referred to UNC insistence on rotation & replacement, and to his side's objection to "interference in internal affairs." UNC repeated posit on rotation and replacement & airfields from record of Dec 15. Hsieh stated the two questions above must be settled. UNC asked if Hsieh had anything new to propose. Hsieh replied no, insisted his side had made many concessions to UNC views, it was UNC turn to make a move. Recessed 1145.

No other significant development at meeting on Item 4 other than agreement by Commies to give POW data. The Commies were told that the UNC sub delegation would not be ready to meet again until it had a chance to study the POW list. Of course the real reason for delaying to meet again is that it is essential to wait for an answer to our msg to JCS. Hodes left today.

Dec. 19 (Thurs [sic; should be Wednesday]): Item 3 sub delegates met at 1100 this date. UNC delivered statement condeming [*sic*] Commies for offering no new proposal, for making no effort to solve disagreements, pointing out great milt. [military] advantages which accrue to Commies during arm. [armistice], as result of cessation of operations of UNC air and naval forces. Hsieh responded with statement claiming concessions by his side, denying UNC concessions. Hsieh said UNC had no love for peace, rather, wailed because armistice in sight. Unless UNC changed its attitude, progress in negots [negotiations] was impossible. After recess, UNC asked what set of principles which includes basic thought of UNC principle 5 would be acceptable to Commies. Hsieh evaded. UNC asked if approval by MAC of any rotation did not constitute a veto power over rotation. Hsieh said approval by MAC was necessary in order to insure no increase of force resulted. Hsieh said UNC [MAC] would approve any reasonable rotation. Regarding airfields, Hsieh said UNC position was unacceptable. UNC asked if Hsieh meant that so long as UNC insisted on principle 5, there could be no arm. Hsieh said 2 main points were in issue:**(1) Rotation, replenishment and (2) interference (airfields).** Hsieh said, as hypothesis, that if UNC gave up insistence in interference (prohibition on airfields) his side would give further consideration to question of rotation. UNC said its position on both points was firm. UNC reminded Hsieh that main cause of lost time in arm. negots was failure of his side to recognize a firm UNC position when confronted with one. UNC said its firm position was for (1) Prohibition of increases of milt. capabilities during armistice, and (2) Effective supervision and observation of arm. Hsieh attacked UNC for refusing to withdraw forces from Korea. **Hsieh charged UNC had been responsible for all lost time in conference. Hsieh repeated offer to exchange rotation for airfields. Airfields are clearly the key issue of the armistice. Recessed 1700.**

Sub-Del for Agenda Item 4 remained at camp analyzing POW data. Sent msg to R. saying ltr would be delivered to liaison officer tomorrow for further delivery to Lee San Jo [Lee Sang Cho] advising him that "**a preliminary analysis of roster of POW which you delivered to us on 18 Dec '51 discloses following discrepancies.**

(a) 31 of 50 names you rptd [reported] to ICRC on 18 Aug '50 do not appear on your roster

(b) 35 of 60 names you rptd. to ICRC on 14 Sept '50 do not appear on your roster

(c) 285 of 713 names of POW whose names are known to have been broadcast over radio Peking & Radio Pyong-yang do not appear on your roster

(d) 335 of 505 POW whose names are known to have appeared in publications in China & NK, or were obtained from other sources such as ltrs to families do not appear on your roster.

The missing names are contained in Inclosures [*sic*].

Information is requested promptly as to status of these POW and as to why they were not included in your roster."

R replied not to release ppsd [proposed] ltr until figures involved can be verified by AG.

Dec. 20 (Thurs): Meeting on Item 3 opened 1100 this date. Hsieh claimed concession made by his side in allowing rotation of 5000 monthly. Hsieh said approval of rotation by MAC would be mere formality. UNC said its posit [position] on rotation and replacement was firm: no limit, except that of no increase in force and material levels. UNC said great concession made to Communists in cessation of UNC air and naval ops. [operations], which would lift a multitude of interferences in internal affairs, and asked only prohibition of airfields. UNC

asked if Commies did not acknowledge minimum nature of interference contemplated in UNC principle 5. Hsieh accused UNC of boasting of its military
strength; said he was trying to settle two major issues, (1) rotation and replenishment (2) airfields. UNC asked if Hsieh was willing to negotiate today on basis of
facts existing today. Hsieh called UNC foolish, deriding UNC concession in
withdrawing air and naval power, in display of anger. **Hsieh asked if UNC could
now assure that a political conference would immediately follow armistice.**
UNC said it could not prophesy about political conference immediately following
armistice, only sought stable armistice. Hsieh said UNC did not desire peace.
Hsieh laid heavy emphasis on matter political conference, saying UNC opposed
this. Hsieh said UNC evaded question of higher level conference. Hsieh contended independent state (N.K.) had inviolate rights to rehabilitate facilities.
Hsieh said provided UNC gave up stand on airfields, rotation would be easily
solved. Hsieh said question of when deadlock was broken depended on UNC,
his side had made all possible effort to resolve deadlock. UNC said UN desired earliest possible solution of K problem. First step is effective stable arm.
[armistice]. This objective best served by Commie agreement to UNC principle.

UNC invited Hsieh to present a set of principles acceptable to him which
include basic thoughts of UNC principle 5[.] Hsieh asserted two opposing forces
were in balance. Hsieh said UNC opposed peace. Hsieh said only if UNC gave
up unreasonable stand was there any hope for arm.

After recess Hsieh said his December 14 proposal was reasonable; that main
issues were (1) rotation and replenishment and (2) airfields. Hsieh asked if UNC
had given up unreasonable demand about interfering in internal affairs. UNC
said it had no intention of giving up prohibition on airfields. Hsieh again offered
to exchange rotation for airfields. **Hsieh said his side would never enter into an
agreement which permitted interference in internal affairs (airfield prohibition).** UNC reworded Commie principle 4 to render it acceptable to UNC. Hsieh
said this was joke. Hsieh questioned good faith of UNC towards armistice. **Hsieh
again said he would exchange rotation for airfields.** Repeated foregoing once
more. Hsieh said next move was set up to UNC. UNC asked if Hsieh was
willing to let staff officers jointly draft a set of principles to submit to sub-
delegates tomorrow. Hsieh agreed provided staff officers used his 14 Dec
proposal as basis of discussion. UNC said agreed provided UNC principle 5 was
incorporated. Hsieh evaded, insisted that staff officers proceed with work. UNC
agreed. Staff officers went into session at 1600, when sub dels recessed.

Sub-Del on agenda Item 4 did not meet. Delegates continued to analyze POW
lists.

Dec. 21 (Fri): Rec'd msg from JCS (JCS 90083) which was in answer to R's
msg outlined in record of 18 Dec. Gist of msg. follows.

"1. Since arm [armistice] will remain controlling agreement for prolonged period, its significance attains greater importance and its character must provide for greater degree of permanency than would otherwise be the case. Arm. agreement must clearly provide that it will remain in effect until superseded by other arrangements.

"2. Appears likely that Commie violations of arm. terms will be disturbances in nature of nuisance demonstrations, threats etc rather than open & renewed aggression.

"3. Safety of UN Forces & major deterrent to renewal of aggression must in last analysis be dependent upon realization by Communists that a renewed aggression in Korea would result in a new war which would bring upon China the full retribution which U.S. and her allies deem militarily advisable. Declaration to this effect under discussion at present. UK shows her support this concept.

"4. U.S. public opinion fully supports an acceptable milt [military] arm. as best of alternatives which confront us in Korea. On issues of major imp. [importance] public in U.S. and allies stand staunchly behind negotiators.

"5. Following are positions you should firmly maintain in negots [negotiations]. Cannot say each one is absolutely final. While complete disagreement on all these positions would be considered grounds for breaking off negots, U.S. Govt is unable now to state that failure to achieve agreement on only one or even several of final posits [positions] given below or elements thereof would in last analysis be considered in itself a breaking point.

"5. (a) [*sic*] *Airfields*. As long-range proposition complete prohibition on any rehab. [rehabilitation] of air fields will be impracticable to enforce. On other hand there must be a prohibition against rehab. of those fields in K. suitable for jet opns [operations], against extension or enlargement of existing runways as well as against constr. [construction] of new fields or runways. Not to exceed an agreed no [number] of specified fields, which no is left to your discretion, may be rehabilitated and maintained subj [subject] to above restrictn's.

(b) *Aerial observation*. Aerial obsvn would be desirable but not essential, particularly after ground obsn teams are in place. Accordingly insistence on aerial obsvn should not be a part of your final posit, and failure to effect agreement to provide for aerial obsvn, even if ground obsvr. [observer] teams are not in place, should not be a breaking point.

(c) *Rotation of personnel*. Rotation of personnel and replenishment of supplies and equipment should be separated. for purposes of negots. We concur in your insistence on provisions for rot. [rotation] of personnel. Unless agreement can be reached on a limiting no. which would satisfy your max. [maximum] requirements for rotation, there should be no limit on no rotated in any month. Under any agreement there must be provision that at no time must overall level of pers. [personnel] be greater than that which existed at time arm. goes into effect.

(d) *Replenishment*. It is desirable that there be no increase in supply levels over those at time arm goes into effect, & you should seek agreement in principle on this point. However, since this would be extremely difficult to monitor, it is not too important **except that there should be a definite prohibition against increase in combat aircraft.** On this specific prohibition you should be adamant.

(e) *Non-combatant observer teams & MAC*[.] Your posit on n.c. [non-combatant] obsvn teams & MAC is approved (parallel organs [organizations]). Regardless of composition of teams, no voting or other procedures should be accepted which would limit agreed freedom of movement or restrict right of reporting by teams or individual members thereof. We concur that obsvr. teams must be located at major ground, sea, & air ports of entry specified in arm. agreement with freedom of movement as required to perform their duties.

6. Armistice should go into effect on an agreed date specified in arm. agreement. It should be keyed directly to having MAC & some obsvr. teams in Korea but not necessarily in place. We recognize risk involved thereby, but feel effective date of arm should not be delayed thru inability to get teams in place. Suggest possibility of aerial obsvn. by non combatant teams on temp [temporary] basis pending complete location of grd. [ground] teams.

7. We consider time has not arrived for you to initiate procedure of announcing and reiterating final posits nor are we able to approve now recom [recommendation] for authority to announce final posits.

7. [*sic*]. As deadline approaches, if progress is still being made and depending upon status of negots you are authorized to propose or agree to an extension for a period not to exceed 15 days.

8. *POWS*. We do not accord priority to civilians over POWs but as suggested your msg. you should not oppose all for all exchange of POW provided a specified no of selected civilians are included by Commies. Actual exchange of POW by UNC for POW and listed civilians by Commies would be on a one-for-one basis, until POW and listed civilians held by enemy are exhausted. **Release of remaining POW would be in accord with principle of voluntary repatriation along gen** [general] **lines outlined in your msg.**

On question of exchange of civilians you should be guided by folg [following]:

   (a) Strong effort should be made to obtain release of UN civilians and ROK govt personnel[.]

   (b) Similar effort, though of lesser priority, should be made to obtain release of all remaining internees & refugees held by Commies.

   (c) Consult Muccio on all phases of exchange of K civilians.

9. *Final POW position*. If not successful in obtaining Commie agreement to posit in above para [paragraph] you should request authority from Wash. [Washington] before taking final posit to secure release of POW only.

Any posit. requiring forced return of personnel held by UNC must have prior approval by Wash.

Agenda Item 5.

Adopt folg statement as initial posit: "The Military Comdrs [commanders] have not considered questions concerning a political settlement in Korea, including unification of Korea under an independent, democratic govt. and other questions arising from but not resolved by arm. agreement. The Milt. Comdrs recommend to govts & authorities concerned that early steps be taken to deal with these matters at a political level." If Commies insist inclusion subject of withdrawal of trps [troops], you are authorized to add words "such as withdrawal of non Korean Forces" to end of first sentence.

R then sent an amplifying msg to above JCS msg. gist of which follows: *Rehabilitation of airfields*[.] "Suggested first position on this subject should be that UNC will not agree in principle to the rehab of airfields for combat operations but as a major concession will agree to the rehab. & maintenance of up to 8 airfields for civil air ops [operations], such rehab. not to consist of extension of runways."

R then listed 22 airfields in N.K. which would be suitable for jet ops. if rehabilitated. Min [minimum] airfield specs [specifications] required for jet ops: length of runway 5000 ft, width—100 ft. Surface—packed earth or better.

"CinCUNC also listed 9 N.K. airfields which could be rehab. without causing undue alarm to UNC. These 9 are considered only operational airfields in N.K. which could be tolerated by UNC under an arm agreement[.]

"*Rotation of personnel:* Alternate posit to be taken at your option will be a limit of 35,000 per mo. under supervision of obsvr teams but without prior consent or concurrence of MAC. When this principle is revised it would be desirable to avoid wording which would prohibit the organization of units in Korea within personnel ceilings existing at time arm. is signed. This is subject which we should avoid discussing with Commies. Suggested wording: "Neither side shall increase the numerical level of milt. personnel existing in K after the effective date of the arm."

"*Replenishment of Supplies & Equipment.* An acceptable wording would be: "Neither side shall increase the numerical quantities of combat aircraft, weapons, ammo [ammunition] & armored vehicles existing in K at time arm becomes effective." The advantage to this position is that it gives us flexibility of logistic support which may be essential if our forces remain in K for a protracted period of time.

JCS msg is interpreted to mean that normal civil air ops. would be permitted. Also that "agreed freedom of movement" is interpreted to mean that movement which the arm. agreement will specifically authorize.

Bear in mind that your proposals must be in complete consonance with guidance contained in JCS msg.

Staff officers meeting on Agenda Item 3. am session. Reviewed principles discussed previous p.m. Agreement reached on principle 1 worded as follows: "(1) All armed forces under control of either side, including all units and armed personnel of the ground, naval and air forces shall cease all hostilities within 24 hrs after the arm agreement is signed and becomes effective[.]"

Agreement also reached on principle 2 worded as follows: "All armed forces under control of either side shall be withdrawn from demilt [demilitarized] zone within 72 hrs. after arm. agreement is signed and becomes effective. Except for such armed forces of a police nature as may be specifically agreed to by both sides, no armed forces of either side shall thereafter enter the demilt zone; nor shall the armed forces of either side commit any acts of armed force against the demilt zone. Each side shall manage in accord with the stipulations of the arm. agreement the admin. [administrative] affairs of that portion of the demilt zone lying on its side of the milt dem [demarcation] line.

Agreement reached on principle 3 reworded as follows: "All armed forces, ground naval & air under control of either side shall be withdrawn, within 5 days after arm agreement is signed and becomes effective, from rear & coastal islands and waters of other side, meaning islands which were formerly controlled by other side and any others specifically and mutually agreed to. If they are not withdrawn within the stated time limit, and there is no mutually agreed & valid reason for delaying the withdrawal the other side shall have right to take all nec. [necessary] action against such armed personnel for maintenance of security & order."

Discussion was had on question of ports of entry. UNC wanted to insert "ground sea & airports." Commies objected said their wording ports of entry was collective and included all types of ports. UNC proposed use of "non combatant" instead of "neutral" teams. Commies said they would consider change.

PM session. UNC explained necessity for prohibition against airfield rehab. Commies stated they did not intend to rehab all airfields, that it was question of internal affairs. UNC asked why nec. Enemy said it involved sovereign rights[.] Commies offered revised principle 4 as follows: "In order to insure stability of milt. armistice so as to facilitate holding by both sides of a political conference of a higher level, both sides undertake not to introduce into K any milt. units, milt personnel, war equipment, and ammo during the Armistice. Such rotation as within the limit agreed upon by both sides shall be reported to the milt arm commission so that the inspecting organ of neutral nations may be entrusted to conduct supervision & insp. [inspection] in ports of entry in rear, agreed upon by both sides."

Enemy claimed big concession made, would not discuss airfield rehab. further. UNC listed concessions. Commies stated air field rehab., air reconnaissance[,] insp. at comm. [communication] centers involved internal affairs sovereign state; such demands must be given up.

Commies reiterated they could absolutely not accept interference in their internal affairs, namely rehab of airfields.

R passed JCS msg to us on subj [subject] POW's. Msg invited attention to incompleteness of list of POW camps furnished by Commies; specifically mentioning that:

(1) 40 to 50 % of U.S. prisoners were sent to China & Manchuria in '51.

(2) Commies list only 11 out of at least 29 permanent camps in N.K and none out of at least 18 permanent camps in China & Manchuria.

(3) Msg gave locations of camps not indicated in Commie list[.]

With ref [reference] to completeness of POW list by name, JCS msg pointed out that:

(1) **Total list of names of U.S. POWs and ROK POWs is too small in comparison with % of missing in action of other nationalities. For inst. [instance] list contains 25% of U.S. MIA [missing in action] and 11.7% of ROK MIA as against 85% of British MIA, 64% of Turkish & 69% of Philippine MIA.**

(2) Commie list names only 40% of those 110 U.S. POW reported by NK Govt to ICRC in Aug 50 to be held as POW[.]

(3) It is estimated Commie list names only about 48% of U.S. mil. [military] personnel who are alive in hands of Commies. Estimate based on % of U.S. names presented on propaganda bcasts. [broadcasts] pub. [published] lists & photos, ltrs recd by next of kin, interr [interrogation] of enemy POW & recovered U.S. personnel.

JCS msg emphasized that in attacking Commie POW data "you should proceed cautiously so as to avoid creating an emotional atmosphere here or a situation from which neither side can withdraw. Furthermore data on this subj. should not be released to press at this time. Also essential that data used by you (R) in disputing Commie contentions must be that from credible sources."

JCS also pointed out there was a possibility that UNC POWs in China & Manchuria may be classified as "internees" by Chinese Govt. This would be consistent with posit. of Chinese Govt that they are not participating in war.

CinCUNC in msg said he was checking intell. [intelligence] sources and will furnish further info as rapidly as it becomes available.

Libby despatched a ltr. to Lee San Jo [Lee Sang Cho] concerning UN POW's which should have been on Commie list. Ltr said at end "In summary, more than 1000 UN pers [personnel] and tens of thousands of soldiers of the republic of K who should be safe in your custody are not included in your POW lists. A complete, proper & satisfactory explanation is reqstd [requested] promptly as to status of the many thousands of ROK army pers unreported by you as POWs."

Dec. 22 (Sat): Summary staff officers meeting Item 3. A.M. Commies said interference in their internal affairs cannot be accepted. Claimed big concession on principle of rotation even though such rot. [rotation] would increase UN milt. [military] capabilities.

Commies presented reworded version their principle 5(b) as follows: "Outside demilt [demilitarized] zone at ports of entry in rear agreed upon by both sides and in places where violations of arm. [armistice] agreement have been rptd. [reported] to have occurred, representatives of neutral nations shall be entrusted to execute the supervision & inspection.''

UNC pointed out that since Commies agree that freedom of movement of non combatant nations insp. [inspection] teams on ground is not interference in internal affairs, aerial reconnaissance & photo flights by these same teams cannot be called interference in internal affairs. Explained that rotation would not increase UN milt capabilities but enemy's rehab. [rehabilitation] of airfields definitely would. UNC presented revised principle 4 reworded as follows: ''In order to ensure the stability of the milt arm. so as to facilitate the holding by both sides of a political conference of a higher level, both sides shall undertake not to increase the numerical quantities of milt personnel, combat aircraft, armored vehicles, weapons and ammo in K. after the arm agreement is signed and becomes effective. Any rotation of personnel shall be subject to on-the-spot supervision by the supervisory organ of non combatant nations and shall be carried out at the ports of entry in rear agreed upon by both sides. The rehab. of a limited no [number] of airfields for civil air operations at specific points shall be agreed, such rehabilitation shall not include extension of runways. No other air fields shall be rehabilitated or constructed.''

UNC stated that above concession was offered even though such rehab. increases greatly Commie milt capabilities.

Commies contended rotation would increase UN milt. capabilities. Claimed aerial obsvn. [observation] and airfield rehab a question of interference in internal affairs. Declined to discuss UNC revision of principle No 4 as it included rehab. of airfields. Commies rejected UN revision of principle 4; stated no progress possible unless UN gives up interference in internal affairs. Commies stated that since no further progress possible staff officers meetings should be terminated, sub dels reconvened. UNC agreed.

Sub dels on Item 3 met at 1400. UNC stated that through staff offs. at this am meeting it had made a proposal designed to solve main issue (airfields) now it was Commie turn to make a move. Hsieh said crucial question was that of his principle 4 (air fields) saying UNC proposal in staff meeting was no concession. Hsieh said quest [question] of air fields should not even be discussed[.] He said his stand on this point was an unshakeable one. UNC said realities must be faced, as in case of solution of agenda Item 2; asked Hsieh accept UNC proposal made by staff offs. for revision principle 4, Hsieh said two forces were in balance; his side would not accept interference in internal affairs. UNC said milt realities must govern solution; that the idea of preserving rough balance now existing was precisely why UNC insisted on prohibiting mil. [military] air fields rehab. Hsieh said UNC must give up interference in internal affairs. UNC said arm. would remove almost all of present interference in internal affairs, leaving only restrict. [restriction] on airfields. **Hsieh said UNC failed to see advantages gained by**

UNC as result of arm. UNC said it was Hsieh's turn to make a move[.] UNC said no progress possible until Hsieh gave up demand to increase his milt. capabilities during arm. Hsieh said UNC sought to deceive world. Hsieh asked if UNC meant that unless he accepted UNC revised principle on airfields, nothing further could be done. UNC said it was willing to listen to any new proposal. Hsieh said sole issue was interference in internal affairs and that there would be no progress as long as UNC insisted on this. Hsieh charged UNC was stalling. UNC recommended Hsieh study concession made in our proposal of today.

Item 4. Sub dels on Item 4 convened 1100[.] UNC opened requesting info as to when it might expect Commie reply to UNC ltr. on discrepancies in POW data. Lee replied that paras 1 & 2 were under study and that a reply would be given following study. Para 3 he said was untenable; one cannot ask from the other side a figure based upon numbers missing in action. Lee criticized POW data provided by UNC on grds. [grounds] that it was in English and that it omitted rank, serial nos. [numbers] & organizations. He stated that whereas the figures from Geneva up to June '51 amounted to 150,476 persons, the list provided by UNC was short by 44,259 names of which 34,786 are from regular army. He requested a satisfactory explanation. In closing he said that now that the data was exchanged there would be no pretext not to discuss the principle [*sic*] quest, the release of all POWs as soon as the arm. is signed.

    UNC introduced a concrete proposal for release & exchange immed [immediately] of all seriously sick or wounded POW under Arts 109 & 110 of Geneva Convention. UNC followed this with a statement referring to General R's letter to Kim & Peng on ICRC and explaining why these visits were considered an essential part of process of release & exchange of POWs.

    Lee said he would take UNC proposal on exchange now of sick & wounded under study and that his Comdrs were considering General R's letter. He reiterated the faults of UNC POW data, particularly the missing 3rd of the Geneva total. He then insisted that UNC had no further excuse for not discussing central problem, the release of all POW.

    UNC replied it would seek clarification of Commie proposal during p.m. session[.]

    P.M. Lee opened asking for a response to his sides proposal to release all POW after arm. signed or an explanation of disappearance of 44,000 POW. UNC replied as follows: Current list includes 132,474 broken down by nationality as follows: N.K. 95,531, Chinese 20,700, ROK 16,243. The last named were domiciled on 25 June '50 south of 38th parallel. They were for most part apprehended by UNC forces under suspicious or hostile circumstances[.] Some were guerillas, some fighting with N.K. army; some were taken into custody as a security measure, others thru the confusion of war. Last spring

UNC held much larger group of these nationals of the ROK. Screening was initiated to separate those who had voluntarily identified themselves with the enemy from those who were innocent of connection therewith or who had been impressed. In cases where these persons were found to be improperly detained as POW they were reclassified and dropped from POW lists. A rpt was forwarded to Geneva. The classification of some 37,000 has been corrected. 16,000 remain who while technically POWs are qualified to retain their status as citizens of the ROK. They are entitled upon release to repatriation within ROK. UNC has no intention of delivering them to other side. The only POWs subject to discussion under Agenda Item 4 are those who were bona fide residents of NK or China prior to 25 June '50. **Lee attempted to refute this statement largely on grds** [grounds] **that it was not a question of where these persons lived but of what side they were fighting for.** He came back to the theme of release all POW now. UNC started exploration of Commie principle of all for all exchange asking Lee to justify his proposal that UNC exchange during arm. 120,000 men in good condition for 11,000 in unknown cond. [condition] thus giving enemy advantage of 12 Divs [divisions]. Reference was made to double milt advantage obtained by reducing Commie POW list by impressment ROK soldiers into N.K. army. Lee evaded quest. of justifying the all for all exchange & repeated former arguments. Col Tsai took up refrain and made a long statement criticizing UNCs evading discussion of principle & disappearance of 44,259 POW. including 34,786 of N.K. regular army. **To say South Koreans were conscripted is to lie. There are large nos of South Koreans in** [N] **KPA to fight for a just cause. It is not a question of their origin. These reasons are unacceptable.**

UNC replied if it is a lie that SKs were impressed it is a lie which they told UNC upon their return. As to correction of classifications, it is a fait accompli. It was rptd to Geneva. If Commies not satisfied UNC invites them to send reps. [representatives] to Pusan area where they will be given opportunity to interview all these people[.] If any of POW wish to go to N.K. UNC will so permit them at proper time.

Comment: UNC by implication revealed its first posit. This will be confirmed tomorrow thru further exploration of all for all principle in light of milt. adv [advantage]. Intend proceed thereafter accord our HNC 611, initially pressing for return of impressed ROK soldiers.

Sent following msg to CinCUNC: "Subject is UNC del plan of action in event of an extension of time for negots [negotiations] beyond 27 Dec. is required. Because of proposed agreement on Item 2, we feel it undesirable for UNC to raise question of extension of 30 day period. We intend to continue along present planned lines in conducting negots. Should Commies introduce the question we will, of course, reluctantly agree to an extension of not to exceed 15 days. UNC del believes only alternative to course of action indicated in para 2 is to adopt a "take it or leave it" position, which of course it is unable to do at this time."

Dec. 23 (Sun): Sub dels on item 3 met at 1100. UNC led off with proposed revisions of 3 remaining disputed principles as follows:

"4. In order to insure the stability of the milt [military] armistice so as to facilitate the holding by both sides of a political conference of a higher level, both sides shall undertake not to increase the numerical quantities of milt. personnel, combat aircraft, armored vehicles, weapons and ammo [ammunition] in K after arm. [armistice] agreement is signed & becomes effective. Any rotation of personnel shall be subject to on the spot supervision by the supervisory organ of non-combat nations and shall be carried out at ports of entry in rear agreed upon by both sides.

"The rehab. [rehabilitation] of a limited no [number] of airfields for civil air ops. [operations] at specified points shall be agreed; such rehab shall not [be taken] to include extension of runways. No other airfields shall be rehabilitated or constructed.

"(5) Each side shall designate an equal no of members to form a milt arm. Com. [Commission] to be responsible for supervising the execution of the arm. agreement & for settling thru negots any violation of the arm. agreement. The functions of supervision & inspection as stipulated in the arm agreement shall be carried out in accord. with the following 3 provisions:

(a) Within the demilt]demilitarized] zone, the MAC utilizing joint teams directly dispatched by it shall be responsible.

(b) Outside the demilt zone, at the port of entry (including air ports) in the rear as agreed upon by both sides, and at places where violations of the arm. agreement have been reported to have occurred, a supervisory organ of reps [representatives] of non combatant nations shall be responsible. A request from the senior member of either side represented on the MAC for an investigation will be referred to the supervisory organ which must see that the inspection is conducted.

(c) Any member of the supervisory organ is authorized to communicate directly with any member of the MAC[.]

"(6) Each side agrees to invite non-combatant nations in the Korean war to send reps. to form a supervisory organ. The supervisory organ shall, when requested by the senior member of either side represented on the MAC, dispatch insp. [inspection] teams of non combatant nations to carry out the functions of supervision & inspection as stipulated in the arm. agreement. at ports of entry in the rear as agreed upon by both sides & at the places where violations of the arm. agreement have been rptd. to have occurred outside the demilt. zone. The supervisory organ shall rpt. on the results of supervision & inspection to the MAC. Both sides shall accord the insp. teams of non-c [combatant] nations full convenience of the main lines of comm. [communication] & transportation in performing above stated functions. In addition, such periodic aerial reconnaissance, observation & photo flights as are required will be performed by the non-c teams."

Hsieh asked what were UNC concessions in revised principles. UNC said its proposal was clear. Hsieh rptd [repeated] threadbare complaints about interference in internal affairs, saying he would absolutely not accept limitation of air fields. Hsieh also attacked aerial observation. Hsieh said if UNC did not drop the above 2 points, no progress could be made. UNC invited Hsieh to make an alternate proposal designed to break deadlock. Hsieh again rptd [repeated] objection to interference in internal affairs[.] Hsieh said if UNC would cancel last passages in principles 4 & 6 all other questions could be settled. UNC again asked for counter proposal. Hsieh attacked restrictions on airfields & said again so long as UNC insisted on such restrictions no progress could be made. UNC said progress depended on Hsieh facing facts as they exist today. After recess, Hsieh said question was whether UNC would give up concluding passages in principles 4 & 6. Hsieh said he saw no reason for inclusion of sub para C in UNC revised principle 5, or for last sentence of sub para (b) in same principle. UNC said these designed to avoid deadlocks in MAC. Hsieh asked if UNC would remove the two pts [points] at issue (airfields & aerial obs. [observation]). UNC said it was for a stable arm., that Hsieh delayed progress by opposing one. UNC said Hsieh should accept fact that UNC would keep on insisting on a safeguard against development of an air threat on other side during arm. Recessed 1600.

#4. Meeting on Item 4 convened 1100 [.] UNC devoted entire am to getting Commies on record with a definite answer to UNC proposal to exchange now the seriously sick & injured in accord with arts 109 & 110 Geneva Convention. This was not accomplished. All that could be established was that they would not agree to our request. In long and evasive responses to UNC questions on this subject Commies raised following points:

1. Commie 5 pt [point] proposal provides for early exchange of sick & wounded. Aim of UNC in raising this question now is to delay rather than expedite exchange of POW.

2. UNC seeks to retain POWs after cessation of hostilities.

3. Where are 44,259 missing persons? UNC admitted yesterday it had detained 37,000.

4. UNC statement that we do not know when arm. negots will be concluded is an expression of its policy towards arm.

5. Does UNC agree to release all POWs held by both sides after signing of arm. agreement?

6. UNC says 16,000 persons in it's [sic] POW camps which it will not release. This is untenable.

7. Regarding sick & wounded, UNC said yesterday that some might decline to return. What does that mean (UNC invited attention to para 3 Art 109 Geneva convention).

8. UNC is afraid to discuss principles because that would disclose its objectives to the world.

UNC refuted all above points.

A list of UNC POWs was handed Commies in which Korean names were written in K characters and chinese in Chinese characters. Recessed 1315.

Reconvened 1500. Lee opened in following vein: Now that POW lists are published the people of the world are anxious for an arm to get POW back. UNC should no longer oppose Commie principle of releasing all POW. The proposal includes early release of sick & injured.

UNC replied: Do Commies mean all POW they have or all they rpt [report]? Have they rptd. all POW camps? Are no prisoners sequestered outside Korea? Where are missing soldiers ROKA?

Lee replied: Perhaps UNC retains POW outside Korea but KPA never does it. The data submitted covers all POWs "held by our side at present." UNC says ROKA has 88,000 missing. UNC cannot ask for POW on this basis. Commies have 188,752 MIA [missing in action] **but dont ask for that many POWs.** It is Commie policy to educate POWs and release them directly at front. This explains why Commies now hold so few. It does not happen in war that one side takes a prisoner for each taken by other side. Thus they should not be released as chattel, one for one. Birth place is not a criterion in determining status of POW but rather in what army did they serve? Nationality is not the basis for release. "In list no civilians are mentioned but we are ready to release the civilians." Accordingly UNC cannot oppose release of 16,243 persons of SK origin because they are from NKPA. UNC implied that because there is a difference in number of POWs held, UNC will release part & retain part. This is intolerable. UNC implied that some POWs do not want to be repatriated because of certain political beliefs. We are not discussing politics beliefs but to what army did POW belong. UNC presented question of increase of milt capabilities. That argument is untenable. Firstly all POW should be released regardless of race, nationality or rank. Secondly NKPA opposes releasing some and retaining others because of difference in figures. Release at front must be considered. Thirdly, NKPA opposes retention [*sic*] of retaining some POW on grds [grounds] of so called political beliefs. Fourthly, NKPA opposes UNC stand of retaining 16,000 persons on grds they are SKs. Fifthly, NKPA opposes retention of POWs on grds of no increase in milt. forces.

UNC inquired if it understood correctly that all POW camps had been rptd. and that no POWs had been transported out of K. Genl Lee answered: "That is all the prison camps we have and accordingly we have none anywhere else."

UNC again inquired: "You said you have not transported any POW outside K, is that correct?" Lee: "None of the POWs is being held abroad—outside the country."

UNC: "You made some reference to release of civilians, reporters and those of other occupations. Will you explain further what you mean by that?"

Genl Lee: ["]That is no more than telling you about our policy toward releasing the POW. For instance, civilians——we are going to release civilians who are not actually POW after signing of arm. and it is, of course, a fact that there are among them also newspaper reporters["] (At this point Tsai spoke to Lee with some urgency.) Lee continued: "That is, at the arm. negots—this is a question which is not related to the quest. [question] of releasing POW. It is not a question within scope of discussions."

UNC asked how many civilians were involved.

Genl Lee: "That is a question not within scope of this meeting. That is something which can be made clear after armistice. Accordingly we hope with that explanation to go over to discussion of main issue."

UNC replied: "We are puzzled as to why you brought the question up when you do not consider it part of main issue." UNC went on. **Difficulty in determining number POW Commies hold arises from conflicting rpts. Commie GHQ releases say one thing, radio something else, and delegates another thing. Commie GHQ officially announced that from 25 June to 25 Dec '50 Commies captured 38,500 POW; from 26 Dec to 25 Mar '51, 26,863. In first half of war 65,363 UN POW. On basis of official figures for 1st 9 mos. alone Commies have failed to account for well over 50,000 POW. These are not MIA figures but official Commie Govt figures. Where are missing? Commies say they do not have as many POW as UNC because they release them at front, thus implying that they may have released in the neighborhood of 100,000. Fact is they have released 177. UNC still wants to know what happened to tens of thousands of POWs the Commies officially claimed to have taken.**

Lee replied: UNC underestimates no [number] released at front. UNC seeks an excuse. Majority of POW were released at front. Some died in air raids; some of illness. Some deserted. **There is also a big difference between figure UNC announced and made propaganda of and the number it rptd.**

UNC replied: UNC is not looking for an excuse but for tens of thousands of POW who must still be in Commie hands since you have given no explanation of their whereabouts. UNC is trying to find the men who will make the Commie proposal of all-for-all exchange honest, no matter how ridiculous it may be from milt standpoint. Even accepting what it understood from Genl Lees remarks, that official govt [government] figures used for broadcast purposes are not accurate, UNC still seeks info on missing men. UNC will pursue this quest. tomorrow.

Genl Lee denied inferring that the announcements of his govt were in any way unreliable and attacked unreliable UNC figures on shortage of 44,259 persons.

Recessed 1540 hrs.

Comment: Many indications as to posit [positions] Commies may be expected to take in subsequent discussion were elicited during this session. These portions are rptd fully above. It is requested that info this despatch not be released until such time as Commie posits are more fully developed.

Dec. 24 (Mon): Hsieh led off sub-del meeting on item 3 with statement that only one question remained on disagreement: Interference in internal affairs. Hsieh said UNC proposal of 23 Dec contained no concessions on this point and submitted following proposal:

"(4) In order to ensure the stability of the milt arm. [military armistice] so as to facilitate the holding by both sides of a political conference of a higher level, both sides undertake not to introduce into Korea any milt personnel, combat aircraft, armored vehicles, weapons & ammo after arm. is signed and becomes effective. Such rotation of milt personnel as within limit agreed upon by both sides shall be rptd [reported] to MAC so that the supervisory organ [organization] of neutral nations may be entrusted to conduct on-the-spot supervision & inspection, and shall be carried out at the ports of entry in the rear agreed upon by both sides.

"(5) Each side shall designate an equal no [number] of members to form a MAC to be responsible for supervising the implementation of the arm. agreement and for settling thru negots [negotiations] any violation of the arm. agreement. The functions of supervision and inspection as stipulated in the arm. agreement shall be carried out in accord with the following two provisions:

"a. Within the demilt [demilitarized] zone, the MAC utilizing joint teams directly dispatched by it shall be responsible.

"b. Both sides agree to invite neutral nations which have not participated in the K war, to send upon their consent an equal no. of reps [representatives] to form a supervisory organ to be entrusted by the MAC to be responsible for carrying out the functions of supervision and inspection as stipulated in para (4) and para (5) of this agreement. Upon the request by both sides or either side on the MAC for carrying out these functions of supervision & inspection, the supervisory organ of neutral nations shall immed [immediately] dispatch inspec [inspection] teams to carry out the functions as stipulated in the arm. agreement at ports of entry in the rear, and at places where violations of the arm. agreement have been reported to have occurred outside the demilt. zone, and shall report on the results to the MAC. In performing their above stated functions, the inspection teams of neutral nations shall be accorded full convenience by both sides over the main lines of communications and transportation as agreed upon by both sides."

UNC pointed out new Commie proposal contained no new points of substance, no concessions whatever. Hsieh said restrs [restrictions] on air fields & aerial obsvn [observation] were firmly opposed by his side. Hsieh said his side felt it was more thorough to use wording "no introduction" rather than "no increase" in respect to weapons & other material. UNC delivered lengthy statement condemning Hsiehs so called concessions and [pointing out] equity of UNC proposals. Hsieh claimed he had made huge concession on rotation in removing specific limit of 5,000 from his proposal.

After recess, Hsieh said he had nothing new to offer, desired UNC comments on his proposal of today. UNC said Hsieh's proposal deserved no more comment than already had been given, and asked if Hsieh considered he had made sincere effort to solve differences. Hsieh defended his proposal as best he could, laying stress on point that words "ports of entry" included all types of ports. Hsieh again attacked air field restriction and aerial observation. Hsieh said whether UNC wished to have an armistice depended entirely on UNC next step. UNC made statement pointing out that loss of some sovereignty was inevitable in arm. the only imp [important] question being whether restrictions were equally applied on both sides. All nations today forfeit a part of their sovereignty. Hsieh said preceding arguments were absurd, deserved no comment. Recessed 1545.

#4. UNC opened as follows: **In his final statement yesterday Genl Lee repudiated his earlier implication that the official pronouncements of his govt for bdcasting** [broadcasting] **were not reliable.** He asserted the official announcements were strictly accurate. Thus he confirms the accuracy of the figures concerning the no [number] of POWs. This means the Commies have failed to account for at least 50,000 POWs on the basis of official figures for the 1st 9 mos of the war. Yesterday Commies said that their total of MIA [missing in action] was 188,000[.] UNC holds at least 116,000 which is some 62%. On the other side of the ledger, the ROKA has a total of 88,000 persons officially rptd as missing in action. Commies rpt holding only 7,142 of these men, less than 9%. The U.S. has 11,500 men missing in action. Commies have only 3,198—only 28%. These % relationships are revealing. 9% of ROKA MIA and 28% of U.S. MIA are in Commie POW lists — — — against some 62% of Commie MIA in UNC custody. If it were assumed that Commies captured 62% of UNC MIA it would amt [amount] to about 62,000. In face of the 65,363 officially rptd by Commie GHQ for 1st 9 mos of hostilities or the 62,000, which is a reasonable estimate based on expected percentages, Commies now list only 11,559 for entire period of hostilities. UNC is convinced that there is no such actual discrepancy; that Commies are holding thousands of POW for whom they have failed to account. UNC requests accounting for a min [minimum] of some 50,000 POW missing from Commie list.

Lee made following pts. [points] in reply: (a) It is unscientific and unreasonable to expect a POW figure corresponding to the MIA figure. (b) This neglects conditions of war, the large scale movement on the front since a year ago Sept. (c) There is also the traditional policy of releasing POWs on the front. (d) Many POWs escaped. (e) Many POWs were released to go home. (f) This policy of releasing POW's, not detaining them, was right not wrong. These people have gone back home and are enjoying a comfortable life. (g) Dont ask us for POWs but congratulate them on their life at home. (h) Where are the 44,259 persons? (i) During hostilities and with propaganda about the atom bomb UNC kidnapped hundreds of thousands of civilians. They live a miserable humiliating life in the ROK. After the armistice proper arrangements must be made for them.

UNC replied as follows: **A reason you give for the extremely small list of POW is that many many POW were released at the front. As a matter of fact exactly 177 POW were so released**. As to escape surely Commies dont contend they mislaid some 50,000 in this manner? It is a safe estimate that not more than 100 at most escaped. With respect to the contention that use of MIA figures as a basis of calculation is unscientific and untenable, admittedly the % ratio is not definitive but it is indicative. With respect to the condition of combat, there were large scale movements on front after Sept '50. In general, and overall since then, Com [Communist] forces have been retiring and defending. It is characteristic of retrograde movement that MIA figure is relatively high. It is high because some soldiers who are KIA [killed in action] are listed as MIA since no one has knowledge that they were KIA and the rearward movement prevents recovery of the bodies. Thus MIA figure of retiring forces tends to be inflated, whereas the MIA figure of the pursuing force, which is able to find all its KIA is low. Thus, under overall combat conditions since Sept 1950, Commie MIA figure is inflated while UNC is low. Yet UNC hold min of 62% of those Commies carried as MIA while Commies admit to holding only 9% of ROKA MIA and only 28% of US MIA. Using most favorable figure, UNC maintains that there are upwards of 50,000 POWs admittedly taken by Commies for whom Commies have given no accounting.

Lee replied: UNC is trying to prove it holds many POWs whereas Commies hold small number. Figure published by Commie GHQ is correct. UNC has forgotten fact that in figure it published and in lists it submitted, many other persons are included. It forgets fact that should figure of kidnapped be included it would be an astonishing figure. UNC says people at front released only 177. This underestimate. If Commies had like UNC detailed all persons captured it might have 50,000 mentioned. They were allowed to go back home. These measures are perfectly right. This is a scheme to justify UNCs retaining part of the POW. **UNC is trying to retain thousands of POW because people of world know how our people are being massacred on account of their political beliefs**.

UNC replied: We are seeking simple factual accounting for people we believe you hold and have not rptd. Commies say they released them at front. But they released only 177. They say they let them go back home. But they are UN and ROK nationals and they are not at home. Where are they? Recessed at 1315.

Reconvened 1500. UNC opened as follows: UNC will suggest where many of the more than 50,000 unaccounted for may be found. Commies captured many thousands ROKA soldiers. Where are they now? Some who succeeded in getting back to UNC lines have told of having been forced to fight against their own army until they escaped.

Thousands of others are still serving in C [Communist] army. Commies say they are volunteers. UNC is by no means sure this is so, in the light of what those returned GIs have rptd. In any case these captured soldiers are and always have been in the status of POWs. They should never have been used for work directly connected with milt. ops. [operations], and Commies should have shielded them from the effects of milt action. Obviously these 2 rights, the right of all POWs not to participate in work contributing directly to the war, and the rt. [right] to be protected against milt. ops. precluded the use of POW to fight against their own army. The Commies have flagrantly impressed POWs and have further violated their rt. as individuals by striking their names from POW list. By this action Commies would deny POWs the rt. to be repatriated during an arm. Having used POW illegally during war they would continue to use them illegally during an arm. Quite apart from the effects of this practice upon individuals immed. concerned is its effect upon basis of exchange of the POWs. It constitutes a transparent and fraudulent attempt to get something for nothing. Having deliberately presented incomplete lists from which many thousands of names are missing the Commies come to the arm. conference and demand an all-for-all exchange of POW. When they include in list all POW they actually hold, then their proposal of an all-for-all exchange, while unsound from a milt point of view in a milt. arm would be at least honest.

Lee replied: History shows no cases where same no of POWs were taken by each side and same no released by each side. UNC insistence on wanting to know where POWs were released is no more than insistence to avoid solving the question. UNC says Commies should have about 20 times as many POWs as they actually have. The fact is that a large no of POWs who were released may be in UNC army or may be living at home. Many after they returned home joined guerillas and fought for people in UNC rear. By releasing many POWs Commies could destroy the anti popular reactionary army. Experience indicates it is successful. UNC considers release of POWs to be increase of milt. forces of other side, but Commies are not afraid of such thing. To release all POWs directly at front during hostilities is possible only for an army which fights for the people. UNC say Commies rob POWs of their rts. by making them join army. Not what Commies are doing but what other side is doing. It uses POWs as spies but many are captured. They can be seen in custody[.] After experience of past & in accord with their consistent policy, Commies consider release of POWs a must & they will do it in future. This is not only a consistent policy but a large no of POWs have been released.

Maybe it is hard to understand that release of POWs is a must at front. Only an army which was brought up among the people and which fights for the people can carry out the policy. Now what about a clear explanation of the 44,000 persons.

UNC replied: We are still trying to find out what happened to the thousands and thousands of POWs that have apparently vanished from face of earth. UNC will not stop until it has a satisfactory explanation of 50,000 POW. As to no of POWs released at front who might be in UNC army or at home, a grand total of 177. None are at home. **Commies say it is policy to educate POWs and release them en masse at front. They must educate them in a hell of a hurry if they turn them loose without getting their names. 177 have come back to UNC lines and unannounced thousands have vanished.** Balance of session was spent in clarifying UNC POW data with particular reference to a Commie figure of 44,259 the origin of which has not been clarified but which does include the approx 38,000 former ROK nationals who have been reclassified. Recessed 1723[.]

At close of morning session today Commies delivered answer to Genl R's letter to Kim & Peng in which he asked that [remainder of this sentence and all of the next emphasized by a bold line in left margin] ICRC be permitted to visit NK POW camps immed. The answer turned down R's request but stated that the ICRC would be given the permission when the arm was signed. Kim & Peng proposed however that joint visiting grps [groups] be formed of reps. of NK & Chinese Red Cross with ICRC to visit camps to assist in delivery of POW after arm is signed.

Commies also presented ltr from Genl Dean [Maj. Gen. William F. Dean, USA; then a POW of Communists] to his wife & requested delivery.

Dec. 25 (Tues): Upon opening of Sub Del meeting on Item 3 at 1100, UNC delivered statement how UNC visualized enemy utilizing increased air capability on rehabilitated air fields, and immunity from aerial observation. UNC stated it would not change its views on these points. Hsieh said UNC did not want peace, that UNC slandered his side. Hsieh said his posit [position] is no threat to UNC. UNC said if Hsieh had no intention to employ air capabilities why did he object to UNC proposal. Hsieh said his 24 Dec proposal was sufficient for a stable armistice. Hsieh said he had no authority to accept unreasonable demands of UNC. UNC asked if this meant Dec 23d proposal of UNC. Hsieh said he did not need to answer. UNC asked if Hsieh had anything new to offer. Hsieh replied no. Hsieh said it was up to UNC to take next step. UNC said it stood firm on its position. UNC asked if Hsieh did not intend to develop an air capability during armistice, why did he oppose UNC principles. Hsieh evaded. UNC proposed recess. Recessed 1210.

#4. Lee opened meeting on Item 4 with rambling statement which included the following points:
   a. Source of figure 44,000 which is number missing from UNC POW list will be given soon.

    b. Release all POW as soon as arm. is signed.

    c. UNC cannot continue to detain 16,000 POWs under pretext their birth-place is in South Korea, nor on the basis of their political beliefs. Neither can UNC retain them on basis of humanitarianism nor adherence to Geneva Conv.

    d. The 30 days expire very soon so a speedy agreement is necessary. UNC should agree to Commie principle.

UNC replied in following vein. While UNC is anxious to reach an agreement, Commies wasted 8 days denying UNC info necessary to make a start on the problem, info which should have been provided during hostilities. The info now furnished is far from complete. The problem is still to find what is meant by "all" in Commie proposal. UNC is not satisfied that all POWs held by Commies are listed. With reference to the 16,000 both Lee & Tsai have advanced the thesis that the place of a persons birth is of no importance in determining his status. With this UNC concurs. Lee & Tsai also said that a persons race or color are of no imp. in determining his status. With this UNC concurs. But they say that the question of status is a quest. of whether the individual belonged to the Peoples' Army or the Army of the Republic of Korea? This of course is nonsense with respect to the nationals of the ROK now held by UNC. **The only criterion for determining the status of these persons is whether they were or not residents of the ROK on 25 June '50. If they were they were of no concern whatsoever to the Commies. They are nationals of the ROK. They will not be included in any exchange of POW.**

Commies may for safety have taken some UNC POW outside of N.K. Info to this effect comes from several sources. POWs from Commie forces have indicated that they have seen or heard of fairly large nos. [numbers] of UNC POWs in China. Perhaps they are back in K; if not they should be rptd [reported] as being interned in China. Can Commies furnish a supplementary list of POWs who have just returned from China or who have been interned in China?

In summarizing, UNC has furnished full info on POWs. Through Geneva Commies have been given full POW info, even on nationals of ROK who might at any time have been identified with Commie forces. Thus Commies can assess whole prob. [problem] of release & exchange of POWs. UNC is still lacking vital info on upwards of 50,000 men who have been in Commie hands as POWs. UNC asks for factual accounting for these people.

Lee replied as follows: About 16,000 POWs. In this conference no political questions should be discussed. Accordingly it is not possible to discuss the nationalities or birthplaces. The key to the solution of the issue is "which Army one belongs to[.]" Political & admin. [administrative] questions should not be discussed. To do so will only make the conference more complicated. Question of 16,000 POWs is very clear. Again today UNC talked about ratio of missing

POW. It is not possible to capture equal no POW on each side. A full explanation has been given as to why the figure of the POW detained by Commies is smaller. It is because they release many POW at front. **This is policy. "As to question of having POW in China for their security, I will now give you a clear explanation. During hostilities we never transported any POW abroad and we have no POW abroad." Recessed 1228.**

Reconvened 1330. UNC opened in follow [following] vein. Commies oppose UNC stand on the 16000 ROK nationals saying we must not discuss political questions. From what [that?] they reasoned that UNC should hand over this grp. [group] of ROK nationals without further argument. A clear distinction must be made between a political & a legal question. UNC position with respect to these 16,000 nationalists is based on law of nations and fact that these people are citizens of ROK. As such they have certain rts. [rights]. Neither rts. nor responsibilities can be abrogated by accident of war. Commies say that nationality & birthplace have no bearing, that only criterion is which army did a man belong to. That did not go far enough. One criterion is which army did a man belong to first. Suppose an N.K. soldier was captured by UNC & he volunteered to fight on UNC side. Suppose further N.K. recaptured that man. Would N.K. under any circumstances hand him over as a POW? Or suppose a known citizen of the DPRK was found in the course of a battle in the ROK. Would Commies under any circumstances turn him over to UNC as a POW?

With respect to POW data. It is true the UNC POW list was deficient in certain details which are being corrected. But it did give an account of every POW the UNC ever held. It is also true that Commie list contained the name, serial no, unit designation & rank of POW; 11,559 of them. There is only one small omission: The names of upwards of 50,000 POW who according to official Commie govt rpts [government reports] have been in Commie hands. These POW were Communists' responsibility under laws of war. Who are they? Where are they? What has happened to them[?] If we can find these 50,000 men the Commie proposal regarding the release & exchange of POWs would begin to be honest. Without them it is a dishonest and fraudulent proposal. As to names & serial nos of these 50,000, obviously they would appear on list of MIA [missing in action] after deletion of POW rptd. There is an easier approach to finding a reasonable portion of these names. Give UNC a list of the ROKA soldiers impressed into DPRK army. **Before denying having impressed ROKA personnel listen to a few facts as rptd by former ROKA soldiers who escaped to UNC lines. Incidentally this conflicts with statement made this am that no POW ever went abroad.** Perhaps Commies get around this discrepancy by your assertion that these are "liberated privates." To UNC they still remain POWs.

In Sept & Oct of 1950 Commies moved bulk of captured ROKA personnel into Manchuria. After indoctrination these POW were assigned to the VI, VII

**& VIII Corps KPA. Some divisions in the Corps contained as high as 30%
former ROKA soldiers. These were compelled to fight against their own
forces in 1951.**

**From Dec 1950 thru Aug 1951 captured ROKA personnel were assigned to
the II, III & V Corps of the KPA. Two of the rgts.** [regiments] **were the 398th
Unit of the III KPA Corps and the 792nd Unit of the V KPA Corps.** Strength of
these rgts. varied between 1,200 & 1,300 depending on no of ROKA personnel
captured.

Captured ROKA personnel rec'd [received] 2 to 3 mos training & indoctrination, prior to assignment to a front line unit. These personnel were never assigned
to any one combat unit in large nos, to facilitate strict surveillance & prevent
desertion.

Though this procedure of impressing captured ROKA personnel may be
labeled "voluntary induction" or as "re-education & release" it is nothing more
or less than forced induction—impressment. It is a violation of the rts of the
individuals impressed. UNC therefore asks that they be restored to POW status
and that their names be added to POW lists. This will account for a considerable
block of the 50,000 persons for whom we are looking.

Lee replied. Nationality these people complicated question. Name of our
republic is DPRK. When it was born it was as a result of an election which
showed the will of the entire people of K. including S.K. Therefore such a
complicated political question should not be discussed. About inaccurate claim of
50,000 persons—most POWs were released. Dont worry about their safety. They
must have gone home long ago. No small no of them must be fighting in your rear
for liberation of S.K.

UNC summarized its arguments on the missing 50,000 and stated when it had
rec'd an honest forthright explanation it could discuss Commie proposal
intelligently. Recessed 1545[.]

Agenda Item 4.

Sub Del. Staff Study. (HNC 654)

Facts Bearing on Problem.

(1) Milt. Arm. [Military Armistice] will be of protracted duration[.]

(2) Probably several hundred thousand civ. [civilian] refugees from N.K. in
territory ROK.

(3) About 117,000 ROK civ in N.K. 1/5 were kidnapped.

(4) JCS have directed strong effort be made to secure repat. [repatriation] of a
list of named ROK civ. and (of lesser priority) to secure repat of other ROK's civ.
held by Commies. ROK govt specially desires return of 3,729 civs held by
Commies.

(5) In connection with subj [subject] of former ROKA soldiers who became
POW and were subsequently impressed into KPA Commies have defended prin.
[principle] of individual choice, though sensitive to it in conn. [connection] with
ROK nationals now held by UNC as POW.

(6) Commies have now accepted mod. [modified] prin. ICRC visits to POW camps after signing of arm.

Discussion.

(7) Consideration might now be given to an add. posit. [additional position] on release & exchange; i.e., *all for all exchange of POW and civs. with* no forced repat [repatriation]. Exchange of POWs to be conducted on one-for-one basis until one side has exchanged all POW held by it who desire repat. Other side shall thereafter repat all who express a desire to be repatriated. All POWs repatriated will be paroled to opposing force, such parole to carry with it the condition that the individual will not again bear arms against side releasing him. Dels of ICRC shall be permitted to interview all POWs in order to insure that choice is freely made. Named UN civs. will be repatriated at time of repat of POWs. All civs. who on 25 June 1950 were bonafide residents of ROK and DPRK respectively, and who are at time of signing of arm., in territory under control of other side shall be repatriated if they so desire. The repat. of civs. will be effected under supervision of ICRC.

8. An important issue in evaluating above proposed course of action is palatability to UN public of subjecting UN POW to screening process and insuring screening is bona fide[.]

9. Another imp issue is that of practicability of estab. [establishing] supervisory organ [organization] for repat of civilians.

After giving advtgs [advantages] & disadvtgs [disadvantages] of above proposed course of action our study concluded that position set forth in para [paragraph] 7 has intrinsic and negot. [negotiable] merit which outweighs its disadvtgs.

We recommended that:

(1) Position be approved for our employment when and if situation warrants.

(2) That a concept of the organ. [organizational] authority & function of supervisory body for use in conn with civ. repat be developed at GHQ & forwarded to delegation[.]

CinCUNC then submitted folg. comments on our staff study: His msg C 60192.

1. Your staff study excellent. Embodies most of desirable features of an agreement and position is in consonance with policies outlined by JCS. However urge you adopt folg revised version which differs from yours in only minor elements:

"All-for-all exchange of POWs & civs. with no forced repat in accord with fol procedure:

(1) POWs of both sides will be exchanged on 1 for 1 basis until one side or the other has completed delivery of those POWs who elect to return to control of opposing force.

(2) When one or the other side has exchanged all of POWs in its custody who desire to be repatriated, such side will proceed to exchange selected civilians named by other side on 1 for 1 basis, continuing until all named civs. who elect

repatriation are returned. (UNC would demand return of UN & ROK named civilians[.])

(3) The side which thereafter holds POWs shall repatriate all those who express a desire to be repatriated and shall then release from POW status all remaining POWs held by it. Those so repatriated will be paroled to opposing force.

(4) All civilians (other than selected named civilians listed in para 2 above) who, on 25 June '50, were bonafide residents of ROK and DPRK respectively and who are at time of signing of arm. in territory under control of other side, shall be repatriated if they so elect.

(5) In order to insure that choice of exchange is made without duress, dels of ICRC shall be permitted to interview all POWs and civs. of both sides at the point or points of exchange[.]

CinCUNC then gave reasons for not separating ROK & UN civs, chief of which was that ROK Govt might rightfully object to arbitrarily placing selected ROK Govt officials & key persons on a lower priority than UN named civilians[.] Also inclusion of selected ROK officials as an integral part of larger grp [group] of Korean civs & refugees would correspondingly decrease our chances of securing their release since this large grp. would be first to be dropped from consideration. Also they should be considered in same category as civs. deprived of liberty by a belligerent for milt. reasons, and entitled to be treated as POWs. Furthermore JCS place them (both groups) on higher priority than remaining internees & refugees.

We commented on CinCUNC's above despatch as follows in our HNC 675:

1. The Del fully concurs that every effort should be made to secure release of those ROK civs. in whom ROK Govt is particularly interested. However, in conn. with this particular posit the Del. recommends against any revision of para 7 HNC 654. for purpose of placing ROK civs. in class by themselves for folg. reasons:

a. Special effort in behalf of selected ROK civs. is inconsistent with principle under which all who desire it will be repatriated.

b. Although ROK Govt has now authorized presentation of selected list to the Commies, the expression of special interest in persons listed may only serve to identify many of them who might otherwise attract no special attention from Commies. More of them might be returned under a proposal for a genl [general] exchange of civs. than by a specific listing, partic. [particularly] if an effective organ can be established to supervise former. In such case, a list of selected ROK civs can be furnished the supervisory organ to enable it to inquire into non return of such selected civs.

c. Avoiding estab. of a special category of ROK civs during negots would avoid estab. of special category for N. Koreans[.]

d. Latest indications are that no ROK list will be avail. [available] from ROK Govt prior to 31 Dec at earliest.

2. Concur in view that interview of POWs be conducted at exchange pts [points] although it will entail considerable purposeless movement of POWs who do not wish to be repatriated. It appears impracticable however to move hundreds of thousands of civs. to exchange pts for sole purpose of indicating their desires on repatriation when many thous. [thousands] would subsequently be returned to refugee camps or to their scattered homes. Prelim. [preliminary] interviews at various locations in both N & S Korea would seem to be desirable so far as civilians are concerned.

3. In view above comment recommend folg revised points para 7 HNC 654 be approved: All for all exchange of POWs & civs with no forced repatriation.

a. Exchange of POWs to be conducted on 1 for 1 basis until one side has exchanged all POWs held by it who desire repat.

b. *The side which thereafter holds POWs shall repatriate all those who express a desire to be repatriated in a 1 for 1 exchange for foreign civs interned by other side, and for civs who on 25 June 1950 were bona fide residents of the territory under that sides control and who are, at the time of the signing of the arm. in territory under control of the other side, and who elect to be repatriated.*

c. *All POWs not electing repat shall be released from POW status.*

d. All POWs repatriated shall be paroled to the opposing force, such parole to carry with it the condition that the individual will not again bear arms against the side releasing him.

e. All remaining civs. who on 25 June 50, were bona fide residents of the ROK and DPRK respectively and who are, at the time of the signing of the arm. in territory under control of other side, shall be repatriated if they so elect.

f. *In order to insure that the choice re. repat. is made without duress, dels of ICRC shall be permitted to interview all POWs at points of exchange, and all civs. of either side who are at time of signing of the arm. in territory under control of other side.*

Changes are indicated by underlined parts[.]

4. Commies give no indication of voluntarily receding from their present proposal. for an all-for-all exchange of POWs[.] The sub del is now of opinion that once quest. of civs. is accepted for discussion under Agenda Item 4 there is considerable negotiatory and propaganda value to be obtained by taking initiative & formally proposing entire UNC posit. stated in para 3 above. While we realize this is deliberately introducing the overall civilian & refugee prob. which is not properly part of a Milt Arm.[,] discussion of it is inevitable in complying with JCS directive. We consider this package proposal constitutes a decisive step by UNC that Commies will have difficulty in countering both in negots and propaganda-wise. It will definitely put them on defensive and will eliminate negot difficulties and time involved in our trying to arrive at this posit. by gradual stages. Moreover a solution involving only named ROK civs. is a less desirable solution than one involving a general exchange of ROK civs. It appears desirable

therefore to press for a broader solution of a general exchange, initially, receding to the narrower solution of named ROK civs. only if the broader solution is rejected.

5. If you concur in paras 3 & 4 above it appears there may be two points which require JCS approval. 1st is the acceptability of submitting UNC POW in Commie hands to voluntary repat. 2nd is the inclusion in arm. terms of overall quest of civilian repat.

CinCUNC in his C 60352 replied to our HNC 675 above as follows:

1. Position which you propose in para 3 ref [reference] msg approved subj to folg:

a. The parole principle will apply only to those POWs released from POW status after a 1 for 1 exchange has been completed, and will not be applicable to those incl. [included] in 1 for 1 exchange.

b. If agreement is secured on the overall civilian-refugee quest. urge most strongly you introduce at earliest opportunity the lists of selected UN & ROK civilians which are available to you.

CinCFE then sent on our revised proposal to JCS with correction as given in in [*sic*] his C 60352, saying he had approved it for presentation to Commies when it appeared desirable.

Dec. 26 (Wed): Sub dels on Item 3 convened 1100[.] UNC asked if Hsieh now had authority to negotiate points in dispute. Hsieh said question was whether UNC continued to insist on interfering in internal affairs, saying his Dec 24 proposal was sufficient for armistice. UNC stated it had before, and once again, rejected Hsieh's proposal of Dec 24. Hsieh said UNC did not make efforts to reach an armistice. UNC made statement criticising [*sic*] Hsieh for refusing to negotiate, invited Hsieh to give more study to UNC proposal of Dec 23. Hsieh derided concession of UNC in respect to civil airfields. Hsieh returned to question of replenishment, objecting to it. Hsieh said provisions in his Dec 24 proposal met all security requirements of UNC. **Hsieh said UNC sought to prolong war, delayed progress, opposed peace, would not remove stumbling blocks (air fields, aerial observation).** UNC said Hsieh's statement included nothing new, nothing which had not previously been refuted. UNC said Hsieh dodged problem; asked why he wished to increase his offensive air capability; whether he had any serious proposal to make looking to solution of differences. Hsieh said first question was slander, distortion, no reply needed. Hsieh said second question was answered by UNC giving up demands on airfields, aerial observation. UNC said it awaited new proposal from Hsieh. Hsieh said up to UNC to break deadlock. Recessed 1200.

Comments: Commies have not brought up subject of the expiration of deadline. It is possible they may wish to sit it out. UNC Del. will not raise question unless brought up by Commies. Tomorrow will present revised UNC principles 4, 5, 6. We have reached a stage where only time & patience will tell.

#4. Sub Dels on Item 4 met at 1100. UNC pressed for an accounting on upwards of 50,000 men who were once in Commie hands as POW's, and who are not on POW list. Asserted that until missing personnel **were accounted for the Commie proposal of all-for-all exchange is fraudulent and dishonest.** It is a proposal to release all POW's except 50,000, to exchange 130,000 for 12,000 while sequestering 50,000.

General Lee was ill and left conference on two occasions. Tsai attempted to refute UNC charges using counter-charges and arguments which have all been outlined in previous reports. In view Lee's illness UNC suggested a recess until pm or tomorrow if other side preferred. Tsai proposed 1100 tomorrow. Near end of session a ltr was received at conference by the Commies and delivered to UNC along with voluminous enclosures. This will be forwarded as soon as it can be translated. Recessed 1310.

Dec. 27 (Thurs): Sub Del Item 3 met at 1100. **Hsieh led off with statement charging UNC delaying progress.** Hsieh reviewed arguments past 30 days. UNC stated it still awaited a serious proposal. UNC asked why Hsieh was unwilling to agree to limitation of airfields, in view his assertion that his side did not intend to threaten UNC with increased air capability. Hsieh said he had already answered quest. [question]. UNC recommended recess until tomorrow. Hsieh said if UNC needed more time, that was up to UNC. UNC pressed inquiry as to why Hsieh refused to agree in writing with what he asserted verbally in conference. Hsieh evaded and accused UNC of delaying.

After recess, UNC again asked why Hsieh was unwilling to put in writing his assertion that his side did not intend to increase its milt air capabilities during armistice. Hsieh said his princ. [principle] 4 answered quest. pointing out prohibition against introduction of combat aircraft into Korea. UNC said this did not answer question. UNC asked if Hsieh considered milt. airfields were part of milt. capabilities. Hsieh evaded. UNC said if Hsieh refused to discuss the prime dispute, recess until tomorrow was in order. Recessed 1355. New UNC proposal not presented today due to inopportune atmosphere of negotiatory situation. Intend to present this proposal tomorrow, if opportune.

#4. Sub Del Item 4 met 1100. Lee opened with long statement which included following points: (1) UNC responsible for lack of agreement on Item 4 within 30 days after agreement on Item 2. (2) Commies broke deadlock by giving POW data although this not necessary to agree on principle. (3) On pretext that UNC MIA exceeds POW held by Commies, UNC refuses to release & repatriate all P.O.W. (4) *Commie policy of release at front results in smaller POW list.* (4) [*sic*] UNC submitted 1000 names for further info. In large part this has been provided. Further investigation being made. (5) UNC should explain discrepancy of 1456 between recap & names submitted on its list[.] (6) ICRC shows 44,205 POW who cannot be found on 18 Dec data. (7) Personnel should be released on basis of army they belonged to, not on basis of residence[.] (8) It is intolerable that UNC openly says it will retain 37,000 on 18 Dec list. (9) In order to speed release all POW original proposal is resubmitted.

UNC replied as follows: As to delay on Item 4 Commies refused for 2 weeks to form a sub-commit [committee] on this item. Then they delayed 8 days in providing data nec. [necessary] to discuss item. With respect to the reply on 1000 names, Commies rptd 726 killed, died, escaped or released. UNC requests (1) Names of POWs who were allegedly killed; the date on which each POW was killed; where he was killed and where he is buried. (2) The data [date] on which POW allegedly escaped; the place of internment from which he escaped. (3) The date and place where each POW was released. (4) The names of POW who allegedly died of disease; the date, and place, and burial place.

As a general comment on Commie principle just reintroduced, it proposes not the release of all POWs as claimed, but the release of all POWs less approx 50,000 who remain unaccounted for. Until the accounting is made the proposal is not a suitable basis for discussion of exchange of POWs[.]

Libby then took Lee to account for his slurring reference to "Syngman Rhees Govt." Lee made feeble reply. He also said neither KPA nor CPV have any POW abroad.

Thruout pm session UNC pressed for an accounting of "50,000 men" who were at one time prisoners of Commies. in conjunction with thesis that, in the absence of such an accounting, the Commie proposal of an all-for-all exchange is not an honest effort to reach a solution to agenda Item 4.

Sent following msg to CinCUNC for his consideration.

1. (a) Item 4 sub Del feels that possibilities of its present stand of confining discussions solely to insisting on full accounting for missing 50,000 is about exhausted, and that to retain initiative we must move on to additional pts. [points] very soon. As [An?] initial step toward new posit. [position] would be to raise question of civilians.

b. We feel best way to open civilian quest and to explore Commie attitude towards discussing civilians under Item 4, and at same time permit us to keep discussion within limits we can control, is to introduce the question of non-Korean UN civilians as a separate entity. This has added advantage of presenting submergence of this grp. [group] into overall Korean civilian repatriation problem, from which it should in our view be clearly distinguished at all times. While delegation recognizes that some elements in Korea may accuse

UNC of favoritism, it is not believed that ROK govt itself will resort to such measures.

(c) The time element further militates against simultaneous introduction of UN and selected ROK lists. A firm ROK list is not yet available and we have no firm commitment as to when it will be.

(d) It also appears most probable that while list, when rec'd [received], will contain a number of govt officials, it will be comprised in the main of a list of persons whose relatives are sufficiently influential to induce ROK govt. to make a special effort to recover them. Undue emphasis by UNC & ROK govt on such a list may ultimately react unfavorably on both.

(e) Furthermore, premature disclosure of a named ROK list in advance of any agreement in principle concerning exchange of civilians may serve to alert Commies concerning the special interest of ROK govt in persons named and thereby increase difficulty of obtaining their ultimate release.

2. If foregoing considerations lead you to conclude that UN list may be presented separately as first step in introducing the issue of including civilians in POW exchange, the delegation requests authority to take this step tomorrow pm. should it appear timely[.] The introduction of a name list of ROK civilians could then be undertaken later if developments warrant[.]

3. As we see it, alternative to above is to sit tight.

CinCUNC answered in folg vein:

(1) Concurred in our proposal as expressed in para 1 above.

(2) Because of quest. [questionable] attitude of ROK Govt in support of our efforts to secure successful arm [armistice], R felt every effort should be made to secure release of ROK civilians in whom ROK govt is particularly interested.

(3.) CinCUNC believed folg course of action desirable in order to prevent a stalemate in Item 4 which could cause unfavorable public reaction:

(a) Introduction of the ques. of release of non-Korean civs. [civilians], not as separate entity, but as an initial step. Stress that many of these persons are missionaries and members religious organs, none of whom posed threat to mil. scty. [security] of Commie Forces and who in fact were interned only as an accident of war. Others reps [representatives] foreign nations, correspondents, and some were in area of invading Commie forces only because personal interests which had no connection with political or mil. sit. [situation] existing in Korea. Their release can neither help nor hinder cause of either side militarily. Be careful with press release.

b. Depending on Commie reaction, the matter of the selected ROK civs. could be brought up as a matter of similar interest, completely divorced from overall civ. internee & refugee prob. [problem].

(c) To plan rebuttal determine from Muccio what key NK. and other Commies ROK is holding.

(d) Because of interest of JCS there is every reason to apply max [maximum] pressure to accomplish release both categories as part of POW exchange. Timing of introducing named ROK civ ques left to your discretion. Must be closely allied to, and fol as soon as pract. [practical] the opening of UN civ. ques.

Dec. 28 (Fri): Sub Del [delegation] on Item 3 met at 1100. UNC opened meeting by asking for answers to questions posed yesterday. Hsieh evaded quests, [questions], stated interference in internal affairs and aerial reconn. [reconnaissance] by anybody will not be tolerated; further stated replenishment is absolutely impermissible. UNC asked why Commies feared aerial observation by non-combat nations. Hsieh evaded question.

UNC pointed out Commie insincerity by insistence on building up milt. capabilities during arm. [armistice]. Cited UNC efforts to expedite negots. Hsieh claimed UNC insistence on simultaneous discussion of Items 3 & 4 was only to further delay negots. Hsieh claimed they have been fighting in defense of peace and will firmly carry on their struggle until peace is achieved.

UNC pressed again in pm session for answers, Commies again dodged & evaded questions claiming UNC assuming role of victor, trying to force them to discuss quests. of internal affairs. Claimed UNC delaying negots. UNC stated since Commies practicing tactics of evasion no progress could be made, and since they had nothing new to offer UNC suggested recess until 1100 tomorrow.

New UNC proposal not presented due to inopportune atmosphere. Intend to continue to press for answers to UNC quests & present new proposal if propitious at next meeting tomorrow.

#4. Sub Dels on Item 4 convened at 1100. UNC cont'd to press for an accounting of missing POWs. The only development of possible significance was one statement from Genl Lee: "About all the personnel of the POWs whom we have captured in the past we are now putting the data in order and checking the data." In view of this the UNC decided to postpone raising the quest. of the exchange of civilians under the release & exchange of POWs. Recessed 1345.

Dec. 29 (Sat): Sub Del on Item 3 report follows:
Morning session UNC asked for answers to quest. [questions] of past 2 days. Hsieh claimed answers given many times. UNC stated Commies refuse to make any effort to solve differences while UNC has agreed to rehab. [rehabilitation] of limited no [number] airfields for civil air ops [operations]. Thus any pretext of interference in internal affairs eliminated. Claimed Commies intend increase mil. [military] air capabilities preventing stable and effective armistice. Accused Commies of hiding this intent under false term "interference in internal affairs," claimed Commies attempting to deceive people of world. **Hsieh refuted UN remarks, made long statement accusing UN of attempting to gain control of all of Korea thru aerial observation during arm** [armistice]. UNC pointed out that

proposal applies equally to both sides, asked enemy to adopt sincere attitude thus enable both sides to reach agreement on existing issues. Hsieh said Commies would accept no unreasonable demands and would continue to defend their sovereign rts [rights]. Asked UN to accept their fair and reasonable proposal of Dec 24. UNC asked for any serious effort which would solve existing differences. Commies stated they had made all efforts, next step up to UN. UN asked if enemy intended to build up air capabilities during arm. Hsieh avoided quest.

P.M. Session. Commies evade & ignore issues remaining & refuse to answer quests. Stated many details left to be worked out after principles agreed to, including agreement on non-combatant nations, supervisory organ [organization], & observer teams; functions rights and support of MAC and supervisory organ; agreement on ports of entry; islands to be controlled by each side; and agreement on ways & means of recovery of war dead. UNC submitted new proposal revising principles 4, 5 & 6; claimed great concession made already on airfields. Reiterated previous concessions on islands; single directing authority, non-combatant inspection teams, rehab. of limited no of airfields for civil air ops. *UNC proposed giving up safeguard of aerial observation only if Commies willing to agree to 3 principles submitted without substantive change.* Commies requested 15 min recess to study new proposal.

b [*sic*]. Hsieh asked 3 quests: (1) UNC interpretation of "reinforcing." Would exchange of weapons on piece-for-piece basis still be permitted? (2) Was it intentional UNC did not take out last passage of principle 4, which refers to rehab. of airfields[?] (3) Would number of neutral nations to be invited be odd or even?

c. UNC answers were as follows: (1) Answer has been given in previous sessions (2) Yes (3) That is a detail; we are now talking about principles.

(d) Hsieh agreed 3 revised principles a step forward but a main stumbling block is still UNC desire to interfere in their internal affairs. Hsieh suggested recess until 1100 30 Dec for more complete study of UNC proposal.

Comment: UNC now at presently authorized final posit [position] and will adopt firm stand on this position beginning tomorrow.

#4. Sub Del on Item 4 pressed all day for data on POWs as yet unaccounted for. Near close of session Lee indicated that Commies would, in exchange for add. [additional] data from UNC to constitute a full rpt [report] on all POWs held thruout war, provide similar data. He stated it would not mean that there would be any increasé in the numbers of POWs now held which has been accurately reported. He indicated further that the new data would be incomplete because of the absence of records and due to their destruction in war. No other significant development[.]

Comment: Tomorrow UNC will attempt to get agreement to restoration of former ROKA soldiers to POW status as an end in itself and as a means of getting a clearer statement from the Commies on individual self-determination in connection with the incorporation of these former POWs into the NKPA. Success in the former is not anticipated but the latter will support a posit. which UNC intends to advance later. If appropriate the question of exchange of UN civilians under POW exchange will be raised and, depending on Commie reaction, possibly the quest of ROK civilians[.]

U.N.C. Revised 4, 5 & 6 Principles (Agenda I.3)

4. In order to insure the stability of the Mil. Arm. so as to facilitate a peaceful settlement by action at a political level, both sides undertake not to introduce into Korea any reinforcing mil. personnel, combat aircraft, armored vehicles, weapons and ammo after the arm. agreement is signed and becomes effective. Such rotation of mil. personnel as within the limit agreed upon by both sides shall be rptd. to the MAC so that the supervisory organ of non-combatant nations may be entrusted to conduct on-the-spot supervision and insp. [inspection], which shall be carried out at ports of entry in the rear agreed upon by both sides.

The rehabilitation of a limited no of airfields for civil air ops. at specified points shall be agreed; such rehab. shall not include extension of runways. No other airfields shall be rehabilitated or constructed.

5. Each side shall designate an equal no of members to form a MAC to be responsible for supervising the implementation of the arm. agreement and for settling thru negots any violations of the arm agreement. The functions of supervision & inspec. as stipulated in the arm. agreement shall be carried out in accord. with following two provisions:

a. Within the demilt [demilitarized] zone, the MAC utilizing joint teams directly dispatched by it shall be responsible[.]

b. Outside the demilt zone, at ports of entry in rear as agreed upon by both sides and at the places where violations of the arm. have been rptd. to have occurred, a supervisory organ of reps. [representatives] of non-combatant nations shall be entrusted to be responsible. Upon the request to the supervisory organ of non-c [non-combatant] nations of both sides or either side of the MAC for investigation of a violation of the arm. agreement, the supervisory organ of non-c nations shall carry out the inspection.

6. Both sides agree to invite nations acceptable to both sides which have not participated in the K war, to send, upon their consent, an equal no. of reps. to form a supervisory organ to be entrusted by the MAC to be responsible for carrying out the functions of supervision and inspec. as stipulated in paras 4 & 5 of this proposal. Upon request by both sides or either side on the MAC for carrying out these functions, the supervisory organ of non-c nations shall dispatch immed. [immediately] inspec. teams to carry out the functions of supervision & inspec. as stipulated in the arm. agreement at ports of entry in the rear as agreed upon by both sides, and at places where violations of the arm. agreement have been rptd to have occurred outside the demilt zone, and shall

report on the results of supervision & inspec. to the MAC. In performing their above-stated functions, the inspec teams of noncombatant nations shall be accorded full convenience by both sides over the main lines of comm. [communication] & transportation as agreed upon by both sides.

Dec. 30 (Sun): During am session on Agenda Item 3, UNC amplified answers to questions Hsieh asked previous pm. Stated "no reinforcing" was a limiting term, permits normal resupply and replacement but no increase, does not include replacement of articles damaged during period of hostilities. UNC explained that number of non-c [non-combatant] nations invited is immaterial but that total number of individuals invited by each side on supervisory organ. [organization] & observn teams will be same. Hsieh asked, regarding principle 4, what is meant by "action at a political level." UNC explained that wording was more expressive than Commie wording of proposal and does not change meaning of sentence. Commies commented on UNC revised proposal. *Stated UNC had expressed agreement to holding of a political conference of a higher level during discussions on Agenda Item 2.* Asked that wording of first sentence of principle 4 not be changed if UNC new version had no intention of changing meaning. Hsieh accused UNC of intent to continue to introduce all types of weapons while Commies insist on no introduction of any weapons. Stated Commies principle of no introduction necessary for effective armistice. Hsieh claimed there should be no increase of mil. forces in Korea and no replenishment. Insisted that last para. of UNC principle 4 regarding airfields was stumbling block, and a demand that absolutely cannot be accepted. Explained measures Commies had taken to dispel UNC fear of growing Commie air power. First: Enemy agreement on no introduction of combat aircraft. 2nd: Provision for inspection of violations by neutral teams in rear. Hsieh claimed Commies sincere, desired stable and effective armistice. Admitted that UNC proposal is a step forward but stated that differences still exist. Asked for UNC opinion for reaching settlement on these differences. UNC suggested that Commies study UNC proposal and amplifying statements, claimed enemy had offered nothing toward solution of remaining differences. Hsieh stated he had pointed out differences. Agreed that no difference exists on principle 4 if UNC agrees to adopt Commie wording of 24 Dec. Insisted that Commie stand on interference in internal affairs is unshakeable. Advised UNC to reconsider if solution is to be reached on remaining issues. UNC stated its proposal very clear and next effort up to Commies[.] UNC suggested recess until 31 Dec unless they had anything to offer. Hsieh stated that differences still exist in 4th principle and that 2nd para. of principle is absolutely unacceptable. Commies agreed to recess until 1100 31 Dec.

#4. During am session on Item 4 UNC concentrated remarks on subject of former ROKA soldiers who became POWs and subsequently were incorporated in KPA. *Lee committed himself further on the principle of individual self determination but gave no indications that Commies could be persuaded to restore this class of personnel to POW status.*

In pm session UNC raised quest [question] of foreign civilians interned by the Commies and requested they be exchanged with the POWs. Lee replied that they would be released after the arm. was signed, but asserted that the matter was beyond the scope of the arm. talks. UNC accepted this assurance that this personnel would be released and stated that this should be stipulated in the arm. agreement. Lee did not directly oppose this, though he did not give his assent. UNC went on to say that it intended to bring up the problem of other civilians, a problem to which Lee had adverted in several occasions during talks. *Lee attempted to extricate himself from any responsibility for* having introduced this subject, saying his remarks had been directed to the fate of the many thousand NK refugees now in ROK. He did not express himself fully on the discussion of civilians under Agenda Item 4. UNC closed saying it saw no reason why civilians should not be permitted to return to their homes during the arm. Recessed.

Comment: After further discussion of the civ. [civilian] problem tomorrow UNC will formally propose its recently approved posit. on the basis for the release and exchange of POWs if time is judged ripe. Since the position embodies the principle of individual self determination regarding repatriation which we feel will be repugnant to the Commies, the proposal will not be introduced at this time unless the Commies have agreed in principle that the repat [repatriation] of civs. be permitted under the arm. agreement.

Dec. 31 (Mon): Sub-del Item 3 convened 1100.

UNC explained that rewording of 1st sentence of principle 4 sets forth true objective—peaceful settlement—while previous wording only indicated conference would be held. UNC further explained meaning of "no reinforcing" as no increase in numerical quantities, only replacement of weapons and articles which become unserviceable during armistice. Stated piece for piece basis for exchange is unshakeable stand. Commies listed existing disagreements: (1) Holding of political conference (2) Replenishment (3) Interference in internal affairs. Asserted that UNC wording was hollow and aimed at dodging issue of political conference. Maintained that the method as well as the objective should be included in principle. Hsieh stated that UNC interpretation of replenishment **only indicated intent to increase mil. weapons and equipment. Asserted that UNC attempts to maintain "state of war["] in Korea to facilitate carrying out war policy thruout world.** Hsieh reiterated previous stand that UNC interference in internal affairs main stumbling block and that Commie position of "no interference["] is firm. UNC charged Commies with insincerity towards effective armistice[.] Asserted that enemy intent is to develop mil. air capability during armistice. Charged that Commie insistence on unlimited airfield rehab [rehabilitation] &

constr. [construction] must be given up if progress is to be made. Col Chang asserted that UNC had admitted that restriction on airfields is interference in internal affairs. Reiterated stand that no combat aircraft be introduced into Korea. Stated Commies may or may not rehabilitate airfields; asserted that this subject is a matter of sovereign rights. Chang said that if either side began to develop airfields on a large scale the other side would immediately know of this fact thru inspec. [inspection] teams. Maintained that Commies are more concerned over their sovereign rights than airfields. Chang stated no concession could be made which involved the surrender of sovereign rts. Charged UNC with placing obstructions in way of progress. Claimed that subject of airfields had nothing to do with present conference for a mil. arm. Hsieh charged UNC with delaying negots. by refusal to remove main stumbling block which is UNC's unreasonable demand to restrict airfields.

#4. Sub-del Item 4 met 1100. **An early remark by Gen Lee which appeared to be a repudiation of his previous agreement to provide data on all POWs held at any time touched off a discussion which occupied most of day.** At its conclusion, it was not entirely clear as to whether or not he would provide the required data. Following this sequence Lee charged UNC with evading the discussion of his proposal to release all POW in the custody of both sides following the signing of the arm. UNC replied that it had been discussing the principle for days on basis of the data which had been exchanged; that on this basis the proposal was dishonest and inequitable. It asserted that it was exploring all avenues in an effort to find a means of making the proposal more acceptable. Lee disregarded several opportunities which were offered him to discuss the question of civilians in response to the trial balloon sent up yesterday by UNC. Recessed 1630.

Comment: Pointed lack of response to UNC trial balloon on civilians led sub-dels. to conclusion that further advance in this direction today would be premature. The subject will be raised again tomorrow. If Commies indicate agreement in principle that civilians be permitted to return to their former homes under the arm. UNC proposal on release and exchange will be introduced.

During the am I made a telecast for the Ed Murrow show.

Jan. 1 [1952] (Tues): Sub del meeting Item 3 convened at 1100. Hsieh asserted that UNC proposal of Dec 29 provided no solution to 3 points of disagreement: (1) Political conference, (2) Replenishment (3) Interference in internal affairs. Stated 3rd point is main stumbling block and that Commies absolutely would not agree to such unreasonable demands. Hsieh charged UNC intentionally raised question of restriction of airfields which has no place in arm negotiations. Stated delay in progress of conference resulted mainly from this unreasonable demand although other points of lesser importance also exist. UNC asked enemy if more time needed to study UNC proposal and explanatory statements. Hsieh reiterated that question of restriction of airfields cannot be settled, therefore UNC delaying negots [negotiations] by insisting on unreasonable demands. Stated Commies had nothing new to offer. Said question is whether UNC will take away unreasonable demands[.] UNC asked: Since enemy has nothing new to offer when should sub-del recess. Hsieh reiterated that question was not to offer something new but rather to cancel something old. UNC charged that Commies delaying tactics wasting time. Hsieh claimed UNC too optimistic over old proposal. stated as this is 1st day of New Year we should divest ourselves of old things, not offer new things. UNC stated Commies objections to UNC fair & reasonable proposal very old and should be divested. Hsieh stated Commie stand firm and unshakeable, absolutely would not accept UNC 2nd para. of 4th principle (airfield restriction)[.] Reiterated that this para must be deleted. UNC stated Hsieh would grow old sitting at this table if he expected UNC to remove any of the parts of principle 4. UNC suggested sub-dels recess and reconvene when enemy has something new to offer. Commies again charged UNC with wasting time by bringing up a question which both sides were unable to settle. Stated would absolutely not permit interference in internal affairs. Agreed to reconvene at 1100 2 Jan. '52. Asked UNC to seriously consider Commies firm & unshakeable stand. UNC asked enemy to study proposal and explanatory remarks.

#4. In meeting on Item 4 Lee gave a clearer statement that Commies will make an effort to provide data on all POWs taken during entire war. Under guise of seeking a more equitable exchange ratio UNC then raised question of including ROK civilians now in NK under POW exchange. As expected Lee raised matter of NK civilians in ROK. UNC expressed view that there should be a provision in arm. [armistice] agreement to permit civilians to return to their homes since acquiesence of mil. [military] authorities would be needed. Lee showed great interest but stated this was a complex problem which required mature consideration and requested a recess until tomorrow. Recessed 1215.

Comment: Unless his consultation with higher authority changes the attitude toward the civilian question indicated by Lee today[,] the stage is set for the introduction of the UNC proposal. It is anticipated that it will be introduced tomorrow.

Jan. 2 (Wed): Upon convening of sub-del on item 3, UNC charged Commies hiding real intent behind false cloak. Pointed out that both sides already have generally agreed to some abridgment of sovereign rights regarding no increase of mil. forces and non-combatant insp. [inspection] teams. Therefore Commie arguments that they could accept no provision involving sovereign rts. [rights] illogical and contradictory. Stated further argument will only delay negots. Charged Commies with intent to build up mil. air capabilities during armistice. Hsieh asserted UNC delaying conference[.] Stated only way to insure against resumption of hostilities is to prohibit introduction of any foreign forces into Korea. *Stated Commies consistent stand is withdrawal of all foreign troops.* Maintained that Commie proposal is sound with complete guarantees for a stable and effective arm. [armistice] and does not interfere with sovereign rts. Said UNC can find no objection to Commie proposal which all the people of the world recognize as fair and reasonable. Claimed UNC has raised point which should not even be discussed at arm. negots. (air field restrictions). Hsieh stated he absolutely would not agree to this point. UNC charged Commies with stalling and delaying negots. Pointed out concessions made (1) aerial observation (2) islands (3) single directing authority for arm. (4) mil. insp. teams (5) airfields for civil air ops. [operations]. Stated UNC will make no further concessions and has nothing further to propose. Said it is clearly and unequivocally up to enemy if progress is to be made[.] Hsieh stated that Commies will continue to oppose UNC unreasonable demands. Said UNC has made no concessions. Claimed both sides must make efforts to solve existing differences[.] UNC asked when would enemy be prepared to make new effort. Hsieh stated had made effort. Claimed UNC had not removed unreasonable demands. Stated as UNC had no new efforts agreed to recess until 1100 3 Jan.

#4. Lee's opening statement accepted the principle that provision should be made in the arm. agreement to permit civs. [civilians] to return to their homes during the arm. On basis of this indication that Commies could not logically oppose UNC posit. [position] on release & exchange of POWs on grounds that it went beyond scope of mil. arm. or of Item 4, UNC del. made following statement introducing a new proposal:

"Certain areas of agreement and certain differences of opinion have emerged from our exchange of views on the POW prob. [problem] during period it has been under discussion. Among them are these:

"First, your side wants all the POWs to be released following the signing of the arm. UNC agrees that this should be done, under an equitable formula.

"Second, your side has incorporated into your army many thousands of our soldiers who fell into your hands as POW's. From your standpoint your action in this connection was in accord. with your traditional policy towards POWs. **According to you, the POWs were "reeducated and released at the front." The fact that practically all of them later reappeared in your own army is explained away by the alleged fact that they exercised their own volition in joining it.**

"From our standpoint, the wholesale incorporation of POWs into your army is contrary to the rules of warfare and a violation of the rights of the men concerned since there is reasonable doubt that the prisoners were free from duress in making this decision. The rules of warfare and the rts of the individual under those rules require that you refrain from using POWs in work connected with mil ops. & that you shelter the POWs. from the effect of mil ops. Manifestly, these requirements are not met by incorporating POWs into your own mil. forces. It is the view of the UNC that all former soldiers of the ROKA who were incorporated into your army through your mechanism of impressment should be returned to their status as POWs[.]

"Moreover, since the outbreak of hostilities on 25 June 50 your side has conscripted many civilian nationals of the ROK and accepted a certain no [number] of deserters from the ROKA into your army. Both of these practices are consistent with your doctrines of warfare. But both are inconsistent with ours. It is our view that deserters just as involuntary captives should be accorded a POW status. The fact that it was with his consent that you placed a deserter from our forces in your army does not change our view that he should now, for the purpose of POW exchange, be placed in a POW status.

"Third, your side takes the position that all POWs should be returned to the side with which they were identified when they were captured. The UNC on the other hand takes the view that all bona fide residents of the ROK as of 25 June 1950 are nationals of that state. From that fact they derive certain rights and have certain responsibilities which are not set aside by the accident of war. Consequently the disposition of persons of this category who have been taken into custody by the UNC while fighting against the ROK is a matter for our side alone to determine. It is of no concern whatever to your side.

"Fourth, the tides of warfare in Korea have displaced many civilians of both sides from their homes. sometimes this resulted from accident; sometimes from mil. necessity. Whatever the cause, many former residents of the DPRK are now in the territory under the control of the ROK & vice versa. Your side has alluded frequently during these discussions to the conditions under which these refugees are living. You have expressed the thought that these displaced civilians should be permitted to return to their homes as soon as the arm. is signed. The UNC, too, sees no reason why displaced civs should not be permitted, if they so desire, to return to their former homes as soon as the arm is signed. Moreover, it considers that failure on the part of the armistice delegations to insert a permissive provision in the arm. agreement would be to disregard the needs of these people unnecessarily.

"In determining its posit on the quest. [question] of release & exchange of POWs the UNC has accorded recognition to the viewpoints of both sides as set forth above & has developed a proposal which in large measure reconciles them. Our proposal provides for the release of all POWs. In this respect it is consistent with the principle advocated by your side. **With respect to repatriation; the UNC proposal differs from yours in that it expressly provides that all repatriation will be voluntary.**

"To accomplish this the UNC proposal embodies the principle, advanced & advocated by your side, that a soldier from one side who becomes a POW of the other side can, upon his 'release', exercise his individual option as to whether he will return to his own side or join the other side. However the application of this principle of freedom of choice as regards repatriation is extended, under the UNC proposal, to include all personnel who are, or should be eligible for repatriation under concepts held by either side. The proposal extends the right of individual self determination to former ROKA soldiers who came under your control and who are now in your army. It extends it to residents of the ROK who were inducted into the KPA following the outbreak of war. It extends it to nationals of the ROK who fought on your side but who are now in our hands as interned civilians or as POWs. Finally it extends it to displaced civilians on both sides. Specifically the principle is applied to the following groups:

(a) Approx 16,000 nationals of the ROK who were identified with the KPA and the CPV and whom the UNC now holds as POWs.

(b) Approx 38,000 nationals of the ROK who were incorrectly classified initially as POWs and who have since been reclassified as interned persons.

(c) All former ROKA soldiers who came into the custody of the KPA and CPV and who were subsequently incorporated into the KPA.

(d) All bona-fide residents of the ROK who were inducted into the KPA subsequent to 25 June 1950.

(e) Approx 11,000 soldiers of the UN and of the ROKA who are now held as POW's by the KPA and the CPV.

(f) Approx 116,000 soldiers of the KPA & CPV who are now held as POWs by the UNC.

(g) Foreign civs. interned by either side.

(h) All civs who on 25 June '50, were bona fide residents of the territory under the control of one side and who are, at the time of the signing of the arm., within the territory under control of the other side.

"The principle of individual self determination is a valid principle only if adequate machinery is provided to insure that the decision of the individual is made freely & without duress. Neither side would be satisfied that persons were accorded an opportunity to express their desires on repat. [repatriation] freely & without duress if the interviewing process was conducted by or under the unilateral aegis of one of the respective belligerents. Thus there is a requirement under the UNC proposal for an impartial neutral organ [organization] to conduct and supervise the interview in which the individual expresses his choice as regards repat.

"The fact that both sides have, to a degree, accepted the services of the ICRC suggests that this agency, which is ideally suited and fully qualified, perform this function. Therefore, the UNC proposal provides that the ICRC be requested to supervise the exercise of the right of individual self determination as relates to both POWs and displaced civs. To afford additional assurances to both sides the proposal provides that, in the case of POWs, the individual expression of choice on repat will be made at the exchange point or points. There the process will be under the close scrutiny of reps [representatives] of both belligerents.

"In order that neither side will gain a milt. advantage thru the exchange of POWs under the arm. agreement the UNC proposal contains a parole feature. Under this provision, POWs repatriated by one side after all POWs held by the other side have been exchanged will be required to give their parole not to bear arms against the captor in the future. The delivery of the POW is subject to acceptance of this agreement by the mil. authorities of the side to whom the POW is delivered.

"The UNC proposal is as follows:—

UNC Proposal

1. POWs who elect repat shall be exchanged on a 1 for 1 basis until one side has exchanged all such POWs held by it.

2. The side which thereafter holds POWs shall repatriate all those POWs who elect to be repatriated in a 1 for 1 exchange for foreign civs. interned by the other side, and for civilians and other persons of the one side who are at the time of the signing of the arm. in the territory under control of the other side, and who elect to be repatriated. POWs thus exchanged shall be paroled to the opposing force, such parole to carry with it the condition that the individual shall not again bear arms against the side releasing him.

3. All POWs not electing repat. shall be released from POW status and shall be paroled, such parole to carry with it the condition that the individual will not again bear arms in the Korean conflict.

4. All remaining civs. of either side who are, at the time of the signing of the arm. in territory under control of the other side, shall be repatriated if they so elect.

5. In order to insure that the choice re. repatriation is made without duress, dels [delegations] of the ICRC shall be permitted to interview all POWs at the points of exchange, and all civilians of either side who are at the time of the signing of the arm. in territory under the control of the other side.

6. For purposes of para [paragraphs] 2, 4, & 5 civilians and other persons of either side are defined as those who on 25 June '50 were bona fide residents of either the ROK or the DPRK.

"In summary, the UNC proposal provides for the release of all POWs including soldiers of the other side who may have been incorporated into the army of the detaining power. Thus it is consistent with the first principle advanced by your side that all POWs be released. As regards repat., it permits freedom of choice on the part of the individual, thus insuring that there will be no forced repat. against the will of the individual. It provides repat. not for POWs alone but for those other victims of war, the displaced civilians. All those who desire it are permitted to return to their former homes. Finally the proposal provides for a supervisory organ to interview the persons involved to insure that, whatever their choice, such choice will be made freely and without duress.

"In advocating our proposal of an all-for-all exchange of POW your side has many times asked the question, 'What could be fairer than the release and repat. of all POW following the arm?' Today in this proposal the UNC gives you the answer to that question. The release of all persons who are or should be classified as POW, and the repat. of those who desire to be repatriated, is fairer than the release and forced repat. of all POW. Moreover, it is fairer to permit displaced civs. who so desire to return to their former homes, under the arm. agreement, than to neglect their interests in that agreement.

"We ask your earnest consideration & early acceptance of this proposal."

Following this statement Lee made usual prelim. [preliminary] objections & requested recess until tomorrow.

Jan. 3 (Thurs): In sub-del meeting on Item 3, UNC opened with solemn statement that arm. negots. [armistice negotiations] were in jeopardy. **Charged Commies do not desire a stable arm. Pointed out that the people of the UN, heretofore only suspicious of enemy intentions, now are certain that Commies intend to build up mil. air capability and that enemy's ultimate objective is not peace, but war.** Expressed thought that sincere hopes of people of UN for an armistice are being eaten away by the cancer which Commies germinated and are currently aggravating. Warned that unless enemy acts soon this disease will be beyond cure; beyond control of the UNC del. Assured Commies of absolute and dangerous truth of statement. Urged enemy to act prudently & quickly. Suggested recess until 1100 4 Jan in order that enemy could study carefully UNC statement.

Hsieh said he would answer UNC statement. Asserted that UNC statement was valuable in that it set forth fundamental differences existing. Claimed UNC only wished to picture Commies as warlike & UNC as peaceful. Stated UNC conclusions were entirely wrong. Charged that UNC assertion of enemy's warlike intentions is a big lie. Alleged that interference of UNC forces in internal affairs of Korea *and endangering the border caused CPVs to enter war.* Stated that righteous defense of sacred sovereign rts. [rights] will be continued. Stated Commie objective is peace by other methods than fighting. Charged UNC caused extension of war. Asserted UNC refused to accept and opposed discussion of Commie fair & reasonable proposal thereby clearly indicating UNC desire to maintain state of war. Claimed UNC assuming attitude of a would-be victor, and not sincere towards peace. *Claimed UNC launched summer and autumn offensive to gain what could not be gained in negots. When offensive failed, UNC returned to negots.* Hsieh claimed UNC wants to prolong state of war in Korea by demanding unlimited rotation & replenishment. and by refusing to agree to political conference immed. [immediately] after arm. Charged that UNC refused to remove stumbling block (airfields) which prevents progress of conference. Commies will not permit interferences with their right to deal with own internal affairs. Hsieh ended his long statement by reiterating that Commies are for peace and an effective arm. but that Commies will fight on in defense of their rights until UNC accepts their reasonable proposal. Stated cancer was engendered by UNC not Commies. Again stated that Commies would absolutely not permit interference in their internal affairs. Charged that UNCs alarming statements are designed to fool people of the world and to block the truth.

UNC stated that Hsieh's illogical rantings only proved that Commies need more time to study UNC statement; suggested recess until 1100 4 Jan. Hsieh said any demand by UNC to interfere in internal affairs absolutely will not be accepted.

#4. Commies opened Agenda Item 4 session by categorically rejecting UNC proposal of 2 Jan. Stated they could not consider UNC proposal, and that shameful attempt of UNC to avoid repatriation and to detail 160,000 POWs on pretexts of "voluntary repatriation" and exchange on "1 for 1 basis" can never succeed. That although UNC verbally agreed to principle of releasing all POWs it openly refuses repatriating them. UNC list of 18 Dec. omits 44,205 Commie personnel; 16,243 other Commie personnel of that list are to be detained by UNC; and 100,000 others are to be detained thru proposed 1 for 1 exchange. Release & repat [repatriation] is not trade of slaves, & UNC absurd and unreasonable exchange on such a barbarous and shameful basis is intolerable. As result of Commie lenient policy large nos. [numbers] UNC personnel released at front. Commies ready, where possible, to provide specific lists & data. No similarity between such lenient policy of Commies & unreasonable UNC proposal which refuses repat of POWs and demands 1 for 1 exchange in order detain overwhelming portion after cessation hostilities. *Further, UNC proposal makes groundless slander that Commies forced civs.* [civilians] *& POWs into Army, and absurdly demands they be handed over as POWs. There is not one single man in Army who is forced to fight.* Army does contain "awakened Korean patriots" who shall never be handed over as POWs[.] More intolerable is proposal of trading civs. on 1 for 1 basis. Commies ready repatriate all civs held by them, & hold that arm. agreement should permit return to homes all displaced civilians. UNC has similar responsibility[.] No justification for exchange civs. on 1 for 1 basis. UNC proposal will be condemned by all POWs. their families and people thruout world, & will block release & repat of POWs & speedy conclusion of arm agreement[.]

UNC replied that all UNC-held POWs electing repat. will be repatriated under UNC proposal. Explained 1 for 1 exchange of POWs and voluntary repat features as applied to both POWs & civilians. Rejected Commie rejection of UNC proposal, on grounds Commies have not sufficiently studied proposal and therefore do not understand it. UNC ready to explain any part of proposal.

Commies repeated earlier arguments concluding that UNC proposal, first mixes civs & POW's; second, permits UNC detain many Commie persons under pretext of "voluntary repat"; third, proposes 1 for 1 exchange which would barter persons as slaves, & block return of UNC-held POWs; and fourth, sets up neutral agency to attempt to carry out impossible task of interviewing POWs. & civs. while interfering in Commie internal affairs. Therefore, UNC proposal is **"a barbarous formula and a shameful design." We absolutely cannot accept it. We firmly oppose it. It is absolutely untenable. Accused UNC of not wanting to settle Agenda Item 4.**

UNC informed Genl Lee his accusation a "flagrant discourtesy and an arrogant untruth." UNC proposal sincere, carefully thought out, and designed as compromise of principles & concepts previously presented by both sides. Obviously Commies misunderstand proposal or deliberately choose to misunderstand it. After again refuting Commie arguments, UNC stated its proposal constitutes best efforts as [at] solution to basis of exchange prob. [problem]. Statements by Commies indicate they have not studied proposal and dont understand it.

Col Tsai, Chinese member Commie del, made long statement in response. Reiterated previous Commie arguments particularly referring to UNC attempt to detain personnel in POW status. Made reference to UNC newspaper accounts of UNC-held Chinese POWs indicating desire to join Chiang Kai Shek forces. Stated such so-called vol. [voluntary] repat. would be only expression of will of Chiang Kai Shek. For UNC to permit this would not only be shameful but dangerous.

UNC closed by stating issues now clearer. Stated UNC concurred all POWs should be released and all civilians desiring to return should be returned unconditionally. UNC was not attempting to "capture around conference table" any personnel in Commie army except those captured UNC personnel who wished to return to UNC side. Explained that 1 for 1 exchange regulated the rate of exchange and not the numbers, that if Commies comply with provisions of UNC proposal they will get back all their people who elect to return. Again explained voluntary provision of proposal as being based on freedom of choice of individual, since the individual, including Chinese was best able to express his own desires for repat. Col Tsai interrupted to state if UNC desired to discuss Formosan prob. he was ready.

UNC informed Col Tsai it had made no reference to Formosa question and that ref. [reference] to Chinese prisoners and Chiang Kai Shek had been made by Col Tsai. UNC could not understand why, nor what he meant, by saying it would be dangerous to permit Chinese POWs to exercise their freedom of choice.

UNC urged Commies take whatever steps were necessary to enable them to understand UNC proposal.

Recessed 1435[.]

Jan. 4 (Fri): Item 3. UNC stated failure to accept UNC fair and reasonable proposal has exposed Commie lack of sincerity towards arm. [armistice]. Asserted enemy desires to maintain & prolong state of war in K. by developing mil. [military] air capabilities during arm. Charged Commies oppose safeguards for stable arm. Cited objections to (1) observers in rear (2) aerial obsvn [observation] (3) single directing head for MAC (4) observation at comm [communication] centers (5) replacement. Stated enemy's intention develop mil airfields indicates ult. [ultimate] objective not peace but war. Refuted enemy's charge that entry of foreign forces into K and their threat to China border caused extension Korean war. Cited resolution Security Council on 25 Jun '50 calling for immed. [immediate] cessation of hostilities and withdrawal of invading forces. Stated that only when Commies ignored proposal did UN call for forces to assist ROK and to restore international peace & security. Stated that subject of why UNC and CPV entered war is not relevant to arm. negots [negotiations] and further discussion will only delay progress. Rec. [recommended] that conference get back on the track[.] Said both sides realize that one major difference (airfields) confronts conference. Pointed out that, technically, a state of war will still exist during arm; therefore, facilities which constitute an increase in milt. capabilities should not return to peacetime status. Stated that both sides have agreed on "no increase in mil forces or equipment during arm["]. Asked if Commies agree that there shall not be an increase of mil. capability by either side during arm.

Col Chang charged that UNC is using conf. [conference] room as a broadcasting station. Hsieh stated interference & infringement in internal affairs absolutely will not be tolerated. Said there should be no introduction of mil forces and strict restr. [restriction] of introduction of mil. equipment into K. Reiterated that no interference in right of Koreans to deal with our own internal affairs can be tolerated. Claimed UNC is intentionally delaying negots. Stated there are two major differences (1) unlimited replenishment (2) interference in internal affairs, and in addition there are certain diffs [differences] of secondary importance. Said question of solving diffs up to UNC. Gen Ferenbaugh said UNC still waiting for suggestions from Commies on how to make progress on solution of main pts. [points] of issue. Hsieh stated that diffs will be solved & progress made if UNC removes unreasonable demands. Again charged that interference in int. [internal] affairs (airfields) should not be discussed. Hsieh said "if you insist upon settling such questions and since form of our present conf. is not proper for doing so, then is it that your side has other suggestions re: form or scope of the conference?'' **UNC asserted Commies had not answered question "do you agree that there shall be no increase of mil capability by either side during arm?''** Hsieh stated Commies subscribe to no introduction of forces from without K., definitely oppose interference in internal affairs, & that Commie proposals provide for stable & effective arm. UNC asked if Commies believe constr. of airfields capable of handling mil aircraft is conducive to stable effective arm.

Hsieh answered, this is a question of sovereign rts. [rights] & cannot be raised in this conf.—again said interference in int. affairs absolutely cannot be tolerated. UNC charged Commies evading quest., asked for a direct answer. Hsieh stated enemy proposal of Dec 24 provides for effective & stable arm. Charged that quest. of airfield restr was attempt by UNC to interfere in int. affairs using airfield subject as a cover.

P.M. Session: UNC asked what is meant by ''form'' & ''scope'' in question asked by Hsieh during morning session regarding discussion of interference in foreign affairs at this conference. Hsieh stated that his question was caused by UNC insistence on interfering in internal affairs. Said UNC in support of such unreasonable demands for interfering in int. affairs had touched on extensive quests. regarding K and even touched on some which override scope of Korea. Therefore, if UNC willing to discuss more extensive quests and considers conference is not fit for such discussions, does UNC have other suggestions with regard to conference.

UNC asked if Hsieh was referring to restrs on airfields. Hsieh answered that UNC had touched on extensive political questions for past several days. UNC charged Commies insist on developing mil. air capability during arm. Stated this would be threat to stability of arm. and security of UNC. Asserted only rational explanation of Commie stand is their intent that arm. will end in resumption of hostilities. Charged enemy with intent to disrupt arm. by employing this capability developed during period of arm. Stated Commie intentions are not peaceful as long as they insist on such menacing intent. Said Commies must recognize that security is prime consideration during arm. and basic security of both sides is assured if there is no increase in mil. capabilities by either side during arm. Accused Commies of delaying progress of negots. by failure to give up ominous demands. Hsieh charged UNC still insisting on interference in internal affairs under pretext of restr. of facilities. Accused UNC of purposely distorting Commie intentions. UNC asked if enemy had any practical suggestions for solving present deadlock. Hsieh stated quest now is whether UNC will accept Commie view and remove UNC unreasonable demand. UNC suggested recess until 1100 5 Jan.

#4. Sub-del Item 4 met in continuous session for 4 hrs 15 min. UNC opened at 1100 with explanation that parole feature in our proposal is necessary to prevent accrual to either side of significant military advantage.

In response to UNC query, Commies stated they had no quests. about UNC proposal because its objectives all too clear. Then launched into attack on our proposal as follows: (a) Asserted UNC wants to get its personnel back first thru device of 1 for 1 exchange. (b) Alleged UNC using POW excess to number held by Commies as hostages coerce Commies into turning back ROK personnel not in POW status. Took opportunity again to deny impressment of ROKA soldiers into their forces, involuntary recruitment of ROK civs into their army & kidnapping of civs. (c) **Charged that UNC principle of voluntary repat** [repatriation] **is device to detain large nos** [numbers] **POWs and then by force & cruel mistreatment to deliver part of them to a certain friend in S.K. and part to a certain friend in Taiwan.** (d) Charged UNC with wanting to detain in misery & humiliation some 500,000 N.K. civs whom they charge we took away by force & intimidation. (e) Labeled UNC chg. [charge] of impressment of POWs into Commie forces "groundless fabrication." (f) rejected concept of considering civs. & POWs together. (g) rejected interviews by ICRC (h) rejected concept of parole on basis that no conditions can be attached to release & repat. (i) Denied that release & repat can be separated.

Commies employed such adjectives as absurd, unreasonable, useless & ridiculous in discussing UNC proposal, and asserted they cannot & absolutely will not agree to it. Again raised quest. of Art 118 Geneva Conv. of '49 & stated that UNC proposal is shameful scheme to trade human beings like slaves in violation thereof.

UNC told Commies they had put worst possible light on our proposal. UNC refuted chg. of taking NK civs by force or intimidation, explaining they had come to our side for refuge. Commies were reminded that any NK refugee who desired could be returned during arm. UNC reviewed evidence of impressment of POWs and conscription of ROK citizens into Commie forces and stated that we wanted back those who want to return.

UNC then outlined proposed handling of POWs not electing repat, stating they would come under jurisdiction of international organ [organization] similar to IRO after release.

Commies repeated attack on UNC proposal with following variations:

(a) Held up Art 118 of Geneva Conv. of '49 as a most reasonable part of Conv. worthy of their respect.

(b) Accused UNC of using POWs as spies.

(c) Stated our proposed handling of non-repatriated POWs would amount only to changing sign on inclosure in which they were confined.

(d) Stated they would not, out of respect for personal integrity of foreign civs. exchange them for POWs.

(e) Characterized interviews by neutral organ as political, not mil matter.

UNC pointed out great differences existing between views of two delegations and stated their resolution would take long time. Therefore proposed again the immed. exchange of seriously sick & injured. Commies demurred.

Comment: In early morning Commies indicated UNC proposal too unreasonable for them to ask quests about it. In pm, they were arguing the merits of the proposal.

Jan. 5 (Sat): Opening Sub del meeting on Item 3 UNC stated Commie air does not threaten UNC forces at present and UNC will not agree to enemy's development of threatening air capabilities during arm. [armistice]. Stated that quest. [question] of rehabilitation of airfields should not be clothed in misleading words such as sovereignty of internal affairs. Pointed out that Commies said they did not necessarily intend to rehabilitate all airfields and that UNC is willing to agree to rehab of limited no of fields for civil air ops. Therefore, quest is rehab of airfields for mil. purpose[.] Asked why Commies insist on developing such fields during arm. if they do not intend to use them. Reiterated statement that UNC will not agree to the development of mil. air capabilities during period of arm. Asked if Commies had anything new to offer. Hsieh stated UNC statement was rude and absurd and had gone too far in vituperation. Charged that UNC lacks sincerity towards negots [negotiations]. Charged that UNC had exposed ugly features of a bandit. Said UNC only desired Commies to give up their sovereign rights and permit UNC to interfere in internal affairs. Charged UNC openly admitted intention to interfere in int. [internal] affairs during the Arm. **Alleged that UNC daily brags about mil forces and had increased these forces during present negots.** Challenged UNC to try another offensive. Stated UNC slandered Commie peaceful posits [positions]. Claimed Commie proposal is fair for effective and stable arm. Charged that UNC sub del. cannot pretend to represent Britain, France and Netherlands or peoples of the world. Stated UNC in recent statements had touched on many extensive quests and showed no sincerity towards these negots.

UNC said statement was intended to bring attention to realities. Said that Commies on various occasions spoke of UNC menace to China. Said UN directive specified mil. action in K only and UNC therefore could have no intent to attack China. Charged Commies with attempting to portray Americans to people of China and America. Hsieh stated that UNC is dealing with quests involving Far East, but that Commies are very willing to discuss these extensive quests. **Charged UNC openly declared intention to cross Yalu River to set up defensive posits. Charged UNC had attacked China. Cited bombing of Antung, artillery and machine gun fire across Yalu. Charged UNC carried out air raids over Mukden China & Shanghai during week of Aug. 23d.** Stated UNC talk of friendship between Amer [American] & Chinese people was attempt at deception. Stated UNC does not represent Amer. people. Charged handful of warlike persons handling Amer. policy only slander Amer. people. Asked why Amer. seized Taiwan and why air raids made on Antung, Mukden. Stated Chinese people will not be deceived. Asserted UNC tactics of deception, blackmail & mil pressure are clear to Commies. Stated UNC must admit that balance of mil. forces exists & therefore, must not make such unreasonable demands. UNC asked if Commies had anything new to offer. Hsieh stated UNC had raised quests. which reveal UNC war policy. Said Commie refutations based on ironclad facts. Stated would continue to refute UNC statements.

#4. Sub del Item 4 met for 3 hrs 10 min. UNC opened with amplification of parole principle of para 2 in our proposal, explaining that intent of parole feature would be reliance on the honor of the Commie Comdrs [Commanders] to carry out promise for parolees not to bear arms against UNC.

Commies briefly brushed off UNC explanation of the parole principle by indicating subject was political. Commies than launched into attack on our proposal as follows:

a. Asserted para 1 does not coincide with spirit of Geneva convention.

b. UNC has created a strange condition stating that: "The exchange of POWs with the civs on basis of one for one after cessation of hostilities is something [with?] which you are going to create an unprecedented incident in the recent history of mankind—a scheme of detaining numerous POW [to?] confine their freedom."

c. Charged UNC under principle of voluntary repat [repatriation] of "creating numerous refugees of the warfare, "prisoners of war who do not elect repat. shall be released in your rear." It is a barbarous content under civilized cloak."

d. Charged UNC with intent to delay release of POWs by introducing in the proposal the principle of interviewing POWs and refugees in order to guarantee voluntary repat. Commies claim the plan of interviewing such great nos. is a "dream," "impossible" and "in a mil. negotiation there is no need to make any such proposal."

e. Charged that in UNC proposal para 6 is a "political question"; that "two states are considered,["] "there are no two states in Korea." "We should not touch on political questions."

f. Charged UNC proposal will "detain further POWs after cessation of hostilities.["]

g. During course of Commie discussion of UNC proposal the ICRC was referred to as "so called neutral." *Excessive use was made of lurid adjectives.* Commies were taken to task by UNC for their evident lack of common courtesy.

UNC told Commies that they had not made a fair analysis of our proposal. UNC refuted the argument that mil parole is a political matter. UNC proposal of exchanging ROK nationals for KPA and CVPA paroled POWs was explained as not bad just because it was without precedent.

Commies were told that UNC does not intend to detain POWs. In view of Commie statement that they could move only 11,000 people in 30 days, the UNC is not too impressed with accusations of delay and detaining. UNC further told Commies, ''that every single man, woman & child of these people from your side—of civs. [civilians] from your side who are now in the territory under control of ROK will be free to go back to you if they so desire, 5 mins after the arm is signed.''

UNC requested Commies to reconsider UNC proposal for the immed. [immediate] exchange of the seriously sick & seriously wounded POW, Commies made no reply.

UNC refuted Commie accusation that UNC was creating refugees in warfare. It was pointed out that, if anything was being created, free men were being created so that they could pursue peaceful lives.

UNC pointed out necessity for organization to interview people to see that they made a free choice for repat without duress. As to practicability for release of nationals of the ROK held by UNC as POW or civ internees, it was pointed out that these nationals will be given the right to express their desire to go to Commie side. Commies were asked to do likewise for the ROK nationals they have in their army and those they have interned.

UNC pointed out Commies faulty analysis and conclusions in study of UNC proposal.

Commies accused UNC of making hostages of KPA and CVP POWs and NK. civilians thru exchange of civs. for POWs. Again they pointed out the impossible task to carry on the individual inquiries required to interview all of soldiers & civilians.

UNC attempted to clarify point on return of NK civs., but Commies evaded explanation by interrupting & discussing at some length the complicated procedure required.

Meeting recessed at 1410.

Comment: Commie attitude more intransigent and rude than usual indicating either lack of instrs. [instructions] on our proposal or instrs. to attempt to goad UNC Del into breaking off negots.

Jan. 6 (Sun): Upon opening of sub del on Item 3, UNC charged Commies continue to evade question of increase in mil. air capabilities and attempt to hide real intent. Stated UNC posit [position] is firm and that arm. [armistice] must be based on mil realities as they exist now. Charged Commies with delaying progress. Said point of issue is rehab [rehabilitation] of airfields for mil purposes, therefore discussion should be focused on this point.

UNC gave statement pointing out sovereign rights were not abridged since all terms of arm had to be agreed between both sides. No specific reaction was noted[.]

Hsieh charged UNC statement was hollow intimidation and another attempt to threaten negots [negotiations] with war. Stated UNC not sincere and deliberately delaying and trying to wreck negots by provocative quests. [questions]. Said UNC attempting to force Commies to accept UNC proposal by coercion, but Commies will oppose forever UNC attempt to interfere in internal affairs.

UNC asserted enemy had offered nothing new since UNC introduced 29 Dec proposal which was great effort to solve existing differences.

Hsieh claimed UNC proposal still leaves greatest obstacle (airfields) in way of progress and UNC refusal to remove this point is reason for delay[.] Charged UNC deliberately introduced airfield quest. to delay conference[.]

UNC asked if enemy intends to construct mil airfields during arm.

Hsieh avoided quest., said it had been answered many times, so quest of internal affairs & sovereign rights therefore should not be discussed.

Recessed at 1315.

#4. Morning session spent in UNC explanation of its proposal, aimed at clarifying apparent Commie misunderstanding of provisions. Points emphasized: (1) Release of all POWs inherent in UNC proposal, but repat. [repatriation] voluntary. (2) Inclusion of civs. [civilians] in exchange has dual purpose of insuring return of civs. from Commie control and of regulating date of return of POWs by UNC.

Afternoon session found Commies informally exploring UNC explanation of its proposal. Apparent aim of Commie exploration was attempt to obtain UNC agreement that our proposal could be changed to provide for release & repat. of all POWs. and that return of civs to their homes could be handled separately[.] Failing in this aim, Commies stated UNC proposal is untenable and they will not agree to exchange civs for POWs.

One point became clear. One Commie objection to UNC proposal is that agreement thereto would involve implied Commie acceptance of fact that some Koreans are citizens of ROK. This contrary to oft-repeated Commie claim that theirs is only legal govt for all of Korea.

Jan. 7 to Jan. 13: **Decided to go back to Tokyo for a conference with R on ways and means to break the deadlock on Item 3, submitting staff study which reworded principle 4 to read: "There shall be no increase in milt. capabilities of either side during the period of the armistice."** Also brought along proposed next step for Item 4 sub del which in effect dropped any intent to try to wheedle the Commies into releasing ROKs impressed into their army and also separated POWs & civilians from each other in any exchange.

Arrived Tokyo about 1600 after quick 3 hr 15 min trip. Learned that R wanted me to see a despatch he had sent to the JCS that day. This msg took a crack at para 4 of JCS 90083 which mentioned the contemplated allied declaration which would be issued upon signing of the armistice to 'scare' the Commies from renewed aggression. Said in effect that UNC as presently constituted would be incapable of any real retribution against Communist China. **Also took a crack at some of the 'leaks' emanating from Wash** [Washington] **especially one date lined Wash Jan 5 which was headlined "America is seen prepared to make new concessions"—an AP despatch.** R's msg ended up with folg. para. "If U.S. Govt should decide to support our present position, even to the breaking point, then I suggest that the sooner the UNC Del. is empowered to inform the Commies to that effect, the sooner might we reasonably expect an acceptable arm."

The next day, the 8th, I conferred with R discussing the staff study on Item 3. Study was later disapproved because it was felt that rewording principle 4 to exclude airfields would only put off the evil day. Also discussed with R the personnel situation of Item 3 sub-del.

On the 11th JCS 91600 was received. This referred to R's msg mentioned above saying it had been given "careful and searching consideration[.]" Said also sufficient agreement had now been achieved on statement mentioned para 4 JCS 90083 to assure it will be issued. Went on to say, "In view of this we attach less importance to a prohibition on rehab. of airfields. On balance, in light of all factors, decision is that you are directed that your final position will be agreement to omission from arm. terms of any prohibition on constr. [construction] or rehab. of airfields if that becomes only unresolved point of issue on armistice agreement. However, we do not feel UNC should adopt this final position unless & until it appears clear that it is final and only breaking point for Commies."

JCS msg then went on to suggest that UNC Del attempt to defer further discussion of airfield quest. [question] until agreement is reached on all other outstanding quests. under agenda items 3, 4, & 5. and requested CinCUNC's comments.

After 4 hr conference on Jan 12th with R, Hickey, Wright, Muse & Darrow a reply was drafted to JCS 91600 the essence of which follows.

Part 1. reiterated R's conviction that with presently available milt. resources this command would be incapable of posing a threat to Communist China sufficient in itself to deter it from renewed aggression.

Part II pointed out that the arm [armistice] agreement must be written in considerably more detail than could result from the incorporation of the agreed principles into one document[.]

Part III said that in conformance with instrs [instructions] your 91600 that subject of airfield constr be isolated and deferred until it becomes only unresolved point of issue, following procedure would be adopted:

UNC Del. at an appropriate time in near future will propose that, in view of continued disagreement upon question of rehab. of airfields, the discussion on this latter quest. be deferred and other topics of items 3, 4 & 5 be discussed & resolved.

Should above UNC proposal be accepted, drafting on staff level of the arm agreement details derived from the agreed principles of Items 2 & 3 will be attempted concurrent with substantive discussion of Items 4 & 5.

Msg then pointed out that acceptance by Commies of this proposal is not probable. Commies may anticipate concession on airfield quest. as result of press release which stated UNC had further concessions to make.

Part IV. said it was important for UNC to know final posits [positions] on exchange of civs [civilians] & voluntary repatriation so that Del. may be in a position to exploit possible Commie agreement to defer airfield question.

Upon return to camp on the 13th (about 1430) after a beautiful 3 hr & 50 min flight from Tokyo the folg. msg from Hickey was awaiting me: "Reference subject of conference yesterday, General R. desires to caution that for at least one week, scrupulous care must be exercised to avoid any indication of shift in position. During that period stand firmly on present position."

Item 3. During this period the debate on the airfield question continued along the same lines as in the past. UNC continued to insist that there be no increase of mil. capabilities of either side during armistice and that there be effective safeguards against such increase. On other hand Commies continued to charge that UNC was intentionally delaying and attempting to wreck negots. [negotiations] by insisting on unreasonable demands, and to contend that an airfield itself does not constitute an offensive military [act?] and that constr of airfields is a question of internal affairs which cannot be discussed at these negots. UNC continued to point out that since enemy states no aircraft have been introduced into Korea and none will be introduced during arm. then there is no necessity for rehab. of milt airfields and Commies cannot object to UNC principle 4. Commies kept reiterating that they are not concerned with airfields but with integrity and independence of sovereign rights.

On 9 Jan the Commies submitted a rewording of our 29 Dec proposal as a new proposal, except that they omitted all reference to restrictions on rehab of airfields under principle 4. **They also substituted the phrase, "the attainment of a peaceful settlement through the holding by both sides of a political conference of a higher level" for our phrase, "so as to facilitate a peaceful settlement by action at a political level."** They also used the words "neutral nations" instead of ours "noncombatant nations." In presenting this proposal Hsieh claimed great concession made in agreeing to necessary replenishment of war equipment during period of armistice.

UNC said new proposal was unacceptable because it failed to include restrictions on rehab. of airfields during arm. Explained UNC stand on airfield issue firm because of our concern for security of forces and stability of armistice.

To show how contradictory the Commies are at times; when UNC asserted that Commies intended to increase their milt. capabilities during the arm. Hsieh vehemently said this was a misrepresentation and a slander. Yet their senior delegate Nam Il said on 2 Dec that Commies intended to reconstruct airfields during the armistice. When confronted with this Hsieh said they were not inconsistent, that whether or not Commies install facilities is a matter of internal affairs [with] which UNC has no right to concern itself.

Item 4. During this period Jan (7–13) debates centered on UNC proposal of 2 Jan. Commies attacked proposal on basis that (1) UNC detains POWs as hostages to assure return of civilians. (2) So called volunteer repatriation principle is a pretext to detain an over-whelming portion of POWs to send them to "the deadly enemy of the Korean and Chinese peoples," (3) UNC has no right to reclassify milt persons of other side. They have already elected way they should take (4) KPA does not cancel mil. designations of it's [*sic*] POWs. It only prepares them for release & repatriation (5) The parole feature is the demand of a victor over the vanquished and is therefore untenable, (6) Voluntary repatriation is a **political question**, (7) It is unavoidable obligation of both sides to release and repatriate all POWs on basis of their original army designation (8) **Since every POW has the inviolate right to be repatriated if he wants to be he must be repatriated even if it is against his will—that it is barbarous to give the POW his right to say for himself whether he desires to be repatriated or not. A strange doctrine!** (9) UNC still wishes to adhere to principle of one-for one exchange of POWs. (10) Instructors from Taiwan are in POW camps to establish free choice. With their aid anti-Communist organizations being created. (11) Contend UNC violating Arts 118 & 7 of Geneva Convention. (12) UNC proposal that ICRC supervise expression of opinion only confirms that voluntary repatriation is only an effort to detain POWs. (13) How will release of POW increase military force of other side. POWs are human beings[.] We must respect their personal integrity and guarantee their freedom and a comfortable life at home following the armistice.

On 8 Jan UNC resubmitted its 2 Jan proposal with revised phraseology. intended to eliminate any grounds for Commie technical opposition to the proposal. Reworded proposal reads as follows:

1. It is agreed that all POWs shall be released as hereinafter set forth.

2. POWs shall be repatriated on the following basis:

(a) POWs held by KPA and CPVs who elect repat. [repatriation] shall be exchanged for an equal no. [number] of POWs held by UNC who elect repat.

(b) Thereafter the UNC shall repatriate POWs held by it who elect to be repatriated in exchange for an equal number of:

(1) Foreign civilians interned by the KPA or the CPV who elect repat; and

(2) Other persons electing repat. who on 25 June 50 resided south of the 38th parallel and who are, under any pretext whatsoever, serving in the KPA at the time of the signing of the arm; and

(3) Other civs. electing repat who on 25 June '50 resided south of the 38th and who are, at the time of the signing of the arm, in territory under the milt. control of the KPA and the CPVs[.]

(c) If after the foregoing exchange has been completed, and POWs remain in the custody of the UNC who elect repat, such POWs shall be repat without delay.

(d) The Supreme Comdr of the KPA and the Comdr. of the CPVs shall solemnly agree that POWs repatriated in accord. with sub paras 2b & 2c above, shall not thereafter be permitted or compelled to bear arms against the UNC.

3. All POWs not electing repatriation shall be released from POW status upon giving written assurance that they will not thereafter bear arms against either side in the Korean conflict.

4. All civs. who at the time of the signing of the arm. are in territory under the milt. control of the UNC and who, on 25 June 1950 resided north of the 38th parallel shall, if they so elect, be permitted and assisted to move to territory under the milt. control of the KPA and CPVs; and all civs. who, at the time of the signing of the arm., are in territory under the milt control of the KPA and CPVs and who on 25 June '50 resided south of the 38th parallel, and who are not repatriated under the provisions of subpara 2b(3) above, shall if they so elect, be permitted and assisted to move to territory under the milt. control of the UNC.

5. The right to elect to go to the territory under the control of the KPA and CPVs shall be extended to all persons held by the UNC who have been classified as civs internees. It shall also be extended to all persons who, although they resided south of the 38th parallel on 25 June '50 are now held by the UNC as POWs.

6. In order to insure that the choice re: repatriation is made without duress, delegates of the ICRC shall be permitted to interview all POWs at the points of exchange, and all persons described in paras 2b(2) above, and all civs of either side who are, at the time of the signing of the arm., in territory under the milt control of the other side. Each side shall cooperate fully with the ICRC in the performance of this function and shall make such logistical and administrative arrangements as are necessary to expedite the process.

When this proposal was introduced Lee noted it and remarked it replaced the unreasonable one for one and national designation with equal nos and north & south of the 38th parallel respectively[.]

In defending our proposal Libby pointed out it imposes upon both sides exactly same obligations; that is to release all POWs. and to repatriate all POWs and displaced civs who elect to be repatriated. The obligations placed upon both sides by UNC proposal are equal but responsibilities placed on UNC in carrying out these obligations are substantially greater than those placed upon Commies and benefits accruing to Commies far outweigh those accruing to UNC. It gives Commies those who elect repat from total of approx 670,000 persons; it returns to UNC side those who elect repat from only approx 200,000 persons.

Substantial differences exist in the viewpoints of two sides on merits of UNC proposal. These differences should be brought out in open. 1st Commies oppose voluntary repat for POWs. 2nd they oppose parole feature. 3rd they oppose giving a choice to ROK nationals in KPA to be repatriated. 4th they oppose gearing return by UNC of POWs to Commie return of civs. Now they oppose individual choice as regards repatriation.

In Item 4 talks in Dec. Commies extolled freedom of choice exercised by the individual in joining KPA. They said it was traditional policy to release POWs from captivity. Later reappearance of POWs in KPA was explained by fact that they had exercised their freedom of choice to join KPA. Deserters from ROKA were given this choice, as were civilian nationals of the areas invaded by KPA. Accepting these assertions at their face value, UNC formulated a proposal for release & repat. of POWs based upon what Commies said was a basic tenet of the new "internationalism." Each is to be given right to decide for himself whether he wants to be repatriated. UNC is surprised Commies now oppose freedom of choice and demand forced repatriation. What is significance of Commie opposition to freedom of choice and insistence upon forcible repat. of all POWs?

1st, they do not trust "volunteers" and "awakened patriots."

2nd, Commies do not dare to expose ROK nationals whom they have incorporated into KPA to true freedom of choice publicly expressed. They are fearful that results would indicate that many had actually been impressed and conscripted into KPA against their will.

3rd, having augmented their forces thruout war by "freedom of choice" they now seek to continue to augment them by its opposite "forced repatriation." **Apparently freedom of choice as practiced by the Communists is a means to an end, the augmentation of their military forces.** To oppose freedom of choice as regards repat and to demand forced repat. is to denounce individual freedom and to advocate slavery.

Commies oppose parole because they regard the arm. not as a bridge to peace but as a prelude to a resumption of hostilities. Why else would they oppose parole, a principle which merely prevents a substantial change in the mil. strength of one side from occurring as a result of the arm?

UNC concludes;

1st[,] Commies are afraid to agree to ICRC interviews of former ROK civs; they fear the results would reveal that thousands would elect to return to their homes.

2nd, they want to conceal the fact that they involuntarily conscripted into the civilian economy and milt service thousands of former ROK. civilians.

3rd, they do not intend to release these thousands who were taken north and who are now serving the Commies because to do so would weaken their milt. potential.

Plain truth is that there is no valid & logical objection to any of the basic issues that can stand the light of day and spotlight of public opinion.

UNC continued during this period in attempt to confine discussion to one subject forced repatriation versus freedom of choice as regards repatriation.

Jan. 14 (Mon): UNC opened sub-del meeting on Item 3 by pointing out that since beginning of the negots [negotiations] Commie efforts have been directed towards attempt to obtain a cease fire rather than a stable armistice. Examples; withdrawal of foreign troops, indefensible 38th parallel as milt. dem. [military demarcation] line, objections to observers in rear areas, attempt to reduce milt. capabilities of UNC thru attrition and current attempt to avoid restriction on milt. air capabilities. Sudden extreme sensitivity on so called sovereign rights and interference with internal affairs is consistent with cease fire only, during which air potential could be developed. A Commie agreement on restrictions on development of airfields by both sides would be first Commie step consistent with a desire for a stable armistice.

Hsieh countered by stating that Commie proposal of 9 Jan completely and reasonably solved two major disagreements on Item 3 and that although he had twice warned UNC not to go too far in its attempt to interfere in Commie internal affairs this warning had been disregarded and instead yesterday there had been deliberate provocation by dispatch of group of planes to NE China. Hsieh intimated that UNC mil. actions were conducted to threaten and intimidate Commies into accepting unreasonable demands. UNC does not learn from experience. Tactics of intimidation cannot frighten people of the world. UNC not strong enough.

Item 4. Commies opened opposing UNC proposal on release & exchange of POWs on grounds that its purpose was to detain POWs hostages for civilians.

UNC attempted to steer talks back to freedom of choice vs. forced repat. [repatriation]. It presented a lengthy statement explaining that UNC proposal was based on a compromise between the conflicting precepts and practices of each side with respect to POWs. If Commie practices alone were accepted as the basis for a proposal there would be no exchange to speak of. UNC would merely incorporate majority of POWs into its armed forces as Commies have thruout war. On other hand if UNC practices alone were accepted as basis of proposal following would result;

a. UNC would retain 54,000 ROK nationals now in its custody[.]

b. UNC would demand return of all ROK nationals inducted into KPA since June '50.

c. Both sides would repatriate all rptd [reported] POWs. Disadvantages to both sides and to individuals concerned under these proposals were pointed out.

Under UNC compromise proposal which is based upon a conciliation of practices of each side the folg. [following] results:

a. UNC retains only those from among 54,000 ROKs who elect to be repatriated to ROK. Those who would prefer to go to other side are free to do so.

b. Commies retain all loyal soldiers among ROKs in their forces while eliminating those who, if given a free choice, would prefer to return home rather than serve in KPA.

c. Both sides repatriate all listed POWs who desire it.

Lee responded heatedly & illogically, touching on all points of diff. [differences] between 2 proposals, in effort to keep discussion from centering on free choice vs. forced repat.

Jan. 15 (Tues): UNC opened with statement pointing out that both sides have agreed there shall be no increase in mil. capabilities during the arm [armistice]. Therefore, there should be restrictions on development mil. airfields. UNC has agreed to rehab. of specified airfields for civil air ops. [operations] therefore Commies have no pretext for stating there is interference in their civil & domestic affairs. Restrictions are only on mil airfields. Commies have stated "there is a balance of mil. forces on both sides[.]'' They must admit their mil. capabilities do not include many operational airfields in Korea. While they have agreed that the mil. balance must not be upset by introduction of reinforcing troops or equipment into K during arm. they refuse to agree that the mil. balance should not be upset by rehab. & constr. of mil. airfields during arm. Commies are seeking to unbalance mil. capabilities. Only by reaching agreement on airfields can both sides be assured that neither side will gain any mil. advtg. [advantage] as result of arm and that arm will be stable and lead to peace.

Hsieh insisted Commie proposal of 9 Jan completely solved 2 major diffs [differences] of opinion on Item 3—replenishment and UNC insistence on interference in their internal affairs. No point in wasting time. Acceptance of Commie proposal of 27 Nov would have resulted in speedy convocation of political conf. [conference]. Commie position had always been farsighted and intended to extinguish war flames in K while UNC's did not. Quest. [question] of constr. of facilities within it's [sic] territory is a matter of internal affairs which is to be decided by sovereign nation itself and Commies will not permit any restrictions on that sovereignty[.]

UNC answered Commies state they want peace only a stable arm. will lead to peace. For a stable arm there must be prohibition on increase in mil. capabilities, including mil. airfields.

Item 4. UNC opened asking justification by Commies of charge made yesterday that UNC proposal was deceitful. Lee replied para 1 (UNC proposal) provides for release of all POWs but under guise of "free choice" UNC seeks to retain POWs. Thus they are not released. Secondly UNC proposal provides for one for one exchange. Thirdly it proposes to exchange civs. [civilians] with POWs, that is, hold the latter as hostages. Fourthly the proposal requires parole from the Commie Comdr but not CinCUNC which is inequitable. Fifthly, it attempts to interfere in internal affairs of KPA by seeking to ask soldiers of ROK origin whether they are serving willingly. There too it violates Geneva Conv. by depriving POWs of their right to be released and repatriated. Deceit of proposal lies here, an equitable proposal must offer equal rts. [rights] and equal obligations but UNC proposal gives UNC rights only and other side obligations only. Such a proposal cannot deceive the world.

With ref [reference] to ROK nationals in KPA Lee said it is not necessary to discriminate between S & N Koreans. "Within revolutionary KPA all are volunteers. In any case UNC will never be able to investigate.["] He continued "Free choice is absurd. It is a violation of Art 118. It is to deprive POWs of their rights. UNC adds word forced to repat. [repatriation] to deceive POWs and people of world. It is better not to misconstrue by such additions. How does UNC justify hostages? How does it request parole from part of POWs only?"

UNC then refuted these arguments.

Lee asked the question, "If our side releases only a part of the POWs and for the remaining requests you to give us civs. in place of POWs. would you agree to it? If not, why impose such conditions on our side?" UNC answered "So long as there are civs. in territory under our control who elect to return to your side, we would have no objection to exchanging them for POWs if you prefer to exchange the POWs you hold for civs rather than POWs. It would make no diff. whatever to us, as we intend to turn over all POWs and civs. who elect to go to your side."

In reply Lee said, "Do you think it is proper to exchange the POWs with the civs who did not join the warfare?"

UNC replied that it was proper to get all POWs and displaced persons who wish to be repatriated exchanged as expeditiously as possible. UNC proposal would do that.

Colonel Tsai took up this theme saying proposal stipulates that after exchange of POWs Commies should deliver foreign displaced civs. and the alleged POWs incorporated in KPA for remaining 165,120 POWs. Commies say civs. should not be treated as POWs or exchanged for POWs. Those in KPA are a fabrication. UNC says balance of POWs will be repatriated when exchange is satisfactorily completed. This is inequitable and unilateral. If UNC was in Commie position would such a proposal appear equitable? Tsai further stated UNC holds we should follow the measure of making hostages of POWs. Commies say proposal is inequitable. UNC says it is equitable. How would UNC feel if positions were reversed? The answer will give both sides a deeper understanding of the nature of the proposal.

Jan 16. (Wed): Hsieh opened Item 3 meeting with statement that before submission of Commie proposal of 9 Jan, there had been two differences: (1) UNC insistence on replenishment, and (2) UNC insistence on so called restriction on airfields which was an attempt to interfere in their internal affairs. The 9 Jan Commie proposal settled these 2 differences in a reasonable manner and includes sufficient conditions to insure a stable armistice. The principle prohibiting introduction of reinforcements into Korea includes combat aircraft. Since there will be no introduction of combat aircraft into K, it is inconceivable that there will be an increase in milt. capabilities during the arm. Why then does UNC assert that Commies intend to increase milt. air capabilities during the armistice? In answer to UNC query as to whether the foregoing statement meant that Commies did not intend to increase milt. air capabilities during the arm, Hsieh countered by asking how it was conceivable that there would be an increase of milt. air capability during arm. since Commies have agreed to restriction on introduction into K. of combat aircraft.

UNC stated Commie proposal of 9 Jan is identical with UNC proposal of 29 Dec except for airfields and minor details. This however does not resolve the diff. [difference] it merely makes it more obvious. Because of the one additional safeguard contained in UNC proposal, Commies brand it "unreasonable" and an interference in their internal affairs. How is it possible for a so called sovereign state to agree to limitations on admission of milt. personnel and equipment and to agree to observn. within its borders by foreign nationals and yet to object on the ground of interference in internal affairs to restrs [restrictions] on increase in milt air capabilities of both sides during the arm. UNC emphasized that restrictions on mil air capabilities of both sides is a prerequisite of the arm agreement. Commie contention that their proposal contains "sufficient conditions" to insure against increase in milt. capabilities during [armistice?] makes it clear that they admit that this is a requirement for an arm. They have agreed to other restrictions aimed at preventing an increase in milt. capabilities. But those are not enough. The restriction on milt airfields is also required. It is a safeguard which must be incorporated into the arm. agreement.

Air power requires communications fuel & ordnance, aircraft & airfields. UNC expects Commies to repair comm [communications]. Fuel & ordnance they could have now. Aircraft can be flown into Korea from outside in a matter of mins. There remains the imp. [important] element of air power—airfields. If neither side can rehabilitate nor construct mil. airfields, the other components of air power will not be a threat to the stability of the arm.

Hsieh repeated that since Commies have agreed to restrs. on introduction of combat aircraft into K, he could not understand why UNC continues to assert that there is no restriction on increase of milt air capability in their proposal.

Restriction on introduction of milt forces into K and supervision by neutral nations involves matters outside of K not matters within K and therefore do not constitute interference in internal affairs. Commie proposal would insure a stable arm. without interference in internal affairs—which is why UNC opposes it. UNC has consistently sought to include political requirements involving interference in internal affairs.

Item 4. Continuing yesterdays session question before UNC Del was this: "UNC is going to release part of POWs and request delivery of civs in lieu of remainder. If Commies were to release part of POWs and request delivery of civs. in lieu of POWs would UNC agree?"

Fearing that Commies were trying to get clear committment [*sic*] from UNC that (1) use of POWs as hostages was proper and (2) that the exchange of POWs for civs was proper, as a basis for a counter proposal involving the use of POWs held by Commies as hostages for DPs from N.K. now in ROK, UNC made a statement crux of which was as follows: "There are no hostages in UNC proposal and no exchange of civs for POWs. The exchange of POWs takes precedence over repat [repatriation] of civs. However, when one side no longer has POWs who desire to be repatriated, then displaced civs should be integrated into the repat process concurrently with repat. of POWs. It is simple logistics prob. [problem] of making the most effective use of transportation to ensure the earliest completion of the overall repat. problem. This explanation is entirely consistent with UNC proposal."

In this manner UNC prepared grd. [ground] to move either way on quest [question] of use of POWs as hostages to regain civs. The proposal as written fits either interpretation. Obviously Commies are not fully satisfied with this explanation. It is believed they will not permit proposal to stand as now written if they can avoid it. However, we hope to be able to avoid the issue coming to a head at this stage by attempting to concentrate on other diffs. i.e. voluntary vs forced repat, parole former ROKA in KPA & ROK nationals in UNC custody.

After recess for lunch UNC said: "Repat. is the act of reestablishing a person in his own country. For the US or Fr. [French] soldier or a soldier of the UN it is clear that repat is effected by returning him to the UNC for eventual return to his own country. Such POWs hold no problem. For a ROK soldier captured by your forces or for a soldier of KPA captured by ours there is a real prob. because he is a Korean and Korea is divided into 2 parts.

"Now we have in our POW camps 3 categories of K soldiers; First, we hold many Koreans who were bona fide members of your army and who desire to return to your side. For such persons delivery to your side would be repat. Second, we hold Koreans who were bona fide members of your army, but who do not desire to return to your side. They are Koreans who want to live under the ROK govt. For such people, delivery to the ROK would be repat. while delivery to your side would be deportation or expatriation. 3rd, we hold approx 16,000 ROK POWs. Of these some may want to remain in the ROK and some may want to go to your territory. Delivery of the 1st group to the ROK and delivery of the 2nd group to you would be repat. Should our side retain all the 16,000 ROK POWs we would be, in effect, repatriating the 1st grp. [group] and expatriating the 2nd grp. Should we deliver all of this grp to you, however, we would be in effect repatriating the 2nd group and expatriating and deporting the 1st group.

"Now in the case of ROK soldiers captured by you, you are confronted with exactly the same prob. and the similar repat policy should apply. You have acknowledged holding only 2,500 approx ROK personnel as POWs. You have given no accounting for the remaining ROK soldiers you have captured and whom we still contend should have been classified by you as POWs. We know that a great many of these persons are actually in your Army. In equity you should apply the principle of "vol. repat" to all ROK soldiers held by you in exactly the same manner that we would apply to Korean soldiers held by us as POWs.

"Vol. [voluntary] repat. provides the only true repat for K soldiers who are held by either side as POWs. and for those ROK nationals in your Army who we again say should be classified by you as POWs. These people are all Koreans; they will all remain in Korea. The imp point is that they should remain in that part of K which they choose, that part of K in which they desire to make their real homes. No thumb rule will fit all these individuals. The only way you can determine what constitutes repat for that man, his inalienable right to be repatriated, is to ask him.

"In the case of the Chinese POW held by UNC the matter of repat is even more complicated. According to you these soldiers are "Chinese Volunteers" who have volunteered to aid your forces against the UNC. They are all Chinese but China is a country with two govts [governments]. Furthermore both Chinese govts are neutral in the Korean war. So just as the K soldiers should have a right to choose to which part of Korea they prefer to be repatriated, so should these Chinese Vols. [Volunteers] have the right to choose where they wish to go. Those who desire to be repatriated to the Republic of China should be so repatriated. Those who desire to be repatriated to the Chinese Peoples Republic should be so repatriated. Our proposal makes provisions for those who desire to go elsewhere. According to you these Chinese soldiers exercise freedom of choice by volunteering to fight for your side. They should be given the same right to exercise the same freedom of choice in electing repat.

"So here again, there is no set of rules that applies to all these persons. The only way you can insure that the individuals rights are not infringed, that his rights are, in fact protected is to have him sent where he wishes to go.

"There is no detention in our proposal. There is no coercion, there is no hostage, there is no deportation, expatriation or enslavement[.] Each person is released. Each person is truly repatriated to the place he wishes to go.

"[*sic*] **Col Tsai's long and general response included the folg** [following] **statement: "The Chinese peoples movement of safeguarding their homes, defending their fatherland, fighting against the American partisans is supported by all the people of the Peoples Republic of China. If anybody dares to hand over any of the personnel of the CPV captured by the other side to the deadly enemy of the Chinese People, the Chinese people will never tolerate it and will fight to the end."**

Jan 17. (Thurs): Opening Item 3 meeting UNC explained how air capability can be increased without intrduction [*sic*] into Korea of reinforcing combat aircraft.

Example cited how additional airfields closer to B.L. [battle line] permitted additional sorties per day by same aircraft. This would be a definite increase in milt air capability even though no reinforcing aircraft were introduced into K. Example cited how additional dispersal air fields provided flexibility in operations. The mere existence of these dispersal fields increase UNC air capabilities. UNC fully recognizes this fact and advocates restr. [restriction] in this regard in order that there be no tension created during arm. Obvious that development of air fields does increase mil air capabilities. No intention yesterday to imply that either side intended to violate arm [armistice], merely illustrating our firm belief that neither side should be given opportunity to increase its mil air capability during arm. Both sides have agreed to various safeguards designed to provide a stable arm; but agreements so far reached have left back door open. Agreement not to develop mil. airfields would close that door. UNC is unwilling to be a party to an agreement which so obviously lacks one very elementary safeguard. Both sides must agree not to increase mil. air capabilities. By addition of this safeguard to those already agreed to, we will have basis for stable & effective arm.

Hsieh attacked UNC statement on basis that it was really the theory of military balance—UNC method of prolonging war. Anything UNC desires is a basic condition to insure a stable arm. Most imp [important] principle for insuring a stable arm. is prohibition against introduction into K. of reinforcing mil forces, including combat aircraft. Of four factors in air power, basic one is aircraft since without aircraft there can be no air power.

UNC reply: Sophistry of Commie argument clearly revealed by its argument that since UNC proposed air field restr. it is responsible for the delay in reaching agreement on Item 3. Commies state UNC wants to prolong state of war. If that is so why should UNC propose restrictions on development of airfields? It is obvious that side which refuses to agree to restrictions on an increase of mil air capabilities is one which desires to prolong state of war. Doesn't the constr. [construction] of airfields which would double the effectiveness of a combat aircraft increase the mil air potential?

Hsieh queried whether UNC admitted that limitations on any facilities carried out by a sovereign state is interference in its internal affairs. UNC replied with comprehensive discussion of fact that agreements on restrictions on sovereign rights, as distinguished from violations of sovereignty and interference with internal affairs, are inherent in a mil. arm., citing as examples agreed restrs. on introduction into K of mil forces. and specified mil. equipment, and for observation by foreign nationals as to who and what enters K. Agreement on restrs on rehab. [rehabilitation] or constr. of airfields would not differ from these other agreements. It would not be a violation of sovereignty nor would it interfere with internal affairs.

Hsieh said UNC answer could have been made in one sentence: "I must interfere in your internal affairs."

#4. No progress was made in Item 4 meeting. Discussed bombing of POW camp at Kang Dong on 14 Jan in which 20 POWs were killed. **We asked whether camp was marked. Commies replied " As it happened at 2100 it didnt make any diff** [difference] **whether it was marked or not. We marked it in past but in spite of that it was raided so we dont make any mark any more."** UNC answered that this reveals Commie disregard for basic humanitarian principles of Geneva Conv., Art 23. Some illuminating mark should have been made. UNC insisted camps be marked & we be given exact geographical locations. Commie reply was a tirade on UNC wanton bombing.

UNC made long refutation Col. Tsai's statement of 16 Jan, stressed advantages of both sides of UNC compromise of 8 Jan and compared respective attitudes of two dels towards voluntary repat. UNC closed its statement by requesting Col Tsai to state in whose name he was speaking when he made statement quoted at end of Jan 16th meeting.

Lee replied with long dissertation which was later characterized by UNC as "a hysterical outburst containing more than usual no. [number] **of flagrant misquotations, and which show no comprehension of what we have said today."** UNC again attempted to force answer out of Tsai who he was representing when he made his statement referred to above. After some bluster Tsai informed UNC sub-del that it knew who was sitting in front of it and that was his answer.

Commies accused UNC of not living up to its promises re submission of data, particularly that on the 44,000 and demanded a clear answer as to when they would receive the data they had requested.

UNC stated it would answer quests [questions] on data tomorrow and would reply to such parts of Lees statement that required any comment.

Commies rptd [reported] that at 0935 today 2 single engine aircraft entered air space over Kaesong from NW. At appreciable interval following passage of plane one 500 lb bomb exploded near small village. No damage or casualties. R directed Feaf [Far East Air Force Headquarters] to make rpt. Prelim. investigation by Murray indicated UNC aircraft involved.

Genl Ridgway visited the camp overnight[.] Upon arrival he discussed with me JCS answer to his CX61348 which read as follows (paraphrased)[:] [JCS message number indistinct and thoroughly crossed out in margin]:

1. We concur your views Part 2a[.]

2. Your comment Part 2b. confirms our doubt on practicability of such procedure, but we wish to reiterate that all practical steps should be taken to reduce to min. [minimum] time between concession on airfields and final agreement.

3. Your planned procedure Part 3 approved.

4. Re Part 4, as a final posit. [position] which is currently approved at highest govt level, *you are authorized to agree to an all for all exchange on mil. POW's,* except that no forceful return of POWs would be required; however, prior to taking this posit, it should be clear that all other possibilities have been exhausted. Furthermore, since the President must be informed prior to actual break off, you should rpt. [report] to Wash [Washington] before precipitating or accepting such a break off in negots. [Brackets on next two sentences are CTJ's.] [It is possible that in face of pressure which could develop on this issue wherein loss of some 3000 POWs is balanced against welfare of an indefinite number of Commie POWs. in our hands, the govt might find it necessary to further modify our stand. Nevertheless you should act as if current position were final position keeping next preceding sentence strictly for your own guidance.]

Note: Bracketed portion not shown anyone in camp.

5. Accordingly, before adopting final posit, you should seek an agreement which makes provision for return of selected UN & ROK civilians. Such provision for return of civs [civilians] need not be on one-for-one basis against POWs. provided by Commies contain names of all UN POWs who can reasonably or account for civilians listed. It is assumed that prior accepting any all for all agreement on POWs, you would make every effort to ascertain that lists of living POWs provided by Commies contain names of all UN POWs who can reasonably be presumed to be alive and all ROK POWs whose return it is practicable to expect. Additionally any agreement on POWs must provide by one-for one exchange, or otherwise, that POWs held by UNC will not be turned over to Commies until satisfied UN & ROK POWs Commies have agreed to return will in fact be delivered to UNC. If in your judgment clearly no agreement whatever on civilians possible to achieve under Item 4, you will include specific reference thereto in formulation under Agenda Item 5, together with an expression on intent by MAC to facilitate and assist within limits its authority return of civilians to their homes. Instructions paras 10 & 12 Part 4 JCS 90083 in conflict this msg hereby rescinded.

6. In order exhaust every possibility obtaining agreement on civilians under Item 4 or, if possible at min. agreement on principle vol [voluntary] repat [repatriation] POWs only, it is suggested that at time deemed appropriate by you and consistent objectives para 4 JCS 91600, **you transfer negots on unresolved issues of *all* Agenda Items to full delegations and handle concession on air field issue in such a manner as to require Commie concession to our final position (para 4 above) on POWs and if feasible, civilians.** Your comment this point requested.

7. In order remove any possible genuine misapprehension that UNC intends utilize vol. repat. principle as pretext retaining all or most of POWs held by UNC and to counter Commie propaganda this subject, request your comments re. possibility of immediate poll of POWs, if practicable under ICRC supervision, to

determine approx number who would definitely desire repat. Commies could then be assured that at least the number determined by such poll would be returned.

8. Re Part 5. Suggest any possible ambiguity last part your proposed formulation would be removed if amended to read as follows:

"The Articles & paragraphs of this Armistice Agreement shall remain in effect until expressly superseded either by mutually acceptable amendments and additions or by provision in an appropriate agreement for a peaceful settlement at a political level."

As a result of my discussion with the Genl he gave me the following memo:

1. Following is substance of my proposed comment requested by JCS on para 6 their msg. and is offered for your consideration:

a. Assuming Commies will agree to initiate discussions now on Sub Del level on Agenda Item 5 we could then expect to delineate issues arising under that agenda item, and determine which, if any, could not be resolved. This having been done, the procedure suggested in para 6 of JCS msg would appear logical.

b. UNC Del believes, however, and I concur, that assumption stated in a. above has no valid basis in Commie conduct to date, and we can expect it to be summarily rejected.

c. If action in b. above should prove correct, then procedure proposed in para 6 of JCS msg could only be followed with understanding that issues which might arise under Agenda Item No 5 would have to be handled after agreement had been reached by mutual concessions on Agenda Items 3 & 4 and might accordingly present issues which would reopen and nullify this agreement.

2. Request your comments by 191200 Jan '52.

Jan. 18. (Fri.): In accord with CinCUNCs memo of last night, and after a conference with Libby Ferenbaugh, Darrow, Murray, Briggs & Galloway the following msg was dispatched:

To CinCUNC

1. Reference your memo handed me last night, the UNC Del. concurs in your proposed comments on para 6 of JCS 92059. We recommend elimination of clause "and might accordingly present issues which would reopen and nullify this agreement" at end of para 1c. It is felt such qualification is unnecessary and might result in needless receipt of additional restrictive instrs [instructions] from Wash [Washington].

2. The folg comments are offered for your consideration in connection para 7 JCS 92059[:]

"One of the strongest points of UNC proposal concerning vol [voluntary] repatriation is that choice is to be expressed by each POW at exchange point in presence of reps. of both belligerents and of neutral observers. UNC Del has vigorously denied existence of any program to influence ult. [ultimate] choice of POW and any coercion in POW camps. Consider Commies could seize upon poll by any agency whatever as basis for further propaganda concerning intimidation and coercion, and would never accept results of poll as fact. Moreover, should poll be taken and additional POWs later elect non-repatriation it would be most difficult not to hand over total number which original poll indicated wanted to go to Commies. Furthermore, poll conducted by ICRC at instigation of UNC might impugn neutrality of that organization, since Commies could not accept invitation to participate in poll without appearing to be giving some consideration to accepting principle of vol. repatriation. Finally not believed here that Commies have any real concern as to numbers who may choose not to return to them; it is the principle which is anathema to them since quest [question] of the individual versus the state is the crux of the difference between democracy and Communism. In summary believed here poll is impracticable, undesirable, unnecessary, and dangerous to UNC position.'' Signed JOY.

In accord with R's instrs to submit a plan showing our strategy and maneuvers by which we would follow out JCS instrs I directed team captains (Murray & Darrow) to appoint a joint Item 3 & 4 committee to study the problem & submit recommendations.

#3. UNC opened Item 3 meeting today with summary of truths & facts. Stated UNC yesterday had proven that additional mil. airfields would be increase in milt. air capabilities. This fact borne out by Hsieh's own statement of Jan 17. Also had shown an agreement to restrict milt. airfields was neither violation of sovereign rights or interference in internal affairs. Any state entering into Arm. [armistice] agreement voluntarily agrees to certain restrs [restrictions] of its own sovereign rights. Pointed out strange logic of Commies who, while accusing UNC of desiring to prolong state of war, would create stress by insisting on right to deal with milt airfields as it sees fit. Repeated UNC objective to reach agreement providing for stable & effective arm. Asked Commies again ''What is your objective in insisting upon right to build milt airfields thereby increasing your milt air capabilities during an arm?''

Hsieh replied UNC again asserts that restr of right of independent & sovereign state is not interference in internal affairs. Such assertion inconsistent UNC previous statements thus UNC must admit such restr. is interference. Insisted UNC must admit this is inter. [interference] in internal affairs in spite of tricks employed to make it sound mutually agreeable. UNC disguise as angels of peace do deceive certain people who voluntarily assume role of "running dogs" to appear volunteers. (Repeated slander of running dogs several times) This method of self deception will not fool Commie side. If UNC real objective is to assure stable arm leading to peaceful settlement, UNC should accept Commie proposal which has all necessary safeguards. Commies asked what justifies restrs on mil. airfields which are entirely a quest of internal affairs? What is UNC real intention in trying to create various excuses to insist on UNC unreasonable stand in spite of Commies firm stand? UNC argument that it does not intend maintain state of war in Korea is inconsistent with UNC refusal to withdrawal foreign troops. Reiterated spread of war due presence foreign forces in Korea. UNC closed eyes to quest. of withdrawal. Posit [position] of UNC to continue war and prolong stationing of foreign forces in K disqualifies UNC arguments. UNC actions subsequent Commie proposal 9 Jan further delay negots & maintains state of war in Korea.

Ferenbaugh stated his impression Commies recognize appropriateness UNC statements, soundness UNC logic and firmness UNC stand since they had to resort to slanderous statements re: UN forces in Korea. Running dog propaganda no answer previous UNC quest.

Hsieh said UNC logic is sound & reasonable to UNC side only. Commies want to uphold right of sovereignty and maintenance of internal affairs for which they have been fighting over a year.

UNC then rptd [repeated] statement that any state entering into an arm. agreement voluntarily agrees to certain restrictions of its own sovereign rights.

Hsieh stated UNC merely contradicts previous statement made in sub committee that restr on milt. airfields is question of internal affairs. Could proceed if UNC would only admit adequate safeguards to insure stable arm. have already been agreed. Most elementary safeguard is not to introduce a/c [aircraft].

#4. Sub dels Item 4 met 1100. UNC objective of concentrating discussion on issue of vol. vs forced repat [repatriation] largely achieved in todays session. UNC held initiative thruout session. No significant developments. Recessed 1330.

Jan. 19 (Sat): UNC opened Sub Del meeting on Item 3 with folg statement: Problem is reduced to single factor—restrictions necessary for stable and effective arm. [armistice]. Commies claim their 9 Jan proposal solved two remaining differences. Commies attempt to solve airfield quest [question] by ignoring it. UNC will continue to insist on arm. provision restricting both sides from increasing its mil air capabilities. It will not accept an agreement that does not insure the stability and effectiveness of the armistice. No validity in Commie reasoning that restriction not to introduce reinforcing a/c [aircraft] into K. is sufficient. Both sides have combat a/c in K. and capabilities these a/c would be greatly increased by additional airfields.

Hsieh answered that UNC is merely repeating its arguments of 16 & 17 Jan. No need to repeat refutation. The prob [problem] can be settled only if UNC realizes there is no purpose in further haggling. All Commie proposals have one basic provision for insuring a stable arm.—the prohibition on the introduction into K of mil. forces. including combat a/c during the arm. If UNC like Commies would carry this out, it is inconceivable that there would be any increase in mil. strength including air power.

UNC replied that Commies had made numerous references to existing balance of forces, with which we had agreed, and had demanded that UNC take attitude of equality and reciprocity. Bearing in mind the existing balance, that it should not be upset by any increase in mil. air capabilities, and that arm. agreement should be one of equality & reciprocity, UNC has consistently maintained that neither side should increase its mil air capabilities by rehab. [rehabilitation] or constr. [construction] mil. airfields. Requested explanation of enemy 17 Jan. statement that the theory of maintenance of mil. balance is unnecessary and impractical. **Commie answer was a masterpiece of specious reasoning and irrelevancies the tenor of which was that they have never favored the principle of maint.** [maintenance] **of balance of forces which is impossible and impractical and would require interference in internal affairs.** Introduced subject of "provocative" acts of UNC in violating territory of Peoples Republic of China, violating Kaesong area, and attack on marked convoy on 18 Jan. [Unclear in Joy's journal whether this is "18 Jan." or "8 Jan." with a number scratched out preceding the "8"]

UNC stated it had already refuted Commie argument that their 9 Jan proposal is a solution to the problem. Both sides well know that the the only way to prevent increasing the capabilities of a/c in K is to prohibit development of mil. airfields. UNC queried how it was conceivable that air capabilities would not be increased if there were no restriction on development of mil airfields & how there could be a stable arm. without such a restr. Hsieh replied that both quests were answered by the principle contained in the 9 Jan proposal prohibiting introduction of mil. forces, including combat a/c, into K since this principle made it inconceivable that there could be any increase in mil. power including air power.

#4. In Item 4 meeting UNC was again able to keep the discussion on the issue of vol. versus forced repatriation and to maintain the initiative. No significant results. Recessed 1600.

Received as info adee [addressee] msg from CinCUNC to JCS which answered JCS 92059 as follows:

1. Ref para 6.

a. Ref is made to Part 3 my msg CX 61348, 12 Jan '52. In order to make the proposal outlined in Part 3a(1) of CX 61348 it will be necessary to convene full del. in plenary session. At that time we will:

(1) Propose that the quest of rehab. of air fields be deferred in view of the continued disagreement on both sides.

(2) Propose that discussion of Agenda Item 5 be initiated at sub del level and conducted concurrently with continued discussion of unresolved topics under Item 4.

(3) Propose that drafting of arm agreement details derived from agreed principles of Items 2 & 3 be initiated at staff level concurrent with the substantive discussion of Items 4 & 5.

b. Should Commies agree to the proposals in a, above, which is considered doubtful it will be possible to definitely establish unresolved issues on all agenda items and then proceed as suggested in para 6 JCS 92059.

Part II answered para 7 JCS 92059 practically with the same wording as our suggested answer.

Jan. 20 (Sun): Hsieh started Item 3 meeting saying he had nothing to say. UNC stated that its posit [position] on airfield restrs [restrictions] had been fully explained and that no further explanation was necessary; that its proposal was sound and its position firm; that it proposed that its 4th principle be accepted; and that if Commies had no quests [questions] & nothing to offer, a recess until 1100 hrs tomorrow was suggested. Hsieh replied that they had many times rejected the UNC 4th principle because it calls for interference in their internal affairs[,] that it was impossible for him to make the Commie posit more clear; and that he agreed to recess tomorrow. Meeting lasted 6 mins.

Delegation believes the foregoing stategy [*sic*] for today and next day or two, to be the most effective we can follow. Our proposal and the basis for our position has been very completely explained & established. At the opening of every meeting recently, Hsieh states that he has nothing to say, thereby compelling UNC to make a statement and afford him an opportunity to give vent to propaganda blasts reiterating allegations of interference in internal affairs in what purports to be a rebuttal of the UNC statement. We shall continue to press for our proposal each day in concise statements which support our firm & unequivocal stand.

Item 4. Lee opened Item 4 meeting with a long prepared statement intended to be a comprehensive review of Communist opposition to UNC proposal. A summary of that statement follows[:]

"UNC proposal is designed to blackmail with the greater number of POWs. UNC has failed to justify its proposal. The false argument that Commies have impressed POWs has almost become a protection for the proposal. It is a false assumption from which UNC cannot depart in trying to explain. It is a slander. Arguments developed from this false position are invalid.

"UNC charges that persons born in the southern part of Korea are in Commie forces involuntarily, and proposes to bring all these people to the exchange point to express their will before a neutral organ [organization]. This is an internal affair in which UNC has no right to interfere.

"UNC attempts to use the POW in excess of the no [number] of POW held by Commies as a means of blackmail. Thus exchange on a 1 for 1 basis and the idea of substituting the POWs with the civs [civilians] and holding POWs as hostages. Under interrogation UNC has 3 times changed its explanation on a 1 for 1 basis; has been altered into an exchange of equal nos. The exchange of equal nos. is further described as simultaneous transportation. But the proposal clearly states that the no of POWs shall be exchanged with an equal no of foreign civs. displaced civs, and the so called POWs who were incorporated into our army.

"If such a position is not equivalent to holding POWs as hostages, then what is it? UNC unnecessarily confuses the quest. of the civs with POW and further assurance by which you attempt to deprive every POW of a part of the right and obligation conferred on him by his country (parole)[.] Our side is resolutely against such a unilateral demand. The shield to cover all this is the high sounding phrase "vol. repat. [voluntary repatriation]" with which UNC rejects principle of unconditional release & repat of all POWs. The instructors from Taiwan enforce the so called Anti Commie Salvation Grp [Group] and force POWs to write so called posits [positions] to express they would rather stay 10 yrs in custody than to return to their homeland. UNC trick is obvious. It is called free will but this has been unmasked with respect to those of the CPVs who have been captured, if they wish to be repatriated to the Chinese Peoples Republic they can go there. If they wish to go back to Taiwan they can also go there[.] This is clear evidence that UNC would hand over to Chiang Kai Shek personnel who have been captured. With respect to the personnel of the KPA it is again clear that UNC would hand them over to the ROK. Commies shall fimly oppose this and oppose this forever. UNC has talked of deportation and expatriation. Is not detaining captured personnel under various pretexts and refusing to repat them to the milt. [military] units to which they belonged deporting them? This is strictly a milt negot discussing the release & repat of POWs. The quest. is very simple. The POWs are milt men. After the hostilities they should be released and repatriated to the other side without any conditions[.] This is their undeniable right. This is the inescapable obligation of both belligerents. Such rights & obligations are not to be altered. In order to prevent either side from detaining the POWs. under the pretext that it is their voluntary will or any other pretext the Geneva Convention stipulates clearly in Art 7 that not even the POW themselves can renounce this right in part or in its entirety. UNC does not hesitate to violate the basic right of the POW and to complicate the quest. to such an extent as to go beyond the scope of strictly mil. negots. UNC says majority of captured personnel will elect back to your side. This is nonsensical remark unrelated to quest. Commies will never give up in their determination to bring about the unconditional release & repat of all POWs."

In reply UNC disregarded Commie reference to hostages and mixing of POWs and civilians inasmuch as we have already given sufficient indication that we might be amenable to modifying UNC proposal in this respect. Commie opposition to parole was refuted. Remaining portion of refutation was directed to issue of vol. vs forced repat. A summary of UNC concluding remarks follows:

"Discussion has centered on freedom of choice which is the basis of the UNC compromise proposal, versus forced repat. which is included in the proposal advocated by Commies.

"UNC has demonstrated that Commies have without adequate safeguards to insure the right of the individual, unilaterally applied the doctrine of free choice during hostilities in Korea. If Commie practice were accepted as a basis for the release & repat of POWs the problem would be reduced to insignificant proportions. UNC would simply incorporate the majority of the POWs it now holds into its armed forces, even as Commies have done thruout war.

"In view of the past practice of Commies this solution would be equitable as between the two belligerents, but it would do violence to the rights of thousands of individuals. Moreover it would be inappropriate to an arm. [armistice] intended as a first step towards a peaceful settlement.

"What is needed is a formula which will protect the interests of the POWs without infringing upon the legitimate interests of either belligerent.

"While the problem of the release of all POWs is not complex, the problem of true repatriation is complicated by the circumstances surrounding this conflict and by the facts that (a) milt persons & civs who are nationals of the ROK have been inducted into the armed forces of the other side; and (b) nationals of the ROK who joined Commies have been recaptured and are now held in UNC custody.

"Under these circumstances, repat of the POWs according to army designation alone would do only slightly less violence to the rights of the individual that [than] the solution under which each side incorporates the POWs it holds into its own forces. This formula, if adopted would expatriate many POWs, not repatriate them[.] Each side would receive from the other many POWs whose loyalty was in quest. Each side would deliver its own loyal supporters to the other side. The inevitable consequences of such an exchange would be the visitation of retribution of many POWs who have suffered enough from the war. The suffering of POWs should not be compounded by revenge & retribution.

"The UNC compromise proposal was drafted to eliminate the shortcomings of a proposal based upon the previous practices of Communists or of repat by army designation alone[.] It extends to the individual freedom of choice and it provides a supervisory organ to insure that the choice will be made freely and without duress or coercion of any kind.

"The equity and humanity of this principle have been widely recognized. Communists however, have attempted every device to discredit it. They have called it political[.] It is not. They have called it a vicious plot by means of which UNC seeks to hold hostages and deliver them to the ROK and Taiwan. It is not. They have called it interference in their internal affairs. It is not. Commies have advocated in opposition to it, the inadequate, inhumane and vengeful doctrine of forced repatriation according to army designation. But they have not advanced one logical, valid argument that can refute the proposal. The principle of freedom of choice stands openly and conclusively as an equitable and humane solution to the prob. of repatriation. Since Commies can no longer defend their opposition to the principle on logical grounds UNC asks that they accept it. The UNC is not going to give up its insistence on this principle." Recessed 1445.

Jan. 21 (Mon): Starting off Item 3 meeting UNC offered Commies the floor. Hsieh stated he had nothing to say. UNC then stated in substance: for past week UNC has patiently explained the necessity for airfield restrs. [restrictions] & how UNC proposal met that requirement. Commie argument has been limited to false allegations that UNC desires to prolong the war and to interfere in their internal affairs. Commies have offered nothing constructive. UNC proposal is clear, sound and firm, but we are always ready to answer any questions concerning it. If none recommend acceptance of UNC proposal. If Commies not ready to accept today, suggest recess until tomorrow at 1100 hrs[.]

Hsieh replied with folg. prepared statement: UNC 29 Dec proposal has been rejected by Commies many times. They will reject it forever. In order to insure a stable arm. [armistice] they have already made all reasonable suggestions toward the wording on the principles on Item 3 and it is impossible to make any more changes. The arm negots [negotiations] in K have already reached basic agreement on all points. The peace loving people of the world recognize this but UNC still insists on its outrageous demand to interfere in Commie internal affairs by restrs. [restrictions] on airfield facilities. Sole purpose is to delay and disrupt the negots.

Comment: The use of the above prepared statement by Hsieh seems to indicate that he anticipated UNC would maintain its firm stand on airfields at least in todays meeting. Unless directed otherwise, tomorrow we plan to tell Commies that UNC would be willing to accept principles 4, 5 & 6 of their 9 Jan proposal as worded HNC (728) provided they add a provision for restr on mil [military] airfields. We are thus accepting Commie wording on "political conference" and neutral nations without a following parenthetical "non combatant[.]" In return, we hope to induce Commies to suggest a revised wording of airfield restrs. part of principle.

Item 4. UNC opened Item 4 meeting with a summary of arguments on forced vs vol repat [voluntary repatriation] charging that Commie objective in opposing vol repat. was to gain milt advantage thru their one sided proposal. Lee made a general refutation. No significant developments. Recessed 1310.

Sent folg msg (HNC 780) to CinCUNC, referring to JCS 91600, CX 6138, JCS 92059 and CX 61892.

"Part 1. In accord with your verbal instrs, and guidance in above refs. [references] **delegation plans to adopt folg procedure in continuing arm negots.**

1. a. Item 3 sub del [delegation] continue to hold firm with present posit. until on or about 25 Jan.

b. Item 4 sub del continue to hold firm with present posit. When appropriate be prepared to revise present proposal to separate POWs and civilians.

2. a. On or about 25 Jan, sub del on Item 3 submit revised proposal in which airfield quest. [question] is separated from principle 4. and made a new principle 7. Sub-del intends thereafter to press for agreement by Commies to settle details of 6 agreed upon principles in staff officer or sub del meeting[.]

b. If Item 3 goes to staff officers:

(1) Negots on Item 4 continue at sub del level reducing issues as soon as pract. [practicable] to major one of vol. repat. When UNC final posit in Item 4 is established and when appropriate, attempt to shift details of agreed issues to staff officers as in Item 3.

(2) At appropriate time reconvene plenary session and propose sub-del meetings for Item 5[.]

3. If Commies refuse to accept UNC proposal in 2a, convene full del in plenary session and propose procedure outlined in para 1a, CX61829:

a. That quest of rehab. of airfields be deferred, in view of continued disagreement on both sides.

b. That drafting of Arm Agreement details derived from agreed principles of Item 3 be initiated at staff officer level concurrent with sub-del discussions of Items 4 & 5. (Details of Agenda Item 2 Final Mil Dem [demarcation] Line cannot be settled until just before signing of Arm agreement.)

c. That discussion of Agenda Item 5 be initiated at sub del level and conducted concurrently with continued discussion of Item 4 at sub del level.

4. If Commies in Plenary Session reject proposal Para 3, press for agreement to sub-del meetings on Item 5 and propose continued discussion on Items 3 & 4 at sub del level. At appropriate time thereafter carry out procedure in para 5. below.

5. Reconvene Plenary Session and submit to Commies a complete draft of Arm. agreement. This draft will include the two major issues, airfields and vol repat, as well as any major point which might arise under Agenda Item 5. It will then be possible to propose at the opportune time settlement of all remaining details of the Arm Agreement on staff officers level, while the main dels discuss the major issues in disagreement.

Part II. UNC Del believes the procedure proposed above to be the most logical one capable of accomplishment in the sequence indicated. The submission of the UNC draft of Arm. agreement as indicated in para 5 would gain for us a large psychological advantage and result in our securing negotiatory and propaganda advantages. However we feel this step cannot be taken until many details of our posit have been discussed with Commies. It is most desirable that every pract effort be made to obtain Commie reaction on these details prior to submitting entire draft in Plenary Session.

Dr Lehner & Mr de Cocoatrix of the ICRC stopped in at the camp for luncheon on their way from Pan Mun Jom to Seoul with reply to their President's msg from Kim & Peng.

Jan. 22 (Tues): Hsieh opened Item 3 meeting, saying: Now 12 days since Commies made 9 Jan proposal. UNC has not been able to raise any tenable arguments in opposition to that proposal. Since 13 Jan on 4 successive occasions UNC has carried out provocative acts in attempt to make excuses for delaying and disrupting negots. Those acts clearly reveal UNC intent. If UNC intends to continue negots it should not insist on its dogmatic attempt to interfere in Commie internal affairs. Responsibility for delay is on UNC.

UNC reply: Yesterday Commies said it was impossible to change wording of their principles. UNC has not suggested changes in wording. UNC willing to accept exact wording Commie principles 4, 5 & 6 if Commies would add a provision for restr. [restriction] mil airfields in order neither side could build up mil. air capabilities. Would welcome proposed wording from Commies, if none forthcoming, suggest they accept UNC wording regarding air fields. If not prepared do to that suggest recess until 1100 tomorrow.

Hsieh closed: UNC statement is continuation of actions of past two days and wastes another day. Commies have pointed out reasonableness their proposal and proven unreasonableness UNC demand. Continue to firmly reject any attempt to interfere their internal affairs. Said senior UNC delegate bragged about renewed mil. activity in US News & World Report by saying, "Maybe only way to break deadlock is renewed mil. pressure, other side only understands bombs & bullets." Thus UNC deserves high vigilance of Commies. People of world realize this. Four provocative acts since Jan 13 prove UNC putting senior del. words to action.

Plan to continue tomorrow pressing for UNC posit on restr. on airfields.

#4. In Item 4 meeting Commies stated they had nothng to offer. UNC made two hour statement which discussed the composition of the various groups entitled to vol repat. [voluntary repatriation] under UNC proposal, and discussed Commie objections to application of principle to each group. The five groups discussed were: Civilians; Civilian internees held by UNC; ROK POWs held by UNC; ROK personnel in KPA; and bona fide POWs held & reported by each side.

Commies gave one hr. refutation. Stated that they would assist civs. returning home thru their administrative organs [organizations] and that they would repatriate them. Foreign civs under their care will be unconditionally and immediately repatriated. POWs as well as displaced civs. will be unconditionally repatriated. Remainder of refutation was repetition of old arguments.

At end of meeting, UNC asked if Commies were ready to convene staff offs meeting on locating & marking POW camps. Commies replied first meeting of staff officers could take place tomorrow following Item 4 sub del meeting. Recessed at 1415.

Recd msg from CinCUNC approving procedure outlined in our HNC 780.

Jan. 23 (Wed): Hsieh opened Item 3 meeting stating UNC suggestion of 22 Jan was no concession in that there was no difference from UNC proposal of 29 Dec. Point of issue is quest [question] of interference in internal affairs against which Commies reiterated their strong stand. Said Commies would not bargain on this point. Reiterated that Commie 9 Jan proposal settled the two major issues fairly & reasonably and that UNC should accept their proposal without hesitation unless UNC desires continues playing tricks to disrupt and delay conference.

2. UNC asked if Commies had anything to propose. Hsieh replied no. UNC then pointed out Commie 9 Jan proposal was inadequate; that Commies were insisting UNC accept arm [armistice] terms which will give Commies free hand to increase milt air capabilities at will; that Commies are insisting upon an ineffective arm. UNC stated UNC would not be party to any such ineffective arm. UNC then accused Commies that, by refusing to recognize importance & necessity of UNC recommendation regarding restrs on mil airfields, they are delaying the conference, prolonging the state of war, desire to create tension during an arm. and intend to increase milt. capabilities during an arm. UNC then asked why Commies would not answer UNC quest by stating they do not intend to increase milt. air capabilities during an arm. Said their refusal to answer question provided whole world with their intentions. UNC suggested recess if Commies had nothing to propose or offer.

#4. Sub del met at 1100 & adjourned at 1350[.] Discussion centered on voluntary vs forced repatriation and produced no significant developments.

Comment: **It is my opinion that the Commies are deliberately stalling on orders from Peking & probably Moscow and that we will make no progress until the UN Assembly adjourns.** Vishinsky will continue in his attempts to transfer the arm conference from Korea to the Security Council. In the meantime the Commies are building up their strength along the front and are becoming more formidable each day. They are using these talks as a tactical maneuver in which to build up for another offensive.

Jan. 24 (Thurs): Hsieh opened Item 3 meeting with lengthy prepared statement in which he said: Commie basic objection to UNC proposal to restrict military airfield development is that it constitutes an interference in the internal affairs of a sovereign state. Subordinate reason for objection is that such restrs are an unnecessary requirement. No merit to UNC argument that Commies refusal to state explicitly that they do not intent to build milt airfields indicates they intend to do so. Whether they will or will not is not pertinent. Quest [question] of restrs on milt airfields is by its very nature not proper subject for mil. arm. [armistice]. He then reviewed Commie version of UNC statements in support of proposal to restrict development of mil airfields and reiterated various Commie arguments in purported refutation of those statements. He concluded that UNC object was to disguise its intent to interfere in Commie internal affairs, leading Commies to believe that UNC objective is also to enable it to retain ability to unleash wanton bombing at time of its own choosing. He again asserted that so-called provocative acts were an attempt by UNC to intimidate Commies.

UNC requested Commies to state clearly whether they intended to increase their mil. air capability during the arm. Hsieh evaded question by stating that his statement had comprehensively refuted UNC posit. [position]. UNC stated that Commies actions were those of one who expected to reap mil benefits from the arm. by calling an increase in mil air capabilities an internal affair. Commies are responsible for causing delay in reaching agreement under the guise of resisting interference in internal affairs. Hsieh replied that he had already refuted the UNC statement.

Intend to execute tomorrow first step of planned action outlined in HNC 780.

#4. UNC opened Item 4 meeting with an attack on Commie formula of "release & repatriation of all POWs" showing effects of application on each of 5 groups of personnel ie civs [civilians], ROK nationals in KPA, ROK nationals now held by UNC as civilian internees, ROK nationals now held by UNC as POWs and all other POWs rptd [reported] held by KPA and held by UNC.

Lees reply is summarized herewith: "Classification of POWs into 5 grps [groups] has no foundation[.] On basis of what law & what facts is such classification made? POWs cannot be regarded as civs. & classified on basis of nationality. First error lies in classification under presumption that there are 2 govts. in Korea & China. Second error lies in disregarding fact that POWs must be classified by army designation. 3rd error lies in trying to settle quest. by confusing civs. with milt persons. 4th error lies in classifying them under presumption there are POWs in KPA which is not true. All these errors spring from fact that UNC reps. [representatives] forgot they are milt. reps, that these are milt negots [negotiations] & that POWs are milt. persons with proper army designations. Thus UNC touches on political quests. which cannot be discussed here. Therefore UNC would deal with POWs not as POWs. but as nationals of certain govts. **Therefore UNC would coerce POWs to express their political standpoints.** Therefore, there are uprisings in the POW camps as UNC organizes anti-Commie Salvation Corps & carves anti Commie slogans on bodies of POWs.

"UNC insistence comes from its effort to justify exchange on a 1 for 1 basis. As UNC thinks 1 for 1 proper it interprets that unconditional release and repat [repatriation] involves an increase of milt force. Therefore UNC develops strange argument on vol. [voluntary] repat. & free choice. UNC explains its improper stand as though it were designed for defense of individual rights when it would violently tread down the inviolate rights of the POWs. The fair stand of release & repat. conforms with Art 118. It conforms with Art 7 which stipulates that the rights of POWs cannot be renounced. It conforms with the effort to make the armistice a bridge to peace.

"The UNC unnecessarily complicates the issue by its 5 group classification. It has no basis in fact. We have already indicated our attitude towards the civs. The POWs held by the UNC are milt persons with army designations who belong to our side and those we hold are milt persons who belong to UNC. Thus, these must be unconditionally released & repatriated. UNC should give up its barbarous insistence on repat on basis of increase of military force, trade of populations, slave trade & exchange of human meat. UNC should accept our proposal to achieve a clear cut rapid solution to Item 4[.]"

UNC refuted briefly.

In closing Lee inquired again as to when data on the 44,000 would be provided. He stated that the world would be very interested in the process by which 34,000 persons of their regular army had been converted into civs.

Recessed 1400.

Jan. 25 (Fri): UNC opened Item 3 meeting. Statement made by Commies yesterday contained nothing new and failed to overcome the firm basis upon which the UNC proposal stands. It indicated that Commies do intend to increase their milt [military] air capability during the arm. [armistice]. This makes UNC stand all the more firm. Hsieh answered with prepared statement reasserting that UNC proposal was illogical, that its allegations were slanderous. He reiterated that restr. [restriction] on introduction into K of reinforcing combat a/c [aircraft] was a sufficient guarantee that there would be no increase in milt air capabilities. UNC stated that Commies had said nothing new and asked if they had anything new to propose. Upon receiving negative answer, UNC stated it was apparent that until Commies accepted UNC proposal or offered an acceptable revision, no progress could be made; and then suggested course of action as planned in HNC 780. (See part 2 for text). Hsieh replied that since their 9 Jan proposal, they do not consider there is any remaining difference between the two sides. They believe there should be agreement on principles before discussion of details. Stated unable to answer UNC suggestion until comparison different translations but that it would be subject to necessary study and suggested recess until tomorrow.

Part II. Complete text UNC statement: "Since 9 Jan, our two sides have been discussing last remaining major issue not settled in Agenda Item 3. We have made no progress during this period. UNC has offered a solution to this problem; however, unless you will accept this solution or offer a revision acceptable to us, it does not appear that we shall make any further progress in the preparation of Arm. terms at this time.

"Our side sincerely wishes to reach a stable and effective armistice as soon as possible. We hope that you are likewise sincere and desirous of making tangible progress as rapidly as possible. You will agree with us I am sure that the hopes of the world would be immeasurably stimulated if we could report some progress instead of the stalemate that now blocks any mutually satisfactory agreement to Item 3.

"With that end in view, we have a suggestion to make which we hope you will consider seriously. True, the suggestion does not immediately solve the main problem that confronts us, but it may pave the way towards an eventual satisfactory resolution of our differences.

["]It is, of course, apparent that there are many details to be worked out under Item 3 even were all principles agreed upon. Each principle must be expressed in wording of the actual arm. document, and some require considerable amplification prior to incorporation in that document. A great part of this work can be done now, thus bringing nearer the time when an arm agreement can be signed once agreement is reached on unresolved issues. With this thought in mind, our side has a suggested course of action to offer which we believe will contribute towards making tangible progress in these negots [negotiations], even though we have not reached agreement on the airfield quest [question].

"Our suggested course of action consists of—immediately turning over to the staff officers the task of settlement of details and the drafting of the wording for the arm agreement, based on tentative agreements which have already been reached under Item 3. For this purpose we are prepared to accept and utilize the agreed principles 1, 2 & 3, principles 5 & 6 as worded in your proposal of 9 Jan, and to use your wording of that portion of prin. 4 on which we are agreed.

"As to the present point of dispute, the air field quest. we propose the selection of one of the folg. [following] alternative courses of action in a continued attempt to resolve this issue:

(a) Continue to conduct sub del discussions on this issue as at present, while the staff offs are meeting to discuss & resolve details of the tentatively agreed upon principles[.]

(b) Temporarily recess the sub-del discussions until the staff offs are ready to submit to the sub del for approval, the results of their efforts.

(c) Submit the airfield issue also to the Staff Offs. for their discussion and recommendation after they have resolved the details of the tentatively agreed upon principles.

"We are willing to accept your recommendation as to which of these alternative actions the sub del should pursue.

"We submit this course of action in a sincere desire to make progress in these negots. and bring them to a successful conclusion in the min [minimum] amount of time. We hope you will join us in this endeavor.["]

#4. Lee opened Item 4 meeting with statement demanding to know when UNC would deliver additional data on POWs. i.e. (a) original list with addition of ranks & unit designations (b) 1456 names omitted from original lists of names but shown but shown [sic] in numerical recap of POWs held (c) 44,000 names taken from Geneva lists but not included in lists submitted by UNC of POWs held.

UNC replied (a) & (b) would be delivered as soon as completed but that delivery of (c) which taken in conjunction with (a), (b) and a list of dead, escapees, etc would constitute data on all POWs ever held by UNC, was contingent upon receipt from Commies of an accounting for the missing 50,000 UNC POWs.

After exhaustive discussion of this subject Lee turned to issue of vol. repat. [voluntary repatriation] with statement summarized herewith:

"As regards the so called 5 groups of persons listed by UNC the first group is the civilian DPs[.] After the arm, both sides should unconditionally all [allow] the displaced persons to return home. There is no necessity to bring them to the exchange points nor is it permissible to mix them up with the POWs for any human barter. The second group, civilian internees held by the UNC, consists largely of our milt personnel taken prisoner by your side who have been reclassified. Since UNC has repeatedly stated that the milt personnel of a party to the conflict who have fallen into the power of the enemy should be taken as POWs, what justification does it have to reclassify as civs. [civilians] our captured milt personnel? Furthermore, what justification has UNC to demand on the one hand to exchange civs. on a 1 for 1 basis with our personnel captured and held as hostages by your side, while on the other hand unreasonably reclassify our captured personnel as civs. in violation of every international law. The 3rd group is the so called ROK POWs held by UNC. These POWs are milt. men of K nationality. They are moreover milt personnel of the KPA and they have the inalienable right to repatriation enjoyed by all POWs.

["]As for the 4th grp. [group] the so called ROK personnel in the KPA all the men in the KPA are milt men of K nationality and there are no POWs in the KPA. Such a group of persons exists only in fantasy. They do not exist in reality.

["]The fifth group is POWs held by both sides. Release and repat. is the inalienable right of each of the POWs. There is no necessity to bring them to the exchange points to cast a vote. Neither is it permitted to infringe on their right to repatriation under any pretext. The so called vol repat is an attempt to deprive the POWs of their right of unconditional repat. It is an attempt to retain our captured personnel. It is an attempt to keep the men of the KPA and CPV to be handed over to their enemies. UNC has had instructors sent over from Taiwan. It has tatooed the bodies of the POW held by it. Uprisings take place again and again in its POW camps. All these fully express the substance of the so called vol repat. Our side absolutely will not permit the violation of the principle of unconditional release & repat of all the POWs under any pretext." In subsequent statement Lee said: "There is no such nationals of the ROK (civ DPs of ROK nationality) among them. If those from the regions south of the milt. dem [demarcation] line want to go home we will assist them in going home." Recessed 1345.

Comment: Data was rec'd at CinCUNC Adv [Advance Camp] this date & (a) & (b) as described in par [paragraph] 2 will be delivered as soon as obvious errors therein can be corrected. Current preoccupation of Commies with data probably reflects a feeling that its poss. [possession] will improve their posit. [position] with respect to the 38,000 former POWs who have been reclassified as civ internees. Increasing effort by Commies to avoid recog. [recognition] of ROK nationals as such probably forecasts grounds on which they will further challenge this reclassification and on which they will press their claim for the ROK POW we hold.

Jan. 26 (Sat): Hsieh opened Item 3 meeting by repeating Commie Jan 9 proposal provided all necessary conditions for a stable arm. Commies do not recognize there are any differences remaining between two sides. Why does UNC persist in attempting to interfere in internal affairs of other side? Responsibility for delay rests squarely on UNC shoulders.

UNC got Commies back on track by asking if Commies needed more time to study UNC suggestions of 25 Jan. Hsieh said UNC suggestion still under consideration but did not consider it related to UNC acceptance of Jan 9 proposal. After prompting by UNC, Hsieh remarked UNC still attempts to postpone agreement on principles and still insists on interference in internal affairs. This attitude requires clear explanation.

UNC explained alternate courses of action given yesterday. Assured Commies UNC had no intention of abandoning requirement of no increase in milt air capabilities during period of arm. [armistice]. Said that if Commies preferred Staff Officers could work on agreed principles 1, 2 & 3 and on Commie revision of 4, 5 & 6 and make the airfield question principle 7 which sub del could (1) continue to discuss now (2) defer until Staff Officers had completed details of other principles (3) defer until Staff Officers made recommendations on principle 7 after completing work on first 6 principles.

Hsieh said listing airfield question as principle 7 did not change UNC unreasonable demand to interfere in internal affairs of other side. Commies stand on this matter perfectly clear. Commies do not consider question of procedure very consequential.

#4. UNC opened Item 4 meeting with 2 statements with folg. theses:

(1) The ROK is a fact and it is a fact that it has nationals. The implications of this cannot be disregarded in these negots. [negotiations].

(2) Commies agreed previously that supplementary data would be exchanged on a reciprocal basis. They now appear to be trying to get data on the 44,000 without providing data on all the POWs they have held.

The folg is a summary of Lee's reply:

"It is inevitable that our viewpoints on political and ideological quests [questions] **differ because our side represents the interests of oppressed masses whereas UNC represents interest of** a group in opposition to them. Let us talk about the regime in which UNC is interested. A definite territory is required for a state. A state must have the support of broad masses of its people. If it cannot sustain the form of a state by itself and must be sustained by the armed forces of foreign interventionists it is no more than a puppet govt under their control. Such a puppet govt. becomes an organ [organization] for the massacre of the people under the interventionists. The regime the UNC defends is such a regime. If the UNC wishes to discuss political quests the delegates should obtain proper credentials from the govts concerned and make appropriate arrangements for such a conference. But they are not so empowered. So I will fight to frustrate UNC's absurd contention (that some of the personnel under discussion are nationals of the ROK[)].

"I am not satisfied with UNC's answer on the data because UNC does not show an attitude of exchanging data on an equal basis and does not discriminate correctly between basic and supplementary data. The 44,000 are milt. personnel of our side. Data on these is basic data which should have been delivered with the other data on 18 Dec. UNC has said the 37,000 reclassified constituted the major portion of the 44,000. But 34,000 of these are regular milt. personnel of our side and upward of 9,000 were irregular milt persons. When they fell into hands of UNC they became POWs. In no way can they be reclassified as civs. [civilians]. This is why data on the 44,000 is important. UNC has no right to withhold this data. Moreover the 16,000 POWs are also our milt. personnel and no one can deny it. Quests asked yesterday on justification for reclassification are repeated. UNC refuses to submit data on our milt personnel and reclassifies them as civilians with apparent intention of handing them over to their deadly enemy under various pretexts such as voluntary repatriation."

UNC response included an explanation and justification of the reclassification of 37,000 nationals of the ROK as civilian internees.

Lees reply was a long tirade summarized herewith:

"What is content of humanitarianism of UNC? The destruction of the peaceful cities of Korea, the villages, the schools, the hospitals, and cultural institutions. For what milt. target were they bombed and in accordance with what law? It is brazen of UNC to claim it observes war regulations. Now about the kidnapped civs, the atrocities in Pyongyang upon UNC withdrawal. UNC made deceitful propaganda to effect that it would drop atom bomb after withdrawal. It said CPV would slaughter citizens. It said that all who remained would be shot by the Commies[.] Therefore thousands took to the road to Kaesong[.] What did UNC do? Its aircraft bombed & strafed them. Its ground troops machine gunned them. When we returned to Pyongyang a tragic sight greeted us at the bridge over Taedongyang. Numberless corpses of civilians massacred by bombs and machine guns of UNC. Such massacres occurred everywhere. The Korean people will talk of this for generations and revenge will live in their hearts. This has aroused the indignation of the world. It is only a shred of the story of the civs kidnapped by the UNC. Where is the humanity in this? Can UNC prove it did not kidnap them. There are numberless orphans in northern Korea and numberless parents without children. What better witnesses are there? Dont tell us such fairy tales.

"UNC attempts to justify vol repat [voluntary repatriation] and reclassifies POWs as civs. What articles of the Convention authorize it? To organize anti-Communist Salvation Corps in POW camps to tatoo slogans on the bodies of POWs is that humane administration. Why are there uprisings in these humanely administered camps? What is the plight in the humane POW camps. Poets & artists of Korea will sing of and paint these humane camps. Historians will record the facts of your temporary rule. These righteous records will rouse the flame of vengeance against you in the hearts of the Korean people.

"As for the question wherein does UNC proposal tread down rights of POWs. It is the right of every POW to be repatriated. UNC proposal opposes this and adds conditions and brazenly calls it voluntary repatriation. It says this is not infringement of rights but an increase in them unprecedented in history and a dvelopment [*sic*] in humanitarianism. Lincoln advocated freeing the slaves unconditionally. Suppose one had risen to give them one more right: that they be voluntarily freed. This would have been deception and would have resulted eventually in no emancipation. Such a one would have been a criminal for trying to infringe upon the rights of negroes. By adding a condition to emancipation he would kill it. Such a thing is the so called vol. repatriation. It does not add to rights of POWs but is a deceitful method of depriving them of their rights[.]'' Recessed 1445.

Recd copy of a personal msg from Collins to Ridgway advising R of a coming high policy meeting between Sec [Secretary] State, Sec Defense and JCS to explore what new actions if any should be recommended to the President in order promptly to bring about an armistice on proper terms in Korea. Invited R to send a representative earliest, suggested Hickey.

R answered that in view of steps being planned he did not feel his representative could contribute anything more for consideration[.] R reluctant to send Hickey but could send Wright.

R then followed up with a second msg giving his opinion "there was a measurable chance of achieving real progress on acceptable arm terms providing there be not slightest indication revealed to Commies from any authoritative, or even normally reliable official source that further UN or US concession is forthcoming or even under consideration." R went on to offer the view "that we should be permitted to pursue the program outlined to you without further directed concessions, new instrs. or even the holding of high level conferences to discuss our negots." He recommended its adoption for approx 2 wks.

In view of R's msgs to the JCS outlined above, I thought it a good idea to inform R of our present thinking in the event that it might become necessary to submit in plenary session our package armistice agreement. Our proposed course of action follows: "Having rec'd the Commie reaction to the overall agreement, we shall divide the resulting issues into categories of major & minor issues. We shall propose that major issues be discussed in plenary session while minor issues are handled by staff officers in separate meetings. With this procedure in view, we intend to submit our package agreement including some issues on which we can afford to concede, so as to provide a negotiating cushion[.] To this end we consider it desirable at the present time to include among others in our package agreement, the following points:

(1) Airfield restrictions

(2) Voluntary repatriation

(3) Civilian repatriation

(4) No definite time limit as to the convening of a political conf. [conference] after the arm

(5) Principle of parole.

"We would initially offer to exchange (1) for Commie concession on (2), (3), (4) & (5). Later we would expect to concede on (1), (4) & (5) in order to gain concession on (2) & (3).

"As a final step, we should be authorized to adopt an ultimatum posit. [position] including (2) above only. Such an ultimatum posit. must be associated with a definite time limit for acceptance by the Commies, and a proclamation from highest sources supporting our posit. should be issued concurrently[.]

"It is highly likely that the Commies will prefer to concede on airfield restrs. [restrictions] rather than on voluntary repat. [repatriation]. If so the delegation will require further guidance."

Sent R a msg concerning Item 5. since Del feels that at proper time inclusion in our proposed wording of Item 5 of a solution acceptable to the Commies might serve to convince them in some measure of the sincerity of our desire to at least initiate the first step towards a permanent settlement of the K problem[.] My msg took exception to the wording authorized by the JCS as it disregarded Commie phraseology and requested certain changes thereto. Msg also asked authority to include a definite time limit for recommending political conference after the armistice. Also said in msg "it would be extremely helpful to know current thinking as to the countries that are to be considered as comprising the "countries concerned[.]"

R came back to say: "I feel that the statement contained in JCS 90083 must be presented as UNC initial position. Our rec. [recommendation] about a definite time limit was under consideration. Countries concerned are considered to be the overt belligerents in K war but avoidance of the question of the identities of the countries concerned is important to preclude defacto recognized govts & authorities concerned."

Jan. 27 (Sun): Hsieh opened Item 3 meeting with prepared statement to effect Commies consider that quest. of rehab. of airfields does not exist since Commie proposal of 9 Jan prohibits the introduction of milt a/c [aircraft] into Korea. during the period of the arm. [armistice] thus preventing the increase of mil air capabilities. Proposed that sub committee meetings be suspended temporarily and staff officer meetings be held on those principles of Agenda Item 3 on which agreement had been reached. Sub committee would be reconvened when staff offs. had completed their work and made recommendations to the sub delegates.

UNC reminded Commies of three alternates which UNC submitted, requested Commies clarify which alternate Commies had chosen. Hsieh evaded direct answer & made folg statement, "It is our proposal that the sub committee meetings be suspended temporarily and that the staff officers of both sides meet to discuss the details and that the sub committee meetings will be reconvened upon agreement reached by the staff offs. on the details and when their agreement is submitted to the sub committee.[''].

Evident that Commies desired record to read as though airfield quest had been dropped altogether; after 15 min recess UNC agreed to put matter into staff off. meeting with folg statement, "We understand that you have proposed to accept alternate (b) of our suggestion of 25 Jan. We are prepared to proceed on that basis with the clear understanding that we reserve the right to return to the subject of airfield restrs as soon as the sub dels. reconvene. We hereby record our unalterable intention to do so. Our staff officers are prepared to meet with yours 10 mins from now."

After reiterating reasons for non-existence of airfield quest, Hsieh agreed to recess. Staff offs met immediately. Report of staff offs meeting follows.

UNC opened staff officers meeting to say purpose of first short meeting was to discuss procedure. UNC intended to present draft of Armistice Agreement for Commie study and comment. This draft considered suitable and in accord with agreed principles Agenda Item 3. Explained that draft did not contain paras. pertaining to Agenda Items 4 & 5 and that provisions relating to milt airfields would not be discussed by staff officers. Presented Commies with two copies of draft revision of 26 Jan. Copies presented to Commies & released to press here contained provisions para 1, CX 62278. Chang [Chang Pyong San] agreed to make thorough study and in meantime tentatively agreed to work in accord procedure suggested by UNC. As for questions to be resolved, stated his understanding that discussions will be based on details of agreed principles of Agenda Item 3. Suggested staff officers recess & reconvene at 28 1100 I. UNC agreed.

#4. Opening Item 4 meeting UNC inquired if other side had anything to say which would assist in the solution of Item 4.

Lee said they had long ago proposed a most fair and reasonable proposal for the solution of Item 4 adding that the item could be easily settled by UNC giving up voluntary repatriation and accepting Commie proposal.

UNC replied that it would not give up its insistence upon vol repatriation. It stated that if other side had nothing further to offer, a recess until 1100 tomorrow was proposed.

Lee replied that principle of unconditional release & repat of all POWs was an unshakeable principle and agreed to recess.

Comment: UNC action in proposing a recess today was negotiatory step taken in consideration of Lees irrelevant tirade yesterday. However, Lee's ready acquiescence to this proposal tends to confirm the conclusion that a stalemate has now been reached on the issue of vol. vs forced repatriation.

Jan. 28 (Mon): Sent folg personal msg to General Hickey: "On 24 Jan Lowell Thomas broadcasted over CBS folg: **The word persists that the allies are getting ready for new concessions** — — — Maj Gen Harrison takes the place of Maj Gen Ferenbaugh. The belief is that Gen Harrison will use more tactful diplomatic approaches, not so fiery as "Fireball" Ferenbaugh. Dispatches keep on intimating that new concessions are now being prepared. The fact that these dispatches are being passed by censors in Korea is taken as a sign that the info is likely to be correct.

Undoubtedly this info originated from article in Nippon Times by Rutherford Poats. As you are well aware articles of this nature can do great harm to our negots. [negotiations]. Suggest every effort to indoctrinate censors in proper screening and PIO's [Public Information Officers] in carefully briefing and educating correspondents.

Staff officers meeting on Item 3 was postponed until tomorrow pursuant to telephone request of Commies.

#4. UNC opened Item 4 meeting by delivering revised rosters of POWs showing 20,720 Chinese & 111,360 Koreans. This total of 132,080 is 394 less than the recap of POWs presented 18 Dec. It was explained to Commies that the 394 were civ [civilian] internees in the POW camps as of 13 Dec who have since been transferred to CI camp and whose names are now on CI roster. UNC stated this constituted all basic data.

UNC then stated that it was prepared on 72 hrs notice to exchange the supplementary data which taken together with the basic data, would provide a complete accounting for all POWs ever held in exchange for similar data from Commies.

Lee noted the receipt of the data and read a short prepared statement summarized herewith:

"To release and repatriate all the POWs is the obligation of both sides and the right of the POWs; yet UNC opposes this principle; seeks to deprive POWs of their rights and produces "vol repat." [voluntary repatriation], "substitute POWs with civilians" and "parole" in an attempt to detain POWs to hand over to Taiwan & S.K. Attempting to justify itself UNC argues that principle of vol. repat. is designed not to deprive POWs of rights but to in [insure?] them. The consequence of it is denial of rights, the preventing of repat. UNC says its proposal is not to substitute POWs with civs nor hold POWs as hostages. Nevertheless, the written proposal includes it. Since UNC holds more POWs it is attempting to use them as blackmail[.] It does not hesitate to deprive them of their rts. It seeks pretexts to serve purpose of blackmail. That is where vol repat, substitution of POWs with civs. and parole had their origin. UNC likes word voluntary. I tell you you cannot attain this purpose.[''']

After brief refutation, UNC introduced proposed wording of armistice on Item 4 with folg statement:

"For a number of days both sides have been discussing the basis of release of POWs, repatriation of POWs and repatriation of civs. Thus far we have achieved no agreement in this regard and during past several days we have made no perceptible progress toward such agreement. The UNC sub-del believes that its compromise proposal of 8 Jan constitutes a very positive step toward agreement on Agenda Item 4. However, you continue to oppose the UNC proposal and adamantly to demand that we agree to the principles of your proposal of 12 Dec '51. In the meantime your side has failed to take any positive steps whatsoever toward resolving the differences between us. Despite this, you continue to assert that you do in fact, desire an early agreement on Agenda Item 4 and on an arm. [armistice]. We too are desirous of reaching an agreement. We believe that if we are to achieve an early agreement on Agenda Item 4, both sides must take positive steps toward resolving the issues which have thus far prevented agreement. [Following sentence crossed out in text: We believe that if we are to achieve early agreement on Agenda Item 4, both sides must take positive steps toward resolving the issues which have thus far prevented agreement.] Pending resolution of our basic differences and in order to facilitate settlement of details concerning points on which we are agreed, the UNC del. has expanded its proposal of 8 Jan to include all items which in our view are essential to constitute a complete solution for Agenda Item 4.

"You will note that this proposal not only contains the basis for the release of POWs, the repat of POWs, and the repat of civs, but also incorporates all pertinent matters listed in your proposal of 12 Dec '51 with exception of forced repat. and the provision for 'release in groups' which we do not understand. In addition, we have included several other matters which we consider essential to the settlement of the overall problem and we have written this proposal in detail so that it is in all respects a complete solution to Agenda Item 4.

"We request that you carefully study this proposed solution and that when you have completed your study you give us your comments as soon as practicable[.]"

Recessed 1212.

Comment: Purpose of presenting draft agreement to enemy at this time was:

1. To attempt to get enemy to respond to indications given previously by UNC that it would reconsider parole feature and exchange of POW with civilians

2. To attempt to secure enemy agreement to non controversial features of Item 4

3. To attempt to narrow area of disagreement in Item 4.

I sent special msg to R (HNC824) which in effect said that instead of calling a plenary session at an early date in order to initiate sub del discussions and obtain Commie views on Agenda Item 5, I now proposed unless directed otherwise to submit a request for a sub del meeting direct to Nam Il by letter. I pointed out this procedure would have advantage of not interrupting progress of present meetings of sub del on Item 4 and staff officer meetings on Item 3 and of avoiding possible stalemate in plenary session. Also proposed to press as an alternative to this meeting that Commies furnish us their proposed first draft of Arts. [articles] for Item 5. Gave draft of ltr to Nam Il which said, ''My reason for recommending the initiation of discussion of Agenda Item 5 at this time is to enable the dels. to develop all major issues confronting us in conn [connection] with an armistice agreement in the hope that these issues may be resolved in context with one another. We have not been able to resolve these issues singly perhaps we can resolve them in conjunction[.]''

R approved msg & ltr. with several minor changes.

Jan. 29 (Tues): At staff meeting on Item 3 staff officers discussed preamble and paras 1 through 13d of UNC draft agreement. In general, Commies showed disposition to accept UNC wording and format in armistice document. The two principle issues were (1) Islands (2) Rotation total. Commies contended that the extension of the dem. [demarcation] line on the west would result in islands listed in para 13b of the arm. [armistice] agreement being assigned to their side. UNC refuted this point. Commies stated they were astonished at enormous rotation figure (75,000). UNC staff officers indicated this could be reduced to 40,000 if rotation was interpreted to include only true replacements, (exclusive of R & R [rest and recuperation] activities, etc)[.]

Meeting was conducted in an atmosphere of serious intent to make progress. Changes in draft agreement suggested by Commies are regarded, in most instances[,] as improvements. Meeting recessed 1545.

#4. Lee opened sub-del meeting on item 4 with comment on UNC draft of Item 4 agreement presented yesterday. Summary of his opening statement follows:

''This detailed draft is not a positive step towards solution of Item 4. 6 out of 14 Arts are identical with 8 Jan proposal. It disregards basic principle of unconditional release & repat. [repatriation]. This renders entire proposal defective. UNC still designs to detain POWs to turn over to its partners. To this we cannot agree. Because of this difference any effort to undertake discussion of details is untimely[.]

"With respect to the ICRC we have stated that the RC of the DPRK and of the Chinese Peoples Republic together with the ICRC could form a joint visiting group which would proceed in separate teams to the POW camps of both sides to make visits and assist in the reparation work at the points where the POWs are handed over and received. Such assistance in the repat work should not be mixed up with the functions of the organ [organization] to be formed by both belligerents for release & repat. of POWs.

"Civilians should not be confused with POWs. Both sides should unconditionally assist DPs to return to their homes. UNC has made a similar statement but its proposal still substitutes POWs for civilians and uses the former as hostages[.]

"As for voluntary repatriation all the POWs should be unconditionally released & repatriated. It is their inalienable right and the recognized principle of all past wars. To depart from it is to infringe on rights of POWs. Vol. repat. so infringes.

"As these are mil. discussions between belligerents it is a matter of course that POWs be repatriated solely on basis of previous army designation. UNC proposal is political and exceeds scope of negots [negotiations].

"UNC says unconditional release & repat would increase Commie mil [military] forces and proposes one for one exchange to avoid this. These absurd arguments have been refuted.

"Judging from this draft there is no desire on part of UNC to make progress. If it does not give up its unreasonable proposition of blackmailing simply because it holds more POWs, no progress will be made at the conference."

In subsequent discussion Lee indicated little disposition to discuss "minutiae" while there was no agreement on the "basic principles." However, it was determined that Commie attitude on draft presented yesterday was in opposition to all but 2 of the 13 Arts.

In response to UNC effort to get Commie views on some form of guarantee as regards the repat of displaced civs. [civilians] in exchange for separation of POWs & civs. in UNC proposal Lee only repeated that it was the obligation of both sides to repatriate the displaced civs.

Following up a msg from us (see Jan 26) R sent a dispatch to the JCS asking for guidance as to "countries concerned" should Commies attempt to name them when discussing Item 5. Also requested guidance about definite time limit, i.e., authority to substitute some such phrase as, "that steps be taken within a period of 90 days" for presently prescribed phrase "that early steps be taken" as outlined in JCS 90083.

Jan. 30 (Wed): Staff officers continued to make progress on details of Item 3. Discussion centered on control of 5 islands, which we maintain must remain under UNC control, and figure of 40,000 for rotation. Commies maintain figure should be 25,000 including R & R [rest and recuperation] & TDY [temporary duty]. Our figure of 40,000 excludes R & R & TDY, 75,000 with R & R & TDY. Commies stated on their part they would dispatch more men out of Korea per month than they would bring in.

#4. Lee opened Item 4 meeting saying that he had already expressed Commie attitude on UNC proposal of Jan 28, and that principles should be determined before details were discussed. He then expressed folg views:

1. Commie posit [position] on ICRC is stated in ltr from Kim to Ridgway
2. Civilian & POW repat [repatriation] should be separated
3. Oppose unconditional release & repat of POWs and advocate so called vol [voluntary] repat which not only deprives POWs of their basic rights but exceeds scope of mil. negots. [military negotiations]. They involve the principle of one for one exchange and blackmail for greater no [number] of POWs held by UNC. They mix POWs & civs. substituting POW with civs and holding POWs as hostages. They advocate unilateral parole. They unlawfully classify Commie mil. pers. [personnel] as civs.

Lee agreed civs should be assisted to return home. However they are scattered widely in homes of relatives and friends. A detailed statistical investigation under present circumstances is impossible. It is also impossible to call them together and repatriate them in groups within a definite period after the signing of the arm.

UNC refuted briefly Commie stand on Red Cross matter. It stated ICRC was neutral and could not be identified with UNC. Membership of a joint activity such as Commies proposed would consist of national RC societies of UN fighting in K along with RC of DPRK and CPR. Such an activity might be formed with profit to the POWs[.] However, it would scarcely take the place of the ICRC in matters concerning the exchange of POWs since national RC societies are not neutral and since their functions are different from those of ICRC.

Turning to the quest. [question] of civ. repat UNC stated that there was need for an arrangement by which each side would be safeguarded against charges from the other side that it was not complying with the arm. [armistice] provision on the return of displaced civs. It stated that UNC proposal contained such a provision, but indicated that it was willing to consider any proposal the Commies might wish to make which would accomplish same purpose.

Lee indicated that foregoing would require more study.

In view of progress being made in meetings of staff offs and Agenda Item 3, I feel it advisable to deliver letter to Nam Il tomorrow and consequently sent R a msg giving him contents of ltr that would be sent. It follows:

"In view of suspension of meetings of sub del on Item 3 of Agenda, and in order to make max [maximum] progress in development of arm terms, I recommend that sub-dels be appointed to discuss Item 5 of the Agenda concurrently with present discussions on Agenda Items 3 & 4. If you agree to this recommended procedure, a UNC sub del would be prepared to meet with your sub del at an early mutually satisfactory time & date.

"I have taken this means of proposing action on Item 5 in order not to disturb the work now proceeding on Item 3 & 4 by calling a plenary session of the full delegations. If you desire to discuss this proposed action rel [relative] to Item 5 in plenary session, however, I am agreeable to meet with you.

"The UNC Del has furnished to your side proposed draft arts of the arm. agreement relating to Items 2, 3 & 4 of the agenda. Since Item 5 of the Agenda was introduced at your initiative, and since the UNC has initially submitted the draft articles for Agenda Item 2, 3 & 4, it seems appropriate that your side propose the 1st draft of arts relating to Agenda Item 5. If you prefer, as an alternative to early establishment of a sub-del for Item 5, our mutual purposes might be as well served by your staff. offs. now working on Item 3 of the Agenda submitting to ours a draft of your proposed arts regarding Item 5.

["]I await your reply" signed C. Turner Joy[.]

R approved my contemplated action.

Jan. 31 (Thurs): Staff Officers meeting on Item 3 continued to make progress; went through para 36. Atmosphere continues very favorable.

#4. Lee opened Item 4 meeting by questioning UNC use of 38th parallel as basis for distinguishing civilians to be repatriated.

Comment: Apparently his desire is to use dem. [demarcation] line as basis in order to avoid recognition of ROK nationality implicit in use of 38th parallel. There is a legitimate objection that the article as written denies the former residents of those areas between the dem line and the 38th who are now on the other side of the dem line an opportunity to return home. To meet this objection UNC will draft a revision of the current wording of its proposal.

Lee continued minimizing the need for any provision to assure observance of the arm. [armistice] agreement with respect to civilian repatriation.

UNC stressed absolute necessity for such safeguard and explored further the possibility of getting Commie agreement on the above issue and on any part of the provision involving the ICRC. In the latter connection the folg exploratory statement was used:

"In Dec, CinCUNC addressed a comm. [communication] to your Comdrs [commanders] requesting them to give favorable consideration to inviting the ICRC to visit your POW camps.

"In responding to this request, your Comdrs undertook to admit the ICRC for this purpose and for the additional purpose of assisting in the repatriation of POWs, on a joint basis with your national RC societies, provided your national RC societies were invited to extend their services to the POW camps under our control.

"As we have previously indicated a truly joint RC activity would include as members your RC Societies and the national RC Societies of nations participating in the UN milt [military] action in Korea—that is a group of National RC Societies from your side and from our side. An organization comprising members from one belligerent and a neutral cannot be a joint organization in the sense that we have been ascribing to the term "joint" thruout these discussions.

"These national societies of our side are already serving the forces in the territory under our milt. control. Insofar as it is appropriate they are assisting the ICRC in the performance of its specialized duties with respect to POWs, duties which are prescribed under the Geneva convention.

"Presumably your National RC Societies are already serving your own camps, even as ours are serving our camps. Moreover if your side desires to operate in this manner behind your lines, it is your own affair and a matter for arrangement between you and the ICRC direct.

"Organization of a joint RC facility to operate in the POW camps of both sides would take some time. Since its organization could not very well get started before the arm is signed and since the camps should be empty within a month or two after that it is doubtful if the facility would be operating in time to serve its purpose. It seems to us that it would be preferable to have the national RC societies of both belligerents continue to serve the POW camps under their control and to assist the ICRC in every way in its own specialized field as defined in the Geneva Convention. However if your side desires to attempt to establish a joint RC facility we are willing to take it under consideration.

"As I indicated, the exchange between our Comdrs. on the subject of the ICRC was related only to its function of visiting POW camps.

"While this function is included in the UNC proposal, that proposal contemplates requesting the ICRC to perform certain additional functions for each side.

"The first is to provide a technical advisor to the POW Exchange Committee

"The second is to provide a technical advisor who will serve as Chairman without vote on the Committee for Reparation [repatriation] of Civilians

"The 3rd is to provide personnel to each side who will be responsible to see that all displaced civs. [civilians] will have an opportunity to state whether or not they wish to go to the other side. This provides each side a safeguard against possible charges from the other side that it has failed to comply with the agreement to repatriate all civs who desire it."

Lee gave no conclusive reply to these proposed uses of the ICRC indicating that they would be studied further as would the UNC comment on a joint RC facility to serve both sides. He also indicated that he would study further the matter of writing into the agreement some language which would provide mutual protection against possible charges of violation of the arm. terms with respect to repat. [repatriation] of civs.

Comment: Should the Commies categorically reject the use of the ICRC in conn [connection] with civilian repat. the UNC will suggest as an alternative the use of neutral observers.

Feb. 1 (Fri): Staff officers continued to make progress in Item 3 meeting. Discussion centered around ports of entry for neutral inspection teams. Commies proposed only 3 ports of entry. In reply to UNC statement that such a limited number of ports was insufficient, Commies pointed out that each side must necessarily assume the good intent of the other to bring in replacements through agreed ports. Otherwise, said Commies, an infinite no [number] of teams would be needed to guarantee against a deliberate effort to circumvent armistice terms. Commies further pointed to authority of MAC to send neutral teams to investigate any reported violation. It appears to the delegation that there is much to the Commie line of thought. After further development of the point, we expect to reduce number of observed ports on each side to the number needed by UNC for it's [*sic*] rotation and replenishment activities during armistice[.] Tentatively our thought is that this number is six.

Commies were not prepared to nominate neutral nations. UNC nominated Switzerland, Sweden & Norway for "Neutral Nations Supervisory Commission." Commies not prepared to discuss acceptability of these nations[.]

#4. UNC opened Item 4 meeting by submitting revised version of para 10 of Item 4 proposal to provide for return to their homes of displaced civilians who were former residents of areas between 38th parallel & Milt Dem [Military Demarcation] line. Commies indicated they would comment after studying translation.

Major part of days discussion centered around UNC proposal for interviewing of displaced civilians in both North & South Korea. UNC stressed point that interviews at adequately located points on both sides were necessary to provide assurance to both belligerents that the other side was carrying out the provisions of the arm [armistice] agreement and to protect each side against unwarranted accusations that the agreement is not being carried out.

Commies stated unequivocally that they intended to carry out fully any agreement concerning repat [repatriation] of civs [civilians]; that interview teams were unnecessary[;] that the ICRC was in their view not neutral and hence could not be acceptable for interviewing[;] that even if real neutrals were available the use of interview teams in their rear constituted interference in their internal affairs; and that good faith & sincerity were the only essentials needed to make the armistice work.

UNC pointed out that good faith was not enough, that like the use of teams in Item 3 each side needed safeguards written into the Arm Agreement to increase the stability of this phase of the arm; that use of neutral teams instead of ICRC should be considered, if Commies found ICRC unacceptable in this role; that safeguards to both sides in preventing charges of breach of Arm Agreement was vital and that either the UNC proposal or one Commies might propose should be brought forward to solve this issue.

Further re ICRC, Commies stated they could not agree to have ICRC representative as non voting chairman or as technical adviser to the Civilian Repat Committee, nor could they agree to ICRC technical adviser to POW Exchange Committee. Communists again stated that ICRC was not considered by them to be neutral.

Comment: It is clear that Commies definitely oppose any impartial role for ICRC and consider that agency definitely favorable and biased towards UNC.

Feb. 2 (Sat): Staff Officers continued meetings on Item 3. Discussions centered on (1) Control of shipping navigating waters of Han River estuary (2) Definition of "coastal waters" (3) Control of 5 islands (4) Rotation. Considerable progress made in that entire document was covered with substantial agreement throughout.

#4. Lee opened Item 4 meeting with prepared statement substantially as follows: Establishment of neutral teams at interview points not necessary, proper or acceptable; this situation different from neutral teams under Agenda Item 3 where it is purely military; interview of civilians is a task for civil authorities; neutral teams add nothing in the way of assurance since good faith and sincerity essential in any case and it would interfere in the internal affairs of his state. Then Lee attacked UNC reworded para [paragraph], defining displaced civs. [civilians] as ambiguous since UNC used both 38th parallel & Mil. Dem [Military Demarcation] line when only consideration should be Mil. Dem line. Noted that element of choice remained in para and stated while not a bad idea he considered it beyond scope of these discussions. Closed by indicating that we should solve principles first; that main obstacle to a solution of this Agenda Item was UNC unreasonable insistence on vol. repat; exchange of equal numbers, unilateral parole etc; that all these points must be given up if Item 4 to be solved; that unconditional release & repat. is right of POWs and an obligation we must fulfill. Then he asked for a change of stand and constructive suggestions from UNC.

UNC replied indicating only UNC had made constructive efforts so far; that UNC must have adequate safeguard on civ. question before arriving at solution of completely separating civilians from POWs. Two solutions had been offered by UNC; Commies should contribute by accepting one or offering alternative. Although UNC assumes good faith that alone not enough. Reaffirmed necessity for safeguard. Then UNC described in detail concept of neutral interview teams and demonstrated that instead of interfering in internal affairs, work by such teams would be invaluable to civil officials of each side. Concerning para. defining displaced civs, UNC amplified and explained it and strongly suggested that instead of merely objecting Commies should contribute by submitting their proposals for study. Closed with 2 questions: (1) How would you define displaced civilians? (2) Suppose UNC expects 100,000 ROK civs. to be repatriated and with good faith Commies send only 1,000 back. How do you propose to satisfy UNC you have carried out terms of agreement under such conditions.

Commies answered with long, rambling pointless statement which offered nothing to solution of civilian problem and attempted to revert to POW quest. [question]. Neither UNC quest was answered. UNC requested answers to quests tomorrow. Commies suggested recess at 1307.

Feb. 3 (Sun): Staff officers continued discussions all Arts Item 3 except airfields. UNC requested Commie views regarding definition of "coastal waters." Commies stated no necessity define these waters since (1) Both sides had agreed cease naval blockade and patrol; (2) Specific items such as minesweeping could be settled thru MAC. Further discussion brought out intention of UNC not to blockade outside coastal waters. Commies strong on this point and apparently needed reassurance. Commies then agreed to define coastal waters & suggested 12 miles. UNC indicted this was too far, but both sides agreed to study matter further.

UNC then reopened quest. [question] of islands. Commies agreed UNC retention of 5 named islands. UNC stated would submit rewording of para to clarify island quest.

Commies indicated it would be necessary include rest & recreation personnel & temporary duty personnel under rotation figures, UNC stated.if such personnel were included and movement was limited to specific ports of entry, 12 such ports would be required by UNC. UNC recommended that since both sides had agreed not to increase cumulative totals in Korea and that exchange would be on man for man basis both sides should agree to strike out ceiling clause on rotation. Commies indicated reluctance to do so, stating principle of limitation had already been agreed by sub dels. Decided to study matter further. Commies reiterated 25,000 was adequate for rotation including TDY and R & R.

UNC indicated 15 Joint Observer Teams would not be too many considering length of line, area of demilt [demilitarized] zone and probability of some teams being used on Han River Estuary. Further recommended figure of 10 be adopted at very min. [minimum]. Commies stated there shouldn't be much difficulty resolving this matter, stated they would like to consider further.

Score to date at staff officers conference follows: Commies have agreed to 39 paras and sub-paras of UNC draft Arm. [armistice] Agreement without change and 22 with minor changes in wording; 11 are agreed generally and under discussion pending agreement on wording; and 7 are under consideration for resolution.

#4. 'In initial statement of Item 4 meeting Commies reviewed history of meetings to date, emphasizing positive steps taken by them versus unfairness and unreasonableness of UNC. Result has been no basic agreement after 52 sessions.

Stated usual arguments against UNC proposal regarding 1 for 1 exchange, vol repat [voluntary repatriation], mixup of POWs and civilians and unilateral parole. [Remainder of paragraph emphasized in text by a bold line in left margin.] Accused UNC of intent to capitalize on larger no [number] of POWs held by it, by using them as blackmail while at same time turning over many POWs to its partners. UNC proposal defined as unprecedented violation of all traditions of warfare and violation of all reason & ethics.

Fundamental agreement on other agenda Items had been reached and all peace loving people of world awaiting agreement on an early armistice. To meet desires of people and to eliminate any possible UNC pretexts, Commies submit a new proposal. The proposal is based on unshakeable and correct principle (release & repat all POWs) incorporates all reasonable propositions of UNC, and eliminates the unreasonable pretexts put forth by UNC. Requested agreement in principle so that both sides can enter into discussion and decide on details and fulfill task assigned by Plenary Session.

Commie proposal follows:

"1. Both sides agree that, immediately after the Milt. [Military] Arm. Agreement is signed and becomes effective, all POWs in custody of each side shall be released and repatriated.

2. Both sides agree to ensure that all their captured personnel shall, after being repatriated, be restored to a peaceful life & shall not take part again in acts of war.

3. Both sides agree that seriously sick & wounded POWs shall be repatriated with priority. Insofar as possible, both sides shall repatriate captured medical personnel at same time when such POWs are repatriated so that latter may be accompanied & cared for.

4. Both sides agree that all the POWs in their custody besides those who are repatriated with priority under par 3. shall be repatriated in grps. [groups] within the period of 2 mos. after the Milt. Arm. Ag. [Agreement] is signed and becomes effective.

5. Both sides agree that Pan Mun Jom within the Demilt. Zone will be the place for handing over and receiving POWs by both sides.

6. Both sides agree that, immediately after the Milt. Arm. Ag. is signed and becomes effective, each side shall designate 3 officers of field grade to form a Committee for Repatriation of POWs, to be responsible, under the supervision and direction of the MAC for specifically planning & supervising the execution by both sides of all the provisions in the Milt. Arm. Ag. relating to the repat. of POWs. If unable to reach agreement on any matter relating to its mission, the Committee shall refer such matter to the MAC for decision. The Committee for Repat. of POWs shall be located in proximity to the Hdqtrs of the MAC.

7. Both sides agree that, immediately after the Milt. Arm. Ag. is signed and becomes effective, civilians displaced owing to the war shall be assisted to return home and resume a peaceful life.

(a) The UNC shall permit and assist those civilians, who originally resided north of the present Milt. Dem [Demarcation] line but have been stranded south of the present Milt. Dem line before the Milt. Arm. Ag. is signed and becomes effective to return home; the KPA and CPVs shall permit and assist those civs [civilians] who originally resided south of the present MDL [Military Demarcation Line] but have been stranded north of the present MDL before the MAA [Military Armistice Agreement] is signed and becomes effective to return home.

b. The Supreme Comdrs [Commanders] of both sides shall be responsible to publicize widely the content of the above agreement in the territories under their control, and to mandate the related civil administrations to give necessary guidance and assistance to all the above mentioned civs who wish to return home.

c. Immediately after the MAA is signed and becomes effective, each side shall designate two (2) officers of field grade to form a Committee for assisting the return of Displaced Civilians to be responsible, under the supervision and the direction of the MAC, for assisting the above mentioned returning civilians to cross the Demilt Zone and dealing with other related matters. If unable to reach agreement on any matter relating to its mission, the Committee shall refer such matter to the MAC for decision. The Committee for Assisting the Return of Displaced Civs. shall be located in proximity to the Hqtrs of the MAC.''

In answer to several UNC quests, Commies stated folg:

1. "Repatriation in Groups," para 4 is purely a technical matter. Transportation facilities not same on either side and nos. of POWs held by each side differ. The numbers of POWs in the groups would depend on the capability of each to deliver & receive. Commies still intend to deliver POWs held by them within 30 days, but realize UNC cannot deliver its larger no of POWs in 30 days & therefore specified 2 mos in their para 4.

2. The phrase "all of the POWs in custody of each side," para 1, means all POWs included in data handed by Communists to UNC, and all POWs included in data given to Communists by UNC. UNC then asked if Commies were thus renouncing claim to 37,000 ROKs held by UNC as civilian internees. Commies stated they had never agreed that UNC should have reclassified these former POWs, and therefore they should be in the UNC POW camps, and should be included in para 1. [Following sentence crossed out in text: However Commies stated they had never agreed that UNC should have reclassified these former POWs and therefore they should be in the UNC POW camps.] However Commies stated that when we had supplied them with data on the 44,205 they can express their viewpoint on whether these are POWs or civilians after they have surveyed the data. UNC informed them such data was available on 72 hrs notice and would be furnished at same time as they furnished us the remaining data they owe us on unreported POWs.

3. In answer to UNC question whether phrase "who wish to return home," para 9b, applied to all civs, Commies stated that all displaced persons who left

their homes because of havoc of war, and who want to go back home, should be assisted and permitted to go home.

I received msg from Nam Il in reply to mine, which said that Commies agreed to discuss Item 5 of Agenda concurrently with discussions on Agenda Items 3 & 4. Considered that an agreement in principle should first be decided upon in plenary session and that afterwards the matter could be handed over to the staff officers.

I replied thru liaison officers that we could meet them at 1000 on 5th but Commies prefer 1000 on 6th.

Comment: Both Darrow and Kinney who are working on Item 3 feel that Commies are sincere in their evident eagerness to make progress. This opinion springs from the Commies unusual reasonableness in trying to reach an agreement on the various paras of Item 3. No doubt their desire to make progress may be occasioned by the UN's action in Paris. A UN Committee has voted to postpone all consideration of the Korean issue until an armistice is reached or a breakdown at Pan Mun Jom forces the UN to discuss stronger action. The general assembly's political, economic and social committees acting jointly voted 51 to 5 yesterday for a resolution to this effect put up by the U.S. Britain & France. The resolution provides for calling a special or emergency session of the Assembly whenever Korean developments warrant one way or the other. The full assembly is expected to give final approval early in the week.

Feb. 4 (Mon): Staff officers, Kinney & Darrow, continued Item 3 meetings with little progress. At end of our daily report msg to CinCUNC folg comments were made:

(a) Current discussions have highlighted the folg. as result of which delegation recommends reconsideration of the number of ports of entry to be specified by UNC:

(1) Neutral teams stationed at ports of entry observe introductions and withdrawals of personnel, aircraft, weapons, vehicles and ammo and that only. No other function is prescribed for these fixed teams.

(2) The number of ports of entry utilized for the above stated purpose provides no intrinsic protection against introduction at other points. For example the entire length of the Yalu could be employed by the enemy for surreptitious entries. Whether there are 6 or 12 ports being observed will not significantly affect this possibility.

(3) In view of the above cited potentialities, it is clear that the number of ports specified need only be that number required by each side for legitimate replenishment and rotation.

(4) Provided the UNC can operate its rotation and replenishment activities thru 6 or 7 ports of entry, it is believed agreement on such a number could be forced on the enemy[.]

(b) Staff offs. are convinced that Commies will not agree to a figure of 40,000 for rotation. However they believe that Commies can be made to agree to rotation figure of 40 to 45,000 including all types of rotation. It is therefore recommended these figures be considered to determine feasibility from UNC standpoint. Additional guidance on this point will be appreciated.

#4. In Item 4 meeting UNC spent first 2 hrs commenting on and exploring Commie proposal.

UNC stated it appreciated forward move of Commies. Could agree some elements; required clarification of other elements; disagreed with certain provisions, particularly those parts of proposal which required forced repatriation. Brief of comments follows:

Para 1. UNC cannot agree to any provision which requires forced repat [repatriation] of POWs.

Para 2. UNC agrees extension of parole to all POWs. Pointed out parole feature should apply only to POWs and only to Korean conflict.

Para 3. Agreed, on assumption that sick and wounded would be given 1st priority.

Para 4. Could not agree to part requiring forced repatriation. No objection to provision that POWs electing repat. be exchanged in groups accordance capability to deliver and receive at exchange point or points; also willing specify time limit for exchange (not to exceed 30 days for Commie held POWs, and 90 days for UNC held POWs)[.]

Para 5. Agreed, subject possible necessity selecting other exchange points than Pan Mun Jom. Recommended Committee for exchange of POWs be empowered select such points.

Para 6. Agreed in principle. Dropped requirement for ICRC representative as technical advisor, in interest of progress. Stated detailed authority of the Committee should be set out in Arm [Armistice] Agreement and requested comment as to Commies views.

Para 7. Stated cannot agree joint visiting groups ICRC and DPRK Red Cross, since ICRC a strictly neutral agency. Indicated Commie proposal could be made satisfactory by (a) ICRC assisted by Commie Red Cross in visiting their camps and our RC in visiting our camps; and assisted by RC from both sides in assisting and interviewing POWs at exchange points; or alternatively (b) truly joint RC teams of both sides to visit all POW camps & assist and interview at exchange pts [points]. Also asked that such teams have rights specified in para 1, UNC proposal.

Para 8. Indicated full agreement subject understanding that all data required on deceased POWs would be exchanged.

Para 9. Indicated several differences. First failure include[d] safeguard for actual repat. civilians and to protect both sides against baseless charges of violation agreement on return of civs. Second indicated term "home" and use of milt. dem. [military demarcation] line as dividing line, undesirable. It prevents loyal supporters of one side who lived in territory now held by other side from returning to the one side; also would require both sides to settle civilians in vital defense areas. Third noted omission any reference foreign civilians and suggested subpara be added to provide for return such civilians. UNC agreed, in spirit of compromise to drop its requirement for ICRC representative on Committee for Repatriation of Civilians[.]

In response Commies indicated UNC comments showed both sides in agreement on many points, but still in disagreement on most imp. quest. [important question] of repatriation. Commies resolutely oppose so called principle vol [voluntary] repat and firmly insist that all POWs be released and repatriated.

Stated that re. parole feature in para 2 what is discussed in this conference concerns arm in Korea, and intent of para 2 is that persons cannot join Korean conflict. Asked if UNC had any concrete opinions for revision this para. UNC stated intent of discussion is to explore differences and clarify misunderstandings with object turning over prob. [problem] to staff offs to agree on explicit wording. Asked if such procedure satisfactory to Commies.

Lee did not answer but continued his remarks. Stated would consider our proposal regarding visiting teams composed of RC each side and that authority of Committee for Repat of POWs can be considered when armistice terms are drawn up.

Regarding para 8 stated data on cause of death etc would be given within limit of possibility.

As to para 9, stated organs [organizations] to supervise & inspect whether civs return home is not necessary and even with such organs question could not be settled. Real guarantee for returning home of civilians depends only on sincerity of both sides to observe and carry out arm. agreement. In order [to] study UNC comments, requested recess[.]

UNC expects to continue exploration of Commie proposal tomorrow. UNC did not raise question of ROK nationals in NKA. Except for this issue and quest of guarantee for return of civs. it appears only outstanding issue which remains is quest of vol. repatriation. Commies appeared unusually cooperative in today's meeting.

Feb. 5 (Tues): Staff officers continued to discuss Item 3. Commies submitted new versions of paras covering graves registration, composition of Neutral Nations Inspection teams and mission of Neutral Nations Supervisory Commission[.]

Rotation & ports of entry discussed. UNC held to figure of 40,000 per month, exclusive of R & R & TDY, and 10 ports. No agreement reached. Commies still say 25,000 inclusive of R & R & TDY and 3 ports sufficient.

Commies maintained Neutral Nations Inspection teams should be given full convenience of inspection to insure replenishing equipment is not reinforcing in character. Teams should not be frustrated under pretext of state secrets. **UNC agreed in principle, suggested that wording already submitted is adequate.** Requested Commies to submit their version.

Commies inquired as to scope of activities of Neutral Nations Inspection Teams in agreed ports of entry. UNC stated it would be difficult to define areas without knowing what ports are involved. Explained to Commies that intent is to provide convenience of movement between city and adjacent points of entry connected with introduction of replenishing supplies & personnel.

#4. In meeting on Item 4 Lee made folg additional comments on Commie proposal of Feb 3.

2nd para. "Captured personnel" means POWS and has nothing to do with "civilians." The phrase "shall not take part again in action of war" means "shall not take part again in acts of war in Korea."

4th para. Any agreement shall be equally binding on both sides. The period of 2 mos is applicable to both sides equally.

6th para. The provisions regarding the functions of the Committee as set forth in UNC proposal do not exceed the sphere contained in stipulation in principle of Commie proposal. After agreement in principle staff offs. can work out details.

7th para. Since ICRC is not a neutral organ [organization] the first measure suggested yesterday by UNC cannot be considered. 2nd measure suggested is impracticable.

9th para. Stipulation of para 9 is entirely adequate. Commies will not consider demand for providing additional safeguards.

Finally Commies are unshakeable on principle of unconditional release & repat [repatriation] of all POW.

UNC inquired if comment on 4th para indicated Commies were going back on their previous commitment to return POWs within 30 days and offered to lower its own requirement to 75 days or to consider 60 days if Commies would agree to make provisions for additional exchange pts [points] should they prove to be necessary.

Lee acknowledged that Commies could deliver POWs short of the prescribed time limit and stated that Commies did not intend to detain any. However, he indicated an unwillingness to enter into any terms which were not identical for both sides.

UNC replied that wording which goes into document should reflect as accurately as possible the actual agreement which we understand to be that both sides will get POWs to the exchange points as rapidly as possible; that it is equitable for Communists to accept commitment to deliver in 30 days while UNC accepts commitment to deliver in 75 days or possibly 60 days if Commies will agree to additional exch. [exchange] pts. if they are found to be necessary.

Lee replied, "We cannot agree that any agreed paras have unequal binding force. As for the regulation of details, that can be done by staff officers." He said again, "We can agree that the POWs will be repatriated as soon as possible within the specified time limit."

UNC referred to Commie reply on ICRC and proposed in view of Commie rejection of ICRC, the establishment of joint teams made up of National Red Cross personnel of two belligerents.

Lee undertook to reconsider his former rejection of joint National RC visits to POW camps.

UNC reasserted the need for a safeguard for both sides on civilian repatriation and stated that both sides must continue search to find one that is mutually agreeable. UNC has proposed two which Commies have turned down[.] It asks Commies to make a proposal. If Commies are unwilling themselves to accept any such advice, UNC may seek to write into the armistice agreement a unilateral safeguard.

Lee replied that a guarantee was unnecessary.

UNC raised the question of displaced civs. whose former homes were in the defensive area. Lee replied that if military necessity prevented the return of displaced civilians to their homes within the positions of either side, this was an internal matter for that side alone to solve.

UNC replied that Commie para on this matter should be amplified to cover this contingency and that appropriate wording could be devised by the staff officers.

Feb. 6 (Wed): At full delegation meeting which convened at 1000 this date Nam Il introduced the following statement and proposal in writing on subject of Item 5 of the Agenda:

(1) Statement. "The fifth item of the agenda "Recommendations to the Govts and countries concerned on both sides" is the last item of the entire agenda of our present negots [negotiations][.]

"During our discussions of other items of the agenda, both sides have expressed again & again that the arm [armistice] in K. should serve as a bridge toward the peaceful settlement of the Korean question.

"Both sides have explicitly agreed that once an arm. is realized in Korea, a political conference of a higher level should be convened quickly by the govts of the countries concerned on both sides to commence the work of a peaceful settlement of the Korean question.

"For this reason, our side formally proposes that we recommend that within three months after the Korean Armistice Agreement is signed and becomes effective, the opposing sides, the govts of the DPRK and of the PRC on the one hand and the govts of the countries concerned of the UN on the other appoint 5 reps. [representatives] respectively to hold such a political conference.

"Since the war in Korea will be stopped there can be no justification for any further stay in Korea of all the foreign forces which have participated in the war and on the other hand, in order to lay a foundation for the peaceful settlement of the Korean quest [question], it is absolutely essential for all foreign forces to be withdrawn from Korea. During our discussions of the agenda, both sides have already agreed that the question of withdrawal of all foreign forces from Korea be referred to a political conference of a higher level of both sides to be convened after the arm. for discussion and settlement. Therefore our side formally recommends that the above mentioned political conference should first discuss and decide upon the withdrawal of all foreign forces from Korea. The withdrawal of all foreign forces from Korea. is a decisively important pre-requesite [sic] for a peaceful settlement of the Korean question. However the peaceful settlement of the Korean question itself contains a series of important issues which require to be settled. Therefore our side formally recommends that the above mentioned political conference to decide in question of withdrawal of all foreign forces from Korea and should also settle through negots. the fundamental principles and specific recommendations regarding peaceful settlement of the Korean question so that the milt [military] arm in Korea will really become a bridge towards the peaceful settlement of the Korean question.

"The Korean question is not an isolated question. The war in Korea has involved many problems beyond Korea. A peaceful settlement of the Korean question will in fact pave the way for the solution of those other problems which are related to the Korean question. Conversely it is only when those other problems related to the Korean question are solved simultaneously that peace in Korea can be consolidated. All arguments which attempt to isolate the peaceful settlement of the Korean question are untenable as well as invalid.

"On June 27, 1950, President Truman of the USA publicly connected the war in Korea with other questions of the east and using the Korean war as a pretext for a series of war like measures in the east.

"The peaceful settlement of the Korean question calls for a simultaneous solution of these other important problems related to the Korean question. It is only when these problems related to the Korean question are solved simultaneously that peace in Korea can be consolidated, that peace in the east which has been breached as a result of the war in Korea can be recalled and that the state of extreme tension in which the world has been plunged as the result of the war in Korea can turn for the better.

"Therefore, our side formally recommends that the above mentioned political conference shall discuss the other problems related to peace in Korea.

"This is the main content of our draft of principle on the 5th item of the agenda. I hope that the plenary conference will seriously consider and adopt this draft principle as the agreed principle of the plenary conference on the 5th item of the agenda."

2. *Proposal* "Draft of the Principle Proposed by the Delegation of the KPA and CPVs on the fifth item of the agenda. 'Recommendation to the Govts of the Countries Concerned on Both Sides.' **In order to ensure the peaceful**

settlement of the Korean question, it is recommended that within 3 months after the Korean Arm Agreement is signed and becomes effective, the opposing sides, the Govts of the DPRK and the Peoples Republic of China on the one hand, and the Govts of the countries concerned of the UN on the other hand, appoint five (5) representatives respectively to hold a political conference to settle thru negots the folg questions:

(1) Withdrawal of all foreign forces from Korea;

(2) Peaceful settlement of the Korean question; and

(3) Other questions related to peace in K.['']

UNC made only one comment on the above, i.e., ''In your statement, you have asserted that agreements have been reached between both sides on several specific matters. In receiving your proposal for the purpose of studying it, I do not imply concurrence in your assertions regarding agreements.'' UNC proposed recess of plenary session until later date with Commies to be notified thru liaison officers. Commies agreed.

After conference with Genl Ridgway, who visited camp over night, folg dispatch was sent to JCS:

''Your instrs [instructions] to me and wording of Commie proposal on Item 5 are in my opinion not far apart.

''Adm Joy and U.S. Del. see strong advtgs [advantages] in our prompt acceptance of as much of the Commie wording as practical. It is believed this would enhance the chances of quick agreement on Item 5, while at the same time expediting progress on other unresolved issues. I concur.

''We have therefore agreed within U.S. Delegation upon the following proposal to be submitted to the Communists:

''The milt Comdrs [Commanders] have not considered questions concerning a political settlement in Korea, including unification of Korea under an independent, democratic govt [government] and other questions arising from but not resolved by this Arm. Agreement. [In the left margin of this paragraph, Adm. Joy has added the following heading in bold letters: ''UNC Proposal Item 5.''] In order to ensure the peaceful settlement of the Korean question, the milt Comdrs recommend to the respective governments and *authorities* concerned, namely to the Govts of the DPRK and of the Peoples Republic of China on the one hand and to the UN and to the Govt of the Republic of Korea on the other hand, that steps be taken within a period of 3 mos to deal with these matters at a higher level in a political conference for a Korean settlement or by such other political means as they deem appropriate, including:

''(1) Withdrawal of non-Korean forces from Korea.

''(2) Peaceful settlement of the Korean question; and

''(3) Other *Korean* questions related to peace[.]

[''] I therefore request as a matter of urgency authority for the UNC Del. to present the foregoing proposal to the Commies at a time of my choosing.''

JCS approved above proposal with exception modifications underlined

above. Gave folg. reasons. "Amendments to first part of sentence above made to cover UN which is not a govt. as well as Commie regimes which we do not recognize as govts. However, no issue need be made in negots of non-recognition question and under suggested amendments Commies will be able interpret "govts" as referring to DPRK and PRC while we would interpret "authorities" as referring to DPRK and PRC as well as UN.

"It appears clear that Commies intend their point 3 to cover discussion of other Far Eastern quests. **US Govt has made it clear that it does not consider these questions are in fact properly related to peace in Korea and that it would not discuss these quests before agreement on a political settlement for Korea.** While we would prefer to see Item 3 omitted, there would be no objection to its inclusion if amended as indicated above. Acceptance Commie proposal for this item without change in light of explanation as to what they have in mind would be interpreted as commitment to discuss other Far Eastern quests. in relation to Korean question and presumably in same conference with same parties[.] **While strictly speaking we might be able to point out thereafter there was no commitment of any kind as this only a recommendation, or that in any event there was no commitment to consider all these questions at same time and same forum, US Govt would be accused of bad faith by Commies and possibly by our allies and our position on these quests jeopardized.** UNC Del can well state to Commies that competence of del already stretched considerably in agreeing formulation Agenda Item 5, and that UNC Del clearly has no competence to even make recs. [recommendations] on quests outside Korea. **If Commies desire discuss other quests there are appropriate forums for raising them which they are, of course free to utilize at appropriate time[**"].

Rec'd folg. from JCS:

"a. Some agreement should be reached at least in principle and incorporated in arm agreement on repat [repatriation] of Korean civilians. This need not include any specific safeguards or machinery to effect such repat.

b. Some agreement should be reached at least in principle on repat of UN civilians held in N.K. While statements of Commies in this regard provide some measure of assurance, it is desirable that a written provision at least in general terms be included in arm. agreement.

Nothing in foregoing is to be construed as changing your current instrs regarding vol [voluntary] repat of POWs. This quest now under review at highest level. Will inform you ASAP [as soon as possible] of any developments[.]"

Also discussed Item 3 & 4 matters with R and members of sub committee teams. In Item 3 we recommend following solutions which we feel we can obtain thru negots[:]

a. A limit of 30,000 persons for pure rotation or 45,000 for all types of rotation per month.

b. Six specified ports of entry on each side. (These ports are to be used for introduction of rotation personnel, combat aircraft, weapons and any munitions. Other supplies may be introduced through non-specific ports.)

c. Acceptance of 10—14 mile definition of coastal waters.

e.[*sic*] CinCUNC verbally authorized reduction number mobile neutral inspection teams from 10 to 8 at my discretion.

Concerning Item 4, we discussed matter of guarantee & safeguard for return of displaced civilians, which will be dropped. Also further attempts to have ROKs in NK army reclassified as POWs. will be dropped.

Beauty Martin also spent the night at the camp.

Staff offs meeting on Item 3 made little progress. Commies still refuse to increase ports of entry from 3 and rotation from 25,000 and are not prepared to nominate neutral nations. UNC submitted new draft Para 15. as follows: "This Arm agreement shall apply to all opposing naval forces, which naval forces shall respect the waters contiguous to the Demilt [demilitarized] Zone and to the land area of Korea under the control of the opposing side, and shall not engage in naval blockade of any kind of the Korean peninsula.["]

#4. Lee opened Item 4 meeting accepting in principle the establishment of a joint RC activity composed of the National Red Cross Societies from the 2 belligerents to visit POW camps. after signing of the arm. and to assist in the repat of POWs. He again rejected the UNC proposed neutral agency as a guarantee and a safeguard for the repatriation of displaced civilians[.]

UNC restated the case for a neutral agency and requested Commie reconsideration of this point.

UNC then stated that it appears except for the basic disagreement on voluntary vs forced repat, a point has been reached where Item 4 can profitably be turned over to staff offs. for the development of arm. agreement phraseology acceptable to both sides. UNC proposed a recess of sub del while staff offs. carry on this task basing their work on the discussions held and the agreements reached during the sub del meetings.

Lee accepted this proposal making it clear that Commies were unshakeable in their stand on release & repat of all the POWs.

Colonels Hickman & Murray were appointed staff offs. for UNC; Tsai & Lee for Commies.

Feb. 7 (Thurs): In Item 3 staff officer meeting UNC reiterated requirement for 40,000 excluding TDY [temporary duty] and R & R [rest and recreation] personnel. Commies agreed to UNC definition of rotation but claimed 25,000 sufficient. They maintain since amount of replacement and replenishment will be reduced, three ports are sufficient. UNC replied difference in rotation figures small and not worthy of attempting to adjust rotation policies of 19 nations on which UNC figure is based. UNC claimed 3 ports of entry restrict flexibility of Comdrs of each side and insufficient for Neutral Nations Teams to carry out their functions.

UNC reiterated necessity for paras 13f & g pointing out these paras apply equally both sides. In order make progress, UNC offered to consider Commie views on 13f & g and the deletion of definition of "coastal waters" in para 13b if Commies would consider UNC view on 40,000 rotation figure. Commies replied that 40,000 for rotation and 8 ports of entry too great & unnecessary. UNC pointed out that 8 ports of entry was not UNC suggestion & that only rotation figure was being discussed[.]

UNC requested Commie comment on no [number] of 10 mobile [neutral inspection teams]. They replied both sides not far apart on this issue but should be decided when no of ports of entry is determined. Commies insisted direct relationship exists between no of ports & rotation figure & attempted to argue that a smaller rotation figure should require fewer ports of entry. UNC maintained that no of ports must be large enough to give Comdrs each side flexibility for logistical & admin [administrative] activities and that diff. [difference] in 25,000 & 40,000 rotation would not influence increase in no of ports.

Commies still not ready to nominate neutral nations.

#4. In order to regain the initiative and to consolidate the agreements in principle adopted by the Commies in sub del during last few days, UNC staff offs. presented comment on Commie counter proposal of 3 Feb. in form of a working draft of appropriate portions of the arm. [armistice] agreement. This draft incorporates the general paragraphing of the Commie counter proposal and some of its wording & ideas. UNC reserved right to modify the working draft at any time.

Commies sought acceptance of their counter proposal of 3 Feb as basis for discussion but agreed to accept the working draft for this purpose and requested a recess to allow them to study it.

In accord with R's instrs I interviewed Mr Lightner of Ambassador Muccios office. Folg developed.

1. UNC dropping guarantee & safeguard for displaced civilians.

Comment: Lightner considers neither guarantee nor safeguard of particular significance to ROK govt. ROK attitude is that Commies will only return those they wish to return anyway. Embassy considers UNC action avoids impossible admin burden.

2. Application term "to return home[.]"

Comment: Considers this a minor matter overshadowed by ROK govt antipathy to entire arm conference.

3. Notification ROK Govt as to UNC action[.]

Comment: Feels no reason to attach special significance to matter by notifying ROK govt and intends, subject to approval of Ambassador Muccio to let events take natural course. (Will inform CinCUNC when Embassy notifies ROK Govt if at all. There is nothing del or CinCUNC should do.[)]

Feb. 8 (Fri): Staff off meeting Item 3. Discussion ensued on Rotation and Ports of Entry but no progress was made during meeting[.] Commies maintained that there exists a close relationship between monthly rotation figure and required ports of entry. UNC pointed out that the mere changing of the monthly rotation figure would not automatically alter the required no [number] of Ports of Entry. Communists reiterated stand that 3 ports of entry on both sides will suffice for the needs of rotation and replenishment after the cessation of hostilities. UN replied that 3 ports of entry on both sides would restrict flexibility of Comdrs of each side and would make impossible the locating of Neutral Nations Inspection Team[s] in strategic areas thruout Korea. Commies stated they will not give consideration to the number of 10 to 12 ports of entry for each side.

It is becoming apparent that the no. of Ports of Entry is the obstacle to further progress in staff officers discussion.

#4. In staff meeting on Item 4 Commies insisted that their wording which provided for both sides ensuring that repatriated POWs would not again take part in Korean war was preferable to UNC wording that no POW after release should be permitted or compelled to take further part in Korean conflict. Commies also insisted that the work "repatriation" was more appropriate than "release" in connection with parole. UNC use of word release is designed to cover 3 classes (1) POWs not desiring repat. [repatriation], (2) ROK POWs desiring transfer to Commie side, and (3) bona fide POWs desiring to be repatriated to Commie side[.]

Commies refuse to accept a shorter period to complete return of POWs in their custody than that prescribed for UNC. Under UNC questioning it appears Commies may intend to delay return of POWs their custody so as to utilize whole of time limit established. Intent is cloaked in terms of damage to their transport system. UNC asked Commies to give estimate of anticipated average daily rate of delivery by them of POWs and also their max. [maximum] daily capacity to receive POWs from UNC.

Comment: Not considered that any of the objections raised by Commies to UNC working draft are insurmountable.

Feb. 9 (Sat): **Plenary session opened at 1000 with folg introductory statement of UNC proposal mentioned in msg to JCS on Feb 6: "The draft principle proposed by your delegation on 5th Item of the Agenda has received our careful consideration. We have found certain matters contained therein with which we are in substantial agreement; others which we had not considered necessary but to which we have no objection; and a few**

modifications primarily of phraseology, which we consider advisable for reasons which we believe will be obvious."

Commies answered by requesting recess until 1000 tomorrow in order to permit them to study our proposal.

#3. Staff officers meeting on Agenda Item 3 convened 1020. Discussion was confined to subjects of rotation & ports of entry but no progress was made during meeting. Commies asked for UNC opinion on Commie proposal of a rotation figure of 25,000 with 3 ports of entry for both sides. UNC stated it was far from meeting UNC initial proposal and did not meet UNC requirements. Commies asked UNC to give serious consideration to their proposal. UNC pointed out that main prob. [problem] is to define ports of entry and that rotation should not be a problem since it is only necessary to agree on a limit and 40,000 is a conservative figure and should not be objected to by Commies. Meeting adjourned 1055.

#4. In Item 4 meeting staff offs. resumed discussion Art III para 4. Commies reaffirmed they would not agree to principle of two different time limits and in answer to UNC question of yesterday, stated that their ability to receive POWs not a cause for concern. Declined to furnish estimate on their rate of delivery because of condition of their transportation system and possible further deterioration before signing of Arm. [armistice]. Discussion of para 5 indicated agreement by Commies for additional exchange points, if needed, but elicited disagreement over name of Committee. Commies wanted "repatriation" substituted for "exchange." Re para 6, Commies agreed fully in principle but questioned mission being set out in such detail on basis Committee may be inclined to perform only assigned functions[.] UNC defended principle of including details in order to expedite operations of Committee and pointed to last assigned mission as saving clause. Commies objected to para 7 as too detailed. Agreed to principle, number of teams & mission but were reluctant concerning sub teams. Suggested that modification their para 7 by including composition of teams and substituting our National RC societies for ICRC should make it acceptable. Throughout discussions difference in interpretation of repatriation recognized but tabled.

Comment: Meeting proceeded on businesslike basis. Still consider no new insurmountable objections encountered.

Feb. 10 (Sun): **Plenary session on Agenda Item 5 convened at 101000** [Feb. 10 at 1000 hours]. Nam Il presented his objections to UNC proposal as follows:

1. The first sentence is unnecessary[.]

2. The phrase "steps be taken" is vague, and provides a basis for evading or indefinitely delaying a political conference.

3. The wording of subpara (3) regarding "other Korean questions" is an attempt to exclude consideration of matters related to peace in Korea, which

matters are inextricably bound up in a thorough peaceful settlement of the Korean question.

4. Not all UN countries are involved militarily in Korea hence the use of that all inclusive term is inappropriate [bold check mark appears opposite this sentence][.]

5. The use of the phrase "and authorities" is improper in view of 4 above.

6. **The phrase "or by such other means as they deem appropriate["] is objectionable since it would permit delaying and obstructing tactics to be employed to avoid a conference, which is the proper and essential action.**

Nam Il emphasized 2, 3 & 6 above very heavily[.]

UNC responded to the above point by point refuting arguments of Nam Il, emphasizing that UNC would not attempt to stipulate the form of political action to be taken nor agree to recommend consideration of matters outside of Korea.

Comment: Tomorrow general position of UNC will be that Item 5 is unnecessary to an armistice, which is the objective of the milt [military] Comdrs [Commanders]. UNC is willing to consider appropriate recommendations to the govts but will not agree to inappropriate recommendations nor to delaying the advent of cessation of hostilities by protracted debate re. Item 5. We will point out that Item 5 is the enemy's own idea, is not integral in a milt armistice and that we have made considerable effort to meet their views. Sent folg to R:

"We request authority to propose the folg wording at the discretion of the delegation:

"In order to ensure the peaceful settlement of the Korean question the milt. comdrs. recommend to the respective govts & authorities concerned, namely to the DPRK and the PRC on the one hand, and to the UN and the ROK on the other hand, that, within a period of 3 mos after this arm [armistice] agreement becomes effective, a political conference for a Korean settlement be convened to deal with the following through negots [negotiations]:

"(1) Withdrawal on [of] non-Korean forces from Korea.

"(2) Peaceful settlement of the Korean question; and

"(3) Other Korean questions related to peace[.]"

"It appears to us that the phrase "a political conference" could be interpreted by our side as meaning any form of activity of the UN, such as that submitted to the General Assembly on 26 Jan.

"It would be extremely helpful for the delegation to be advised at the earliest possible moment.

Ridgway sent msg on to JCS concuring· [*sic*] in our recommended change in the phrasing.

#4. Staff officers continued Item 4 discussions[.] Commies contend primary purpose of RC is to assist in repat [repatriation], UNC that primary purpose is welfare. Commies objected to inclusion of reservation concerning resettlement of civs. [civilians] in defense areas as an internal matter. UNC explained this reservation necessary because of acceptance of Commie idea of returning home as contrasted to UNC expression "to other side." Commies claimed inclusion of comm. [communications] lines in this reservation appeared unreasonable. UNC indicated it would reconsider this. Commies questioned necessity of including foreign civs but will consider that point further. As expected safeguard on civilian repatriation was turned down flatly. As prelude to dropping safeguard, UNC indicated still thought safeguard desirable and requested Commies to suggest alternative for accomplishing desired result. No serious divergence in views concerning paras discussed today.

#3. In staff offs. meeting on Item 3 today UNC stated that after considerable study of requirements for ports of entry as determined by logistic needs of Comdrs of both sides, flexibility of supply and strategic location of inspection teams UNC would consider reducing requirements to 8 ports of entry. Commies argued that the limited rotation and replenishment necessary during armistice and the defining of rotation so as to exclude temporary duty personnel, drastically reduce no [number] of ports of entry required. Furthermore, the use of mobile neutral nations inspection teams provides adequate fulfillment of duties of neutral nations supervisory commission. Commies therefore still maintain 8 ports of entry far in excess of requirements. UNC stated definition of rotation in no way affected no of ports required and that neutral nations sending inspection teams would undoubtedly desire at least 8 ports of entry for observation in order to properly fulfill their tasks. UNC took strong position that reduced logistic requirements during arm, in no way made valid Commie arguments for only 3 ports, also stated Commies had no reason for objecting to ceiling of 40,000 monthly rotation.

Further discussion explored relationship between no of stationary neutral nation insp teams at agreed ports of entry and mobile teams at other ports in rear. No definite proposals or results obtained.

Feb. 11 (Mon): **Nam Il lead off plenary session which opened at 1000 with a refutation of my statement of yesterday.** He contended that both sides had agreed to leaving political questions, such as withdrawal of foreign forces, to be decided by a political conference. He also contended first sentence of our proposal was unnecessary. **He took exception to our phrasing "steps be taken within 3 mos," and ["]appropriate political means" saying it is improper to bury such recommendations in ambiguous & hollow words. He pointed out that the Korean question is not an isolated quest [question] and that the consolidation of peace in Korea hinges on other quests.** He ended by saying "in order to eliminate all the pretexts which may be employed as objections, our side proposes to change the wording of "other questions related to peace in Korea" into "other questions directly related to peace in Korea."

In my statement rebutting his two statements of yesterday I pointed out that Item 5 was really not necessary for an armistice agreement [word "conference" written in and then crossed out.] I said that rather than make inappropriate recommendations we would prefer to make none at all. We had agreed to discuss the question of recommending a political conference but we had never reached an understanding that the political settlement of the Korean question should be realized by a political conference of a higher level. I pointed out that the first sentence of our proposal was meant to disclose beyond question that the milt comdrs [military commanders] had not attempted to invade the political field. **Regarding Commies objection to the use of the term United Nations on the ground that not all members of the UN have sent troops to Korea to take part in the war, I pointed out this raises an interesting question i.e. the status of PRC** [People's Republic of China]. If the sending of troops to K by a nation is the criterion for determining which nations shall be named to receive the recs [recommendations] from the milt Comdrs and to participate in the subsequent discussions, does the PRC qualify? **PRC has repeatedly insisted that Chinese units engaged in hostilities are 'volunteers' and that their sudden appearance in Korea was completely unrelated to any official action on the part of their political authorities. I then went after their 3d recommendation saying that it was far beyond purview of the conference.** Was an attempt to introduce extraneous issues which are not pertinent to the armistice and which have no direct relation to a peaceful settlement of the Korean problem. Pointed out there are political channels to use for initiating discussion of the many probs [problems] besetting Asia. **I also refuted their objections of the phrasing "steps shall be taken within a period of 3 mos" and "or by such other political means as they deem appropriate" by saying that it is not for the milt Comdrs to dictate to the political authorities the nature of the forum which will undertake to bring peace to Korea.** Ended up by saying we have already stretched our views to the utmost. But there are limits beyond which we will not go. (See HNC902)

#3. At staff meeting on Item 3, in response to the UNC proposal of 8 ports of entry for both sides Commies maintained figure was still too high. As counter proposal they offered to consider the UNC figure of 5 mobile teams for each side provided the number of ports of entry could be limited to 3. UNC stated that 3 ports of entry for each side is unacceptable since that number would limit the needs & functions of the milt Comdrs, the Neutral Nations Supervisory Commission and the Neutral Nations Supervisory teams. On rotation Commies reiterated previous stand that the monthly figure of 25,000 is adequate. UNC maintained the monthly rotation figure of 40,000 is essential in order to carry out planned rotation schedules. Commies reiterated figure of 40,000 is too high and is unnecessary.

#4. Staff officers on Item 4 continued to discuss question of joint RC teams. UNC submitted revisions of Art 3, Arm [Armistice] Agreement.

Feb. 12 (Tues): **At plenary session on Item 5 held 12100 Feb Nam Il made statement in which he attempted to refute points in UNC statement of 11 Feb.** Concluded by saying Commies are revising their proposal and desire to recess plenary session until a date to be agreed on by liaison officers. **I responded by taking exception generally to the distortions contained in the Commie statement and then agreed to request for recess.** We did not submit the new proposal we were authorized to make.

#3. No progress in Staff Offs. meeting on Agenda Item 3 except that Commies upped their rotation figure to 30,000 and proposed 4 ports of entry instead of 3. Manpojin was proposed for NK and Yosu for SK. UNC said 30,000 & 4 ports too few to meet min [minimum] needs. Commies were again not able to name their neutral nations.

#4. In staff offs. meeting on Item 4 discussion centered around RC teams. Commies questioned use of teams enroute to exchange points, granting of privilege to visit freely at any time all POW camps and our stipulation concerning sub teams. Reiterated concept of primary mission as assistance at exchange pts [points]. UNC reaffirmed necessity of inclusion of these provisions and restated UNC concept of primary mission as welfare & morale. Both sides briefly reiterated firm stand on major issue of voluntary versus forced repatriation.

Since Commies requested a recess of the plenary session I decided to return to Tokyo during the interim to discuss with R our plans for the final showdown.

Feb. 13 (Wed): **Left camp about 1000 and arrived Tokyo about 1430. Conferred with R at 1600. Explained to him that we were approaching the final phase of the conference and that we should begin to lay definite plans for the final showdown when only two major issues, i.e. airfields & vol [voluntary] repatriation, remained unsolved. Gave him opening statement and msg to JCS we had prepared on subject. Msg pointed out importance of holding firm on our final stand and making it unmistakably clear to Commies that it was our final position, even to the breaking point. Authority to do so was also requested. I also reviewed our sessions with the Commies on Item 5 pointing out their latest move in calling a recess of several days to work up a revised proposal might mean several things: (1) They are really concerned about Item 5, and the holding of a political conference, and want to submit a proposal which is more palatable to us.**

Our last tough statement may have scared them into it. In short a satisfactory solution to Item 5 may be of great import to them & more vital than we have heretofore thought. (2) They may have our same idea, the bargaining of the two main issues (airfields vs vol repatriation). (3) Or they may have the idea of presenting a complete packaged arm. [armistice] proposal.

R said that Gen Hull & a Mr Johnson from the State Dept were arriving tonight to discuss POW question and would probably like to confer with me tomorrow. He would let me know.

#3. In staff meeting on Item 3 UNC proposed to reduce number of Ports of Entry to seven for each side and suggested that paras 13f and 13g might be deleted if Commies would consider UNC figure of 40,000 for rotation. Col Chang stated he had hoped his proposal of 30,000 for monthly rotation & 4 ports of entry would have solved the major problem in Item 3 but evidently this had not been so[.] Commies argued that their proposal figures on rotation & Ports are adequate to meet max. [maximum] needs of armistice. UNC maintained that UNC will require a min. [minimum] monthly rotation figure of 40,000. UNC also stated that 7 Ports of Entry will be required to support normal logistical activities. Commies were not able to name their neutral nations.

#4. In staff meeting on Item 4 Commies indicated that no differences in principle on Item 4 remain except voluntary vs. forced repatriation. Heretofore they have appeared reluctant to commit themselves on exact wording. They agreed today to undertake this task at tomorrows session.

Feb. 14 (Thurs): At 0900 I met with Ridgway Gen Hull, Mr Johnson, Hickey, Wright & Milburn at the Dai Ichi Bldg to discuss a suggestion brought out by the Washingtonians with regard to the solution of Agenda Item 4. Beforehand R asked me into his office and made the startling statement that he would support me to the hilt if the subterfuges that I might hear shortly went against my grain to such an extent that I felt I could no longer continue as senior delegate.

The proposition, or suggestion, or whatever you might call it, that Hull & Johnson advanced can be summarized as follows. The Chinese & NK POWs held by the UNC were to be screened as to their wishes re: repatriation and all those not desiring to return to the Communist side were to be released. Then when we had the final showdown we could agree to Commie proposal (forced repat [repatriation]) but say that the POWs who did not wish to return had already been released. In short we would only return the POWs who wanted to go back to the other side even though the Commies had not agreed to the principle of vol. [voluntary] repatriation. We would confront the Commies with a fait accompli. I was asked what the Commie reaction would be to a fait accompli.

I condemned the idea vehemently pointing out how such an action would jeopardize the return of our own POWs held by the Commies. I claimed that it would be a breach of faith on our part which would wreck the conference. In my opinion the Commies would react violently to any such subterfuge. It would have dire consequences and the more I thought about it the less I liked it. Hickey & Wright felt the same way. Ridgway claimed we were abandoning the principle of voluntary repatriation by such an action. I feel sure the idea is killed, though one never knows. Hull seemed a little embarrassed over having to propound the idea.

We then went on to discuss Item 5 and the tactics for arriving at the final "showdown." I explained what the delegation thought should be done. The majority felt we should agree to any reasonable revised proposal in order to get along with the conference and not complicate matters with another unresolved issue for the final "showdown[.]" An early agreement, besides, would have a salutary effect by providing the Commies with an incentive to quit haggling and get on with the negots [negotiations]. Some however felt that we should capitalize on the Commies evident intense desire to be assured of a post armistice conference and hold out on agreement to give us another issue to bargain with in the final showdown. Hull & Johnson felt this way, though the rest of GHQ thought we ought to settle Item 5 as soon as possible.

I asked Hull to give me his opinion whether we would be authorized to stand firmly, even to the breaking point, on the issue of vol. repat. His answer consisted of reading a memo from Acheson [Secretary of State Dean G. Acheson] to the President which in effect said public generally supported our position on voluntary repat. but that, should the conference break as a result of our stand on this issue we would not be supported in retrospect.

When I left the conference I reminded Hull that we were no longer negotiating from a position of strength as we had been doing prior to 27 November when the 30 day truce period went into effect. We were now negotiating from the position of a military stalemate.

#3. Staff meeting on Item 3 made no progress. Each side reiterated its views on rotation & Ports of Entry. Commies still insist that rotation figure of 40,000 and 7 ports of entry are too high. UNC stated 4 ports totally unacceptable. UNC agreed to prepare a map showing coastal island locations to be attached to Arm [Armistice] agreement. Commies proposed that para 43c read: "The inspection of combat aircraft, armored vehicles, weapons, and ammo by Neutral Nations Inspection Teams will be such as to enable them to properly insure that reinforcing equipment is not being introduced into Korea." They further stated that the insp. teams should have the full & unrestricted right to inspect as necessary to perform their tasks and that the additional phrase "but this shall not be construed as authorizing inspections or exams. [examinations] of any secret designs or characteristics of any combat aircraft, armored vehicle, weapons or ammo" is unnecessary. Commies had previously stated at earlier sessions that inspection teams should not inspect secret equipment and gain milt. [military] intelligence.

Comment: It became apparent as meeting progressed that Commies were deliberately stalling. From the arguments they presented, it appeared they were trying to find points on which they could disagree with UNC views. Nevertheless, the general attitude of discussions was amicable.

#4. Commies presented their proposed wording for Item 4. Discussion centered on changes in para 2. which read "Both sides agree to ensure that all their captured milt. personnel shall not, after being repatriated, take part again in acts of war in the Korean war." UNC urged Commies to accept a wording which is neutral with respect to basic difference between the two sides. Commies showed unwillingness to agree to any version in this and subsequent paras. which would intend to imply a departure from their stand on unconditional release & repatriation.

Commies asked for a plenary session tomorrow. We said we would not be ready until the 16th which date was agreed upon.

This evening I attended a dinner given by Col & Mrs. Hysong at the GHQ club. After dinner I told Doyle Hickey and Pinkie Wright that the more I thought of the plan advanced by Hull & Johnson the less I liked it. I also told them emphatically that if I was directed to carry it out I would ask to be relieved.

Feb. 15 (Fri): I was summoned to the Dai Ichi Bldg by R just as I was leaving Qtrs 404 for the airfield. Upon arrival I was ushered into the conference room where R was having an arm. [armistice] conference with his staff on POWs. Col Salisbury was expounding at a great rate on how the Commies had been practicing the principle of vol. [voluntary] repatriation by the impressment of ROK's into the NK army and the failure to account for missing POWs[.] R emphasized how important it was to keep on demanding an accounting of missing UNC POWs who were at one time known to be in Commie hands. We should continue to demand such an accounting right up until the time the arm is signed.

Left Haneda in the Constellation at 1030 arriving K16 (Seoul) at 1430 and at camp about 1500.

#3. Staff meeting on Item 3. Discussion limited to rotation, ports of entry but no progress made. Commies asserted that to increase rotation figure above 30,000 would annul significance of any limit. They also continue to maintain that seven ports are excessive of needs. UNC reiterated stand that rotation figure of 40,000 is essential to needs of UNC and will not annul rotation limit. UNC stated that both 4 & 7 ports are small in number and that the latter no [number] is required for strategic location of Neutral Nations Insp. Teams and to permit flow of authorized personnel and materiel to needed areas with a min [minimum] of trans shipment[.] On para 43c, Commies stated that neither side should use milt.

[military] secrets as a means of restricting inspections of NNITs. UNC pointed out that its draft version authorized adequate insp. of milt equipment and provided for a safeguard to prevent NNITs from using insp. activities as a pretext for gathering milt. intelligence.

#4. UNC opened staff meeting on Item 4 with general discussion of Commies 14 Feb proposal citing 2 major unacceptable items other than basic diff. [difference] of vol [voluntary] vs. forced repatriation: (1) Interjection of idea of forced repat. [repatriation] in paras other than para one; (2) insistence on use of word "repatriation" unqualified to apply to all POWs including ROK nationals held by UNC. Then proceeded with para by para discussion of minor differences[.] Most significant development during subsequent exchange of views elecited [*sic*] that Commies still refuse to recognize re-classification of civ [civilian] internees.

Feb. 16 (Sat): At 1000 plenary session Nam Il presented folg. revised draft of their Item 5 proposal:

"In order to insure the peaceful settlement of the Korean question, the milt cmdrs [military commanders] **of both sides hereby recommend to the govts of the countries concerned on both sides that within three months after the arm** [armistice] **agreement is signed and becomes effective, a political conference of a higher level of both sides be held by reps.** [representatives] **appointed respectively to settle thru negots** [negotiations] **the questions of the withdrawal of all foreign forces from Korea, the peaceful settlement of the Korean question, etc."**

Nam Il then went on to make the folg explanation[:]

"Firstly, an independent democratic unified Korea is what the Korean people aspire to see, but in the first sentence of your proposal made by your side on Feb 9, this demand is brought forth virtually as a political proposal and the method by which your side put forth this demand contains a hidden intent which your side cannot make public. It goes beyond the scope of the agenda and to it our side absolutely cannot agree[.]

"Secondly, recommendations to the [']govts concerned on both sides' is the original wording of the 5th item of the agenda[—]no change is to be allowed. **In view of this the wording of the 2nd sentence in your proposal of Feb 9th, is obviously in violation of the original wording of the agenda item already agreed upon.** In order to adhere strictly to the original agreed wording of the 5th item of the agenda and eliminate your pretexts for continued haggling, in the revised draft of our side, the present revisions are made regarding this question.

"Thirdly, with respect to holding of [']a political conference of a higher level' it has been explicitly brought forth by your side in the proposal submitted at a committee meeting on Agenda Item 3 on Dec 23, '51 and has

now been incorporated in the agreed principle 4 on Agenda Item 3. Hence the proposal of our side that 'a political conference of a higher level['] of both sides be held by reps appointed respectively is made on the basis of mutual agreement. This is beyond any dispute.

"Fourthly, by foreign forces in our revised draft, is meant non-Korean forces.

"Fifthly, in order to settle peacefully the Korean quest. [question] it is a matter of certainty that other quests which are directly related to peace in Korea would be touched upon. However, owing to the fact that your side insists on an unreasonable objection to the content of the 3d item of our original draft, our side now makes an alteration by using the term 'questions etc' which does not commit the future political conference so as to facilitate the holding by both sides of a political conference."

I replied: "Your proposal and statement have been duly noted. In order that we may consider your statement & proposal very carefully, we suggest a recess until tomorrow at the same time".

#3. Staff meeting Item 3. Commies nominated Poland, Czechoslovakia & Soviet Union as their neutral nations and then formally proposed that both sides agree mutually and simultaneously to the neutral nations nominated by both sides. UNC reps stated they were authorized to accept the nomination of Poland & Czechoslavakia [*sic*] but that Soviet Union was not repeat not repeat not acceptable. Commies said that they could not understand reasons for UNC rejection of any nation nominated by their side. UNC answered that it should be obvious why the Soviet Union is not acceptable and reasons for nonacceptance will be presented at next meeting[.] UNC called attention to Principle 6 which states that "Both sides agree to invite neutral nations acceptable to both sides which have not participated in the Korean War." UNC stated that there are many neutral nations which the Commies could invite which would be acceptable to the UNC but the Soviet Union is not one of them.

At staff session 17 Feb Commies will be informed that nomination of Soviet Union is summarily rejected as UNC Delegation does not consider this nation a neutral. No additional explanation will be made.

Both sides reiterated views of past sessions on rotation & Ports of Entry but no progress was made.

Commies submitted new draft on matter of graves registration.

#4. In staff meeting on Item 4 UNC objected to Commie use of word "repatriation" by itself in most of their paras. of their 14 Feb proposal. What was needed was a word or a phrase which would describe return of Commies of NK and Chinese POWs as well as the sending to Commies of ROK POWs transferred to Commies. UNC had initially used "repat [repatriation] or transfer" but had shifted to word "exchange" in other paras than first, since it was felt "exchange" in other paras would be acceptable to both sides[.] Unless Commies agreed to "exchange" or some other word could be found, UNC would continue to use words "repatriate or transfer[.]"

Commies continued to insist on use of "repatriate" thruout their proposal.

Commies proposed provision be made for (1) respective comdrs to provide security in their area for RC teams; (2) means whereby teams could communicate with their parent side; & (3) total of additional members of RC teams. Commies implied add. [additional] members would be necessary in providing the comm [communication] needs of the teams.

UNC would study need for security & comm provisions in para 7. though it questioned need for add RC members since teams could utilize comm facilities of the respective comdrs[.]

I sent folg. msg to CinCUNC concerning new enemy proposal for Item 5: (HNC924).

"The general nature of the wording of the new enemy proposal seems to afford widest latitude in interpreting its application. All specifics of the new proposal appear to be consistent with instrs [instructions] received by UNC Del. **Accordingly, it is our intent unless otherwise directed to accept the new wording, accompanying our acceptance tomorrow with folg statement for record:**

"We have carefully considered your revision of the principle proposed by you as the solution of Item 5 of the Agenda. The UNC Del is prepared to accept it as the solution of this Item of the Agenda[.]

"So that there may be no question regarding the understanding of the UNC Del as to the meaning of your proposal we deem it advisable to make certain explanations at this time. First, we desire to point out that this recommendation will be made by CinCUNC to the UN as well as to the ROK. Second, in accepting the term 'foreign forces' we are doing so on the basis of your statement that this term means 'Non Korean forces.' And third, we wish it clearly understood that we do not construe the word 'etcetera' to relate to matters outside of Korea.

I then added to the msg "Since the matter is merely a recommendation, It [*sic*] is believed that the foregoing statement provides an adequate basis for any interpretation the US Govt would wish to employ."

CinCUNC passed my above msg on to JCS for approval which was given.

R also concurred in our rejecting Soviet Union as one of the Neutral Nations giving as reason that the country was not neutral passing his msg to us to JCS also. JCS came back with folg:

"Opinion here is to concur in summarily rejecting Soviet Union as nominee but consider it inadvisable to give as reason UNC does not consider Soviets as neutral. Proof of Soviet participation difficult to substantiate. Also, consider it better to present Commies with reason whose validity they can accept rather than one the validity of which they cannot admit. Therefore suggest that either no reason at all be given or one along these lines: "Believe it to interests of all concerned that members of supervisory organs [organizations] should be drawn from those nations not in close proximity to Korea[.]''

[''']Regarding public statement opinion here is that rejection Soviet Union should for present be treated factually without overemphasis or indication it is absolutely unalterable position in order to retain negotiating flexibility for both sides.['']

My comment—A craven message!

Feb. 17 (Sun): **I started the plenary session by saying: "We have carefully considered your revision of the principle proposed by you as the solution of Item 5 of the Agenda.** In order to give you concrete evidence of the sincerity of the UNC Del and to eliminate entirely any pretexts for further delay on your part in reaching agreement on unresolved issues in Items 3 & 4, the UNC Del accepts your proposal of 16 Feb as the solution of this item of the agenda, subject to the folg remarks[.]''

I then gave the explanation of UNC understanding as given in my msg to CinCUNC of yesterday (HNC924).

Commies requested 40 min recess at end of which Commie Senior Delegate stated: **"We have made a preliminary study of your statement of this morning but in order to make a careful study of your statement we propose to recess until 1000 tomorrow.** UNC agreed[.]

Our plan for tomorrow is to stand on our statement. If Commies disagree with our interpretation of their proposal, I plan to make a statement substantially as follows: "You have expressed dissatisfaction with the remarks we made in explaining the basis of our acceptance of your proposal. Our remarks stand as a matter of record. **They represent our understanding of your proposal.** If you are going to make an issue of our interpretation of your proposal we will reconsider both our acceptance of the proposal and the whole question of the necessity for any recommendation.''

#3. In staff meeting on Item 3, in response to Commie request ror news on yesterdays proposal, UNC stated that according to the principle mutually agreed upon, both sides agreed to invite neutral nations acceptable to both sides. The Soviet Union is not acceptable to the UNC[.] Commies retorted that the UNC has no justification nor can it give any for the rejection of any neutral nation that they may nominate[.] Commies further stated that all of their nominated neutral nations are consistent with the definition of neutral nations. They alleged that the rejection of their nominees shows a deliberate attempt on the part of the UNC to prolong the Arm. [armistice] negots. [negotiations].

Each side reiterated its stand on rotation & ports of entry. No progress made.

I told R [following inserted below the line of text: ''and he concurred''] that if matter of Neutral Nations becomes stalemated, one possible solution to the prob. [problem] of Neutral Nations, if feasible, is that UNC drop one of its neutral nations and propose to the Commies that only 2 Neutral Nations be nominated by each side, provided the Commies will stipulate that the Soviet Union is not one of the nations to be nominated.

#4. Staff meeting Item 4. Not much if any progress. UNC attempted to get clarification of Commies statement that RC teams should carry independent comm. [communication] equipment. Remainder of discussion fairly general and covered no new ground. Commies stated that they will soon submit revised wording of some paras of their 14 Feb proposal covering some of the points discussed during past 3 days[.]

Feb. 18 (Mon): **Had long discussion with Mr Johnson & Col. Matthews, who came up from Seoul, about the plan we had previously discussed in Tokyo when Hull, R, Hikey [*sic*] and Wright were present.*** Also present in my tent were Libby, Galloway & Briggs. Later, when he returned from Pan Mun Jom, Hickman took part.

Johnson first explained the plan as follows[.] We were to go ahead as planned resolving all issues except the two major ones, i.e. airfields & voluntary repatriation. If the Commies refused to buy our final proposal, the swap of airfields for voluntary repatriation, we were then to go ahead and release our POWs [following inserted below the line of text: "who did not wish to be repatriated"] announcing to the Commies our action and saying that we would return all others. In short we would confront them with a "fait accompli." Our reason for doing this (we would tell the Commies) is because they had already exercised the principle of voluntary repatriation when they released their ROK POWs at the front.

---

* A memorandum for record was prepared after these discussions and a copy of it is in the Joy archive. Because the Defense Department history of the negotiations (Walter Hermes, *Truce Tent and Fighting Front*, Washington: Office of the Chief of Military History, U.S. Army, 1966) identifies "Mr. Johnson" as Assistant Secretary of the Army Walter Johnson, I wrote to Ambassador U. Alexis Johnson to confirm that it was really he who had participated in the talks with Admiral Joy. On February 18, 1976, I received a letter from Ambassador Johnson that confirmed this and went on: ". . . in my capacity as Deputy Assistant Secretary for Far Eastern Affairs, I accompanied General John Hull, then Army Vice Chief of Staff, to the Far East on a mission to assist in determining the facts with regard to their attitudes towards repatriation and to make recommendations on the disposition of prisoners of war held by the UNC. On occasion, in company with General Hull, and on other occasions by myself or with Colonel Matthews, we conferred with officers of the UNC in Tokyo and Seoul, visited Munsan–ni and the prisoner-of-war camps in Korea, as well as met with the Ambassador and officers of our Embassy in Korea.

"For your information, I never saw the UNC memo for the record until recently, when I was in Washington. It was shown to me as an item being requested under the Freedom of Information Act. I had no objection to its release, although it was written entirely from the standpoint of the UNC, and I am very clear in my recollection that, in my conversations at Munsan–ni, as well as elsewhere, I only raised the possibility of a unilateral release of prisoners of war as one of the alternatives that might be considered and was not sounding out opinion solely upon this alternative, as implied in the memorandum."—Ed.

I then asked Johnson who had originated the plan. He said it had sort of grown out of consideration of the entire subject on a high level. The JCS knew about it though they did not unanimously agree with it. It is known in Wash [Washington] at the highest level even by the President who feels very strongly that some solution be accomplished that does not require the forced return of unwilling Chinese & NK's[.] The idea of not getting involved in forced repatriation came originally from him. Hull's and Johnson's mission out here is exploratory only. I elicited the info that the Del's dispatch recommending against the principle of vol. [voluntary] repatriation had already been taken into consideration.

After plying Johnson with questions we proceeded to take his plan apart on the basis that the Commies would retaliate by not returning all of our POWs that they hold. In short we would sacrifice our men for a bunch of Chinese & NKs who were formerly our enemies and who had shot at us. Libby mainly carried the ball. He emphasized emphatically that he would not be a party to carrying out the plan as I did to Hickey before I left Tokyo. We all pointed out the bad precedent it would set for the future should the Commies ever defeat us and capture a large no [number] of our men[.] And what would our own soldiers say if [we] would now desert our 3,128 US etc captives in the hands of the enemy. Furthermore we are on record as having said we would abide by the Geneva Convention. In addition as R said in Tokyo by adopting such a plan we were in reality giving up the principle of vol repatriation, since we would not be standing by it to the end.

Johnson asked if we had any other alternative to suggest. Lovett seems to think Yankee ingenuity can solve the problem. Libby pointed out it was too late. We had already gone too far and committed ourselves too deeply.

I said there was no other alternative but to stand firm for our principle. We must go into our final position with the complete backing of the President and make it clear to the Commies that we were willing to break off negots [negotiations] rather than give in on vol repat. Or we must abandon our principle soon. There was no other choice. I also told Johnson if we did stand firm we had a 50-50 chance to win out and get an armistice on our terms. Libby is more pessimistic.

As we broke up I asked Johnson if we would continue the war should the Commies refuse to return our men. He said yes we would fight for them. Then said I what have we to lose by standing unmistakably firm for voluntary repatriation.

#3. At staff meeting on Item 3 Commies again brought up the subject of the Soviet Union as one of their nominated neutral nations. They contended that the neutral nations nominated by their side were consistent with the [following inserted above the line of text: "neutral nations"] definition in that their combatant forces had not participated in the hostilities in Korea. They said we could not give any reason why the Soviet Union should not so serve. "The

Soviet Union is one of the United Nations which is not only most strictly opposed to intervention in the K war but also is most strongly in favor of a peaceful settlement of the Korean question. If the Soviet Union could not be nominated as a neutral nation, there would be no neutral nation at all existing in the world."

UNC made no comment.

Each side reiterated its views on Ports of Entry but no progress was made.

I said the folg in my rpt [report] to CinCUNC: "The restraint on UNC Del. not to discuss reasons for unacceptability of Soviet Union results in enemy making propaganda statements lauding SU while UNC is unable to refute these assertions. The fact that UNC does not refute assertions of Soviet neutrality can be used by enemy to bolster his propaganda. Accordingly, it is believed desirable to make folg or similar statement at tomorrows meeting:

"The reasons why the S.U. is unacceptable as a member of the Neutral Nations Supervisory Commission have been set forth at length during the meetings of the Security Council of the UN. & are well known to the world at large. If your side is actually in doubt regarding the reasons for rejection of Soviet Union, you can secure copies of the minutes of the Security Council meetings and inform yourself. The essential facts, however, are that the SU. is wholly unacceptable to the UNC and that the agreed prin. [principle] #6. provides that 'both sides agree to invite neutral nations acceptable to both sides who have not participated in the Korean war.' The S.U. does not qualify under these agreed criteria. Therefore your nomination of the SU in this connection is formally rejected[.]"

R sent above on to JCS saying he was in full accord with proposed statement but was withholding permission for it to be presented as it appeared to depart somewhat from previous JCS instrs [instructions].

JCS replied saying Del should present statement along folg lines instead: "Agreed prin #6 provides that both sides agree to invite neutral nations acceptable to both sides who have not participated in K war. S.U. is unacceptable to UNC and therefore does not qualify under these agreed criteria. UNC believes that it is in interest of all concerned that members of supervisory organs [organizations] should be drawn from those nations not in close proximity to Korea and without a record of past participation in Korean question."

JCS added "This statement is substituted until strength of Commie insistence becomes clear. Line of argumentation you suggest may well be useful later."

My comment—another craven msg!

#4. In staff meeting on Item 4 Commies submitted changes to their proposal of 14 Feb which appear to eliminate majority of minor objections. Sections dealing with vol vs forced repatriation and improper use of word repat unchanged. Commies stated that they are still considering questions of independent comm [communication] equipment for RC teams.

Feb. 19 (Tues): **Nam Il opened plenary session at 1000 with folg. statement:** "We have carefully studied the statement made by your side day before yesterday re the revised draft of our side. I must point out that the stumbling blocks standing in the way of complete agreement on Items 3 & 4 of the Agenda are created by your side. **Since the 5th Item of the agenda has attained its solution in principle, as a result of the reasonable revised draft submitted by our side, it is all the more improper for your side to continue to insist on your unreasonable proposition and demands of the 3d & 4th Items of the agenda thus delaying the advent of the Armistice in Korea.**

"The draft of the principle submitted by our side on the 5th Item of the Agenda is very clear in itself. There can be no misunderstanding whatsoever. **By 'the govts of the countries concerned on both sides' in our draft principle is naturally meant the govts of the countries concerned on the part of the KPA and the CPVs and the govts of the countries concerned on the side of the UNC.**

"By 'foreign forces' in our draft principle is naturally meant non Korean forces. And the meaning of 'questions, etc' in our draft of principles is also very clear. **It neither binds the forthcoming political conference to the discussion of certain specific questions nor excludes the possibility of other quests [questions] by this political conference.**

"I propose to turn over the work of drafting the details of Arts [articles] in the 5th Item of the Agenda to the Staff Officers. The time for the Staff Officers meeting can be determined thru negots [negotiations] by the Liaison Officers of both sides[.]"

U.N. "You have suggested that Item 5 of the Agenda now be referred to the staff officers[.] It appears to us that the agreement which we have reached is a full solution to this Item of the Agenda. We would like to hear what action you contemplate the staff offs. would be expected to take. In other words, what would be the terms of reference to the staff officers?"

Commies: "We have reached an agreement in principle on Item 5. In order to formulate the terms of the agreement which we reached on the principle, we propose to turn it over to the Staff Officers Meeting for proper wording and insertion in the Arm [armistice] agreement[.]"

U.N. "No details are considered necessary. There is nothing for the Staff Offs to do. Including the draft as it stands in the Arm Agreement will constitute a complete solution. We formally propose that the two delegations agree that the wording proposed by you be accepted as Item 5 of the Agenda and that as a properly numbered para, It constitute Art IV of the Arm Agreement."

Commies: "Then you mean that you oppose turning the matter over to the staff offs?"

UN: "I mean that we see no reason why it should be turned over to the staff offs. We propose that it be adopted as it stands.["]

The Commies then asked for a 40 min recess. Evidently our proposal was totally unexpected and contrary to their planned procedure. Consequently it threw them for a loss. Whether they intend to elaborate on the agreed upon principle which needs no elaboration, or whether they are only concerned about deviating from their planned procedure and have no real alteration to make, remains to be seen.

When they returned from the recess Nam Il gave us the choice as to whether the draft they would draw up of the article should be submitted to the Staff Offs. for discussion or to the plenary session. I answered, "I have no objection to turning over any further mechanical details to the liaison officers with the understanding that there will be no change in or addition to the agreed wording which we consider complete in itself.["]

After batting the ball back & forth some more I finally said: "We have already told you that we dont consider that your draft proposal requires rewriting. We have accepted it as you drafted it for inclusion in the Arm. Agreement. We agree to recess with the understanding that Item 5 is to be turned over to the Staff Offs. to complete any necessary mechanical details. Our staff officers will not be authorized to change the agreed wording.["]

Nam Il said: "Leaving the matter with the Staff Offs meeting to discuss the formulation of the article of the Arm. Agreement on the principle agreed upon, we will let you know the time for the Staff Offs meeting.["]

UN: "We agree to the Staff Offs. meeting to discuss the mechanical details of framing the Arm Agreement on Item 5. I suggest a recess.["]

Nam Il agreed.

#3. Staff meeting Item 3 [appearing in the margin is the designation "HNC 949"]. Regarding Soviet Union, the enemy stated UNC could give no reason for opposing Soviets since there was no reason for such opposition. UNC stated enemy staff officers were failing to comply with agreed prin [principle] 6. which required them to name neutral nations acceptable to UNC. This failure on their part to carry out agreed principle placed blame for delay on their shoulders. UNC said there was no requirement that number of neutral nations nominated by each side be equal, the principle provided only that the total no [number] of neutral nations reps [representatives] on each side be equal. Reiterated that S.U. was unacceptable to UNC. UNC staff offs. did not utilize argument that SU is in close proximity to Korea, since such a statement implicitly agrees that other criteria, such as neutrality and non participation in war, did fit the S.U. It is considered opinion of delegation that unless the S.U. may be objected to on the grounds of participating in the K war, it is preferable to offer no reason for unacceptability of Soviets.

Staff Offs suspect enemy may be attempting to shape up deal whereby they offer concessions on ports & rotation in return for acceptance of Soviets by

UNC. It is the unanimous opinion of the delegation that the Commies should be informed definitely that the SU will never be accepted as a neutral nation. Such an unequivocal stand should be adopted at once, else the enemy will be led to believe that the UNC position on this point is soft and uncertain. Furthermore if Commies are convinced of firmness of our stand on this point before they involve their prestige irrevocably, there is a better chance of their withdrawing the nomination of the S.U.

The above rpt [report] of staff meeting was sent on to R. who in turn forwarded it to JCS concurring strongly with last sentence of 2nd para above and with above para, with deletion of words "as a neutral nation" in 2nd sent. [sentence]. He also requested authority to proceed along lines indicated in above para.

#4. Staff meeting Item 4 little progress. Made effort to agree on minor differences in wording last Commie proposal. UNC agreed to Commie proposal that RC teams be composed of 60 members 30 from each side. Question of communications for these teams still unresolved pending further study by Commies.

Feb. 20 (Wed): Staff meeting on Item 3. UNC proposed 35,000 rotation figure in attempt to make progress in the negots [negotiations] and to settle this issue. Commies continued to insist that 30,000 was an adequate figure.

Both sides reiterated their views on ports of entry. Chang stated that 7 ports would be suitable for war conditions but not armistice conditions.

On matter of UNC rejection of Soviet Union as a neutral nation, Chang made folg statement: "I would like to call your attention to the fact that how could your side possibly resolve this question if your [side?] is only engaged in exchanging the matters which result in the form of refusals instead of giving any concrete reason at all to the proposal that the other side has made with regard to the matter of the nominations of neutral nations. Therefore our side submitted the proposal that both sides shall agree mutually and simultaneously to the proposals by both sides regarding the nominations of neutral nations. I therefore am against your attitude in refusing the proposal that our side has submitted with regard to the question of the nominations of neutral nations without giving any reasonable justifications for your refusal. Accordingly I request that your side should retract such a stand which is only blocking the progress of the negots unreasonably. I make this request with a view to facilitate the resolution of this question as soon as possible.

UNC remarked that, as the Commies have stated many times, the neutral nations, the reps [representatives] of the neutral nations and the Supervisory Commission will have the status of guests in the area under the control of both sides. UNC had agreed to this viewpoint. UNC pointed out that now the Commies are attempting to force an unwanted guest on its side; not only are Commies attempting to force an unwanted guest on UNC but they are also asking for reasons why this particular person is an unwanted guest. UNC stated that this action of the Commies is quite inconsistent with the proprieties. Furthermore the Soviet Union does not fit the criteria established by agreement between the delegates, and the failure of the Commies to nominate a nation which does not fit those criteria, including the criterion that the nations shall be acceptable to our side, is in direct violation of the agreement reached between the delegates and in violation of the instrs given to the staff meeting.

UNC also explained that it was the Commies who first suggested that neutral nations be used and that the neutral nations which would be invited would be agreed to and acceptable to both sides. With this understanding the UNC agreed to Commie suggestion of inviting neutral nations, which would be acceptable to both sides. UNC then stated that the Commies are now asking UNC to disregard this original understanding and accept a nation that is not acceptable to the UNC.

Comment: After today's attempt to make progress without results, it is becoming increasingly apparent that the Commie nomination of Soviet Union will block further progress until this matter is settled.

#4. In staff meeting on Item 4 Commies presented revised wording of their 14 Feb proposal which reflected discussion of past 5 days concerning minor matters.

In order to permit UNC to eliminate personal difference remaining in several paras [paragraphs] over meaning of word "repatriation" UNC offered new para 1 as follows: "For purposes of this Arm. [Armistice] agreement the act of delivery of a POW by one side to the other side shall be called repatriation notwithstanding the nationality or place of residence of such POW." This para. was summarily rejected by the Commies on the absurd grds. [grounds] that it was arguing our basic stand and that it was related to the question of civ internees. UNC refuted these arguments and suggested that Commies study implicatons of our proposed new para 1. Commies countered with statement: If your side will not make any suggestion re. the settlement of this entire item of the agenda, I think no progress can be made in our staff offs. meeting.

CinCUNC referred to our HNC949 of yesterday in forwarding JCS reply which follows: "Previous instrs remain applicable. Our position with respect to unacceptability Soviet Union should be stated firmly and unequivocally and along general lines previously supplied you."

R then went on to add: "I have carefully reviewed JCS instrs in msgs. The intent of these msgs. is clear. The UNC is not authorized to adopt at this time as a final posit [position] the rejection of the S.U. If we are to give any reasons for the unacceptability of the S.U. then I believe they should be given at the earliest date. Consequently unless you have cogent reasons to the contrary a statement along folg. lines should be made at time of your choosing:

"At the meeting of 18 Feb '52 you said 'your side cannot give any reason nor does it have any reason to object to any of the neutral nations nominated by our side. Your side cannot give any reason nor does it have any reason to object to the nomination of the S.U. by our side as one of the neutral nations.' We have carefully considered your statement. The UNC does have reasons for rejecting the S.U. as one of the nations to participate in the supervisory organ [organization]. The reasons are clear, cogent & irrefutable. I should like to point out however that neither side is obligated to state reasons for the acceptance or rejection of any particular nation. The principle simply and clearly states that both sides agree to invite neutral nations acceptable to both sides. The acceptability or non acceptability of any given nation therefore is a unilateral matter beyond the purview of these discussions. In the furtherance of understanding, however, and so that our position may be unmistakably clear to you, we will give our reasons for stating unequivocally that the S.U. is not acceptable to our side. The UNC holds that it is in the interest of all concerned that members of the supervisory organ should be drawn from those nations not in close proximity to Korea and without a record of past participation in the K question. This is not the introduction of a new principle. It is our rightful and unilateral application of logic to the problem of selecting nations acceptable to both sides. I repeat: the S.U. is not acceptable to our side."

R added: In event Commie side attacks this statement along usual lines e.g. "What do you mean by K question? How then do you justify Sweden?" etc it is considered that UNC reps should answer in substance as follows: "Our statement is clear and stands on its own merits. We do not propose to enter into endless discussion of matters which are self evident. We strongly recommend that you give our statement your thoughtful consideration[.]"

Feb. 21 (Thurs): Staff meeting on Item 3 opened with discussion of figure of rotation. Commies reiterated figure 30,000 was reached after much consideration and represented more than enough for UNC purposes. Any more would be impermissible. UNC stated 30,000 was completely inadequate and that UNC views remained completely unchanged.

Neither side had any offers or comments regarding ports of entry.

Discussion of neutral nations followed. After Cols Chang and Pu had pressed him for a reason Col Darrow finally gave the statement authorized yesterday by CinCUNC.

Col Pu Shan & Col Chang then attacked Darrows "so called reasons" asking "What is the logic upon which your side attempts to exclude nations who are in close proximity to Korea as a neutral nation?" "If the neutral nations nominated by our side have any record of participation in the Korean question that is a record that they strongly oppose any intervention in the Korean war." "Can your side deny that the S.U. is a nation which is most strongly against any intervention in the K war and which is most strongly in favor of a peaceful settlement of the K question?"

Darrow stood his ground saying that he did not propose to enter into endless discussions of matters which are self evident.

Chang said in effect that if the S.U. wasn't considered neutral there were not any neutral nations at all in the whole world[.]

Col Kinney pointed out that the delegates had agreed in principle that both sides would nominate neutral nations acceptable to the other side. Commies had failed to live up to the agreement. Therefore responsibility for delay wholly Commies.

Comment: **Attitude of Commies remained intransigent and completely disinterested on reaching a compromise. When UNC pointed out that it had made all the last moves Commie reply was to effect that revisions to unreasonable and illogical ideas could not be considered and in effect that move was still up to UNC.**

Commies statements today suggests that their strategy may be to permit no further progress even on minor details of Item 3 until UNC accepts Soviet Union or until complete concept of inspection in the rear is abandoned. Commies contend if Soviet is not neutral, no nation is neutral. The logical extension of this position would be that if the Soviets are unacceptable in Neutral Commission, all nations are unacceptable, hence no neutral commission can be formed. If this proves to be the enemy's strategy, UNC may be soon faced with choice of Soviets in Neutral Commission, or no neutral commission i e no inspection in rear areas. This is, of course speculative but a distinct possibility.

#4. Staff meeting Item 4. Discussed and adjusted several minor items in wording in Commies revised proposal. UNC then indicated agreement with Commies paras 5 thru 9 dependent on Commies acceptance of UNC definition of repatriation and its inclusion in Arm [armistice] agreement. Commies acknowledged for first time that there was a difference in meaning of repat [repatriation] in English from that in Chinese & Korean. They stated that in English it meant return to the homeland, while in Chinese & Korean it just means—"That a person returns or is sent to or returns to some place." They considered it redundant in Chinese & Korean to include any such definition in the Arm Agreement. In order to overcome Commies objection that this definition was redundant in Korean & Chinese and to indicate the necessity for it in English, UNC submitted for consideration the folg. revised wording of proposed definition para: "So that there may be no misunderstanding owing to the equal use of 3 languages, the act of delivery of a POW by one side to the other side shall, for the purpose of this Arm. Agreement, be called 'repatriation' in English, 'Song Hwan' in Korean and 'Chien Fan' in Chinese, notwithstanding the nationality or place of residence of such POW." UNC then stated that inclusion of this definition would make possible acceptance of Commie para 3 and also implied that paras 2 & 4 could be agreed upon perhaps with some rewording. Commies stated they felt it was unnecessary to include a definition of repatriation in the Arm Agreement, but in view of UNC insistence, they would consider both its inclusion and its location in the Armistice wording.

Feb. 22 (Fri): In Staff meeting on Item 3 Commies made opening statement re. ports of entry in which they offered to increase this number of ports of entry to five. Statement also reiterated idea that limit of rotation should be fixed at 30,000 as previously proposed by Commies.

UNC replied that Commie statement represented an effort on their part, and that UNC staff offs. were authorized to suggest 6 ports of entry and rotation limit of 35,000 as the solution to the 2 problems. Suggested Commies accept these figures.

Commies replied that the new proposal they had made was final and that UNC consider their proposal as a solution.

UNC stated for second time that 6 ports and 35,000 monthly rotation figure was as far as UNC would go.

Darrow then introduced new para about withdrawal from coastal islands with accompanying map showing islands remaining under UNC control—Paeng Yong-Do [Paengnyong-do], Taechong-Do, Sochong-Do, Kunyonpyong-Do & U-Do.

Col Chang then took up the cudgel again about their nomination of the S.U. as a neutral nation, requesting that UNC withdraw its unreasonable objection to "our" nomination of S.U. Claimed reasons UNC gave in objecting were untenable. UNC's two unilateral and ingenious arguments were in fundamental [contravention?] of agreed principle. No justification at all to say that S.U. is in close proximity of K and it would deprive it of qualification of a neutral nation. Because of S.U's mighty milt [military] power it drove Japanese aggressors from K, therefore it has strongly upheld a peaceful settlement of K question. Because of S.U.'s record, more than any other nation it should be invited to participate in Neutral Nations Supervisory Commission.

Darrow of course stood his ground and refused to enter into debate. Said if both sides strictly adhere to principles agreed upon by the delegates in sub committee to nominate neutral nations acceptable to both sides, this problem would not be difficult to solve. Repeated once again, the S.U. is not acceptable to our side.

Col Pu Shan then carried the ball along the same lines as Chang. Contended UNC reasons for objecting to S.U. would not stand debate—which they want!

Darrow ended battle by referring to remarks of his of yesterday in reply.

Comment: Issues remaining in Item 3 which require solution can be summarized as follows: (1) Ports of entry (2) Limiting figure for rotation (3) Nomination of S.U. (4) Question of examination of secret items of equipment during insp. [inspection] by neutral teams (5) Number of Neutral Nation mobile insp. teams (6) Agreed lines of comm. [communication].

#4. UNC submitted complete draft of Arm [Armistice] wording. Commies indicated agreement to paras 4, 6, 7, 8 & 9 & 10 subject to exact comparison of wording with Commie paras 3, 5, 6, 7, 8 & 9 as amended in 21 Feb meeting.

Commies likewise indicated general agreement to wording of para one, definition of "repatriation," but stated it should not be a separate para. They suggested that the definition wording might better be inserted in para of Article III of Arm Agreement where the word "repatriation" is first used. UNC concurred, though no definite decision reached on this point[.]

Commies indicated that if UNC agreed to use word "all" in UNC paras 3 & 5, as it appears in the corresponding paras 2 & 4 of Commie proposal, then it would not be then it would not be [sic] difficult to reach agreement on these two paras. During remainder of meeting UNC attacked Commie insistence on inclusion of word all in 2 paras in question. UNC stated that UNC paras 3 & 5 are consistent with concepts of both sides regarding the issue of repatriation and that both sides could adopt the two paras with full knowledge that they are suitable to points of view of either side on basic question[.] Commies continued to insist on it's [sic] inclusion, stating that repat [repatriation] of all POWs should be expressed and stipulated in the two paras. In this discussion Commies stated they had made all the efforts to solve Item 4; that they had exhausted all their efforts; and that unless UNC makes corresponding efforts, with respect to basic issue, there would be no possible solution even if another 70 days are spent in discussion.

Feb. 23 (Sat): Staff meeting Item 3. Commies stated in order to insure progress they wished to make "final" compromise offer of monthly rotation figure of 35,000 & 5 ports of entry.

UNC unable to understand Commie continued haggling over one port of entry, stated that as brought forth yesterday UNC not authorized accept less than 6 ports of entry[.]

Further discussion brought no results. UNC brought forth facts that UNC had met more than halfway the Commie ideas by decreasing no [number] of ports by 6 whereas Commies had only increased their number by 2. UNC proposed that 6 ports be adopted with proviso that number could be reduced by agreement of senior members of MAC.

Commies replied only way to reach agreement today would be to accept their proposal of 35,000 and 5. Commie argument based on reasonableness of Commie proposal and extent of Commie concessions. Stated in effect there would be no other solution but evaded reply to direct question as to whether their stand was in effect an ultimatum[.]

Then followed a lengthy discussion along the same lines as yesterday over the Commies nomination of the S.U. as one of the neutral nations. Some of it follows:

Col Kinney: "In accord with the agreed principle and instrs [instructions] of the dels, it is your duty to present the names of nations acceptable to both sides. You have been fully and repeatedly informed that the S.U. is not acceptable. The obligation devolves upon you to either present the name of an alternate national acceptable to both sides or to elect to draw the total representation for your side on the Neutral Commission from the two nations which you have been informed are acceptable to our side. If you elect to do so you can continue to delay progress in this matter by failing to carry out the agreement and instrs. of the delegates. We cannot compel you to follow those instructions in that agreement but there can be no doubt as to where the responsibility for such delay lies[.]"

Col Chang: "In your statement which you have just made every word is in violation of the principles agreed upon between both sides[.] There exists not a single word nor phrase nor thought in cooperating in the principles agreed upon by both sides and the definition re. the neutral nations, by which you can oppose a neutral nation which is in full compliance with the definition. Therefore the responsibility for delaying the negots [negotiations] and leaving the quest [question] unresolved is solely resting on your side, who with an unreasonable opposition goes counter to the principles agreed between both sides."

Col Darrow: ["]It appears I must point out again that our side agreed to this principle suggested by your side. If the interpretation that you place upon this principle is correct, the prin. [principle] should read 'both sides agree to invite neutral nations which must be accepted by both sides[.]' The principle however does not read that way. It reads 'both sides agree to invite neutral nations acceptable to both sides.' The wording is very clear. It cannot be [mis?]interpreted and we have given you our opinion re your proposal. We are not violating the principle agreed to by both sides. I have nothing further today."

The matter of allowing insp [inspection] of secret equipment has not been discussed recently. In order to be prepared to secure agreement on this matter, the folg sent [sentence] is suggested as a possible solution: "In event majority of the members of the Neutral Nations Inspection Team agree that certain secret designs or characteristics must be inspected to insure that reinforcing equipment is not being introduced into Korea, this fact shall be rptd [reported] to the MAC and the matter settled thru negots."

#4. In Item 4 meeting Commies indicated acceptance of paras 4, 6, 7, 8, 9 & 10 of UNC proposal of 22 Feb. On basis that parole provision and time limit for completion of exchange are closely related to prin. governing repat. [repatriation), Commies rejected UNC paras 3 & 5 due to omission of word "all" as relating to POWs. Suggested UNC abandon stand on vol. [voluntary] repat. and accept their proposal.

UNC requested that definition of "repat" contained in present UNC para 1 be placed in parenthesis immed. [immediately] folg 1st sent. of para 2 and that all para be renumbered to permit parallel numbering of paras. in Commie & UNC proposals.

UNC suggested rewording paras 2 & 4 (as renumbered) to include phrase "as required by para 1 hereof," where appropriate to definitely indicate connection between these paras & renumbered para 1. Commies agreed to consider this. During discussions Commies stated that their side absolutely cannot consider our para 1 (as renumbered) in any conference but apparently did not intend to refuse to discuss it. They implied that their acceptance of the principle of parole and a time limit for repatriation of POWs was contingent upon UNC acceptance of forced repat. Commies then presented to the delegation a formal protest against recent incident occurring at Koje Do wherein 69 civilian internees were killed by our troops in a Communist inspired riot. Protest follows: "I am instructed to lodge a serious protest with your side for the sanguinary incident of barbarously massacring a large number of our personnel captured & interned by your side at Koje Do.

The latest massacre fully testifies to the brutal inhumanity with which your side treats our captured personnel. It belies all your claims at this conference table about the good treatment rec'd [received] by our personnel in your custody. It further proclaims before all people with a conscience thruout the world the utter bankruptcy of your absurd principle of so called "vol repatriation[.]"

"Our side never recognized the reclassification of our personnel captured by your side as civilians. Our side urges that your side submit full data concerning the more than 44,000 personnel of our side captured by your side, including full data concerning those personnel of our side massacred by your side. It is imperative that your side give a clear account for the slaughter of these personnel of our side. You absolutely cannot cover up your flagrant crimes with such frauds as reclassification. We will continue to accuse your side before the whole world. I hereby solemnly declare that our side reserves the right to pursue further into this intolerable sanguinary incident."

"[sic] UNC noted protest and inquired if the sentence therein referring to data meant that the Commies were prepared to carry out exchange of data agreed to by both sides on 1 Jan. Commies replied that they were instructed to lodge the protest and were not prepared to discuss any questions mentioned therein.

I should mention that yesterday I addressed a note to R. voicing the Delegations concern over the recent turn of events which has injected Soviet Russia directly into the arm. [armistice] negots as a possible neutral nation. Said we are emphatic in our belief that if we give way on this point, our negot positions on other remaining issues will be irrevocably impaired. Ended by saying: "Finally I desire to rpt that the U.S. members of the Del present are unanimous in feeling that unless UNC intends to achieve a milt arm. entirely on Commie terms the UNC Del should be authorized at very earliest to take an unalterable final stand and tell Commies categorically that Soviet Union will never be accepted by the UNC.''

R in reply said he was "in full and sympathetic accord with your views" and that he had "initiated further effort which may result in authorization to take desired position or other means to remove this point from further arm discussions." "Meanwhile you are hereby authorized at your discretion to announce UNC Del. refusal to enter into any further discussion whatever of Commie proposal[.]''

Feb. 24 (Sun): Staff meeting Item 3. In reply to Commie question, UNC stated it had nothing new on issues of ports & neutral nations. UNC stated 5 ports were inadequate for purpose of arm and recommended both sides agree on 6 ports. Commies reiterated UNC had no reason to object to their nomination of neutral nations and asked UNC to withdraw unjustifiable objection. UNC replied prin [principle] 6 requires neutral nations be acceptable each side; that Commies can solve this issue by either substituting another nation or withdrawing nomination of S.U. Commies reiterated statements of past days on this matter and claimed term "acceptable to both sides" is formula for indicating mutual respect for nomination of neutral nations by each side. UNC declared Commies statement was just for record & requires no refutation since UNC views have already been stated.

#4. In staff meeting on Item 4 UNC asked Commies their reaction to proposed changes submitted yesterday to para 2 (concerning parole) and para 4 (concerning the time limit for repatriation of POWs). Commies stated revised paras not acceptable and that only way to solve them was to solve the basic issue. They continued to imply that their acceptance to the principle of parole and a time limit for exchange of POWs was contingent upon UNC acceptance of forced repatriation.

Commies at every opportunity stressed their desire to discuss repatriation and finally UNC in a forceful summation of the issue reiterated its firm stand on the principle of vol. repat [voluntary repatriation]. Keynote of this statement was that Commies had in effect embraced this principle during course of hostilities for their own ends and now were trying to deny UNC same right. Remainder of session devoted to discussion of this issue with nothing new evolving. Commies closed by stating that their continued efforts to solve Agenda Item 4 had reached a limit. No answer to Commies formal protest of 23 Feb was submitted since subject not introduced in todays meeting.

Conferred with Col Salisbury who came over from GHQ with a plan to implement the Johnson "fait accompli" plan. Plan was accompanied by a ltr from Doyle Hickey saying that R expected to submit the plan to Wash. [Washington] and wanted our comments thereon. Plan would be used as a vehicle to express CinCUNCs & Delegations strong disapproval of the idea. Our comments were in effect not to submit the plan but instead to let Wash know how strongly we were against it. See my personal file for details. [In Admiral Joy's personal files at the Naval Historical Center in Washington, D.C., there exists a Memorandum for the Record on this subject. It is now being reviewed for declassification. A copy of it will be on deposit in the Joy Archive at the Hoover Institution.] When Salisbury left I expressed the opinion that there were only 2 possible courses of action, either to drop the whole position of vol repat as soon as possible (on the sub del level) while it was still deemphasized or to fight for it to the breaking point in the Plenary session[.] He said he would carry my views to CinCUNC.

Feb. 25 (Mon): Beginning staff meeting on Item 3. Commies reiterated their proposal to agree to UNC rotation figure of 35,000 and suggestion of 5 ports of entry was final. UNC urged Commies to accept 6 ports since 5 ports are inadequate and will un-necessarily restrict UNC activities during period of armistice. UNC pointed out difference of one port reduces port facilities by 20%.

Neutral nations. UNC suggested para 37 be revised:

(1) Changing no [number] of senior officers to compose Supervisory Commission to four with two being appointed by neutral nations of each side.

(2) Stipulating Neutral Nations of Sweden, Switzerland, Poland and Czechoslovakia. Commies made no direct comment to suggestion, claimed UNC had no reason to object to S.U. stated issue could be solved by both sides agreeing simultaneously to 6 nations nominated or for each side to nominate nations without requiring formality of approval. UNC replied it is obvious Commies intend delaying negots [negotiations] if they cannot accept UNC equitable solution.

Para 26g. UNC presented rewording in view of agreements reached by staff offs. on Agenda Item 4: "Give general supervision & direction to the activities of the Committee for Repatriation of POWs and the Committee for Assisting the Return of Displaced Civilians hereinafter established." Commies will consider.

Para 43c. In reply to Commie query re last sentence UNC claimed it could see no reason for deleting last clause and suggested sentence read as follows: "The inspections of combat aircraft, armored vehicles, weapons and ammo [ammunition] by the NNI Teams will be such as to enable them to properly insure that reinforcing equipment is not being introduced into Korea; but this shall not be construed as authorizing inspections or exams [examinations] of any secret designs or characteristics of any combat aircraft, armored vehicles weapons or ammo.'' Commies asked UNC give further consideration to their previous views.

#4. There was no progress in Item 4 staff meeting. UNC again indicated advantages of both sides agreeing to wording of paras 2 (concerning parole) and 4 (concerning the time limit for repat of POWs) but Commies continued maintain these 2 paras dependent on agreement that all POWs must be repatriated. After further brief exchange of opinion on basic issue of vol [voluntary] vs. forced repatriation meeting recessed 1157. Translators & interpreters of both sides were to meet during the p.m. to eliminate minor wording differences in Chinese & Korean versions of paras 3, 5, 6, 7, 8 & 9.

Feb. 26 (Tues): Staff meeting Item 3. UNC insisted that 5 ports are inadequate and can see no reason for Commies not accepting six since it will not affect or inconvenience them. Commies claimed their agreeing with UNC 35,000 rotation figure & suggesting 5 ports is their final compromise proposal; declared both sides understand each other's views, therefore it is only technical procedure for UNC to agree to 5 ports. UNC replied Commies must have reason unknown to UNC for insisting on 5 ports; pointed out principle states replenishment and rotation shall be carried out at ports agreed to, therefore sufficient ports must be provided to satisfy this requirement. Commies maintained 5 ports more than adequate since amount of rotation personnel & replenishment will be greatly reduced during period of armistice.

In reply to UNC query on proposal to invite only four nations, folg is quoted from record:

Col Pu Shan: ''Re question of neutral nations, it must be pointed out that there can be no reason to object to the nations nominated by our side completely in accord with the definition of neutral nations agreed upon, nor are there any reasons at all to object to the nomination by our side of the S.U. as one of the neutral nations. The point now is therefore not the number of members on the NNSC. It is a quest. [question] that one side cannot give any reason for objecting to the nations nominated by the other side in complete compliance with the definition of neutral nations. Our side has already proposed two alternative methods for solving the quest which are both reasonable. **That is either both sides will agree simultaneously and all at once to all the nominations of neutral nations of the other side** or we should follow the stipulation of para 38 of the draft arm [armistice] submitted by your side. **That is both sides nominate their neutral nations respectively and without going thru any procedure of approval''.**

Col Darrow: ''Your methods of solution to para 38 are not acceptable and have been rejected. No matter how you phrase your methods or how many methods you call them, in the last analysis it amounts to your asking us to accept the S.U. as one of the nations to be on the supervisory commission. We have told you repeatedly that the S.U. is not acceptable. Are you prepared to comment on our proposal of yesterday?['']

Col Pu Shan: "Re the quest of neutral nations, we have long ago pointed out that your side is unable to advance any tenable reasons nor does your side have any reasons to object to any of the nations nominated by our side in complete compliance with the definition of neutral nations. Your proposal yesterday is a further attempt to exclude, without any justification, the S.U. as one of the members of the NNSC. We have already pointed out yesterday that your side has no justification at all to object to our nomination of the S.U. as one of the neutral nations. Our side absolutely cannot consider and will categorically reject any objection without justification to the nominations of our side which are completely in compliance with the definition of neutral nations. Our side has already proposed reasonable solutions for this question. We recommend that you again seriously consider our proposal and withdraw your unreasonable objections to the nominations of neutral nations by our side."

Col Darrow: "In regard to your comments of the neutral nations, you have not given me any comment re the proposal we made yesterday in an attempt to solve this problem. We submitted this proposal for the purpose of solving the problem of para 38."

Col Pu Shan: "Our side has not only categorically rejected your proposal yesterday re the neutral nations, but has also fully explained the reason why we categorically rejected this proposal of yours. Any objection without justification to our nominations of neutral nations completely in compliance with the definition, will also be categorically rejected by our side. We recommend that your side further consider our reasonable proposals and that your side accept our solution so that progress can be made in these negots [negotiations]."

I added the folg to our daily rpt [report] (HNC980) to R: "The strong and unequivocal statement made today by the enemy in support of their nomination of the S.U. leaves no room for reasonable doubt that this point has become a major issue. Consequently the delegation continues to feel strongly that we must at the earliest be authorized to reject categorically and finally the S.U. as a nominee for the NNSC (Neutral Nations Supervisory Commission).['']

#4. Entire staff session on Item 4 occupied by discussion of questions of wording in Chinese & Korean of six paras. previously approved in English by both sides. No substantive changes involved.

Sent folg msg (HNC979) to CinCUNC: "Staff of Agenda 4 has reached point where only remaining topic for discussion is voluntary vs forced repatriation. Current instrs [instructions] to delegation are to stand fast on this issue and staff is proceeding on this basis. Failure to pursue question agressively [*sic*] on staff level or on sub delegation level if Commies propose return to sub-del almost certain to be taken by Commies as indication that we are weakening in our stand.

"Renewed discussion of this issue on either staff or sub del level sure to be reflected in press and again place issue in limelight. It is obviously undesirable to restress this issue if there is any likelihood that we are not going to stand firm to the breaking point if necessary. Furthermore if concessions are to be made it is preferable to make them on the staff level before the issue is again highlighted.

"Delegation present unanimously of opinion that early decision from Wash [Washington] to adopt an unalterable final position on POW question is imperative[.]" [Following inserted in margin: "Para 3 HNC 979."]

Feb. 27 (Wed): We were info adee [addressee] on folg msg CinCUNC sent to JCS: "Strength of Commie insistence on inclusion of USSR as a member of the neutral supervisory commission is now believed crystal clear as indicated in part 4 of HNC 980. Therefore respectfully request authority to inform Commies that UNC refusal to accept the Soviets is irrevocable and no longer subject of discussion[.]"

CinCUNC also sent folg to JCS: "JCS requested to furnish decision in para 3 of HNC 979[.][''']

In staff meeting on Item 3 Commies opened by presenting a prepared statement which summarized past discussions on ports of entry, rotation and neutral nations. Commies pointed out that their side had agreed to UNC figure of 35,000 for rotation with 5 ports of entry and, therefore UNC cannot justify its demand for Commies to make another concession on the number of ports at a time when both sides have approached agreement on these two questions. On the problem of neutral nations, Chang made the folg statement:

"Your side has advanced arguments the absurdity of which can find no comparison in an attempt to exclude the Soviet Union as a member of the NNSC under the pretext of what you call close proximity—of record of past participation in the Korean question. *But upon what logic can your side deprive a nation of its status of a neutral nation simply because it is in close proximity to Korea?* **What justification does your side have to exclude the USSR which has consistently advocated a peaceful settlement of the Korean question from being a member of the NNSC? The USSR more than any other nation should be invited to participate in the NNSC. Any unreasonable objection to the nations nominated by our side which are fully in compliance with the definition of neutral nations, any attempt to exclude the S.U. from participating in the NNSC, no matter what form they may take, absolutely cannot be considered and will be categorically rejected by our side."**

UNC stated that it had [seen?] nothing new in Commie statements; that it was apparent that Commies were more interested now in arguing the merits of the

S.U. than in reaching an Arm [armistice] agreement. UNC explained that its proposal on NN [neutral nations] eliminated any pretext for arguing reasons; further UNC has accepted the nomination of Czechoslovakia & Poland, and both sides can reach a speedy agreement on this matter if the Commies are interested in making progress in these negots [negotiations].

Commies made folg closing statement: "The only possible progress in these negots can be made when you put aside your unilateral demand and frankly come back to deal fairly with a view to solving these pending issues. Until such a time should come, there would be no progress in these negots."

#4. In staff meeting on Item 4 agreement was reached on Korean, Chinese & English versions of all agreed paras with the exception of one item, the Korean version of "United Nations." NK representatives desire to use Yon Hap Kuk in place of UNC proposed Kuk Chae Yon Hap. UNC suggested both be used in document. Commies will consider.

Folg agreement on wording Col Tsai made a statement substance of which follows: Long discussions on Item 4. Commies have made many concessions. Their efforts have reached the limit. Remaining stumbling block is UNC's unprecedented and absurd proposal of vol. [voluntary] repatriation. This has been thoroughly refuted, proved to be notorious & categorically rejected. Hereafter, whether there will be any agreement on Agenda Item 4 or any progress depends on whether UNC will give up its unreasonable proposition.

Col Murray replied as follows: "I agree with many parts of Col Tsai's analysis. We have had a long discussion in reaching agreement insofar as we have been able to reach agreement up to this time. Many concessions were made by both sides in so doing. It is for that reason that I regret to note your statement that efforts by your side have come to a limit. When an unshakeable [sic] position is opposed by an unshakeable [sic] position the inevitable result is a stalemate. Col Tsai indicated a few days ago that he was prepared to discuss for 70 more days in support of your position. I must tell you frankly that 70 more days of talk will not provide a solution. Neither will the problem be solved by asserting that the proposal of the other side is absurd or that it has been fully refuted, for such assertions are a matter of opinion only. Col Tsai knows that many probs [problems] in connection with the arm. have been solved in the staff offs. [officers] meeting but he knows that they are not solved by such an approach as was made in his initial statement.

"One issue remains between us. If approached in the same manner as the other issues we have solved, a solution may be possible. If it is not the inevitable result is a stalemate.

"The only remaining difference regards the repatriation of the POWs. The initial proposal made by the UNC on this subject was a compromise proposal in the sense that it was an effort to harmonize the conflicting doctrines and practices of the two sides with respect to the treatment of POWs in an equitable solution. However by comparing this initial proposal with the current proposal of the UNC, you will discover that many additional concessions have been made to your point of view. Let us examine some of these.

"From the standpoint of our side, the 37,000 civilian internees and the 16,000 POWs of South Korean residence are nationals of the Republic of Korea. Their disposition is an internal affair of our side. This stand is fully sanctioned by the law of nations & laws of all national states. Conversely there is no authority, no sanction, no precedent in the law of nations nor in the law of individual states to support the stand of your side that these persons of S.K. residence should be treated as POWs. and be turned over to your side under the Arm Agreement. Nevertheless, we have by our acceptance of an unprecedented definition of the word "repat," [repatriation] paved the way for such persons to go over to your side, as many of them who wish to do so. Whether they will be permitted to do so or not rests with you.

"The traditional policy of your side with respect to the treatment of POWs. was well described by your spokesman during the early days of our meetings on Agenda Item 4. It involved the so called 'release at the front.' It also involved the incorporation of personnel of our side, both milt [military] and civilian into your milt forces on what was called a volunteer basis. In consideration of these doctrines and practices of your side, freedom of choice as regards repat. was included in the initial proposal of the UNC. Moreover this right was extended to certain specified categories of personnel such as former ROK Army soldiers who are now serving in your armies and to civilians of SK who were incorporated into your forces during their advance into the areas south of the 38th parallel on the grds [grounds] that there had been no neutral agency to determine the validity of your contention that the first choice had been freely expressed. Such specific listings of persons are not included in the current version of our proposal.

"Our side by no means agrees with your contention that freedom of choice as regards repat. during an arm. is political whereas freedom of choice to volunteer during active hostilities is not. Nevertheless we have taken your views into consideration and rephrased our current proposal in such a manner as to remove from it the implications of a political choice between the two sides. The current version does not propose 'freedom of choice as regards repat,' & it does not propose 'repat of those who so desire.' It expresses the UNC position in min [minimum] terms. That is that 'there shall be no forced repat.' What does this phrase mean? It means that every POW will be repat except those few who oppose it, that is those who would have to be forced to cross the line. What assurance does your side have that this is so? Your RC reps [representatives] will be in the POW camps where they can check the method of promulgating the provisions of the Arm Agreement to the POWs. In fact that procedure could be made the subject of a joint agreement between us. The NN observers and your own reps will be at the exchange point to determine that all POWs will return to or go to your side except those who would have to be forced.

"In summary, in preparing our current proposal, we have made every [word inserted above line] effort to devise wording which will provide a suitable vehicle for a negotiated solution of the one remaining diff [difference]. If you are interested in negotiating this issue we are prepared to discuss it here in the staff officers meeting. If you are not interested in negotiating it, but only in talking about it for another 70 days, it might be well to refer our differences back to the sub-delegation. There we can discuss the issue of forced repat. for 70 days or for twice that length of time if you so desire. There is no possibility that our side will ever abandon the position that it will not deliver those persons to your side who must be forced to go there."

Tsai replied in substance as follows: "Commies have done their best to discuss diffs even unreasonable proposal of UNC. The difference cannot be settled if the quest. [question] of repat. is not dealt with according to army designation. UNC attempts to evade Commies reasonable principle cannot be successful regardless of level on which discussions are held. Arguments of UNC will be no better on a different level on which discussions are held. Apparently UNC has not decided to expedite the solution nor to give up its unreasonable proposition. Therefore, I agree to refer this quest. to the sub-committee for discussion. Inquiry is made on when we may expect an answer to our protest of the incident at Koje Do on 18 Feb."

UNC replied that is regrettable that other side should have taken the decision to refer the unsettled item to sub del [delegation] without allowing itself time to give full consideration to UNC statement of this am. UNC then gave reply on Koje-Do protest as follows:

"Your protest of 23 Feb is based upon a false premise. The incident involved personnel who were not of your side. You must understand that this incident did not occur among POWs but among the Civilian Internees led by Commie agitators. These civilian internees have been legally so reclassified & so rptd [reported]. Therefore the whole matter is an internal affair of the UNC and no proper concern of yours.

"The Senior Del of the ICRC which is a truly neutral body internationally recognized as such, was promptly notified and the ICRC delegates are now present at Koje-Do."

Col Tsai noted the protest and stated: "I have noted your answer to our protest. Our side has never recognized the illegal reclassification of POWs made by your side. The basic data relating to POWs can absolutely not be mixed up with the civilian data relating to POWs. I must point out that any pretexts of your side cannot cover up or escape your serious responsibility for this barbarous massacre.''

Tentatively sub dels will meet Friday.

Feb. 28 (Thurs): Staff meeting Item 3. UNC reviewed record of concessions & compromises prior to present stalemate on ports of entry. Pointed out that majority of concessions had been made by UNC. Commies maintained their original stand was to prohibit all introduction of milt [military] personnel and war material into Korea which would eliminate all need for any ports of entry. Thus Commie proposal of rotation of 35,000 and 5 ports of entry and concessions leading thereto were not to be disturbed by sophistry. Both sides remained firm.

Commies remain adamantly against UNC objection to Soviet Union and against UNC proposal for 4 nation NNSC[.]

Col Chang: ['']No matter what kind of cunning formula you adopt, no matter how you advance that formula, our side is adamantly opposed to your opposition to the nominations of neutral nations which our side, by our proposal, prepared to invite on the NNSC. Therefore, I now propose that either both sides agree simultaneously, all at once, to the nominations of neutral nations of the other side or else each party should nominate their respective neutral nations. For the sake of interest of the armistice I now urge your side to give serious consideration to this proposal of ours which is fair & sufficient to resolve the difficulties pending.''

Col Levie: ''Our proposal called for the designation of 4 neutral nations. Two—Poland & Czechoslovakia, nominated by you. Two[—]Switzerland & Sweden[,] nominated by us. All 4 of those nations are acceptable to both sides. All 4 of those nations meet the requirements of the principles and of acceptability. Agreement on our proposal would remove all basis for any further dispute on this matter. Continued objection to our proposal only indicates a lack of desire to reach an agreement. I formally propose that you accept our suggestion for a 4 nation NNSC composed of the 4 nations I have mentioned.['']

Col Kinney: ''We have nothing more to say[.] Unless you have other matters to discuss I suggest we recess until tomorrow.['']

Col Chang: ''Everyone of your attempts or so called proposals refusing our entirely fair and thoroughly agreeable proposal of the nominations of neutral nations, which are fully in compliance with the agreement between both sides does not merit any refutation. Such proposals or attempts of your side have been rejected by our side already in the past; and I now reject them and will do so in the future. This stand should be clearly understood by your side. The only result that you would bring about by your unreasonable refusal to accept our proposal will be a further delay of the Arm [armistice] negots. [negotiations]. If your side is sincerely interested in the progress of these negots, I I [*sic*] urge again as I said before, that both sides agree simultaneously to the nomination of neutral nations all at once made by the other side, or both sides designate their respective neutral nations respectively in pursuance to your proposed version of para 38. We have this alternative at hand now. I again urge your side to give serious consideration to our proposal for the sake of progress of the negots & the interest of the arm. If your side is reluctant to carry on the discussion I agree to recess until tomorrow.["]

Col. Kinney: "Your proposal to which you just alluded has already been formally rejected. I need not repeat that rejection. In the interest of progress and in order that we may more speedily reach an armistice I urge that your side agree to the 4 nation proposal which we have made, which proposal adequately and completely fulfills the requirement stipulated in the principle that a neutral Nations Commission be established.

"Nothing more is needed. To continue to argue over an issue which is unnecessary to the complete fulfillment of the requirement for a NNC is to delay progress toward an arm. You now bear that responsibility."

#4. Staff meeting Item 4. Both sides presented English, Chinese & Korean version of Arm. Agreement on Agenda 4. Numerous minor discrepancies were noted & corrected. Others follow:

Korean phraseology for "United Nations" tabled for present since it does not pertain to Item 4 alone[.]

Commie drafts contained provisions for the dissolution of Committees on Repat [repatriation] of POWs & return of Civilians upon completion of functions for which organized. UNC accepted.

Commie drafts omitted definition of word repat as used in agreement. UNC stated its agreement to use of word repatriation was contingent upon acceptance of the definition and that without the definition UNC made a reservation on each para. [paragraph] in which the word "repat" occurred. Col Tsai stated that this was understood; that the definition had not been included because there was no agreement on para one and no final agreement on the definition.

Commies asked that para 9b. be expanded to include return to them of foreign nationals in UNC territory. UNC replied no objection if there were in fact any such persons. UNC took this opportunity to present a revised and completed list totalling 57 foreign civilians now in Commie custody and requested any additional data on them which might have become available. UNC suggested Commies might have a similar list of names to indicate the need for a provision such as was requested[.]

Then followed a harangue by Tsai on the Koje Do incident. Claimed personnel involved were milt personnel of Commies. Took up quest [question] of data saying our side has not submitted complete data whereas Commies had.

Murray came back saying UNC responsibility limited to POWs of your side we hold. Our side has no responsibility to yours of ROK nationality. Asked for data on approx 50,000 persons, former milt personnel of UNC for whom no accounting has been given. "You said that this data would be given to UNC in due course contingent on our giving you complete data on all POWs taken by UNC. **We now have available complete data on all POWs taken by our side thru 31 Jan '52.** This includes a detailed accounting for the list of 44,000 names which you handed over on 26 Dec. We can have this data here tomorrow am. Are you ready with your complete and detailed accounting of all POWs your side has taken?"

Tsai dodged question of exchange of data and harangued some more about the "massacre" at Koje Do. Claimed UNC had illegally reclassified captured personnel of Commies.

Rec'd folg msg from CinCUNC. Ref [reference] HNC980 (see Feb 26)[.]

JCS 90216 [designated as CX 64445 in margin] is passed to you for info & compliance at times & manner of your choosing as follows:

1. "You are authorized to make it entirely clear to Commies that UNC refusal to accept Soviet Union as member of neutral supervisory commission is absolutely firm & irrevocable. There is no propaganda problem in regard to our position on this question. Therefore we consider amplification of basis for UNC rejection of S.U. not necessary beyond that required to make it clear to Commie delegation that UNC position this regard is entirely firm.

2. ["]**We believe that a position along folg lines might be set forth by UNC Del at your discretion, if you believe agreement can be advanced thereby. The UNC initially proposed that insp.** [inspection] **teams be composed of the belligerents of both sides. This proposal was rejected by the Commies. The Commie proposal for neutral supervisory agency consisting of neutral nations acceptable to both sides was accepted by UNC but the Commies failed to comply with the terms of their own proposal. As a solution the UNC could propose that an arm supervisory organ** [organization] **and insp teams be constituted to consist of nations selected by each side regardless of their combatant status in the Korean hostilities. UNC Del should make clear that under this proposal it would feel free to select any countries participating in hostilities under UNC which would include the US & Commies would have similar rights to include USSR.**"

CinCUNC added: Ref part 1 above. To extent that you deem practicable, would like to know in advance positions you plan to take with respect to this point, but do not wish to restrict you in any way in taking full advantage of quoted JCS msg in situations as they develop.

With ref to above msg, last para, I replied: Intend to take action along folg line at staff off [officers] meeting on Item 3, 29 Feb:

Point out to Commies their insistence on nominating a nation not acceptable to UNC is in violation of principle 6 to which both sides agreed. Further Commies have reversed themselves re: need for nations nominated to be acceptable to both sides. This will be followed by statement that USSR is categorically rejected as member of NNSC and UNC stand is firm & irrevocable.

It is planned to follow theme above for as long a period of time as considered practicable. Will advise you of contemplated procedure before adopting line of action outlined in para 2 of JCS 902160.

Feb. 29 (Fri): Staff meeting Item 3. Ports of entry were discussed with both sides reiterating previous views and remaining firm on current respective no [number] of ports.

Folg is transcript of statements relative to neutral nations [entry emphasized in text to this point by a bold line in left margin]:

Col Darrow: "On 4 Dec in reply to quests [questions] by UNC Delegates concerning the meaning of your proposal to invite neutral nations, your side provided written answers. In these answers, you used the phrase and I quote: 'both sides can immediately work out, through negots [negotiations] a list of neutral nations agreed upon by both sides.'

["]In order that our side would clearly understand your proposal, our delegates asked additional quests on the folg day. Gen Turner asked if your side would consider Switzerland, Sweden & Denmark as neutral nations. Gen Lee replied that nations which have not dispatched their troops to Korea, such as Switzerland, could be considered neutral nations. Gen Turner then asked if you would consider Switzerland acceptable to your side. Gen Lee replied and I quote: **'I do not mean that we would accept any such nation as the neutral nation, but that is just in accordance with the definition of neutral nations used for an example.'**

"Your explanation was clear. We agreed to your proposal on principle 6 with the understanding that each side would invite neutral nations acceptable to the other side.

"Now it is your side which defies your own proposal. It is your side which does not live up to your own explanation of your proposal. It is your side which is demanding that a nation which is not acceptable to our side be permitted to send representatives in our rear. If you will not live up to your own principle, if you will not stand back of your own explanation, how can we expect to reach any agreement?

"I now tell you formally, unequivocally & with the fullest authorization that the UNC's decision to reject the S.U. as a member of the NNSC is final & irrevocable. Further debate on this subject will be completely futile. I repeat, the decision of the UNC to reject the USSR as a member of the NNSC is absolutely firm & irrevocable. Under no circumstances will there be a change in the decision of the UNC to reject the S.U. as a member of the NNSC.

"I suggest we recess until the usual time tomorrow in order that you may carefully consider the statement I have just made."

Col Chang: "I have one thing that I must make very clear to your side.

"Your side must be aware that the side with whom you are dealing right now, namely the KPA and the CPVs will refuse, reject and pick [apart?] **any unreasonable, arbitrary, cunning and threatening attitude of your side and any attitude apart from one corresponding to the fair & reasonable attitude of the other side.** No fantastic entertainment, nor any other speculation will be permitted to find any place in the reception by our side. **If your side is really interested in an arm.** [armistice] **and if your side is aware of the fact that you are dealing with the Korean Peoples Army & CPV's, your side ought to retract & withdraw such an unreasonable, arbitrary aloof attitude along together** [*sic*] **with the statement you made this am. No further arguments will make any avail or consequence, and they will be of no use at all.** To the extent that your side rejects unilaterally, arbitrarily, absurdly our fair and reasonable compromise proposal, a proposal which has already prepared to draw a mutual agreement closer to a point of substantial agreement, to that extent your side is obviously not interested in the progress of this arm negots and that is all that your side is implying to our cognizance. I must tell you the fact that all you can expect us to do is [to expect?] that your side accept the proposal that our side has presented with an utmost effort."

Col Pu then took the ball and categorically rejected Darrow's statement. Said that discussions in sub committee meetings proves [*sic*] that UNC has no reason to object to nominations which are in compliance with the definition of neutral nations. When delegates were discussing definition of neutral nations it was not a time to discuss whether either side would accept any particular nation as a neutral nation.

Col Darrow: "Our attitude is only that of maintaining strict compliance with the agreements reached by the delegates. It is your side which is assuming the attitude of vitiating the agreements already reached. Unless you intend to adhere to the agreements reached by the delegates, the staff officers cannot make progress in this matter. I suggest you seriously consider the proposals we have made in this regard in order that we may settle this problem in accordance with the principles agreed to by both sides.["]

Col Chang chimed in to say that "the KPA and CPVs have rejected and now rejects and will reject any statement or any formal proposal of your side which is in opposition to the fair & reasonable proposal of our side of the nomination of the neutral nations of the NNSC which are fully & completely in compliance with the definition of neutral nations.["]

Col Kinney: "I understand your statement to be that if our side wants an armistice in Korea, we must choose to adopt one of the two methods proposed by your side both of which include the S.U. as a member of the NNSC. These baroque statements & bankrupt arguments accomplish nothing but delay in the progress towards a cessation of hostilities in Korea. It is with utmost gravity that we urge you to give very careful & serious statements made by Col Darrow this am[*sic*].["]

Col Chang: ["]The statement that your side made this am offers no gravity no worthiness to be given consideration by the side of the KPA and CPVs. I once again inform your side of our rejection our firm rejection of your statement. If your side is really interested in the arm. negots and the progress of it I once again urge your side to give a further serious consideration to the method of solution that our side suggested in the form of a fair & reasonable proposal.

"If your side is deliberately delaying the negots and finally wreck[s] them, the whole responsibility rests on your side.

["]I agree to recess.["]

#4. In Sub Del meeting on Item 4 both sides ratified paras 3, 5, 6, 7, 8 & 9 of agreements reached by staff officers (revised 28 Feb attached to transcript of meeting for that date)[.] UNC ratification was made contingent upon Commie acceptance of definition of word "repat" [repatriation] as set forth in UNC para 1 but omitted from Commie version. Commies did not oppose this but appear unwilling to commit themselves fully on definition pending further developments on remaining issue. Commies said para 9b should be expanded to provide for return to their side of foreign civilians in custody of UNC. UNC replied it was not unwilling but knew of only one person in that status, a national of the USSR the facts concerning whom have already been reported to Soviets. Commies skirted this case but insisted para 9b be made reciprocal. UNC agreed to consider any wording Commies might propose.

Lee read a long statement which attacked voluntary repatriation using the Koje Do incident to bolster his arguments "that free choice constantly advocated by your side is free choice at the point of guns and bayonets.["] Ended by saying: "In order that agreement may be reached at an early date, I wish to remind you that your side should reconsider your unreasonable stand and carefully study and accept our fair and reasonable principle of release and repat of all POWs so that the agreement in principle, which should have been reached long ago, will not longer be delayed indefinitely."

UNC replied as follows: "The day before yesterday, when substantial agreement had been reached in staff off. meetings on the matters we have ratified here today, the quest [question] of the single remaining issue was raised.

["]Our staff, for its part, made a statement indicating its hope that both sides would approach this remaining issue in the spirit of negotiation which has resulted in our reaching agreement on so many issues. Col Murray indicated where concessions towards your point of view on repat had already been made in our current proposal. He indicated areas in which further negots on this issue might be feasible. Finally, he stated that if your side was interested in negotiating this issue it might be done in the staff offs meeting where so many stormy issues had already been resolved. Your side responded to this effort on the part of the UNC rep. [representative] with the statement that you were not interested in further negotiation. You stated that you had reached the limit and that there could be no agreement on the remaining issue nor any progress towards the solution of Agenda Item 4 except by the UNC's acceptance of your demands. Thus the remaining issue was referred back to the sub dels as a result of your refusal to approach the issue in a spirit of negotiation or to consider any viewpoint except your own.

"I note with regret your statement of this morning that confirms our understanding of your present attitude, which is that you are unwilling to settle the remaining issue by negotiation and that no agreement is possible except thru our capitulation to your demands. I must further state that despite your assertion that your opening statement was not a propaganda speech we find that it is. It is inflamatory [*sic*], it is contentious, and it is not factual. It contributes nothing toward any possible solution of the issue now between us. We must remind your side that a refusal to negotiate is absolutely fatal toward progress. If you are not unwilling to bring about an armistice in Korea you must reconsider your attitude on the single issue that now prevents complete agreement on Agenda Item 4. If you desire to persist in that attitude today, and are unwilling to negotiate the issue, we propose a recess until tomorrow, for there is no possibility that our side will ever abandon our position that we will not deliver to your side those persons who are forced to go there."

Following a brief statement asserting the willingness of the Commies to negotiate as shown by past agreement, Lee agreed to recess expressing the hope that the UNC would give up its "unreasonable position[.]"

Mar. 1 (Sat): In staff meeting on Item 3 Commies indicated that they may want TDY [temporary duty] and R & R [rest and recreation] personnel introduced into Korea on basis of a man for man exchange. Such personnel would not be required to enter thru specified ports nor be subject to insp. [inspection] by Neutral Nations Supervisory teams. Commies preparing new draft.

On the selection of Neutral Nations Chang again rejected UNC's "unreasonable attitude" and declared that "our side will eternally reject your opposition until you withdraw your unreasonable objection[.]"

In refutation Darrow again pointed out that UNC action was in full compliance with principle agreed upon by both sides and if Commies will strictly adhere to agreements reached by two sides, we should have no difficulty in solving this problem.

Chang came back with another strong statement again firmly & decisively rejecting UNCs statements & attitude. "And we will do so in the future as well.

In the interest of an armistice our side *demands* that your side withdraw your unreasonable opposition. If your side is really interested in achieving an arm [armistice], the only way of solution of these quests [questions] is that either both sides agree simultaneously and mutually to the nominations of neutral nations of the other side, or each side designates neutral nations respectively that they deem qualified to invite.''

Darrow: ''In regard to your statement on the neutral nations you said that you demanded that we withdraw our objection to the U.S.S.R. I think Gen Hodes made it very clear to Gen Hsieh Fang that your side does not demand anything from our side. We have a perfect right in accord with prin. [principle] #6 to accept or not to accept any neutral nations you nominate. When Gen Lee gave his explanation of this matter he made it very clear that there were two items to be considered in regard to nominating neutral nations for the NNSC. One was that it must live up to the definition agreed to by both sides. The second was that the nations nominated must be acceptable to the other side. I am sure that if we had nominated certain nations, your side would be quick to state they were not acceptable and we would have agreed with you that you had the right to accept them. The matter before us is strictly a matter in complying with the agreements already reached by the delegates of the two sides. Unless both sides will adhere to those agreements we shall find it very difficult to make progress. I think you will find it difficult to reject our statement of yesterday since a statement cannot be rejected. You may choose not to consider it, but a mere statement of rejection does not change the validity of any statement we make.''

Chang: ''I do not believe that you have to make unnecessary reiteration of the statement that you previously made. Your statement in itself was so preposterous, arbitrary & hollow that it not only disapproved itself but was also such that it was detrimental to the interests of the arm, therefore, invited due refutation from our side. The folg remarks of mine will refer to the negots [negotiations] and to the negots of the Staff Offs [officers] of opposing belligerents. It is a known fact that the only basis for resolving quests, particularly under such circumstances as we are now fighting each other, that both sides require a certain criteria, that is, a certain fundamental condition by which both sides may be able to work their problems. The basic link, that is to say the core of it, is the definition of the neutral nations upon which both sides made an agreement. Only by this criteria questions could be resolved. Apart from this criteria, that is the definition of the neutral nations, no other argument nor reason, no matter how far traced and solved by one side will make any use to resolve this quest. and will leave the distance still far from settlement. It is easier that both sides adopt certain form or formula in deference to the other side's views in making an agreement to accept—to agree and accept a given problem. *Consequently, it is impermissible for any party to seek the right to disagree and refuse without giving any reason nor having any reason a proposal which is fully in compliance with the definition of the neutral nations & which again constitute the basic condition for agreement.* It is therefore ideal for resolving this question by such an attitude. I and Col Pu in the negots of these staff meetings, not to speak of our delegates in the past, all had no idea of rejecting any proposal of yours as long as it was in compliance with the definitions of the neutral nations that your side had submitted. When viewed from this angle, our nomination of the S.U. on the NNSC is entirely in compliance with the agreed principles of both sides and is fully in compliance with the definition of neutral nations. We are simply wondering the reason why your side is still objecting to the proposal that our side has submitted which is fully in compliance with this definition of the neutral nations—a definition which was agreed upon by both sides. Such an objection only is the cause for creating a stumbling block in these negots. Therefore I once again urge your side to remove those stumbling blocks that your side has established.''

#4. In sub del meeting on Item 4 UNC maintained position that delay in solution of Agenda Item 4 is due to Commie refusal to negotiate.

UNC raised point that Commie POW camps are not yet marked as they had agreed. Commies replied they were informed that the camps were marked; that perhaps the markings were covered by snow when reconnaissance was made. They undertook to look into the matter.

UNC proposed again the immediate exchange of seriously sick & injured POWs[.] Commies refused.

UNC proposed arrangement for delivery of RC comfort packages to POWs. Commies refused and charged UNC was attempting to delay the conference with propaganda issues.

UNC refuted this and accused Commies of refusing without reason to exchange sick & injured now in order to use these unfortunate victims of war as a means of forcing UNC to accept Commies position.

Following Commie statement that there could be no reason for refusing to agree now to the unconditional release & repat [repatriation] of all POWs, the UNC turned once again to the 50,000 milt [military] personnel of our side whose capture had been rptd [reported] by the other side but whose names did not appear in the POW data.

Commies attempted to dismiss this argument on grds [grounds] these were hypothetical bogies. UNC gave sample statistics to show large nos [numbers] of former ROKA personnel now in KPA.

This led into discussion of POW data. Commies maintained UNC should immediately give them data on the 44,000 as well as a satisfactory explanation of the Koje Do incident, after which they would discuss the exchange of the supplementary data. UNC reviewed earlier agreements on exchange of data and reaffirmed that it was ready to exchange data on that basis on 12 hrs notice[.]

Commies protested this; rejected UNC arguments on ROKA personnel in KPA, and abused UNC for depriving POWs of the opportunity to go home. They refused to exchange data in accord with previous understanding but insisted that they be given the data on the 44,000 even if 72 days late.

UNC noted for record that Gen Lee had repudiated his previous promise on exchange of data.

Mar. 2 (Sun): Left camp for Tokyo at 1130 arriving Haneda via P2V at 1600. Flying time 2 hrs 58 min for 795 miles. Not bad! Saw Dunc for a while before he left for Osaka.

Staff officers meeting on Item 3. UNC opened with: **"We note with grave concern that your side yesterday, in the next tent, repudiated your agreement of 29 Dec & 1 Jan to furnish to our side an accounting for all the POWs captured by your side.** At the same time your side in this tent has repudiated the agreement reached with respect to nominating neutral nations acceptable to both sides. As a result of these 2 instances of flagrant violation by your side of agreements already reached our side has serious doubts as to whether it is worthwhile to continue with our attempts to reach further agreement. Certainly it is pointless to reach agreement if your side intends to repudiate **such agreement at your own convenience. I hope that your side, this am, will have something constructive to offer by which we may make progress in these negots** [negotiations]."

Commies claimed UNC attempting to wreck negots by arrogant threats[.]

UNC reiterated Soviets not acceptable as member NNSC; our objection final & irrevocable. Urged Commies give serious consideration to 3 UNC alternative solutions. Challenged Commies to show where in record any other interpretation than UNC's of principle 6 could be justified[.]

Commies evaded issue. Submitted redrafts of a number of paras i e 13b. 13c (stating they agree UNC figure of 35,000 for rotation provided UNC accepts 5 ports of entry) 13d, 13i and 15. Latter read "This Arm [armistice] Agreement shall apply to all opposing naval forces, which naval forces shall respect the waters contiguous to the Demilt [demilitarized] Zone & to the land areas under the control of the opposing side, and shall not engage in blockade of any kind of the opposing side.

#4. No progress in sub del meeting on Item 4. Libby made same statement as Darrow's opening one in Item 3 meeting. UNC accused Commies of unwillingness to negotiate placed blame for delaying meetings on them and attacked them strongly on question of data on POWs not yet accounted for. Commies turned down UNC proposal for exchanging Red Cross packages and immediate exchange of seriously sick & injured.

Commies submitted new para 9b on subject of return of civilians of foreign nationalities. UNC agreed to consider.

Mar. 3 (Mon): Attended turn over ceremony of 7th Fleet at 1100 and buffet luncheon thereafter at officers club Yokosuka. Then had a session with dentist. Had an appointment with R which was postponed by him until tomorrow at 0830.

Staff officers made no progress on Item 3. Col Chang again brought up issue of neutral nations urging UNC "to withdraw unreasonable opposition to the proposal of our side which is fully in compliance with the agreed principle and particularly is in full conformity with the key of the principle, that is, the definition of the neutral nations."

Darrow replied: "There is nothing you can say which changes the fact that the S.U. is not acceptable to our side as a member of the NNSC. No matter what you say that statement is valid and can be changed only by your side. I have told you that the decision will not be changed and the statement is irrevocable."

Chang insisted we were blocking progress because of our groundless objection, and stated they would always reject our objection. Again proposed that both sides agree simultaneously to the nomination of the neutral nations—or both sides respectively designate, as provided under UNC draft version of para 38, members to be invited on NNSC without requiring other party's approval. No other method will be able to break the deadlock.

Darrow again pointed out that UNC had proposed 4 neutral nations which could be accepted by both sides right now and make progress in these negots [negotiations].

#4. In sub del on Item 4 Communist attitude was extremely intransigent and exhibited no desire to move toward solution of the problem.

Lee was very nasty. Accused UNC of deliberately delaying negots by introducing quest. [question] of early repatriation of seriously sick & injured and of using data "concerning our captured personnel" (44,000 reclassified civs [civilians]) as an instrument of blackmail. Again attacked UNC on subject of Koje Do incident. Claimed UNC massacred their POWs because they refused to accept illegal interrogation & screening. Requested an accounting.

Libby again pointed out that incident did not involve POWs but ROK nationals. An internal affair of UNC. Said there would be no further accounting by UNC to Commies of this purely internal affair now or later[.] Again clarified quest of exchange of data stating UNC readiness to exchange supplementary data, that is data on all POWs it had ever held in exchange for similar data from Commies. This would include data on 50,000 persons who had been rptd [reported] as captured but whose names had been omitted from the data handed over by Commies.

Lee then after a tirade said UNC must be held responsible for Koje Do incident. Again demanded an accounting. Said UNC has falsely accused Commies of repudiating promise in agreement in order to cover up its failure to deliver data which should have been delivered 70 days ago. He then interpreted record to show that he had not agreed to the exchange of data as UNC had claimed. On contrary UNC has violated its undertakings in connection with the exchange of data.

UNC accused Lee of taking remarks out of record and quoting them out of context to build up a case to the effect that we have changed our position on the quest. of the data. Libby forcefully pointed out that satisfactory resolution of issue of reporting 50,000 captured ROKs was as much a prerequisite of full solution of Agenda Item 4 as the agreement on vol [voluntary] vs. forced repatriation. Libby said: "All military personnel of our side who are in your power must be included in POW exchange except those persons who were on 25 June 1950 residents of that portion of Korea under your milt [military] control. You are obligated by rules of warfare to return them[.]"

Mar. 4 (Tues): Met with R at 0830. Discussed JCS suggestion that we propose NNSC composed of members not necessarily neutral i.e. Russia & USA. Agreed with him it would be better to stick to our guns on present tack that USSR was unacceptable and that our position in this respect was firm final and irrevocable. Also discussed Libby's memo recommending that we be authorized to drop pressing Commies for an accounting of the missing 50,000 POWs. because data would be worthless. He agreed. **Then asked R to recommend to Wash.** [Washington] **that U.S. Govt make a strong public announcement to effect that decision to reject USSR as a member of the NNSC was irrevocable[.] R said he would consider it.**

#3. Chang opened Item 3 meeting with a statement alleging that Commies nomination of neutral nations was in accord with definition of neutral nation as agreed to in prin. [principle] 6 by sub del. Pointed out the only two alternative methods which can settle quest. [question] reasonably. Either both sides will agree simultaneously and all at once to all the nominations by the other side or both sides nominate respectively neutral nations in compliance with the definition agreed upon by both sides without going through any procedure of approval.

UNC stuck to its guns saying decision in matter was firm & irrevocable. Suggested UNC proposal of four neutral nations Czechoslovakia, Poland, Sweden & Switzerland, or suitable alternate for USSR, be adopted.

Commies then went over their old arguments ending up by saying they rejected firmly attitude of UNC. Emphasized that there would be no solution of quest. as long as UNC does not withdraw its unreasonable refusal[.]

Staff offs. then went over Commie versions of paras. 13b, c & d. In par 15 on Naval blockade Commie version had deleted ref [reference] to Korean peninsula. It is conceivable that at some future date the claim could be made that the Peoples Rep [Republic] of China was on one "side" in Korean war and that therefore a blockade of that country is prohibited by this para.

#4. The sub del meeting on Item 4 devoted the entire time to debating the question of repatriation of POWs. Libby made long statement pointing out there remained not one vital issue between the two sides but two. Both closely related. One is the status of the 50,000 of our people impressed into Commie army, other is question of no forced repatriation. 50,000 must be included in exchange of POWs. The 54,000 ROK nationals in our custody are not subject to exchange other than under principle of vol [voluntary] choice to go to Commie side if they so desire.

Lee in reply claimed UNC fabricated existence of 50,000 who do not exist. Said there was not two points in dispute only one—question of principle of repatriation[.] Attacked classification of POWs into civs. [civilians]. Again brought up Koje Do incident in attempt to prove our failure to coerce civs. into vol repat [repatriation] & free choice. An example of respecting human rights. Vol repat is absolutely unacceptable, etc. Obstacle to solution of Agenda Item 4. Only one fundamental issue remaining.

Mar. 5 (Wed): Spent most of day with Radford & had him for dinner that night[.] Discussed Navy matters—he did not once bring up my assignment to USNA [U.S. Naval Academy, which CTJ later headed]. He made trip to Tokyo mainly to discuss with CinCFe turnover of responsibility for Formosa from CinCFe to CinCPac[.]

#3. In staff meeting on Item 3 neither side had any new ideas re. Neutral Nations & Ports of Entry. Recessed after 15 mins.

#4. In sub del meeting on Item 4. UNC presented supplementary lists of 174 US names with statement that evidence shows they were taken as POWs. although Commies did not list them in POW data. This aggregates 1621 names so presented.

UNC again pressed Commies on subject of missing 50000 UN personnel captured during first 9 mos of war. Vast majority of these being forced to serve in your army[.] Former ROKA personnel have rptd [reported] **in detail how Commies denied them rights as POWs. UNC accusations based on facts. In Sept & Oct of 1950 your side moved bulk of ROKA personnel into Manchuria. Out of 9 Divs** [divisions] **7 still have ROKA personnel. Your attempts to politically reindoctrinate ROKA personnel not uniformly successful. Hence assigned to labor regiments etc.** 11% of all POWs captured by UNC during Feb. were of this category. These are the "awakened patriots & volunteers['] whom you maintain you released at front & who you maintain are serving voluntarily in your armed forces.

Your inability to disprove these facts is reason you repudiated your agreement to account for the 50,000 milt personnel of our side whom you failed to list as POWs. Your phsychological [*sic*] forces disprove what you say. To illustrate one of your broadcasts on Mar 2 1952 said: **"I am an ex ROK soldier who has been captured by KPA and furnished the training as a member of the KPA. I am leading an easy life with the KPA[.]"**

Lee in answer claimed Libby was distorting facts and fabricating non-existent facts. He then attacked our reclassification of civs. [civilians]. Brought up Koje Do incident again to try and prove incident was caused by UNC's coercion of POWs to the political choice of vol repat [voluntary repatriation] at the point of a bayonet. POWs insisted on their rights & opposed UNC's measures.

Lee ended up by saying "Both sides can and ought to establish first the principle of release & repat of all POWs held by both sides after an arm. [armistice] is realized on the basis of the data concerning the POWs in the custody of both sides which have already been exchanged."

Libby retorted Lee was inconsistent. "On the one hand you reject our having reclassified certain persons from POWs to civ internees. On the other hand you apparently propose an all for all unconditional exchange on the basis of the POW lists already exchanged. The POW list we gave you include some 16,000 ROK nationals who should have been, and in the natural course of events can be expected to be, reclassified as civ internees. Either you are making a proposal that we hand over to you all the POWs plus all the civ. internees or you are proposing that we base the exchange on the POW lists which we exchanged on 18 Dec."

Libby then explained the process of reclassification.

Lee replied there was nothing inconsistent in his statement.

Mar. 6 (Thurs): In staff meeting on Item 3 UNC submitted new draft of para 13d for Commies consideration. This para deals with the introduction into Korea of combat aircraft, armored vehicles, weapons & ammo, and replacing worn out equipment on piece for piece basis of same effectiveness & type. Rpts [reports] made to MAC NNCS [NNSC] shall conduct inspection of replacements at ports of entry.

Discussed para 42c. UNC claims there should be no unnecessary insp [inspection] of secret equipment & phrase covering this. Commies claim should not be any such stipulation which would prevent NNSC from seeing that improved equipment is not substituted for worn out material.

Neither side had any new ideas re Neutral Nations & Ports of Entry.

#4. In sub del meeting on Item 4 UNC asked if Commies had any constructive ideas for solving the Item. Lee replied: "the statement we made yesterday was a statement with clear intent. It is not ambiguous. Of [sic] your side has any constructive opinion, we are ready to hear it[.]" Recessed after 10 mins.

Comment: Lee's statement of yesterday could be interpreted as an offer to exchange all for all on the basis of data exchanged 18 Dec. That is Commies would not insist on delivery of civ [civilian] internees.

Mar. 7 (Fri): Returned to Munsan-ni from Tokyo leaving Haneda 1000 arriving Seoul 1400 and camp about 1445. Radford came with me to airport.

#3. In staff meeting on Item 3 Commies submitted draft of agreed paras on Item 3 in Korean & Chinese. Interpreters will meet in future to eliminate any discrepancies in 3 language versions.

Most of discussion centered on para 15. UNC claimed UNC wording most appropriate and suggested that areas referred to thruout Arm [armistice] agreement specify "Korea" where appropriate[.] Commies inferred that Arm Agreement would apply to all territory controlled by either side no matter whether that territory is within Korea or outside Korea. Some pertinent parts of discussion follow.

Col Pu: "We are sure that your side agrees it is inconceivable that after realization of the arm, ground forces & air forces of one side should not respect the territories controlled by the other side, no matter whether those territories are within or outside of Korea. Therefore, there is no necessity to add such words as you have suggested in para 15 & other paras."

Col Darrow: "As you know, the purpose of the staff offs. meetings is to prepare a draft of the arm agreement which will be accurate, legal & clear. Your statement leads me to believe you are not aware of the nature of the conflict in Korea. The UNC is fighting only in Korea. I understand from statements made by your side that the KPA and the CPVs are fighting only in Korea. The arm agreement as we have stipulated is for the purpose of ceasing all hostilities in Korea. In order that the document be strictly legal and subject to no misinterpretation, our side feels that we should wherever necessary clearly specify the limitations of this agreement."

After further exchanges Darrow ended by saying: "I think Col Pu knows as well as I know that the only way the conflict in Korea could be transferred to another area when hostilities cease in Korea is for action to be taken on the political level by the govts [governments]. Certainly the Comdrs [Commanders] who are negotiating this arm in Korea have no authority to transfer the conflict to another area. You need not concern yourself with the apprehensions of our side. We are here to prepare a draft of an arm agreement for the cessation of hostilities in K and nothing more. The agreement must be specific & clear. Our side will not agree to paras which are subject to misinterpretation."

#4. In sub del meeting on Item 4 Commies accepted UNC proposed revision of para 9b which has to do with the movement of civilians between the two sides after arm is signed.

UNC made folg statement: "If our understanding of your statement of 5 Mar is correct you suggest the exchange of POWs on the basis of the data exchanged by both sides on 18 Dec[.]

"Such a proposal does not provide a suitable vehicle for negotiating the remaining issues on Agenda Item 4 for several reasons.

"First, it neglects to make provision for the 50,000 milt [military] persons of our side whom you rptd. [reported] that you had captured but whose names you failed to include in the POW data exchanged on 18 Dec.

"Second many of the civs [civilians] whom we have interned wish to go to your side and we are prepared to respect their desires. Your proposal would require us to retain all these persons and deny them the opportunity to go to your side.

"Third, some of the POWs whom we hold and possibly some of those you hold would violently oppose return to the other side under any circumstances. Your proposal would require the forced return of all such persons to the other side.

"These three shortcomings can be overcome by your favorable consideration of the proposal which was made to your side in the staff offs meetings."

Lee replied to Libby as follows: "You insist that the unidentifiable 50,000 persons were incorporated into our army. That does not coincide with the facts.

"If you want to speedily reach an agreement on Item 4 you should not bring forth this unfounded matter. By requesting us to recognize this unfounded fact you contribute nothing to the progress of negots [negotiations].

"However firm you may insist on it it will not be accepted because it is not existent[.]

"Our side has never recognized reclassification of upward of 37,000 captured personnel of our side. As data on more than 44,000 captured personnel of our side has not been received, the basic data exchanged can only be the basis of agreement in principle on release & repat [repatriation] of all POWs. It is not the list of all the POWs who should be repat.

"The list of all POWs who should be repatriated still has to be checked by the staff offs. of both sides after the principle is determined. Our side has already clearly stated our stand.

"Our side absolutely opposes your principles of so called vol [voluntary] repat and so called no forced repat, which in fact, is an attempt to retain the captured personnel of our side. Our side also opposes your re-classifying at will the captured personnel of our side into civs. Our side has never recognized reclassification of upwards of 37,000 captured personnel of our side. It is more impossible for our side to concede to any attempt at carrying out reclassification among POWs listed in the basic data already submitted. Our side considers that in order to obtain progress in the meeting, both sides ought to establish first the prin [principle] of release & repat of all POWs after the arm on the basis of the data already exchanged.["]

Libby next attacked Commies for failure to account for non-ROK POWs—a total of 1621, who according to available evidence have been or are now in your custody as POWs. and insisted upon an adequate and proper accounting. Summed up his remarks by saying UNC posit. [position] of no forced repat is our absolute min. [minimum] beyond which UNC will not go. Also said UNC far from satisfied that Commies have rptd anywhere near the actual number UNC personnel they hold. Another unresolved issue is their refusal to recognize as legal and proper our reclassification of our men into correct category of civ. internees[.] Said finally: "Apparently our understanding that your statement of 5 Mar represented willingness on your part to negotiate these remaining issues was a misconception.["]

Lee had the crust to say UNC had incorporated their personnel into our army. Again said UNC principle of so-called vol. repat or no forced repat. is a principle which we cannot absolutely accept.

Comment: Commie proposal appears to be to agree in sub del to principle of release & repat of all the POWs and then pass the problem to staff off level to determine to whom principle applies. Some indications that they might drop claim on civ. internees, but most likely only those who are not on their military rolls, that is those who were interned by mistake or for reasons of internal security.

Mar. 8 (Sat): In staff meeting on Item 3. UNC asked Commies to accept insertion of ref [reference] to Korea in paras 13b, 13g, 14 & 16 for purposes of clarification. Commies maintained that opening statement & preamble clearly express intent of Arm [armistice] Agreement and that the paras as written are clear enough. However, Commies stated they would take UNC desires under consideration. Relevant discussion follows:

Col Chang: "Basically as long as our understanding pertains to the content of that provision, there is no difference between both sides inasmuch as the preamble itself of the arm. agreement clearly expresses to that effect. If such is the case, I believe that these particular paras fully express what is intended to be expressed, even if insertion of the wording Korea not be included."

Col Darrow: "I am not sure I understand you Col Chang. Did you say that both sides are in agreement that this armistice agreement pertains to the belligerents in Korea and solely to Korea? Is that correct?"

Col Chang: "In view of my answer to this question, I would like to read the beginning sentence of this draft armistice agreement: 'Agreement between CinCUNC on the one hand, and our Supreme Comdrs of the KPA and CPVs on the other hand, concerning a milt [military] arm in Korea.'"

Col Darrow: "That was my understanding, that this was an arm. in Korea. However, yesterday I was not quite sure that both sides had the same views. Apparently we now are in accord and if so, your side would have no objection to inserting a reference to Korea in those paras. Is that correct?"

Col Chang: "Even if we do not insert the wording Korea the substantial meaning of the arm. agreement shall not be affected at all. However if your side insists upon the insertion, our side may give to it consideration. We will put it under our consideration when we revise the wordings of the arm agreement draft."

Col Darrow: "Since this agreement will be used by a great number of people, it is the opinion of our side that we should make each specific article and para. as clear as we can in order that unnecessary misunderstandings may not arise. If you agree, then we can let the interpreters take this matter up when they are adjusting the drafts of the paras in relationship to the 3 languages.''

Col Chang: ''I do not believe there exists a great difficulty pertaining to this quest [question] and I'm sure that we would have further opportunities to make consideration.''

Discussion notable for apparent willingness of Commies to eventually include references to Korea[.]

#4. In sub del meeting on Item 4 UNC (Libby [''Libby on POWs'' also appears at top of diary page] opened as follows:

''After further study of your statement of Mar 5 we reiterate yesterday's reply. Your suggestion does not provide a suitable basis for negotiating the remaining issues of Agenda Item 4.

''The UNC will not be a party to the forcible repatriation of individuals opposed to being returned to the other side. We have made our position in this regard unmistakably clear. I shall repeat it. We will not agree to any procedure which would require us forcibly to repatriate anybody.

''Furthermore, we know definitely that you have not accounted for even a respectable percentage of all the personnel of our side whom you have captured. The preponderance of evidence points undeniably to the fact that many of these captured personnel are still in your custody[.] They should be included in the POW exchange.

''In spite of your vehement denials & charges of fabrication the testimony of individuals who have returned and who **continue to return to our control indicates that you have incorporated captured milt personnel of our side into your army. Your front line propaganda broadcasts confirm this fact. You have not repudiated this fact: you only deny it.**

''We also have convincing evidence that you are holding POWs outside of Korea without having rptd [reported] them to our side. This evidence has reached us from too many sources to be ignored or lightly dismissed. For example milt personnel of our side whom we have captured have related that they were members of details which escorted UNC personnel to POW camps in China. One such individual described in detail a POW processing center in Harbin to which he had helped escort captured UNC personnel[.]

''Let me outline to you the basis on which we are willing to negotiate the remaining issues:

'' 'All the captured milt personnel of our side in your custody who want to return to us *must* be returned.

'' 'We have no desire to detain personnel of your side but we will not force any to return to your side who violently oppose being turned over to you.'

"We are willing to turn over to you those ROK nationals whom we hold, whether as civ. [civilian] internees or as POWs who wish to go to your side. **"We are anxious to settle this problem. We are not building up issues to delay such settlement. But we insist that the prob.** [problem] **be solved on a factual, sound, humanitarian and equitable basis."**

In reply Lee accused UNC of fabricating non-existent facts & spreading rumors. He then read from prepared statement as follows[:]

"In order to solve the only basic differences now on Agenda Item 4, our side on Mar 5th made a proposal adequate for a reasonable solution of this issue. That is, to establish first the principle of release & repat [repatriation] of all POWs. on the basis of the already agreed or already ascertained data concerning the POWs. However, much to my regret, your response yesterday to the proposal of our side was to continue to insist upon the so called vol [voluntary] repat. During the long period of our discussions we have repeatedly refuted your proposition of the so called vol repat. and made it clear & definite that it is absolutely unacceptable to our side. If your side is sincerely willing to solve the quest. and if you have carefully studied my important statement of Mar 5th I see no point for you to cling longer to this artificial obstacle.["]

Lee then went on to attack the principle of vol. repat. saying, "it is the inalienable right of every POW to be repatriated after the signing of the arm. yet you are trying to abolish that right. Now it has become clearer than ever that what you call voluntary is in fact to coerce them to express their 'voluntariness' in line with your wishes, enabling you to retain our captured personnel." He then tried to prove again that the Koje Do incident supported his contention that 'voluntarily' has become not only a term for detaining all POWs but for the massacre of POWs[.]

Lee also brought up the "Taiwan instructors" to prove that UNC was coercing POWs. Said voluntary repat was coercion, intimidation, resistance & massacre.

Libby ended session by saying: "We are unable to comprehend why you persist in your failure to recognize that we shall never be a party to the forcibly repatriating to your side of POWs. We are particularly unable to understand it in view of the statement you just made 'it is known to all that every POW desires to be repatriated.' If that statement is true there is no problem. I must repeat, one of the criteria on which we insist that this issue be settled is that it be settled on a factual basis."

Sent folg msg to CinCUNC: It is believed that a statement by the President or Secretary of State firmly rejecting the USSR as a neutral nation would be most helpful to negots [negotiations]. The Del is not able to assess the chances of the enemy withdrawing their nomination of the Soviets, with or without such a statement. From past experience on the issues of "withdrawal of troops["] and the "38th parallel" it seems certain that any existing chance of the enemy conceding on this point would be enhanced by such a statement. We strongly recommend one be made.

Mar. 9 (Sun): In staff meeting on Item 3 neither side had anything new to discuss on the remaining unresolved probs. [problems].

#4. Gen Lee opened sub del meeting on Item 4 with a virulent propaganda statement which outdid most of his previous efforts in vituperativeness. Accused Libby of fabrication. "Apparently your side is attempting by means of fabrication to make the question now under our discussion go beyond the scope of the Korean war and is attempting by means of fabrication to make our present armistice negots [negotiations] to exceed their due purview."

Lee also said: "To realize your scheme of retaining our captured personnel, your side while making a hullabaloo about so called vol. repat. [voluntary repatriation] is conducting at the same time the so called reclassification of our captured personnel. We will never recognize such illegal reclassification. Our stand is firm & immovable."

Lee accused UNC of conniving & conspiring with Chiang Kai Shek to carry out large scale intimidation & coercion against Commie personnel. Said they "absolutely cannot tolerate such completely inhuman and barbarous acts of your side." Ended by saying: "In order to settle Item 4 of agenda, our side has made tremendous efforts, submitting on 5 Mar a reasonable proposal which would adequately solve the question. If your side still disregards our reasonable proposal, if you continue to disseminate rumors & slander and cling to your absurd proposition & refuse to solve the quest [question], the responsibility for delaying the conference rests solely with your side."

Libby then said[:] "We note your remarkable statement of this am. Your statement is a deliberate insult to the UNC and the UNCD. It consists of completely unfounded accusations. It is fraudulent from beginning to end. [All of above quotations pertaining to Item 4 emphasized by bold lines in left margin to this point.] You reiterated the threat you made yesterday that if we do not stop our lawless activities in our POW camps, their [?] development will go beyond the scope of the Korean question. I am instructed by my Senior Del [delegate] to inquire as to what your side means by this statement."

Lee claimed his statement did not insult UNC or UNCD, **"only exposed your fraudulent fabrications and exposed plot to expand the issue. Together with the vicious gangs sent by Chiang Kai Shek, your side is hatching a plot at your POW camps together with your hangmen friends of S.K.** Should you develop from such illegal activities of yours, it will naturally lead beyond the purview of the Korean Arm. [armistice] negots."

Libby said Lees answers completely unsatisfactory and unspecific. Still wanted to know what was meant by threats[.] Corrected two of the more glaring misstatements[—] "First we do not and never have owed you any further data. We have never promised to give you any further data and as I have said, you will get it on an exchange basis in accord with our standing agreement or you will not get it at all. We have made our position clear. **We told you yesterday the basis on which we would further negotiate these probs. We shall not change that basis. No amount of insult or irresponsibility on your part will change our determination."**

Mar. 10 (Mon): In staff meeting Item 3 both sides agreed to meeting of interpreters tomorrow to check language of agreed paras of arm. [armistice] agreement. Both sides stated they had nothing new to offer re. unresolved issues. Meeting recessed at suggestion of enemy.

#4. In sub del meeting on Item 4, Libby lit into Lee for his statement of yesterday. Said it was difficult to understand what Commies hoped to accomplish by reading into record such an outrageous agglomeration of misstatements of facts, groundless accusations and thinly veiled threats. Accused Commies of having denied incorporating in their armed forces, thru political indoctrination and intimidation a great number of the 50,000 milt [military] **personnel of UNC whom they reported as captured and of holding in Korea more than 11,559 POWs whose names they gave us on 18 Dec. Also accused them of denying they ever held UNC captured personnel outside of Korea despite evidence to contrary. These personnel must be accounted for.** Accused Lee of repudiating agreement made on 29 Dec to exchange data on 50,000 for data on 44,000 civ [civilian] internees. Said: "We have set forth for you in clear, consise [*sic*], form the basis upon which we believe both sides can negotiate a solution to our existing differences. Your side flatly rejected these efforts in staff meetings, by stating you had made your last efforts and that you were willing to talk 70 more days to force us to capitulate to your demands."

Ended up by warning that their threats to intimidate UNC will not succeed—only further delays proceedings. "You cannot dictate terms of Arm & you cannot hope to achieve any progress in these meetings by resorting to threats & unfounded accusations. Unless & until you decide to negotiate we see no hope for any actual progress in resolving issues confronting us. The next move is up to your side."

Gen Lee in reply again accused UNC of resorting to fabrication regarding our actual handling of POWs. "On Mar 8 you went even further in your fabrication by falsely accusing that our side has shipped POWs to the Peoples Republic of China. Such irresponsible slandering by your side only serves to prove that you have failed to find any presentable argument to support your position and cannot but resort to outright fabrication to delay the negots [negotiations] by such slander."

Lee also accused Libby of promising data on 44,205 civ internees on 31 Dec. He then again attacked vol repat. [voluntary repatriation] as device to retain Commie personnel in captivity. Will not accept, nor tolerate this absurd principle. "[It is?] Only because of your insistence on principle of so called vol. repat. that this issue blocked further progress in these meetings and had to be turned back to the sub-committee."

"Again it was our side that presented, for the purpose of breaking the deadlock on 5 Mar a proposal which is adequate to solve the existing quest. [question] reasonably."

"You even made the absurd allegation that our side does not represent the entire Korean & Chinese people. This is obviously a deliberate insult to our side, which our side absolutely cannot tolerate. It is even more obvious that your hatching of plots among our captured personnel to refuse them repat. by using the Chiang Kai-Shek gang, are activities which go beyond the scope of the Korean question and for which your side must bear full responsibility[.]"

Ridgway visited the camp and discussed the situation with us, particularly our HNC 1027. This msg recommended to CinCUNC the folg steps to bring matters to a head[:]

(1) To present as soon as practicable in plenary session a complete arm. document accompanied by an ultimatum or as an alternate;

(2) To present as soon as practicable in plenary session a draft document containing UNC min [minimum] positions and immediately recess the meetings until the enemy is prepared to accept the full document without substantive change. (We can justify the recess on the grds [grounds] that all issues have been thoroughly discussed and the appearance of a break off is avoided by maintaining liaison contact and by our statement of willingness to agree to an arm. at any time on the basis of the document we presented[.]

(3) Concurrently with the action of the delegation, Wash [Washington] should issue a strong statement and max [maximum] milt. pressure should be initiated & maintained.

R frowned on this course of action primarily because of the lack of reserves to initiate a strong milt action or pressure. Thought we ought to exhaust other possibilities before attempting it. Accordingly it was decided that best course for present was to try and remove the USSR as a road block and continue on our present course of action. In order to convince enemy we were firm in our rejection of USSR a public announcement from Wash might help. Folg msg therefore sent to JCS (HNC 1033).

1. Folg summary of current status of Arm negots has been prepared after full discussion with all US. Dels & senior members of Del staff.

2. a. We do not presume to know whether Commies desire or do not desire an armistice.

b. We do not presume to know Commie intentions with respect to any particular currently unresolved issues.

c. We deem it dangerous to assume that we do know his intention with respect to the foregoing and even more dangerous to the attainment of our objectives were we to base our plans on assumed Commie intentions which intelligence in our possession does not support.

d. With 3 major and several minor unresolved issues now existent; with the attitude of the Commie negotiators on all these major issues remaining obdurate without any indication of willingness to make concessions thereon; with the demeanor of the Commie negotiators *becoming increasingly arrogant and threatening and their language intemperate;* the position of the Del. verges on one of humiliation, derogatory to our national dignity, without discernable probability of improvement and in fact with positive indications of the probability of further deterioration in negotiatory strength of our position.

e. There are I think two courses of action either of which may arrest this deterioration, restore some measure of bargaining power to our Del. and relieve these honorable high-principled reps. [representatives] of the USA who compose the Del, of the rankling humiliation of having their Govt. the UN *and the principles for which both stand daily subjected to vituperative venom & falsehood.*

f. The 1st of these 2 courses of action is to reveal to the Communists the determination of the U.S. to stand inflexibly on stated min. posits. [positions] with respect to the major issues. The benefits to be derived from following this course will depend upon whether or not the Communists still desire an Arm. We should at least obtain an answer to this essential quest by so doing. If the publicly announced statement of its posit by the U.S. can be concurrently supported by like public statements from our principal UN allies, its effectiveness will be greatly increased.

g. The 2nd course of action is to apply the one influence which the Commies the world over recognize, and that is force.

h. I consider the 2nd course as one of last resort, and that the situation has yet to reach the point where it would be in order for me to submit to you my detailed views.

i. I consider adoption of the first course now imperative in order to arrest the very evident present deterioration in our negotiating posit. and permit progress with some measure of amelioration of the adverse influences under which we now negotiate. Removal of the USSR as an issue is a prerequisite to resolution of the other remaining major issues ie air fields & vol repat.

3. *Accordingly I recommend, the UN Del unanimously concurring, that the* **U.S. *Govt.* with the least practicable delay, publicly announce, and with concurrent like public announcements by as many of its principal UN allies as**

practicable, its decision irrevocably to reject the S. U. as a member of the NNSC.

4. It would be very helpful to know soonest the authoritative reaction of the U.S. Govt to this recommendation.

Mar. 11 (Tues): In staff offs meeting on Item 3 Commies asked if UNC had anything constructive to offer on unresolved issues. UNC replied that its constructive solutions of these issues had been presented and discussed on many occasions. Commies suggested recess to which UNC agreed after arranging for interpreters to meet today.

#4. At Item 4 meeting Commies presented 3 lists of POW names totalling 1036 for whom they requested an explanation[.]

List one contained 802 names not included in rosters of UNC held POWs submitted on 18 Dec & 28 Jan but from whom Commie families had received ltrs [letters]. List two contained 182 names included in 18 Dec roster but not in Jan 28 roster. List 3 contained 52 names which had appeared twice in 28 Jan roster.

Commies then read short prepared paper in which they reviewed past 11 days of sub-del meetings to support their contention that UNC is delaying conference. Commies again accused UNC of voiding its promise to furnish data on 44,000. They also called attention to the great effort they had made toward breaking deadlock by submission of their 5 Mar proposal. Stated, "Our proposal of 5 Mar adequately provides a reasonable solution of the existing quest. [question]. The question has to be settled. Whether conference makes any progress is entirely up to your side[.]"

UNC attacked Commie statement calling Commies attention to 28 – 29 Dec & 1 Jan records re. standing agreement on exchange of data. Called attention to fact there exist 2 unresolved issues, the second being that of the 50,000 unaccounted for milt. [military] personnel of UNC. Stated delay in meetings was due inability of 2 sides to agree on 2 basic issues. Told Commies their 5 Mar proposal not understood as fwd [forward] step since it appears to be complete negation of 3 principles set forth by UNC as basis of negotiating solution to basic differences. Suggested Commies explain differences between content of 5 Mar proposal and UNC three principles. Recessed 1144.

Mar. 12 (Wed): In staff meeting, Item 3, Commies asked for UNC view re quest. [question] of rotation, ports of entry, members of the NNSC and authority of the NNI Teams. UNC replied that its views were well known and were: rotation, 35,000; ports of entry 6; Soviet Union, unacceptable. When Commies raised question of extent of inspection by NNI Teams, UNC stated it would not impose upon members of these teams the function of gathering milt [military] intelligence in the course of insp [inspection] activities. UNC requested Commies to state position on para 15 (naval blockade). They objected to use of term "Korean

Peninsula." When UNC suggested substitution of term "of Korea," Commies stated the problem should be capable of solution by the interpreters. Interpreters met after staff offs. meeting.

Added folg to daily rpt [report].

In accordance with Genl R's verbal authorization of 10 Mar re. the insp. of replenishment material, the del will submit folg draft of Para 42c to Commies at time deemed appropriate: "Observe thru its members and its NNI Teams, the carrying out of the provisions of sub paras 13c, 13d & 13e of this arm [armistice] agreement at the ports of entry enumerated in para 43 hereof; and carry out the special observations and inspections provided for in para 28 hereof at those places where violations of this Arm Agreement have been rptd to have occurred. The inspections of combat aircraft, armored vehicles, weapons & ammo by the NNI Teams will be such as to enable them to properly insure that reinforcing equipment is not being introduced into Korea."

As directed by CinCUNC the JCS directives on file at CinCUNC (Adv) have been carefully reviewed. The foregoing para is in accord with such directives[.]

#4. Commies opened 12 Mar Item 4 sub del meeting with prepared statement. Accused UNC of attempting to make two issues out of one basic issue on repat [repatriation] by groundless fabrication of 50,000 captured persons UNC accuses Commies of holding. Stated UNC must face facts. There is only one issue. With regard to that issue the UNC 3 basic principles are not basis upon which issue can be solved. As previously stated they have no intention of retaining UNC personnel. They intend to return all personnel of UNC in their custody. It is actually UNC which is using so called reclassification as a pretext to refuse repat. to Commie personnel in captivity. UNC should not forget that Commies do not recognize existence of the so-called 50,000 persons fabricated by UNC, and do not recognize UNC so-called reclassification.

Commies closed by stating, "Our side maintains that the facts that we have not as yet been able to decide upon ways of solution on a number of quests, that does not affect what we have already agreed upon. In other words we should push fwd [forward] step by step as a basis, instead of standing still or even going backwards. Therefore I feel that my statement on 5 Mar pointed out the path that we should follow. I wish to repeat here a para of that statement of mine: 'The proper way to a solution is not to retrogress and overthrow the already agreed data, but to go forward upon the basis of the already agreed data so as to tackle it step by step.['] Therefore, it is our opinion that both sides can and ought to establish the principle of release & repat. of all POWs by both sides after an arm is realized, on the basis of the data concerning the war prisoners of both sides which have already been exchanged."

UNC asked Commies why they are unable to see they make it impossible for us to solve the problem, since they refuse to recognize existence of facts. First, that there are upwards of 50,000 milt personnel of UNC admittedly captured by

Commies whom they have not accounted for, and second that UNC has reclassified 37,000 persons who were erroneously classified as POWs and who are not now and never were personnel of their side. UNC is not going to unclassify them and no amount of argument can change them into persons of their side.

UNC stated that Commie 5 Mar proposal still appears to be a complete negation of all the bases upon which the prob [problem] can be negotiated. In actuality Commie proposal provides for UNC to return all POWs it holds plus all civ. [civilian] internees, for 1/6th of UNC personnel held by Commies. Further it requires UNC to agree to a principle which violates second of UNC basis, which is that UNC will not be a party to forced repatriation. The 5 Mar proposal is no advance from initial proposal presented by Commies on 12 Dec.

Mar. 13 (Thurs): In staff off. meeting on Item 3 discussion included questions of ports of entry, nominations of neutral nations, & authority of NNI Teams to inspect classified equipment. No new arguments were advanced and no new proposals were made[.]

Continued Commie emphasis on right of NNI Teams to inspect equipment without restriction could be with the intent of building up this issue for later bargaining purposes. In order to credit the UNC with the latest move designed to advance the arm [armistice], UNC staff offs. will on 14 Mar introduce wording given in yesterdays msg with respect to insp. [inspection] by NNI Teams, unless otherwise directed by you.

#4. UNC opened sub-del meeting on Item 4 by reiterating that the quest [question] of the captured personnel of our side is intrinsic to any basis of release and repat [repatriation] of all POWs in the custody of both sides. Stated again that Commie proposal of 5 Mar was not clear and appears to be the same as that advanced on 11 Dec '51. UNC remarks included folg. statement:

"So much of your statement of Mar 7 which reads, 'The list of all POWs who should be repatriated still has to be checked by the staff offs. of both sides after the principle is determined,' we feel this puts the cart before the horse. The first step should be to establish a bona fide list of bona fide POWs complete and acceptable to both sides, so that subsequent discussion of the basis for release & repat would have a definite meaning."

UNC concluded that Commies' proposal of 5 Mar was only a path to the Commie objective of attaining unconditional repat of all POWs we hold in exchange for a small portion of those that Commies hold. UNC would therefore not agree to it. Next step up to Commies.

Commies stated that the question of the UNC missing captured personnel has already been answered, and that if it is a part concerning the supplementary data, it can be handled in accordance with terms already agreed upon.

Commies then gave prepared statement in which they criticized the negative attitude and actions of the UNC Del during past 14 days and accused UNC of ignoring their 5 Mar proposal and of evading discussion of this proposal. Stated UNC principles are not an attempt to solve the question, and are inconsistent with the state of discussions between both sides on the existing question. Stated further that lack of progress resulted from UNC offsetting Commie positive efforts by UNC various kinds of negative actions. Commies concluded by stating:

"If your side is really interested in realizing an arm in Korea, and is sincerely desirous of an early materialization of an arm in Korea, your side must abandon such negative attitude and actions of offsetting the positive efforts made by our side. In the interests of the aspirations for peace of the peoples of the whole world, our side hopes that your side will seriously reconsider such a stand of yours. Your side should be thoroughly aware that actions of retaining our captured personnel under the guise of such catch words as 'voluntary repatriation' or [']no forced repat.' will not be acceptable to our side, and that insistence on this is no way to solve the questions thru negots [negotiations].

"Next as to the question of who will take the next step further. It is your side who should take the step[.]"

UNC stated that our side is determined to adhere to our principle and to 3 bases for negotiation. That delay in conference will continue until both sides reach agreement. Recessed 1140.

Mar. 14 (Fri): In staff officers meeting on Item 3 Commies proposed deletion of sub paras 13f & 13g (5 Feb Draft of Arm [armistice] Agreement) claiming UNC had previously agreed to do so. UNC denied this and raised question of inclusion of words "of Korea" in para 15 and other paras. Commies refused to give reasons for their objection to these words and, when directly questioned as to whether they were attempting to make the arm. applicable to the mainland of China, gave evasive answers. They did however strongly imply that if UNC would delete sub paras 13f & 13g, there would be no difficulty re our insistence on inclusion of words "of Korea," and suggested simultaneous settlement of all "minor issues."

UNC suggested going a step further & attempting to reach simultaneous agreement on *all* remaining issues and enumerated in addition to those mentioned above, ports of entry, and the authority of the NNI Teams. Commies requested elaboration of this suggestion. UNC stated: "If your side is willing to reconsider it's [sic] position regarding certain of the issues which I have enumerated." Commies stated their position concerning ports of entry was well known.

#4. UNC opened sub del meeting on Item 4 with folg statement:
Our two sub dels have been meeting for 15 days without any positive progress toward solution of our remaining differences. Your side has made a proposal of

5 Mar which you seem to believe offers a basis for negotiating a solution of these differences. Our side on 6 Mar. stated 3 bases on which we stated we could proceed to negotiate a solution of these differences. As yet both sides have been unable to reach any mutual agreement on the basis of either or both of these proposals.

"It is still not clear to us just what there is about your proposal which makes you think it can possibly be a basis for the solution of our differences. At the same time we have been unable to obtain your agreement to a solution on the basis of our three principles. It is possible that we can in time, and on sub-committee level, achieve the mutual understanding required. We are ready to continue on the sub-del level if you so desire.

"However, it is apparent that we have reached a situation in these sub del meetings where progress will at best be extremely slow. It is quite possible that neither side is fully cognizant of all the implications of the expressed position of the other side. If such is the case, further clarification and exploration is essential to progress. Perhaps this can best be handled on the staff level. In any case this procedure can do no harm, since we seem to have come practically to a stand-still on this level. We therefore suggest that we instruct our resp. [respective] staffs to meet for the purpose of further exploring the stated positions of each side with a view to their further clarification, and with a view to seeking, and recommending to us, means by which progress can be made toward a solution mutually satisfactory to both sides. This referral of the questions to the staffs, and their subsequent discussions, would of course be without prejudice to the stated positions of each side. Do you concur in this suggestion?"

Commies replied that they considered proper way to achieve solution to existing diffs [differences] was to first agree on principle of release & repat. [repatriation] of all POWs on basis of already ascertained data. Details could then gradually be worked out. Stated they would consider UNC suggestion for staff officers meetings[.] Recessed 1125.

Rec'd msg from Eusak reporting another incident at Koje Do. At approx 0930 on 13 Mar. a POW detail from compound 92 was passing compound 92. This detail was preceded by a formation of ROKA soldiers which was in no way connected with the work detail. As the work detail passed compound 92 rocks thrown by the inmates of 92 showered on the POW detail and the ROKA formation. The ROKA troops, without order, fired on the inmates of compound 92 resulting in 10 POW dead, 28 POWs[,] 1 Korean civilian and 1 US off [officer] wounded.

Sent folg msg HNC 1048 to CinCUNC. In event Commies agree to refer remaining Agenda Item 4 issues to staff offs. UNC Del plans to explore possibility of deal under which list of POWs in UNC custody would be so adjusted as to permit acceptance of principle of unconditional release and repatriation of all POWs on agreed lists. In event Commies agree to such a deal we will need timely info on POWs who would resist being returned to Commie control[.]

Request info as to whether classification of POWs as suggested in Part II, HNC 398 has progressed far enough to permit deletion from UNC list those POWs violently opposed to repat and addition to list of CI's [civilian internees] who desire to return to Commies.

Delegation recommends against interviews to determine those who would oppose return to Commie control, unless they can be conducted in absolute secrecy and without any likelihood of resulting bloodshed.

Mar. 15 (Sat): Staff meeting Item 3. Entire meeting devoted to attempt to obtain firm proposal from Commies covering all issues remaining for decision by staff offs. except quest [question] of Soviet Union. While Commies avoided definite commitment they made it obvious that if UNC will agree to 5 ports of entry and deletion of sub paras 13f & 13g they would agree to UNC proposal for restrictions on inspection of classified equipment and inclusion of term "in Korea" in relevant paras. including para 15.

It seems apparent that continued insistence on six ports of entry will result in protracted delays of the negots [negotiations] **whereas agreement on 5 ports of entry will involve securing for our side the exemption of classified equipment from exam** [examinaton] **by neutral teams, and the clear specification that the arm** [armistice] **terms including prohibition of blockade, apply only to Korea.** Consequently in accord with authority already granted Del. [Delegation] I have directed UNC staff offs. to reach an agreement in accord with above, making it clear however that such agreement is subject to agreement on specific port complexes and to wording of all paras of Arm Agreement pertaining to the issues involved.

#4. Sub Del on Item 4. Folg verbatim report of statements exchanged: Libby: "I am instructed by my senior Del [delegate] to inform you that on Thurs, Mar 13 an incident whereby a large no [number] of unruly POWs of your side attacked cooperative POWs, occurred at the UNC POW camp, Koje Do Island, resulting in the death of 12 and the injury of 26 POWs of your side. One American officer & one ROK civ [civilian] were also injured.

"The UNC is conducting an investigation to disclose the full facts. An independent investigation is being conducted by reps [representatives] of the ICRC."

Gen Lee: ["]We will deliver to our senior delegate the text from your senior del. rel. [relating] to the sanguinary incident in which our personnel, now in custody of your side, were illegally killed by your side. We indicate that we reserve all the rights of our side concerning this matter.

"Our side has repeatedly pointed out that our side cannot tolerate any attempt to retain our personnel in captivity. Our side has also pointed out, moreover that the conspiratorial activities perpetrated by Chiang Kai Shek among our captured personnel will lead to serious consequences[.] In a dispatch from Koje Do dated 14 Mar the Central News Agency of the

Kuomintang openenly [*sic*] stated that the great majority of the volunteers of our side in captivity and [are?] being tattooed and signing petitions in blood, showing that preparations are under [way?] to turn over large numbers of our people to the Kuomintang gang. The dispatch reveals to the whole world the seriousness of the activities being perpetrated among our captured personnel. I point out once more that the continued development of inciting of, and conniving at, conspiratorial activities will necessarily lead to serious consequences. In the interest of the Korean Arm, I deem it necessary to make this matter clear here.

''As our side has told your side, the way to solve reasonably the question does not lie in retreating from, or repudiating, the results already obtained between both sides, but lies in going fwd [forward] step by step on the basis of the already attained results and thus settling the questions. The most reasonable way to reach agreement is to settle first the principle of releasing and repatriating all POWs held by both sides, on the basis of the data exchanged already between both sides at the sub committee, and then turn it over to the staff officers meeting and settle the quest step by step on the basis of the principle already agreed upon. That is what we think and the proposal of our side is based upon this spirit.

''Your side insists that we should immed [immediately] turn the matter over to the staff offs meeting and let them discuss and clarify it & find a way for the settlement of the issue. It is the most reasonable way to first determine the principle and then settle the specific questions step by step. But if both sides have sincerity for the settlement of all the quests, the way of agreement and method of procedure should not be quests. for dispute. Since your side deems it more appropriate to utilize the staff officers meeting, we agree to your proposal and agree to turn over the unsettled questions to the staff offs. meeting.

Recessed 1200 until again requested to convene by staff offs or upon call of either side. Staff offs reconvene 16 Mar at 1100[.]

Rec'd msg from CinCUNC asking that I be available in Tokyo for conference with CinC Mon morning 17th. Msg directed no further action be taken with ref [reference] to HNC 1048 (see yesterdays notes) until CinC discusses matter with me.

Mar. 16 (Sun): In response to a summons by Ridgway I left camp at 0930 for Tokyo. Took off in my P2V from K-16 at 1100 arriving Haneda at 1430. Libby, Galloway & Ball accompanied me. Conference with R tomorrow at 0900.

In staff offs meeting on Item 3, UNC requested Commies to confirm its understanding that the naming of a city as port of entry included the railheads, airheads, and seaport facilities associated with and supporting that city. Commies stated that both sides had reached a general understanding in this regard on 5 Feb. UNC then made folg statement:

''I now propose the folg disposition of 5 issues which are preventing progress toward an armistice:

1. That the nbr [number] of ports of entry be agreed upon as 5.

2. That Para 42(c) (secret equipment) dealing with the authority of the neutral nations inspection teams be exactly as proposed by the UNC.

3. That paras 13(f) & (g) of the UNC draft be dropped from further consideration.

4. That the words, 'in Korea' or 'of Korea' as appropriate be inserted in the introduction to the preamble, Paras 13(B), 13(F) of your version (Graves Registration) and Paras 14, 15 & 16.

"This proposal is contingent upon agreement being reached on the nominations of ports of entry and the areas involved in conn. [connection] with each port and is automatically withdrawn as a proposal in the event that agreement is not reached on those points.

"In addition, if there is any evidence of evasion of commitments in conn with Para 42(c) and the paras specified in relation to the words 'in Korea,' this proposal is automatically rescinded.

"The opportunity to sweep aside these barriers to progress toward an arm. [armistice] agreement is now before your side."

[Sentence preceded by "Para" and then a number, both crossed out and the latter illegible.] Commies asked a nbr of quests. [questions] and then requested a recess after which, while objecting to reservations made by UNC, they accepted our proposal, stating that they had the right to the same reservations.

UNC then stated burden was now on Commies to solve issue of nomination of neutral nations. Commies asked if UNC had any practical solution in this regard. UNC stated that 2 neutrals from each side would meet all requirements. Commies replied with same statement they have made many times concerning their two alternative proposals. When questioned they admitted that under either alternative S.U. would be on neutral nations supervisory commission[.] UNC stated its opposition to USSR was irrevocable. Commies stated their position was well known.

#4. In Item 4 Staff meeting UNC requested Commies to outline in as much detail as possible their concept of how their 5 Mar proposal is intended to work as a solution to differences remaining between the two sides.

Commies stated they believed that UNC understood very well their 5 Mar proposal. However, Commies indicated willingness to answer any specific quests UNC might have. Stated they believe each side fully aware each sides posit [position] as developed in preceding days. They do not believe UNC 3 points can solve problem. It would, therefore be helpful if UNC proposed a constructive opinion adequate for solving the remaining quests. as Commies have done.

UNC informed Commies that UNC was not seeking a principle but an end product; that is, the peaceable return to the other side of POWs. Any method, procedure or understanding that can effect this end product is gist of our prob [problem]. Informed Commies that UNC would submit quests. designed to obtain detailed explanation their 5 Mar proposal. Stated that in our present view Commie proposal same as theirs of early Dec. However on assumption 5 Mar proposal is different UNC will submit specific questions.

Commies stated they would consider quests but felt it more important that UNC give any constructive opinion they had on a solution to differences between both sides. They then submitted a formal protest from their senior del [delegate] to UNC senior Del. concerning the "barbarous massacre" of their POWs at Koje Do on 13 March. We will not reply to this protest pending results of investigation being conducted by UNC and ICRC.

Mar. 17 (Mon): Met with R to discuss JCS msgs recently rec'd, one dated 28 Feb (JCS 902159) directing implementation of the Johnson plan as the final Govt position, the other (JCS 903687) in answer to HNC 1033 which requested comments on a JCS proposed package solution. This latter msg required that CinCUNC make the proposal to the two Commie Comdrs [commanders]. It incorporated the Johnson plan, dropping our insistence on restrs [restrictions] of airfield constr. [construction] and gave commies 3 choices for solution of USSR issue. Morning session devoted to discussion of JCS msgs and tenor of proposed reply. Afternoon session starting at 1600 and lasting until 1815 was spent in going over two msgs prepared by GHQ staff. One commented on JCS proposed package deal (see C-65430) and recommended HNC 1033 be carried out (strong public pronouncement by Wash [Washington] saying U.S. Govt would never agree to USSR). Other recommended we explore Commies Mar 5 proposal (see CX65424) to see if it would be possible to exchange POWS on the basis of revised lists which would not contain names of POWs who were violently opposed to return to other side.

#3. In staff offs meeting on Item 3 UNC opened with folg statement: "To begin with this am I think it best to state the views of our side re the port complexes to be specified. They are as follows: On your side, Sininju, Chongjin, Hamhung including the port facilities of Hungnam & the airfields; Manpojin; Pyonyang [Pyongyang] including the port of Chinnampo and the airfields associated with Pyonyang. On our side, Seoul including the port of Inchon and the airfields associated with Seoul; Kangnung, including port of Yangyang and the associated airfields; Kunsan Taegu and the port complex of Pusan including the dock facilities at Munsan [Masan] and the air fields in the area."

Commies stated they could see no reason for changing the recommended ports of entry in their area, but that they were willing to consider the ports of entry on our side which we had proposed.

Commies then insisted that it had been agreed that "the scope of each specified port is confined to the city limits and to the points of entry belonging to the city and used for handling rotation and replacement. Therefore any specified port should not include more than one city." UNC denied that any such interpretation could be placed on the discussion of 5 Feb and pointed out that UNC had then referred to Seoul as including Inchon, and associated airfields & railheads. Commies insisted that agreement on 5 ports of entry could not be changed by including 2 cities as one port of entry. They then stated that Hungnam could not be included with Hamhung; Pyongyang was not a port of entry; and that Chinnampo was "out of the question."

Repeated objections by Commies to UNC proposal to substitute Pyongyang for Sinanju with statement that they would consider UNC proposal as to UNC ports of entry, make it appear possible that they are leading up to the proposal that each side designate the ports of entry in its own rear.

#4. In Item 4 meeting Commies rptd. [reported] an incident of alleged bombing of POW camp on 16 Mar by UNC aircraft whereby one British POW was wounded. Commies contended camp was conspicuously marked and said: "Such continued murder by your side of captured personnel of both sides makes people doubt whether your side has the sincerity to settle actively the quest. [question] of POWs[.]"

Commies then stated this and past incidents require both sides to immediately adopt the principle which their side has proposed since the first day of the meeting and thus avoid further suffering of captured personnel of both sides.

During exchange of views on bombing incident Commies several times requested UNC to state any constructive opinion it had regarding basic question. UNC asked first of its prepared questions quoted hereafter. Commies requested all quests be submitted at once in order that Commies could study them and submit their considered answers. UNC then submitted 7 quests as for example[—]

"Just what data do you refer to when you state that the proper way to a reasonable solution is to go forward on the basis of the already agreed or already ascertained data so as to tackle the question step by step?

"What do you mean by the phrase tackle the question step by step?

"Is it your view that the UNC should at bayonet point or in shackles force ROK POWs we hold to go to your side against their strong objection after the arm. [armistice] becomes effective?"

Mar. 18 (Tues): Commies proposed Sininju, Manpojin, Chongjin, Hungnam (instead of Hamhung) and Sinanju for ports on their side and Inchon, Pusan, Kangnung[,] Kunsan and Suwon on our side. Commies made folg statement concerning Pyongyang-Chinampo [*sic*] quest [question]: "As we are not going to have any rotation or replacement thru Pyongyang so Pyongyang cannot be proposed here and we absolutely cannot agree to it. We do not think of carrying out rotation or replacement thru Chinnampo and so Chinnampo cannot be proposed here[.]"

Statements to same effect were repeated during course of meeting. UNC queried as to why Suwon had been substituted for Taegu but was unable to obtain any answer other than that UNC had indicated that it intended to conduct rotation & replenishment thru Suwon[.]

Commies again asserted that discussion of 5 Feb and the alleged agreement reached then preclude our present position regarding port complexes. UNC denied Commie assertion.

Commies again indicated that they would probably agree to ports of entry desired by UNC in its rear if we would agree to ports desired by them in their rear. One statement was as follows: "You want us to respect your opinion about deciding the ports of entry for your requirement of rotation and replacement and precisely in accord with that you should respect our opinion of deciding the ports of entry in accord with our requirement and you should agree to it."

Harrison added folg rec [recommendation] to the daily rpt [report]: It is believed that the folg course of action would produce the most favorable outcome of the port quest [question] for the UNC.

(1) Agree that each side accept the other sides nominations of its own five named ports[.]

(2) Agree that the scope of activity of the teams located in NK ports be restricted to the city limits and to facilities actually associated with the named city.

(3) Seek agreement to the port complex scope desired by UNC for ports in S.K.

Step 2 will possibly remove the apparent fear of the enemy that if he agrees to a wide scope of activity for teams in Korea he will be compelled to agree to a wide scope of activity for teams in N.K. Thus chances of enemy agreement to the port complexes in S.K. could be enhanced.

#4. In staff offs. meeting on Item 4. Col Tsai stated he was not yet fully prepared to respond to UNC questions presented yesterday, but that he in turn had certain questions to ask. UNC accepted the folg quests. for study and the preparation of answers.

(A). "In your statement of Mar 16th re. the question of release & repat. [repatriation] of POWs you said, "What our side is seeking for is not the principle but the end result" & your side said further, 'The gist of the question on this phase is the method, procedure and understanding which will effect such end result.' Your side did not give any explanation of such statement on Mar 16th. We feel that that statement is rather ambiguous. I would like to ask you to tell me what the clear meaning of such a statement is and I would like to you to give me sufficient explanation of it."

(B) "What do you refer to by saying 'the principle and end result as our side proposed' and what is the difference between such 'end result' and the result of determining the principle of releasing & repatriating all POWs on the basis of the basic data exchanged at present?"

(C) ''What methods, steps or procedures do you have in mind to obtain the result of the settlement of the questions under the conditions of not impairing the principle?''

Plan for tomorrow is to obtain Commie answers to our quests submitted yesterday[.] Do not intend to be ready to submit our answers until further developments.

Mar. 19 (Wed): UNC opened staff offs Item 3 meeting by proposing that the Commie 5 ports of entry be Sinuiju, Chongjin, Hamhung, Manpojin and Chinnampo with the Pyongyang airfields; and that the 5 UNC ports of entry be Inchon, Pusan[,] Taegu, Kangung [Kangnung] and Kunsan all with associated airfields. Commies replied they had substituted Hungnam for Hamhung and would not change again; that as they did not intend to use Chinnampo they would not accept it as a port of entry; and that they saw no reason for substituting Taegu for Suwon.

UNC stated it would agree to exclude Suwon from the Inchon port complex, that it would not use Suwon for introduction of rotation or replenishment and therefore proposed Taegu instead of Suwon. During progress of meeting it was apparent that this would be acceptable to Commies on a reciprocal basis. They reiterated several times that they did not intend to use Chinnampo or the Pyongyang airfields, for rotation or replenishment and that they would not agree to name it as one of their 5 ports of entry[.]

Commies declined UNC suggestion that staff offs. proceed at this time to delineate area of agreed ports of entry.

The enemys statement today that he does not intend to use Chinnampo or the Pyongyang airfields for rotation or replen. [replenishment] provides basis for dispatching mobile neutral teams to inspect these places if such use is rptd [reported].

In view of opposition of enemy to port complex concept, it is believed desirable to resolve quest [question] of named ports and associated facilities in enemy rear before the enemy so far commits himself on subject of port complexes as to render agreement to UNC complexes (particularly Inchon) a major reversal of his position. Accordingly authority is requested to initiate action tomorrow as outlined in HNC 1062.

#4. Fol'g is gist of record in staff officers meeting on Item 4.

UNC: asked for answers to questions submitted yesterday.

Commies said that 3 questions they had submitted should be answered first[.] UNC answers would be helpful to understand 7 questions submitted by UNC. Commie 3 quests involve not only proposal of our (C) side on 5 Mar. but also 3 bases declared by UNC on 8 Mar. Actually they are also closely related to UNC statement of 16 Mar.

UNC: "I should like to state that we are not standing on ceremony or protocol in not giving you answers to the 3 questions propounded by you yesterday. We appreciate that both sides would prefer, if possible, to have explanations made first to their quests. We are not sparring on that ground, however, and we frankly do not have the answers ready. Although there are some of the quests we asked you which relate solely to your proposal of 5 Mar, we understand that you may not desire to discuss our quests piecemeal. If you are able, or wish, to discuss answers to any of our questions we should be glad to hear them[.]"

Commies: "We are here to make a joint and careful study and exploration of the propositions of both sides to try to find out any way of solving the issues thru exploration. It would be better for the staff offs meeting not to care too much about formality, and we are glad to know that your side is adopting the same attitude. I believe, of course, your side understands the fact that we are not unwilling to give answers to your quests. We only feel that if the 3 quests submitted by our side can be clarified first, it would be helpful to us to understand your quests. and so it would be helpful to us to give answers to the quests presented by your side. Since the answers to the questions are not ready yet, apparently it would be pointless for us to continue discussion now."

When I talked to Briggs last night he mentioned that there were rumors originating on the press train that Commies were hinting secret discussions might be one way of resolving current problems. I told him to send CinCUNC a dispatch on the subject. The folg is gist of dispatch rec'd today.

1. Commie correspondents have been casually vague but persistently optimistic over early settlement of remaining issues of arm [armistice]. Secret discussions one way to resolve them they say.

2. Item 3 as good as settled. Commies give impression they are prepared to yield on nomination of USSR at appropriate time or USSR may ask her name be withdrawn[.] No mention made of air field issue. 3 to 4 wks [weeks] for arm they estimate.

3. Commie correspondents indicated Mar 5 proposal means they are willing to forget about 44,000 names if UNC forgets about 53,000[.]

4. Also hint they would be agreeable to staff offs working out new POW lists from which would be eliminated all those not desiring repat [repatriation]. **Appear to be highly sensitive to idea of NK or Chinese PWs publicly denouncing Communism at exchange pts.** [points] **and will do much to avoid this possibility. They also appear to recognize as a practical fact that there are PWs in UNC camps who will resist repat violently if necessary.**

Mar. 20 (Thurs): Ridgway held conference to determine how much if any of above msg (HNC 1067) should be sent on to JCS[.] After much discussion he finally decided, after strong rec [recommendation] by me & Libby, to send on all of it. It went out as CX 65592.

#3. In staff offs meeting on Item 3. agreement was reached on folg ports of entry: On UNC side, Pusan, Inchon, Kangnung[,] Kunsan, & Taegu; on Commie side, Sinuiju, Chongjin, Manpojin, Hungnam & Sinanju. UNC made it clear airfields were included giving as examples Yongpo for Hungnam & K14 & K16 for Inchon.

UNC then proposed to begin delineation of specific areas. Commies were not prepared to do so and it was agreed that at meeting tomorrow each side would submit to the other side maps delineating areas & routes of comm. [communications] applicable to its own 5 ports of entry.

UNC presented to Commies for consideration a map showing proposed routes of comm. for neutral Nations Insp. [inspection] Teams. from Pan Mun Jom to ports of entry. Commies agreed that if either side desired and NN Insp Teams were willing team could be air transported to or from ports of entry.

#4. In staff offs meeting on Item 4, after preliminary sparring Commies gave preliminary answers to UNC's 7 quests, [questions] gist of which follow.

1st quest.—Our side shall release & repat [repatriate] all your POWs— 11,559 persons and your side shall release & repat the captured personnel of ours in your custody—132,474 persons. In short on basis of data exchanged on Dec. 18.

UNC commented saying: "settlement on basis of your principle rather than our principle would require considerable adjustment. We are sincere in trying to reach a settlement but that does not mean we are willing to agree to every point of view of your side for the solution of the problem."

Re 2nd quest Commies said: "In our proposal of Mar 5 we clearly proposed a procedure for settling the question. That is to determine first the principle of releasing & repatriating all POWs under the custody of both sides on the basis of the data already exchanged or also ascertained by both sides and then to discuss & settle other quests re. to the releasing & repatriating the POWs. That is a procedure of tackling the problem step by step. On Mar 16th your side said & I quote, 'The gist of our problem is in the method, procedure or understanding which would effect such end result. We would like to know what kind of method or procedure does your side have in mind which would enable the settlement of the quests under the condition of not impairing the principle by our side."

After UNC said he was unable to answer quest. just raised Commies answered 3d quest regarding the difference between the data exchanged and the list of POWs to be repatriated. "It is apparent that the above two are different. It is because it is possible that POWs die in their captivity. Therefore the basic data exchanged naturally would be different from those who actually should be repatriated. Furthermore beside the 132,474 persons in your custody there is still the quest of other captured personnel of our side to be repatriated which must be settled thru negots [negotiations]. Now to answer the 4th quest. it has been our consistent proposition that our side is to release & repat unconditionally all the captured personnel of your side in our custody and our side is not going to retain any of the captured personnel of your side under any pretexts.''

Commies said: "With respect to your 5th quest. concerning the so called civilian internees it should be settled step by step according to the procedure proposed by our side. The only way to actual settlement of this question is to discuss it after the principle of releasing & repatriating all POWs is determined on the basis of the basic data exchanged. We consider that any concrete discussion of this question at present is unprofitable."

"Here is my answer to the 6th question raised by your side. According to our proposal of Mar 5, both sides should determine the principle of releasing and repatriating the POWs under the custody of both sides on the basis of the data exchanged. *According to our proposal, the captured personnel of our side under your custody, namely 132,474 persons who are listed in the data submitted by your side on Dec 18 should all be repatriated to our side.* This is also the consistent proposition of our side. From our point of view such question raised by your side is unthinkable. Our side cannot agree to any of your attempts or practices to retain the captured personnel of our side under any pretext."

"Our proposal on 5 Mar is very concrete, entirely realistic and is positive. Our proposition concretely proposes that we should first establish the procedure to settle the questions step by step. It points out what is the principle to be determined first. It proposes the basis for the determination of the principle and provides the procedure to settle the other questions in accord with the present conditions. It is a definite step forward[.]["]

Recessed 1304.

Mar. 21 (Sat): Shortly before Libby & I were to leave for Haneda to return to Munsan word came through from GHQ than [*sic*] an answer to CinCUNC's CX 65424 and his C-65430 had been rec'd from the JCS. and that R wanted my comments on the answer before I left for Korea[.] Therefore I decided to remain over for another day in Tokyo.

Gist of the JCS answer (JCS 904101) follows.

1. **Concurred in CinCFEs view that every effort should be made to determine whether our two objectives of obtaining prompt return of UNC POWs and of avoiding forced repat** [repatriation] **can be attained by agreement with Commies prior to taking action directed in JCS 902159.** They further concurred that action proposed in CX 65424 may offer remote possibility of accomplishing this and in any event may serve as possible gauge of Commie reaction to action directed in JCS 902159. However JCS have grave concern over certain implications of CinCUNCs proposal on which they would like addl [additional] comment prior to making final decision.

2. JCS afraid if they (Commies) accept UNC proposal they could then have an agreed principle on which to base further reclassification & downward revision of lists of UNC POWs already furnished. That is in spite of efforts made to avoid such result UNC would have in effect agreed to Commie retaliation against UNC POWs, thereby seriously weakening our future position on this question. JCS believed if Commies acquiesce in UNC proposal they would also acquiesce in action directed in JCS 902159 modified as proposed in JCS 903687.

3. Msg also requested comments on other points on which elaboration here is unnecessary. Tenor of msg showed anxiety to wind up armistice negots as soon as possible. Implications of proposed Johnson plan which was incorporated in their package deal proposal (JCS 903687) seems to have been overlooked or ignored. They dont appear to understand that an agreement beforehand on the exchange POWs would provide safeguards for UNC POWs return which the fait accompli Johnson plan totally lacks.

CinCUNC in his reply (C 65655) pointed out that it would be made very clear to Commies that the agreement to exchange POWs is contingent upon acceptance by each side of the revised lists of POWs to be exchanged. This agreement to revise the lists and the checking of the revised lists before accepting them as the bases for exchange is a safeguard which would eliminate the chance of Commie retaliation against UNC POWs. whereas implementation of plan set forth in JCS 902159 provides no guarantee whatever and would leave our POWs at mercy of Commies.

CinCUNC also objected both ideologically & practically to acceptance of USSR as a member of a supervisory organ [organization] under any circumstances. Strongly reaffirmed HNC 1033 which asked for public pronouncement against USSR as a member of NNSC.

(See C 65650 for further details.)

#3. In staff offs meeting on Item 3 Commies agreed with 2 minor variations, to main lines of Comm. [communication] between ports of entry & Pan Mun Jom.

The Commies then outlined facilities they intended to use at their ports of entry. Said main use of facilities at Sinanju, for example, would be airfield. Said also "When your side in sub del meeting demanded restrictions on the rehab. [rehabilitation] of airfields, our side counteracted by saying that we can include airfields in the ports of entry in the rear if your side will retract the demand." Commies also stated that each port of entry included everything within the city limits.

Commies method of marking maps to delineate areas in ports of entry consisted of only one small mark to show RR [railroad] station.

UNC pointed out that inspecting teams should have access to all facilities of entry associated with named ports of entry. Delineation of areas should include access to all facilities of entry.

Commies stated they had marked all facilities they intended to use.

#4. Commies opened staff meeting on Item 4 by asking for clear and accurate explanation of UNC statements. Reiterated that they consider Commie proposal of Mar 5 suitable for settlement of remaining issue. Requested detailed answer to their 3 quests [questions]. Made folg statement: "In order to enable your side to clarify further your yesterdays statement, I would like to raise folg 2 questions. You said yesterday: "In order to make progress in negots we are always anxious to see whether there is any way we can subscribe in general to your proposal of Mar 5th. The settlement on the basis of your principle not of our principle requires considerable adjustment." What do you mean by the word 'adjustment' and what kind of adjustment do you have in mind? You also said that you may subscribe in general to our proposal of Mar 5. Do you mean that you would subscribe to the way our side would release & repatriate all the POWs in our custody that is roughly 11,500 persons and your side shall release & repat the POWs in your custody that is roughly 132,000 persons."

"We (C) think that if both sides have the sincerity in settling the program on the basis of the confirmation of our proposal of Mar 5, the possibility of the adjustment on the basis of the proposal exists."

In the absence of clear authority to go ahead Hickman could do nothing but stall when he replied. He said that it was generally his intent to explore the situation in an attempt to see in what way UNC might embrace any part of your (C) 5 Mar proposal. Also that "the reconciliation of fundamental issues naturally require full examination & careful consideration of your points of view as they affect ours."

Commies then proposed an hours recess to consider whether they had any further questions to bring up. After recess they said: "After considering your statements our side now submits a provision in principle on the basis of our proposal on 5 Mar. If your side agrees to this basis of the provisions in principle we are going to submit, *and if your side has any opinion about the form of the meetings as the discussion of details,* we would like to hear them" Commies then submitted folg titled, "Principle for the arrangements of POWs."

"After the Arm [armistice] agreement is signed and becomes effective, the KPA and the CPV shall release & repatriate all the 11,559 POWs in their custody and the UNC shall release & repatriate all of the 132,474 POWs in its custody. The lists of the names of the POWs stated above shall be finally checked by the staff offs of both sides."

Meeting recessed after Hickman said "We will study your provision in principle and will let you know our comments later[.]"

Comment: Item 4 negotiating situation is becoming increasingly difficult in absence of a reply to CX 65592 (see Mar 20). Not only are staff offs⁻unable to respond to apparent current efforts of Commies to solve Item 4 but retrogression of discussions to UNC previous stands and arguments appear undesirable in view of current Commie attitude and favorable negotiating atmosphere.

Mar. 22 (Sun): Returned to Korea today in R's Constellation leaving Haneda at 1035 and arriving back at camp at 1430. Guy Chevalerie and Gen Wild Bill Donovan [Maj. Gen. William J. Donovan, USA] came along with us as far as Seoul. Gingrich accompanied Donovan.

#3. Commies opened Item 3 staff meeting by saying: "After considering the views of your side, our side agrees that the 3 specified ports of entry of Sininju, Chongjin and Hungnam include the airfields. As I pointed out yesterday, the delegates of our side stated unequivocally in the sub committee meetings that the inclusion of airports in the specified ports of entry must have as it's [*sic*] prerequisite the abandonment **by your side of your insistence on restricting airfield facilities in Korea which is an internal affair. I must state once again that it is contingent upon this prerequisite that our side has proposed the airfield at Sinanju as one of the ports of entry and has agreed to include in the three** specified ports of entry Sininju, Chongjin and Hungnam the air fields and their respective facilities[.]"

UNC, "As you know I am not authorized to comment on the subject of air field restrictions. We will study your delineations of the port areas[.]"

#4. UNC opened Item 4 meeting by asking Commies for their views on the form of the meetings.

Commies replied: "What I said regarding the form of the meeting applied to the staff offs' [officers] **meetings.** *It would be profitable if our discussions can be made freely, informally, without reservation and on a broad basis. If your side has any proposal re. the news release of the procedure of the meeting that certain measures should be taken for the purpose of facilitating the discussion of both sides, our side is willing to give consideration."*

UNC then asked whether Commies thought holding the meetings in executive session would help in reaching a solution.

Commies replied if that would help and we thought it necessary they were willing to study the question.

UNC then said it was studying the principle the Commies submitted yesterday in an endeavor to find what adjustments UNC might suggest to make principle more compatible with UNC's views.

Commies then elaborated on their new principle, which would be used to substitute for the original para 1 of Art 3 of the Arm. [armistice] Agreement. Said: "Of course it is apparent that our basic position towards the question of the POW is the unconditional repatriation of all of them. *However we appreciate that there may be certain special cases. Among the captured personnel of our side there are those who originally resided in the area of your side and has some particular situation as your side said before. We are now considering whether there is necessity to make some special arrangements for such special questions together with the special quests re those who are said to be reclassified by your side, but such reclassification has not been recognized by our side. You mentioned about the question of adjustments. We think that if your side agrees to this provision in principle we may submit our points of view on this phase before the checking of the lists for further negots* [negotiations] *with your side*[''']

Meeting recessed at 1155 after Commies said they hopd UNC study could be completed as soon as possible.

Comments: Delegation appraises foregoing as indicating Commies will agree to UNC retention of civilian internees. Moreover statement provides a definite indication that they might be brought to agree to (1) UNC retention of POWs of ROK origin and (2) possible adjustment of lists by substitution of CIs (and possibly POWs of ROK origin) who wish to go to KPA for POWs of NK origin who oppose repat. There is no indication of willingness to adjust similarly list of Chinese POWs. [Paragraph emphasized in text by a bold line in left margin.]

Commies recognize that neither side will wish to take initiative in proposing off the record discussions. They may well consider today's discussion as adequate to accomplish such sessions. Intend however to crystallize understanding tomorrow by stating we concur in Commies suggestion that staff meet in executive session for next few days. This may be responsible for the fuller discussion shown in their final statement. Del considers it desirable to cooperate with them in this respect by not publicizing any concessions they make during current discussions in Item 4. Consequently press briefing today was generalized. It will continue to be so so long as it appears desirable.

Advised R by dispatch that we would issue a statement on press policy if it was decided to go into Executive session tomorrow. Would revert to procedure we kept from July 10 to Aug 23 when no details of sessions were given out.

Mar. 23 (Mon): Rec'd msg from CinCUNC (C65730) which quoted JCS 904385 for compliance. Gist of JCS msg, which referred to CinCUNCs C 65650, follows:

"As indicated in JCS 904101 we have no objection to your making further efforts to obtain agreement with Commies on an acceptable basis for POW exchange. We feel that Communists position should be explored as carefully & thoroughly as possible. Suggest you do so on more informal approach than embodied in para 6 of CX 65424. Private meetings best. Hold in abeyance specific proposal pending further exploration. and until further exploration of Commie position shows definite possibilities for settlement of Agenda Item 4 without danger of downward revision of POW list of UNC POWs held by Commies.

["]Pending outcome of above approach final decision on your other recommendations outstanding as well as approach outlined in JCS 903687 is withheld.["]

#3. In staff meeting on Item 3 UNC presented maps of Commie ports of entry outlining areas we believe should be included in each case. Commies stated that some of the differences appeared to result from discrepancies between maps indicating UNC ports of entry.

#4. In staff officers meeting on Item 4 UNC proposed that henceforth meetings be regarded as in Executive session "until of course, one side or other desires to resume open meetings in Item 4 sessions."

Commies said they would consider & give answer later. Asked for UNC opinion on their "provision in principle" and for concrete proposal by UNC for settlement of present issue.

UNC said "I have hopes of being able to respond more fully in future."

Commies said they would give consideration to more time for UNC studying their proposal—recess for certain period if necessary.

Recessed at 1130 after UNC said it had no proposal to make today.

Sent fol'g msg (HNC 1082) to CinCUNC[:]

1. "In view of recent developments at Pan Mun Jom statement outlined in CX 65424 is obsolete. Commies have made their position as clear as they are likely to unless & until UNC indicates a willingness to talk in concrete & specific terms. It is vital that we take advantage to Commies present apparent willingness to make a deal and evident to Del that further indefinite & vague "exploration" can serve no purpose. Requisite degree of informality is in our view implicit in the fact that staffs rather than sub dels are conducting discussions, & that starting tomorrow these will likely be executive sessions. The stage is set for getting right down to cases. We are convinced that this should be done now. Commies made us a proposal on 21 Mar. Experience has proved that the best way to progress is to submit them a counter proposal or a revision of their proposal.

2. "To this end, and in consonance with JCS 904385 we propose to proceed along the folg lines at staff offs meeting on 24th[:]

a. Give a statement couched generally as follows:

Careful consideration has been given to the discussion of the past several days & particularly to the proposal of 21 Mar and to the further exposition made of it on 22 Mar[.] These have encouraged hope that a solution acceptable to both sides is not beyond the realm of possibility.

The proposal of 21 Mar with proper adjustments might well constitute a suitable basis for such a solution. Obviously, however neither side can agree to a proposal without a thorough understanding of its contents and of its implications with respect to its minimum objectives. Consequently, agreement in principle must follow rather than precede a general understanding on the details of the proposal. Our side is interested only in the end result and in the welfare of the POWs. This need not be inconsistent with the result to be obtained thru application of the principle of repatriating all the POWs in the custody of both sides at the time the arm [armistice] agreement is signed.

We seek to insure the return to our side of all the captured persons of our side & to insure the return to you of all captured personnel held by us except those released because they originally resided in the area of our side or because they are subject to a special situation such as you referred to on Mar 22.

In this connection the figure 132,474 set forth in your principle of the 21st does not fully reflect all pertinent factors. This figure included approx 16,000 persons who are residents of the area of our side. Therefore it should be reduced by this number. Some additional adjustment might be needed to accommodate POWs released because they are subject to a particular situation. What, if any, such additional adjustment might be we cannot estimate[.] However our side will make every effort to insure that any such additional adjustments will be reasonable. [The next two sentences are ruled out and bracketed by Joy to signify deletion by R as noted below:] Such an indefinite answer may not be satisfactory to you as a basis for an agreement. If an accurate estimate would be helpful we are willing to suspend discussion of the 21 Mar proposal until such time as it can be prepared.

Once the numerical adjustments are agreed to, it would be desirable to revise the lists of POWs previously submitted to reflect such adjustments, as well as deaths escapees and so forth. On the basis of these revised lists there should be no trouble in agreeing upon a principle of repatriating all POWs in the custody of each side, [word "when" deleted] at the time the Arm. Agreement is signed. [Next sentence deleted:] We are prepared to submit a revision of the 21 Mar proposal which should be acceptable to both sides.

b. If Communists reaction to foregoing is favorable, submit to them at appropriate time the folg revision of their 21 Mar proposal:

"The KPA & the CPVs on the one hand and the UNC on the other shall release & repatriate all POWs held in custody at the time the Arm Agreement is signed and becomes effective. The release & repat of such POWs shall be effected on the basis of lists which shall be checked by ["staff officers of" deleted], and be mutually acceptable to, both sides prior to the signing of the Arm agreement."

3. ["]In summary, we are convinced that only by being specific to this lmtd [limited] degree can any progress be made. Even if Commies reject our ideas we have lost nothing; and if they accept we have gained much. On the other hand further temporizing can serve no purpose, confuses the issue, and may result in loss of favorable opportunity to settle this issue.

4. ["]Request any additional instrs [instructions] you deem necessary prior to 240800 I Mar if possible."*

R. replied to above by making corrections as noted. He further said: "No accurate estimate should be offered to Commies at this time. Consider here that no reasonable estimate can be made by UNC without actually screening and

---

* "I" is the designator of the time zone in which Korea is located; CTJ is asking here for instructions before 0800 hrs Korean local time on the 24th.—Ed.

segregating POWs concerned. If Commies ask for an estimate or if agreement cannot be reached without furnishing them an accurate estimate, appropriate recommendations will be made to JCS from here.

"The proposal contained in your para 2b should be held in abeyance until reaction of the Commies to the above approach is determined.

"Commies should also be informed that revisions in existing lists will be determined discreetly & without publicity.[''']

Since above msg from R was not rec'd until 1230 on the 24th it was necessary to put off the Item 4 meeting until 1400.

Mar. 24 (Mon): Opening Item 3 meeting Commie staff officers presented maps redesignating areas accessible to Neutral Nations Inspection Teams in ports of entry of North Korea. Preliminary study indicates these areas in accord with UNC recommendations.

Regarding areas accessible to NNI Teams in ports of entry in South Korea Commies declared they would comment simultaneously when UNC comments on NK ports of entry.

Commies further proposed that highways would be considered the main lines of comm. [communication] and that motor vehicles would be the primary means of transportation but that Comdrs [Commanders] of either side may provide other modes of transportation as appropriate. This includes a/c [aircraft] when actually needed by the NNI Teams and when agreed to and provided by the Comdr over whose territory travel is to be performed.

Comment: Tomorrow intend to accept Commie versions of ports of entry in NK and then explore Commie viewpoint of Neutral Nations for possible change in stand.

#4. Commies opened Item 4 meeting at 1400 with folg statement:

"With regard to your proposal of yesterday concerning the form of these Staff Officer meetings from now on, our understanding is that your side proposes that we turn those sessions from now on into meetings of an executive nature, that is the specific contents and current results of our discussions shall be made known only to official sides and furthermore such a form shall continue until either side wishes to resume the open sessions.

"On March the 21st, our side indicated that on the basis of your agreement to the draft provision on the principle submitted by our side, we were willing to consider the views you might have re. the form of meetings for discussing the details of the principle. On Mar 22, our side further indicated that if your side demanded the necessity to change the form of our meetings, our side will spare no efforts of cooperation if only the change is conducive to the progress of the conference. Therefore, on the basis of the above stated understanding our side agrees to your proposal of yesterday that our meetings should hence-forward be considered by both sides as meetings of an executive nature until such time as either side may wish to resume the open sessions. If your side has no further opinions about this question, we will from now on hold our meetings under such new understanding.''

UNC staff offs agreed to conditions set forth in para 1 of this statement but refused to agree to first sentence of 2nd para as one of terms of reference for executive session. Balance of session was spent in discussion of this issue with progressive weakening of Commie stand but no clear agreement that no conditions would be attached to passing into executive session other than those stated in para 1 of Commies opening statement.

Comment: This was a disappointing day from our standpoint as we had not expected that the Commies would attach the condition of UNC agreement to their draft provision on their principle to passing into executive session. Jim Murray thinks this move of theirs was purely to test our negotiating strength. I am inclined to agree with him.

Mar. 25 (Tues): In staff meeting Item 3 UNC advised Commies that there was substantial agreement on areas for their ports of entry & gave them UNC maps with areas from Commie maps transported [transposed?] thereon.

UNC proposed to Commies that where necessary paras [paragraphs] **include clear provision that rotation personnel & restricted items "shall be introduced into Korea only thru agreed ports of entry." Commies concurred.**

UNC raised prob of neutral nations, proposing that the problem could easily be solved by agreement on the 4 nations which are acceptable to both sides. Commies stated they considered it unnecessary to repeat their views on this matter which had already been clearly stated. UNC replied that Commie proposals were not in accord with the agreed principle which requires nations nominated to be acceptable to both sides and that the only obstacle to complete agreement by staff offs. is Commie unreasonable insistence on the S.U. which is not acceptable to the UNC. UNC further stated that its stand on the matter was irrevocable & final.

Copies on [of] English, Korean & Chinese versions of arm. [armistice] agreement were exchanged for cross checking.

#4. In Item 4 meeting, under pretext that yesterdays difficulties in terms of reference for executive sessions were due to language difficulties, Commies agreed that no conditions would govern such sessions except those stated in first para of their yesterday statement to which UNC had agreed.

Substance of record after going into Executive session follows: UNC then gave statement reported to CinCUNC on Mar 23d in HNC 1082 and corrected by him. At end of statement UNC asked "Is not this concept of revised lists essentially the idea your side had in mind in the last sentence of your 21 Mar proposal?

"Agreement to this concept would be contingent upon the acceptability of the revised lists to both sides.[''']

After 30 min recess requested by Commies they replied: "With respect to the question you raised in your statement, I think this is the question of what is the meaning of the last sentence of our proposed provision on principle on 21 Mar. We maintain that after both sides have agreed on the provision on principle as proposed by our side on 21 Mar. we will enter into the stage of concrete and specific checking of the lists of the POWs.

"In your statement it appears that your side maintains that the principle should be determined after the lists have been agreed upon by both sides. That being the case, obviously both sides have different ideas about the procedure or the steps regarding this question. Therefore, if your side considers that the lists should be determined first and the principle later, and if your side has any concrete proposals about how to determine the lists, we should like to have your side submit the proposal."

UNC: ["]We set out our concept of revising the lists in order that it might be more evident as to what our two sides mean prior to making the agreement on the principle. We will study your remarks concerning a more concrete exposition & give your suggestion serious consideration. We think a general tentative agreement is worth while to be achieved, however, before new lists are prepared. Otherwise the work and delay attendant upon the preparation of the lists would be wasted.

"In other words, what I am saying is that we are not advocating full. agreement on the details before reaching a tentative agreement on the principle. I am indicating that we are not going to the other extreme of waiting to the last to decide on the principle, as Col Tsai apparently understood from my remarks.

"Perhaps I might clarify the situation a little bit by stating that the last sentence of my earlier statement, prior to the recess, could be amended as follows: 'Obviously final agreement on this concept would be contingent upon the acceptability of the revised lists to both sides.' In other words we think it would be pointless to proceed with the revision of lists without a degree of tentative agreement in principle."

Communists: "I think I have understood in general the meaning of what you said. Now I would like to make some preliminary remarks about your statement of this morning.

"In answering your seven quests, [questions] our side has clearly stated the necessary premise to our proposal of 5 Mar. I believe your side understands this point. After formally submitting our proposal of the provision on principle on 21 Mar, on 22 Mar we made an additional explanation of it.

"Since our provision on principle submitted on 21 Mar is made on the basis of our proposal of 5 Mar, the necessary premise of the proposal of 5 Mar is still required as with the proposal of 21 Mar.

"On 22 Mar, in the additional explanation we stated that among the captured personnel of our side under your custody, namely, approx 132,000 or more persons, there are persons who were former residents in the area of your side. If

there is any special situation re. some of those persons—of course it is not necessary that there must be, or should be any specific situation—we may consider
such special [paragraph emphasized to this point by a bold line in left margin]
conditions & special questions re. some other group of persons outside that of the
132,000 persons. The latter group of persons are those who are reclassified by
your side, but such reclassification has not been recognized by our side. When we
are considering those two kinds of special quests. we will consider them together
for a reasonable settlement of such questions.

*"However, it is inconceivable that among the rest of the captured personnel of
our side there could be any special situation.* **Our position towards this is clear
and cannot be changed. I think that if your side has sincerity to settle the
quest, the earlier you understand this point the more profitable it would be to
the progress of our meetings."**

Mar. 26 (Wed): In staff meeting on Item 3 Commies agreed to corrected versions
of sub paras 13c & 13d presented to them yesterday and to legends for maps.

Discussion of proper translation into Korean of term "United Nations" left
matter unsolved.

UNC again proposed that problem of Neutral Nations be settled by agreement
on a Neutral Nations Supervisory Commission consisting of the two nations proposed by Commies which are acceptable to UNC and the two nations proposed
by the UNC. Commies stated their position on this matter was well known and
did not require repetition.

**Fol'g was added to daily dispatch: "The Neutral Nations problem is the
only substantive matter left for determination by the staff officers in Item 3. It
is believed here that the public statement recommended in HNC 1033 would
be propitious and extremely helpful at this time."**

#4. Staff offs Item 4 met in executive session and thoroughly explored
positions of both sides relative to the Commies proposal of 21 Mar. Summary of
transcript of record follows.

Commies started in by attacking Hickmans statement of yesterday. "Frankly
speaking, that statement does not represent a step fw'd [forward] towards a
solution of the questions confronting us. Your stated view of making adjustments
on the basis of our proposal is still the proposition upon which your side has been
insisting depite [*sic*] our firm opposition, thus rendering it impossible to solve the
existing problem up until now. In reality, your side has not made any concession
for the sake of a solution."

**Commies then claimed their proposal of 21 Mar was a compromise
proposal. Yet UNC claims 16,000 should be deducted from total of Commie
POWs. "Then, if my understanding is not wrong another so called additional
adjustment will be made; that is to say, the principle upon which your side has**

been unreasonably insisting, and to which our side is opposed would be thoroughly applied to all the captured personnel of our side. Thus your side is insisting on your unilateral proposition and suggesting that further adjustments be made to our reasonable compromise proposal. Such an attitude cannot be considered in any sense as an attitude of negotiating in an effort to solve the question. We cannot agree to your unilateral views."

Commies then made 3 points of Hickmans statement of yesterday. First, that they have never conceded that persons who originally resided in UNC areas should not be captured personnel of their side (refer to 16,000 ROK POWs). Second, they have never recognized our "reclassification" of captured personnel. Third, UNC misinterpreted Commie remarks "by seeking to extend the special cases, which may possibly but not necessarily exist among the 16,000 of our captured personnel who originally resided in your area to cover all the captured personnel of our side. This is an erroneous interpretation and an erroneous application totally inconsistent with the facts. Our side decidedly cannot agree to it."

UNC then pointed out that we had conceded much by abandoning former principle advocated by UNC and the acceptance for inclusion in the arm. [armistice] agreement of your principle. Secondly, in his statement of yesterday Hickman attempted to set forth the means by which an estimated figure of captured personnel to be repatriated to Commies could be arrived at. Hickman also said he had no intention yesterday to repudiate UNC expressed willingness to send to Commie side persons who desire to go to your side. He also referred to the 50,000 who were released at the front, suggesting a realistic approach in this respect. "A practical viewpoint would require by UNC recognition of the fact that captured personnel released at the front by you may not be available for return to us. Similarly, practicality would call for recognition by your side that personnel released by us, because they are subject to special conditions, might not be available for return to you.

No intentional mis-interpretation. English translation your remarks about special situation was couched in broad enough language to give it the implication we thought it meant.

Hickman went on to say, "Your comments today make it appear that you are not willing to give even partial emphasis or consideration to our views with regard to those of the captured persons among the 132,474 who are not among the approx 16,000 but who are subject to a particular situation. A true compromise solution needs to take into consideration our views with regard to these captured persons who are subject to a particular situation. Our solution would take this group into consideration and it would do so discreetly, reasonably, quietly. Our statement was designed to reflect all of the opposing views of both sides. It highlights some issues and it submerges others."

Commies: "I consider that the proposal in your yesterday's statement seems to be an acceptance of the principle of repatriation of all POWs but in substance it is entirely your principle of the voluntary repat [repatriation] to all POWs. It is no compromise[.]''

Tsai said they would not consider a reduction of 16,000 from the 132,000 nor so called additional adjustments for special situations. Intent of his statement was that figure of 132,000 is reasonable since for those of the 16,000 ROK POWs who refuse to go to N.K., civilians who were reclassified from POWs could be substituted.

Hickman reiterated regret that "our two sides cannot today find your proposal a suitable vehicle for solving our problem. We feel it could be made satisfactorily to cope with the min [minimum] needs of our side but it has not done so.''

Commies said: "I believe that if you carefully study our proposal of Mar 21 in connection with subsequent statements regarding it, you will understand that the proposal of ours is a compromise of the position and opinions of both sides. We do not agree to the additional adjustments as your side proposed. That is from our minimum position[.]['']

UNC: [''']It is unfortunate that your minimum position and a min position of ours clash to prevent your solution of 21 Mar from being acceptable to our side.['']

Mar. 27 (Thurs): Staff meeting Item 3 opened with discussion of proper Korean phrase to use for UNC. UNC maintained it customarily uses Kuk Cho Yon Hap Kun for other UNC activities in Korea & that Arm [armistice] agreement should use same phrase when referring to UNC. Commies stated that Yon Hap Kuk Kun was proper translation of UNC. Discussion ended without decision. UNC pointed out that it was the right of UNC to designate title in Korean by which it desired to be known.

UNC then stated that the phrases Chosen and Han Kuk as names for Korea had equal significance and precedence and suggested as a compromise solution that both phrases be used in the Arm Agreement with one of the two appearing in parenthesis. Commies continued to reject usage of Han Kuk.

#4. In executive session of staff on Item 4 Tsai opened meeting by attacking UNC claims of making concessions in Hickman's statement of Mar 25. Said: "we have failed to find any point on which your side has abandoned your principle of vol. repat [voluntary repatriation].'' Their efforts & concessions are clear. "In order to settle the 4th Item of the agenda our side yet makes another effort and submits under the overall provision of our principle of Mar 21st the fol'g understandings relative to the principle of adjustments for the specific planning of repat of POWs. First, all the non-Korean POWs of the UNC in the custody of the KPA and the CPV as well as all of those Korean POWs in the custody of the KPA and the CPV whose residence was in your area shall be repatriated. All the non Korean POWs of the CPV in the custody of the UNC as well as all those Korean

POWs in the custody of the UNC whose residence was in our area shall be repatriated.

"Second, all the Korean POWs in the custody of the KPA and the CPV whose residence was in our area and all the Korean POWs in the custody of the UNC whose residence was in your area shall be repatriated with the exception of those who desire to return to the area of their original residence. I must clearly and unmistakably point out that it is upon the condition that your side agree according to the principle of the repatriating of all POWs to repatriate all non-K POWs and captured Korean personnel of the other side who originally resided on the other side that our side agrees to the repatriation in accord with the principle of vol repat of all the captured personnel held by each side who belonged to the other side but who originally resided in the territory of the detaining side."

"In order to solve the quest [question] thru negots [negotiations] our side has as much as possible accepted your views. In accord with the above stated understanding the number of POWs whom each side should repatriate under the provision of our draft principle of Mar 21 will remain generally the same as the round figures given in our draft principle of 21 Mar. This is because among the POWs whose homes are in the areas of the detaining side the number who desire to return home would not be great and the number so deducted from the 132,000 of our captured personnel certainly will not be greater than the total number of our captured personnel not covered in the figure 132,000 who desire to return to our side." - - - [here, through March 31, and later, CTJ uses three (or two) hyphens apparently as a substitute for a dash or perhaps ellipses] "Our side - - - agrees that the principle of vol repat advocated by your side be adopted in conn. [connection] with the repat by both sides of the captured personnel of the other side whose homes are in the area of the detaining side. In this way by repatriating the POWs in their respective custody both sides will adopt a solution which applies the unconditional repat. to part of the POWs. and applies vol. repat. to the other part of the POWs, a solution which constitutes a compromise, an arrangement which is realistic and adequate for the settlement of the question[.]["]

UNC: - - - "Your statements yesterday and this am. that our side has made no concessions towards a solution of Agenda Item 4 represent a misconception that I wish to correct in order to assist in our making real progress. I wish to review frankly our thoughts on concessions[.]

"There are in excess of 50,000 residents of our area in the custody of the UNC. Some are classified as civ. [civilian] internees. The names of others were included in the data exchanged on 18 Dec. because their erroneous classification as POWs has not yet been corrected. It has been the position of our side that the disposition of all such persons is an internal affair of our side. Your side has been reluctant to recognize this indisputable right. Now as an apparent concession your side has offered to recognize vol. repat. for this class of persons. This represents your sole effort of a concessive nature.

"What efforts have been made by our side? First, we have indicated a willingness to accept the principle advanced by your side for inclusion in the arm. agreement. Second, in discussing the concession which your side feels it has made respecting persons whose residences are in our areas we noted the fact that you would like to receive those among this group who wish to go to your side. We are willing that they go but not as an isolated action. The delivery to you of persons of this group is a concession by our side which is contingent upon a concession by your side which has not yet been indicated.

"Third according to your own statements your side has released or otherwise disposed of some 50,000 milt [military] persons of our side who had fallen into your custody[.] Our side cannot overlook your disposal of these persons many thousands of whom are known to have been incorporated into your armed forces. However, as a part of a practical realistic approach to a negotiated solution of Item 4, our side is prepared to consider that these persons may be beyond our reach in the same sense that personnel released by our side because they are subject to a special situation would be beyond the reach of your side. Thus this concession by us is related to the release by us of those persons in our custody who are subject to a special situation.

"A fourth concession, which is implicit in our response to your 21 Mar proposal and your amended proposal of this a.m. is the criteria for and the procedures to be used in determining what personnel should be accorded treatment as special cases. - - - In contrast to this, our side now contemplates use of min [minimum] criteria to the end that only those whose repat. could not be effected without physical violence will be regarded as special cases.

"A concession on your part similar in nature to the 4th concession made by our side is the key to the resolution of the remaining difference. It is nothing more than a realistic recognition that special cases may and do occur among POWs of all categories, special cases which your side has in the past recognized and accommodated. It is nothing more than realistic recognition that no criteria or procedure which might be employed by either side will erase the fact that special cases do occur."

"In your proposed revision and understandings of this am, you have failed to take into consideration our consistent stand that approx 53,000 captured persons who originally resided on our side, that is 16,000 prisoners of war and 37,000 civ internees are personnel of our side and are an internal affair of our side. Any statement that we have made at any time re. the possibility of sending to your side some of these persons has always been contingent upon your acceptance of the application of the basic principle of our side to all POWs. In actuality you are making no concession. You are merely attempting to make it appear that your willingness to accept the concession of the UNC is in itself a concession by you. Also in return for your apparent concession in accepting our concession with regard to such captured persons whose residence is on our side, you demanded forced repatriation of all other POWs held by us. **You attempt thereby to obtain**

two concessions from us without any real concession by your side - - - I must again very frankly assure you that our side cannot participate in forced repat of those POWs of your side who would violently oppose such repatriation. The sooner your side realizes that this is a minimum position of our side, the sooner we can reach an agreement to this Agenda Item.

- - - "As I have indicated we have receded from our position of giving the POWs from your side a choice. Instead we put it on the basis of returning all to you except those who will forcibly resist repatriation. And it is the end result of not having to forcibly repatriate that we have as a minimum position."

Commies: "Among the 44,000 of our captured personnel held by you from 37,000 to 39,000 of them are the regular milt personnel of our side. The affairs of these persons cannot be your internal affair. How can you say that our agreeing to get back those of them who are willing to come back to our side is a concession made by your side? Furthermore, in order to settle the question speedily our side proposes that the vol repat will be applied to those among the 132,000 persons, that is a number of approx 16,000 persons whose original residences were in your side. How could you say that such concession by our side is a concession by your side? - - - It is very clear that we have made a compromise to your vol repat. in the understanding submitted today. - - - If there is a bar in the way of reaching an agreement that bar is your attempt to demand our side to the surrender to your principle and I have to point out to you clearly that it is completely impossible."

UNC: "In your recognition of vol. repat. for residents of our side now in our custody there is no full compensation for the 50,000 persons of our side because in the first place there will be sent to your side all of our people [preceding 16 words repeated in text and then crossed out] in our custody who desire to go to your side whereas none of the 50,000 are to be returned to us except those few we have already received who were released at the front. In the 2nd place by unilateral action you were able to take at the time, you have solved the problem with respect to persons among the 50,000 who might constitute special cases among the personnel you hold. You were able to make adjustments similar to those which we consider essential now to our min. posit [position]. - - - Thus we cannot consider that your current proposal compensates for the action which your side has already been able to take with respect to our people who might be POWs."

Commies ended session by saying they agreed "to apply the prin. [principle] of vol. repat. to the group of about 40,000 captured personnel of our side." Only did so to settle questions & differences between both sides.

Mar. 28 (Fri): In staff meeting on Item 3 Commies suggested compromise on translation problem under which they would accept Kuk Che Yon Hap for "United Nations" if UNC would accept Chosen for "Korea." UNC stated it would give its opinion on this suggestion tomorrow.

UNC stated neutral nations problem was the only one remaining for agreement by staff offs, pointing out there was already agreement on four nations & that this number was adequate. Commies replied again that their views were well known and did not require repetition. When told that this would not solve the problem they stated they could not understand why UNC would not accept one of their two alternate proposals. UNC replied that both Commie proposals required UNC to accept a nation which was not acceptable and that this violated the agreed principle. Commie answer was in vague generalities[.]

It is opinion of the staff officers that Commies desire to clear up all odds & ends and then return to sub del meetings for discussions of Soviet Union simultaneously with discussion of airfield restrs [restrictions]. Commies apparently do not wish to further highlight the neutral nations problem at this time by extended arguments.

#4. UNC started off Item 4 meeting by attacking Commies' understanding of yesterday in which they applied prin. of vol repat to personnel whose disposition is a UNC internal affair. Although it appeared to be bilateral it actually is not. Pointed out that Commies already had eliminated from consideration those people who oppose returning to our side. Of the more than 65,000 of UNC people who were captured by Commies only some 11,000 are rptd as POWs. It is clear that prin of vol repat to these grps [groups] on both sides is not truly bilateral. Accused Commies of eliminating in their POW camps POWs of our side who were opposed to returning to our side. "We are seeking to accomplish only that which your side has already accomplished."

UNC: "We hope you understand our firm min. posit [minimum position]. We will not be a party to the forced repat of any individual who violently opposes it. On this basis your proposed understanding is not acceptable for the solution of Agenda Item 4[.]"

UNC: "You should recognize that our side should be able to accomplish a portion of what your side has already accomplished with respect to POWs held by you who would have been violently opposed to repat. had they been faced with the problem or the opportunity."

Commies: "It was entirely correct for our side to release large numbers of the captured personnel of your side when the existing situations then were changing greatly. The action taken by our side cannot be any pretext for your side to oppose the principle maintained by our side."

Tsai then attacked our concessions. "The first concession you made is the willingness of your side to accept and write into the Arm. Agreement the prin. advocated by our side, but in fact, your side while accepting our prin. is actually trying to apply your prin to all of our captured personnel. The only diff. [difference] being that this will be done quietly and without publicity." Tsai again claimed that we had really made no concessions since the 44,000 civ. int.

[civilian internees] & 16,000 ROKs were actually captured personnel of their side. Called our principle a 'camouflaged principle.' Asked what is substantive difference between no forced & vol repat. Except for the 44,000 & the 16,000, "there exists of course no circumstance which could warrant their non-repatriation and there is also no reason whatsoever to raise any question of this kind."

Tsai: "Among the captured personnel of our side there is a no. [number] of milt [military] personnel of the CPV's. In connection with these there cannot be any situation which warrants non-repat. If your side insists on refusing to repat. the captured personnel of the CPV the only possible explanation is that your side wants to use 'non-forced repat' as a guise & in fact retain them & turn them over to Chiang Kai Shek brigands on Taiwan. This attempt found its specific expression the other day (incident on Koje Do). Such an attempt shows that your side is determined not to settle the quest [question]. Our side has pointed out to you many times that the continuing development of this course of action on your part will cause grave consequences. I hope you will take full note of this fact."

["]I must point out again that it is upon the condition that your side agrees that both sides repatriate all non K POWs in its custody and all those Korean POWs in its custody who originally resided in the areas of the side to which they belong that our side can agree to the application of vol repat to those captured personnel who originally resided in the areas of the other side. It is entirely based upon reciprocity and practicality. The repat of all those captured personnel of the KPA who originally resided in the areas of our side and of all the captured CPV personnel is indisputable, and most reasonable, as is the repat. to your side of all non-K members of the UNC and all Korean members who originally resided in your area. This stand of ours is firm & unshakeable."

Tsai went on to say: - - - "Therefore by summarizing your proposition about the principle of the repat of the POWs it is clear that actually you are still holding to the so called vol. repat. It is not only that your side refuses the repat of all captured personnel of our side who originally resided in your area, but your side intends to retain by force the captured personnel of our side. The intent of such proposition of your side is entirely not for the reunion of the POWs with their families[.] It is only for the purpose of enlarging the war and to get more cannon fodder."

Hickman then rebutted Tsais remarks such as the one that it was correct for Commies to release UNC POWs at the front. Also Tsai's allegation that UNC has engaged in educational program or coercion of POWs held by UNC.

Mar. 29 (Sat): In staff offs meeting on Item 3. UNC proposed as an administrative matter that each side prepare 3 original sets of the Arm [armistice] Agreement; one each for its own use, the use of the other side, and the use of the MAC.

Each set would contain English, Korean & Chinese versions and be signed by the signatories. Commies reserved comment until later.

UNC then stated that for the Korean version of the MAC to be legally binding to both sides, Korea should be referred to by using both Han Kuk and Chosen wherever appropriate. Lengthy discussion then ensued without decision. Commies still maintain Chosen is valid and sufficient.

Referring to its recently submitted para re. Neutral Nations, UNC maintained that solution whereby each side nominate only two Neutral Nations (USSR excluded) is in full compliance with agreed principles, is fair to both sides and should be immediately adopted by both sides to avoid further delay. Commies stated that their position was well known and would not enter into discussion of the matter. Meeting recessed 1300.

#4. In opening statement in Item 4 meeting, Hickman pointed out that UNC has made major concessions in attempting to solve the POW quest. [question] and reiterated our position on no-forced repat [repatriation]. UNC explained at some length between vol. [voluntary] repat. & no forced repat.

In reply Commies accused UNC of "verbal acrobatics beyond the scope of logic." Reiterated old song that "by agreeing to include nominally the principle of our side in the Arm Agreement, your side said such an acceptance of your side of the name of the principle is a concession by your side. This is inconsistent with the facts in any respect." Tsai again tried to make it appear that they were making an important concession in agreeing that, of the 44,000, "those whose residences are in your area & wish to return to their original residences may not be repatriated to our side." Tsai also said: "Contingent upon your not raising any more the question of the 50,000 persons, our side in our proposal of 21 Mar did not include the 44,000 persons of our side in the figure given in that proposal." Tsai also said: "As to the difference between your "vol repat" and "no forced repat" we consider that there is no substantive difference between the two. Regardless of the criteria—as your side has said, whether it is min [minimum] or max [maximum]—we can only conclude that such criteria maintained by your side is for the purpose of retaining the captured personnel of our side." **Tsai went on to say:** *"Our side even possesses the info which proves that Americans are assisting the gangsters from the Chiang Kai Shek brigands to do the forced tatooing in your POW camps[.]"* Said also: *"Any tattooing would not prevent the captured personnel of our side from returning to us."*

Tsai again: "According to your proposition and under your principle of so called 'vol repat' your side in fact attempts to retain our captured personnel by various means of intimidation and coercion and to prevent them from returning to the places where they originally belonged and resided, to rejoin their families and resume a peaceful life."

Tsai also made this veiled threat: *"I must seriously point out here, once* *again, that your attempts to retain our captured personnel of the CPV and to turn them over to Chiang Kai Shek at Taiwan is fraught with grave danger for the current question to develop beyond the scope of the Korean Armistice.* - - - According to your proposition and under your principle of so called vol repat, your side is in fact, not in the least concerned with your own captured personnel. While our side has indicated thruout our willingness and proposed to repatriate to your side all of your captured personnel who originally resided in your areas you, on your part, have been rejecting the total repatriation of them including the non-Korean personnel of your side. - - - *It is very clear that the content of your proposition is to retain our captured personnel and reject the total repatriation of your captured personnel who originally resided in the areas of your side.*"

Tsai again: "I believe that if your side is really concerned with the welfare of the POWs and seriously desires a settlement of the prob. so as to realize an arm at an early date, you will recognize that your proposition cannot stand publication before the POWs of either side and that it cannot settle the question. - - - Frankly speaking in a milt [military] conference on the basis of equality & reciprocity, any condition by either side of trying to demand the complete capitulation of the other side to the proposition of the one cannot work[.]"

UNC then rebutted Tsai's statement that we are not interested in return of our own POWs. Said: "We do not think there is a single one of our people now in your POW camps who is not going to be hilariously glad to return to our side[.]"

Commies again upheld their stand, saying: - - - "We have even agreed that the 16,000 persons who are clearly and definitely ours as POWs. on the lists submitted by your side to be treated as a similar problem with that of the 44,000 captured personnel of our side in order to reach a solution of the issues. Certainly you are aware of the fact that in our proposal of Mar 21st we have not included the 44,000 captured personnel of our side in the total figure given in that proposal. On our part this is done reluctantly. - - - For the solution of the present issue confronting us, our side has already made the reasonable compromise. Whether your side is willing to cooperate or not in order to obtain agreement, is up to your side[.]"

Mar. 30 (Sun): I sent folg msg to Muccio info CinCUNC.

"Statements of the nature made by Foreign Minister Pyun concerning transfer of Chinese POW[s] to Formosa extremely damaging to negots [negotiations]**, since they give substance to Commies charges that UNC is plotting to hand over CPV personnel to "bitter enemy of Chinese people." The quest.** [question] **of non return of certain Chinese POW[s] now appear to be principal bar to obtaining an arm.** [armistice] **agreement.** Commie hatred of Nationalist China so intense as to border on psychotic, and any evidence of this nature pointing to likelihood that CPV personnel will end up in Nationalist hands intensifies the difficulty of reaching agreement and may well remove any possibility of so doing.

"Delegation urges that every effort be made to prevent further statements of the nature made in referenced dispatch during present critical stage of negots.[''']

#3. In staff meeting on Item 3 Commies agreed to UNC proposal of yesterday that each side will prepare 3 sets of the original Arm Agreement for signature. Each set to contain English, Korean & Chinese version[.]

Commies had nothing to offer towards solution of prob. [problem] involving use of Chosen or Han Kuk in Korean version of Arm Agreement to designate the territory of Korea[.]

Discussion re Neutral Nations disclosed no change in Commie position.

#4. In staff meeting Item 4 Col Tsai began by saying: "You stated yesterday that in determining & carrying out the repat [repatriation] of POWs, the possible adoption of different standards would result in increase or decrease of nos [numbers] of POWs who desire to be repatriated. Such a way of thinking shows that your side holds the view that the repat of POWs. may be influenced & manipulated by your side by various methods as you choose. - - - Facts show that your side is not only attempting to manipulate the repat of the captured personnel of our side but you wanted to prevent suicide & other violence. It is strange that you already foresee violence. However it is not strange. In Dec the Taiwan brigands already ordered their underlings to organize in your camps so called suicides & hunger strikes, signing of petitions with blood & other violences. Since these underlings have been able to carry work in the POW camps you can foresee what they are going to present.

"Your side has admitted that captured personnel have been tattooed in POW camps[.] Their tatooing is by no means an indication of their objection to repat. but is instead evidence of the conspiratorial deprivation of their right of repat. All of our captured personnel except for those who originally resided in your areas, and who desire to go home, following the arm of course, want to return to our side. This is our stand. *It is not affected by their being tattooed compulsory* [sic]. None of our captured personnel would be unwilling to return to their motherland. - - - You have recently dropped by air a no of our captured personnel, who have been tattooed, in our rear to gather milt [military] intell. [intelligence] but they are unwilling to be used by your side. Some have returned to our side, reporting in detail of the compulsory tattooing by your side. This proves that your side has forced our captured personnel to be tattooed and forced POWs to carry on milt. activities."

UNC: "We have likewise received info about what has taken place in your rear. There is no need to go into details now, about the many people of your side who have been placed in your re-education and re-orientation camps—people of both Korean & non-K origin.

- - - "Since you have engaged in the reeducation of POWs thruout the war it is no surprise to you that the attitude of POWs can be affected by the treatment they receive in POW camps. Some of the over 50,000 were disposed of more or less voluntarily because of your practice of re-educating them. Others were coerced[.]

"Based on your experience it should be known to you that many POWs cannot be influenced. Some are so fixed in their opposition to repat. that they could not be repatriated without application of force. You removed any such cases by releasing them from POW status[.] We still have such individuals in custody. We do not desire to deny any POW the right to repatriate but we are unwilling to force them to go. In this respect we are asking for less than you have already taken for yourself."

Commies then reviewed the so called efforts they had made including their alleged concessions re the 44,000 & the 16,000. Said UNC efforts cannot be compared to theirs. Their principle of 21 Mar & their understanding of Mar 27 afford a reasonable compromise[.] "The Mar 21 proposal and the understandings of Mar 27 require the application of our principle to a part of the captured personnel and the application of your principle to the other part of the captured personnel. Our side cannot move further, since such a proposition is the only real compromise solution. Your side insists on the application of your principle to all the captured personnel. That is impossible."

UNC: "We do not wish to utilize time in unnecessary discussions. You are aware that you can bring these executive sessions to an end in case you feel it is impossible to make progress."

Hickman then reviewed the so called Commie concessions pointing out that the quest of the 44,000 is an internal affair of our side. Also pointed out that the 50,000 unreported personnel of our side should be considered. When UNC raises question of their disappearance you cry 'fabrication.' Hickman then took Tsai to task for his yesterday's statement [that follows]: 'It is obvious that your side is interested in retaining our captured personnel and preventing them from returning home and rejoining their families, **more than in the return of your captured personnel who originally resided in your area.'** Said he [i.e., Hickman]: **"Ever since that day more than 3 mos ago when your side reluctantly submitted to us your entirely inadequate list of our captured personnel, the whereabouts and welfare of our captured personnel not listed has been a major consideration of our side. We have done everything possible to persuade you to abandon your false pretenses and report all of our captured personnel. We have pointed out the places to which our unlisted people have been taken and the uses to which they have been put. In answer we received only prompt and categorical denial.** However in spirit of compromise and in greater interest of achieving an armistice we have attempted to hasten a solution by indicating a willingness to approach the prob. of these persons in a spirit of negotiation. This attitude is premised on attaining a satisfactory solution to agenda Item 4.

"To avoid any possibility of misunderstanding on your part I will state again our attitude concerning all of our captured personnel in your custody[.] Based on the premise that solution is reached we are willing to consider the prob of this group realistically and practically. This attitude represents a real and substantive discussion.''

Somewhat mollified the Commies (Tsai) said: ''We are willing to continue the discussion in the spirit of settling the quests. Of course your side may say anything you like in the Exec [executive] sessions[.] However it might be more helpful if we could more unreservedly negotiate for the solution of the issue between both sides.''

Tsai then contended that the 44,000 were milt personnel of their side. Not an internal affair of UNC. Defended again their proposal of 21 Mar & understandings of 27 Mar. ''which clearly set forth that the principle of 'repat of all POWs' be applied to a part of all the POWs whereas the other part, those whose original residences are in your area and who desire to return to their homes, need not be repatriated. That is a reasonable compromise.

''In short,'' said Tsai, ''your side holds that we should accept the unilateral proposition on the principle and, in fact, our side should agree to let your side retain a great no [number] of the captured personnel of our side. Such a position of your side cannot possibly be accepted.''

UNC countered by going over the same ground again pointing out the various UNC concessions ie (1) Agreement to drop the issue of the missing 50,000 whom Commies rptd [reported] captured but whose names were never given. (2) Although somewhat more than 50,000 in UNC hands were an internal affair of our side we were prepared to apply vol. repat to this group of personnel. ''We ask your side as a contribution to a negotiated solution to recognize, among the 116,000 POWs, that such special cases (those who physically resist repat) should be excluded from the unconditional exchange of such POWs.'' - - - ''We are willing to accept as a fait accompli your unilateral disposition of 50,000 of our personnel during the course of hostilities and are willing to deliver to your side all who wish it of the people we hold whose disposition is an internal affair of our side, in exchange for your recognition that we cannot deliver POWs who violently oppose it and who could not be delivered without the application of force. Finally the propositions in this statement are qualified. They are contingent upon the realization of a negotiated solution to the diffs [differences] now remaining with the POW problem.''

Commies ended session by saying: ''We cannot accept the complete proposition of your side. We can only settle the problem by compromise. That is, to a part of the captured personnel of both sides your principle of repat will be applied and to the other part of the captured personnel of both sides our prin. [principle] will be applied.''

Recessed 1403. Comment: I intend to pursue present course of action for 2 or 3 days.

Mar. 31 (Mon): In staff meeting on Item 3 Commies agreed to UNC version of areas of ports of entry in rear of both sides in which NNI Teams might operate.

Both sides agreed on interpreters meeting to arrive at suitable legends to be printed on the final versions of the maps.

Neither side had further proposals to offer on selection of Neutral Nations or on solution of problem re choice of Han Kuk and/or Chosen in Korean version of Arm [armistice] Agreement.

Commies then proposed staff off meetings be recessed and all remaining unsolved problems. together with solutions already reached be handed over to sub del level at 1100 tomorrow morning. UNC stated staff offs. not yet completed their work but that Commie suggestion would be relayed to Senior Del. for decision. Informed Commies that decision of Senior Del would be relayed to them at 0900 Item [3 meeting?] tomorrow.

Comment: Will delay holding sub del meeting as it is probable Commies may want to propose swapping USSR issue for airfield issue. It would be preferable to settle Item 4 before discussing such a trade.

#4. In Executive session of Staff meeting on Item 4 Hickman started the ball rolling by enquiring: "Now that there is a tentative agreement to extend vol repat [voluntary repatriation] to the people in our custody whose homes are in our area, we would like to know why your side objects to the extension of vol. repat to the 50,000? I make specific ref [reference] for the sake of narrowing the quest [question] to the personnel in the units of our side who deserted to your side & were incorporated in your army.["]

Col Tsai: "Our position is that we should not mix up the quest. of the POWs ever captured by either side with the POWs now held. The 44,000 & the 16,000 are in your POW camps. In order to settle the quest. those people must be discussed and the quest re them must be settled."

- - - "You mentioned about the quest of 50,000 persons. During hostilities our side released great nos [numbers] of captured personnel. Since they have already been released discussion of the quests re them could not provide any other solution of that question.

- - - "In order to reach speedy settlement of the questions, our side proposed the principle of Mar 21 and the understanding of Mar 27. We consider such principle & understandings to have taken care of the opinions of both sides. If your side agrees to that principle then we may determine roughly the round figure of the POWs. to be repatriated by both sides[.] Then both sides can proceed to check the lists of those POWs to be repatriated. We think that if we are going to do it in this way, the quest re POWs can be settled.

"Frankly speaking we do not feel satisfied with your attitude in the discussions because your side said that you would accept our principle to have it included in the Arm. Agreement but actually your side wants to have your principle applied in dealing with all the POWs. We cannot accept that.

"Speaking about figures, your side repeatedly indicated that your side is willing to solve a problem within the framework of our 21 March proposal.

However according to what you have indicated before, some figures more than 10,000 persons in the difference from the figure given by your proposal exists [*sic,* whole sentence]. How can we settle the problem in this way?["]

UNC: "We did not intend to mislead you in the statements we made on the utilization of the 21 Mar provision of principle. We meant we could subscribe to that principle so that it could be included in the principle in the Arm Agreement. provided we made factual adjustments to eliminate the probs. [problems] which we have in accepting it. Your side in fact lead us to believe that such adjustments could be made. Let us grant that we misunderstood your allusion to the adjustments which you meant would be acceptable.

"As to the actual figures we have been cautious in attempting to give you a figure because we do not have a realistic one. Rather than guess at a figure we felt it more nearly accurate to speak only in terms of "adjustments." Actually we do not know how many, or even in general terms of a percentage, of the 16,000 odd S.K. POWs. in our custody wish to go to your side or to settle in their home areas in S.K. Nor do we know how many civ. int. [civilian internees] wish to return to their homes in S.K., nor how many wish to go to your side. We have not polled these groups to determine their individual preferences. We do know that there are factions among them; that there are grps. [groups] who generally represent people favorable to your side & grps. favorable to our side.

"Wherever possible we have striven to separate general groups to prevent inter group strife, rioting & bloodshed. You have made statements charging us with stirring up such strife but actually our officials in the camps try in every possible way to prevent it. Actually, of course, in a group which may be in a compound predominantly favorable to your side, there will be some individually favorable to our side & vice versa. Compound leaders or POWs reps. [representatives] as they are called in the Geneva convention, are elected by the majority vote of the POWs in the compound.

"The same prob. is present with the compounds containing members of the CPV and KPA. We have not polled them & we have no idea how many of them would forcibly resist returning to your side. But we feel reasonably certain that there are some of these groups. who would forcibly resist repat. Therefore our side has been unwilling to hazard a guess as to the numerical figure to replace the one used in your 21 Mar proposal. The preparation of new lists and examination thereof fol'g their exchange would disclose the numbers.

- - - "We cannot accept the proposition that one side can do as it pleases while the other side must respect this base for determining whose people belongs [*sic*] to whom. Essentially your side contends we should forget entirely about the 50,000 persons of our side whom your side has disposed of by unilateral action and that we should solve the problem now on the basis of the POWs now in custody. We cannot agree, particularly in view of the fact that many of our people are known to have been incorporated in your army. Essentially the stand of your side with respect to personnel of our side who went to your side must be based upon your assumption that all are violently opposed to returning to our side and that none would return to our side if given a chance; otherwise you would not deprive them of the right to return home. We doubt if your assumption is correct. However we admit that some of them might be violently opposed to repat. Your side has solved this prob by unilateral action. We seek to solve this problem now. The distinction between people now held & those ever held is not a valid one. When one side has accomplished an objective at one time it cannot then say to the other side, 'Oh no! we have different rules now. The old rule we used must now be abandoned.' ''

Tsai: ''I am not going to refute quests already reviewed many times. The present differences between both sides now are as follows:

''First, both sides have not reached a contingent agreement with respect to this principle although your side said that you were willing to settle the quest. within the framework of this principle.

''The next is the quest. of how to make the adjustments under this principle. With respect to this quest, our side proposed our position of making adjustments on Mar 27. Our position is stated in the understanding submitted on the 27th. If both sides can reach a tentative agreement under this principle & the understandings, we may then first determine in general the number of POWs to be repat. by both sides, and then specifically check the lists of POWs, so that the numbers close to the figures given in the principle might be reached [sentence emphasized in text by a bold check mark in the margin]. Your side wants our side to accept your proposition completely. Such a proposition of your side cannot possibly be realized in any respect.

''Speaking about figures given in the provision of principle in our Mar 21 proposal, we consider that the figures given in that provision are in general accurate. Very obviously those among the 16,000 captured personnel of our side who originally resided in your area and desired to return to their homes in your area would not be more than those of the 44,000 persons of our side who desire to return to our side. The 44,000 figure is about 3 times that of 16,000. Of course after the specific checking of the lists, *there might be small discrepancies between the figures*. However if those newly added POWs are added to the final figure, the figure can possibly be more than the figure given in the principle.

''With respect to your instigation or coercion of our captured personnel to resist repat. we have warned you several times that to allow the brigands from Taiwan to continue such instigations in your POW camps would inevitably involve a 3rd party, which has nothing to do with the present Korean war, into the question concerned. This would complicate the quest and we do not wish that such consequences would occur. However in the conference your side insists on our acceptance of your principle & proposition, yet in the POW camps allows these people to do such instigations freely[.] Therefore, the only conclusions we can draw from these facts is that your side intends to retain large nos of the captured personnel of our side.

"We propose a recess until tomorrow because of our feeling that from your statement we do not see that your side is attempting to settle the quests speedily[.]"

Comment: Hickman will continue along present lines tomorrow possibly submitting a proposed revision of principle of 21 Mar and associated understandings if atmosphere is favorable.

Underlined portion may possibly be an indication of a willingness to accept moderate adjustments affecting the 116,000 POWs.

It might help Commies to accept current UNC negotiatory effort if all Taiwanese were removed completely from the general are[a] and from all contact with UNC POW camps and if UNC staff offs. could so inform the Commies soonest in executive session.

Todays meeting gives some slight encouragement to the view that the Commies are sincere in their efforts to settle Item 4.

Apr. 1 (Tues): In reply to our msg of Mar 30 Muccio gave fol'g opinion re. use of Chosun [*sic*] vs Han Kuk in Korean copies of arm. [armistice] agreement. "On basis previous experience believe ROK would object strenuously to exclusive use of Chosun. ROK extremely sensitive in this point: At time formation of republic, national assembly, voted overwhelmingly to adopt name Tac Hun Min Kuk, rejected Chosun as identified with periods of foreign domination while Leftists here cling to term Chosun. In setting up N.K. regime Commies incorporated term Chosun in title Democratic Peoples Republic, Chosun Inmin King Hwa.

Believe Commie insistence on term may be motivated by thought it's [*sic*] exclusive use in agreement might be interpreted, in propaganda, at least, as implying legitimacy of Democratic Peoples Republic Korea while denying legitimacy of ROK. Recommend retention both terms in text if feasible."

Sent CinCUNC a msg (HNC 1109) giving our study of our negotiatory situation and recommending that I be allowed to introduce a package or integrated proposal, at a time deemed propitious by me, which would include (a) Deletion of airfield restrs [restrictions] from Arm. Agreement; (b) Deletion of USSR and Norway from the list of Neutral Nations; (c) Agreement on all for all exchange of POWs based on lists of POWs actually in custody of each side at time arm is signed. Item (c) presupposes that UNC lists will be revised to exclude all POWs and civ [civilian] internees of ROK residence who do not desire to go to the other side and all other POWs who violently resist returning to the enemy and that such personnel will be assigned a status other than that of POW prior to the signing of the armistice.

My msg to R also proposed a dispatch to the JCS requesting approval of the action outlined "as a matter of urgency."

#3. In staff meeting on Item 3 UNC said that it did not consider that sub-delegate meeting was appropriate in view of fact that staff officers had not completed their work on substantive & technical matters. However UNC agreed to sub dels meeting to be held at 031100 I. Commies said they too regretted the existence of major issue (Neutral Nations) but since the staff offs. had been unable to resolve the issue they could find no alternatives but to refer the matter to the sub-delegates. Commies stated they would relay UNC suggestion of time of sub-delegates meeting to their senior delegate.

Regarding usage of words Han Kuk & Chosun, UNC maintained Commie stand is unilateral and unacceptable. UNC proposal accommodates the views of both sides. Commies said that this was merely a technical matter, however since the word Chosun is appropriate and its interpretation free of ulterior motives and possibility of misunderstanding, no other word could be considered. UNC stated that both words (Chosun & Han Kuk) were appropriate and must be used in arm document for legality reasons.

UNC stated both Commie methods of solution of Neutral Nations problem involve Soviet Union, and thus violate the agreed principles and are both unacceptable. UNC asked Commies again carefully analyze the problem and consider the UNC solution. Discussion on problem of Neutral Nations did not make any progress.

Commies produced map showing agreed area of Han River estuary to be under the supervision of the Milt [military] Arm Agreement.

#4. Commies began Staff meeting on Item 4 by accusing UNC of vagueness and not being factual. Said: "Your side is even unwilling to express your opinion about a round figure (no [number] of POWs to be repatriated). Such an attitude is not only consistent with repeated statements made by your side but also is preventing our discussion from going further."

UNC: "We have prepared what amounts to a revision to some extent of your 21 Mar proposal. Together with two understandings explaining the provision of principle it sets forth a practical & realistic way to settle Agenda Item 4. It utilizes the principle expressed in your 21 Mar proposal. It utilizes the system of checking lists. It leaves in abeyance for the time being the quest [question] of definite numbers.

"On the quest of numbers, the exact numbers would of course be indicated ultimately by the lists, which lists would need to be acceptable to both sides. As I indicated yesterday, our side has been reluctant to attempt to secure a poll or census of the people in our custody in order to make even rough estimates of the numbers involved in the various categories. We indicated at the beginning of our executive sessions that 132,000 failed to take into consideration all pertinent factors, and, therefore was likely to be too high. We indicated that possibly 116,000 would more nearly indicate the magnitude of the exchange but that we could not say that this number would reflect all considerations. In short, we did not want to mislead you or ourselves in attempting to guess at a figure, the development of which would require several days.

"The proposed revision reads as follows: 'The KPA and the CPV on the one hand, and the UNC on the other shall release all POWs. held in custody at the time the Arm Agreement is signed and becomes effective. The release & repat [repatriation] of such POWs shall be effected on the basis of lists which shall be checked by and be mutually acceptable to both sides prior to the signing of the armistice agreement. The definition of repatriation would follow.

"This proposed revision of your revision of principle could with perhaps a change or two in tense of verbs be made suitable for inclusion as a para. [paragraph] in the Arm. Agreement.

"At the same time I should like to present to our [sic] side the fol'g understandings for consideration in connection with our proposed revision and with the preparation of the revised lists mentioned therein.

"First, all POWs and civ internees held by either side whose residence on 25 June '50 was in the area now under the control of the detaining side shall be repatriated with the exception of those who desire to remain in the area of their original residence.

"Second, all other POWs held by either side shall be repatriated except that those who could not be repatriated without the application of force shall be released by the detaining side and resettled in so far as practicable in a location of their own choosing where they can lead a peaceful life.['']

Commies noted the revised provision & understandings & "found nothing new in them." Same as UNC has been saying. "At first your side was willing to obtain a round figure & then check the lists. Now you indicate that such round figure should be omitted and your side was not willing to indicate any clear and definite round figures. Therefore we consider it difficult to consider and study your proposal. Furthermore, when we are aware of your activities in your POW camps, we cannot but feel that your attitude toward this quest is still insincere."

UNC: "It is of course true that our proposed revision omits a figure for the reasons that I indicated yesterday and this morning. I agree that an approx round figure would make the revision more capable of complete assessment and appraisal at this time, but that deficiency of complete appraisal would be supplied from the numbers furnished in the revised lists. I consider that it might be possible to agree at an earlier date if we were able to supply a round figure, inasmuch as agreement under our revised principle would be contingent upon the acceptability of the revised lists—the preparation of which, so far as our side is concerned would require several days."

Commies: "Frankly the provision & understandings proposed by your side this am have a diff [difference] in principle with what was proposed by our side and also has a numerical difference with what was proposed by our side. Your side even entirely omitted the round figure given in our proposition. Your side repeatedly states that your side is willing to settle the quests under the framework of our proposal. Now where is our framework?''

UNC: "It includes your statement of principle of releasing all POWs in custody at the time of the signing of the armistice. That is the basic part of the framework of your provision. It also provides, as did you for the checking of the lists. By making the checking of the lists and the acceptance of the lists by both sides a part of the plan there is the capability of supplying the figures, if such be desired, before the Arm Agreement is signed. We omitted the round figures because as I indicated we do not know what those round figures are today.

"In short our proposed revision includes all the elements actually or potentially of your 21 Mar proposal except that it postpones a final figure, but makes such figure unnecessary at the present time because of the requirement for acceptance of the revised lists.''

Commies: "Your side has to take these points into your consideration. Is there anything new in your proposal, which so far I have not discovered, of course I will make a study of it[.]''

Comment: Commies interest in round figure is apparent. It may not be possible to proceed with UNC plan without some figure. This may develop further tomorrow. One step which could be taken now, and is recommended in[is] screening of civilian internees and if practicable the 16,000 ROK POWs.

Apr. 2 (Wed): In staff meeting on Item 3 UNC returned Commie version of maps showing ports of entry in the rear and area of Han River Estuary under supervision of Milt [military] Arm [armistice] Agreement. These maps agree with UNC version except for minor technical matters which interpreters settled after today's meeting.

UNC reaffirmed its insistence on usage of both Han Kuk and Chosen in Korean version of Milt Arm Agreement[,] said that it is not a quest. [question] for argument & debate, Han Kuk is the legal name used by our side and must be included. Commies continued to argue that until recently UNC continually used Chosen in official papers and conversations and thus recent insistence on inclusion of Han Kuk is not understandable. UNC made it clear that it would insist upon use of both terms since they were legally adopted items of both sides.

UNC reiterated firm stand on Neutral Nations and informed Commies that UNC position will not change either in sub del meetings or in plenary session. Commies replied their stand had been made clear, but did not press the discussion further.

Commies concurred in meeting of sub del meeting to be held at 1100 3 Apr.

#4. In staff meeting on Item 4, fol'g a general exchange Commies introduced a new proposal in the fol'g statement:

["]Just as I pointed out yesterday and this am, there exists a great difference between the draft principle of our side and that of your side, as well as between the principle of adjustment put forth by the two sides respectively. **We maintain that with all factors taken into consideration, the number of POWs whom your side should repatriate to our side should not be far from the figure of 132,000.**

"We also hold that only in this way can it be consistent to your repeated claims that a solution will be sought within the framework of the proposal of 21 Mar of our side[.]

["]In connection with the prin [principle] of adjustment, I must also point out that among the POWs in the custody of either side there exists a fundamental diff. [difference] between the non-Koreans and those Koreans who originally resided in the area of the other side on the one hand, and the other Koreans who orginally resided in the area of the retaining side on the other hand.

"The principles of our side in dealing with both these categories of POWs are well known to your side, and we completely cannot agree with the 2nd item of the understandings submitted by your side.

"Now, both sides have already submitted their draft principles and understandings and a great difference has been found between what have been submitted respectively by the two sides. We think that if we continue to spend our time on argument over the principles and understandings themselves, we may not be able to get any results speedily, but viewed from another angle, the contents of the principles and understandings will necessarily be reflected in the specific lists which must be agreed upon by both sides before they become valid. **Therefore, in the interest of progress in these conferences, we would rather recommend that instead of spending time on argument over the principles, we may as well be realistic and enter immediately into the work of checking the lists, and that discussions of principle be resumed after the lists have been checked.** We think that such a procedure will be more beneficial to the progress of the conference and to an early solution of the prob [problem].

"Of course, when both sides are preparing the lists, it is not necessary to wait until the preparation of the lists are completed, then resume the discussions[.] We consider that when both sides are able to present a round figure, discussions may be held first. If you agree to this proposal, we may now recess until the time when either side has completed its preparation and notified the other side thru liaison offs [officers] and then we will determine the time for the resuming of conference."

UNC preliminarily agreed to this procedure but stated that it would study Commie statement & reply tomorrow[.]

I then informed R by dispatch that we intended tomorrow to agree to Commie proposal as set forth above. I also strongly rec. [recommended] screening of all POWs and CI's be initiated forthwith. Basic criteria for those not to be repatriated are:

a. Civ int. [civilian internees] & POWs of ROK residence "prefer to be repatriated to area of their homes."

b. All other POWs; "violently oppose repat [repatriation] and could not be repatriated without the application of physical force."

My msg went on to say: "Commie acceptance of an exchange based solely upon the content of revised lists will be affected by the numbers of each category of POWs to be returned. *This is particularly true of Chinese*; accordingly, recommend use of min. [minimum] standards in screening process.

"Commie reps [representatives] have repeatedly stated that all POWs will upon repat be permitted to return to their homes & resume a peaceful life. Further they have stated that personnel marked with anti Commie tattoos will not be discriminated against on these grounds[.]"

R answered above in personal msg to me as follows: "Desire you continue staff officer sessions without recessing and without commitment to Commie proposals, pending further development of discussions. Will discuss subject with you tomorrow at CinCUNC (advance)[.]

Referring to an article in News Week [*sic*] (Mar 31 issue) entitled "Steps Washington is Planning To Achieve a Truce in Korea." I sent a msg to R ["HNC 1113" is crossed out in text] pointing out strongly the harmful effect the article would have on the truce negotiations. CinCFe in turn sent a strongly worded despatch ["CX66304" is crossed out in text] on the subject to the JCS pointing out the impairment to prestige and personal position which the UNC Del will suffer as a result of the last para of this art [article]. R also recommended "that the US Govt without delay issue an official denial or discredit the official concerned. In either case I suggest a U.S. Governmental expression of confidence in the integrity & ability of our negotiators be issued earliest."

On the 4th the fol'g msg was received from the Pres [President] of USA: "I want you to know that I view with grave concern the breach of security referred to in your ["CX66304" crossed out in text]. The art. was of course not based on an authorized release & I have directed that every effort be made to discover source.

["]At press conf. [conference] this pm I will issue statement to effect that I & responsible offs. of Govt have complete & unequivocal confidence in integrity & competence of our negotiators at Pan Mun Jom."

The offending article appears below. [See reproduction of original diary, p. 348.]

[At the top of the diary page on which the April 3 entry begins there appears the note "798 & 799 sent to Kinney," a reference to the fact that the pages describing Joy's reaction to the Newsweek article were shown to Col. Andrew J. Kinney.]

Apr. 3 (Thurs): Sub-Del meeting on Item 3.

UNC announced that Maj Gen Harrison & Major Gen Turner would represent the UNC[.]

————————THE KOREAN WAR————————

Mar 31 Issue of News Week.

Steps Washington Is Planning
To Achieve a Truce in Korea

Peace may be closer than you think. Despite the surface gloom in Korea, at top-level interdepartmental conferences in Washington discussions were under way on measures that conceivably could produce a Korean truce with startling suddenness. The following authoritative report gives as much as can be revealed at this time on what is taking place at these secret meetings:

1—A decision has been made to abandon opposition to the Soviet Union's serving as one of the "neutral" powers supervising the armistice. Unless developments in Korea cause this decision to be reviewed, the United States is ready to propose that the supervising governments be appointed by both sides without respect to neutrality, nationality, or the other side's approval. In sending instructions to make such a proposal to Gen. Matthew B. Ridgway, the timing is to be left to the U.N. commander's discretion.

2—The possibility of making a direct appeal to Moscow to break the deadlock is under discussion although no decision has yet been reached. The advocates of a direct appeal say that, since the Russians started the armistice talks, it is only logical to ask them point-blank whether or not they intend to bring them to a successful conclusion. A strong hope exists in Washington that the Russians may be eager for a Korean truce when the Japanese peace treaty comes into force. Then Japan will again become a sovereign state. Therefore any nation conducting military operations against China from Japan will become an "ally" of Japan within the meaning of the Sino-Soviet treaty of mutual assistance. Russia is assumed to be anxious to avoid a full-scale war in the Far East. Accordingly it is expected to urge the Chinese to liquidate the Korean adventure and thus remove a pretext for invoking the mutual-assistance treaty.

3—A possible compromise on the prisoner-of-war issue has been discussed. Under it, the United Nations would agree in writing that all POW's listed by either side would be exchanged. But—the U.N. also would make an oral reservation that this exchange is to be voluntary and that no POW's are to be repatriated against their will. The written agreement, under such a compromise, would save the Reds' face. The oral reservation could even be kept secret. This week the POW talks at Panmunjom were put on a confidential basis in order to provide more leeway for working out a face-saving compromise. **March 31, 1952**

4—Some criticism has been voiced by American and other U.N. officials regarding the competence of the U.N. truce team at Panmunjom. The team may possibly be strengthened by the addition of some professional negotiators. The chief U.N. negotiator, Vice Admiral C. Turner Joy, is scheduled to come home anyway, sometime during the coming summer, to become superintendent of the Naval Academy at Annapolis.

note my from President Truman on reverse side.

Commies stated the Staff Offs had solved the major portion of the paras & sub paras with the problem of nomination of Neutral Nations still remaining. Further proposed that the tech [technical] quests [questions] of terminology be left for settlement by interpreters at later time and remarked that this settlement should not prove difficult.

Commies then reviewed the proceedings leading up to nomination of Neutral Nations and reiterated their past arguments against UNC stand on non acceptability of USSR. Commies recommended UNC seriously consider the two proposals made by Commies re settlement of the quest of Neutral Nations. UNC recessed 15 mins.

After recess UNC stated that the major prob. [problem] on airfield restrs [restrictions] also remains unsolved, and that it is UNC unalterable stand to insist on such restrs. Constr [construction] & rehab [rehabilitation] of airfields constitute an increase of milt [military] air capabilities of both sides to which UNC is firmly opposed. In deference to Commie views UNC has already proposed a limited air field program for facilitation of civil air activities only. UNC stated that USSR would never be acceptable as a Neutral Nation, that agreed principle clearly provides that nominee must be acceptable to both sides. UNC recommended acceptance of UNC 4 nation supervisory commission without delay.

Commies said air field prob. no longer existed since both sides had long ago agreed not to introduce milt aircraft into Korea, hence inconceivable there would be any increase in air strength during arm [armistice]. Constr of facilities is entirely a matter of int. [internal] affairs. When all items of agenda are so close to solution, attempt of UNC to interfere in internal affairs is a deliberate attempt to slow progress of negots [negotiations]. Regarding Neutral Nations Commies said their proposals clear.

UNC repeated previous stand re air fields & Neutral Nations. Said arguments of both sides had been exhausted, explored and repeated many times. What is needed is not further debate but progress. Commies then requested 15 min recess.

After recess Commies replied that interference with int affairs absolutely unacceptable and that Commie stand on Neutral Nations is already clear. If progress rather than debate is desired UNC should adopt Commie proposals on both matters.

Comment: Both sides were sparring today.

At 1530 Ridgway visited the camp with Van Fleet, Dodd (C.G. at Koje Do) Young (CG 2nd Log Com) and Milburn for the purpose of discussing the advisability and practicability of screening and segregating all POWs who were violently opposed to forced repatriation. We first held an Item 4 conference in which Hickman, Libby and I explained why we thought it necessary to proceed immediately to accomplish this screening. We pointed out that we had explored the solution to Item 4 as far as possible and that it would be impossible to make further progress unless our proposal could be accompanied by a round figure. Libby said he thought we could come to an agreement with the Commies if we could give them back about 110,000 people. Dodd estimated that only about ½ of the total no [number] of POWs plus civ [civilian] internees would want to return to the other side without being forced. That meant only about 85,000 persons which in my opinion the Commies would never buy[.]

Upon completion of the Item 4 conf [conference], which resulted in the decision that we would go ahead with the screening, Dodd explained his plan for accomplishing the screening. One plan consisted of broadcasting a tough statement to the POWs over the loud speaker and then, 24 hrs later simply taking a poll to determine the prisoners wishes as to repatriation. It was finally decided that a further screening would be conducted of the POWs who did not want to return in order to determine more definitely whether they were violently opposed to repatriation[.] Each POW in this category would be questioned for 10 minutes. Dodd estimated it would take 7 days approx to complete the entire screening process.

After supper we held another conference to determine what course of action should should [sic] be pursued from now on. As a result a despatch was framed to the JCS. which in essence was as follows (see HNC 1118)[.]

Part I. Request immed [immediate] authority to go ahead with the screening & segregation of POWs to determine how many would not be repatriated except by force. Dispatch pointed out that "discussions with Commies on POW question have reached the point where we are convinced that no further progress is possible unless & until we can give them a reasonably accurate estimate of how many POWs would be returned to them under our proposal."

Part II outlined our proposed course of action from now on. Briefly this is as follows:

(a). Present our figure of POWs to be repatriated to the enemy & receive their corresponding figure. The UNC revised list will exclude (a) POWs & civ internees of ROK residence who do not desire to go to the other side & (b) other POWs whose repatriation would require the application of force. The excluded personnel will previously have been assigned a status other than POW. The UNC will insist on the enemy list being substantially the 11,559 UNC POWs previously submitted.

b. Seek agreement on the figure in (a) above. If successful we would have disposed of Item 4 of the agenda, and would then be in a position to trade air field restrs. for withdrawal of the USSR issue thus completing the armistice.

c. If unsuccessful, present a package proposal including the fol'g points:

(1) Deletion of airfield restrs from the arm agreement.

(2) Withdrawal of USSR & Norway from the lists of nominees for the NNSC, thus establishing a four nation Neutral Commission composed of Sweden, Switzerland Poland & Czechoslovakia.

(3) Agreement upon all for all exchange of POWs based on revised lists.

Msg then went on to say: "This course of action requires that at the time the UNC Del. presents the above proposal, it inform the Commies that the proposal must be accepted or rejected in toto; that debate on these subjects is unnecessary since all have been exhaustively explored by both sides and that therefore UNC will not debate them further. The Del will represent its proposal as an equitable compromise solution which is the final stand of the UNC on the unresolved issues. The UNC Del will, of course, make plain its willingness to continue meeting with the enemy del. for the purpose of discussing non-substantive changes in its proposal and will avoid any appearance of terminating negots. Thus if the enemy breaks off negots rather than accept the UNC proposal, the break off will involve enemy rejection of a patently fair solution & will conform with your desire that such a break be over a multiplicity of issues[.]"

In HNC 1120 we followed the above msg by the fol'g to the JCS. "The UNC Del sense that recent developments in the arm negots indicate that with prompt & vigorous action on our part the chances of early agreement are favorable. HNC 1118 was intended to reflect this feeling of prudent optimism, urgency & the need for decisive action."

The JCS approved Part I of HNC 1118 & also Part II with exception that they urged consideration of alternative posit [position] on SU as a member of supervisory comm. [commission] if "neutral" designation is eliminated and US is also member. Not considered concession to Commie position on this point.

Apr. 4 (Fri): Commies began Sub Del meeting on Item 3 by saying: "Our side has fully & clearly explained our stand on the question of nomination of neutral nations and the two reasonable solutions proposed by our side.

"With regard to the demand once again raised by your side for the so called restr [restriction] of airfield facilities in Korea, our side has many times pointed out that such a demand for interfering in our internal affairs is what our side absolutely cannot accept. Since both sides have already agreed not to introduce into Korea any reinforcing milt [military] forces. including combat aircraft during the period of the arm. [armistice] it cannot be conceived how there could be any increase of milt. strength and even less could this be used as an excuse for continued insistence on the demand to interfere in our internal affairs which renders it impossible for the conference to make any progress.

"Your side stated yesterday and I quote, [']What is needed now is not further debate but further progress.' To this we fully concur. *In order to make progress in these conferences our side considers that your side withdraw the demand to interfere in our internal affairs."*

UNC: "Since you have apparently nothing new to offer, I wonder why you suggested we have the sub del meeting.["]

Commies: "We have stated clearly yesterday in our first statement on the resumption of the sub dels meeting that the quests [questions] which the staff offs. [officers] have not been able to settle were referred to the sub-committee for settlement.

"Regarding the stand of our side on those quests. and our proposed solutions, we have made clear explanations and there is no need to repeat them.

"As for the demand of your side which you have raised once again and the so called restr of airfield facilities in Korea our side considers that it ceased to exist long ago. We have explained this point very clearly in our statement yesterday and also our stand in this regard in my statement this am."

UNC: "We are aware that our position in these matters is fully understood by both sides.

"Since neither side has apparently anything new to say, I suggest we recess until tomorrow at the usual time."

Commies: *"We recommend that you study our statement this am.* and I agree to recess."

Comment: Considered likely that todays meeting contained veiled proposal for concessions between airfield restrs and inclusion of USSR on NNSC. UNC Del intends to continue along present lines on 5 Apr.

#4. In executive session of staff meeting on item 4, UNC began by saying: "Our side agrees to begin the preparation of revised lists in accord with your proposal of 2 April. We will notify you thru liaison officers when we have a round figure. If your side is then ready, we can proceed to further discussions in executive session in accord with your suggestion. We assume that your side is willing to maintain the executive session concept to our activities until further notice. If this assumption be correct, it would assist in minimizing speculation if a statement were issued today. We plan to issue a statement substantially as follows:

"The staff offs of agenda Item 4 have agreed to recess until a time to be determined later thru liaison offs. in order for both sides to develop additional avenues for discussion of the remaining probs [problems]." Is there any objection to such a release? Obviously the newsmen are going to know that we are not meeting from day to day.

"One final point, on Mar 30, you made a statement which indicated that your side would, in effect, grant amnesty to all POWs held by our side who are repatriated to your side.

"We appreciate that as spokesman for your side you can bind your side with respect to its commitments to the UNC. There is somewhat of a hiatus in the situation once the individuals have returned to the control of your side. For example, a POW who has tattooed himself may be reluctant to trust himself to return to your side without some authoritative statement from your authorities that he would be accorded good treatment on being repatriated and that the tattoo for example will not be made a basis of disciplinary action against him. **It is possible that your side might wish to prepare some form of signed authoritative statement concerning this matter and might wish to transmit it to us thru liaison offs. in time for us to use it for what purpose it could serve in attempting to allay feelings of alarm among some of your captured personnel in our custody."**

Commies (after 30 min recess): "With respect to the quest of the recess for the preparation of the lists by both sides, I have no additional opinion other than what I suggested in the statement made the day before yesterday proposing that recess.

"Our side at present has not considered any change of the form of the staff offs meetings. With regard to your proposal in conn. [connection] with a general news release, our side agrees and prepares to make a similar news release.

"With respect to the captured personnel of our side before they are repatriated, our side has also been concerned with their health & safety. It is unthinkable that after they have been repatriated our side would not be concerned with their peaceful life and the security of their lives in our area.

"As to the activities of the captured personnel of our side when they are in your POW camps, some of the activities such as tattoos, have never been considered by our side as their own responsibility. Therefore, such activities of those people of our side would not affect at all their restoration to a peaceful life after they have returned to our side. Your side has suggested that our side could make a written statement about this quest. We will give consideration to your suggestion and will inform you of the results thru our liaison offs.

"I propose that we recess until both sides notify each other thru liaison offs. We will then determine the date of the resumption of the staff offs meeting.

"Does your side have any general estimate of the duration of the recess?"

UNC: "My comments concerning an authoritative statement which your side might wish to make was merely an effort on my part to attempt to find add [additional] means which might affect the round figure.

"I know you appreciate some of the probs with the population in our POW and civ [civilian] internee camps being what it is. My preliminary estimate of the duration of the recess would be one week[.] We of course will do our best to make it as short as possible."

Recessed 1201 indefinitely.

Comment: Delegation strongly urges strict adherence to news blackout agreement in all echelons. Speculation by press sure to be made concerning Item 4 recess, and info of screening at Koje do apt to leak out thru native channels. Nevertheless UNC Del has agreed to program of secrecy, and recommends strict adherence to this commitment.

Apr. 5 (Sat): Sub Del meeting Item 3. UNC stated Commie statement of yesterday does not offer any solution to remaining prob [problem]. UNC declared restr [restriction] on airfields is vital to a stable arm. [armistice] and pointed out that airfields are essential to air power. If Commies agree to restr on airfields it cannot be considered an interference in their internal affairs. With reference to Commie statement of yesterday pertaining to agreement of both sides not to "increase milt [military] forces, including combat aircraft during the arm," UNC stated that no agreement can be better than the intent to carry it out; by the insistence that UNC accept Soviet Russia as a representative on the NNSC, the Commies are violating an agreement by both sides.

Commies replied they found nothing new in UNC statement and pointed out their views on Neutral Nations and air field restriction issues have been clearly stated[.]

In reply to Commie quest [question] as to anything constructive to offer, UNC answered negatively and suggested recess until usual time tomorrow.

Meeting adjourned 1120 hours.

Gen Dodds plan for screening POWs and civ internees was received (see CG Eusak advance CX5264) which CinCUNC approved in his CX66471. He directed CG Eusak (adv) to begin operation SCATTER morning of Apr 8th.

Mar. 6 [April] (Sun): Sub Del meeting on Item 3 convened for 2 mins. Since neither side had anything new to offer UNC agreed to Commie suggestion to recess until usual time tomorrow.

Apr. 7 (Mon) until Apr. 14 (Mon): Since no progress was possible and no further negotiatory moves can be made pending final outcome of the screening process, I decided to return to Tokyo and hide out at Kawana for a few days of rest & relaxation. Left the camp at 0930 to take passage in my P2VZ from K-16. However the plane met with an accident upon landing, blowing out 2 tires, which necessitated taking a C-47 to Tokyo. Arrived Tokyo about 1615 and at Kawana about 2100. Returned to Tokyo from Kawana Fri pm the 11th. Libby accompanied us on our visit to Kawana and stayed at House 404 until we returned to Korea.

At 1000 Sat 12th held a conference with R and his staff to discuss progress of the POW screening, about which Briggs had kept me informed. I expressed my concern over the small number to be repatriated and stated emphatically that the POWs, particularly the Chinese, should be rescreened. But I was over-ruled just as emphatically. However, as a result of the conference CinCUNC sent C.G. Eusak a despatch (CX66816) directing him to develop, as a matter of urgency, plans to screen about 12,000 hospitalized POWs and CIs as well as approx 44,000 NKs, SKs and CIs who have either refused screening or are in compounds where the leaders refuse to allow screening. R also suggested that, in order to facilitate implementation of the plan, the POWs & CIs who are to remain in UN custody be moved as soon as practicable to the Pusan camp area.

That evening I interviewed at my house Lieuts Wu & May (our Chinese interpreters) whom Briggs had sent over to give me firsthand info on the screening of the Chinese POWs. Also present were Millburn & Libby. The picture Wu & May gave us was not pretty. It seems that the compounds with pro nationalist [pro Chinese Nationalist] leaders were completely dominated by those leaders, to such an extent that the results of the screening were by no means indicative of the POWs real choice. Wu & May believed that removal of the leaders, coupled with a period of indoctrination of the POWs, would bring the percentage in those pro nationalist dominated compounds of those wishing to return to the enemy up from 15 to 85%. Wu & May gave as an example a labor battalion compound which was not so dominated. In this compound of 1500 POWs 85% elected to be repatriated. Wu & May also told of a mock screening which had taken place in compound 92 prior to the regular screening. The leaders had asked those who wished to return to step forward. Those doing so were either beaten black & blue or killed. Wu & May also said their experience watching Chinese POWs at the polls convinced them that the majority of the POWs were too terrified to frankly express their real choice. All they could say in answer to the questions was "Taiwan" repeated over & over again. They were convinced that many more would be anxious to return to their own authorities if given a real chance to express their preference—an opportunity not influenced by the terrifying dominance of their pro nationalist leaders. In their opinion however a 6 week indoctrination period would be required to wean them over to a point where they would feel free of the terror that presently gripped them.

As a result of this conference with Wu & May I asked Millburn to arrange another conference with R the fol'g am. At this conference Wu & May again told their story which convinced R enough for him to direct Millburn & Bryan to proceed to Korea and arrange with Van Fleet for a rescreening incident to the move [from Koje-Do] of the POWs (who are not to be repatriated) to the mainland. During the rescreening process all compound leaders are to be removed and the POWs placed in compounds of not more than 1000 persons each. Conference arranged at 0830 tomorrow to discuss results of Millburn's & Bryan's session with Van Fleet. Murray also went along with them to represent the delegation.

At conference the fol'g day, Mon, it was apparent than [*sic*] Van Fleet had convinced Millburn & Bryan that it was futile to attempt a rescreening at this time chiefly because of the bloodshed that would ensue. **Lack of facilities and MPs also a factor. Consequently R gave the decision that we would go ahead with discussions in Item 4 reporting to Commies that approx 70,000 POWs will be repatriated. He would withhold decision to rescreen Chinese which we had particularly urged since these nationals were the nub of the question in our opinion.** Bryan also said Van Fleet was of opinion it would take 2—3 weeks to build enough additional compounds that would permit splitting up the POWs into groups of 1000. R said 2 weeks was much too long to wait. Van Fleet & Dodd also of opinion that dominating influences in compounds were people who could not be identified and were not necessarily the compound leaders. I made the remark that I considered it essential to regain control of the compounds. At present it would appear the POWs are in control. UN personnel must first obtain permission from the POWs before entering some of the pro-Communist compounds. An intolerable situation.

In 7 pro-Commie compounds comprising a total of 37,872 POWs. screening was refused by the leaders who claimed that the process violated the Geneva convention. Anyway, said they, everyone in the compounds desires to return to NK so screening is unnecessary. What to do about this situation is a problem. since attempt to use force would result in much bloodshed.

Dodd feels strongly that screening is accurate within 10%. Results to date (Apr 13th) as follows:

	NKs	CCF	SKs	CIs	Total
Total pop [population]	95,474	20,786	16,000	37,740	170,000
Screened	51,491	17,593	14,616	21,303	105,003
To go	21,102	3,075	3,559	2,628	30,746
To stay	30,389	14,126	11,057	18,675	74,247
Not yet screened	*44,345	3,193	1,384	18,015	

*Includes 37,872 Commies who refuse to be screened.

It will thus be seen that only 70,000 to 75,000 will elect to return to the Commies. without being forced. An impossible figure as I told R.

Upon completion of the conference I, with others of the delegation returned to Korea, leaving Haneda in the Constellation at 1100 and arriving back at the camp at 1530.

Item 3. (Apr 7−14). No progress made and very little of substance discussed. **On Apr 9th Commies said: "It was exactly because your side continued to insist on the unreasonable demand for restrs** [restrictions] **on airfield facilities and refused to discuss and settle this quest** [question] **in the staff meetings that our side recommended the resumption of the sub-committee meetings** *so that this so-called question of restriction on airfield facilities could be settled together with the question of the nomination of neutral nations."*

Comment: It is the feeling of the Del. that the Commies are attempting to settle the remaining issues in Item 3 entirely separate and apart from Item 4. By insisting on holding the airfield & neutral nations problems together, it continues to appear as, though they are trying to negotiate a deal whereby the USSR will be dropped in exchange for lifting restrs on airfields[.]

Other than above nothing of interest transpired in Item 3 meetings. Harrison has the definite feeling that the enemy like us is waiting to see how the negots [negotiations] in Item 4 turn out before making another move.

On 13th Commies asked whether we were ready to resume Item 4 staff off. meetings. Their side now fully prepared.

Apr. 14 (Mon): Upon return to camp I held a conference to draw up plans for meeting Commies again. As a result it was decided that we should not meet with them until the 16th and in the meantime acquaint CinCUNC with our planned procedure. Accordingly the fol'g msg was sent to R. (see HNC 1147)

"1. Pursuant to decisions reached in Tokyo 14 Apr. intend to inform Commies in executive session of staff offs on 16 Apr that (a) screening has not yet been fully completed; (b) an estimated 70,000 will not forcibly resist repat. [repatriation]; (c) completion of screening process will require approx 2 more weeks; and (d) estimates are that between 4 & 5,000 additional returnees will result from completion of the screening process.

"2 As I indicated at your conference we believe that Commie reaction to the very low figure of POW to be repatriated will be extremely unfavorable. We therefore deem it essential that we be fully prepared to move forward rapidly toward submission of final package proposal. Any appreciable delay between successive steps beyond that necessary to obtain definite indication of Commies reaction to each step would in our opinion react most unfavorably, since it would serve merely to solidify their opposition and perhaps force them to take positions from which they could not recede.

3. We further are convinced that the next figure (after the initial 70,000) must be as valid as it is humanly possible to make it, and that it must not thereafter be substantially changed. If they get the impression that we might be able to increase the number to be returned to them by further refinements in the screening process, they can be expected to hold out indefinitely. Furthermore, final agreement will be predicated upon checking of POW lists, the presentation of which will at best take some appreciable time.

4. The Del considers that the decision outlined in para 4 of CX 66900 is a wise one, (Note: This directs that, concurrently with the relocation of the POWs who are to stay, POWs & CIs who have elected to remain in UNC custody be given another opportunity to return to Commie control) since it will ultimately strengthen the position of the UNC in the eyes of the world by insuring that it has in fact acted in good faith with respect to the CPV POW.

5. We therefore consider it of the utmost importance that the screening process outlined in CX 66900 be expedited all possible; that the preparation of the final rosters be started forthwith with a view to their earliest possible completion; and that a decision from Wash [Washington] on the matter referred to in C 66891 be sought as a matter of urgency (this has to do with the protective custody concept whereby disposition of POWs violently opposing repat is determined by

the political conf [conference]). Should a reply there to not be forthcoming within a matter of a few days, it may in our opinion be necessary to proceed to submit the final package proposal without the protective custody alternative having been submitted to or considered by the Commies. This would of course mean that it could not later be submitted to them, since any substantive change in the package proposal would destroy its effect and reopen the whole field of negotiations[.]

6. In summary, we believe that the submission of the initial POW figure tomorrow will in effect start a chain reaction which we must be prepared to counter swiftly & definitely with positive moves culminating in the submission of the package proposal, on which we are ready to stand or fall."

Sub Del on Item 3 met for less than one min. Neither side had anything to discuss.

Apr. 15 (Tues): Rec'd fol'g msg from R. (see C 66954):

1. "Postpone staff offs [officers] meeting on Item 4 until further instrs [instructions] from me. After further consideration I have determined that the introduction of a proposal to move any part of Item 4 negots [negotiations] to a political conf. [conference] is not desirable. It might reopen the entire scope of Item 5 and provide Commies with an opportunity for developing a series of unrelated political matters which could seriously compromise not only our negots but the entire US posit [position] on the Korean problem as well.

2. "Re para 1 HNC 1147. After securing JCS approval on our procedure as outlined in CX-66953. I desire that discussions be confined to the figure of 70,000 without any statement which would reveal that the screening program is incomplete or that an upward revision of the basic figure is probable. I concur with your analysis in para 3, HNC 1147, that the Commies would delay indefinitely if they thought that further screening would increase the number to be returned.

3. I would appreciate your views & recs. [recommendations] on a careful and coordinated plan for handling pub [public] relations aspects of this problem as soon as knowledge of screening and results thereof become public. I intend to submit our recs to the JCS on this subject as soon as possible."

CX-66953 to Deptar from CinCUNC is quoted herewith:

For JCS. Ref [reference] JCS 906314.

"1. Results Operation Scatter to date and best estimates of those not yet screened indicate that about 70,000 persons will be available for return to Communist control. Plans are now being formulated as a matter of urgency for relocation of non-repatriates from Koje Do and possible rescreening to determine those who have changed their opinions and desire to be included in the exchange. Further plans, also as a matter of urgency, include screening of non cooperative compounds after additional data has been obtained as a result of this relocation. This is necessary as a preliminary step for preparation of rosters listing those to be returned to Commie control. However firm conviction here that the 70,000 figure will not be materially changed[.]

"2. Request asp. [as soon as possible] authority to implement, at a time of my choosing, the folg planned procedure which with the possible exception of para e is believed to be in full accord with the spirit & letter of your instrs:

a. Reconvene at earliest opportunity staff off executive session.

b. Inform the Commies that as a result of screening it is anticipated that there are about 70,000 persons in UNC custody who will not require forced repat. [repatriation] to their side.

c. If their reaction to this large reduction from rosters initially exchanged 18 Dec '51 is unfavorable, every effort will be made to convince them that we have the max [maximum] possible no [number] of NKs and Chinese to return to their side.

d. In addition the UNC Del will agree that any NKs & Chinese who previously have declared their violent objection to repatriation and who reverse their decision would be returned to their control at any time until the exchange is completed.

e. If Commies continue to maintain opposition UNC will offer a bilateral proposition that will permit rescreening of those persons who have indicated violent opposition to repat by:

(1) Any international neutral body, such as but not confined to, ICRC, together with milt. [military] observers if desired, or

(2) Joint Red Cross teams with milt observers from each side if desired.

f. If Commie position still appears to be irrevocable, our del will propose a recess of staff offs exec [executive] session & will propose that discussions move to plenary sessions.

g. If accepted, introduce package proposal at plenary session as outlined in HNC 1118.

3. Ref para 3 your msg. Public relations aspects of this entire prob. [problem] are being carefully analyzed & our plans on this subject will be submitted to you as soon as pract [practicable].

JCS 906314 to CinCUNC is quoted below:

"Have read your rpt [report] and note large numbers of those who would forcibly resist repat. Request your views & recs. as to future procedure including necessity or desirability of further attempts to screen those compounds whose leaders refuse cooperation.

"2. Since large numbers opposing repat. may be expected stiffen Commie resistance to any acceptable agreement on POWs, request your views re our negotiating position when screening completed. Suggest consideration be given to proposing agreement on POW issue be reached on all for all exchange based on UNC determination of those willing accept repatriation, those opposing repat to be subject to rescreening after arm [armistice] enters into effect by any appropriate international neutral body such as but not confined to ICRC, together with observers from each side if desired. Any who as result such rescreening indicate willingness accept repat. would then be repatriated by UNC[.]

"3. Consider that most careful & coordinated plan required for handling pub. relations aspects of this problem as soon as knowledge of screening and results thereof become public. Request soonest your views and plans for meeting this[.]"

Apr. 16 (Wed): Item 4 team worked up fol'g msg to CinCUNC concerning C 66954 and CX 66953: (See HNC 1152).

"1 On the assumption that the procedures outlined in CX 66953 are directed prior to completing the initial screening of POWs, the delegation submits the fol'g observations on that dispatch for your consideration.

"2 a. As indicated in para 3 of HNC 1147 and concurred in by you in para 2 of C 66954, under the plan of CX 66953 an indefinite delay in the signing of the arm. [armistice] would result if Communists believe that further re-screening would increase the number to be returned. For this reason we feel that the formal and successive steps outlined in subpara 2(d) & 2(e) of CX 66953 should be avoided if possible. Subpara 2(d) may well be interpreted by the Commies as an indication of our recognition that the screening already completed was not truly effective and final; and subpara 2(e), if accepted by the Commies, will serve as a means whereby they can insist that screening go on indefinitely until such time as they decide that no more returnees can be obtained. We therefore strongly recommend proceeding directly to the package deal after carrying out steps 2(a) through (c) inclusive.

"b. However, if in executive session we are to offer the Commies an opportunity to verify our screening or to participate in a re-screening, the Del believes it preferable to make the Commies the proposal outlined in para 2 of JCS 906314, but further to predicate this offer upon their signing of the Arm. agreement and their prompt return of all our POW in their custody.

"3. With reference to para 2 of C 66954, Del feels strongly that it would be on much firmer ground in presenting the 70,000 figure if at the same time the Commies are informed that the initial screening was not yet completed. It is probable that Commies are aware that screening is incomplete, and they may actually have fairly accurate knowledge of the percentage of total prisoners thus far screened. For UNC to refrain from admitting incomplete screening, or give false impression that screening is complete, would place us in a precarious position and invite charges of dissembling which we could not refute. On the other hand, by informing Commie[s] that the screening was not complete we would lay the groundwork for any subsequent increase resulting from rescreening and from completion of initial screening, without the implication that the screening already accomplished was in any way unsatisfactory. This procedure would, furthermore, enable the UNC to set a definite terminal date for the screening process and at that time present the Commies with a firm and reasonably valid figure of returnees.

"4. We therefore respectfully request reconsideration of para 2 of C 66594 & authority to inform the Commies, when presenting the 70,000 figure, that the initial screening is not yet complete[.]''

See HNC 1151 for Del's views concerning plan for handling pub [public] relations of problem as soon as knowledge of screening and results thereof become public.

In his GX 5438 Van Fleet submitted his plan for rescreening POWs and CIs who have elected to remain in UNC custody (see CinCUNCs 66900 also). In his plan each screenee would have read to him the fol'g[—] "You are now to be shipped to a new camp. This is your final opportunity to return to control of authority representing CPV Army at the time POWs are exchanged. If you elect to return you will be removed to a new compound immediately where you will be protected and housed only with those who make the same decision. Do you wish to return?''

R finally approved Van Fleets plan after first proposing a tougher statement to the POWs (see CX 7002) which Van Fleet protested in his GX 540. R directed VF [Van Fleet] to follow the same principles in screening NK POWs to be moved from Koje Do. CI's need not be given specific opportunity to reverse their decision not to return to Commie control (see CinCUNCs CX 67032)[.]

As a result of 1st day's screening of hospital compound (non patients), 2,208 persons elected to return to Commie control while 1003 elected to remain in UNC custody.

Apr. 17 (Thurs): Sub Del meeting on Item 3 convened for approx 1 min. After both sides had indicated they had nothing new to discuss, Commies asked UNC to relay msg to Staff Offs [Officers] of Agenda Item 4 requesting expected date of resumption of Staff Offs meeting on Agenda Item 4. UNC agreed to relay this verbal msg.

Sent fol'g msg to CinCUNC (see HNC 1154)[—]

"Since strong potentiality exists that current estimates of final figure, following rescreening may be much too low and in view of vital importance of end figure to outcome of negots [negotiations], Del recommends that Item 4 staff offs. delay further meetings until completion of all screening and rescreening.

["]Commies apparent anxiety to resume Item 4 talks can in our view be capitalized on by waiting for firm final figure. It is felt that it would be salutary to keep them on the anxious seat for a reasonable period[.]''

CinCUNC rec'd fol'g msg from JCS (JCS 906539) which he passed to Del.

"Re your CX 66953 and CX 67005.

1. We note with approval that you are giving consideration to rescreening by UNC. We consider that this should be done, if practicable from your viewpoint

and time permits prior to submitting any revised figure to Communists. Such rescreening, if undertaken, should be done under the most stringent criteria designed to verify number of POWs who would actually forcibly oppose repatriation. However, if you consider it impracticable to rescreen POWs prior to submitting revised figure to Commies you are authorized to proceed without such rescreening.

"2. Proposal for neutral re-screening non-repatriates fol'g armistice probably as acceptable to Commies as proposal for neutral re-screening prior to arm [armistice]. View here is that in event Commies acceptance, screening fol'g arm. offers us many advantages. Proposal for screening proposed in para 2e CX 66953 prior to arm. would appear give Commies opportunities for further delaying entry into effect of arm.

"3. Therefore, suggest you give consideration amending para 2e, CX 66953 so as to make it clear that at least initial UNC Del proposal will be that any neutral re-screening non repatriates take place fol'g entry into effect of arm by either method mentioned therein. If you concur with foregoing suggestion you are authorized implement plan of procedure set forth para 2, CX 66953 with subpara e thereof appropriately amended. However, if there are clear advantages not apparent here to rescreening proposed in para 2e taking place prior to the arm. you are authorized to implement plan of procedure set forth para 2 your CX 66953. Planned procedure outlined your CX 67005 also approved for implementation at time you consider appropriate."

Comment: The above JCS despatch conforms to the Delegation's views.

Apr. 18 (Fri).: Yesterdays recapitulation of screening of patients in hospital compound resulted in total to return to Commie control—59[.] Total to remain—111. Screening started at 1513 and stopped at 1700.

Rec'd msg from CinCUNC (see CX 67066) directing us to:

a. Reconvene at earliest opportunity staff off. [officers] executive session.

b. Inform Commies that as a result of screening it is anticipated there are about 70,000 persons in UNC custody who will not require forced repat [repatriation] to their side.

c. If their reaction to this large reduction from rosters, initially exchanged 18 Dec, is unfavorable every effort will be made in such manner as you see fit to convince them we have encouraged the max [maximum] possible numbers of NKs & CCF to return to their side.

d. You have discretionary authority to introduce or to omit a proposal that the UNC Del. will agree that any NKs & Chinese who previously have declared their violent objection to repat. & who reverse their decision will be returned to Commie control at any time until the exchange is completed.

e. If Commies continue to maintain opposition, suggest you offer a bilateral proposal that will permit rescreening of those persons who have indicated violent opposition to repat, such screening to take place *after* the signing of the arm [armistice] agreement, and *after* the completion of the initial exchange of POWs by both sides. Rescreening will be done by:

(1) Any international neutral body, such as but not confined to, ICRC, together with milt [military] observers from each side, if desired, or,

(2) Joint Red Cross teams with milt observers from each side if desired.

f. Whether or not the rescreening proposed in para 1e above is introduced, you will notify me and await further instrs [instructions] when in your judgment, negots [negotiations] have reached a stage at which staff offs meetings should be suspended and discussions moved to plenary sessions.

CinCUNC went on to say: "Re para 4. HNC 1152 & HNC 1154. After careful consideration here, I feel that the optimum course for us to follow is to introduce the 70,000 figure without reference to the state of completion of our screening program, & to emphasize the fact that the 70,000 figure is a reliable estimate. The relocation of non-repatriates and the screening of those NK POWs who initially refuse to be screened will take about one month. This delay when balanced against unfavorable public reaction and growing impatience would not justify delay in negots. Despite initial results of the screening at the hospital compound, Pusan, an overall analysis of the results to be expected from screening those not yet screened, and the small no. [number] who might change their mind as a result of rescreening, indicates there will be little or no significant change in our estimate of 70,000.

"3. *[sic]* If after full consideration of the foregoing, there are in your opinion, overriding reasons for contrary courses of action report them without delay, awaiting further instrs."

In another msg (see CX 67067) CinCUNC advised the JCS that he had directed the Del to implement without delay the procedure outlined in para 2 CX 66953 as modified above.

He also explained, as he had to us, why he had decided to introduce the figure of 70,000 as a round number without screening being completed.

After consultation with others of the Del I then sent the fol'g msg (HNC 1157) to CinCUNC:

"1. In accord with instrs contained in CX 67066. Commie liaison off has been notified that UNC is prepared to resume meetings of staff offs. on Item 4 at 1100 on 19 Apr.

"2. In addition to the possible effect that the low round figure of 70,000 will have upon the attainment of an arm, the Del continues gravely concerned as to the possible effect that this low figure will have upon the percentage of our own personnel which the Commies may in retaliation attempt to retain in their custody.

"3. As pointed out in HNC 1147 it is believed here that the implementation of the procedure outlined in CX 67066 will have a chain reaction effect which will make it necessary within a few days thereafter to submit the package proposal at a plenary session. As I indicated during my recent visit to Tokyo I plan to make an opening statement along the general lines contained in the draft which I left with you. Modifications necessitated by subsequent developments will of course be made.''

R sent the fol'g reply (see C 67092) to my msg above: ''Your HNC 1157, para 2. I share your concern as to two possible effects you describe. I am unable however, in the light of the most thorough analysis by all interested parties, to see any reasonable prospect of any increase in the total figure which we could expect to result in any more favorable Commie reaction. Even assuming the increase was on the order of 10,000 I do not believe the overall effect would be materially different. Therefore, I am unable to perceive any way in which the possible retaliatory action which the Commies might take could be lessened. If you or the Del have any concrete views on these points, other than views already fully considered here, I would like them submitted as soon as possible this date.''

To the above I replied (see HNC 1159):

''1. We appreciate your C 67092 and realize fully that you have considered all views. The intent of para 2 HNC 1157 was to express our estimate of Communist reaction to the round figure which we will present to them. Since the Communists on 28 Mar expressed the view that non Korean POWs should be repatriated on a reciprocal basis, the Del. feels that if an all out re-screening effort conducted under the most stringent criteria resulted in a majority of the CPVs. indicating a desire for repat. the retaliatory action which the Commies might take against our POWs would be considerably lessened and the chances of attainment of an arm. enhanced[.]

''2. By informing the Commies tomorrow that the 70,000 is a firm figure, the Del in effect closes the door on the possibility of later submitting a larger figure.''

Sub Del on Item 3 met for 8 mins. UNC said: ''We relayed your msg (on Item 4)[.] As for Item 3 we have nothing to say. Your side asked for these meetings and since the beginning, seem curiously unable to say anything further; therefore there is no progress.'' In answer to their query on the matter, Commies were informed that they could expect a reply very soon on the resumption of discussions on Item 4.

Commies made fol'g statement on Item 3: ''You have referred to the question why these sub-committee meetings were convened. You also raised the so called reason for the lack of progress in these meetings. I am sure your side remembers fully well that we have already explained clearly why these meetings were recalled.

''Regarding the two remaining major issues on the 3rd item of the agenda, we have repeatedly and fully explained the position of our side and the two solutions for these questions. However, your side still insists upon your unreasonable demand and refuses to accept our fair & reasonable proposals, therefore preventing any progress in these meetings. It is therefore very clear that the responsibility for lack of progress in these meetings is on your side[.]''

Apr. 19 (Sat): Results of screening of Hospital Compound (Encl #10) from 1730 17 Apr until 1700 18 Apr.

Total to return to Commie control — 2,503

Total to remain [—] 624
includes 288 Chinese to go out of 296, & 1873 NKs out of 1965[.]

Referring to my HNC 1159 of yesterday R sent me fol'g personal msg (C-67126):
''1. I consider that the program which has been placed in effect for rescreening CCF POWs prior to their removal from Koje Do is as thorough as can be devised under the circumstances. Van Fleet has given me his personal assurance that he and his responsible officers will make every effort to retain only those who plainly indicate that they would forcibly resist return to Communist control. I have full confidence in all these senior commanders, whose integrity, judgment and devotion to duty have been exemplary.
''2. Re para 2 HNC 1159, as I have stated previously, I do not believe that the possibility of acceptance of any round number by the Communists would be enhanced by relatively minor changes in our 70,000 figure. However if the 70,000 is presented in the way of an estimate, without ref. [reference] to the detailed screening of Operation Scatter, it should leave sufficient leeway for any subsequent increases, which might occur. A careful presentation of the 70,000 estimate will probably produce as true a reaction of Commie intent as would any figure short of previously established totals of NK and Chinese POWs initially exchanged.
''3. Fully recognize your deep anxiety and personal interest consistently displayed in this problem. These feelings are fully shared by all of us. I once again express my appreciation for the splendid efforts which you have made thus far, and have every confidence in the ability of the Del to conduct the remainder of these exceedingly difficult negots [negotiations] with the same degree of excellence.''
Before the above msg was received I had sent R. the fol'g (HNC 1161):
''Fol'g yesterday's screening our figures show: 43,807 in Commie dominated compounds not yet screened. 35,526 to be repatriated 5,822 in hospital to be screened. Assuming the similar results from screening of remaining 5,822 in hospitals approx 4,300 will desire repat [repatriation]. This will give 83,633 to go of whom 43,807 are not yet screened. In view of previous low estimates of non returnees in this latter group. & prospective gains from rescreening of CPV and KPA do you still desire us to use 70,000 as firm estimate.''

After receiving R's 67126. I sent fol'g short msg: "Please disregard and cancel my 1161. Appreciate your desires and assure you we are carrying out your wishes wholeheartedly[.]"

Referring to HNC 1118 CinCUNC sent us fol'g msg (C 67156):

"1. In view of expected Communists objection to settlement of repat. issue on all for all exchange based on revised lists, study continuing here on possible negotiatory measures to reduce such objections. Would appreciate your comments on fol'g possible measures:

a. At an appropriate time in Item 4 executive session indicate strongly but short of an actual offer, that settlement of the POW issue on basis of UNC position would, in effect, mean rapid achievement of an arm. [armistice] agreement, as the UNC would then be willing to settle the remaining issues by trading UNC concession on airfield restriction for Commie agreement to a 4 nation supervisory commission.

2. This negotiatory step would:

a. Present advantageous aspect of Commie agreement to UNC posit [position] on POW issue.

b. Provide sounding board for future Commie reaction to package proposal.

c. In effect, constitute a pkg [package] proposal without the psychological disadvantage of of [sic] confronting the Commies with a defacto ultimatum.

3. The suggested action, above, would not constitute a departure from the course outlined in paras 1b & c, part II of HNC 1118 and CX 66953. It would be an additional step within the general framework, to be accomplished just prior to the final resort to a package proposal. It is considered that the UNC presentation in this regard could be so worded as to remain within the terms of reference of agenda Item 4 meetings and still indicate unmistakably UNC intentions. Request your comments[.]"

Item 3. Commies opened sub del meeting on Item 3 with reiteration of their position on Neutral Nations and airfield issues and stating that no progress is being made in sub committee meetings because of UNCs unreasonable demands on these issues. Commies then said: "In view of your indication that your side does not object to handing the question of nomination of neutral nations and the so called restr [restriction] on airfield facilities in Korea over to the staff offs. [officers] for discussion, our side now proposes that the staff offs meetings be resumed from Apr 20th so that the staff offs. may try anew to seek a settlement of all the remaining issues on the 3rd item of the agenda."

UNC agreed to Commie proposal and stated UNC staff offs. will continue to maintain the posit UNC has taken thus far. Commies replied their stand would be as set forth at beginning of their statement this am.

Item 4. Staff offs Item 4 reconvened in executive session. Substance of record follows:

Commies: We have recessed for 2 weeks[.] I believe that both sides have made sufficient preparation for resumption of the work of the staff offs meeting. In order to facilitate the further discussions of both sides as we have agreed upon at the time of the beginning of the recess, I would like to suggest that both sides first exchange the totals and sub totals of the POWs to be repatriated by both sides after the arm. and then both sides exchange opinions about the figures. After that, we will exchange the revised lists. By 'sub total' I mean that on our side in addition to giving you the total of the repatriated POWs we will give you the sub-totals of the Korean POWs as well as non Korean POWs of the UNC. Your side would give us the total of the POWs to be repatriated and the sub-totals of the captured personnel of the KPA and the CPV respectively. If your side has any other opinion re such procedure, or if your side has any statement about other matters, I would like to hear it."

UNC: "We have no statement about other matters at this time and we agree to your general outline of presentation of round figures."

Communists: "Do you mean you are going to present a total and the sub totals of each group or you will only give one round figure[?]"

UNC: "A total and a sub-total broken down by CPVs, NKA personnel, POWs whose residence is south of the 38th parallel, and CI's [.]"

Commies: "Would you like to speak first[?]"

UNC: "Very well. When we recessed on 4 Apr. both sides agreed that the discussions in the exec [executive] sessions would be resumed when both sides were in a posit. to present a round figure based on a checking of the POW lists. In accord with your suggestion and in the interests of continued progress, we have not awaited completion of all our work and of the preparation of revised POW lists before returning to the meetings. The preparation of these lists is now in progress. Because of the magnitude it is estimated they will be completed in from 2 to 3 weeks, at which time we can give you a final roster of all the POWs and CIs to be returned to your side.

"As a result of our screening we now anticipate that there are approx 70,000 persons in UNC custody who will not require forced repat. to your side. This round figure of 70,000 who will go to your side was developed thru a carefully considered and painstaking application of the understandings submitted to you on 1 Apr. As a part of the screening process each was informed of your amnesty declaration of Apr 6.

"We consider this 70,000 figure to be a reliable estimate of the number of captured persons of all categories to be returned to your side. The breakdown of the 70,000 is estimated as follows:

Civilian Internees	7200
POWs of ROK residence	3800
KPA	53900
CPV	5100["]

Commies: "I approve a one hour recess."

Commies: (After recess reading from prepared statement). "Having studied the total and and [*sic*] the sub totals of the captured personnel of our side whom your side is prepared to repatriate to our side, our side considers that this figure bears no relation whatsoever with the figures in our proposal of Mar 21st and this figure by no means can be a basis for further discussion.

"If your side is willing to negotiate for a solution of the POW matter on a fair & reasonable basis, we request your side to reconsider fundamentally this estimated figure. *I repeat, this figure absolutely by no means can be a basis for further discussion.*

["]I propose a recess until the usual time tomorrow[.]"

UNC: "Is your side willing to present now the figure which your side indicated it was willing to give us?"

Commies: 'According to the provision in principle submitted by our side on Mar. 21, the total of the POWs to be repatriated by your side should be a round figure of 132,000. Your side repeatedly indicated that your side is willing to solve this question within the framework of our proposal of Mar 21st. However your side now submitted the figure of 70,000. If our side adopts the same way as your side has done—that is, if our side were to discount the figure of the POWs by the same rate as your side has done—we consider that such a similar manner would not be able to solve the question.

"However, in order to solve the issue speedily and in order to reach an armistice agreement speedily our side does not do in the same way as your side does. The captured personnel of your side to be repatriated by our side will be around 12,000. Among them are around 7,700 Korean POWs and around 4,400 non-K POWs."

UNC: "We agree to a recess."

*Comment:***Immediate request for an hrs recess and obvious efforts of Col Tsai to maintain self composure upon hearing UNC estimate of number of POWs to be repatriated suggest that Commie instrs [instructions] did not encompass the possibility of an estimate in this low range.** Fol'g recess Commie rejection of UNC figure as basis for solving Item 4 was given without vituperation but with an obvious effort on part of spokesman to control his feelings.

In HNC 1165 I answered CinCUNC as follows:

"1. Concur in the analysis and proposal outlined in C 67156.

"2. In addition it is believed that prolonged discussion of the figures may crystallize enemy's opposition to them to the point where give & take respecting this issue may become impossible. We consider it desirable to give an early indication that UNC is willing to make a substantial concession in return for Commie acceptance of our position under Item 4.

"3. Exploration could be accomplished somewhat along the fol'g lines: "As the staff offs. responsible for Agenda Item 3 have stated many times our side can never accept the USSR as a member of the NNSC. The achievement at any time of an arm. is dependent on your side withdrawing this artificial barrier to an arm. which your side has needlessly and capriciously erected[.] Aside from this only two major diffs [differences] stand between our two sides and our common objective, the attainment of an early arm. One is in Item 4, the other is in Item 3. It is the feeling of the staff offs of our side that agreement on Agenda Item 4 would open the way to early resolution of the only diff of substance in Item 3."

Apr. 20 (Sun): In staff meeting on Item 3 Commies reaffirmed their previous stand on the neutral nations and airfield issues.

UNC in rebuttal contended that neutral nations problem was in reality no problem at all since a solution for it existed in accord with previous agreements. As for the airfields it is the main problem[.] It is a military matter we must solve in order to establish a truly stable & effective armistice. Cannot be brushed aside by excuse that it is interference in internal affairs. Our side is interested only in preventing any instability arising from the fact that either side might construct milt. [military] airfields or rehabilitate old fields. "In regard to this prob. [problem] your side has offered no solution whatsoever."

Item 4. Substance of staff offs [officers] meeting follows:
Communists: "It is completely impossible for us to consider your estimated number of 70,000 of our captured personnel whom your side was prepared to repat. [repatriate] fol'g the arm [armistice]. You said that figure was the result of the application of the understandings put forth by your side on Apr 1st. But you should know that our side has long since declared that we definitely cannot agree to para 2 of the understandings put forth by your side. Your side averred repeatedly that you were willing to settle the problem within the framework of our proposal of Mar 21st. Your side also indicated in the exec. [executive] meetings that the no [number] of our captured personnel whom your side was going to repat. would be close to 116,000[.] The round no of 70,000 submitted by your side loses all connection both within the framework of 132,000, which you said you were willing to accept and with the fig. [figure] of 116,000 which you specifically indicated. Such a self contradictory course of action can only make us gravely doubt whether you have any intention of negotiating & settling the quest. [question] on the basis of fairness. It was only due to your repeated indications of willingness to settle the quest. within the framework of our proposal of 21 Mar that a common basis was found between both sides from which a way could be sought toward the solution of the 4th item of the agenda. The estimated figure submitted by your side yesterday has actually overthrown that common basis which is fair & reasonable.

"I would repeat what I said yesterday[,] the figure of 70,000 submitted by your side absolutely cannot serve as a basis for our discussion. If you are still interested in negotiating and settling quests on the basis of fairness and reasonableness it is requested that your side consider this estimated figure all over again.''

UNC: ''I should like to review briefly our agreement reached in early April.

['']The UNC counter-proposal to your statement of principle and your under-standings did not contain a round figure for either side. We stated several times that we were unable to arrive at a figure inasmuch as screening had never been attempted among personnel in our custody. We stated that it would be necessary for us to effect a screening to arrive at a figure. There is no question that the higher the figure the easier it would be to arrive at a solution. Your principles for settling the issue and our principles had clashed and were contrary as we both know and still know. It was therefore agreed that both sides would tentatively defer discussion and consideration of principles while making a round-figure determination. This was done in the hope that an agreeable and acceptable solution could be achieved as the result of our screening process. Our side did not accept the 132,000 figure nor the 116,000 figure. If the eventualities of determining numbers to be returned to your side fitted either of those figures, it was of course indicated to you that such figures would be acceptable to us. The figure we gave you yesterday is the result of the application of the principle and the associated understandings which our side presented to you on April 1st.

''From your statement at our meeting on the 2nd of Apr. I am sure your side understood that it was our intention to apply our understandings in the screening process. This fig. is a valid estimate of the no. of POWs who will return to your side without the application of force, or in the case of the ROK personnel who will go to your side under the principle of vol. [voluntary] repat [repatriation]. Our side is willing of course to allow to return to your side those POWs who may change their present attitude towards repat. between the time of their initial expression of their views and the completion of the overall exchange of POWs between the two sides. Putting it another way we are completely willing & anxious for all POWs meeting the criteria established by our two understandings of 1 Apr to go to your side.

''The screening by the UNC was conducted with fairness and impartiality under the general methods and procedures discussed in prior Item 4 meetings. The length of time employed by our side in reaching the estimate reflects the thoroughness of the procedure. The fact that the figure was not one which either your side or our side may have anticipated does not indicate that it was not done thoroughly and conscientiously in accord with the principles enunciated in our understandings.''

Communists: ''You are very aware of the fact that we completely cannot agree to the 2nd para. of the understandings submitted by your side on Apr 1st. On Apr 2nd in my statement in the meeting I pointed this out clearly. I pointed out that in connection with the prin. [principle] of adjustment[.] I must also point out that among the POWs in the custody of either side—that is among the captured personnel of the one side held by the other side—there exists a fundamental difference between the non-Koreans and those Koreans who originally resided in the area of the other side on the one hand, and other Koreans who originally resided in the area of the detaining side on the other hand. The principle of our side in dealing with both these categories of POWs is well known to your side, and we completely cannot agree with the 2nd item of the understandings submitted by your side.

"As to the results of the so called screening there [*sic*; they?] are only a clear exposition of your intention to retain our captured personnel as well as an exposition of the result of the illegal control managed by your side. In this meeting your side has openly admitted that by different methods, different results could be obtained. The result of your screening is just the reflection of the facts produced under your control. Our side absolutely cannot agree with such results managed by your side.

"With respect to the figure your side stated day in and day out that your side was willing to settle the quests within the framework of the provision on principle proposed by our side on Mar 21st. However the figure presented by your side yesterday has completely repudiated the basis of our discussion and completely departed from the provision of principle proposed by our side on Mar 21st. Nobody with sound intelligence could understand that within the framework of the figure 132,000 means the figure of 70,000.

"Here I can only say that you flagrantly repudiated what you have said before[.] You are not willing to settle the present issues and you are not willing to reach a reasonable agreement on the issues. Under such conditions I propose a recess until the usual time tomorrow[.]'"

The rescreening of POW camp #1 on 19 Apr showed very disappointing results; only a handful changed their minds and indicated a desire to return to Commie control.

In reply to my HNC 1165, R sent fol'g [designated as "C 67236" in margin][:]

"1. Authority to use the proposal outlined in C 67156 is withheld until further notice[.]

2. In event I do grant such authority the timing of its use will be made discretionary with you but will not be delegated by you.

3. Therefore, would like you to give me one days notice in advance of your estimated need for this authority[.]'"

Referring to above msg I sent folg (HNC 1169)[:]

"1. Communists initial reaction to 70,000 figure gives strong indication that this low number is entirely unsatisfactory to them. If this appraisal of their reaction continues to hold, it is apparent that Item 4 cannot be settled independently. However, a broad indication given in connection with Item 4 that the UNC would concede on the airfield question in exchange for settlement of the POW question might induce the Commies to accept. Therefore, provided our appraisal is confirmed within the next day or so, the Del. strongly feels that there is no advantage to continuing the discussions within Item 4 without giving this indication. Furthermore, extended discussions confined solely to the POW quest may well serve only to crystalize [sic] Commie opposition to the point where any bargaining involving the present figure of 70,000 may be extremely difficult if not impossible.

"I therefore recommend that I be authorized to give an indication at an early time of my choosing that the air field issue can be solved in conjunction with the POW issue. It is recognized that this indication may not terminate discussion of the POW issue and that we may eventually consider it desirable to take step outlined in para 1e CX 67066 (note: this step is the rescreening after the arm is signed). However, it is thought that such a step will not by itself result in a resolution of the item and therefore that we should not resort to it unless & until it becomes evident that the Communists will not accept the solution of Item 4 which is outlined in para 1 above."

In his CX 67235 which he sent to the JCS, R pointed out that an official public announcement supporting a final package proposal would be of incalculable value in securing early Commie agreement. Accordingly he recommended that any package proposal which we may present be immediately supported by authoritative public statements of the US Govt and of as many other UN Nations as possible.

In his msg R also gave the statement he proposed to issue from Tokyo when the package proposal was presented to the Commies.

Apr. 21 (Mon): In staff offs meeting on Item 3 each side presented its views on problems of airfield restrs [restrictions] & neutral nations but no progress was made.

Item 4. In staff officers executive session on Item 4 Hickman started off by a rebuttal of the Commies contention that UNC had repudiated the basis for "our earlier discussions." He said: "We indicated before our long recess that our side could not prophesy a round figure, that only a screening process could disclose the number to be repatriated to your side." — — — Actually, the figure has turned out to be an estimated 70,000. That figure has resulted from a carefully worked out screening process. It has not worked out as a result of any desire on our part to retain your people for the sake of retention[.] It has resulted from the application of the understandings which we presented to you on 1 Apr.

"It is the figure which we could not prophesy and it is the one disclosed by the facts. Now, we are aware that your side never agreed to accept as such our second understanding of 1 Apr. Similarly your side is aware that our side never agreed to accept your understanding that all POWs whose residence was not in the area of the detaining side should be unconditionally repatriated. On the other hand your remarks on the 2nd of April indicated to us your appreciation of the fact that our side would employ our principle and our understandings of Apr 1 in connection with the UNC screening processes. I quote from the 2 Apr record: "[*sic*] **We think that if we continue to spend our time on argument over the principles & understandings themselves, we may not be able to get any results speedily, but viewed from another angle, the contents of the principles & understandings will necessarily be reflected in the specific lists, and both sides have agreed that such specific lists must be agreed upon by both sides before they become valid.**' In the light of these remarks of your side there does not seem to be any basis for your indications of a repudiation. That you did not expect this figure is beyond our control. The figure merely represents the facts; that is all.''

Communists: "In your statement this am & yesterday you said that the figure of 70,000 submitted by your side on 19 Apr was obtained on the basis of the principles & understandings put forth by your side on Apr. 1.

"As I pointed out yesterday, our side clearly told your side on Apr 2 that our side could not agree to Item 2 of your proposed understandings. Item 2 of your proposed understandings of Apr 1 is in actuality an application to all of our captured personnel of your so-called 'vol repat [voluntary repatriation]' or 'no forced repat.' That is tantamount to requiring our side to yield completely to the views of your side.

"Our side is always willing to settle quests [questions] thru negots [negotiations], but settlement of quests must be sought on the basis of fairness & reasonableness. Any yielding to the views of your side is absolutely impossible. As I pointed out yesterday the round number of 70,000 submitted by your side has lost all connection with the framework of our proposal of 21 Mar which your side indicated many times that you were willing to accept. It was because your side gave repeated indications that you were willing to accept our proposal of Mar 21, and to seek a solution within the framework of our proposal, that is a solution in the vicinity of 132,000, and because your side specifically indicated that a total no [number] of personnel whom your side would repatriate to our side would be close to 116,000 that our side suggested that our side suggested [*sic*] that both sides should first determine tentatively the rough no of persons to be repatriated so as to seek a reasonable compromise within the figure of 132,000 and 116,000 and then reach an overall solution step by step on the basis of the round number. The figure submitted by your side on Apr 19 however entirely overthrows the basis and the premises of this manner of determining the figure of the rough number. Therefore your figure of 70,000 definitely cannot serve as a basis for our discussion of the round numbers[.]

"Your side surely is aware that any agreement takes two sides. It is impossible and impracticable to expect that in these milt arm. [military armistice] conferences conducted by both sides on an equal footing, our side would completely yield to the unilateral views of your side by actually accepting totally your 'vol repat' or 'no forced repat.' Our side has always been willing to settle quests thru negots—such is still our attitude. However if you should take our willingness to settle quests thru negots as a sign of weakness on our part you will be mistaken— gravely mistaken[.] I would like to tell you unequivocally that our side absolutely cannot accept your round figure of 70,000. Furthermore, I wish to point out that your round figure of 70,000 has overthrown the basis for further negots. In the interest of an arm. I would again recommend that your side consider all over again the round figure submitted by your side on Apr 19.''

UNC: ''I have a few comments to make. Firstly, I think your reactions to the 70,000 figure ignores the dismay with which our side heard the figure of 11,559 on 18 Dec.

''I am not meaning to imply that the figure of 70,000 represents in any measure or in any degree a retaliatory process because it is not. It represents instead a fair and honest exposition of the application of our principles & understandings. It represents as conscientiously as we are able to determine not how our side feels about the matter, but how the captured personnel themselves feel about it.

''Our side does not expect you in these conferences to yield except to accept those arm. provisions which are reasonable[.] On the other hand, not going into detail on the point, we do not expect you to apply one principle for personnel you have captured during the war and then say that we cannot apply a similar principle while the negots are in progress. You have already rec'd [received] your quid-pro-quo unilaterally & in advance. I need only to remind you that percentage- wise the 70,000 figure represents a much higher % of people to be returned to you than the approx 20% you would return of the captured people of our side. Again I wish to emphasize that the 70,000 figure is not an arbitrary one and is not one picked by us to achieve any percentage of any arbitrary retention of your personnel. I mention this because of your reference to the fact that it would be tantamount to your yielding to a unilateral view of our side.

''Our side of course is always willing to negotiate. That is why we are here to attempt to resolve our differences. In our negots however the 70,000 figure is a firm one.

''As to willingness to concede, we agreed to accept your principle of releasing & repatriating all POWs at the time of the signing of the arm. I shall not labor that point other than to say that wars have many times been fought over principles no more important than this. It was our understanding that your side realized that our side was going to apply in the preparation of our revised lists our understandings and principle of 1 Apr. We thought you realized that we were going to utilize these provisions contained in our understandings to achieve for the individual captured personnel in our custody on an informal basis what your side had accomplished as a major milt policy.''

Commies then accused UNC of holding fast to principle of vol repat and of not willing to compromise or negotiate. Accused us of entirely overthrowing basis for negots because we said on Mar 28 that UNC believed the question could be solved within framework of Commies Mar 21 proposal. And on Apr 21 UNC said: "We indicated that possibly 116,000 would more nearly indicate the magnitude of exchange." Commies claim that "only after your side made those indications did we, on Apr 2, propose that we start our work on checking the lists.["] Also claimed that 70,000 figure is a result of UNC manipulation. Ever since beginning UNC has been intending to retain large number of captured personnel of our side (Commies) under all pretexts. Again sincerely recommend that your side reconsider the round figure submitted by your side on Apr 19.

UNC then defended screening process, pointing out that our screening of ROK POWs and civilian internees was designed to afford these two grps [groups] a choice, that is the principle of vol. repat [voluntary repatriation], whereas processing of CPV and KPA personnel was designed to separate those who would not violently oppose repat. from those who would not [*sic*]. Processes designed to determine the greatest number who could be sent to your side without application of force. "Had a sincere effort not been made, or less stringent standards been employed the number would have been much smaller. Therefore I (Hickman) reiterate that the 70,000 figure is now a fact to be reckoned with in future negots necessary for achieving an arm. agreement." Hickman also said: "We are not asking you as a negotiator to agree to our now doing what your side has already done, but instead we are asking that you merely accept our right to do what your side has already unilaterally accomplished."

Tsai ended session by saying[:] "If your side has sincerity for an armistice and if your side is for the interests of the POWs incl. [including] the captured personnel of your side, you must consider all over again the figure submitted by your side on Apr 19."

Comment: (a) Impression is that Commies are sincerely seeking to negotiate a solution to Item 4. It does not appear possible to settle POW issue within Item 4 short of a much higher figure than 70,000.

(b) UNC affirmed and reaffirmed the finality of 70,000 and indicated that that figure must be accepted as a fact in connection with any further negotiation.

(c) Since UNC figure is approx firm, Del [delegation] considers it desirable to interpret Commies stated willingness to further negotiate as being opportune basis for UNC to indicate that Item 4 might be solved in connection with Item 3.

Rec'd folg from R (C 67270): My C 67159 was an exploratory msg to develop additional actions which might be taken by you to improve the prospects of an early and satisfactory arm agreement.

After further study of the proposal and full considerations of your comments, I have reached the fol'g conclusions:

(a) It would be a premature and piecemeal exposure of the pkg [package] agreement[.]

(b) It would be presented without the force & effect of a final posit [position], which will be an ultimatum, and without the refusal to further debate & discuss the issues.

(c) It could force the Commies into a firm posit which would make more difficult their acceptance of the pkg agreement.

(d) It could result in publicity of our willingness to trade the airfield issue for the repat issue. That posit is not endorsed by many of our allies. Premature publicity could develop a serious attack in the Allied press which might cause the Commies to reject the pkg agreement in the belief that a better agreement can be obtained because of allied pressure on the U.S.

I realize that the proposal might be favorably rec'd by the Commies. If so there would remain the single issue of Russia with a capitulation by the Commies on this issue as the only means whereby an agreement could be reached. I do not believe this would be the most favorable negotiating position for us.

In view of the above conclusions I cannot feel that the proposed action is our best course and have therefore decided that it will not be taken.

If you have strong contrary views which have not been presented previously I will be glad to have them.

Since we had no strong contrary views, but only the belief that it would be more palatable to the Commies to get our airfield or package proposal concession during the closed sessions than during open plenary sessions, no answer was sent to the above.

Apr. 22 (Tues): In staff offs [officers] meeting on Item 3 both sides held firm to their previous stands on issues of airfield restrs [restrictions] & neutral nations. No progress made[.]

Item 4. Sent fol'g msg to CinCUNC (HNC 1176)[:] "The Commies indicated today that failure to resolve the POW issue on the basis of the 21 Mar proposal—by which they mean willingness by us to repatriate approx 116,000 POW—would result in their return to the lists of 18 Dec as the basis for further negots [negotiations]. In view of their stiffening attitude I consider that there must be the min [minimum] possible delay in moving to plenary session and introducing the pk'g [package] proposal, since reversion by the enemy to the 18 Dec lists as the basis for solving Item 4 may destroy every chance there now is of his acceptance of the pkg solution.

"Re para 1 (f) of CX 67066, I consider that we should now suspend staff offs. discussions and move to plenary session for the purpose of submitting the pkg proposal. I would like to discuss this action with you on 24 Apr.

"Meanwhile, I have instructed the staff offs to offer the verification and rescreening proposal (supara [*sic*] 1(c) CX 67066) at the 23 Apr session of Item 4. While we feel such an offer by itself will not solve Item 4, it may assist in keeping discussions fluid until the plenary session is convened."

In view of the stiffening attitude of the Commies and their implied threat I decided a conference with R was in order to talk over ways to continue the executive Item 4 sessions and our possible move to plenary sessions[.] I also considered it desirable to talk over publicity releases when results of Operation Scatter become public and releases immediately after presentation of pkg proposal becomes public. It is UNC Del's [delegation's] views that premature release of POW exchange may endanger the securing of an armistice. I also wish to obtain final approval of our statement to go with the presentation of the final pkg proposal. In addition General Yu has asked me for authority to tell Pres [President] Rhee of the pkg proposal. I told him Pres Rhee should be informed thru Gen R & Muccio and not by Gen Yu since he was under Gen R's command. I would transmit his request to Gen R.

Apr. 23 (Wed): Left camp shortly before 1000 with Libby, Briggs & Nuckols, arriving Haneda via P2V2 about 1400. Held conference with R at his qtrs (Strat's old place) at 1500. Also present were Hickey, McDowell, Salisbury, Larden in addition to above three. I started things going by explaining why the Del had liked the idea of exploring the pkg [package] proposal deal in the Item 4 Executive sessions. Said impact of pkg proposal will not be so drastic—gives them time to think about it—Commies wont think we are trying to force pkg deal down their throats in a dictatorial manner. It presents proposal in manner Commies like. Also exploratory idea will keep talks fluid and, together with our rescreening idea after arm [armistice], might turn the trick whereas each one unsupported by the other might not. At this point Hickey interrupted to suggest that recent JCS msg (which we had not seen) be read. This msg (JCS 906923) said: "In view of rel. [relative] success of exec [executive] sessions of staff offs Item 4 view here is that there would be considerable advantage in proposing that Exec sessions of plenary delegates be held at time of presentation of pkg proposal." Msg also requested CinCUNCs views on proposed statement to be made by R when pkg proposal was presented. In addition msg said: "As stated in para 2d(2) and (5) JCS 903687 considered here that any statements issued in connection with introduction of pkg proposal should while reflecting final & irrevocable reconcilliation [*sic*] opposing points of view and willingness of UNC Dels to continue to meet whenever Commies desire [*sic*, whole sentence]. Therefore statement should not be couched in terms which could be interpreted as an ultimatum that decreases probabilities of Commie acceptance and, in event of Commie rejection, raises domestic and international expectations of prompt decisive milt [military] action. In light of foregoing, consider that statements to be made at time of introduction of pkg proposal while clear and firm, should not assume Commie rejection or be so worded as to make acceptance thereof difficult for Commies."

R answered this msg (see CX 67399) saying he had authorized Del. to explore the pkg proposal deal in Item 4 Executive sessions. He went on to say: "If

Commies indicate an interest in this exploratory suggestion, the continuation of the discussion will be suggested at level desired by them. If plenary session is selected, it will be suggested that this discussion be conducted in Exec session under this condition. I believe best interests UNC dictate avoidance of publicity that might provide unfavorable reaction.

"If Commies indicate no interest in the suggestion, or categorically reject it, there is no advantage in keeping our proposal secret. Hence we should propose open plenary session, present pkg proposal, and concurrent therewith issue a statement essentially as suggested by you in reference msg."

JCS approved this procedure in their JCS 907037.

Item 4. Hickman proposed the rescreening of Commie POWs after the arm. which was completely ignored by the enemy Del except that they did say: "Today you attempt to delay the dealing of the quest [question] of the release and repat [reptriation] of more than 100,000 captured personnel of our side to the time after the arm. It not only indicates that your side is still asking our side to yield completely to your principle of forced repat. It also would earn more time for your side for your side [*sic*] to accomplish the work of instigation by your side in the POW camps."

Record of meeting much the same as previously. It is becoming increasingly apparent that the Commies will never accept the 70,000 figure. They exclaim vehemently that UNC is attempting to retain forcefully the captured personnel of their side.

Comment: UNC today introduced the idea of verification & rescreening after the arm. No direct response made to this proposal. In spite of it enemy opposition to negotiating on basis of 70,000 continued as they repeated that the UNC by its 70,000 estimate had overthrown the current basis of negotiating. Since the idea of verification and rescreening has been advanced the enemy will know that he can obtain this feature, if he desires it, in connection with the pkg proposal.

Item 3. Commies opened meeting with a prepared statement which reiterated views presented in meetings for past several days. UNC pointed out that Commie proposals offered no solution to the remaining issues.

Apr. 24 (Thurs): Item 3. Much the same as yesterday, no progress. UNC accused Commies of evading main issue & repeating arguments which do not pertain to the problem. Commies said there would be no progress until UNC changes attitude.

Item 4. Commies opened Item 4 session by saying UNC had completely overthrown basis of negots [negotiations] and had openly violated Geneva Convention. Then said: "Our side wishes to notify your side formally that the form of the Exec [executive] session is abrogated from now on and open negots. are accordingly reinstated.[''']

Hickman then expressed the opinion that abrogation of these sessions will unquestionably delay the attainment of an arm.

After 15 min recess which they asked Commies returned to say they were willing to continue in Exec sessions if UNC is willing to return to basis of their Mar 21 proposal. Both sides agreed to continue discussions tomorrow.

In the report of the meeting to CinCUNC the fol'g comments were submitted:

(a) Item 4 staff offs [officers] tomorrow intend to:

(1) Flatly reject any quid pro quo for continuance of exec sessions

(2) Tell Commies that continuation of exec sessions is up to them and shall not be taken to indicate anything other than a more favorable medium for negotiating

(3) Determine at meeting, if exec sessions are continued, whether occasion is opportune for exploration as outlined in HNC 1165.

(b) In light of todays apparent original intention of Commies to discontinue news blackout and to exploit low figure of repatriates, probability of Commie interest in exploration (HNC 1165) is not high.

Therefore, if exploration is attempted and Commie reaction is hostile plenary session should be called promptly[.] Decision could be made on day of plenary session whether it should be proposed as exec or open[.]

(c) It is recommended that the press releases be made ready for immediate release in event Commies abrogate staff offs exec sessions either at tomorrows meeting or suddenly at any other time.

After consulting with me thru Col Larden R sent fol'g msg to CinCUNC Adv. (Advance) concerning above comments: ''Concur with your comments and recs [recommendations] except for sub para c which is under consideration[.]

[''']In event Commies announce that they refuse to continue in executive session you will immediately ask for a recess and inform them that our liaison officers will contact theirs to arrange for the next meeting.[''']

Rec'd word from Hickey that conference tomorrow would be unnecessary. Consequently I gave word that we would leave Haneda at 251100 Item.

Apr. 25 (Fri): After rough trip in Constellation which iced up considerably at 16,000 ft. we arrived back at camp at 1530. Hickman greeted us with the news that the Commies had abrogated the Item 4 Executive sessions which had been indefinitely suspended. Summary of Item 4 sessions follows:

Hickman opened up by saying: ''You of course realize that our side cannot make any substantive agreement or any concessions as to conditions precedent to remaining in executive session. We merely feel, regardless of the topics or trend of the negots [negotiations] in the next few days, that progress can be more rapidly and successfully made in executive session than in open session. We urge continuance of exec [executive] sessions for the present.''

Commies answered: ''Unless you present a proposal which would be sufficient for the resumption of the basis of negots based upon our Mar 21st proposal, we do not see any reason for the continuation of the exec sessions. After hearing your statement this am, we consider that it is time for us to resume the open sessions. Therefore I now declare that we enter into the open sessions.''

Tsai then blared forth with a long statement outlining the Commies position on the POW question and claiming that their Mar 27 proposal, or principle of adjustment was only reasonable compromise. In accordance with this principle vol repat [voluntary repatriation] would in effect be applied to a portion of the POWs (CIs & ROKs) in the custody of both sides and unconditional repat apply to the remainder (CCF & NK)[.]

After noting Tsai's long statement Hickman requested an indefinite recess which Tsai opposed on basis that UNC was trying to delay the proceedings. Hickman replied that he was willing to meet tomorrow if Tsai insisted. and said perhaps he could give a counterpart tomorrow of Tsai's long propaganda statement of today. Tsai then backed down and agreed to recess until notified UNC would be willing to resume meetings.

Upon receiving rpt [report] of Item 4 session and abrogation of executive sessions, R sent us fol'g msg: ''Desire you submit to Commies this pm a demand for a plenary session at earliest date you are prepared to meet.

[''[W]e are now preparing for press release soonest a full statement embodying the substance of HNC 1156 and CX 67448 modified as we think appropriate in the light of such Commie broadcasts and releases and their interpretation by our press as we are able to secure without unduly delaying our own release. Release will be made concurrently at Munsan & Tokyo at date & hour to be specified.['']] (Note see CX 67538 for this press release.)

Kinney then informed Chang that UNC wanted a plenary session meeting at 1100 on the 27th. Commies agreed after asking what was subject of meeting which Kinney said was the Arm [armistice] Agreement[.]

Item 3 staff meeting produced nothing[.] UNC asked what reasonable solution Commies had proposed on airfield issue and stated progress could not be made until they suggest a reasonable solution or accept UNC solution. Commies replied that UNC demand for restr [restricting] airfields is only to interfere in their internal affairs and basically has no place in the negots.

Apr. 26 (Sat): This am a msg was sent to CinCUNC (see HNC 1190) giving the opening statement I intend to make tomorrow at the plenary session. This statement follows:

''For more than 9 mos. our two Dels [delegations] have been negotiating for an arm. which will bring a cessation of hostilities in Korea. We have progressed to a point where only 3 issues remain between us and final agreement on an arm. [armistice]. These 3 issues concern first, whether there will or will not be restrictions on the rehab [rehabilitation] & constr [construction] of milt [military] airfields; second the basis of exchange of POWs; and 3rd, the nations to compose the Neut [neutral] Nations Supervisory Commission.

"As for the 1st issue, for many wks. [weeks] the UNC Del has stated that in order to maintain the stability of the arm. & prevent the creation of tension which might lead to a resumption of hostilities it is highly desirable that restrs. [restrictions] be placed on the rehab. & constr of milt airfields. Your side has opposed this limitation on what would be a manifest increase of offensive potentiality upon the grd. [ground] that it would constitute interference by one side in the internal affairs of the other. Yet, if your side is moving in good faith toward an arm you should have no hesitation in agreeing not to build up your milt. air potential.

"As for the 2nd issue I have referred to, for many wks. the UNC Del. has stated that all POWs must be released but that only those should be repatriated or turned over to the other side who can be delivered without the application of force. Your side has opposed this principle and has, instead, insisted that certain POWs must be repatriated even if physical force is necessary, asserting that to accord respect to the feelings of the individual prisoner is unprecedented and deprives a POW of his rights. Your current attitude on this quest [question] is inconsistent with the historical facts that during the Korean war your side has followed the practice of inducting captured personnel into your armed forces and that you have in this and other ways disposed of approx 4/5th of the milt personnel of our side who fell into your custody.

"The UNC holds as POWs some 116,000 North Koreans and CPVs. 59,000 or more than 50% of this number held by our side will return to your side without being forced. In addition, some 11,000 ROK citizens now in our custody have elected to go to your side under the principle of free choice. This is in marked contrast to the 12,000 captured personnel of our side whom you have stated you will repatriate, a figure which is less than 20% of those you have admitted having taken into custody.

"The foregoing figures are now a basic factor in the POW quest. It was with the full concurrence of your side that the POWs in our custody were screened to determine their attitude as regards repatriation. Once screened POWs had to be segregated in accordance with their individual determination. No action can now be taken by either side to alter materially this situation[.] It is an accomplished fact. For you to pretend otherwise would be completely unrealistic.

"Moreover our side has indicated our willingness to send to your side any POWs who may change their views on repatriation between the time of the initial determination and the completion of the exchange of POWs. We have also informed you that, if you wish, you may verify the results of our screening processes after the arm is signed. Your side can at that time interview those persons held by the UNC who have indicated that they would violently oppose being returned to your side.

"Lastly, in regard to the 3rd issue, although both sides agreed to nominate mutually acceptable nations to compose the NNSC, you have continued to insist on membership for a nation which the UNC will not accept.

"The issues are clearly drawn. The discussions of the past several months have clearly defined the differences on the issues, but such discussions have failed to develop any common meeting ground for resolving these differences. Within the limit of these discussions each side has indicated that its posit [position] is firm and unshakeable. We believe that because of the strong views already set forth by both sides in the respective meetings, we will only prolong the stalemate on each of the 3 differences if we attempt to discuss them further or to settle them separately. Therefore we believe it absolutely essential that the 3 remaining issues be settled together. It is evident that if both sides remain adamant in their present posit. on the 3 issues, these negots will be deadlocked indefinitely. If an arm agreement is to result from our efforts here, if we are to bring about the long awaited cessation of hostilities in Korea, if we are to build the bridge which is to lead to a solution of the Korean problem, the 3 issues must be resolved at the earliest practicable date. There are 2 ways to accomplish this objective. Either one side could concede on all issues, or each side could accede to the position taken by the other side on some of the remaining issues. The only alternative to the foregoing is for these Dels to admit that they have failed to accomplish their mission.

["]I state categorically that the UNC will not accede to your demands on all matters at issue. I assume that you would make a similar statement on behalf of your Del. It is clear, then, that unless you are willing to accept the entire responsibility for the failure of these negots, you must join us in seeking a compromise solution which both sides may accept in the interest of reaching an early agreement on an arm.

"The UNC has carefully reviewed the posits taken by both sides on the 3 issues. It remains our conviction that the stability of an arm. would be increased by restricting rehabilitation and reconstruction of milt airfields. We are fully aware that you consider that any such restr. constitutes interference in your internal affairs. We utterly disagree with your contention in this regard, since this is a milt. arm. designed to freeze the milt situation in status quo pending a final peace settlement. However in the interest of reaching an early arm agreement we are willing to accede to your stand that no restr. be placed on the rehab & reconstr of airfields.

"I must make it absolutely clear however, that our acceptance of your posit regarding airfields is contingent upon your acceptance of our posits. regarding POWs and the composition of the NNSC. As you know our position re. POWs is the exchange of 12,000 POWs of our side for approx 70,000 of your side. You also know that our posit. re. the NNSC is that this Commission shall be composed of representatives from the four Neutral Nations which are acceptable to both sides.

"The UNC Del submits a draft wording for the entire arm. agreement. This draft wording incorporates all the agreements hitherto reached on Agenda Items 2, 3, 4 & 5. It omits any restr. on the rehab & constr of milt airfields. It provides a specific agreement on the nations composing the NNSC. Lastly it provides a practical & realistic basis for the exchange of POWs.

"We formally propose that this draft arm. wording be approved in toto by our Dels. and that the liaison offs. [officers] be directed to prepare the formal arm agreement for signature by our respective Comdrs [commanders]. Our liaison offs. will be prepared to discuss details concerning minor changes in wording and necessary admin [administrative] matters.

["]The UNC has now made its final offer in an effort to reach an arm. The UNC Del desires to make it unmistakably clear to you that we will not agree to any substantive change in this proposal, and that we are absolutely firm that this proposal must be considered as a whole. The fate of this arm conference, and future peace in Korea now rest fully and exclusively with you."

Nothing new in Item 3 meeting today[,] no progress. Item 4 sessions recessed.

Also sent fol'g msg to CinCUNC (HNC 1191)[:]

1. Para 51 of arm agreement, to be included in pkg proposal follows:

'51. All POWs held in custody of each side at time this arm agreement becomes effective shall be released & repatriated as soon as possible. The release & repat of such POWs shall be effected in conformity with the lists which have been exchanged and have been checked by the respective sides prior to the signing of this arm. agreement. (Here follows definition of repat [repatriation]["])

2. Above change is necessary as a result of recent developments in Item 4 staff meetings.

Apr. 27 (Sun): About 0845 this day just as we had completed all arrangements for the plenary session with the Commies at 1100 the fol'g JCS msg [message] to CinCUNC was passed to us by R:

1. JCS msg JCS 907347 is quoted for your info.

"Ref [reference] Z 38735 (CinCFE's quote of HNU-208) Not clear here whether plenary session called for in ref msg. will be open or exec [executive] in nature. Since Commie reaction to approach mentioned in para 1 CX 67399 (note: the exploratory idea) has not been developed, belief here is that exec session would offer most favorable atmosphere for introduction of pkg [package] proposal. Unless proposal for exec session is clearly rejected by Commies prior to holding of plenary session urge that proposal for exec sessions be made at opening of plenary."

2. Instrs [instructions] will follow immediately[.]

R's instrs follow: (He sent this info JCS)

1. Consider compliance with last sentence of JCS 907347, passed separately, is mandatory and I so direct.

2. Two methods of doing so occur to me. One is to propose exec sessions immediately upon convening and prior to any disclosure whatever of your intended plan of procedure.

   b. The other is to make in open session that part only of your opening statement to include para which begins with the phrase "I state categorically that the UNC," withholding remainder pending result of a proposal you would then make that the meeting would thenceforth be conducted in exec session.

3. You are authorized to use either or any other variant at your discretion, providing you comply with para one herein.

4. Please rpt [report] intentions soonest.

I rptd that I would use procedure in para 2b.

After thinking matter over (after conferring with Briggs & others) I phoned Hickey about 0930 and suggested that we postpone the plenary meeting. Said we were in a tailspin as result of JCS msg and we needed time to pull ourselves together. Delay might show indecisiveness to Commies but it was better than a false move. 15 mins later Hickey called back to say R had authorized postponement of the plenary meeting. Commies were immediately advised by phone that due to unavoidable circumstances we desired postponement and would let them know later when we would be ready to meet. They agreed.

In order that Commies would not get too suspicious I ordered Darrow to arrange an Item 3 meeting which he did.

Later on in the am I sent the fol'g msg (see HNC 1199) to R in accordance with Hickey's urgent suggestion:

"Reference tel. [telephone] conversation between Hickey & Joy this date the fol'g is our analysis of the proposal made by JCS 907347 to suggest to the enemy that we enter executive plenary session.

"(1) This proposal appears to be based on JCS 90692. Since the dispatch of this JCS msg the negotiatory situation has been fundamentally altered by the enemy's unilateral abrogation of the exec sessions on agenda Item 4. By this action Commies indicated their intention to try the POW case in open forum before world public opinion. Any attempt now to avoid meeting the enemy in their chosen forum prejudices negotiating posit [position] of UNC.

"(2) A proposal to enter executive session is wholly inconsistent with our objective which is to avoid substantive discussion of the pkg [package] proposal elements. It is implicit in the idea of exec sessions that full and free discussion will be encouraged, in fact is the very purpose of exec session which invites fullest exchange of points of view[.]

"(3) To present the pkg in an executive session proposed by the UNC tends to indicate we are fearful of public reaction to it in its present form. The enemy would be justified in drawing the inference that the pkg did not in fact represent our "final" posit. and that further concessions by the UNC might be expected. (If this is the intent of the JCS, in order to plan properly we should be advised what these further recessions from present min [minimum] posits might be.)

(4) All separate elements of the pkg proposal have been fully publicized individually particularly the POW question, which the enemy has thrown before the world. The nature of the compromise proposed in our pkg has unfortunately been repeatedly suggested in the press.

(5) To cover in a cloak of secrecy the equitable solution offered in our pkg deprives us of the public support induced by its fairness, and by the fact the UNC has made a major concession in a sincere effort to reach an armistice[.] Secrecy of our offer invites speculation by press of the free world that UNC may be abandoning its actual POW position, a position which has been strongly supported by US free press. Ultimate disclosure of unchanged UNC posit in this regard may not correct lack of public support at time it is most needed.

(6) There is now no particular inducement to the enemy implicit in the executive session, since their acceptance of the pkg would immediately result in an armistice, with attendant full publicity of the agreement reached.

(7) There is no guarantee that the enemy would agree to executive session. Yet regardless of whether the enemy accepts or rejects the executive session, the mere proposal of it by the UNC weakens our position.

Part II. It is therefore strongly recommended that pkg proposal be presented in open plenary session.

Part III. If however the decision is that exec sessions are to be proposed request authority to make the proposal along the fol'g lines after having delivered full opening statement presenting pkg proposal:

"It is not the inclination of our side to withhold the fair & equitable proposal we have made today from the people of the world. However if it is your side's opinion that to consider our proposal as having been made in exec session would expedite progress in our negots [negotiations], our side is willing to consider this session & further meetings as exec in nature.

R sent the above msg (less Parts II & III and bracketed [CTJ means parenthesized] portion in para 3) on to JCS in his C 67643 with fol'g added two paras:

"I concur in above, but far more than that, I feel the action I am urged to take for the stated purpose of developing the Commie reaction to an approach already rendered meaningless and sterile thru the swift sequence of events since the idea of that approach was first suggested, would gravely prejudice such chances as exist for the successful accomplishment of our mission. All our actions had been carefully planned coordinated & approved with the clear recognition that each was an essential link in one strong chain connecting our principles with our pkg proposal. To me delay or hesitation at this stage would expose us to grave loss of confidence by our friends and ridicule by our foes.

"I therefore urge with all earnestness that you at once grant me full authority to proceed with action as planned, reported and approved prior to receipt of your 907347.''

Apr. 28 (Mon): As a result of R's strong msg, given above, I went to bed last night confident that we would not have to present our pkg proposal to the Commies in a closed session. It was difficult to see how the JCS could turn him down. Our peace of mind was short lived however because early this morning R forwarded the fol'g JCS dispatch to us, with which he directed compliance: (JCS 907378)

''Your 67643. Based upon UNC Dels [delegation's] previous comment in HNC 1182 (which said decision could be made on day of plenary session whether it should be proposed as open or closed) understanding here was decision as to form of plenary to be proposed was being held in abeyance until immediately preceding opening session plenary. Also view here was that since dispatch of JCS 906923 desirability of proposing exec [executive] sessions plenary has increased for reasons set forth in detail below, and therefore JCS 907347 was dispatched to gave you full benefit of latest thinking here. Although most careful consideration has been given points made in your C 67643 view here is that advantages of at least proposing exec sessions of plenary delegates are overriding.

''We realize that likelihood of Commies acceptance of pkg proposal under either procedure is questionable at best. However we feel any chance Commies acceptance our min [minimum] terms as contained in pkg proposal is enhanced by presentation in exec session.

''If Commies accept exec session & breach understanding in an attempt gain initial propaganda advtg [advantage] we feel this places on them clear onus for failure to reach agreement and would in effect improve our propaganda posit [position]. If Commies refuse proposal for exec sessions, thus reflecting another clear effort by UNC to prevent negots. [negotiations] falling into propaganda morass, Commies incur serious additional onus[.] This will facilitate important objective of maintaining allied unity & support for posits taken in pkg [package] proposal as well as continued support U.S. Govt policies in event negots [negotiations] are suspended or broken off by Commies.

''Therefore, we desire you instruct UNC Del to proceed as directed by you in CX 67613. If Commies reject proposal for Exec sessions you are authorized to drop proposal, and to proceed at once in open session with action as planned and approved prior to receipt of JCS 907347. Consider it highly important begin plenary session soonest, if possible on morning Apr 28 your time.''

1. Delegations convened in plenary session at 1100 I 28 Apr. Substance of record follows:

2. UNC: ''We intend to propose today an overall solution of the probs. [problems] remaining to be settled. We consider the Exec session form of

meeting to be the most suitable for this purpose and recommend your concurrence. Do you agree?['']

3. Communists: (following 30 min recess) ''Our side is willing to settle probs in any form of meeting. The settlement of problems depends, not on the various forms of meetings, but on the sincerity of both sides to settle problems.

''Since your side considers the exec form of meeting will be helpful to the overall settlement of the quests [questions], our side agrees to adopt the form of exec meeting in order to reach a reasonable settlement of all quests. When either side wishes to terminate the form of exec meeting, the Exec meeting should then be ended. Let's now go over to the exec session.

''Now we wish to hear your ways of overall settlement of your side.''

4. UNC: (statement contained in HNC 1190, see Apr 26)[.]

5. Communists: ''Your statement has been duly noted. The stand of our side as well as the reasonable solution of it has been fully discussed in other meetings in several forms on the remaining issues of each of the items.

''In order to make a study of your statement as well as your proposal I propose to recess until 2:30 this pm[.]

6. Communists: (fol'g recess) ''In order to reach an armistice, our side has no objection to discussion and settlement of the unsolved issues of the various items of the agenda altogether. The attainment of agreement depends upon efforts of both sides. But the remaining issues must be settled on a reasonable basis according to the nature of the various issues. Your side should be well aware of our stand on the remaining questions. Our side has consistently held that the so called restriction on airfield facilities is a question which has no relation with the armistice. Re the question of nomination of neutral nations, our side has already proposed a reasonable solution. In order to solve the quest of POWs, our side has made great efforts and submitted the prin [principle] of repat [repatriation] of POWs on 27 Mar which is a compromise principle and accommodates views of both sides. Our side fails to see how your proposal of this am. can really be of help to an overall settlement of all the remaining issues. Those are my preliminary comments on your statement made this am. In order to make a further study of your statement, I suggest we recess, the time for reconvening the Plenary Session will be notified through the liaison officers.''

7. UNC: ''I wish to emphasize once more that the UNC offer which I gave you this am is our final and irrevocable effort.''

Meeting adjourned at 1437[.]

Comments: (a) There was no noticeable reaction on part of Commies to UNC proposal. (b) Commies have released record thru para 3 to the press. I have done likewise.

Apr. 29 (Tues): The news came out over the 0700 radio broadcast of R's appointment to succeed Eisenhower. As a consequence I decided to return to

Tokyo to discuss conference matters with R and arrange for someone to relieve me should the conference drag on indefinitely. Now that we have made our final offer there is little left for me to do. But if there is any chance for an armistice before 1 June I should of course like to see the job through and sign the document.

Left K-16 in P2V2 at 1515 with Galloway, Hickman, Darrow & Wagner, arriving Tokyo about 1830. Spent quiet evening at home.

Apr. 30 (Wed): Conferred with R at 0830[.] Also present were Galloway and Hickey[.] Told R that it was Del's [delegation's] opinion Commies would make a counter proposal when plenary session reconvened. Proposal will probably be to concede on USSR but to stand pat on POW issue under contention they have, by their Mar 27 principle of adjustment, already made a compromise proposal on POW issue. My intention was to reject out of hand any Commie counter proposal that does not come close to ours. A firm and immediate rejection shows them that we have rec'd [received] our final orders and that our final offer of Sunday is irrevocable. We must take JCS instrs [instructions] at their face value and continue to indicate by unmistakable firmness that our offer is truly final.

R agreed with me and said I had authority to reject out of hand any Commie offer that is not acceptable in my view.

I also brought up the question of holding in custody those POWs who had violently opposed returning pending the political conference. Said I did not like advocating the idea to the JCS until they showed signs of receding or adopting a much weaker stand. R agreed.

Also told R that if Commies desired to abrogate the closed sessions we should not protest but should say it was immaterial to us whether they did or not.

Was informed to the effect that a rumor had been going the rounds Commies had broadcasted intimation of defection of UN POWs in their hands to Communism. We discussed this and possibility Commies might claim only a percentage of our people desired to return to us. It was agreed that I would ask Commies, if they made any proposal which did not include return of all our 12,000, whether their proposal carried with it the willingness to have our people rescreened by a neutral body or joint RC teams immediately after the arm [armistice] is signed. If they answered in the negative I could then reject their proposal at once. If in the affirmative I would play it by ear.

I also asked R to line up a relief for me should it become apparent that the arm. conference would drag on indefinitely. Suggested Weyland. But I said that I would prefer to stay on until our final offer became public. Would not like to leave during these secret sessions. He agreed and assured me he would take the matter in hand.

That evening Martha [Mrs. CTJ} & I attended a dinner for Mr Murphy at the Rs [Ridgways]. Only the Weylands, Hickey & the Bonds were present.

I should also mention that I had an hours interview with Lindsay Parrot [correspondent for the *New York Times*] in the afternoon. Spoke "off the record" to him on several aspects of the conference, chiefly that I had protested to no avail against the present secret plenary sessions. R had supported us but Wash [Washington] had ordered them. Parrot has been directed by the Times to write a profile about me.

May 1 (Thurs): **Returned to camp leaving Haneda with Wagner in the P2V2 at 1100 and arriving Munsan at 1530.**

No sooner had I gotten squared away than Kinney came in to announce Commies want to meet tomorrow. He had accepted. I told him to notify Tokyo which was done. I then held a short conference with the Delegates & Kinney & Murray and told them what I had accomplished in Tokyo.

The fol'g article appeared in this ams Nippon Times. [See reproduction of original diary, p. 390.]

May 2 (Fri): 1. Delegation met in exec [executive] plenary session at 1100. Substance of record follows:

2. Commies: "In order that agreement may be reached on various items of agenda, our side has made great efforts. However your side still refuses to adopt a reasonable attitude to settling unresolved questions so that an arm [armistice] as yet cannot be realized. Responsibility entirely yours. Our correct stand on 3 major remaining issues and our reasonable solutions for these issues well known to people of world.

"Firstly re airfield question. As early as 5 mos ago when you raised question our side pointed out clearly that it was a matter of our internal affairs with which not slightest interference is permissible.

"Question should not have been raised at all. Yet for 5 mos you persisted in this demand on pretext of placing restrs [restrictions] on milt [military] forces. This pretext untenable. It was exactly to eliminate your apprehension concerning the growth of our milt strength, especially air, that our side agreed that there shall be no reinforcing from without Korea of the milt strength of either belligerent party and that our side further agreed to stipulate explicitly that there shall be no introduction into Korea of any reinforcing combat aircraft. It must be pointed out that since both sides have agreed not to introduce into Korea during the period of armistice any reinforcing milt forces including combat aircraft, it is already insured that both sides will not increase their milt air strength during the arm. Therefore the quest [question] of restricting the milt forces of both sides during the arm has long since attained a reasonable settlement.

"Secondly, re question of nomination of neutral nations our side has in accord with the agreement reached between both sides nominated 3 nations in full compliance with the definition of neutral nations to participate in the NNSC.

*Itold him & notify Tokyo which was
done. Ithen held a short conference
with the Delegates & Kinney & Murray
and told them what I had accomplished
in Tokyo.*

The folg article appeared in this ams Nippon Times

U.N. SEEN READY TO YIELD ON ISSUE OF AIRFIELD BAN

But Allies Want Reds to OK Return of Only 3 of 5 Prisoners

Kyodo-UP

PANMUNJOM, April 30—Red truce delegates were still silent at noon today as for the third day they mulled over the U.N. "package" offer to settle the Korean war. Hopes for an armistice agreement rose steadily.

Kyodo-UP

WASHINGTON, April 30—The United Nations Command has urged the Communists to agree to the return of only three out of five Red prisoners as part of a new secret formula to break the deadlock in the Korean truce talks, it was learned Tuesday.

Informants said the Allies in return indicated willingness to retreat on their proposal to ban

Kyodo-AP

WASHINGTON, April 30—The United Nations package deal on remaining Korean truce issues is "about the last offer we can make," Allied diplomats said Tuesday. Whether it will lead to an armistice or a breakdown depends on the Communist response and on decisions which American officials are convinced may be made as much in Moscow as in Peiping.

*And
we
were
directed
& hold
executive
sessions!*

*Another
example
of state
Department
leaks?*

construction of airfields in Korea after an armistice.

They also indicated Allied determination not to force repatriation of any Red prisoners in Allied captivity unwilling to return to the Communist fold.

The Allies apparently are prepared, however, to grant the Reds face-saving concessions where possible. But it was understood the United Nations refused to relax opposition to Red insistence that Russia serve as one of the neutral nations which would check on truce observance.

The Allies unveiled their new settlement proposal at a secret plenary session of truce negotiators at Panmunjom Monday. The Communists have asked for time to prepare their reply.

The three-out-of-five formula apparently would correspond to the proportion of Red prisoners who are willing to return to Communist control.

The Allies hold about 173,000 prisoners, including North Ko-
(Continued on Page 2)

U.N. Seen Ready To Yield on Issue Of Airfield Ban

(Continued From Page 1)
rean and Chinese Communist soldiers, South Koreans who served with the Red forces and South Korean civilian internees. Fewer than half of these say they want repatriation, according to a United Nations poll. But a number of prisoners were reported undecided and these presumably would help fill the three-fifths total indicated by the formula.

Your side cannot deny that all the nominations of neutral nations made by our side are in full compliance with the def. [definition] of neutral nations agreed upon by both sides. Therefore your side has no justification at all to object to any of nations nominated by our side. However your side has been unreasonably opposing our nomination of n.n. [neutral nations] under pretext of procedure of mutual approval of n.n. made by other side.

"As our side has pointed out the procedure of mutual approval of the nom. made by the other side is a formality showing mutual respect between two negotiating parties. Should not be used for rejecting noms. [nominations] made by either side in full compliance with the def. of neutral nations.

"In order to eliminate every possible excuse our side has further proposed that if a procedure of approval is required, both sides should approve simultaneously and at once all the noms. of n.ns. made by other side; otherwise each side can nominate n ns. respectively without going thru any procedure of approval. It is obvious that our proposal is a reasonable solution to this quest.

"Lastly, the question of POWs should not have become an issue. The fact that this quest has become an issue & is yet to be resolved is entirely due to your insistence upon a completely unjustifiable proposition which violates the Geneva Convention of war prisoners.

"Once active hosilities have ceased, it is the unmistakable obligation of belligerents to repatriate unconditionally all the captured personnel of the opposing side in its custody. This is of course beyond dispute. Yet your side fantastically raised the unreasonable proposition of the so called "vol repat" [voluntary repatriation] or "no forced repat," thus converting this indisputable and self evident question into one of the major obstacles in the way of an arm.

"Your so called "vol repat" is in substance forced retention. Your side unlawfully classified ¼ of the captured 176,000 of our side as civs. [civilians] & removed them from the POW lists submitted to our side.

"Everybody knows that these captured personnel of ours who were abstracted by your side are in the custody of your side. Your side absolutely cannot make these people disappear by the simple method of reclassification. Your side has tried to shirk the responsibility for retaining ¼ of our personnel by resorting to the excuse that our side released POWs during war movements. But your side should be aware that those captured personnel of your side whom we released had been released long before both sides exchanged POW lists and that their release definitely cannot be confused with the release & repat of the captured personnel of our side who are in your custody. The retention by your side of our captured personnel is illegal. In order that the deadlock of long standing on the quest. of POWs might be broken and that a settlement might be reached on the basis of mutual compromise, our side proposed on 21 Mar to lay aside for the time being the quest of the ¼ of our captured personnel who you abstracted from the POW list and that both sides agree to establish the prin [principle] of unconditional release & repat by each side of POWs in its custody but on the basis of the lists exchanged on Dec 18th, '51. That was a great con [concession] made by our side on the number of personnel to be repatriated. Under such circumstances, there was no necessity for our side again to modify in any way the principle of unconditional total repat. However in view of the repeated indication of your willingness to reach a settlement within the framework of the above mentioned principle submitted in writing by our side on 21 Mar and in order that a compromise solution may be sought for every aspect of the problem, our side again submitted a compromise principle of adjustment on Mar 27th. According to this principle of adjustment both sides must mutually repat all the non K captured personnel of the UNC and CPV. Both sides also must mutually repatriate all those captured personnel of the SKA who are natives of SK. and all those captured personnel of the KPA who are natives of NK. The only captured personnel who can be exempted from repat by either side are those Koreans who are natives, whose homes are in the area under the control of the detaining side & who desire to return to their native place & resume a peaceful life. It was in accord with this compromise prin. that our side proposed that both sides proceed to check the POW lists exchanged on Dec 18 '51. Had your side had the sincerity to reach settlement thru negots [negotiations] the question of POWs should have obtained a reasonable settlement within the framework of our demand of Mar 21st and on the basis of our proposal of adjustment of Mar 27th. Yet following such great concession made by our side, your side not only gave no indication of readiness to make some concession but on the contrary thru the compromise prin. according to which your side had indicated a willingness to negotiate repudiated your specific promises to seek a settlement within the framework of our prin of Mar 21 and to submit a figure close to 116,000 for the captured personnel of our side who would be repatriated. By applying the so called prin of "vol repat" to all the captured personnel of our side you produced the round no [number] of 70,000 for the POW whom you would repat. to our side and attempted to retain more than 100,000 of our captured personnel. Your side claimed that the rd. [round] no of 70,000 was the result of screening carried out by your side. It must be pointed out with emphasis that our side has never approved your so called screening. The result of so called screening has no legal validity whatsoever.

"The present situation of the POW problem is that your side has in your custody 176,000 captured personnel of our side. Your side is willing to repat only 70,000. Your side wants to retain 60% of the total of our captured personnel[.] On the other hand, our side has in our custody 12,000 captured personnel of your side and our side is prepared to repatriate all of them to your side.

"Our side decidedly cannot agree to your unilateral proposition of applying the so called prin. of vol repat to all the captured personnel of our side and to your outrageous attempt to detain more than 100,000 of our personnel. In order that a settlement may be reached thru negots [negotiations] our side has already made great efforts by submitting the draft prin. of Mar 21st. and the compromise proposal of adjustment of Mar 27th. Our side firmly and unswervingly maintains that those are the only reasonable solutions to the quests of the POWs.

"The above are the posits [positions] of our side on the 3 unresolved quests. It is obvious that the responsibility for the lack of agreement rests entirely upon your side. As our side stated on Apr 28th. in order to reach an arm. [armistice] our side has no objection to the settlement of the 3 issues together. Yet they must be settled on a reasonable basis. According to the nature of the various issues, it is perfectly clear that on the POW quest. our side has already made tremendous efforts and has submitted reasonable compromise solutions. If your side truly realizes that in these negots conducted by both sides on an equal footing, probs. [problems] can be solved only on a reasonable basis and thru mutual concessions, if your side is truly interested in reaching an arm. our side cannot see how your side can still imagine that our side would accept your unreasonable solution completely and can still refuse to adopt the reasonable compromise solution by our side. It is equally clear that the quest. of so called restrs on airfield facilities is itself a question which has no relation with the arm. negots. It is only because your side is bent upon delaying the arm. that it has been made an unresolved issue. In order to reach an arm. in Korea your side must give up this unreasonable demand to interfere in our internal affairs[.]

"Re. neutral nations, our posit on this quest is absolutely reasonable. Each of 3 n.ns [neutral nations] nominated by our side is in full compliance with def. [definition] of n.ns. agreed by both sides. Our side firmly maintains that your objection to our nominations of n ns is completely unjustifiable. **Your side has not been able to produce any tenable objection nor is it possible for your side to do so**. However in order to reach an arm in K at an early date to meet the primary wishes of millions of peace loving peoples all over the world, on this question of n ns our side is willing to consider the acceptance of your proposal for the NNSC to be composed of 4 n ns contingent upon your acceptance of our reasonable compromise proposal of POWs and your abandonment of restrs on airfield facilities within Korea, which constitutes interference in our internal affairs.

"I must make it unmistakably clear that our proposal is an integral whole. Our concession on the nomination of n.ns must follow the indisputable prerequisite that your side abandon the unreasonable demand for restricting airfields and adopt our compromise proposal on the quest of POWs. I must make it unmistakably clear that our proposal is a proposal for making a genuine compromise on a reasonable basis. Our solution to the POW quest is in itself a compromise solution accommodating the views of both sides to which your side has had no justifiable objection. And now when our side has again made a great effort on the quest of the nom [nomination] of the neut nats. [neutral nations] your side can have no justification at all to oppose our compromise solution to the POW quest.

As you are aware our solution to the POW quest is set forth in our draft principle of Mar 21st. and our proposal of adjustment of Mar 27th. The total of our captured to be repatriated by your side is 132,000, and the total of captured personnel to be repatriated by our side is 12,000. Our side has always been striving for an early arm. in Korea. This is clearly borne out by the great efforts made by our side on the various items of the agenda. However, our side decidedly will not, on account of this succumb to your unilateral and unreasonable demand[.]

"Now the question of whether an arm in Korea will be reached speedily is entirely up to your side.["]

3. UNC: ["]I have noted your statement[.] Your proposal is a modification of our solution of 28 Apr.

"You apparently did not understand the statement accompanying the UNC proposal of 28 April. At that time I advised you that it must be absolutely clear that the proposal of the UNC must be considered as a whole and that the UNC would not agree to any substantive change. Further I advised you that the UNC proposal was the final & irrevocable effort of the UNC.

"We will entertain no compromise of the integral solution we have proposed[.] Your proposal is, therefore, formally rejected. And again I repeat in the clearest language possible: The UNC proposal of 28 April is an integrated whole. It is firm. It is irrevocable and final.

"Whether or not we have an arm in Korea is a decision that rests entirely with you. That is all.["]

4. Commies: "I must point out with emphasis that our proposal has been submitted as an integral whole. Our concession on the nomination of neut. ntns [nations] must follow the indispensable prerequisite that your side abandon the unreasonable demand to restrict airfield facilities in Korea and agree to our compromise solution to the quest of POWs[.] On the question of POWs our side has exerted our utmost effort and submitted a compromise solution which is entirely reasonable. On the other hand, your side has in substance never made the slightest concession since Dec 11th last year but has on the contrary, gone a step backward by repudiating your own indication that you were willing to seek a settlement within the framework of our Mar 21 principle and that the nos of POWs whom your side would repat to our side would be close to 116,000. It must be pointed out that it was exactly such an attitude on your part of refusing to reach a settlement on the basis of the executive session of the staff offs on the 4th item of the agenda. In these negots conducted by both sides with an equal footing, it is necessary that within reasonable bounds both sides make mutual concessions in order that a problem may be settled. It is impossible for either side to require the other side to yield completely to its unilateral demands. If your side is interested in the settlement of the prob and in reaching an arm agreement, I

recommend that your side make a careful study of our statement today and seriously consider and accept our proposals.''

5. UNC: ['']Your proposal needs no further explanation or discussion. We understand it fully and reject it formally & finally. We have made our final integrated compromise offer. We shall not compromise further.

['']It is unmistakably clear that you have not had sufficient opportunity to study completely the statement that I gave you on 28 Apr. In order to give you time for further consideration of our fair proposal, I propose a recess until such time as you may elect or until tomorrow—whichever you prefer[.]''

6. Communists: ''I have already clearly explained our stand. Does your side mean there is nothing left to negotiate? I request a clear expression of your side[.] In order to reach an arm our side has already made tremendous efforts[.] In order that your side seriously consider the proposal of our side we will wait for the resumption of the meeting until we get a notification from your side.['']

7. UNC: ''You have our proposal. It is firm & final. Decision now rests with you[.]

''I propose that we meet tomorrow at the same time.''

8. Commies: ''We agree to your proposed recess and I suggest that you reconsider our reasonable proposal of today and accept it.''

Meeting adjourned at 1218[.]

I then sent fol'g comments along to R in a dispatch (HNC 1211):

''Part I (a) Now that UNC pkg [package] proposal has been presented in exec session, and has been met by an enemy counter proposal which in effect rejects the UNC pkg. the Del [delegation] is strongly of the opinion that authority should be granted to suggest reverting to open sessions. As long as we remain in exec session the enemy is unlikely to be convinced that no further UNC concessions are to be expected. Since the UNC took the initiative in placing the meetings in exec session the enemy will cling to the idea that the truly final UNC posit has not yet come forth[.] On the other hand if we revert to open sessions, the enemy is more likely to recognize that our posit is firm & unalterable.

b. If authority to suggest open sessions is granted we will propose this to the enemy at a time I deem appropriate. Once in open session, we will reiterate our pkg proposal as an equitable compromise solution and declare it to be firm & final. We will then tell the enemy that we are willing to meet at any time to explain or amplify our pkg proposal but since we will not in any event agree to substantial change in it, we propose a recess of the plenary sessions subject to recall at any time the enemy desires.

c. When the above action has been taken it is considered that an authoritative public statement should be issued in Wash. [Washington] confirming the final nature of our pkg proposal, if indefinite stalemate is to be avoided.

''Part II. In respect to the enemys question ''Do you mean there is nothing further to negotiate?'' I propose to answer this quest, if repeated as follows:

"If by negotiation you mean further concessions or compromises by the UNC the answer is no, there is nothing further to negotiate. If by negotiation you mean further explanation or amplification of the UNC proposal, we are willing to enter into such at any time and to any extent desired.''

May 3 (Sat): R answered my above msg by saying: "It is my sensing that we having expressly proposed "exec sessions" should not on our own initiative propose their abandonment in so brief a period. Were we to do so, free world public opinion might well conclude we have been unduly hasty and had failed to explore fully in exec session Commie reaction to our pkg [package] proposal. I therefore conclude we should continue in exec sessions for at least 2 more days even though sessions should be limited to mere asking if Commies have accepted our proposal and in event of negative answer, recessing. Keep me informed[.]

["]Desire you avoid use of "final" & "irrevocable" in future statements[.]''

R sent this msg info JCS who came back and said: "Your instrs [instructions] to Joy approved except there should be no restr [restriction] on Joy using words "final & irrevocable[.]''

Note: The JCS for once seem to be on our side!!

JCS also sent CinCFE a msg indicating that the White House, Secretary of State, Secretary of Defense as well as Ridgway would all make statements supporting the pkg proposal as soon as it was brought out in the open.

Delegations met in exec session at 1100. Substance of record follows:

Communists: "Yesterday our side refuted your statement and proposal of Apr 28th and submitted our fair & reasonable overall solution to all the problems yet to be resolved. Yet your side repeatedly stated that your proposal of Apr 28th was final & irrevocable. Such an expression made by your side was designed to delay and attempt to break the negots [negotiations] and was inconsistent with a proper attitude toward the negots and represented an intended threat to our side.

"If your side was determined to adopt an attitude of refusing to reason & negotiate your side should make an open and explicit indication and be prepared to shoulder the full responsibility for all the consequences of your action. If your side aims at using this as a threat to our side, I have to tell you frankly that such a threat from your side does not have any effect on the KPA and the CPV. If your side is still interested in continuing these conferences on a reasonable basis & thru negots, your side must abandon such an attitude of refusing to reason and refusing to negotiate. Your proposal of Apr 28 can in no sense constitute the basis for an overall solution to the problem. You claim that your side has made great concession. As a matter of fact your concession is merely the withdrawal of the unreasonable demand to interfere in our internal affairs in connection with the quest. [question] of so called restrs on airfield facilities within Korea a demand which should have been withdrawn by your side long ago. On the quest of POWs your side has made no substantive concession at all since Dec 11th last year. Furthermore, after your side indicated that you were willing to settle the quest. by compromise, repeatedly stated that you were willing to settle the quest within the framework of our draft principle of Mar 21st. and made the specific promise that the no [number] of captured personnel of our side whom you were to repatriate would be close to 116,000 your side has now made a retrogression and produced the rd. [round] no. of 70,000, insisted on the unreasonable proposition of applying the so called prin [principle] of 'vol repat' [voluntary repatriation] to all the captured personnel of our side and outrageously attempted to retain more than 100,000 of our captured personnel. You should be clearly aware that such a unilateral and unreasonable proposition and outrageous attempt of your side are what our side absolutely cannot consider under whatever circumstances.

"On the other hand, the quest of neut. [neutral] nations, on which our side made a concession in our May 2nd proposal, is an imp. question of substance. Our side has also made a major concession on the question of POWs in our draft principle of 21 Mar. and our compromise proposal of adjustment of Mar 27th. Your side has no ground at all to require our side to accept your unilateral and unreasonable proposal. Our proposal is completely fair and reasonable. Your side has no justification whatsoever to refuse to consider and accept it. The next step in these negots is now entirely up to your side.

"I must point out once again that if your side wishes to delay or disrupt the negots, your side should make an open and explicit expression—no ambiguities are permissible at this conference."

UNC: "We do not propose to enter into debate with you on posits [positions] which have been adopted in the past and which are well known to both sides. We have made our ultimate negotiatory effort with regard to the 3 issues involved; namely, airfield restriction, membership in the Neutral Nations Supervisory Commission, and the basis for the exchange of POWs. We stand ready to amplify or explain our proposal, but that is all. This is the firm position of the UNC.

"After studying your statement made yesterday, we found it unworthy of any more comment than has already been made. That is, your proposal is absolutely and finally rejected. Your statement of this am adds nothing new. The proposal made by the UNC Del on 28 Apr. is one which makes substantial concessions to the views of your side and which constitutes an equitable solution of the issues remaining before us. If your side sincerely desires an arm [armistice] in Korea, you will accept that proposal without further delay, debate or counter proposal which will avail nothing. There will be no substantive change in our proposal. No alternate proposal embodying substantial differences from the UNC Del proposal of 28 Apr. can ever be accepted by our side. The necessity to decide now confronts you. You cannot evade or compromise with it. The fate of these negots depends on whether you join with us in the fair and reasonable compromise solution proposed by us on 28 Apr.

"If you have nothing further to add, I propose a recess until tomorrow at the same time.["]

Commies: "It is obvious that your side has still no intention today to settle the quest. by adopting an attitude of reasoning and negotiating. Your attitude is no attitude of negotiating at all. Our side is firmly opposed to this attitude of yours. Your side must bear all the responsibilities for the consequences of such an attitude.

"In order that your side may have sufficient time to reconsider the attitude of your side, I agree to recess until tomorrow at the usual time."

Meeting recessed at 1123.

May 4 (Sun): R transmitted fol'g msg (JCS 907962) from JCS to us for info: "Assume you will inform Wash [Washington] prior to instructing UNC Del to take initiative to abandon exec [executive] nature of plenary sessions. However, this should not preclude UNC Del, if it desires from readily acquiescing in Commie proposal abandon exec nature sessions if record clear that initiative taken by Commies. While UNC Del should continue posture of full willingness to meet at any time Commies desire, not considered here that this requires UNC Del take initiative at this time in proposing subsequent daily meeting of delegates unless it considers useful negotiatory purpose would thereby be served. However, in absence of other action by Communists such as press release or radio broadcasts clearly in violation of agreement on exec sessions, do not consider that any failure of dels to meet should in itself be interpreted as abrogation exec nature of previous plenary sessions.["]

Delegations met in exec session at 1100. Substance of record follows:

Communists: "Our side has thoroughly refuted and hence also rejected categorically your proposal and statement of Apr 28th. In the spirit of settling probs [problems] on a reasonable basis thru mutual compromise and in accord with the nature of the questions themselves, our side submitted on May 2nd a completely reasonable overall solution. If your side is really sincere toward an early arm. [armistice] you should have no justification to refuse to consider and accept our proposal of May 2nd thereby settling all the remaining questions. Yet in your statement of yesterday you still adopt the attitude of refusing to reason and to negotiate and asserted that any further debate of counter-proposal would avail nothing and that your side refused to consider any compromises. I must tell you frankly that your peremptory attitude of refusing to reason and to negotiate and attempting to force our side to accept your proposal is of no avail on the del. of the KPA and the CPVs. If your side still wants to continue these negots [negotiations], you must withdraw this attitude of refusing to negotiate. Otherwise your side should openly declare that you now do not want to conduct the negots any further. Our side has already submitted a completely reasonable over-all solution. The next step in the arm negots is entirely up to your side. That is all for the moment.''

UNC: ''Your side overlooks the fact that our 28 Apr proposal was in itself, a compromise of the diffs [differences] outstanding between us. It may require more time, but ultimately your side will come to realize that the equitable com-promise solution proposed by the UNC cannot undergo substantive change and must, therefore, constitute the final agreement between us. The agreement we have proposed is the final compromise between the stated views of each side which the UNC will entertain. It is firm & unalterable[.]

''If your side is not prepared to accept this fair solution today, I suggest we recess until tomorrow or until such time as you may desire in order to give you further opportunity to study our position.''

Communists: ''Our side has thoroughly refuted and categorically rejected your proposal & statement of Apr 28th. Since today your side still obdurately refuses to reason & negotiate any attempts to push thru at this conference your unilateral and unreasonable proposition, it is obvious no progress can be made. In order that your side may have the time to reconsider carefully your position, I agree to recess until tomorrow at the usual time.['']

Recessed at 1113.

Comment: Re JCS 907962, it may not be possible for UNC delegation to avoid proposing daily meeting without giving Commies excuse to allege UNC has broken off negots.

May 5 (Mon): CinCUNC sent us the fol'g instrs [instructions] in a despatch (CX 67977) he sent the JCS.

''1. In view of your JCS 907962 I have today transmitted fol'g instrs to UNC Del:

''1. In light of developments plenary session 2–3 May concur with you that continuation of exec [executive] sessions is inimical to further progress in negots [negotiations]. Accordingly, you are authorized to propose termination of exec plenary sessions at any time you deem appropriate on or after 6 May[.] If at any time the Commies clearly propose termination of exec sessions you are authorized to accept at once at your discretion[.]

''2. In the event of UNC proposal for termination of exec sessions I be-lieve it important that Commies be given adequate opportunity to consider such proposal prior to termination; one method of accomplishing this would be a UNC statement in plenary session substantially as follows: ''In the light of events obtaining during the executive sessions on and subsequent to 2 May, I see no further purpose in continuing exec sessions. I therefore propose we recess and reconvene in open session in 20 mins unless at that time you have a different proposal.''

"3. In event of agreement on UNC proposal to terminate exec sessions arrange to inform me by fastest means possible and using code word which I will transmit by separate msg. If I receive this code word I intend to release a public statement from here outlining contents of pkg [package] proposal and UNC posit [position] thereon and you are authorized to release your prepared statement. If situation develops so that use of code word is insufficient you will ask in a secure manner & without delay for instrs."

[''']2. I feel it necessary to delegate this discretionary authority to Adm Joy for 2 primary reasons. First, to meet without delay the contingencies of Communist violation of agreement on exec session without warning and in that event to gain max [maximum] favorable attention of free world press by immediate publication of our prepared press release, and second, because if by 6 May, in his discretion no further substantial progress appears probable, believe added pressure of pub. [publicity] of UNC proposal will increase chance of Commie acceptance.['']

Delegations met in exec session 1100[.] Substance of record follows:

Communists: "If you have any statement to make, please go ahead; we are ready to hear it."

UNC: "I have no statement to make except to propose that our fair offer of April 28th, which represents a real & substantial concession to your point of view, be adopted at this session in order that an early armistice may be realized."

Communists: "There is nothing new in your statement. I clearly point out again that your attitude is no attitude for negots.

"In your statement of yesterday your side again asserted that your proposal was final and unalterable and even declared that it must constitute the ultimate agreement.

"I must point out once again that this attitude on your part of threat and refusing to reason and negotiate can have no avail on the delegation of the KPA & CPV. Our side has thoroughly refuted and categorically rejected your unilateral and unreasonable proposal of Apr 28th. Our side will continue to refute and forever reject that unilateral and unreasonable proposal of yours.

"Your side claims that your proposal is an equitable compromise proposal. As a matter of fact, the only concession made in our proposal is your withdrawal of the demand to interfere in our internal affairs in connection with the quest [question] of so called restrs [restrictions] on airfield facilities within Korea—a demand which your side should have withdrawn long ago. But after our side has made a great concession on the question of nominations of neutral nations, your side still insists upon your unilateral and unreasonable proposition on the quest of POWs, refuses to consider and agree to a reasonable compromise solution to the question of POWs and attempts to retain more than 100,000 of our captured personnel. Your proposal is in no sense equitable and is therefore what our side absolutely·cannot consider.

"In your statement of yesterday, your side openly expressed that your side would take more time in continuing to insist upon your unilateral and unreasonable proposition. It is obviously your objective to delay the arm [armistice] negots. It is our consistent aim to achieve an early arm in Korea and it is for this purpose that our side has been reasoning & negotiating with your side patiently. However, if your side should take this as a sign of weakness, on our part, you will ultimately come to realize your mistake. Our side has already made every effort on our part. The next step of the armistice negots is entirely up to your side.

"If you have nothing new to propose, in order that you may have enough time to reconsider your stand and accept our proposal, I propose to recess until 1100 tomorrow."

UNC: "I state again that our proposal is final & irrevocable. We agree to recess."

Recessed at 1111[.]

Comment: At tomorrows session UNC will explore termination of executive sessions in accord with CX 67977. If Commies show reluctance to terminate exec sessions UNC will not press for open sessions at this time.

May 6 (Tues): I sent the fol'g msg to CinCUNC[:]

"In view of JCS approval not to screen Commie dominated compounds at Koje Do it appears that the number of POWs to be repatriated to the Commies will be 80,000 to 85,000 in lieu of 70,000. While we cannot estimate what effect notification of an increase of 10,000 to 15,000 potential repats [repatriates] would have upon the Commie attitude toward the UNC posit [position] in the POW quest [question], we feel that the facts should be furnished them forthwith.

"b. The major disadvantage of such notification is that Commies may assume that UNC is weakening in its posit, and that further delaying tactics on their part might produce additional increases in repatriates.

"c. Balanced against this, is the possible increased chance of Commie acceptance resulting from (1) a substantial increase in the no. [number] of repatriates that is, approx 20% and (2) a change which could be interpreted by the Commies for their own purposes as a concession by the UNC, thus a face saver in the presence of the current firm attitude of the UNC. Moreover, if the negots [negotiations] were to be prolonged indefinitely or to be broken off over the POW issue it would be most difficult to explain to the world why the figure of 70,000 had been allowed to stand when the actual no to be repatriated was known to be 10,000 to 15,000 greater.

"Part II. The Del [delegation] considers that the possible advtgs [advantages] of presenting a new figure outweigh the poss. [possible] disadvtgs [disadvantages], and that the new figure should be given as soon as it is known. Accordingly the fol'g plan is submitted for your consideration[.]["]

I then outlined a plan for the liaison offs [officers] to inform the Commies of the firm figure. The figure would be introduced an [as] an administrative matter[.]

R replied there was considerable merit in our proposal outlined above; but that it could not be favorably considered at this time, because, although JCS had approved plan not to screen Commie dominated compounds at Koje Do, they directed that rosters containing names of unscreened personnel would not be submitted to Commies at this time.

R went on to say that until we have the final decision from JCS as to which names shall be included on the rosters, it is inadvisable to furnish Commies with any number in excess of 70,000.

Delegations met in exec [executive] session at 1100 today. Record follows:

Communists: "If you have any statement to make, please go ahead. We are ready to hear it[.]"

UNC: "I have nothing to add to what I have said previously. I again propose that our fair and reasonable solution which represents a reconciliation of both points of view be adopted without further delay[.] The next move is up to you."

Communists: "Your attitude of today also is no attitude for negots. There is nothing new in your statement. Since our side submitted our May 2nd fair & reasonable counter proposal, your side has taken an attitude of refusing to reason and negotiate in these conferences attempting by this means to force our side to accept your unilateral and unreasonable proposal of Apr 28th. I would like to tell you frankly that your side will not be able to reach your aim by so doing. Our side has thoroughly refuted and categorically rejected your unilateral and unreasonable proposal of Apr 28th and will continue to refute and reject that proposal of yours. Your attitude of refusing to reason and negotiate only serves to show that your side is determined to delay and even to disrupt the arm [armistice] negots.

"In the interest of an arm. I recommend that your side carefully reconsider your posit. Our side firmly maintains that our proposal of May 2nd is the only fair and reasonable proposal for the settlement of all the remaining issues. If your side has nothing further to say, I suggest a recess until the usual time tomorrow."

UNC: "The UNC Del recommended that these plenary sessions be of an executive nature because of the possibility that this type of session would facilitate progress toward the final agreement. Since this hoped for agreement has not materialized during more than a week, we see no point in continuing exec sessions. What are your views?"

Communists: "Do you mean to propose that we stop the exec session and go over to the open meeting?"

UNC: "I asked your views. What are your desires?"

Communists: "The executive session of the plenary session is originally a form which your side has proposed. Your side said that the form of the executive session would be helpful to the overall settlement of the unsettled issues but in fact your side has been assuming an attitude of refusing any negotiating and by assuming an unreasonable unilateral attitude in these meetings, your side has not made any progress. I want to know clearly your attitude about making the meeting open.''

UNC: ''I have just given you my attitude. I have said since this hoped for agreement has not materialized during more than a week, we see no point in continuing exec sessions. (Since Commies displayed surprise and indecision in consulting among themselves Adm Joy added the fol'g statement)[—]If you would like to give us your answer tomorrow, we now accept your proposal to recess until then.''

Communists: ''We agree to recess.''

UNC: ''It will be understood that we are still in closed session until tomorrow. We agree to recess.['] Meeting recessed 1115.

Comment: (a) Should Commies tomorrow leave the decision on termination of executive sessions with the UNC I will inform them that we will henceforth consider the executive sessions as terminated[.]

(b) In case (a) materializes or if Commies agree to terminate executive sessions I intend to propose a recess until such time as they desire to meet again, adding that we are ready to meet with them at any time should they desire further explanation or amplification of our proposed solution.

May 7 (Wed): R sent us JCS 908093 for info the gist of which follows:

''Fully appreciate difficulty of pro Commie compounds Koje Do & approve plan to list all POWs therein for return to Commie control. Assume no list will be given enemy until after agreement in principle is reached to arm. [armistice] terms[.]

''Concerned about deletions from list which might subject UNC to Commie propaganda charge of abrogating part of agreement & possible adverse on prompt return UNC POWs in Commie hands. Suggest feasibility of announcement to inmates compounds stating UNC assumes they all want to be repatriated and that this will be done. Desirable also to give them opportunity to express sentiments if possible.['']

R then asked 8th Army to develop plan for providing basis for an estimate of total no [number] of POWs & civ [civilian] internees in unscreened compounds to be returned to Commie control in case arm agreement is reached.

He then asked us if we had any suggested changes in procedure recommended in my msg to him of yesterday.

Delegations met at 11001. Gist of record follows:

Communists: ''When your side proposed on Apr 28 to hold the executive sessions of the plenary conference of the delegations, your side stated that you considered the exec [executive] form of meeting to be the most suitable form for the purpose for the overall settlement of the remaining issues. Yet since the exec form was adopted on Apr 28, since your side submitted your proposal and our side submitted on May 2nd our reasonable counter proposal, your side has taken consistently the attitude of refusing to negotiate and attempted to force our side to accept your unilateral and unreasonable proposal so that no progress can be made in the conference.

"During the staff offs. [officers] meeting on the 4th item of the agenda & during the plenary sessions, your side twice recommended to adopt the form of exec session and yet in these exec sessions your side repeatedly took the attitude of refusing to negotiate so that the form of executive session only serves to cover up the facts of the negots [negotiations] from the people of the world but could serve no useful purpose[.]

["]Our side has always been of the opinion that the settlement of the problems does not depend at all on the form of meeting but on the sincerity for settling problems and the attitude of negotiating no matter what form of meeting is so ordered providing there exists sincerity thru problems. Problems can be settled thru negots. Therefore, our side formally proposes to terminate the exec sessions and to enter from today into open sessions of the plenary conference of the delegations[.]["]

The Commies then went into a long harangue on their "just and reasonable proposal" as contrasted to our "unilateral and unreasonable proposition."

The fol'g passages are worthy of note and perhaps should be refuted to set the record straight.

"On the contrary after your side has indicated that you are willing to settle the questions (POW) within the framework of our Mar 21 principle of repatriation of POWs and stated that the figure of 116,000 was the approx total of the POWs whom your side were to repat. [repatriate] to our side, your side overthrew completely your own explicit indication & specific promise and cont'd [continued] to insist on your unreasonable proposition of applying the so called principle of vol. repat. [voluntary repatriation] to all captured personnel.

"The unilateral and unreasonable solution to the question of POWs as once again set forth in your proposal of Apr 28, only serves to show that your side is not in the least concerned with the interests of the captured personnel of your side and that your side is determined to delay and even to disrupt the arm. negots.

After Nam Il had finished his long review of their proposal which was only a repetition of what he had said before, I then said:

UNC: "I note that you agree with our statement of yesterday that no useful purpose shall be served by continuing the exec sessions. We accordingly consider the closed session terminated & that both sides are free to present the record to the world.

"Our position is clear, final & irrevocable[.] The issues are thoroughly understood & it is pointless to debate them further.

"Unless you have something new to offer, I propose we recess until such time as you desire to meet again. We are ready to meet with you at any time should you desire further explanation or amplification of our proposed solution."

Communists: "Our side has unmistakably clearly explained our position. Our side firmly holds that our proposal of May 2d is the only reasonable compromise proposal for the overall settlement of the remaining unresolved issues. But our side does not consider that there is any necessity to suspend (TN [Translator's Note]. The Korean word is synonymous with recess for a period of time) the conference. Your such [*sic*] attitude of threatening with a suspension of the conf. only serves to show that your side is determined to delay or even to disrupt the arm negots.

"Our side proposed that the plenary session of the Dels [delegations] continue to meet at 1100 tomorrow and that negots be open."

UNC: "Very well we agree."

Meeting recessed 1140.

Comment: Current instrs [instructions] are interpreted as requiring UNC del to meet in daily sessions as requested by Communists. In such sessions we will continue to refuse to debate substantive issues; offer to explain and amplify UNC solution and reiterate that our final position is final & irrevocable.

Note: The above indicates that the Commies want very much to continue the negots. The reason can be twofold: either they are preparing to concede or they wish to continue the talks as a smoke screen for their next offensive which they are not yet quite ready to launch. I believe the latter is the more probable because it is difficult for me to believe they will ever concede to the return of only 70,000 of their people.

After the plenary session today I made the fol'g statement to the press:

"After 5 days of executive meetings, it became abundantly apparent yesterday that no useful purpose would be served in continuing the sessions behind closed doors. Therefore the UNC yesterday proposed that the temporary agreement be terminated forthwith. The Communists today agreed.

When we called for the plenary session on April 28, it was with high hopes that our equitable overall solution would reconcile the divergent views of both sides. The quest [question] of the Soviet Union as a member of the Supervisory Comm. [commission] was never a real issue[.] It was an artificial one, created by the Communists for bargaining purposes only.

The milt [military] airfield issue and the POW issue represented the crux of the prob. [problem] with which we were faced.

Therefore our pkg [package] proposal, which represents our firm & ultimate proposal was introduced. We were willing to accept the Commies views on milt airfields if they would accept the fact that the UNC would not be a party to forced repat.

The purpose of the UNC suggesting initially that the talks be conducted temporarily in closed session was threefold:

1. To attempt to convince the Commies that our proposal was truly sincere, and was not merely a propaganda vehicle[.]

2. To permit them to modify their previously expressed stand without public attention, thus facilitating their acceptance of our compromise proposal.

3. To avoid the inevitable propaganda morass which the Communists have created around open discussions in the past.

The Communists have so far rejected our final, unalterable compromise. It was obvious that nothing more could be accomplished in exec session, and we now release the details of the recent series of plenary sessions.

As I told the Commies yesterday, the next move is up to them.["]

May 8 (Thurs): Delegations met in plenary at 1100. Substance of record follows:

Communists: "I point out once again that the KPA and the CPVs categorically rejected your proposal of Apr 28th. Your unilateral and unreasonable proposition to retain more than 100,000 of our captured personnel is what our side can absolutely not consider.

————"Your proposition to apply the so called principle of "vol repat" [voluntary repatriation] to all the captured personnel of our side is an attempt to retain more than 100,000 of our captured personnel goes against every international law and constitutes an outright violation of the explicit stipulation of the Geneva convention. As everybody knows, there does not exist any amt [amount] of freedom in your POW camps. The so called screening carried out by your side among our captured personnel is utterly absurd. Your so called result of screening is completely invalid. Your suggestion that "on the spot" investigation be conducted after the signing of the arm. [armistice] into the so called result of your screening is doubly absurd. To put forth such a suggestion—who should have known clearly that it is totally opposed by our side—shows that your side has no other objective than to deceive the world.

"On the question of POWs. your side has not made the slightest concession since Dec 11th last year. etc etc————This proves that your side has not the least concern with the interests of your own captured personnel————.

Usual propaganda about Chiang Kai Sheks brigands & coercion of their people. Then went on to say: "In what way is your side qualified to invite investigation after the signing of the arm? The people of the world have seen thru the deceiving tactics of your side. To release & repat all the POWs so that they may return home is an explicit stipulation of the Geneva convention, an inescapable responsibility and obligation provided for in all international laws————.["]

UNC: ["]I have no statement to make. Our posit [position] should be very clear to you by this time. If you have nothing constructive to offer, I suggest we recess until such time as you may desire.["]

Commies: "Your attitude of refusing to reason and to negotiate once again exposes your deliberate intention to delay the arm. negots [negotiations]. If your side should imagine that such an arbitrary attitude could force our side to accept your unilateral and unreasonable proposal, I advise you that the sooner you give up your illusion the better. Such an attitude of your side will serve no purpose except to delay the armistice negots."

"In order that your side may reconsider your stand I propose to recess until the usual time tomorrow.['']

Generals Ridgway, Clark* and Van Fleet visited the camp today from about 1530 to 1800. After attending a ceremony in which R decorated a nurse with the bronze star we repaired to my tent for conferences.

I was astounded to hear that General Dodd had been captured in one of the Communist compounds and was being held hostage while Commies were demanding all sorts of privileges. R gave orders that force was to be used as necessary tomorrow am in order to regain control and rescue Dodd if possible.

Discussed the folg with R: (1) Giving Commies additional info concerning the 10,000 to 15,000 more POWs who wish to return to them. R agreed with me that it ought to be done on liaison level as an administrative matter as soon as possible when lists are ready to be checked. Figure should be given as a firm final figure.

(2) Our tactics at Pan Mun Jom. I said we will avoid substantive debate and simply reaffirm again and again that our position is firm, final & irrevocable[.] Commies will probably attack our stand on POWs on basis we are more concerned about their POWs in our hands than our own in theirs. 1 will refute this in press statements but not at conference table. R agreed with me[.] Also read type of statement I would give daily which he also agreed with.

Discussed my relief by Harrison in two weeks with which both he & Clark agreed. Collins will not give Harrison another star but Clark will give him a Corps later on. Clark OK'd Libby being relieved provided I found a suitable relief.

I was indeed sad to see R depart. His support of the Dels [delegation's] effort throughout these negots. has left nothing to be desired. We shall sorely miss his loyalty, wise counsel and guidance.

May 9 (Fri): Plenary session commenced at 1100. Gist of record follows:

Communists: "Since 2 May your side has persistently taken at these conferences the attitude of refusing to reason & negotiate. This fact fully proves that your side has no reason whatsoever with which to argue for your unilateral and unjustifiable proposal. Your side attempts by means of your refusal to negotiate to force our side to accept your unilateral and unreasonable proposal, but I can

---

* Note: Lt. Gen. Mark W. Clark, USA, Chief of Army Field Forces, replaced Ridgway as CinCUNC on April 28, 1952.—Ed.

assure you your side will not be able to achieve your attempt. No matter what the tactics are, *inside or outside* the conference you will not be able to convert your unilateral & unreasonable proposal into a fair & reasonable one. Our side has categorically rejected your unilateral & unreasonable proposal."

Then followed a tirade against UNC violation of Geneva convention, vol repat [voluntary repatriation], **and screening of Commie POWs.** Also: "The endless series of bloody incidents occurring in your POW camps clearly proves that your so called screening is only a means of returning forcibly captured personnel of our side."

Usual ending that their side's solution is only fair & reasonable solution to all issues yet to be solved.

UNC: "The firmness & finality of the UN position should be unmistakably clear to you by this time. I have nothing else to add. We agree to recess."

Recessed 1110.

No news from Koje Do.

May 10 (Sat): Just before starting for Pan Mun Jom the fol'g JC msg (JCS 908433) was reenciphered to us for action:

"1. Considered here imp. [important] that in any subsequent meeting of delegates, Commies not gain any propaganda advantage or initiative from such sessions, which from their statement, it is apparent they will attempt to do. In subsequent open plenary sessions UNC should present in clear emphatic terms reasonable nature of its proposal in endeavor [to] keep Commies on defensive propaganda wise and to maintain widespread support for UNC position in negots [negotiations][.]

"2. In such presentation desirable UNC delegates include repetition in each session willingness UNC to submit to an impartial rescreening of POWs in accord with proposal of 28 Apr and reasonableness this proposal as resolution of POW issue. Believe this affords UNC strong and positive issue commanding worldwide support and forcing enemy into increasingly weak posit [position] propaganda wise. Repetition this fair & impartial proposal coupled with firm stand on overall UNC proposals should serve [to] keep strong negotiating and propaganda position for UNC."

Upon return from Pan Mun Jom I sent fol'g msg to CinCUNC (HNC 1228).

"1. No action was taken on (ref a [*sic*] JCS 908433) at todays session due to lateness of receipt of cited msg. In JCS 903687 the UNC del was directed to avoid substantive discussion of the elements of our pkg [package] proposal. In accord with this latter directive the Del has for ten days tersely refused to debate the elements of our Apr 28 proposal. JCS 908433 however seems to direct abandonment of this procedure. It is the opinion of the del. that to enter into substantive discussion of the POW issue at this time will induce a conclusion on the part of the Commies that our position is weakening. We had expected to accomplish the results sought by JCS 908433 thru releases to the press and comments of the Senior Delegate to the press at Pan Mun Jom while continuing to refuse substantive discussion in the conference tent. We believe that this procedure best maintains the firmness of our position while allowing us the advantage of propaganda initiative. In the last 2 days a notable diminution of Commie propaganda speeches re. our Apr 28 proposal has occurred in the conferences.

"2. We consider that the above procedure together with an occasional carefully worded short statement in plenary sessions attacking the Communist failure to accept the UNC proposal, will achieve the objectives sought by JCS 908433[.]

Fol'g is record of plenary session today:

Communists: "Before the opening of the plenary session, I want to make a notification. I am authorized by the Comdrs [commanders] of our side to convey to your side the fol'g notification:

"During the time when our captured personnel are in the custody of your side, your side is systematically taking a series of barbarous measures to attain your long deliberated objective of forcibly retaining our captured personnel. These criminal acts committed by your side under the name of "vol repat" [voluntary repatriation] thoroughly violate the Geneva convention relating to POWs and repudiate the min [minimum] standard of human behavior. The resistance of our captured personnel against these unlawful and perfidious acts of your side is entirely justified. The sanguinary suppression, one after another, perpetrated by your side cannot shake the firm will of our captured personnel to demand their right to repatriation. However when your side has not yet given a responsible account for the sanguinary massacres of our captured personnel of Feb 18 & Mar 13, the Comdr of your side openly declares on May 9 that yet another massacre will be carried out against the bare handed captured personnel of our side. This is not to be tolerated[.] Your side should be clearly aware that it is the inescapable obligation of the Comdr of each side to ensure the safety of the POWs under his custody and to respect their personal dignity[.] Your side must bear the full and absolute responsibility for the safety of our captured personnel. Now I will hand over the notification I have mentioned in writing[.]"

UNC: "Your notification being entirely unfounded in fact is categorically rejected."

Communists: "Under such pretext, you cannot avoid your due responsibility for your POW camps."

UNC: "The UNC has always attempted to exercise humane methods in controlling the POWs in its custody. However some of these POWs have taken advtg [advantage] of these humane policies, have instigated riots and violence among themselves and have now seized the camp comdr. whom they are holding hostage. The UNC will take whatever measures are necessary to eliminate this intolerable situation and restore control over POW compounds."

Communists: "Under whatever pretext you cannot evade your responsibility for your criminal acts. In our notification we have clearly said that any denial of your side cannot cancel your responsibility for the captured personnel of our side.

"Now lets go over to the plenary sessions[.]"

"Our side has thoroughly refuted & categorically rejected your proposal of Apr 28th. Our side has submitted a reasonable compromise solution to all the issues yet to be resolved. If your side has anything new to say we are ready to hear it. If not we propose to recess until the usual time tomorrow."

UNC: "We agree." Recessed 1112 I.

R sent on gist of my msg (HNC 1228) to JCS asking for reconsideration of JCS 908433 (see his CX 68269).

Dodd was released by Commies at 2130[.] No violence[.]

May 11 (Sun): JCS reply (JCS 908528) to R's CX 68269 of yesterday was reinciphered [*sic*] to us for action. Gist of msg follows:

"Some misinterpretation of JCS 908433 appears to exist on your part. Msg was not intended to modify in any way the procedures outlined in JCS 903687 to the effect that in plenary sessions UNC del would refuse to be drawn into debate on individual points of final UNC proposal, nor should these instrs [instructions] be interpreted as restraining the UNC del on its own initiative from reiterating as appropriate its firm posit [position], or any part thereof, if in so doing Commies could be placed in position of refusing to agree to our fair & reasonable solution. View here is the reiteration by UNC of its proposal for impartial rescreening of POWs would not be considered by Commies as weakness and disposition toward compromise, but would be opportunity for us to capitalize on strongest aspect of UNC position. Re emphasis of this proposal need not require UNC Del to become involved in substantive debate on entire POW issue[.]"

There follows the record of the plenary session this date:

UNC: "We have been meeting here daily at your request, since the 2nd of May. In nine consecutive meetings nothing has been accomplished. No progress has been made simply because your side is not yet willing to face acceptance of the rights of the individual.

"The longer your side delays acceptance of the UNC compromise proposal of Apr 28th, the more the world is convinced that you will not face the truth. Your side even fears the results of a joint, open verification of the screening of POWs. Your fear of this rescreening process can stem from only one consideration: your side knows it cannot face up to truthful results of such rescreening even when verified by your own representatives. Therefore you are guilty of delaying these negots [negotiations] because you dare not face the facts.

"Let me say once again: the equitable compromise proposal of the UNC is firm, final & irrevocable. We shall not recede from it. Any delay in reaching agreement is due entirely to the refusal of your side to recognize this fact. We shall not vary or recede from this posit. If you are not prepared today to accept our proposal, I suggest a recess until your side desires to meet again."

Communists: "In your statement of today there is nothing new at all. The so called rescreening and reconsideration which you talked about is not tenable. It is nothing else than your attempt to deceive again the people of the world under such pretext. We categorically rejected your unilateral and unreasonable proposal of Apr 28. There is only one thing which blocks the realization of an arm. [armistice] in Korea, that is your unilateral and unreasonable proposition on the quest [question] of POWs.

"Your side, in thorough violation of the Geneva convention and repudiating the min [minimum] standards of humane behavior employs all sorts of barbarous measures against our captured personnel, conducts activities of the so called screening which are totally impermissible and attempts to retain forcibly our captured personnel under the name of so called "vol repat" [voluntary repatriation].

"What your side calls humane methods in control of POWs are in actuality the use of whatever force is necessary. In order to manufacture your so called results of screening, your side does not hesitate to employ openly measures of massacre to coerce our captured personnel into tattooing, submitting appeal, writing petitions in blood, fingerprinting & so on.

"These acts committed by your side not only lack any features in common with the principles of humanity but are precisely antagonistic to humanitarianism and constitute direct violation of arts 13 & 14 of the Geneva convention.

"Your side shoots hundreds of our bare handed captured personnel every month and constantly carries out bombing against your own captured personnel. Your side completely disregards the natural desire of captured personnel of both sides to be repatriated. Your side systematically creates obstacles to prevent the settlement of the quest. of POWs to prevent the cessation of the Korean war and to prevent the POWs of both sides from returning to their homes.

"The just resistance of our captured personnel against the atrocities perpetrated by your side has already exposed to the world the true essence of your so-called 'vol repat.' The del. of the KPA & the CPV is firmly and unshakably opposed to your unilateral and unreasonable proposition. [Preceding two sentences emphasized in text by lines in margin at 45° angles.] Our side has made great concessions on the quests of POWs and submitted an entirely reasonable compromise proposal. I am ready to hear anything new you may wish to say. Suggest recess until tomorrow at usual time."

UNC: "Your statement is nothing but a tedious repetition of your flagrant propaganda. It has no basis in fact. It is only further confirmation that your side dares not face the facts which would be produced by an impartial verification of the screening process.

"Your position is based on fear of the truth. We agree to your recess until tomorrow."

Communists: "As I have said already the so called re-screening & reconsideration which you are talking about are nothing other than your attempt to deceive the people of the world."

Meeting recessed 1120.

May 12 (Mon): Gist of record of plenary session follows:

UNC: "It has long been evident that your side dares not admit before the world that some of your captured personnel could not be returned to you without the use of force. It is obvious you are not willing to verify this fact for yourselves by participating in an impartial re screening, after the signing of an armistice, to prove beyond cavil that the personnel who have refused to return to you have done so of their own free will. You know that the results of such action on your part would completely destroy the basis for your propaganda by the simple process of requiring you to acknowledge the truth[.]

"In order to avoid facing up to the truth, your side apparently is quite willing to delay indefinitely the settlement of this issue and the attainment of an armistice, and meanwhile to continue to utilize these plenary sessions to trumpet your propaganda[.] Thus your side, by its unwillingness to meet the challenge of incontrovertible facts openly and impartially arrived at, condemns itself and its false assertions beyond any quest. No more conclusive proof of your guilt in delaying an armistice has ever come forth in these negots [negotiations]."

Communists then lodged a protest with us over the strafing by 4 milt [military] aircraft of their No 8 POW camp at Kangtong [Kangdong?]. Their protest was accompanied by their usual propaganda line on our "humanitarian treatment."

Then followed one of their most vicious propaganda statements in rebuttal of our remarks of yesterday. Said we would not allow news reporters at Koje for on the spot investigation of POW camps. Said "**In order to camouflage your outrageous attempt to retain forcibly the captured personnel of our side and to practice your habitual tactics of deceiving the whole world, your side again brought up in your statement of yesterday the position of the so called impartial and joint rescreening of POWs and the partial re-screening process. Our side has thoroughly exposed and rejected categorically this deceitful proposal of your side long ago.**" — — — "**Activities of the so called screening are in themselves a direct violation of the Geneva convention relating to POWs[.]**"

"Art 118 of the Geneva Convention explicitly provides that POWs shall be released from incarceration and repatriated without delay after the cessation of active hostilities.[']"

Commies also quoted Art 7 of the Geneva Convention: "prisoners of war may in no circumstances renounce in part or in entirety the rts [rights] secured for them in the present convention." in contending that UNC is depriving POWs of their inalienable right to repatriation.

————"Ever since May 2nd your side has not hesitated to resort persistently to means which may cause a break down in negots. in an attempt to force out side to accept your unilateral and unreasonable proposal. *I must point out to you frankly that if your side is determined to disrupt the arm.* [armistice] *negots. you should formally declare the breakdown of the negots.* Otherwise our side will insist on holding the meetings continuously and our side will at these meetings continue to oppose firmly and unswervingly reject the unilateral and unreasonable proposal of your side.

"Yesterday your side declared once again from your unilateral and unreasonable proposal. I would like to ask you again does this mean that your side is prepared to break up the arm. talks? Your side should be clearly aware that these threatening methods of your side only prove to the whole world that your side has no sincerity toward the negots[.] Both in the conference and in the battle field your threatening methods have encountered persistent defeat. If they persist the very end will be even greater defeat. Today you again proposed a recess sine die. I must point out that such repeated proposal for an indefinite recess is merely a design of your side to delay and even to disrupt the arm. negots. If your side attempts to use indefinite recess as a means to coerce our side into accepance of your unilateral and unreasonable proposal, your side will never achieve your aim. Our side is firmly opposed to an indefinite recess. But if your side wishes to decide unilaterally on an indefinite recess, while not prepared to disrupt the negots your side should say now when these conferences will be reconvened. Your side must also bear full responsibility for the delay of the arm negots which may arise therefrom.

"If your side is not prepared unilaterally to decide on an indefinite recess, or to declare openly the termination of the arm negots, our side is opposed to your action of delaying the arm negots under the disguise of an indefinite recess and insists that the plenary conferences of the dels [delegations] should continue and meet tomorrow at the usual time.["]

UNC: "These meetings are being called daily by your side. It is to be expected that the side which calls for the plenary sessions has something progressive to offer toward arriving at an arm. The UNC called for the initial meetings in this current sequence of plenary sessions in order to present our reasonable compromise solution of the remaining issues. We have presented this fair solution and have nothing further to offer. Your side however, continues to call plenary sessions daily without presenting any constructive thought, without accepting the compromise proposed by the UNC, and solely to attempt to conceal your weakness in transparent, false propaganda. Thus it is made clear to the world that your intent in calling these meetings is one of propaganda, not one of achieving an armistice. Because you fear confirmation of the truth implicit in the UNC proposal for joint or neutral re-screening after the arm of all personnel who refuse to return to the other side, you continue to attempt to hide behind the smoke screen of the propaganda you release at these meetings[.] The UNC del. will continue to meet with you at your request but the UNC formally disassociates itself from the propaganda purposes for which you are now utilizing these meetings.

"Your remarks concerning the 11 May incident are noted. Your protest is also noted and appropriate investigation will be made. We agree to your proposal to meet again tomorrow."

Commies: "Our side has resolutely rejected your unilateral and unreasonable proposal of Apr 28th. On May 2nd. we presented our fair & reasonable proposal.

"We are not making any propaganda before the people of the world but we are merely making them know clearly the truth of the conferences. By doing so we expose your tactics of deceiving the people of the world. Our side opposes firmly and unshakably your unilateral and unreasonable proposal, but we have been consistently and patiently carrying on the negots with your side. Since your side does not firmly declare the disruption of the negots our side will insist on the usual proceding [*sic*] of the conferences and our side will firmly oppose your unilateral and unreasonable proposal. It is exactly your side which does not dare to face the facts. Our side will continue to reveal thru these conferences to the people of the world these undeniable facts and expose your false[hoods?][.]

["]Now let us recess until 1100 tomorrow.["]

Meeting recessed at 1152[.]

After a conference upon return to camp I sent the fol'g msg (HNC 1236) to CinCUNC[:]

"Part I. It has become evident that the Communists will continue to use further meetings solely as a propaganda vehicle and that they have no intention of accepting the UNC proposal at least not for the present. In effect, the Commies have laid down a challenge to the UNC to either back up its statements of finality re. our pkg [package] proposal, or compromise the POW issue. Today the Commies in effect challenged the UNC to terminate the conference unless we are willing to meet daily.

"It may be that the Commies do not expect a concession by the UNC but are instead seeking to provoke the UNC into breaking off the conference, i.e. they are unwilling to meet our terms in order to get an arm, but wish to put the onus for breaking off the talks on the UNC. We believe the issue must now be squarely faced. It appears to the del that the time for decisive action is here; that a determination must be arrived at to risk the onus of a possible breakoff of negots in a final effort to achieve an armistice. To continue along the present lines of action is to exhibit serious weakness at a time when a posture of strength is imperative. **In view of the strong statements made by the President and other**

high officials of the UN that our present position is final, the del. considers we should be authorized to announce unilaterally a suspension of the conferences until the Commies are ready to accept the UNC proposal of 28 Apr without substantive change. We would accompany this announcement with a statement that the liaison officers would maintain contact during the period of suspension. We recognize that the Commies could utilize this action to support a charge that the UNC broke off negots. We also recognize that even were the Commies to break off negots themselves they would charge the breakoff to the UNC.

"If the Communists will ever accept an arm on our terms, the action recommended will not cause them to break off negots. If they are determined not to accept our terms, no action by UNC short of capitulation to their position will gain an armistice. Further discussion of the remaining issues is futile since all have been exhaustively and thoroughly discussed. The UNC del cannot thwart the Commies intent to utilize the plenary session as a propaganda outlet so long as these sessions continue.

"Part II. Two courses of action are open, (1) We can continue to meet daily at Commie insistence. This is an evidence of UNC weakness and follows Commie initiative and desires. (2) We can unilaterally suspend further meetings until the Commies are willing to accept our 28 Apr proposal without substantive change. We would in this course of action maintain contact thru the liaison offs [officers].

"Part III. The del unanimously recommends implementation of course (2) at the discretion of the Chief Delegate[.]"

In his CX 68355 Clark sent above msg to JCS heartily concurring in the views of the del and strongly recommended that he be authorized to implement course of action (2) at his discretion.

Deptar (G-3) replied saying recommendation under consideration. ["]You will be advised as soon as possible. In interim you are to continue under existing intrs [instructions].["]

May 13 (Tues): [At top of page appears the note: "Colson's Statement."] This morning in a press statement Clark gave out the details of the Dodd incident at Koje Do. In this press statement the fol'g reply of Brig Gen Colson to the Communists' demands was published. As Clark said Colson (who had relieved Dodd as Camp Comdr [commander]) apparently acted on his own initiative.

"I do admit there have been instances of bloodshed where many POWs have been killed or wounded by UN Forces. I can assure you that in the future the POWs can expect humane treatment in this camp according to principles of int [international] law. I will do all in my power to eliminate further violence & bloodshed. If such incidents happen in future, I will be held responsible.

"Regarding your item 3 pertaining to forcible investigation (screening) I can inform you that after Gen Dodds' release unharmed there will be no more forcible screening or any rearming of POWs in this camp, nor will any attempt be made at nominal screening.''

From our standpoint no more damaging statement could possibly have been issued.

Clark attempted to tone down the impact of Colson's reply by saying that any violence that has occurred at Koje has been the result of deliberate and planned machinations of unprincipled Commie leaders. But the damage has been done!*

There follows gist of record of plenary session:

Commies started off by protesting attack on supply trucks of Del [delegation] by one of our aircraft which killed one working personnel. Trucks on way from Pyongyang to Kaesong. Requested that UNC deal with incident speedily and responsibly.

Commies then went into usual long propaganda tirade on subject of our forcibly retaining their personnel. Although we claim to abide by Geneva convention we still cling to absurd proposition of so called vol repat [voluntary repatriation], designed for forced retention of POWs. ''Your side refuses to carry out your obligation to repatriate your POWs and in effect your side also contradicts the wishes of your own captured personnel to return home & rejoin their families.''

Also accused us of refusing to negotiate[.] ''You only stress arbitrarily that your unilateral and unreasonable proposal is firm final & irrevocable.''

UNC: ''For 12 consecutive days we have met at your request. The only valid reason for holding these plenary sessions is to attempt to reach an arm. **Your side has however cont'd to utilize these meetings solely as a device by which to put your vicious propaganda before the world.** These propaganda statements of your are calculated not to facilitate agreement but to widen the breach between our 2 sides. There is one primary inescapable fact your side has no[t] yet been willing to face & that is: The UNC compromise proposal of 28 Apr is final, unalterable and irrevocable.

''Since there is nothing left to discuss all the facts are known & the issues clear, we agree to recess until tomorrow[.]''

Commies: ''Our side continues to explain our reasonable proposal and to refute your unilateral and unreasonable proposal on the basis of unshakable facts & in accord with clear logic. In order to develop the discussion this is entirely necessary. Your side cannot cover up with any pretext the unreasonable attitude of your side, of refusing to reason, refusing to negotiate, and refusing to conduct discussions which in effect entirely negates the purpose of these negots [negotiations].

---

* At later meetings the Communists refer to the statement of the ''commandant'' and also the ''former commandant'' of the Koje Do camp, meaning Colson's statement. Dodd testified later that he modified Colson's original draft to satisfy his captors and this reply was then signed by Colson.—Ed.

"To make the facts and the truth public to the people of the world can only be of help to the negots. What blocks progress in these negots is your absolutely unreasonable attitude of totally refusing to negotiate.

"It is your side which does not want to face the facts to settle the question. It is precisely your side which is afraid of facing our reasonable and compromise proposal of May 2nd."

["]Lets recess until tomorrow.["]

May 14 (Wed): The gist of the record of the plenary session follows:

Commies: "After your side submitted your proposal of Apr 28th our side submitted our entirely fair and reasonable counter proposal of May 2nd. But since then, your side has persistently taken the outrageous attitude of refusing to reason and refusing to negotiate, avoided discussion and attempted to force our side to accept your unilateral and unreasonable proposal by tediously reiterating that your proposal is "final, unalterable and irrevocable."

"I must point out again that your outrageous and threatening attitude be speaks [*sic*] your deliberate intention of delaying and even disrupting the negots will not be capable of producing any effect on the KPA and CPVs but only serves to show that your side has no sincerity to reach an agreement on the quest [question] of POWs and to bring about an arm. [armistice] in Korea.

————["]Unless your side openly and explicitly declares that your side has decided to break off the arm. negots [negotiations], our side will continue to insist upon the normal holding of conferences and continue to explain in these conferences our proposal and refute your proposal on the basis of logic and facts. The undeniable facts are that your side applies all sorts of inhuman treatment against our captured personnel and resorts to every means of violence to push through the totally impermissible activities of the so called screening among our captured personnel so as to create your so called results of screening[.]

"In his reply to our captured personnel re: the dark instance the comdt [commandant] of your POW camp openly admitted, "There has been bloodshed; many POWs have been killed & wounded by the UN forces. I can give you assurance, and it should be confined to the POWs in the camps, that they can expect humane treatment in the future in accord with the principles of int [international] law. I will do all within my power to eliminate further violence & bloodshed." The comdnt of your POW camp also promised that, "There will be no more forced screening or any rearming of any POW in this camp."

"The official reply of the comdnt of your POW camp, openly admitted treatment of POWs inconsistent with int. law. and in violation of the Geneva convention, admitted acts of violence, admitted forced screening, and conclusively testified before the whole world to the iron clad fact that your so called "vol repat" [voluntary repatriation] is solely the result of violence & forced screening. This is the primary and inescapable fact.

"Yesterday your side went to the length of saying that your assertion that your Apr 28 proposal was final, unalterable, and irrevocable was a primary and inescapable fact and yet an arbitrary assertion repeated by your side does not represent any fact. It only shows that your side does not yet desire to reach an agreement on the question of POWs, so as to bring about an arm. in Korea. The final, unalterable and irrevocable facts are the determined resistance of our captured personnel against your inhuman treatment and the righteous struggle of our captured personnel against your forced screening; they are that your side will never be able to succeed in your attempt to retain our captured personnel as your cannon fodder.

"Your side stated that to make the facts public to the whole world would not facilitate agreement but would only widen the breach between our two sides but the facts are not to be covered up or pushed aside. The reason why a breach exists between our two sides, and why an agreement cannot be reached has nothing to do with publication of facts, but is because your side has taken the outrageous attitude of refusing to reason and refusing to negotiate and insisting upon your unilateral and unreasonable proposal.['']

UNC: "It is apparent that you are still not yet ready to accept the UNC equitable compromise proposal of 28 Apr. without substantive change but wish to continue to propagandize from this tent rather than to act seriously in the interest of an armistice. It is equally apparent that the major reason for such destructive tactics is your fear of an open, joint re-screening of POWs conducted under fair & equitable circumstances. Each day adds to your already heavy guilt in delaying an arm. We agree to your recess until tomorrow."

Meeting recessed at 1122 hrs.

May 15 (Thurs): Gist of the plenary session follows:

Commies opened by bringing up alleged violation of Kaesong neutral zone on 14 May whereby milt [military] aircraft of our side dropped flares & straffed [*sic*] Kaesong neutral zone. Then said that series of incidents exposed UNC design to delay or disrupt negots [negotiations].

Nam Il then went on with a long propaganda statement claiming that statement made by Brig Gen Colson to POWs was proof that UNC had carried out violence against Commie captured personnel. and pushed through "so called screening by force in attempt to retain our captured personnel as cannon fodder." If it were not so he would not have made promise to discontinue these criminal acts.

As I told the press later they also accused the UNC of perpetrating every crime in the book. including germ weapons and atomic bombs.

"To retain our captured personnel for your murder and slavery is the substance of your unilateral and unreasonable proposition on the question of war prisoners embodied in your proposal of Apr 28."

Nam Il railed on about our open and joint rescreening proposal claiming it is in violation of Arts 118 & 7 of Geneva Convention and therefore impermissible. Only a direct design to deceive the people both on our side & your side. He also brought in the Colson episode again to prove we were forcibly screening and detaining their people.

UNC: "The alleged incidents of your protest are already being handled by the liaison offs. [officers]. What you seek to gain by taking up the time of the plenary session, other than to waste our time and avoid facing the main issue is not clear.

["]It has been our thought that in a very short time your propaganda would become so transparently ridiculous as to condemn itself. Your statement today confirms that judgment. Since you refuse to agree now to put your wild charges to the test of fact by conducting joint re screening in the demilt [demilitarized] zone under conditions of strict equity between both sides, the world dismisses your statements as obviously springing from fear of the results of impartial screening. What you object to is not the screening process, in which your side acquiesced, but its results; which you fear to face or verify for yourselves.

"As long as you continue to have nothing constructive to offer, I suggest a recess until such time as you desire to meet again."

Nam Il then said: ———"In accord with our consistent stand for an arm [armistice] in Korea, our side insists on the normal holding of conferences. However, I must point out that the conferences are held thru agreement by both sides. If your side is determined to disrupt the negots [negotiations] your side is free to declare that you are not coming to meet with us. But unless your side openly announces the disruption of the conferences, our side will continue to insist upon the normal holding of conferences to explain day after day our reasonable proposal and to insist upon settling the issues confronting the conferences thru reasoning & negotiating. Our side proposes meeting at usual time tomorrow.["]

UNC: ["]Very well we agree.["]

Meeting recessed 1148 hrs.

May 16 (Fri): Commies opened plenary session with another propaganda tirade much the same as previously. Claimed that unconditional repat [repatriation] of POWs is their inalienable right and inescapable obligation of the comdrs [commanders] of the belligerents. Anything else violates Geneva Convention. "Under resolute & just resistance of our captured personnel your absurd principle of so called vol [voluntary] repat has collapsed in utter bankruptcy.

"The facts confessed by the comdnt [commandant] of your POW camps before the whole world have proved incontrovertibly that the so called 'vol repat' and the so called screening are only cunning devices for the forceful retention of our captured personnel as your cannon fodder."

Accused UNC of attempting to restore bankrupt principle by repeating proposition of so called "joint screening in demilt [demilitarized] zone under condition of strict equality."

UNC: "We again reject formally and finally your utterly unreasonable May 2nd proposal. Your remarks this morning only convince us the more that you are afraid to face the truth. Otherwise, your statement consisted only of tedious repetition and is unworthy of notice."

Commies then again accused us of refusing to reason, refusing to negotiate and refusing to conduct any discussion attempting thereby to force our side to accept your ultimatum. Responsibility for delay rests on UNC. "We resolutely reject your unreasonable and unilateral proposal."

They also said: "Since you are insisting upon your absurd proposition you will not be able to escape the inevitable consequences of such insistence. ————The Comdnt of your POW camp has already declared to the whole world the utter bankruptcy of your proposition."

UNC: "We are here to attempt to gain an arm. [armistice] and not to engage in an exchange of false propaganda, invective or recrimination.

"We will continue indefinitely to stand firm on our reasonable and equitable compromise proposal. If you have nothing constructive to add, I suggest a recess until such time as you desire to meet again."

Commies: "Unless your side formally declares the termination of the arm. negots [negotiations], you have no justification to object to the normal holding of conferences[.]

["]It is the duty of both sides to come here to hold conferences; therefore, we suggest that the conferences be cont'd at the usual time tomorrow."

UNC: ["]We agree.["]

May 17 (Sat): Last night Clark sent us for info a despatch he had already sent the JCS. The msg gave a breakdown of screened and unscreened personnel. Totals screened & unscreened to return to Commie control:

| Screened | - | 39,485 |
| Unscreened | - | 43,803 |

The unscreened 3500 in the hospital compound will be placed on an addendum roster to be furnished to Commies at time of repat [repatriation].

Clark's msg added the fol'g para:

To attempt to break the present deadlock in the arm negots [armistice negotiations] I plan to take the fol'g action:

a. No more individual screening will be attempted on Koje-do.

b. As soon as practicable inform Commies thru liaison offs [officers] that approx 80,000 individuals will be returned to their control, indicating that rosters containing at least this number will be available in a short period of time if the Commies agree in principle with the revised figure[.]

c. If gen'l [general] agreement is reached on the 80,000 figure, submit to the Commies rosters outlined in para 4 above.

d. If both sides accept the revised rosters, we will repat. all POWs and civ. [civilian] internees whose names appear on the rosters which we submitted to the Commies.

This dangerous plan of action advocated by Clark occasioned the fol'g immediate msg from us: "Considered here absolutely essential that any new figure given Commies must be a firm, repeat, firm figure rather than an approximate figure such as planned in your msg. The submitting of a new and larger approx figure by UNC would encourage Commies to assume that a further period of denunciation & delay on their part would again cause UNC to revise this new figure upward; the giving of a new approx figure would, in short, be fatal to the apparent firmness of UNC posit [position]. In addition it would predispose Commies to consider it an arbitrary approximation arrived at for our own purposes, and would tend to support their previous charge that we have manipulated the figure.

"The final firm figure should, however be presented earliest, since, as pointed out in HNC 1233 (which recommended that firm final figure should be given Commies earliest as matter of record before any possible breakoff or termination of negots) it is essential that the final figure be given Commies before a possible break off of negots. In light of recent Commie attitude Del [delegation] has little hope that increased figure will cause Commies to accept UNC proposal.["]

This am the fol'g msg came thru from JCS (JCS 908998) to CinCFE which he reens [re-enciphers] to us:

"1. In view of confused and unsettled attitude of public toward recent events involving POWs held by UNC, we do not consider it advisable to approve at this time recommendation for unilateral suspension of meetings contained in HNC 1236 (see May 12). Possible advtgs [advantages] of unilateral suspension set forth in HNC 1236 are recognized. However, it is considered that present disadvtgs of unilateral suspension are overriding in terms of need for cont'd domestic and international support for UNC. Also among other disadvtgs, is fact that unilateral suspension by UNC would require Commies to take initiative for any subsequent meetings and thus make it more difficult for them to concede to UNC posit [position].

"2. In view of above contd sessions afford ex [excellent] opportunity to intensify propaganda pressures on Commies to put them increasingly on defensive. To maintain and utilize present strong world wide support for UNC position on POWs for purpose of achieving arm, considered here essential UNC Del make full and appropriate statements at every session, emphasizing basic humanitarian principles of UNC posit and utilizing fol'g themes which bring out most vulnerable weaknesses of Commie posit:

(a) Screening entered into in good faith with tacit approval of Commies and screening procedures were scrupulously fair.

(b) UNC impartial rescreening proposal as direct refutation of Commie statements on forceful retention of POWs[.]

(c) Commies are seeking to compel UNC to jeopardize lives of POWs by insisting UNC use force and violence in sending POWs to Commies against their will.''

Gist of todays plenary session follows:

UNC: ''It is quite apparent that your side does not understand the nature or the fairness of the UNC proposal of 28 Apr. In the sincere hope that further explanation this am may lead to progress in these negots, I shall briefly review the substance of our proposal.

''The UNC presented its proposal on 28 Apr after careful consideration of all factors involved. The great concessions we made to your views were done for the purpose of bringing the negots to a rapid conclusion. With this purpose in mind, we conceded to your views to the max [maximum] extent possible, and this action obviously causes the UNC proposal to be our last and final negotiatory effort. In the interests of achieving peace, we have met you more than halfway.

[''']First, we conceded to your views re the restrs [restrictions] on constr [construction] & rehab. [rehabilitation] of milt. [military] air fields. The efforts of your comdrs [commanders] during this conflict to build new milt air fields and to rehabilitate old air fields attest to the significance your side places on them as a milt potential. Although both sides know that the stability of the arm. would be substantially increased by restrs on milt air fields, in the interest of achieving peace, we have agreed to accept your views on this matter.

''Secondly, we have not insisted on the return of more than 50,000 POWs whom you admit having captured during the first 9 mos of hostilities and for whom you have since failed to account. Yet our side offers in the interest of an early arm. to refrain from raising this obvious & well documented demand.

''Thirdly your side in complete repudiation of an agreed principle, insisted on nominating the Soviet Union as a participant in the NNSC, even though in accord with agreed principle our side stated S.U. was not acceptable. Although we had nominated 3 neut. [neutral] nations who were acceptable we agreed to drop one of the neut nations we had nominated in order to eliminate the artificial prob. [problem] you have created. Again it was our side that made a real concession toward solving the problem.

''And fourth, in the matter of exch [exchange] of POWs held by our side we have offered you an opportunity to participate in a joint, impartial investigation of those persons who have stated they would forcibly resist repat to your side. We have offered to have this impartial re-screening take place either at our POW camps or at the exchange pt. [point] in the demilt [demilitarized] zone.

''I have informed you briefly this morning of the major factors in the final negotiatory posit of the UNC. Our proposal of 28 Apr. was made with full and mature consideration being given to all these factors. No amt [amount] of propaganda engendered by your side and no prolonged period of delay can operate to change the finality of our 28 Apr proposal, which fairly and reasonably takes into account all the viewpoints and past actions of both sides.

"The UNC will not concede further. We have made our final negotiatory effort in the interest of an early arm. We will not consider further concessions or counter proposals. If your side sincerely desires an arm. you will cease your procrastination and recognize the UNC proposal as the only equitable overall solution."

Commies then tried to refute above statement with same old threadbare remarks as—"The question of the 50,000 persons is a quest [question] which does not exist at all.["] Colson episode again thrown in our faces. **"Former comdn't [commandant] of your POW camp has openly admitted before world that your side subjected our captured personnel to inhuman treatment, carried out forcible screening among them and re-armed them to serve as your cannon fodder.** There is not only no sign that your side has discontinued these criminal actions, but the newly appointed comdnt of your POW camp* even asserted that the just demands raised by our captured personnel did not hold water under the Geneva convention, thus implying that your side is going to persist in this inhuman treatment of our captured personnel, persist in forcible screening and persist in impressing them to serve as your cannon fodder,["] etc, etc ad nauseum [*sic*].

UNC: ["]Your statement consists of nothing more than repetition of your hysterical propaganda, designed to conceal your fear of facing up to an impartial re-screening of POWs.["]

Commies: "For several days your side has attempted to evade the facts enumerated in our statement by calling the statement made by our side at these conferences 'propaganda.' This is because your side is afraid of your atrocities against POWs being exposed before the people of the whole world. This is only a lame excuse put up by your side in an attempt to dodge your responsibility for the unredeemable intolerable crimes committed by your side. If your side dares to face the facts, I would like to ask you which particular point or points in our statements made here is not a fact.

"Is it not a fact that the former comdn't of your POW camp pledged to our of your POW camp by openly repudiating your assurance implied that your side would persist in carrying out inhuman treatment and forcibly screening of POWs?

"Is it not a fact that your side carried out all kinds of atrocities even including mass massacre against our captured personnel in disregard of the Geneva Convention and repudiated the min [minimum] standard of human behavior?

---

* Colson was relieved of command at Koje-do shortly before. The newly appointed commandant was Brig. Gen. Hayden L. Boatner, USA, Assistant CG of the 2d Division.—Ed.

"Is it not a fact that the former comdn't of your POW camp pledged to our captured personnel that no futher criminal acts would be perpetrated?

"Is it not a fact that the comdn't of your POW camp promised our captured personnel, and I quote, 'There would be no more forcible rescreening[']['']?

UNC: Your tactics attitude and irresponsible words reveal an insincerity and ill will which make increasingly difficult the consummation of an arm, and lead all the world to suspect that you have never genuinely desired an armistice. Distortion and invective can only destroy the elements of good faith essential to any agreement. I suggest you re-evaluate your present behavior in the light of the tragic situation you are creating."

"We agree to recess."

We added fol'g comments in a separate msg (HNC 1249): "The UNC statement made at commencement of plenary session 17 May was in compliance with JCS 908998. Enemy reaction was one of gratification & relief that UNC had apparently relaxed its firm and adamant attitude. While effects cannot be foretold, del. is more than ever of opinion we now face a protracted period of enemy propaganda releases from Pan Mun Jom. While the del. is not in a position to judge the problem of retaining public and allied support for our position, from a negotiatory standpoint we are firmly convinced that only by a display of determined strength as indicated in HNC 1236 (see page 964 [of diary; entry of May 12]) can the Commies be convinced of the finality of our position. Since this course of action is not, however, approved we strongly recommend adherence to the intermediate course recommended in HNC 1228 (see page 949 [of diary; entry of May 10])."

May 18 (Sun): Commies led off in plenary session meeting by attempting to refute our statement of yesterday. Claimed in effect that our concessions were hollow. POW question only one blocking realization of an arm [armistice] in Korea. Our forcible detention at fault. Our criminal acts impossible to hide[.] Colson incident again brought up as proof. CinCUN has had effrontery to claim treatment of POWs in accord with Geneva Convention[.] "As long as your side continues to say your proposal is final you are declaring before whole world that you do not want arm." "Our proposal only reasonable basis[.]"

UNC: "It is a peculiar characteristic of your ideology that in order to gain your own ends, you deny the existence of facts and truth when these are unfavorable to you. In these negots [negotiations] you have, however, overreached yourselves. Your recriminations over the past two weeks have been devoid of any foundation in fact; have denied the truth and have consisted solely of a series of trumped up charges so fantastic and so ridiculous that they have defeated their own purpose. The acts with which you have charged the UNC are so completely out of character, so foreign to the known historical characteristics and

practices of the nations represented by the UNC, that no informed person anywhere could place the slightest credence in your charges.

"You do not even believe them yourselves; it would be a reflection upon your
intelligence if you did. **Nevertheless you mouth this nonsense in the hope that
your own misguided subjects will thereby be deceived and will continue to
remain supine while you lead them, and the world, into more bloodshed &
destruction.**

"There remain, however, certain hard facts which you dare not face and dare
not publicly acknowledge. The facts are these:

"For months you have been well aware that the UNC would not and could not
participate in forced repat [repatriation] and that the UNC proposal is the only
possible humanitarian solution to the POW question.

"The screening of the POWs to determine those persons who forcibly will
resist repat was entered into in good faith and was done with your full knowledge
and acquescence [*sic*].

"Because the results were unexpectedly unfavorable to your side, you now cry
"fraud" and loudly scream that the process was illegal. You dare not admit that
the results represent the firm conviction of the individuals concerned, and that
they must stand.

"No amnt of ex post facto accusations on your part can change the result or
alter the truth that many thousands of personnel formerly under your control
would choose death in preference to returning to your side. This fact is now
known to the world. The myth that all your people are volunteers is forever
shattered, nothing can restore it.

"Only your dread of public acknowledgment of the inescapable truth stands in
the way of an arm. There is no other issue. If you persist in blocking an arm
through sheer perversity and refusal to face the truth, the full responsibility to the
world is yours and yours alone. That is your choice."

Commies: "As you are afraid of the facts which we are exposing to the world,
of your criminal acts against our captured personnel, you try to cover them up
under the pretext of refutation. That will not work. What do you mean by calling
it "not a fact"? It is precisely your side which does not face the fact. Your side
dares not make public to the world the fact that your side has resorted to
measures of bloody violence to seek forced retention of our captured personnel.
The facts that are mentioned are known to all the peoples of the world and even
the comdn't of your POW camp could not but admit them in public.

["]No news blackout order by your side outside the conference can hide these
facts. No amount of sophistry put forth in this conference can wipe them out.

"If your side is still interested in settling the prob [problem], your side must
face these undeniable facts, and must give up your unilateral and unreasonable
proposal which has already gone thoroughly bankrupt.

"The facts have proved that your criminal acts to screen our captured personnel and retain them as your cannon fodder have become utterly bankrupt. Our side is firmly opposed to any screening and re-screening."

UNC: "As long as you do not seem to have anything more constructive to offer, I suggest a recess until tomorrow."

Recessed 1144 hrs.

CinCUNC passed to us for info msg he sent to JCS which included our HNC 1249 (see p. 988 [of diary; entry of May 17]). He added fol'g para: "Observation of enemy reactions are based on results of a single session operating under instrs [instructions] contained in JCS 908998 (see p. 981 [of diary; entry of May 17]). I plan to follow next two sessions closely prior to forwarding further comments & recs [recommendations].

May 19 (Mon): Commies led off plenary session again with the same old propaganda line[.] Some of their lies and distortions follow: "You attempted and you now still attempt desperately to increase your citadel for extending the war by the myth that our captured personnel refuse to be repatriated." "Your activities in employing barbarous methods in an attempt to retain our captured personnel by force have already reached such an extent as makes it impossible for you to hide or deny them." "The former comdn't [commandant] of your POW camp openly admitted that your side used all sorts of violence to screen our captured personnel by force in an attempt to retain them as cannon fodder. The newly appointed comdn't of your POW camp openly implied that your side would continue to treat our captured personnel inhumanly, continue to screen them by force and to retain them as cannon fodder[.]"

"To strengthen your rule of bloodshed and violence over our captured personnel, your side recently moved large amounts of reinforcing forces to the locality of your POW camps for further suppression of the just resistance of our captured personnel. The fact now placed before the people of the whole world is that in spite of your such barbarous measures you violated the will of the captured personnel of our side. Thousands of them would rather die than yield to your forcible retention. Your side dares not face this fact. In order to cover up this fact your side has invented the myth that our captured personnel were not willing to be repatriated. But when the comdn't of your POW camp admitted before the world that your side screened our captured personnel by force, your such [*sic*] myth was already shattered, never to be restored.

"It is inconceivable and nobody would believe that our side, who is firmly opposed to the retention of our captured personnel by your side, under whatever name, could have agreed directly or indirectly to your so called screening."

UNC: ["]On 17 May, we presented to your side a review of our compromise proposal of 28 Apr. That proposal represents the final position of the UNC[;] no amount of invective on your part and no prolonged delay by your side can cause us to recede from the provisions of this equitable and realistic proposal. You do not like this proposal because it requires you to face the results of the screening of POW.

"Let us review the steps leading up to the screening of POWs by the UNC. In the secret Item 4 sessions, your side sought a compromise round figure as a basis for settling the POW problem. Although our side was anxious to find a means for settling Item 4 we nevertheless repeatedly informed your reps. [representatives] that we could not furnish an arbitrary figure, that an individual poll or canvass of POWs would first have to be made. On Apr 4 when you agreed to recess the Item 4 meetings your side was well aware that our side would require at least a week to complete the screening nec. [necessary] to determine the new round figure to replace that of 18 Dec. Your side was well aware that we were going to use our statement of principles and our "understandings" of 1 Apr in our screening process. Your side knew that we would encounter trouble in getting some of your people to agree to non forced repat. [repatriation] because you furnished our side for use in our screening process a statement of amnesty from your official sources. In short, you knew that screening was to take place, you acquiesced in its accomplishment, and only when its result was not to your liking and expectation did you decide to object to it. Had the results been to your liking you would have enthusiastically welcomed the product of the screening.

"Thus it is clear that your complaint that the screening of POWs was illegal is a hypocritical complaint, based on your unwillingness publicly to acknowledge the truth. It is equally clear to the entire world that the UNC proposal of 28 Apr. is an equitable compromise of all remaining issues. We stand on it irrevocably.

"Unless you wish to make another propaganda speech I suggest we recess until tomorrow."

Commies: "We have rejected your unilateral and unreasonable proposal of Apr 28 and will continue to reject it.

"Our side has always been opposed to your screening of our captured personnel. Our side opposed it in the past, and will oppose it in the future. But you had the audacity to say that and I quote 'the screening of POWs was entered into in good faith and was done with your full knowledge and acquiescence.'

["]I must point out with emphasis that this is complete fabrication & slander. The record of the discussions of the POW quests [questions] thoroughly belies such unfounded fabrications of yours. It is precisely your side which dares not face up to the fact that the captured personnel of our side would rather die than yield to forcible retention by your side."

Commies then went into tirade with a series of quests, such as: "Is it not a fact that the Comdn't of your POW camp pledged to our captured personnel that no further criminal activities in violation of the Geneva Convention would be perpetrated? Is it not a fact that the comdn't of your POW camp promised our captured personnel that there will be no more forcible screening?["]

UNC: "Your quests are formally ignored[.] They have been answered fully and adequately outside this tent. We will recess."

Later in the evening I sent the fol'g msg to CinCUNC (HNC 1255).

"1. a. On the assumption that our assigned objective remains to obtain an arm. [armistice] at the earliest possible date, it is the unanimous conviction of the Del. that we could not make a worse tactical error than to continue daily plenary sessions.

"b. We are constrained to go on record as saying that in our judgment and in the light of months of personal experience in dealing with the Commies, our inability to accept the Commie challenge to suspend negots [negotiations] has convinced them that our posit [position] is not in fact firm. We believe that by far the strongest move we can make is to emphasize the finality of our stand by recessing the plenary sessions until the enemy is ready to accept our proposal of 28 Apr. It is obvious that Commies will not accept the POW situation unless they want an arm. badly, and the mere fact that they would have to so indicate by calling a plenary session would not in our opinion be controlling[.] On the other hand, daily meetings subject the UNC and the nations it represents to a stream of vituperation and abuse which, although unfounded, leaves the Del with the only alternative of becoming mired in a propaganda morass which the JCS in their 907378 indicate a desire to avoid. The stand of the UNC has been firmly and fully stated and is well known to the free world. It can be reinforced but little by repetition. In contrast the Commies, unhampered by any considerations of truth or scruples, have every advantage in the propaganda exchange and will exploit it to the utmost. The Koje Do situation has played directly into their hands and gives them a plausible basis on which to build propaganda which however false, will by sheer force of repetition work to the eventual detriment of the UNC posit.

"c. In summary, we believe that only by the display of determined strength can the situation be salvaged; and that the strongest act we can perform now is to proceed as rec [recommended] in HN 1236 (see pg 964 [of diary; entry of May 12]).

"2. This is being forwarded in advance of our meeting at Eusak, 20 May as Harrison and I wish to discuss this subject with you."

May 20 (Tues): Today we were subjected to the most vicious propaganda we have heard in the 10½ months of the negots [negotiations]. Gist of plenary session follows:

Commies first tirade again contended confessions of comdn't [commandant] of POW camp "have killed and buried myth that our captured personnel refused to be repatriated[.] The comdn't of your POW camp could not confess before the whole world your inhuman treatment and murderous violence against our captured personnel and the criminal and unlawful acts committed by your side in screening and rearming POWs by force."

Quoted their amnesty proclamation in attempt to show they did not acquiesce in screening process. Said: "Your clumsy method of flagrant distortion of facts only serves to show to what low depths you have degenerated in an attempt to salvage your thoroughly bankrupt absurdity of voluntary repatriation[.]"

Brought up again secret Item 4 meetings and their Mar 21 proposal which they claimed we had agreed to and violated.

UNC: "If you were to come to this tent with a list of upwards of 65,000 POW instead of a meager 12,000 then your proposal for an all for all exchange would at least be honest. As it is, your proposal is as fraudulent and hypocritical as your statement this am.

"The UNC, which this del. represents at this conference, is guided by the principles of the UN. One of the basic principles of the UN is to achieve international cooperation in solving international problems of an economic, social, cultural or humanitarian character, and in promoting and encouraging respect for human rights and for fundamental freedom for all without distinction as to race, sex, language or religion. In the preamble to the UN Charter the peoples of the UN reaffirm their faith in fundamental human rts. [rights] and in the dignity and worth of the human person. It is upon this fundamental doctrine that the UNC based its humanitarian proposal of Apr 28th.

"Your side should be fully aware that the UNC cannot & will not accept a solution to the POW problem unless that solution provides for and respects human rts. and fully considers the dignity and worth of the human person. The UNC has proposed such a solution[.] It must be obvious to you that the UNC cannot accept any compromise in its basic and fundamental principles. It must also be obvious to you that the UNC proposal of Apr 28 by its very nature, is firm, final, and irrevocable.

"During the Item 4 Staff Offs. meetings, our side entered into in good faith an arrangement to determine the approx nos [numbers] of POWs held by our side who would not forcibly resist returning to your side. The procedures used by our side to accomplish this were scrupulously fair. No amount of slander and false allegations by your side can change the truth of this matter. Nevertheless our side has stated many times our willingness to have the results of our survey examined and verified by an impartial group and witnesses by your side. In order that your side can have no excuse to avoid the witnessing of this procedure, our side has stated its willingness to have it conducted at the exchange point in the demilt [demilitarized] zone. For your side to refuse this reasonable proposition is to deny the human rights of individuals[.]

"The counterproposal your side made on May 2nd is one which would compel the UNC to jeopardize the lives of the numerous human beings by using force and violence in sending them to your side against their will. The UNC will not accede to such an inhuman proposition. To do so would be to repudiate one of the purposes and principles upon which the UN is founded.

"It should be quite clear to you now that the UNC cannot accept your inhuman counterproposal of May 2nd. It should be quite clear to you now that the UNC solution to the POW problem proposed on Apr 28 is the only solution which can be accepted by the UNC[.] It should be obvious to you that the UNC proposal of 28 Apr cannot and will not be other than its firm, final & irrevocable position[.]"

Commies: "I have noted your illogical and unrealistic statement of today. I have one thing to ask you. You mean the criminal acts you perpetrated in your POW camp on Koje-do are humanitarian according to your definition? Can you give me an answer to this question?"

UNC: "You got your answer to that question yesterday."

Commies—Accused us of not daring to answer the question. Our answer would fundamentally overthrow "the statements you have made already." Repeated again "that so called screening of our captured personnel has been designed to retain the captured personnel of our side and no method of retaining of our captured personnel is permissible."

"Your side dares not face these undeniable facts and cannot answer my questions. Yet you audaciously stated that your side has given your answer outside the tent. But what is your answer outside the tent?

"A few days after the former Comdn't of your POW camp gave his assurances for the min [minimum] standard of treatment of POWs, your CinC [commander in charge] openly tore them to pieces and clearly implied that your side would continue to use violence. to push through forcible screening and rearming POWs by force and to attempt to retain our captured personnel as your cannon fodder. The new Comdn't of your POW camp went one step further by calling your inhuman treatment of our captured personnel "far too lenient" and claimed that "we are going to impress upon them that we are strong." Your side concentrated large amounts of forces and tanks in the locality of your POW camp for further suppression of the righteous resistance of our captured personnel. This is the answer given by your side outside of the tent. But your side must bear full and absolute responsibility for every act of yours taken against our captured personnel outside of this tent.

"Everyone of your arguments, deceits and lies made in this tent have been shattered to pieces by the facts happening outside of this tent which are known to all the people of the world.["]

Commies then asked us: "What qualification do you have to continue to raise here the principles of "vol repat" [voluntary repatriation], "fundamental human rights" and "individual dignity"? and to suggest so called "screening" and joint rescreening?"

UNC: "Your attitude this am again proves conclusively to the world that because of your fear of the truth you are seeking every vicious means at your disposal to block an armistice. If you seek to perpetuate the stalemate you will continue on your present pointless course of action. The responsibility is yours. If you have nothing to add I suggest the usual recess until tomorrow."

Recessed 1201 after Commies agreed. Fol'g comment was added to msg reporting session: "The record of todays meeting indicates clearly that the Commies will continue to use the plenary sessions solely as a vehicle for their vicious propaganda and in the opinion of the Del confirms the desirability of deciding at the earliest date to carry out the course of action recommended in HNC 1236 (p. 964 [of diary; entry of May 12]).

May 21 (Thurs): Gist of Plenary follows:
UNC: "Your side continues to display crass hypocrisy on POW issue. Have you for example, undertaken to settle the problem of the more than 50,000 milt [military] persons of our side whose capture you reported, but whose names you have omitted from the lists of POWs to be exchanged? Have you undertaken to restore to these 50,000 POWs the rights accorded them by the Geneva Conv [convention]? Have you rptd [reported] their capture to the Info. Bureau at Geneva as required by the Convention on POWs? Have you opened your POW camps to visits by neutral benevolent societies as required by the Geneva Convention? Have you agreed to the exchange during hostilities of the seriously sick and injured as required by the Geneva Convention? Have you undertaken to refrain from using captured personnel in a milt capacity or in labor directly contributing to milt. ops. [operations] as is required by the Geneva Convention or do you adhere to your announced policy of incorporating captured personnel into your milt forces? Have you undertaken to restore to POW status those captured personnel whom you have incorporated into your armed forces or have transported to China or elsewhere? You have not.

"Never before in modern history has a belligerent displayed less regard for the rights & welfare of POWs. Never before have the rights of POWs been so fully and completely violated. Never before has a belligerent unilaterally disposed of 4/5ths of the captured personnel of the other side before sitting down at the conference table.

"Under the existing circumstances no solution of the POW question which is truly equitable as between our two sides is feasible. A wholly equitable solution would abrogate the rights of the prisoners we now hold, since it would involve the immediate release of 4/5th of the prisoners in our custody and the incorporation of the majority into our armed forces. Our side does not ask for such equity at the expense of the welfare of the prisoners. Their rights and their welfare are paramount in the solution proposed by our side. That solution puts humanity before other considerations, the welfare of the remaining POWs before the full satisfaction of our legitimate claims against you for your illegal and inhumane disposition of the captured milt personnel of our side.

"If our refusal to use force to deliver to you POWs who oppose returning to your side results in delay in the attainment of an arm. [armistice] then make the most of it. Our stand in this issue is firm & final."
Commies: "I have noted your unfounded, illogical argument.

"Your so called question of the 50,000 people is a question which does not exist at all. Our side released large nos [numbers] of POWs during the movements of war. But you are fully aware that those people were released long before your side and our side exchanged lists of POWs and that they should not under any circumstances be mixed up with the POWs who are now in the custody of either side. You have only mentioned this non-existent question once again in an attempt to cover up the absurdity of your proposition to retain our captured personnel who are now in your custody.

"Today you brazenly insisted that you will incorporate 4/5ths of our POWs into your army whom you hold in your custody. With this you declare that you will commit a criminal action, but that is absolutely untenable."

Commies then went into song & dance about "rptd massacre of our captured personnel" although "comdn't [commandant] of camp pledged to discontinue inhuman treatment.["] Then brought up "sanguinary incident of May 20," in which 86 of their POWs were injured which "exposed before the whole world that your so called vol. repat. [voluntary repatriation] and screening are a great hoax and your so called respect for 'fundamental human rights' and [']personal dignity' and [']humane principles' is a big lie."

Then went on in usual vein trying to prove we were forcibly detaining their personnel. "After your design to retain our captured personnel by force collapsed in bankruptcy on account of their righteous resistance on Koje do, you have taken a series of measures of terror against them in seeking to retrieve your bankrupt design."

Nam Il lodged protest against 20 May incident.

————"The charter of the UN solemly [sic] declares 'respect for the obligations arising from treaties and other sources of international law.' However your side does not hesitate to violate the charter of the UN nor hesitate to violate all international laws including the Geneva Conv. by using violence against our captured personnel and screening them by force in an attempt to deprive them of their basic rts. [rights] of repat after the arm.

"Your special agents mauled or beat our captured personnel unconscious and then dipped their hands in their own blood to put their fingerprints on your lists of so called POWs resisting repat. Is that your consideration of the dignity of the human person?"

And on & on!

UNC: "The only progressive move your side can make is to inform us when you are ready to consummate a cessation of hostilities in Korea by accepting our proposal. No other remarks by your side will achieve anything except more delay in bringing this about. As long as you wish to continue this delay, you are of course free to continue to make yourselves ridiculous by persisting in your childish distortions. In fact, you have no other course, since the truth will in no way serve your objective. We suggest the usual recess."

Communists: "In your statement you said we distorted facts. I want to ask you what facts have we distorted? You mean your repeated criminal acts on Koje Do are no facts? You mean the sanguinary acts committed just yesterday at Pusan are no facts[?] Now I request your answer."

UNC: "Every statement you've made since May 2 as a fact has been distorted. That is my answer."

Communists: "You cannot make any direct answer and you are not qualified to do so either. I have one more thing to ask. Does your forcible screening of our captured personnel constitute your respect for the fundamental human rights? I request your answer."

UNC: "I will not answer distorted questions. You know that.["]

Commies: "That is not a distortion but a fact; you are not able to give an answer to it. I have another question[.] Does your repeated sanguinary massacre of our captured personnel for the purpose of achieving forcible retention constitute your respect for the worth of the human person? I have another question to ask. How did it happen that on 20 May there was such sanguinary incident that you killed our captured personnel in Pusan?* I have another question. Do your repeated murders of our captured personnel and repeated massacres indicate respect for humanity, human rights, and human persons? Why has your side not yet given a responsible account for the repeated bloody incidents committed in your POW camps on Koje-do?"

UNC: "Your questions are designed solely to generate enmity within this tent and to block an armistice. As I have told you before, such questions have been answered fully outside this tent, in public statements. We will continue in our refusal to answer them in here. Whether this satisfies you or not is immaterial to us."

Commies: "No evasion could whitewash your criminal acts of sanguinary massacre one after another.

"Your side must be held fully & absolutely responsible for every unlawful criminal act perpetrated by your side against our captured personnel.["]

We agree to recess.

Comment: Comments on meeting of 20 May apply equally to today's session.

[Here CTJ inserts an article from *Time,* April 28, 1952 (reproduced, p. 434) and adds:] This hits the nail on the head. I should have put it in before.

---

* Throughout 1952, incidents in which Communist POWs were killed also occurred in camps at Pusan and Cheju-do.—Ed.

1015

This hits the nail on the head.
I should have put it in before.

Time April 28th

STRATEGY

The Reason

Why has no truce agreement been reached in Korea? Beneath the weird and interminable welter of words at Panmunjom, the reason is plain even to the newest soldier on the front.

When the truce talks got under way last July, the U.N. knew what brought the Reds to the conference table: they were suffering heavy losses on the battlefield and they faced the prospect of defeat. U.N. spokesmen said insistently that only by continued pressure could the Reds be brought to sign an armistice. But U.N. strategists lost sight of that fact.

Last summer the Communists set out to test U.N. determination by breaking off the talks for two months. The result was to bring Matt Ridgway's army down on them with almost as much weight as before, and the Reds came meekly back to the table and gave up their demand for a truce line on the 38th parallel. Washington might have learned a lesson. Instead, it all but stopped the pressure. U.N. settled down to a wait & see campaign. Casualties fell off, but over the past ten weeks the U.S. has still suffered a weekly average loss of 60-plus killed, 140-plus wounded. The cost of the war went on at roughly $5 billion a year.

Since the lull on the battlefield, the Red negotiators have been wholly intractable. The U.N. has no policy except to try to wear down the Reds at the conference table. In the game of waiting, the U.N. is up against the champs. Once, the U.N. had the advantage in Korea; now it has got into a contest in which the advantage is with the enemy.

MY LAST DAY

May 22 (Thurs): Commies began plenary session as follows: "Since our side made our entirely reasonable compromise proposal on May 2nd, your side has persistently refused to conduct discussions and attempts to force our side to accept your unilateral and unreasonable proposition as if you were tendering an ultimatum.

"After the substance of your so-called vol repat [voluntary repatriation] and screening was declared bankrupt by public confessions of the comdnt of your POW camp, your side not only refuses to give at these conferences any account for the atrocities which continue to be perpetrated by your side but also fails to give any answer to our question by brazenly denying the facts in an attempt to thereby achieve your completely bankrupt proposition. But the facts are not to be denied. The facts prove incontestably that your proposition of so called vol repat and your so called screening activities are the plots laid by your side for retaining our captured personnel to serve as your cannon fodder and to subject them to your disposal and slavery.["]

Commies then made usual accusations about Chiang Kai Sheks gangsters and Syngman Rhees agents.

"In the face of the resolute struggle of our captured personnel, the comdn't of your POW camp could not but confess before the world that your so called screening is sheer coercion and that the aim your side pursues is to re arm our captured personnel to serve as your cannon fodder. Can you deny the fact that the Comdn't of your POW camp admitted openly that you treated our captured personnel inhumanly, slaughtered them, screened them by force and rearmed them? Can you deny the fact that the comdn't of your POW camp pledged to our captured personnel not to treat them inhumanly, not to screen them by force, and not to rearm them in the future? Can you deny the fact that another comdn't of your POW camp resolutely refuted that pledge and implied that you would continue to treat our captured personnel inhumanly, continue to screen them by force and continue to rearm them? Can you deny that you are now resorting to opened armed suppression to retain our capt. [captured] personnel by force?———

"You have moved large amounts of armed forces to the locality of your POW camp for further slaughter and atrocities. According to your own official rpts [reports] on May 15 your side wounded one of our captured personnel by shooting and on May 17 your side shot dead one of our captured personnel. On May 20 your side inflicted 86 casualties on our capt. personnel in the POW camp at Pusan. But your murderous acts against our capt. personnel cannot suppress the righteous protest of our capt. personnel. They cannot retrieve your utterly bankrupt position. On the contrary they only serve to expose more fully that your filibuster that our capt personnel refuse to return home to lead a peaceful life is an out & out lie. Iron clad facts are not to be covered up. Your side will not be able to escape the full & absolute responsiblity for each of the murderous atrocities, each of the criminal and unlawful acts. Your absurd proposition of the so called vol repat [voluntary repatriation] & screening are thoroughly bankrupt beyond recovery. Your side must completely abandon your absurd proposition to retain our captured personnel[.]"

Then came my valedictory as follows: "At the very first Plenary Session of our two delegations, on the 10th of July of last year, I said: 'The success or failure of the negotiations begun here today depends directly upon the good faith of the delegations present.' These words constituted both a promise and a warning—a promise of good faith by our side and a warning that we would expect good faith from your side. Today at the 65th Plenary Session, my opening remarks on the subject of good faith are more than ever pertinent.

"It has become increasingly clear through these long drawn out conferences that any hope that your side would bring good faith to these meetings was forlorn indeed. From the very start, you have cavilled over procedural details; you have manufactured spurious issues and placed them in controversy for bargaining purposes; you have denied the existence of agreements made between us when you found the fulfillment thereof not to your liking; you have made false charges based on crimes invented for your purposes and you have indulged in abuse and invective when all other tactics proved ineffective. Through a constant succession of delays, fraudulent arguments, and artificial attitudes you have obstructed the attainment of an armistice which easily lay within our grasp had there been equal honesty on both sides of this conference table. Nowhere in the record is there a single action of your side which indicates a real and sincere desire to attain the objective for which these conferences were designed. Instead you have increasingly presented evidence before the world that you did not enter these negots. [negotiations] with sincerity and high purpose, but rather that you entered into them to gain time to repair your shattered forces and to try to accomplish at the conference table what your armies could not accomplish in the field. It is an enormous misfortune that you are constitutionally incaple [*sic*] of understanding the fair and dignified attitude of the UNC. **Apparently you cannot comprehend that strong and proud and free nations can make costly sacrifices for principles because they are strong; can be dignified in the face of abuse and deceit because they are proud, and can speak honestly because they are free and do not fear the truth.** Instead you impute to the UNC the same suspicion, greed and deviousness which are your stock in trade. You search every word for a hidden meaning and every agreement for a hidden trap. It would be charitable for me to say that you do these things by instinct, but you are people of intelligence and it is probably truer to say that you do these things with purpose and design.

"From the very first the UNC has had but one objective in Korea: To bring an end to the Korean war so that a permanent and enduring peace might be established as quickly as possible[.] This has been the precise objective of the UNC Del [delegation] in these negots. This is what we meant by good faith on our part. You have but to examine the record to see the many evidences of our restraint, our constructive suggestions, our willingness to conciliate and compromise, and our patience. There is very little evidence of similar contributions by your side. As an answer to the question: "which side has brought good faith to these meetings?" Nothing could be more impressive than a comparison of the actions of the two delegations during our 10 mos of these conferences. They are as different as day and night. No amount of propaganda however oft repeated can hide your ignoble record. That these meetings have continued this long and that we have, after a fashion, resolved our differences to the point where only one major issue remains is testimony to the patience and dedication of the UNC.

"Now our negots. have come to the point where the POW issue stands as a formidable barrier to the accomplishment of an armistice. Casting aside any pretense of humanity, you have made the demand that the UNC must return to your side all POWs in its custody, driving them at the point of a bayonet if necessary. You even have the colossal impertinence to document your position by referring to the Geneva convention. What could be more ironic than your attempt to found your inhuman proposition upon an international agreement whose purpose is to defend and protect the unfortunate victims of war. These are strange words for you to employ. You who have denied the International Red Cross access to your POW camps, who have refused to furnish lists of POWs to the POW Bureau, and who cannot even account for over 50,000 UNC soldiers whom you officially boasted as having in your custody before the Korean war was 9 mos old. After months of conciliation, of meeting you more than halfway on issue after issue, the UNC has told you with all firmness and finality that it will not recede from its position with respect to POWs. On the 28th of April we offered you an equitable & specific solution to the issues remaining before us. We told you then, and we tell you now, that we firmly adhere to the principles of humanity and the preservation of the rights of the individual. These are values which we will not barter, for they are one and the same with the principles which motivated the UNC to oppose you on the battlefield. No amount of argument and invective will move us. If you harbor the slightest desire to restore peace and to end the misery and suffering of millions of innocent people, you must bring to the solution of this issue the good faith which, as I said at our first meeting would directly determine the success or failure of our negots. The decision is in your hands.

After 10 mos and 12 days I feel that there is nothing more for me to do. There is nothing left to negotiate. I now turn over the unenviable job of further dealings with you to Major General William K. Harrison, who succeeds me as Senior Delegate of the UNC Del. May God be with him.["]

I then left the tent.

Admiral Joy's Chronology
of the Negotiations

Date	Subject
Date	*Subject*
[1951]	
July 10–25	The agenda debates.
July 26	Agenda formally adopted.
July 27– August 16	Plenary sessions on demilitarized zone.
August 4	Company of Chinese violate neutral area.
August 10	Plenary sessions reconvene.
August 17–22	Sub-Del [delegation] dead locked on demilt [demilitarized] zone.
August 22	Alleged UNC bombing of Kaesong; Commies suspend talks.
August 24	Possible reasons why Commies suspended talks.
August 29	R. replies to Commie's protest.
September 1	Another alleged bombing incident.
September 2	Commie's reply to R's msg [message].
September 3	I return to Tokyo [from weekend at resort].
September 6	R. replies to Commies suggesting new site.
September 12	Commies reply to R.
September 18	R. replies to Peng and Kim, admitting incident of 10 Sept.
September 20	Commies propose return to Kaesong.
September 21–23	R. replies to Commies.
September 24	Commies reply to R. reiterating their former stand that negots [negotiations] be resumed at Kaesong.

Date	*Subject*
September 26	Hassle with Wash [Washington] over Kaesong issue.
September 29	Bradley & Bohlen visit Tokyo.
September 30	Conference with Bradley & Bohlen & decision reached on UNC initial proposal on Item 2.
October 3	Last conf [conference] with Bradley & Bohlen.
October 4	Commies reject meeting Songhyon ni.
	R. replies suggesting site of Commie's choice.
October 7	Commies suggest Pam Mun Jom [Panmunjom].
October 10	I return to Korea.
October 10–24	Liaison offs [officers] battle over conditions for resuming conference at Pan Mun Jom.
October 24	Nam Il signs admin [administrative] agreement & suggests we resume meetings.
October 25	We resume meetings with Commies & throw Item 2 into Sub Del [sub-delegation].
October 26	I return to Tokyo (Molly leaving on 28th) [CTJ returns to Korea October 29].
November 7	Commies propose present l of c [line of contact] for dem. [demarcation] line–in effect de facto cease fire.
	JCS suggest time limit.
November 10	JCS don't like R.'s inflexible posit [position] re l of c as dem [demarcation] line upon signing arm [armistice].
November 11	My statement to press on train.
November 14	JCS urge acceptance Commie proposal earliest—present l of c [line of contact] only valid for 1 mo.
	R. urges JCS to reconsider "more steel and less silk."
November 15	JCS direct acceptance Commie proposal—present l of c to be valid for approx 1 mo.
	Commies appear licked.
November 17	UNC sub del [sub-delegation] gives JCS proposal, l of c.
November 19	Commies recess to meet Nov 20 with reply & I return to Tokyo.
November 22	I return to camp with Barkley and R.
November 23	Agreement reached over Item 2.

Date	*Subject*
November 24	Staff offs [officers] meet to determine l of c [line of contact].
November 26	Staff offs reach agreement on l of c.
November 27	Plenary sessions start on Item 3 & we exchange principles.
December 3	Nam Il proposes NNSC idea.
December 4	Sub Committee takes over Item 3 & UNC proposes sub com [committee] for Item 4.
	We request guidance concerning NNSC.
December 11	Commies finally agree to sub del meeting on Item 4.
	Commies propose all for all exch [exchange] of POWs.
	JCS agree to neut [neutral] nations proposal of Com.
December 12	Battle starts on exch of POW data.
	Commie proposal on POWs exchange.
	CinCUNCs prelim [preliminary] views on vol [voluntary] repat [repatriation].
December 13	JCS agree to our insistence on exch POW lists before beginning subs. discussion.
December 14	We give our views on vol repat.
	We plug for visits by ICRC to POW camps.
December 15	Our rec [recommendation] initial posit [position] re POWs.
December 18	R.'s estimate of situation, sent to JCS−(1) Gen [general] situation (2) Points of disagreement (3) Rec. [recommendations on] final posits [positions].
	Insistence on vol repat a dangerous precedent.
	R.'s views on vol repat.
	Commies give us list of POWs held by them.
December 21	JCS answer R.'s msg [message] of 18th giving positions we should firmly maintain.
December 22	We propose release [of] seriously sick POWs.
	Plan of action if negot [negotiations] go beyond 27 Dec.
December 23	Commies deny any POWs held outside Korea.
	Commies say missing POWs released at front.

Date	*Subject*
December 24	Libby attacks Commie figures on POWs. Commies turn down visits of ICRC. Our staff study & recs. on POW issue.
December 26	Battle over airfields continues. We press for accounting 50,000 missing POWs.
December 27	We ask Commies why they won't put in writing what they said verbally about milt [military] air capabilities. #4—We continue to press for accounting 50,000 missing POW. Take up quest. [question] of civilian return with CinCUNC.
December 28	Hsieh evades quest on airfield restr [restrictions] & aerial obs [observation] by neut [neutral] nations. #4—we continue to press for accounting of POWs.
December 29	#3—We introduce revised principles 4, 5, 6, giving up aerial obs. if Commies will agree to 3 principles without subs [subsequent] change. #4—Lee indicates he will provide add [additional] data on all POW held during war.
December 30	#3—Wrangle and explanation over prins. [principles] 4, 5 & 6. We take up quest of release of civs [civilians].
December 31	#3—Hassle on airfield restr continues. Chang contends it is infringement of sovereign rts [rights]. #4—Lee repudiates agreement to provide data on all POWs held at any time. He disregards trial balloon of yesterday re. return of civs.
[1952]	
January 1	Commies continue adamant on airfield restrs [restrictions]. #4—Lee says they will make effort to provide data on all POWs taken. Shows interest in return of civs.
January 2	#3—Hsieh again brings up quest [question of] withdrawal [of] foreign troops. Airfield wrangle continues. #4—Lee accepts prin that civs be allowed to return home. *We introduce for the first time our proposal incorporating vol* [voluntary] *repat* [repatriation].
January 3	#3—We accuse commies of bad faith in desire to build up airfields. #4—Lee rejects our Jan. 2 proposal. UNC personnel released at front. Our 1 for 1 exchange proposal intolerable, a barbarous formula. Tsai joins in

Date	*Subject*
	about UNC wanting to turn CCF POW over to Chiang Kai Shek.
January 4	#3—Hsieh dodges quest [question].—Is reconstr [reconstruction of] milt [military] airfields conducive to stable arm. [armistice]? Wrangle over airfields continues. #4—Lee continues violent attack on UNC proposal. Refuse again to let ICRC interview POWs.
January 5	#3—Wrangle over airfields branches out into political quests. #4—Lee continues virulent attack on UNC exchange proposal. Libby takes him to task for lack of courtesy. Enemy attitude more rude than usual.
January 6	#3—We accuse Commies of evading issue on milt airfields & attack their sovereign rts [rights] stand. #4—Commies explore our proposal with evident idea of separating civs and POWs in exchange.
January 7–13	I return to Tokyo & discuss ways & means to break deadlock. JCS msg [message] about declaration when arm [armistice] was signed and final position on airfields—omission from arm [armistice] agreement if it turns out to be breaking point. R. asks JCS for final posit [position] on civ. [civilians] return & vol repat [voluntary repatriation]. #3—no progress except Commies submitted new proposal, omitting ref to airfields but agreeing to replenishment of war material during arm [armistice]. #4—we resubmit our Jan 2 proposal to eliminate any grds [grounds] for Commie technical opposition to proposal.
January 14	UNC accuses Commies of striving only for a cease fire rather than a stable arm [armistice]. Hsieh contends we are deliberately trying to provoke them. #4—Lee contends we are attempting to detain POWs as hostages, trys to keep discussion off vol repat [voluntary repatriation].
January 15	#3—UNC accuses Reds of seeking to unbalance milt. [military] capabilities by insisting on no airfield restrs. No side must gain advtg [advantage] during arm. #4— Lee attacks "deceitfulness" of UNC proposal. Vol repat violates Art 118 of Geneva Conv. Asks number of quests [questions] concerning exch. of civs. for POWs.

Date	*Subject*
January 16	Hsieh defends their 9 Jan proposal. UNC contends Commies have agreed to other restrs which infringe on sov. rts. [sovereign rights]—why object to airfields? #4—We answer quests of yesterday and defend prin of vol repat.
January 17	#3—We explain how rehab. [rehabilitation] of milt airfields can increase milt. capabilities without introducing a/c [aircraft]. We point out how infringement of sov. rights is inherent in any arm. #4—Wrangle over bombing of POW camp. Another hysterical outburst by Lee. R. visits camp and discusses JCS msg [message] which authorizes all for all exch [exchange] of POW provided there is no forced repat. JCS also broach subj. of transferring all unresolved items to full del [delegation] & handle concession on airfields in such manner as to require Commie concession on our vol repat position.
January 18	I give memo to R. on subject of POW poll by ICRC and direct committee to prepare plan for carrying out JCS directive. #3—We ask if you are sincere for peace why insist on rt. [right] to build airfields? We get "running dog" answer. #4—no significant development.
January 19	#3—We continue to attack Commie Jan 9 proposal. Requested explanation Commie statement that maintenance [of] milt balance during arm [armistice] impractical. Commies answer a masterpiece of specious reasoning. Hsieh said proposal not to introduce a/c made it impossible to increase air power. #4—No significant results. UNC still on initiative on vol vs. forced repat. R. sends JCS msg [message] on how we intend to proceed with unresolved issues.
January 20	#3—short session. UNC emphasizes firm posit [position] on airfields. #4—Lee in long statement charged UNC attempting to use excess of POWs as blackmail. Attacked UNC proposal on basis not in accord Geneva Conv. Art. 7—not even POWs themselves can renounce right. UNC stresses humanitarian aspects vol. repat. Pointed out again that Reds have already exercised principle in releasing POWs at front.

Date	*Subject*
January 21	#3—We continue firm stand on airfield quest [question]. Hsieh keeps on about interference in internal affairs. #4—no developments. *We send HNC 780 to CinCUNC outlining proposed future course of action.*
January 22	#3—We say we are willing to accept Commie version of prins 4, 5 and 6 if Commies add prov. for restr milt airfields. Hsieh balks; mentions my U.S. News & World Report interview to show our warlike intent. #4—We discuss groups entitled to vol. repat. Lee repeats old arguments.
January 23	#3—Hsieh rejects UNC suggestion of 22 Jan, saying it was no concession. We accuse Reds of trying to maintain state of tension during arm. Ask why they won't answer quest whether they intend to increase milt air capabilities during arm. #4—No developments—Commies probably stalling while Vyshinsky attempts to transfer conf. [conference] to Security Council.
January 24	#3—Hsieh still on old interference in int [internal] affairs argument. UNC wants to be in posit. [position] to unleash wanton bombing at time of its choosing. UNC again asked Commies to state their intent re: increase milt capabilities. #4—UNC attacks Red prin unconditional release showing effect on each of 5 grps. [groups] civs; ROK nationals, etc. Lee accuses UNC of bringing up political quests at milt. arm. conf. UNC would deal with POWs not as POWs but as nationals of certain govts [governments].
January 25	#3—We propose first step of HNC 780—i.e., abandoning discussion on prins and concentrating on drafting wordings on agreements already reached—staff offs [officers] to take over. #4—Lee presses us for add. data on POWs and continues attack on vol. repat.
January 26	#3—We press for acquiescence to our proposal of yesterday to have staff offs draft details of agreements reached. Hsieh said still under consideration. #4—Lee goes off on a tangent on subject of politics and then into long tirade on inhumanity of UNC & vol. repat. I send msg to R. about future tactics & Item 5.

Date	*Subject*
January 27	#3—Hsieh agrees to turn meetings over to staff offs, but tries to brush off airfield quest [question]. UNC makes it plain question will be brought up again after staff has completed their work. #4—Stalemate on vol repat continues and is becoming more apparent.
January 28	I complain about broadcast by Lowell Thomas intimating that UNC will make further concessions. #3—meeting postponed. #4—We deliver revised roster of POWs, and give them expanded version of our 8 Jan proposal. R. approves my suggestion to initiate discussion Item 5 by letter to Nam Il.
January 29	#3—Commies show disposition to accept UNC wording and format. Islands and Rotation two principal issues. #4—Lee attacks revised version of our proposal submitted yesterday. I ask R. for guidance on Item 5.
January 30	#3—Staff makes progress. Rotation figure main bone of contention. #4—Lee takes exception to ICRC and states civs and POWs should be separated in exchange principle. Vol repat continues main sore point with Reds. R. approves my suggested ltr [letter] to Namil [Nam Il] for discussions on Item 5.
January 31	#3—Progress contd [continued] thru para 36. #4—Discussion on use of 38th parallel for distinguishing civs. We again bring up ICRC this time as technical advisors and to assist displaced civs to return home. Lee will study.
February 1	#3—Progress continues. Commies propose only 3 ports of entry. #4—Commies oppose any impartial role for ICRC. *Consider agency biased towards UNC.*
February 2	#3—Considerable progress made by staff offs. #4—Lee turns down safeguards for repat of civs. Dodges questions on subject.
February 3	#3—Commies allergic to blockade & suggest 12 miles for coastal waters. Discussion on rotation ceiling. UNC proposes 15 joint observer teams. #4—Commies submit new proposal, which still insists on forced repatriation.
February 4	#3—Discussion continues on number of ports of entry, function of neutral teams and figure for rotation. We recommend to Genl R. figure of 40 to 45,000 for rotation and only enough ports of entry for legitimate re-

Date	*Subject*
	plenishment and rotation. #4—Exploring Commie proposal. Minor agreements reached. Commies appear unusual [*sic*] cooperative.
February 5	#3—Commies insist on 3 ports of entry and 25,000 for rotation and replenishment. We hold out for 10 ports and 40,000/mo. exclusive of R&R and TDY. #4—Exploration of Commie proposal of Feb 3 continues.
February 6	Full delegations meet to consider Agenda Item 5. Nam Il insists Korean question not an isolated one and that other problems should be discussed by political conference. Gives us proposed draft. Matter discussed with Genl R and msg sent to J.C.S. Item 3 little progress.

#4—turned over to staff officers. |
| February 7 | #3—No progress. #4—Staff offs present working drafts of appropriate portions of arm. agreement. |
| February 8 | #3—No [number] of ports of entry continue as obstacle to progress. Commies want 3 we want 10–12. #4—Discussion centered on parole and rate of exchange of POWs. |
| February 9 | #5—UNC presents modification of Commies draft.

#3—No progress. #4—meeting continued on business like basis. |
February 10	#5—Commies objection to our proposed modified draft of their proposal. #3—We propose 8 ports of entry. No results. #4—Commies turn down safeguards for civilian repat.
February 11	#5—Nam Il refutes my statement of yesterday and I do likewise. #3—No progress. #4—No progress.
February 12	#5—Commies say they have new proposal which they will present later. #3—Commies up rotation figure to 30,000 and ports to 4. We say too little. #4—Discussion centered around RC terms.
February 13*	Conferred with R on final phase of negotiations. Airfields and voluntary repatriation last obstacles and discussed need for firmness in our final position. Item 3

---

* Two gaps in 1952 exist in Admiral Joy's chronological index to the negotiations. These cover the period from February 13–March 15 and from May 7–22, his last day at the Korean Armistice Conference. The "entries" for those periods, consequently, were prepared by me and in a manner that I thought consistent with the one that Joy himself had prepared.—Ed.

Date	*Subject*

staff meeting—UNC proposed 7 ports of entry and 40,000 rotation figure. Commies stuck to their figures. Item 4 staff meeting—Commies accepted in principle (except for vol. repat.) and agreed to work on wording tomorrow.

February 14   Met with R, Hull, Mr. [U. Alexis] Johnson, Wright, Milburn on Washington proposal for Item 4. The "proposition" was to present Commies with a fait accompli: screen and release all Chinese and NK POWs who did not want to return and then agree to forced repat. Condemned idea because it would threaten safe return of our POWs and wreck conference. Item 5—majority favors reaching quick agreement. Told Hull we were no longer negotiating from position of strength but from military stalemate. Item 3 staff meeting—no progress. Item 4 staff meeting—Commies refused all UNC wording proposals.

February 15   Last minute conference with R who wants to keep pressure on Commies to account for missing UNC POWs. Returned to camp at 1500. Item 3 staff meeting—no progress. #4 staff meeting—no progress on wording.

February 16   Full delegation met on Item 5. Nam Il proposed that within 3 months of armistice, political conference decide withdrawal of all foreign forces. Asked for recess to study this proposal. Item 3 staff meeting—Commies propose Poland, Czechoslovakia, and Soviet Union as their neutral nations. UNC said not authorized to accept Soviet Union. No progress. #4 staff meeting—hints at flexibility in wording. I ask Washington for instructions, Washington authorizes us to continue to reject Soviet Union but says we can't give as reason that we consider it not a neutral nation.

February 17   I accept Nam Il's proposal subject to UN and ROK approval, agreement that "foreign forces" means non-Korean forces, and clear understanding that proposed conference would deal only with Korea. Commies ask for recess. Item 3 staff meeting—Commies told Soviet

Date	*Subject*

Union not acceptable and they claim we are delaying the conference. No progress. #4 staff meeting—no progress.

February 18

Another discussion with Johnson and Col. Matthews on Washington plan to present Commies with a fait accompli on the repatriation issue. Again told Johnson that such an act would endanger our POWs. Emphasized we must stand united and firm on principle of vol. repat. or give it up entirely and soon. I told Johnson we had 50-50 chance of winning if we stood firm. Libby more pessimistic. Item 3 staff meeting—no progress. Complained to R that not being able to give reasons for rejecting Soviet Union gives Commies propaganda advantage. Washington refuses to change its position on this. Item 4—Commies submit wording changes that eliminate majority of minor obstacles.

February 19

Nam Il appears to accept our stipulations and proposes that details of wording articles on Item 5 be turned over to staff officers. I see no reason to do this and propose we accept Commie wording as is. Commies surprised and ask for recess. We reconvene and they finally agree that staff officers meeting will not rewrite section but meet to discuss mechanical details. Item 3 staff meeting—staff officers suspect enemy may be attempting to arrange a deal: UN acceptance of Soviet Union for concessions on ports and rotation. #4 staff meeting—little progress.

February 20

Item 3 staff meeting—UNC proposes 35,000 rotation figure. Chang accuses us of delaying conference by not giving reasons against Soviet Union. No progress. #4 staff meeting—no progress.

February 21

Item 3 staff meeting—deadlock. #4 staff meeting— some basic definitions agreed on.

February 22

Item 3 staff meeting—no progress. #4—UNC submitted complete draft. Commies indicated general agreement, but still a deadlock on repatriation.

February 23

Item 3 staff meeting—Commies accepted 35,000 rotatation figure but would agree to only 5 ports of entry. Then pressed their case for the SU as a neutral nation.

Date	*Subject*
	#4 staff meeting—no progress. Commies protest Koje-Do riot that resulted in deaths of 69 prisoners.
February 24	Item 3 staff meeting—no progress. #4 staff meeting—no progress. Conferred with Col. Salisbury on the Johnson "fait accompli" plan. Restated my views again.
February 25	Item 3 staff meeting—no progress. #4 staff meeting—no progress.
February 26	Item 3 staff meeting—no progress. #4 staff meeting—Chinese and Korean wording of approved English-language paragraphs discussed.
February 27	Item 3 staff meeting—no progress. # 4 staff meeting—agreement on wording discussed yesterday reached, but still deadlocked on vol. repat.
February 28	Item 3 staff meeting—no progress. Item 4 staff meeting—no major progress. Language of Korean, Chinese, English versions compared and corrected.
February 29	Item 3 staff meeting—no progress. #4 sub-delegation meeting—paragraphs worked out by staff officers ratified.
March 1	Item 3 staff meeting—no progress. #4 sub-delegation meeting—deadlock.
March 2	Left for Tokyo. Item 3 staff meeting—no progress. #4 sub-delegation meeting—no progress.
March 3	Item 3 staff meeting—no progress. #4 sub-delegation meeting—no progress.
March 4	Met with R on latest Washington proposition NNSC—to accept non-neutral nations on it. Agreed to stick to our guns. Item 3 staff meeting—no progress. #4 sub-delegation meeting—no progress.
March 5	Meeting and dinner with Radford. Item 3 staff meeting—no progress. #4 sub-delegation meeting—no progress.
March 6	Item 3 staff meeting—no progress. #4 sub-delegation meeting—no progress.
March 7	Returned to Munsan-ni. Item 3 staff meeting—no progress. #4 sub-delegation meeting—Commies accept wording of another paragraph. Commie proposal on

Date	*Subject*
	repat. appears to be to agree in principle at sub.-del. level and let staff officers meeting decide to whom forced repat. would apply.
March 8	Item 3 staff meeting—Commies agreed to consider UNC proposal to insert references to Korea that make clear specific limits of armistice. #4 sub-delegation—no progress.
March 9	Item 3 staff meeting—no progress. #4 sub-delegation meeting—no progress.
March 10	Item 3 staff meeting—no progress. #4 sub-delegation meeting—no progress. R visited camp. Status of negotiations reviewed.
March 11	Item 3 staff meeting—no progress. #4 sub-delegation meeting—no progress.
March 12	Item 3 staff meeting—no progress. #4 sub-delegation meeting—no progress.
March 13	Item 3 staff meetings—no progress. #4 sub-delegation meeting—no progress.
March 14	Item 3 staff meetings—no progress. #4 sub-delegation meeting—UNC proposed that we return to meeting at staff officers level in effort to break deadlock. Commies said they would consider this.
March 16	I return to Tokyo. Item 3—UNC pkg proposal settles all issues except USSR. Item 4—We tell Commies UNC not seeking principle but an end product.
March 17	I discuss Johnson plan & JCS proposed pkg solution with R. Item 3—discusses port complexes. Item 4—UNC explores basic question & Commies Mar 5 proposal.
March 18	Item 3—discussion continues on port complexes. Item 4—More on Commie Mar 5 proposal.
March 19	Item 3—more on port complexes. Item 4—continuing discussion on Mar 5 proposal of Commies. Briggs phones of hints by Commie correspondents.
March 20	In conference with R we decide to give JCS gist of Commie correspondents hints. Item 3—agreement reached on ports of entry. Item 4—Commies propose

Date	*Subject*
	settlement on basis of basic data exchanged, i.e., 132,474 for 11,559.
March 21	*JCS come thru with despatch on subject of agreement of POW exch. on basis of revised lists.* R points out that revised lists would be checked before UNC agrees, & objects again to USSR. Item 3—Minor matters. Item 4—Commies hint on secret meetings & make proposal on POW exch on basis revised lists.
March 22	I return to Korea. Item 3—Airfields at ports of entry discussed. Item 4—*Commies again hint on Exec* [Executive] *sessions & elaborate on their new principle.*
March 23	JCS say to go ahead with efforts to obtain agreement with Commies on an acceptable basis for POW exch— explore carefully. Item 3—map discussion. Item 4—*we propose exec sessions & send msg to R proposing counter proposal. R agreed with slight changes.*
March 24	Item 3—lines of comm. discussed. Item 4—Commies agree to Exec sessions but attach condition to it, namely that UNC agree to draft provision on their prin [principle].
March 25	Item 3—UNC states position on neut nations irrevocable & final. Item 4—goes into Exec sessions. We give counter proposal (see Mar 23) & discuss procedures for checking the POW lists.
March 26	Item 3—UNC again proposes, & is rejected, that neut [neutral] nations prob be settled by agreeing on 2 nations for each side. Item 4—more exploration of Commie proposal of Mar 21. Wrangle over status of 16,000 ROK POWs. UNC contends they are a special situation.
March 27	Item 3—Wrangle over what Korean translation should be for Korea & UN. Item 4—Commies submit prin [principle] of adjustment which applies prin of vol repat to some POWs and not to others. *We say again "no forced repat."*
March 28	Item 3—Commies propose solution for translation of Korea & UN. Item 4—Both sides hold to their posits.
March 29	Item 3—no progress. Item 4—Commies wish us to forget 50,000. They'll forget 44,000; made it clear we must turn over all CPV POWs.

Date	*Subject*
March 30	Item 3—no progress. Item 4—Both sides stick to their guns. UNC asks special cases (those who resist repat) be excluded in exchange. Commies stick to prin that part of capt. pers. [captured personnel] must be repat (CPV) while other part (Koreans) abide by prin "no forced repat."
March 31	Item 3—some progress on areas for ports of entry. Commies propose transfer unsolved probs to sub-del [sub-delegation]. Item 4—Commies start talking about round figures and checking lists so that nos close to figs in prin might be reached. *Commies appear to be sincere in efforts to solve Item 4.*
April 1	Muccio's despatch about use of Chosun for Korea. I sent R msg on proposed pkg [package] proposal. Item 3—we agree to return to sub del. Item 4—We make counter proposal. Commies want rd. [round] figure. We say 116,000 would more nearly indicate magnitude of exch.
April 2	Item 3—More about Chosun & Horn Kuk [Han Kuk]. Item 4—Commies propose immediately enter into checking of lists. We send msg to R on subject. Newsweek editorial. R. replies to continue with staff meetings.
April 3	Item 3—Sub dels do some sparring. Item 4—R visits camp and we discuss screening with him, Van Fleet, Dodd, Yount & Milburn. Estimate only 85,000 would not be violently opposed. Msg to JCS requesting authority to go ahead with screening & outlined our proposed course from now on.
April 4	Item 3—Commies hint in sub del meeting they will agree to our solution of neut. nations if we will agree to drop airfield restrs. Item 4—Agreement reached to recess exec sessions to "check lists" for rd. figure. News blackout continues.
April 5	Item 3—Nothing new, we ignore hints by Commies of yesterday. Dodds plan for screening POWs approved.
April 7–14	I return to Tokyo for rest at Kawana. Conference with R on progress of screening. I recommend rescreening and am overruled. Wu and May tell R about screening

Date	*Subject*
	process. Millburn [Milburn] & Bryan visit Van Fleet to get views on rescreening. Van Fleet says 2−3 weeks. R says too long. Item 3—no progress. Commies would like to trade airfields for USSR.
April 14	We send msg to R. concerning future action to bring matters to a head. Necessary for speedy action on pkg proposal step. Chain reaction will be started when figure of 20,000 is submitted for repat to Commies.
April 15	Msg from R to confine discussions Item 4 to 70,000. Also msg from R to Deptar outlining future recommended course of action including introduction of pkg proposal in plenary session. J.C.S. reply also rec'd.
April 16	Our rec [recommended] course of action in which we recommend authority to inform Commies screening not complete when figure 70,000 is given them.
April 17	We rec. delay in further Item 4 meetings until screening completed. J.C.S. despatch concerning rescreening and neutral screening which conforms to Del's views.
April 18	We are directed by CinCUNC to reconvene staff offs [officers]. Executive sessions earliest and give Commies 70,000 figure because it would take another month to relocate POWs and rescreen those refusing to be repatriated. I express my views on low figure to be returned vis à vis the return of UN POWs.
April 19	I get a vote of confidence from R. and another msg from R. asking my views on desirability of offering to trade airfields for USSR provided Commies settle on UNC basis for POWs. Nothing new Item 3. Staff offs reconvene in Exec session on Item 4. Hickman gives Commies figure of 70,000 broken down into sub-totals. Commies ask for 1 hr recess & return to say figure can not be used as basis for further discussions.
April 20	Item 4—Commies reiterate figure of 70,000 cannot be used as basis for further discussions. Was not a settlement under framework of their Mar 21 proposal. Accused us of indicating 116,000 would be returned and of repudiating what we said before. I exchange msg's with R on further course of action.

Date	*Subject*
April 21	Item 4—Hickman rebuts Commie contention we had repudiated basis of earlier discussions. Commies are adamant that 70,000 can never be used as basis for further negots. Received msg from R. which gives his decision not to prematurely disclose pkg. proposal. We agree.
April 22	Item 4—Commies attitude stiffens. I recommend to R. that we move to plenary session & present pkg proposal with minimum delay. Said I would like conference with him on Apr 24th.
April 23	I return to Tokyo and confer with R on future course of action. We discuss plenary session for presentation of pkg proposal. Item 4 meeting showed that Commies would never accept 70,000 figure.
April 24	Item 3—nothing to report. Item 4—Commies abrogate Exec sessions but said they would continue if UNC were willing to return to basis of their Mar 21 proposal.
April 25	I return to camp. Hickman reports Commies had abrogated Item 4 Exec sessions. We request plenary session on Apr 27.
April 26	I send R. msg giving my opening statement at plenary session and a change to par 51 of arm agreement (exchange of POWs).
April 27	Just as we had completed arrangements for plenary session, which was to be an open one, msg was rec'd from JCS to hold Exec session. After approval from GHQ we postpone meeting with Commies until tomorrow. I then send msg to R. giving reasons why we should meet in open session, which R sent on to JCS strongly concurring.
April 28	J.C.S. turn down R. and direct us to meet in Exec session. We meet at 1100 and propose an overall settlement in Exec session. After recess Commies agree and I give the overall solution. Commies after unencouraging preliminary statement ask for recess.
April 29	I return to Tokyo for conference with R. Radio announces R will relieve Eisenhower in Europe.
April 30	Had conference with R. Upon my request was given authority to reject out of hand any counter proposal of

Date	*Subject*
	Commies, such as airfields for U.S.S.R. which left POW question unsettled.
May 1	I return to Korea and receive word from Kinney Commies want to meet tomorrow. He had agreed.
May 2	We meet in Exec session and receive Commie counter proposal which was what we thought it would be, they agree to drop U.S.S.R. but stand pat on POW question referring to their Mar 21 principle & "compromise" proposal of adjustment of Mar 27. I send msg to R. telling of Commies rejection of our pkg and recommending open sessions for future.
May 3	R says to keep on with Exec sessions for a while at least 2 days. He also recommended I not use words final and irrevocable but J.C.S. says to use them. J.C.S. also indicate all top levels will support pkg deal with public statements when matter is brought out in open. Nothing new at Exec sessions. Commies hold fast and so do we.
May 4	Msg from J.C.S. requesting to be informal before Del goes to open sessions. R advises J.C.S. he will give Del authority to call off Exec sessions on or after May 6 at my discretion. Nothing new at Pan Mun Jom. Both sides stand fast.
May 5	No progress.
May 6	I recommend figure of between 80 & 85,000 of POWs to be repatriated be given to Commies as an administrative matter. R turns down idea for present. At Pan Mun Jom we propose abandoning Exec sessions. Commies ask for recess until tomorrow, are surprised.
May 7*	Delegations met at 1000. Commies criticize us for not negotiating seriously in executive sessions we requested and propose open plenary sessions. I agree and say since our proposal is final we will only meet when Commies have something to say. Commies want meetings to go on as smoke screen for their next offensive.
May 8	Plenary session—Commies take familiar line on repatriation. I say I have no statement to make since our posi-

---

*See the editor's note related to the February 13 entry.

Date	Subject
	tion is clear. R, Clark and Van Fleet visit camp for conference.
May 9	Plenary session—no progress. Recessed after ten minutes.
May 10	JCS want us to stop making terse statements that our position is final and engage in substantive review of our proposals at plenary session. I think this might lead Commies to think we are weakening. R asks JCS to reconsider. Plenary session—no progress. Recessed after 21 minutes.
May 11	JCS still wants us to make substantive reviews for propaganda purposes. Plenary session—no progress.
May 12	Plenary session—UNC subjected to vicious propaganda attack. I advise R that we appear to Commies as negotiating from weakness and that we should be authorized to announce unilaterally a suspension of talks until Commies ready to accept UNC April 28 proposal.
May 13	Gen. Colson, in statement to press after Koje-Do incident, says he will end all POW screening. This most damaging statement to us that could have been issued. Plenary session—no progress.
May 14	Plenary session—no progress.
May 15	Plenary session—Nam Il claimed that Colson statement proof that UNC had engaged in POW screening by force.
May 16	Plenary session—no progress.
May 17	Clark proposed to JCS that to break deadlock no more screening would be done and that we agree to repat. approximately 80,000 prisoners. We sent message opposing this on grounds that any revised approx. figure would just encourage Commies to assume that further period of denunciation and delay would cause UNC to revise figure again upward. JCS won't approve our May 12 proposal to suspend the talks. Plenary session— no progress. But longer statement we made today along lines of JCS instruction visibly relaxed and gratified enemy. Del. is more than ever of opinion we now face a protracted period of enemy propaganda.
May 18	Plenary session—no progress.

Date	*Subject*
May 19	Plenary session—no progress. Del. sends another message to R arguing against continuing plenary sessions.
May 20	Plenary session—most vicious propaganda we have been subjected to in 10-1/2 months.
May 21	Plenary session—no progress.
May 22	My last day. Plenary session—as valedictory, I reviewed UNC goals, stand on POWs, and good faith in the negotiations. Said decision up to Commies now since there is nothing left to negotiate.

Recapitulation of Military Armistice Negotiation Sessions, Korea (through May 22, 1952)

Agenda Item #1

Plenary session (only)
Total no. of days   10
Total no. of hours   23.5

Agenda Item #2

a. Plenary session
Total no. of days   17
Total no. of hours   34.3

b. Sub-delegates
Total no. of days   37
Total no. of hours   110.3

c. Staff officers
Total no. of days   11
Total no. of hours   42

Agenda Item #3

a. Plenary session
Total no. of days   8
Total no. of hours   17.2

b. Sub-delegates
Total no. of days   71
Total no. of hours   104.9

Agenda Item #3 (con't.)

c. Staff officers
Total no. of days   77
Total no. of hours   117.5

Agenda Item #4

a. Plenary session (none)

b. Sub-delegates
Total no. of days   71
Total no. of hours   196.6

c. Staff officers
Total no. of days   50
Total no. of hours   98.6

Agenda Item #5

Plenary session (only)

Meetings from April 25–May 22

Plenary session (only)
Total no. of days   22
Total no. of hours   14.1

Who Was Who at the Korean Armistice Conference

Allen, Leven C., Maj. Gen., USA: Chief of Staff, Eighth Army

Ammon, William B., R. Adm., USN: Commander, Battleship Division Two

Ball, George C., Lt. Comdr., USN: Staff Officer, UNCD

Bohlen, Charles E.: Counselor, U.S. Department of State

Bolté, Charles L., Lt. Gen., USA: Deputy Chief of Staff (Plans) UNC

Bradley, Omar N., Gen., USA: Chairman, Joint Chiefs of Staff

Briggs, H. M., Capt., USN: Staff Officer, UNCD

Bryan, Blackshear M., Maj. Gen., USA: Deputy Chief of Staff, Far Eastern Command

Burke, Arleigh A., R. Adm., USN: UNCD Delegate to the Korean Armistice Conference

Chang Chun San, Col., (N)KPA: North Korean Liaison Officer for the Korean Armistice Conference

Chang Pyong San, Maj. Gen., (N)KPA: North Korean Delegate to the Korean Armistice Conference

Chung Tu Hwan, Maj. Gen., (N)KPA: North Korean Delegate to the Korean Armistice Conference

Clark, Joseph J., V. Adm., USN: Commander, Seventh Fleet

Clark, Mark W., Gen., USA: CinCUNC, April 28, 1952–October 7, 1953 (succeeded Ridgway)

Collins, J. Lawton, Gen., USA: Chief of Staff, UNC

Colson, Charles F., Brig. Gen., USA: Chief of Staff, I Corps—appointed by Van Fleet to negotiate the release of General Dodd at Koje-do POW camp

Craigie, Laurence C., Maj. Gen., USAF: UNC Delegate to the Korean Armistice Conference

Darrow, Don O., Col., USAF: Staff Officer, UNCD

Dodd, Francis T., Brig. Gen., USA: Commandant, Koje-do POW camp—
appointed by Van Fleet in late February 1952 to
restore discipline to the camp, held hostage by
prisoners May 7−10

Duncan, Dunc: *see* Joy, David Duncan

Edwards, Norman B., Lt. Col., USA: Staff Officer, UNCD

Everest, Frank F., Maj. Gen., USAF: Commander, Fifth Air Force

Fechteler, William M., Adm., USN: Chief of Naval Operations

Ferenbaugh, Claude B., Maj. Gen., USA: UNCD Delegate to the Korean Armistice Conference

Galloway, D. H., Col., USA: Staff Officer, UNCD

Goldhamer, Dr. Herbert: Analyst, the RAND Corporation. Special Adviser to
Admiral Joy during the fall of 1951

Harrison, William K., Jr., Lt. Gen., USA: Deputy Commander, Eighth Army
—joined UNC delegation in February 1952 as re-
placement for Ferenbaugh and became the Senior
Delegate, succeeding CTJ on May 22, 1952, and
serving until the armistice agreement was signed
on July 27, 1953.

Hickey, Doyle O., Lt. Gen., USA: Chief of Staff, UNC

Hickman, George W., Jr., Col., USA: Staff Officer, UNCD

Hill, Harry, V. Adm., USN: Superintendent, U.S. Naval Academy

Hodes, Henry I., Maj. Gen., USA: UNCD Delegate to the Korean Armistice
Conference

Hsieh Fang, Maj. Gen., CPV: CPV Delegate to the Korean Armistice Conference

Hull, John E., Gen., USA: Vice Chief of Staff

Hurr, Arthur, Col., USAF: Staff Officer, UNCD

Hyong Keun Lee: *see* Lee Hyung Koon

Jacoby, Oswald, Lt. Comdr., USN: Staff Officer

Johnson, U. Alexis: Deputy Assistant Secretary of State for Far Eastern Affairs

Joy, C. Turner, V. Adm., USN: Senior Delegate, UNC Delegation to the Korean Armistice Conference, July 10, 1951—
May 22, 1952

Joy, David Duncan, 1st Lt., USA: 4th Signal Bn, Eighth Army (son of CTJ)

Kiland, Ingolf N., R. Adm., USN: Commander, Task Force 95, the UNC Blockading and Escort Force

Kinney, Andrew J., Col., USAF: Staff Officer, UNCD

Latoszewski, E. J., Col., USAF: Staff Officer, UNCD

Lee, Col., ROKA: aide to Paik Sun Yup

Lee, Hyung Koon, Maj. Gen., ROKA: UNCD Delegate to the Korean Armistice Conference

Lee Sang Cho, Major General, (N)KPA: North Korean Delegate to the Korean Armistice Conference

Levie, Howard S., Lt. Col., USA: Staff Officer, UNCD

Libby, Ruthven E., Adm., USN: UNCD Delegate to the Korean Armistice Conference

Lightner, Edwin A., Sr.: Deputy Chief of Mission and Counselor of the U.S. Embassy, Republic of Korea

Lovett, Robert A.: U.S. Secretary of Defense

Martin, Harold M., V. Adm., USN: Commander, Air Force, Pacific Fleet

Merchant, Livingston T.: Special Assistant to the Secretary of State for Mutual Security Affairs

Molly: Mary M. Joy Roll (daughter of CTJ)

Muccio, John J.: U.S. Ambassador to the Republic of Korea

Mudgett, Gilman C., Col., USA: Staff Officer, UNCD

Murray, James C., Col., USMC: Staff Officer, UNCD

Muse, George R., Commander, USN: Staff Officer, UNCD

Nam Il, Lt. Gen., (N)KPA: North Korean Senior Delegate to the Korean Armistice Conference

Nitze, Paul, Director: Policy Planning Staff, U.S. Department of State

Nuckols, William P., Brig. Gen., USAF: Staff Officer UNCD

Ofstie, Ralph A., V. Adm., USN: Chief of Staff, Naval Forces Far East

Paik Sun Yup, Maj. Gen., ROKA: South Korean Delegate to the Korean Armistice Conference, CG, ROKA I Corps

Peng Teh-huai, General, CPV: Commander, CPVs

Pien Chang-wu, Gen., CPV: Communist Chinese Delegate to the Korean Armistice Conference

Pu Shan, Col., CPV: Staff Officer, North Korean delegation to the Korean Armistice Conference

Radford, Arthur W., Adm., USN: CinCPac

Ridgway, Matthew B., Gen., USA: CinCUNC, April 11, 1951 – April 28, 1952

Robertson, Sir Horace, Lt. Gen.: Commander, British Commonwealth Forces in Korea (until November 1951)

Roper, John W., V. Adm., USN: Commandant, 11th Naval District

Shepherd, Lemuel C., Lt. Gen., USMC: Commander, Fleet Marine Forces in the Pacific

Teng Hua, Lt. Gen., CPV: Chinese Communist Delegate to the Korean Armistice Conference

Tsai Chen Wen, Col., CPV: Communist Chinese Liaison Officer for the Korean Armistice Conference

Turner, Howard M., Maj. Gen., USAF: UNCD Delegate to the Korean Armistice Conference

Underwood, Horace G., Lt., USN: Staff Officer and Interpreter, UNCD

Underwood, Richard F., Lt., USA: Staff Officer and Interpreter, UNCD

Vandenberg, Hoyt S., Gen., USAF: Chief of Staff, USAF

Van Fleet, James A., Lt. Gen., USA: CG, Eighth Army

Weyland, Otto P., Lt. Gen., USAF: Commander, Far East Air Forces

Wright, Edwin K., Brig. Gen., USA: Director, Joint Strategic Plans and Operations Group

Wright, George C., R. Adm., USN: Head, New Developments Branch, Office of the Chief of Naval Operations

Wu, Kenneth, Warrant Officer, USA: Staff Officer and Interpreter, UNCD

Young, Robert N., Maj. Gen., USA: CG, 2nd Division

Yu Chae Heung, Maj. Gen., ROKA: UNC Delegate to the Korean Armistice Conference

Certain persons who were not at the Conference are included above because of their participation in related events in Korea and Japan during the period. Other persons are identified in the text insofar as seems necessary or helpful, and some whom CTJ mentions only in passing are left with no more identification than he provides.

Abbreviations and Glossary

ADV, adv	Advance, advance headquarters
AG	Adjutant General
AP	Associated Press
B.L., b.l.	Battle line
CCF	Chinese Communist Forces (participating in the Korean War)
CinCFE	Command in Chief, Far East
CinCPac	Commander in Chief, Pacific
CinCUNC	Commander in Chief, United Nations Command
CG	Commanding General
Commie	Communist
CPV	Chinese People's Volunteers
CTJ	Vice Admiral C. Turner Joy
DA	Department of the Army
Deptar	Department of the Army
EUSAK, Eusak	Eighth U.S. Army, Korea
GC	Geneva Convention
GHQ	General Headquarters
ICRC	International Committee of the Red Cross
IRO	International Refugee Organization
Item 2, #2	Agenda Item #2 (demarcation line and demilitarized zone)
Item 3, #3	Agenda Item #3 (arrangements for cease-fire and armistice)
Item 4, #4	Agenda Item #4 (prisoners of war)
Item 5, #5	Agenda Item #5 (recommendations concerning political settlement of the conflict)

JCS	Joint Chiefs of Staff
Johnson Plan	Plan proposed in February 1952 by General John E. Hull (Vice Chief of Staff) and U. Alexis Johnson (Deputy Assistant Secretary of State for Far Eastern Affairs) to release all UNC-held North Korean and Chinese POWs who did not wish to be repatriated, as against Communist demand that all POWs be repatriated regardless of preference
JSPOG	Joint (Army, Navy, Air Force) Plans and Operations Group established by General MacArthur in 1949 under Brig. Gen. Edwin K. Wright; UNC's planning agency that drafted plans for the opening of truce talks
K	Korea
K16	Seoul
Kansas line	Forward defense line established by the Eighth Army after the Spring 1951 offensive
KPA	*See* NKPA
L of C, line of c	Line of contact
MAC	Military Armistice Commission
MP	Military Police
NK	North Korea, North Korean
NKA, NKPA	North Korean Army, North Korean People's Army (officially, North Koreans refer only to KPA)
NNSC	Neutral Nations Supervisory Commission
Operation Scatter	Screening process to determine POWs' wishes as to repatriation
PMJ	Panmunjom
POW	Prisoner of War
R	General Matthew B. Ridgway
RC	Red Cross
ROK	Republic of Korea (South Korea)
SK	South Korea, South Korean
SU	Soviet Union
UNC	United Nations Command
UNCD	United Nations Command Delegation (to the Armistice Conference)

UNCSD   United Nations Command Sub-Delegation (to the Armistice
             Conference)

In addition, various common abbreviations and others improvised by CTJ
for brevity or adapted from military usage appear in the diary text. All are spelled
out, in brackets, at first occurrence and fairly often thereafter, according to the
editor's judgment as to their usefulness as a reminder.   In some instances
bracketed words are inserted to avoid a flow of telegraphese, not on the assumption that the reader has forgotten what the abbreviations mean. All text in
parentheses is CTJ's own.

Index of Names

Index of Names

---

*First name unknown.